Learning from Imbalanced Data Sets

Alberto Fernández • Salvador García • Mikel Galar
Ronaldo C. Prati • Bartosz Krawczyk
Francisco Herrera

Learning from Imbalanced Data Sets

 Springer

Alberto Fernández
Department of Computer Science and AI
University of Granada
Granada, Granada, Spain

Salvador García
Department of Computer Science and AI
University of Granada
Granada, Granada, Spain

Mikel Galar
Institute of Smart Cities
Public University of Navarre
Pamplona, Spain

Ronaldo C. Prati
Department of Computer Science
Universidade Federal do ABC
Santo Andre, Brazil

Bartosz Krawczyk
Department of Computer Science
Virginia Commonwealth University
Richmond, VA, USA

Francisco Herrera
Department of Computer Science and AI
University of Granada
Granada, Spain

ISBN 978-3-030-07446-3   ISBN 978-3-319-98074-4   (eBook)
https://doi.org/10.1007/978-3-319-98074-4

This Springer imprint is published by the registered company Springer Nature Switzerland AG
The registered company address is: Gewerbestrasse 11, 6330 Cham, Switzerland

To my beloved wife, my family, friends, and close colleagues. For their support since the very beginning.

Alberto Fernández

To my family
Salvador García

To my family
Mikel Galar

To my family
Ronalo C. Prati

To my family
Bartosz Krawczyk

To my family
Francisco Herrera

Preface

Learning with imbalanced data refers to the scenario in which the amounts of instances that represent the concepts in a given problem follow a different distribution. The main issue when addressing such a learning problem is when the accuracy achieved for each class is also different. This situation occurs since the learning process of most classification algorithm is often biased toward the majority class examples, so that minority ones are not well modeled into the final system. Being a very common scenario in real-life applications, the interest of researchers and practitioners on the topic has grown significantly during these years.

Based on the experience of the authors after several years focused on imbalanced classification, this book aims at offering a general and comprehensible overview for anyone interested in this area of study. It contains a formal description of the problem and focuses on its main features and the most relevant proposed solutions. Additionally, it considers the different scenarios in Data Science for which the imbalanced classification can suppose a real challenge.

After a gentle introduction to the KDD process and current state of Data Science in the first chapter, the book then stresses the gap with standard classification tasks by establishing the foundations and reviewing the case studies with a direct application in this area in Chap. 2. Then, Chap. 3 introduces the main ad hoc evaluation metrics to be considered in this area of study. The book also covers the different approaches that have been traditionally applied to address the binary skewed class distribution. Specifically, it reviews cost-sensitive learning (Chap. 4), data-level preprocessing methods (Chap. 5), and algorithm-level solutions (Chap. 6), taking also into account those ensemble-learning solutions that embed any of the former alternatives (Chap. 7). Furthermore, it focuses in Chap. 8 on the extension of the problem for multi-class problems, where the former classical methods are no longer to be applied in a straightforward way.

The book includes in Chap. 9 some notes on data reduction, being provided in order to understand the advantages related to the use of this type of approaches. Then, Chap. 10 focuses on the data intrinsic characteristics that are the main causes which, added to the uneven class distribution, truly hinders the performance of classification algorithms in this scenario. Finally, this book introduces some novel areas of study that are gathering a deeper attention on the imbalanced data issue. Specifically, Chap. 11 considers the classification of data streams, Chap. 12 the non-classical classification problems, and finally Chap. 13 discusses the scalability related to Big Data. To sum up, some examples of software libraries and modules to address imbalanced classification are given in Chap. 14.

This thorough review on the current and future state of imbalanced classification aims giving this topic the significance it deserves. In particular, the interest of research and academia is clearly shown by the rising number of publications and citations year by year. In the foreseeable future, it predictably will continue expanding with novel significant developments, as many contemporary real-world applications must be addressed from the viewpoint of imbalanced classification.

The intended audience of this book are developers and engineers aiming to apply imbalance-learning techniques to solve different kinds of real-world problems, as well as researchers and students needing a comprehensive review on techniques, methodologies, and tools for learning from imbalanced data.

We wish to thank all our collaborators of the research group "Soft Computing and Intelligent Information Systems." We are also thankful to our families for their helpful support.

Granada, Spain   Alberto Fernández
Granada, Spain   Salvador García
Pamplona, Spain   Mikel Galar
Santo Andre, Brazil   Ronalo C. Prati
Richmond, VA, USA   Bartosz Krawczyk
Granada, Spain   Francisco Herrera
June 2018

Contents

Acronyms

ADASYN	Adaptive synthetic sampling
AL	Active learning
ANN	Artificial neural network
AUC	Area under the curve
AUC_{ROC}	Area under the ROC curve
AUC_{PR}	Area under the precision-recall curve
CV	Cross-validation
CNN	Condensed nearest rule
DM	Data mining
DR	Dimensionality reduction
EC	Error concentration
EM	Expectation-maximization
FCV	Fold cross-validation
FS	Feature selection
IS	Instance selection
KDD	Knowledge discovery in data
KEEL	Knowledge extraction based on evolutionary learning
KNN	K-Nearest neighbors
LLE	Locally linear embedding
LVQ	Learning vector quantization
MCC	Matthews correlation coefficient
MDS	Multidimensional scaling
MI	Mutual information
MIL	Multi-instance learning
ML	Machine learning
MLL	Multilabel learning
MLP	Multilayer perceptron
MV	Missing value
NCL	Neighborhood cleaning rule
NN	Nearest neighbor
OSS	One-sided selection

PCA	Principal components analysis
PU-learning	Positive and unlabeled learning
RBFN	Radial basis function network
ROC	Receiver operating characteristic curve
SMOTE	Synthetic minority over-sampling technique
SONN	Self-organizing neural network
SSL	Semi-supervised learning
SVM	Support vector machine

Chapter 1
Introduction to KDD and Data Science

Abstract Nowadays, the availability of large volumes of data and the widespread use of tools for the proper extraction of knowledge information has become very frequent, especially in large corporations. This fact has transformed the data analysis by orienting it towards certain specialized techniques included under the umbrella of Data Science. In summary, Data Science can be considered as a discipline for discovering new and significant relationships, patterns and trends in the examination of large amounts of data. Therefore, Data Science techniques pursue the automatic discovery of the knowledge contained in the information stored in large databases. These techniques aim to uncover patterns, profiles and trends through the analysis of data using reconnaissance technologies, such as clustering, classification, predictive analysis, association mining, among others. For this reason, we are witnessing the development of multiple software solutions for the treatment of data and integrating lots of Data Science algorithms. In order to better understand the nature of Data Science, this chapter is organized as follows. Sections 1.2 and 1.3 defines the Data Science terms and its workflow. Then, in Sect. 1.4 the standard problems in Data Science are introduced. Section 1.5 describes some standard data mining algorithms. Finally, in Sect. 1.6 some of the non-standard problems in Data Science are mentioned.

1.1 Introduction

Recent technological advances imply that the capacities to generate and store data are increased everyday. Among the factors that influence this reality we can highlight the widespread use of bar codes and QR reading, the automation of all type of transactions (commercial, business, economic, scientific) and the advances in data collection, among others. In addition, the Internet has rapid access to information, where both data and results can be easily obtained by others equipment. In this sense, current organizations although distant in the space, are very close in the cyberspace. All of these has led to strong economies of scale through the pooling of databases, theoretical knowledge and successful results. Furthermore, in the last decades there has been a change in the organizational environment that has caused

© Springer Nature Switzerland AG 2018
A. Fernández et al., *Learning from Imbalanced Data Sets*,
https://doi.org/10.1007/978-3-319-98074-4_1

a strong competition. This implies a need for organizations of all kinds to be able to survive in such changing environments.

Besides, the evolution of mass storage devices (in relation to price – storage capacity), such as hard disks that can store gigabytes of information at a reduced price, has led to companies and organizations to store all kinds of information. Citing some examples, we may refer to the data of customers and their transactions, to telemetry data, patients, price evolution in markets, among others. In the beginning, this information was stored in files that were difficult to handle, but with the advent of database management systems this difficulty was reduced. With the time, the amount of data that was stored began to grow and, although the tools to perform the data management was suitable, the significant relationships existing between them, began to surpass the human capacities for analysis. At the same time, database systems had begun to be decentralized, hence the decisions lacked credibility, inefficiency and lack of productivity.

All this explosive data growth generated, in the late 1980s, the emergence of a new field of research called KDD [15]. Under these acronyms hides, as suggested by Fayyad et al. [9], "the non-trivial process of discovering valid, new patterns, potentially useful and understandable in large volumes of data". The KDD process has served to unite researchers from areas in principle dispersed as Artificial Intelligence, Statistics, Visualization Techniques, Mathematics, Automatic Learning or Databases in the search for efficient techniques and that help to find the potential knowledge that is immersed in the large volumes of data stored by organizations on a daily basis [10].

Although the name with which this area of research appeared was that of KDD, other names have been used for this same concept. Some of them are *Knowledge Discovery, Data Discovery, Discovery Information, Knowledge Extraction, Data Extraction, Pattern Discovery, DM, Data Science*. At present the names that enjoy greater acceptance have been the DM and Data Science [2, 29]. Both processes need smart methods to extract information from data and to optimize the results. In the beginning, DM was only used to refer to the stage of the process in which they are applied techniques and pattern discovery algorithms. However, currently it is used to refer to the overall process of extracting knowledge from the data. Similarly, the term Data Science is currently used to generalize the DM and KDD terms into a new discipline which encompasses techniques and theories drawn from many fields within the broad areas of mathematics, statistics, information science, and computer science.

The great increase of data that the organizations have to analyze not only resulted in the appearance of Data Science, but at the same time Big Data concept emerges. One of the great problems of Data Science is that the data was never stored thinking that as a consequence, prior to the analysis, is necessary a process of integration and cleaning of data that in many cases results more expensive than the analysis itself. However, the appearance of the Data Warehouses as repositories of centralized information allows the processes can not be performed on data sets that have been previously integrated and subjected to cleaning processes.

For researchers in the fields of knowledge named previously, these two recent areas of research pose a great challenge to find a new way of thinking, designing, and implementing both the basis as the data analysis.

1.2   A Definition of Data Science

The diagram in Fig. 1.1 illustrates the idea that the KDD is a process [22], that is, it is a set of tasks or stages, which will be analyzed in detail throughout this chapter, and among which include:

- Establishment of a relevant problem.
- Selection of the appropriate data to solve the problem.
- Exploration and cleaning of data.
- Processing and modification of data.
- Application of modeling techniques (algorithms for the discovery of patterns).
- Obtaining and interpreting the models obtained.
- Use of knowledge obtained.
- Generation of new data from your application in the real world.

But how does the Data Science process differ from the analysis that other disciplines perform? Traditional systems of data exploitation are fundamentally based on the existence of previous hypotheses or models. Once the hypothesis is formulated, it is analyzed empirically from the information in the available data and the results obtained are interpreted as a response to the initial hypothesis.

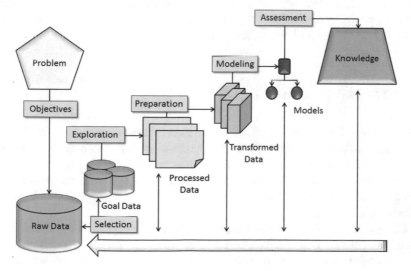

Fig. 1.1 KDD process

However, in common use, this methodology raises two problems. On the one hand, the individual who formulates the hypothesis must guess or know for certain what is the necessary information to accomplish the task. On the other hand, given the complexity of stored data and their interrelations, model verification is nowadays inadequate in many fields for decision making. The interpretation of results will thus be limited for its true quality.

Therefore, supplementing the above analysis with the possibility of discovering in an inductive manner for information and key hidden patterns in data is the main feature of Data Science. For instance, some examples are:

- *Automatic prediction of trends and behaviors.* Data Science automates the process of obtaining predictive information in big databases. Some issues that have traditionally required complex calculations can now be answered directly and quickly from the data. A typical example of a predictive problem is targeted marketing. Data Science uses data from past promotional campaigns to identify the objectives that are most likely to make future campaigns. Other examples of predictive problems include prediction of financial risk, identification of segments of the population likely to respond identically to certain events, etc.
- *Automatic discovery of previously unknown patterns.* The Data Science tools filter the data contained in large databases and identify previously hidden patterns. An example of pattern discovery is the analysis of sales data to identify apparently unrelated products that are often purchased together. Other problems of pattern discovery include detection of fraudulent transactions with credit cards and data identification anomalies that could represent input errors [7].

Data Science techniques can provide the benefits of automation on existing software or hardware platforms and can be implemented over new systems as existing platforms. When Data Science processes are implemented on high-performance parallel process systems, they can analyze very large databases in a few seconds, achieving the category of Big Data analytics.

1.3   The Data Science Process

In the initial definition of Data Science, the data refer to a set of facts or cases that confound the database. A pattern does reference to an expression in some language that serves to describe a subset of the data or a model applicable to that data. That is, a pattern is an instance of a determined model. Therefore, the extraction of patterns is understood as the extraction of a model for some data, that is, any high-level description of the data.

This process implies that Data Science is a conjunction of steps, although it is not trivial, because it is assumed to require a complex analysis. The patterns must be valid, with some degree of certainty, and novel, at least for the system and, preferably, for the user, to which should report some kind of benefit.

Everything indicated above implies that some set of measures can be defined to evaluate the patterns obtained. These measures may for instance to evaluate the goodness, utility, simplicity and certainty of the patterns. The Data Science process, as discussed above, is the process to apply in some database the required operations of selection, exploration, sampling, transformation and modeling methods for extracting interesting patterns that will represent knowledge.

The KDD process is an iterative and interactive process due to the fact it includes numerous steps in which the user has to make decisions. It is iterative because it may be necessary to access from any of the above, and interactive because the process is monitored and controlled by the user in a direct way.

Even though there are different alternatives described in the literature, the process consists of the following four main stages:

- **Selection of Goals:** in this phase, the problem has to be studied and we have to decide what is the goal of the project. It is also desirable to have expectations of success or failure of the project given that these concepts are relative. For example, depending on the problem, a model capable of successfully predicting the 70% of cases can be considered as a failure in absolute accuracy, but a great success if the procedure used previously only achieved a correct prediction of the 60% of the cases. With a good approach of the problem, It is easier to discover the data sources and the most suitable DM algorithms to be applied. A bad approach to the problem can lead us to wrong results. At this stage, the costs and economic benefits of the project have to be also estimated for the sake of achieving the best solution as possible.

- **Data preprocessing:** this stage of the KDD process is the one that most effort requires [25]. This phase consists of four main steps, although there could be more interpretations:

  - *Selection of the data:* the internal or external data sources are identified and the necessary subset of data is selected, either relations of one database or text files.

  - *Preparation of the data:* once the data to be used have been identified, we must understand the meaning of the attributes to detect integration errors, such as the existence of repeated data with different names or same data with different formats. These problems arise because the data may come from different sources, and not all of them store the same information in the same way. After this preprocess, what we will have is a data set suitable for the correct functioning of the remaining phases of the Data Science process [13].

  - *Transformation of data:* once analyzed the type of problem and the type of available data, we have to choose the algorithm or set of algorithms to be applied. As each algorithm requires a different format in the input data, we must transform the data to adjust the requirements of the selected algorithm/s.

  - *Reduction of data:* these techniques can be applied to achieve a reduced representation of the data set which will be much smaller in volume and tries to keep most of the integrity of the original data [11]. The goal is to provide to the later DM algorithms with a mechanism to produce the same (or almost the same) outcome when it is applied over reduced data instead of the original data, at the same time as when mining becomes efficient.

- **Construction of the model:** it is the main stage because it is where the different data analysis algorithms are apply to the data, which were transformed, prepared and possibly reduced in the previous stages. During this stage, the patterns present in the data are searched. Depending on the algorithm selected, a different form will be obtained at the output. At this stage it is possible to use several times the same algorithm or even we can use different kinds of algorithms.
- **Analysis of the results:** it is the moment to interpret and evaluate the results obtained in the previous stage. Different techniques for visualization are often used to display the results obtained. Once the results are visualized, the user must interpret them, and if they do not meet their expectations, she must reapply the algorithms with other parameters, and even to run other algorithms to try to obtain more desirable results. All this makes the process of Data Science iterative. At this stage, we have to specify how to use the obtained results. They may be either integrated into an expert system or implemented as procedures in a database management system to make decisions.

1.3.1 Selection of the Data

At this stage, it is first necessary to assess the present problem we want to address. We will thus have to study the antecedents on how the problem has been solved by other organizations and to point out the advantages and shortcomings of the procedure that it is currently applied. Then, the objectives we want to approach with a Data Science process should be posed. Among others characteristics, we can stress quantifiable, realistic, relevant, multiple objectives clearly defined with a list of priorities.

Once the objectives have been defined, we must draw up an implementation plan specifying: the temporal duration, a budget, an analysis of monetary and opportunity costs as well as expectations of benefits, elaboration of a schedule and identification of possible external factors that are key to the organization.

It is worth to recall that this phase is key to the success of the Data Science process. Frequently, researchers and inexperienced analysts tend to think that the data are the origin of a Data Science process. This error usually ends with unproductive results and therefore a waste of time and resources. A thorough knowledge of the problem and the formulation of objectives are therefore vital in any Data Science task.

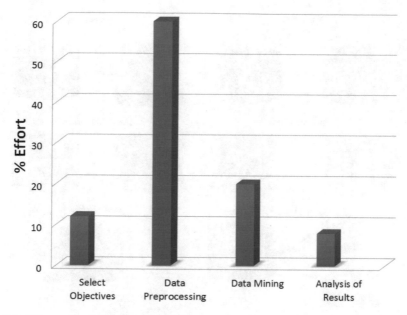

Fig. 1.2 Effort required for each stage in KDD

1.3.2 Data Preprocessing

Often, in organizations involved in Data Science projects, there is an excessive rush in the application of powerful analytical techniques for the extraction of hidden knowledge in the data. To use such techniques and tools, as explained above, it is necessary to develop one of the key parts of the project and of the longest time, which is the phase of Preprocessing prior to the application of the analysis algorithms [13]. Figure 1.2 shows the effort required at each stage of the KDD.

1.3.2.1 Why Is Preprocessing Required?

Inconsistencies, null values, extreme values and noise are properties of all data sets and relations in data bases. Incomplete data are generated for different reasons, for example, the attributes of interest are not always available or the information you have is erroneous. Other data are not stored because at the time of entering the data they were thought to be of no interest. Noise is again available for different reasons such as a simple problem in data collection instruments and personnel, other times it is due to transmission mechanisms or simple inconsistencies in code naming and assignment policies. In this way, data cleansing routines (Fig. 1.2) will help fill in the null values, identifying outliers and solving inconsistencies. Uncleaned data creates confusion for the scanning procedures and although some algorithms include

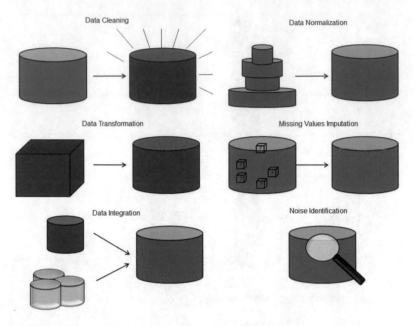

Fig. 1.3 Forms of data preprocessing

routines for cleaning these mechanisms are often not robust, so it is preferable to clean them beforehand.

However, returning to the problem that we wanted to solve, it is important to remember that we can have data from different sources, branches or organizations and that in each one of them possibly have data in more than one database. As a consequence we will need to integrate the data from multiple databases before proceeding with the analysis (Fig. 1.3), otherwise we will encounter redundancies and inconsistencies due to integration.

Finally, once we have the data ready for the analysis, we will find that we have the algorithm that we were going to apply requires categorical input of data and that our variables are given as numerical, which will lead us to transform the data before proceeding (Fig. 1.3).

1.3.3   Stages of the Data Preprocessing Phase

Each of these subphases is explained in detail below, analyzing the techniques that are applied to correct the defects that the data can present.

1.3.3.1 Selection of Data

The target of the selection stage is the identification of the available data sources and the extraction of the necessary data for a preliminary analysis, thus at the end of the phase you have the data that will be prepared to be submitted to Data Science techniques. It is obvious that the selection of the data depends on the type of problem to be solved and the goal pursued. Assuming that the data are gathered, the first task is to check the quantity and quality of the data. A good amount of data is needed to build robust models. But having large amounts of data is not enough, you will have to study each field, data types, maximum and minimum values in order to have large amounts of data with the highest quality.

Since the set of data to be selected will consist of a series of samples that will be described by means of a series of variables, it will be necessary to analyze the metadata (data about the data) associated with each variable to understand what each one means. Metadata not only provides a definition of the data or variable from the perspective of the business, but must provide information about data types, potential values, original source, format and other characteristics that have to do with the definition of the variable.

All this information is very important to take into account as it will be fundamental in later stages. Note that the type of algorithm to be applied will not only depend on the type of problem to solve but will depend on the type of variables used to describe the data. These types are usually divided into:

- Quantitative. They are subdivided into:

  - Discrete (number of persons, number of vehicles ...).
  - Continues (salary, length, benefits ...).

- Qualitative. You can distinguish:

  - Nominal. Name the object to which they refer without being able to establish an order (civil status, gender, colour, race, ...)
  - Ordinal. An order can be established in its values (high, medium, low).

In this way it is usual to speak of qualitative variables and quantitative variables or of categorical and continuous variables. The nominal variables are at the most qualitative end, while the continuous variables stand out on the more quantitative side. Note that certain variables such as scales or rankings can be treated as discrete or ordinal variables depending on the case and therefore their definition may be less clear. When selecting the data, another important consideration is the life time of the variable, that is, to establish the period of time from which the variable will have lost its semantics or will no longer be significant.

1.3.3.2 Exploration of Data

The purpose of this subphase is to ensure the quality of the data that has been selected. As discussed above, the fact that data is clean and free from inconsistencies is a prerequisite for a successful Data Science project. On the other hand, the more and better the data is known, the easier it will be to know where to look in the modeling phase. The first task that must be done is a supervision of the structure of the data to be able to provide a first measure of the quality of the same.

In order to carry out this task, the visualization tools and statistical methods are usually employed. For categorical variables, the estimation of the frequency distributions of the values is the best way to understand the content. Simple tools like histograms or pie charts can help you visualize the distribution of each variable identifying null values and values out of range. When dealing with quantitative variables, it will be necessary to analyze measures such as the minimum and maximum values, the mean, the variance, the mode (value that occurs more frequently), the median (mean value), among others. Combining all these estimated, it will be possible to establish if a variable should be analyzed before continuing. Other useful tools are box-plots, histograms, or QQ-plot charts to study the distribution of variables and to show the distribution of one variable agains another different variable to analyze their relationship.

Once the data have been analyzed with the available tools, two of the tasks that are most frequently performed for each variable are the elimination of noise values, the processing of MVs and the detection of inconsistencies.

- *Noise Data:* noise is a random error or variance in a variable. Consequently, the variables affected by the noise will have values that fall outside the expected values for those variables. If these extreme values that are out of range are called outliers. Outliers can represent an opportunity to continue searching or simply be incorrect data. There are different types of and each one should be treated differently. Thus, for example, an outlier possibility is due to human errors in data collection. In this way an individual can appear with age over 1,000 years or with the negative salary. This error must be corrected. Another type of outliers is the one that is generated because certain operational changes have not been reflected in the Data Science environment. Clearly in this case the only action that has to be carried out is to update the metadata. Nevertheless, most of the noise involves little changes in data and advanced techniques must be applied in order to identify, remove or fix it [27].
- *Missing Values:* In most of the Data Science projects, when we face data analysis we find that many of the tuples (samples) have no value for certain attributes. Hence, two questions arise: what to do with that tuple? and, how can we fill in those values that we do not have? For this there are techniques ranging from ignoring the existence of these MVs, manually fill the data or use simple statistics such as average or correlations to obtain new values. The most advanced techniques and possibly the best approaches are the MV imputation based on predictive DM techniques. However, it should be remembered that no technique is perfect and that one has to be careful to avoid introducing more noise when eliminating MVs [21].

1.3.3.3   Transformation of Data

It represents a crucial phase because the success and accuracy of the models that will be obtained in the DM phase depends on how the data analyst decides to structure and present the input to the next phase. On the other hand, in this phase is when the data have to be codified to be a suitable input for the DM algorithms that will be used. In this way, if the algorithm to be used requires numerical input and the data selected are categorical or vice versa, it will be at this stage when the data is transformed so that they acquire the appropriate format. In addition, it is very common for new variables to be derived at this stage.

1.4   Standard Data Science Problems

The modeling phase is the central stage of the discovery process in which knowledge extraction algorithms are applied to previously preprocessed data. Actually, this step is inseparable from the next step in the chain of results analysis. In fact, often the analysis of the results obtained causes that it goes back again to the preprocessing phase in order to obtain more data or more attributes. In order for the process to be correct, it is essential that the analyst has the pre-processed data set, the corresponding metadata and all the data information that has been previously extracted in the previous steps of the analysis. What will happen in this stage will depend on the type of goal to be achieved. That is, it is not the same if the final result is a characterization of data or if the goal pursued is a predictive model where possibly the process will be longer and more complicated. The analysis of the results is one of the most important steps of the process.

For those who are first approaching a Data Science process, the number of existing algorithms to solve the same type of problem can lead to many confusions. Although it is difficult to establish a classification of the possible complications we can find in Data Science, it is even more difficult to find a procedure that establishes the algorithm suitable for each type of problem. In spite of all this, we will try to establish a guide that will help us to find the best types of algorithms to apply depending on the problem to be solved (goal) and the type of data that we are dealing with in each moment.

A first and general categorization of the problems will lead us to distinguish between descriptive problems (unsupervised learning) and predictive problems (supervised learning). Nevertheless, there are more complex problems assumed to be hybridizations, derivations or restricted formulations of the two mentioned basic problems. More details about them can be found in Sect. 1.6 of this chapter.

1.4.1   Descriptive Problems

In this context, we understand as a descriptive problem that whose goal is simply to find a description of the study data. These types of problems belong to the example of knowing the clients of an organization (characteristics of the customers), or finding the products that are often bought together, or the symptoms of diseases presented together. The goal of all these problems is a description of the source data set. Nevertheless, analyzing these examples more in detail we observe that although both try to discover characteristics of the set origin, in the first case, (description of the clients) what is intended is to organize the clients into groups more or less homogeneous and extract the characteristics of these objects. However, in the second type of queries (products that are bought together or symptoms of diseases presented together), although the problem remains descriptive, the type of description required is different, since what is sought is to find associations between the values of attributes or properties of these objects. This causes a more detailed division of the descriptive problem into:

- *Clustering Analysis:* It refers to problems where the goal is to find homogeneous groups in the source population. These problems are also called profile segmentation. The typical example of segmentation is to segment customers.
- *Association Analysis:* It refers to the problems in which it is sought to obtain relationships between the attribute values of a database. The most typical example is to analyze the shopping cart.

1.4.2 Predictive Problems

On the other hand, there are problems of Data Science whose goal is to obtain a model that in the future can be applied to predict behaviors. These types of problems are called predictive or, in Artificial Intelligence environments, they are called supervised learning problems because the analyst provides the system with the desired response. However, once again we can analyze these problems with more attention to observe that the variable to be predicted can be a categorical variable (whether or not to buy a product). However, in the case of loans, the variable to be predicted is the probability of delay in payment, which is a numerical variable.

This distinction in the type of variables that the model predicts leads us to distinguish the predictive problems in:

- *Classification Problems:* They refer to the problems in which the variable to be predicted has a finite number of values, i.e. the variable is categorical. An example of such problems would be to find a model that, in the light of a history of customers classified as "good", "regular" and "bad", establishes what type of customer is a new one.
- *Regression Problems:* They refer to the problems in which the variable to be predicted is numerical. As an example, we could have the case of finding a model that establishes the likelihood that a client who is asking for a loan will repay it or not, or the probability that some symptoms are described or may or may not present a disease.

1.5 Classical Data Mining Techniques

The techniques are specific implementations of the algorithms that are used to carry out the operations of construction of the model. Not all algorithms designed to solve a given DM problem are the same and each one will have a certain number of advantages and disadvantages.

The convenience of applying a particular algorithm depends not only on the type of problem we are facing but also to a great extent on the type of data being processed. In this sense, it is convenient to analyze the different approaches and algorithms that exist in the literature, because in real life we find that the publicly available tools offer a whole range of possible algorithms and the end user is who has to decide which one to use. So unless you have a knowledge of these algorithms and an experience in their use, it will be very difficult to find the best solution to a given problem.

The following is a brief list of the DM techniques that can be applied to solve the described Data Science problems.

- **Predictive Models. Classification:** The classical supervised learning is used in these models. Decision trees [26], rule induction [11], instance-based learning [4], logistic regressions [30], SVMs [28] and ANNs [5] are often used. These models use a set of training data to create the model, which is then used to classify unknown individuals.
- **Predictive Models. Regression:** For the prediction of numerical values, linear regression and non-linear regression are used, along with regression versions of the previous methods seen in classification.
- **Standard Clustering:** Here, each data example is compared to all clusters by using a certain distance measure among them with the clusters already created. Then each input data example is assigned to the corresponding cluster. The number of clusters can be either automatically adjusted or not. The K-means algorithm is the best representative technique belonging to this family [3].
- **Hiercharchical Clustering:** This type of DM technique is appropriate when we do not know or have any information about the groups in which the clusters are classified. Hierarchical algorithms such as agglomerative or divisive are often used. ANNs based on non-supervised learning, such as the Kohonen maps, are also used.
- **Analysis of relationships. Associations:** The objective of this technique of DM is to find elements that imply the presence of other elements within the same transaction. The result of this technique are rules of the type "if X then Y". In the rules, X is called the antecedent of the rule and Y is called the consequent. One of the most commonly used association algorithms is Apriori [1]. It is based on counting the occurrences of all possible combinations of elements. What it does is to count the occurrences of all the elements present in the transactions of the database and to create a vector where each of its elements carries an account of an element of the database. Those cells of the vector whose value is below the support level (threshold) are ignored.

- **Analysis of relationships. Sequential patterns:** It tries to discover patterns between transactions in which one set of elements is followed by another set of elements spaced apart for a given period of time [23].
- **Time Series Forecasting:** This technique is intended to discover occurrences or sequences similar to those data that stores information that represents a time series, such as the evolution of market prices or telemetry data from a sensor.

1.6   Non-standard Data Science Problems

Some Data Science problems clearly differ from the standard ones and even some can not even be categorized into one of two possibilities of descriptive or predictive problems. As a result, this section will provide a brief description of other important non-standard problems that are well known and pose a challenge in the Data Science community.

We establish a dichotomous division based on the nature of the Data Science problem. When the problem involves a clear extension on the acquisition or distribution of data, restrictions imposed on the models or the implication of more complex procedures to obtain the adequate knowledge, we refer to a derivative or more restrictive problem. On the other hand, when the problem can only be understood as a mixture of descriptive and predictive problems, we refer to the hybrid paradigm. Note that we only mention some learning paradigms of the universe of possibilities and their interpretations, assuming that this section only intends to introduce the theme.

1.6.1   Derivative Problems

This type of problems are those based on a extension or restriction of the original Data Science problem.

1.6.1.1   Imbalanced Learning

It is an extended supervised learning paradigm, a classification problem where the data has exceptional distribution on the target attribute [8, 16, 20]. This issue occurs when the number of examples representing the class of interest is much lower than that of the other classes. Its presence in many real-world applications has brought along a growth of attention from researchers. This book is thought to give all the insights on this topic and here is not the right moment to give more details. Maybe, the impatient readers could jump to the rest of chapters to get into this exciting field.

1.6.1.2 Multi-instance Learning

This problem assumes an extension based on constraints imposed on models in which each instance is a bag of instances rather than an instance alone [19]. The assignment of labels is done at the stock exchange and at the individual level. There are two main ways to solve this problem, whether converting multiple instances to single instances by data transformations or by updating single-case algorithms.

1.6.1.3 Multi-label Classification

It is a generalization of the traditional classification, in which each processed instance is associated not to a single class, but to a subset of classes at the same time [18]. In the last years have appeared different techniques that, through the transformation of the data or the adaptation of classic algorithms, try to give a solution to this problem.

1.6.1.4 Data Stream Learning

In some circumstances, not all data is available at a particular time, so it is necessary to develop learning algorithms that treat the input as a continuous data stream [12]. The basis of this problem is to assume that each instance can be inspected only once and then must be discarded to make room for incoming instances. This problem is an extension in the way of processing the data in on-line mode and is oriented for both descriptive and predictive problems.

1.6.2 Hybrid Problems

1.6.2.1 Semi-supervised Learning

This approach emerges as a hybrid between the task of predictive classification and descriptive analysis based on clustering [31]. Here, the model design is performed considering both labeled and unlabeled data. Mainly, developments in this field use unlabeled samples to alter or re-change the formulation obtained from the labeled samples. Both the semi-supervised classification and the semi-supervised clustering emerged from the traditional perspectives including unlabeled or supervised examples, respectively.

1.6.2.2 Subgroup Discovery

It is formed as the result of another hybridization between predictive and descriptive tasks, namely between classification and association of patterns [17]. A method of subgroup discovery aims to extract interesting rules focused on the examples that belong to a particular class. Other terms denoting this problem are Contrast Set Mining and Emergent Pattern Mining.

1.6.2.3   Ordinal Classification/Regression

In this context, labels present an ordering relation according to the variable meaning [14]. For example, financial trading could be assisted by ordinal classification techniques predicting the amount of investment according yo several categories such as "no investment", "low investment", "medium investment" and "huge investment". Here, to make a wrong prediction of a no investment label with huge investment must be associated a higher cost than with little investment. Thus, the sense of ordinal classification is to accomplish this kind of problems by exploiting the ordinal relations among the label values and forcing this constraint in the modeling.

1.6.2.4   Transfer Learning

It aims to extract the knowledge from one or more origin sources and to apply the knowledge obtained to a different destination task [24]. Traditional learning algorithms assume that training data and test data are extracted from the same source and they more or less maintain the same distribution and feature space. But if this distribution changes, these methods need to rebuild or adapt the model in order to work well. The so-called data set shift problem [6] is closely related to transfer learning.

References

1. Adamo, J.M.: Data Mining for Association Rules and Sequential Patterns: Sequential and Parallel Algorithms. Springer, New York (2001)
2. Aggarwal, C.C.: Data Mining: The Textbook. Springer Inc., Cham (2015)
3. Aggarwal, C., Reddy, C.: Data Clustering: Recent Advances and Applications. Chapman and Hall/CRC Data Mining and Knowledge Discovery Series. Taylor & Francis Group, London (2013)
4. Aha, D.W., Kibler, D., Albert, M.K.: Instance-based learning algorithms. Mach. Learn. **6**(1), 37–66 (1991)
5. Bishop, C.M.: Neural Networks for Pattern Recognition. Oxford University Press, Inc., New York (1995)
6. Candela, J.Q., Sugiyama, M., Schwaighofer, A., Lawrence, N.D.: Dataset Shift in Machine Learning. The MIT Press, Cambridge (2009)
7. Chandola, V., Banerjee, A., Kumar, V.: Anomaly detection: a survey. ACM Comput. Surv. **41**(3), 15:1–15:58 (2009)
8. Chawla, N.V.: Data mining for imbalanced datasets: an overview. In: Maimon, O.Z., Rokach, L. (eds.) Data Mining and Knowledge Discovery Handbook, pp. 853–867. Springer, New York (2005)

9. Fayyad, U.M., Piatetsky-Shapiro, G., Smyth, P.: Advances in Knowledge Discovery and Data Mining. From Data Mining to Knowledge Discovery: An Overview, pp. 1–34. American Association for Artificial Intelligence, Menlo Park (1996)

10. Friedman, J.H.: Data mining and statistics: What's the connection? In: Proceedings of the 29th Symposium on the Interface Between Computer Science and Statistics (1997)

11. Frunkranz, J., Gamberger, D., Lavrac, N.: Foundations of Rule Learning. Springer Inc., London (2012)

12. Gama, J.: Knowledge Discovery from Data Streams, 1st edn. Chapman & Hall/CRC, Boca Raton (2010)

13. García, S., Luengo, J., Herrera, F.: Data Preprocessing in Data Mining. Intelligent Systems Reference Library, vol. 72. Springer, Germany (2015)

14. Gutiérrez, P.A., Pérez-Ortiz, M., Sánchez-Monedero, J., Fernández-Navarro, F., Hervás-Martínez, C.: Ordinal regression methods: survey and experimental study. IEEE Trans. Knowl. Data Eng. **28**(1), 127–146 (2016)

15. Han, J.: Data Mining: Concepts and Techniques. Morgan Kaufmann Publishers Inc., San Francisco (2011)

16. He, H., Garcia, E.A.: Learning from imbalanced data. IEEE Trans. Knowl. Data Eng. **21**(9), 1263–1284 (2009)

17. Herrera, F., Carmona, C.J., González, P., del Jesus, M.J.: An overview on subgroup discovery: foundations and applications. Knowl. Inf. Syst. **29**(3), 495–525 (2011)

18. Herrera, F., Charte, F., Rivera, A.J., del Jesús, M.J.: Multilabel Classification – Problem Analysis, Metrics and Techniques. Springer, Switzerland (2016)

19. Herrera, F., Ventura, S., Bello, R., Cornelis, C., Zafra, A., Tarragó, D.S., Vluymans, S.: Multiple Instance Learning – Foundations and Algorithms. Springer, Cham (2016)

20. López, V., Fernández, A., García, S., Palade, V., Herrera, F.: An insight into classification with imbalanced data: empirical results and current trends on using data intrinsic characteristics. Inf. Sci. **250**, 113–141 (2013)

21. Luengo, J., García, S., Herrera, F.: On the choice of the best imputation methods for missing values considering three groups of classification methods. Knowl. Inf. Syst. **32**(1), 77–108 (2012)

22. Nisbet, R., Elder, J., Miner, G.: Handbook of Statistical Analysis and Data Mining Applications. Academic, Amsterdam (2009)

23. Ong, K.: Frequent Pattern Mining. VDM Publishing, Saarbrücken (2010)

24. Pan, S.J., Yang, Q.: A survey on transfer learning. IEEE Trans. Knowl. Data Eng. **22**(10), 1345–1359 (2010)

25. Pyle, D.: Data Preparation for Data Mining. Morgan Kaufmann Publishers Inc., San Francisco (1999)

26. Rokach, L.: Data Mining with Decision Trees: Theory and Applications. Series in Machine Perception and Artificial Intelligence. World Scientific, Singapore (2007)

27. Sáez, J.A., Luengo, J., Herrera, F.: Predicting noise filtering efficacy with data complexity measures for nearest neighbor classification. Pattern Recogn. **46**(1), 355–364 (2013)

28. Schölkopf, B., Smola, A.J.: Learning with Kernels: Support Vector Machines, Regularization, Optimization, and Beyond. Adaptive Computation and Machine Learning. MIT Press, Cambridge (2002)

29. Steele, B., Chandler, J., Reddy, S.: Algorithms for Data Science, 1st edn. Springer. Berlin/Heidelberg (2017)

30. Vapnik, V.: Statistical Learning Theory. Wiley, New York (1998)

31. Zhu, X., Goldberg, A.B., Brachman, R., Dietterich, T.: Introduction to Semi-supervised Learning. Morgan and Claypool Publishers, San Rafael (2009)

Chapter 2
Foundations on Imbalanced Classification

Abstract Class imbalance is present in many real-world classification datasets and consists in a disproportion of the number of examples of the different classes in the problem. This issue is known to hinder the performance of classifiers due to their accuracy oriented design, which usually makes the minority class to be overlooked. In this chapter the foundations on the class imbalance problem are introduced. Section 2.1 gives a formal description to imbalanced classification and shows why specific methods are required to deal with this problem. Section 2.2 is devoted to an overview of different application domains where imbalanced classification is present. Finally, Sect. 2.3 presents several case studies on imbalanced classification, including several test beds where algorithms designed to address imbalanced classification problems can be compared. Some of these case studies will be considered in the remaining of this Book in order to analyze the behavior of the different methods discussed.

2.1 Formal Description

Any dataset with an unequal class distribution is technically imbalanced. However, a dataset is said to be imbalanced when there is a significant, or in some cases extreme, disproportion among the number of examples of each class of the problem. In other words, the class imbalance occurs when the number of examples representing one class is much lower than the ones of the other classes. Hence, one or more classes may be underrepresented in the dataset. Such a simple definition has brought along a lot of attention from researchers and practitioners due to the number of real-world applications where the raw data gathered fulfill this definition. For instance, applications that are known to suffer from this problem are, fault diagnosis [84, 88], anomaly detection [37, 74], medical diagnosis [54], e-mail foldering [10], face recognition [49] or detection of oil spills [42], among others.

Most of the imbalanced classification literature has been devoted to binary classification problems, where one class significantly outnumbers the other (which is therefore underrepresented). Nevertheless, there are also multi-class problems with skewed-class distributions [25, 79]. Chapter 8 addresses the imbalanced multi-

© Springer Nature Switzerland AG 2018
A. Fernández et al., *Learning from Imbalanced Data Sets*,
https://doi.org/10.1007/978-3-319-98074-4_2

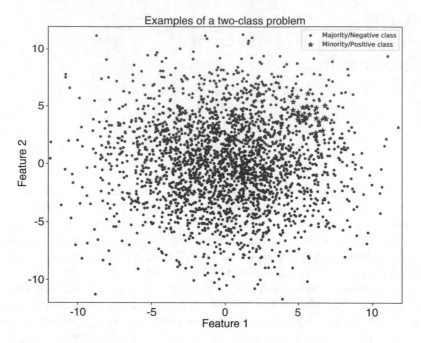

Fig. 2.1 Example of a two-class imbalanced problem with ratio 1:100

class classification problems even though many of the concepts introduced in the subsequent chapters focused on binary classification are also valid for multi-class problems.

In two-class problems the minority (underrepresented) class is usually referred to as the positive class, whereas the majority class is considered to be the negative one. These terms are used interchangeably in the literature.

In the following, we will illustrate the problem of imbalanced classification with a simple synthetic dataset, which is shown in Fig. 2.1. This is a two-class problem with ratio 1:100, that is, for each positive/minority class example there are 100 negative/majority class examples. Positive examples are presented with a blue star '*', whereas negative ones are represented by a red dot '.'. One can clearly observe that the positive class is underrepresented and that one has serious difficulties to define a decision boundary to separate both classes.

Different from the 1:100 notation, another common way of referring to the degree of imbalance of a two-class problems is the Imbalance Ratio (IR) [57]. The IR is defined as the number of negative class examples divided by the number of positive class examples, and can be used to sort different datasets depending on their IR. Hence, in the case of our example the IR is 100. Anyway, as we will explain later, one must take into account that the IR does not always give a good estimation of the difficulty of the dataset.

One of the main issues in imbalanced problems is that usually, the underrepresented class is the class of interest of the problem from the application point of view [12]. For example, following Fig. 2.1, one could think that we are dealing with a medical application where we should differentiate between benign and malign tumours of a specific type of cancer using two different features that have been measured after a biopsy. In this case, it is much more important to correctly identify malign tumours than benign ones, since the consequences of undetected malign tumours can be fatal, whereas a false positive when the tumour is benign would not be as harmful. Obviously, one would want a 100% of accuracy for both classes. However, the truth is that classifiers are usually far from being perfect and they tend to have a great accuracy for the majority class while obtaining poor results (closer to 0%) for the minority class.

Standard classifier learning algorithms are usually biased toward the majority class, since rules correctly predicting those instances are positively weighted in favour of the accuracy metric or the corresponding cost function. Otherwise, specific rules predicting examples from the minority class can be ignored (treating them as noise), because more general rules are preferred. As a consequence, minority class instances are more often misclassified than those from the majority one. In order to illustrate this problem, Fig. 2.2 presents the decision boundaries obtained by two models for the problem in Fig. 2.1. Notice that we have generated a test set for the problem with the same data distribution and IR in order to properly estimate the accuracy of each model. On the left side, Model 1 has learned that it should label every example as negative, that is, it is a trivial model. In fact, such a simple model achieves a 99.01% of accuracy (percentage of correctly classified examples) in test data, but obtains a poor 0% of accuracy in the positive class examples. That is, all the examples from the negative class are correctly classified while no example from the positive one is correctly classified. On the right side, Model 2 is different, it has learned that part of the feature space belongs to the positive class (as it can be observed attending at the decision boundary), which seems to be much more desirable given that the positive class is our class of interest. However, looking at

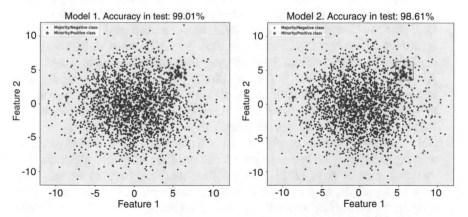

Fig. 2.2 Example of two models learned from the data in Fig. 2.1. Test data is obtained from the same distribution and with the same IR. The decision boundaries of each model are depicted

its performance, the accuracy obtained over the test set is 98.61%, lower than that obtained by Model 1. Despite being less accurate in terms of global accuracy, this second model is able to distinguish both classes, which Model 1 was not able to do.

Two lessons can be learned from this example.

1. Accuracy is no longer a proper measure in the imbalance scenario, since it does not distinguish between the numbers of correctly classified examples of different classes. Hence, it may lead to erroneous conclusions, i.e., a classifier achieving an accuracy of 90% in a data-set with an IR value of 9, is not accurate if it classifies all examples as negatives. Therefore, more informative measures in this context are required in order to assess the quality of the models, for instance, ROC, geometric mean, f-measure, precision or recall. How to measure the quality of the models in this framework is discussed in Chap. 3.
2. We need to somehow construct classifiers that are biased toward the minority class, without being harmful to the accuracy over the majority class. Hence, this book will show how this can be achieved in order to find meaningful models for imbalanced data; for example, as the Model 2 obtained in our toy example.

A large amount of techniques have been developed in order to achieve the objective of correctly distinguishing the minority class. These techniques can be categorized into four main groups, depending on how they deal with the problem.

1. *Algorithm level* approaches (also called *internal*), try to adapt existing classifier learning algorithms to bias the learning toward the minority class [7, 47, 50]. In order to perform the adaptation a special knowledge of both the corresponding classifier and the application domain is required so as to comprehend why the classifier fails when the class distribution is uneven. More details about these types of methods are given in Chap. 6.
2. *Data level* (or *external*) approaches aim at rebalancing the class distribution by resampling the data space [9, 24, 56, 70]. This way, the modification of the learning algorithm is avoided since the effect caused by imbalance is decreased with a preprocessing step. These methods are discussed in depth in Chap. 5.
3. *Cost-sensitive learning* framework falls between data and algorithm level approaches. Both data level transformations (by adding costs to instances) and algorithm level modifications (by modifying the learning process to accept costs) [13, 48, 86] are incorporated. The classifier is biased toward the minority class by assuming higher misclassification costs for this class and seeking to minimize the total cost errors of both classes. An overview of cost-sensitive approaches for the class imbalance problem is presented Chap. 4.
4. *Ensemble-based* methods usually consist of a combination between an ensemble learning algorithm [59] and one of the techniques above, specifically, data level and cost-sensitive ones [27]. Adding a data level approach to the ensemble learning algorithm, the new hybrid method usually preprocesses the data before training each classifier, whereas cost-sensitive ensembles instead of modifying the base classifier in order to accept costs in the learning process, guide the cost minimization via the ensemble learning algorithm. Ensemble-based models are thoroughly described in Chap. 7.

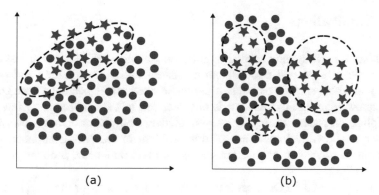

Fig. 2.3 Example of difficulties in imbalanced data-sets. (**a**) Class overlapping. (**b**) Small disjuncts

We have presented several ways in which the class imbalance problem can be addressed. However, we must stress that skewed data distribution does not hinder the learning task by itself [34, 71]. Hence, as mentioned earlier the IR is not truly useful to understand the difficulty of an imbalanced problem. The real issue is that usually a series of difficulties related with this problem turn up.

- *Small sample size*: generally imbalanced datasets have a lack of minority class examples. In [36], the authors reported that the error rate caused by imbalanced class distribution decreases when the number of examples of the minority class is representative (fixing the ratio of imbalance). This way, despite the uneven class distribution, the patterns defined by the positive class examples can be better learned. However, this fact is usually unresolvable when dealing with real-world problems.
- *Overlapping* or *class separability* (Fig. 2.3a): refers to the fact that examples from both classes are, at some degree, mixed in the feature space, that is, the decision boundary cannot be clearly established. When overlapping is present in the dataset the induction of discriminative rules becomes harder. As a result, more general rules are extracted, which misclassify a low number of instances (minority class instances) [29]. One should take into account that in case of no overlapping between classes, the class distribution of the instances becomes less important, since any simple classifier learning algorithm would be capable of solving the classification problem independently of the IR.
- *Small disjuncts* (Fig. 2.3b): this problem occurs when the concept represented by the minority class is formed of subconcepts [81]. In most of the problems, small disjuncts are implicit and their existence usually increases the complexity of the problem because the amount of instances among them is not usually balanced.

In this chapter we have briefly introduced the problems arising in the class imbalance framework. Due to the importance of these difficulties, all these problems are discussed in depth in Chap. 9.

2.2 Applications

In this section we review several application domains where class imbalance is present. We will present the different use cases found in each area and refer to the papers where specific techniques to handle class imbalance have been applied. We acknowledge that this section is not intended to be a thorough review of all the application papers dealing with class imbalance but rather an overview of them in order to show the importance of this problem in real world application. For an exhaustive review of application where the class imbalance problem is present please see [33].

We have focused on the most recent publications except for the works of Kubat et al. [40–42]. These papers are known to be the pioneers in dealing with the class imbalance problem. They dealt with the detection of oil spills from satellite radar images. In satellite images oil spills have less reflectance and hence, they can be identified in the images. However, the problem is that there are other reasons different from oil spills that cause the reflectance to become lower. This is the case of rain, algae or wind, for example. This negative class is known as lookalike and makes the differentiation of oil spills difficult. Moreover, there were many more lookalikes (896) in their dataset than oil spills (41) reaching an IR of more than 20. The authors described a series of difficulties found in the development of their system and presented possible solutions. First, they proposed a data sampling method named as one-side selection [40], which is a modification of Tomek Links method [76]. Afterwards, kNN was applied. Second, they developed a specific algorithm (internal approach) called SHRINK where the g-mean performance measure was introduced in the learning algorithm in order to improve the performance on imbalanced problems whose classes were overlapped [41].

The rest of the applications range from 2012 to 2018, we will describe them in different sections depending on their application area. Before going through each work, Table 2.1 presents a summary of the application papers considered. They are

Table 2.1 Applications of ML and DM where the class imbalance problem is present

Year	Domain	Subcategory	Application	Data-level	Internal	Cost-sensitive	Ensemble	Reference
1997	Engineering	Satellite radar images	Detection of oil spills in satellite radar images		×			[40]
1997	Engineering	Satellite radar images	Detection of oil spills in satellite radar images	×				[41]
1998	Engineering	Satellite radar images	Detection of oil spills in satellite radar images	×	×			[42]
2012	Information technology	Software	Software defect prediction	×			×	[72]

(continued)

Table 2.1 (continued)

Year	Domain	Subcategory	Application	Data-level	Internal	Cost-sensitive	Ensemble	Reference
2013	Bioinformatics	Protein identification	MicroRNA precursor classification	×			×	[45]
2014	Medicine	Quality control	Prediction of the post-operative life expectancy in lung cancer patients			×	×	[91]
2014	Bioinformatics	Protein identification	Five datasets that represent four different bioinformatics applications. These include miRNA identification, protein localization prediction, promoter identification from DNA sequences, kinase substrate prediction from protein phosphorylation profiling.	×				[85]
2014	Information technology	Text mining	Text categorization	×			×	[82]
2014	Bioinformatics	Cell recognition	Mitotic cells recognition in Hep-2 images	×			×	[35]
2014	Medicine	Diagnosis	Lung nodule detection	×			×	[11]
2014	Information technology	Software	Software defect prediction	×		×	×	[62]
2014	Security	Video surveillance	Face re-identification	×			×	[60]
2014	Information technology	Network analysis	Botnet traffic detection	×		×	×	[30]
2014	Information technology	Network analysis	Network traffic classification				×	[80]
2015	Medicine	Diagnosis	Breast cancer classification from thermogram images			×	×	[38]
2015	Information technology	Software	Software defect prediction				×	[43]
2015	Bioinformatics	Protein identification	Contact map prediction in protein structure prediction	×			×	[78]
2015	Business management	Finance	Stock market prediction, credit card/loans approval, fraud detection		×			[64]
2015	Medicine	Diagnosis	Automatic polyp detection	×			×	[6]

(continued)

Table 2.1 (continued)

Year	Domain	Subcategory	Application	Data-level	Internal	Cost-sensitive	Ensemble	Reference
2015	Medicine	Quality control	Prediction of long stay patients in emergency department				×	[4]
2015	Bioinformatics	Protein identification	Protein data classification				×	[18]
2015	Medicine	Diagnosis	Diagnosis of diabetes mellitus	×				[14]
2016	Business management	Customer relationship management	Customer churn prediction	×				[3]
2016	Medicine	Diagnosis	Breast cancer malignancy classification				×	[39]
2016	Medicine	Diagnosis	Bleeding detection in endoscopic video	×			×	[20]
2016	Education	High school	Early dropout detection	×	×			[53]
2016	Security	Video surveillance	Face re-identification		×		×	[68]
2016	Engineering	Semiconductors	Fault detection in semiconductors	×		×	×	[44]
2016	Medicine	Diagnosis	Thyroid nodule classification	×				[1]
2016	Medicine	Diagnosis	Breast cancer classification from Magnetic Resonance Images (MRIs)				×	[52]
2016	Security	Biometric authentication	Multimodal biometric authentication				×	[77]
2017	Engineering	Energy	Short-term voltage stability assessment	×		×		[90]
2017	Business management	Customer relationship management	Customer churn prediction	×		×	×	[89]
2017	Information technology	Network analysis	Mobile malware detection	×		×		[15]
2017	Engineering	Semiconductors	Fault detection in semiconductors	×			×	[32]
2017	Medicine	Quality control	Prediction of the survival status of poly-trauma patients	×				[65]
2017	Medicine	Prognosis	Prediction of bone fractures to prevent osteoporosis	×				[5]
2017	Medicine	Diagnosis	Prediction of chronic kidney disease progression	×				[16]

(continued)

Table 2.1 (continued)

Year	Domain	Subcategory	Application	Data-level	Internal	Cost-sensitive	Ensemble	Reference
2017	Medicine	Prognosis	Donor-recipient matching prediction in liver transplantation	×				[58]
2017	Security	Video surveillance	Still-to-video face recognition			×		[8]
2017	Medicine	Diagnosis	Detection of microaneurysm				×	[61]
2018	Engineering	Rotating machinery	Fault diagnosis in wind turbines	×		×	×	[63]
2018	Information technology	Computer vision	Object recognition in images				×	[87]
2018	Engineering	Rotating machinery	Fault diagnosis in wind turbines				×	[73]
2018	Security	Video surveillance	Face re-identification				×	[69]
2018	Engineering	Rotating machinery	Fault diagnosis in wind turbines				×	[83]

sorted by year of publication. For each work, apart from the year of publication, the application domain, its main objective, the kind of technique used to deal with the class imbalance used, and the reference are presented.

2.2.1   Engineering

Apart from the work of Kubat et al. [42] aiming at detecting oil spills in satellite radar images, there are other engineering applications requiring specific approaches to handle data imbalance. Among them, defect detection in semiconductors have been addressed in [32, 44]. Fault or defect prediction in general is another typical example for the class imbalance problem, since there are usually much fewer faulty products than correctly produced ones. However, in manufacturing industry it is important to correctly detect which products are faulty in order to avoid customer dissatisfaction and returns.

In the work of Lee et al. [44], a study over two different problems of defect detection in semiconductors was developed. The first one consisted of etching process data, whereas the second one dealt with chemical vapor deposition process data. Several variations of kNN and SVMs were considered for the study. Three types of methods were tested to tackle the skewed data distribution: data-level using random undersampling, SMOTE and NCR; cost-sensitive approaches and ensemble based models such as SMOTEBoost. Additionally, one-class classification [75] was considered as an alternative to learn from positive class data.

In the case of [32], the authors addressed defect detection from images, designing a complete system to inspect semiconductors starting from their images. These images were used to extract several features using different approaches. In order to overcome class imbalance, a new modified version of SMOTE was proposed. This modification was introduced into an ensemble mechanism where classifiers were pruned and fused by the use of stacking.

Another challenging use case was published by Zhu et al. [90], where power system short-term voltage stability assessment was considered. One should take into account that these kind of prediction mechanism can help in avoiding blackouts due to the dynamic load of power usage. Obviously, the misclassification of power system instability can lead to irreversible voltage collapse or catastrophic outage, whereas mislabeling stable cases has a much lower expense. That is, a class imbalance problem must be tackled. To do so, a forecasting-based nonlinear SMOTE was proposed together with a cost-sensitive decision tree algorithm so as to bias the decision to those scarce, yet valuable unstable cases.

In [63], the authors dealt with wind turbine failure prediction. This is an important task because most of the operational costs of wind farms are due to their maintenance and the distance between farms and industrial areas. Being able to automatically monitor, diagnose and predict the state of wind turbines is the best way for reducing maintenance costs. In this work, the authors studied the problem of class imbalance in this scenario, where usually there are much more data available from normal functioning than from failures. To do so, different models for addressing class imbalance were tested (data resampling, cost-sensitive and ensembles). Their analysis focused on the influence of the imbalance ration on the prediction capabilities of the system and showed that an ensemble based on rotation forest modified with a cost-sensitive approach was the most robust approach. The same engineering problem was considered in [73], however, in this case the authors proposed a cost-sensitive large margin distribution machine to alleviate the class imbalance problem. Otherwise, an hybridization between SMOTE and EasyEnsemble was developed in [83].

2.2.2 Information Technology

We have differentiated the applications on information technology into four different subcategories: software defect prediction, network analysis, text mining and computer vision.

Software defect prediction is becoming a necessary tool for quality assurance teams in order to detect possible failures. Software size and complexity are increasing and hence, efficient methods for inspection and testing are required. In this case, the idea consists of obtaining different metrics from the source code in order to differentiate between defective and non-defective components. The NASA published several datasets in their Metric Data Program in which a number of metrics were considered as features for the classification problem. These datasets have been used in the application papers we have reviewed due to the great difference between the number of non-defective and defective modules[43, 62, 72].

In [72] the original imbalanced binary-class datasets were transformed into several balanced multi-class datasets, which were afterwards addressed by decomposition strategies [26] (three different decompositions are used, random correction code, one-vs-one and one-vs-all). Differently, Rodriguez et al. [62] studied the effect of different approaches for tackling class imbalance in software defect prediction. At data-level, random undersampling and oversampling together with SMOTE were considered. A cost-sensitive approach was also tested and the study was completed with ensemble-based models (SMOTEBoost and RUSBoost). Rather than considering a specific technique to deal with class imbalance, the authors of [43] claimed that the average probability ensemble model (in which the probability given by each base classifier is averaged) combined with a FS scheme was enough so as to be robust in such a difficult scenario.

There are also a number of use cases dealing with network data analysis. In [30], the authors dealt with the problem of differentiating P2P botnet network traffic from normal traffic. The problem was imbalance because there were more normal traffic examples than abnormal (botnet) traffic ones. They considered the use of Random Forest together with random undersampling and cost-sensitive learning (introduced into Random Forest) as a tool for overcoming class imbalance.

Network traffic classification, where the traffic over the Ethernet network should be classified into different classes was considered in [80]. This problem is clearly imbalanced because most of the network traffic is HTTP or HTTPS (web traffic), whereas there are many other types of traces corresponding to different applications. In order to improve the performance in this scenario, the authors proposed a new ensemble strategy using Adaboost and balancing the dataset in each iteration.

The authors in [15] dealt with a challenging problem falling between network analysis and information security. They designed a system for mobile malware detection from network traffic analysis. To do so, different techniques for the class imbalance were used such as SMOTE followed by a SVM, a cost-sensitive SVM and a cost-sensitive C4.5 decision tree. Moreover, a new internal solution named as Imbalanced Data Gratitation-based classification was presented.

In other respects, ForesTexter [82] was specifically developed to classify text data. In text classification it is not uncommon to find datasets with 20–40 classes and hence, the likelihood of one of them being underrepresented is high. In this method the authors proposed a modification of RandomForest algorithm to tackle imbalanced text mining problems. First, different features were sampled depending on their discrimination capabilities for the majority and minority classes, respectively. Then, instead of learning with the classical RandomForest algorithm, a SVM classifier was used for the data partitioning in each node of the tree.

Computer vision is also affected by class imbalance in many of its applications. In [87] the authors dealt with the problem of object recognition from images. The solution proposed by the authors consisted of a combination of transfer AdaBoost and a modified weighted version of SMOTE. As it is usually done in many computer vision tasks, transfer learning was considered requiring a proper adaptation of SMOTE to this context.

2.2.3 Bioinformatics

In bioinformatics and biotechnology protein research is one of the fields to which researchers have paid attention in recent years. The identification of the protein structures and functions is a very important problem in this field of research since they are directly related with the functioning of an organism. Protein classification is one of the most efficient ways to solve the problem, but protein datasets are always imbalanced and therefore specific techniques are required. However, protein identification is not the only application where imbalance is present in bioinformatics. As an example, we will also show an application of cell recognition where class imbalance is found.

The detection of micro RNA (ribonucleic acid) precursors can be looked from the classification point of view as it was done in [45]. Micro RNAs play a crucial role in very complex genetic processes related with post-transcriptional regulation of gene expression of plants and animals. In [45], after the process of creating the classification problem from the data, the resulting dataset having a skewed class distribution was preprocessed using a FS method in first place and followed by an hybrid preprocessing (SMOTE + different runs of random undersampling) in order to create several balanced datasets. Finally, three different base classifiers were trained (SVMs, RF and kNN) to form an ensemble of 12 classifiers (since 4 different undersampled datasets were created with the different runs of random undersampling).

Yang et al. [85] rather than focusing on a single bioinformatic problem, considered several imbalanced bioinformatic problems in order to test their newly developed method in imbalanced domains. More specifically, they considered four different use cases: miRNA identification, protein localization prediction, promoter identification from DNA sequences and kinase substrate prediction from protein phosphorylation profiling. All these problems were treated with the sample-subset optimization technique that was proposed by the authors. This method is an undersampling model focused on selecting the most useful instances from the majority class to intelligently undersample the dataset.

The authors of [78] dealt with a different problem known as contact map prediction, which is a part of protein structure prediction with only around 2% of positive examples. Given the number of examples in the dataset, the authors considered a MapReduce [19] based system to overcome the problem that was considered to be a big data problem. In several MapReduce phases an evolutionary feature weighting approach was performed after extremely oversampling the dataset with random oversampling. This extreme oversampling consisted of having a dataset with many more instances from the minority class than then number of instances from the majority class due to the special characteristics of the dataset. Finally, a RandomForest classifier was considered to learn the final model.

The work of Dai [18] was focused on protein data classification. Given that there are a huge number of classes, the multi-class problem was reduced to multiple binary classification problems (as many as the number of classes). Once this transformation was performed, the imbalance ratio of each new binary problem was highly increased given that one class should be distinguished from all the others (whose total number of examples becomes much larger). In order to address this problem, the authors considered the usage of inverse random undersampling, in which the majority class is severely undersampled multiple times in such a way that datasets with many more instances from the minority class are created. Afterwards, each dataset is used to learn a new fuzzy SVM used to form an ensemble.

The last bioinformatic use case reviewed consists of a cell recognition problem [35], where mitotic cells (those which are in mitosis phase, that is, when chromosomes are being separated into two nuclei) should be detected in HEp-2 images obtained after an indirect immunofluorescent assay. Such kind of analysis is interesting in order to detect connective tissue diseases. Mitotic cell recognition is an imbalanced problem because the most common state of a cell is not mitosis but interphase. For example, the dataset considered in this work had 70 mitotic cells, which contrasted with the 1457 interphase cells. The dataset was balanced using different techniques such as random undersampling, SMOTE and one-side selection; besides, specific ensemble methods were considered in their experiments.

2.2.4 Medicine

Applications dealing with medical problems are typical examples of imbalanced class distributions. There are several subcategories where these types of problems can be found such as diagnosis, prognosis, monitoring or quality control. Hereafter, we review some examples where class imbalance plays a key role in order to obtain a successful decision support system. We will start with quality control works, followed by applications on prognosis and diagnosis.

2.2.4.1 Quality Control

Quality control refers to those problems aimed at improving health care services by the usage of DM techniques. In [91], the authors developed a system aimed at predicting the post-operative life expectancy of lung cancer patients. Considering the sort period used for prediction (1 year), the number of patients surviving the assumed interval was significantly higher than the number of deceases. Moreover, the misclassification of deceases as survivals is much more harmful than making the mistake in the opposite direction. These kind of systems can help clinicians in deciding which patient should be selected for surgery and also to identify the patients with the greatest risk after surgery. This problem was addressed by the authors using a modified SVM capable of managing costs for each example, which was also introduced into a Boosting mechanism for addressing the imbalanced classification problem. Authors put a great effort on extracting interpretable rules from their model in order to obtain a white-box model.

The work of Azari et al. [4] was focused on emergency services. They developed a system for predicting how long will a patient be in the emergency department of a hospital. Patients staying long (more than 14 h) account for most of the beds and costs, while being less than 10% of the patients. Hence, it is interesting to understand who and why will stay for long in order to improve resource management in the emergency department and the hospital. It is clear that the authors dealt with an imbalanced problem for which they designed a new ensemble method where k-means clustering was combined with random or SMOTE oversampling.

A way to evaluate the quality of emergency services is by means of comparing the service outcome for poly-trauma patients with the expected outcome obtained by an intelligent system. In order to improve these types of intelligent systems, in [65] the authors developed a study of different data-level techniques to deal with the class imbalance existing in the prediction of the survival status of poly-trauma patients (where luckily, there are more patients that survive than those who die). The authors mainly focused on developing an interpretable model by means of C4.5 decision tree. However, they needed to take advantage of different external methods ranging from SMOTE to Tomek Links in order to deal with the skewed class distribution in the data.

2.2.4.2 Medical Diagnosis

Medical diagnosis is by far the application area and subcategory where more imbalanced examples can be found. As a first example, in [11] a computer-aided system for lung nodule detection in computer tomography images was developed. Pulmonary nodules are important clinical indication for early-stage lung cancer diagnosis. Fortunately, there are many more images where nodules are not present, creating an imbalanced classification problem. The authors developed a complete system where the combination of a hybrid probabilistic sampling using oversampling and undersampling with random subspace method for constructing classifier ensembles was proposed.

Similarly, in [1] the authors dealt with nodule classification, but in this case for thyroid nodules. A complete system was developed were nodules were classified into malign or benign classes. Again, this is the classical example of imbalanced classification where there are much more patients with benign nodules than those with malign ones. In order to balance the dataset before learning the different classifiers (SVMs, C4.5, kNN and MLPs) four preprocessing strategies (3 oversampling and 1 oversampling) were considered, namely, SMOTE-TL, SPIDER, SMOTE-RSB* and Safe-Level SMOTE.

The case of breast cancer detection considered in [38] is similar to the previous ones, being many more examples from the benign class than from the malign one.

Likewise, the cost associated with missing a cancer case are much higher than those for mislabelling a benign case. In this work, the authors considered medical thermography technology. In thermogram images an infrared camera is used to study the region of interest. The authors tackled the skewed class distribution by a cost-sensitive decision tree combined with a genetic algorithm that performed simultaneous FS and classifier fusion.

Rather than focusing on the detection of breast cancer, the authors of [39] focused on grading the breast cancer malignancy. This problem is unbalanced since the highest malignancy grade is the most important even if it is the one with the lowest number of cases. In order to handle the uneven class distribution, the authors made use of EUSBoost, which is an evolutionary undersampling boosting method that generates an ensemble of classifiers. Instead of using random undersampling inside the boosting process, a genetic algorithm is considered to select the most appropriate examples.

Breast cancer detection can also be performed from Magnetic Resonance Images (MRI) as it was done in [52]. A new computer-aided diagnosis system for breast cancer detection from MRI was presented in this work. After the feature extraction phase from the MRI images, the resulting imbalanced dataset was addressed with an ensemble of randomly undersampled datasets. Each one of the new datasets was used to learn a model where FS and adaboost was used together with C4.5 decision tree.

Polyp detection in endoscopic or colonoscopic images is another problem where ML can help clinicians. However, due to the diversity of polyp types, expensive inspection and the labor-intensive labeling tasks, polyp datasets tend to be imbalance, with much greater number of examples from non-polyp class than from polyp one. In the work by Bae and Yoon [6], a data sampling-based boosting framework was proposed to learn a classifier managing the skewed class distribution. The sampling scheme considered generates synthetic minority class examples (using SMOTE) and then eliminates hard to classify majority class examples (using Tomek Links). This resampling mechanism was introduced into AdaBoost algorithm in order to create an ensemble of classifiers.

Capsule endoscopies are a patient friendly alternative to traditional wired endoscopies and play a significant role in the diagnosis and management of gastrointestinal tack diseases. However, during their battery lifespan they generate thousands of images that require a lot of effort from the clinicians to be analysed. For this reason, in this work the authors aimed at developing a system capable of detecting bleeding in this kind of endoscopic videos. Since there are many images but few where bleeding is present, the problem suffers from class imbalance. The authors studied the influence of different degrees of imbalance. To simulate such scenarios, they considered the random undersampling of the majority class. Several classifications methods were tested such as SVMs, ANNs, decision trees and kNN. They also compared the robustness of those methods against an ensemble based model (RUSBoost).

Diabetes is known to be the most common endocrine disease across all population and age groups, being one of the leading causes of death in developed countries.

The authors of [15] designed a system to ease the diagnosis of this illness where class imbalance took an important role. As in other medical problems, there are more examples from people who is healthy than from those who are diabetic. Hence, a new data-sampling technique based on a back-propagation ANN was developed, whose resulting dataset was then used to learn a SVM classifier.

Also related with diabetes, the detection of microaneurysm is important in order to reduce the possibility of a patient becoming blind due to diabetic retinopathy, which is a progressive disease. In [61], the authors developed a computer-aided detection system for microaneurysm detection aiming at reducing the number of false positives present in previous works. In order to do so, the class imbalance problem was addressed by over-sampling (an adaptive SMOTE was proposed) the minority class in combination with different ensemble techniques (Boosting, Bagging, RSM) using Extreme Learning Machines as base classifiers.

In other respects, the authors of [16] addressed the problem of predicting whether a patient suffering from chronic kidney disease at stage 4 will advance to level 5 in the next six months. This problem is unbalanced because there are more patients staying in stage 4 than those progressing to stage 5. These kind of system do not only allow one to predict the state of a patient in the future but it also helps in understanding why a patient may progress from one stage to the next. In order to cope with the data skew, the authors consider the usage of random undersampling. The balanced dataset is used afterwards to learn a model with C4.5 and CART decision trees, SVMs and Adaboost.

2.2.4.3 Medical Prognosis

Regarding medical prognosis, we have classified two works in this category. The authors of [5] developed an study on over- and under-sampling techniques to deal with the class imbalance problem that was present in their data in order improve the screening of patients who may suffer from osteoporosis. In order to do so, they gathered data from almost 1000 womens and they aimed at predicting whether they had suffered any bone fracture or not. This system allows them to better select the patients who may have osteoporosis problems. Since the people who had not had bone fractures was much less than those who had it, the authors performed an study of several data-level techniques (random undersampling, edited nearest neighbor and SMOTE with different degrees of oversampling). After the preprocessing, several classifiers were learned such as C4.5 decision tree, Naïve Bayes, kNN and other ensemble models (Random Forest, Bagging and AdaBoost).

In the work by Prez-Ortiz et al. [58], a new donor-recipient allocation system for liver transplantation was presented. In order to build such a complex system, the authors developed a prediction model where the graft survival after transplantation was predicted. In this way, not only the severity of the patient waiting for the transplant was taken into account but also whether such a transplant will be successful or not. The class distribution was skewed due to the fact that they had recorded many more cases of successful transplants than those which did not ended well. Aiming at tackling this problem, a new approach based on generating data (it can be considered as a data-level approach) was presented, but in this case, the generated data was unlabeled and hence, they addressed the problem with unsupervised classification.

2.2.5 Business Management

In this category we have gathered two different use cases where the distribution of the classes becomes a problem that needs to be taken into account. On the one hand, Sanz et al. [64] dealt with several finance problems where this problem affected the accuracy and interpretability of fuzzy models. They designed a new interval-valued fuzzy rule-based classification system capable of dealing with imbalanced data without altering the rules extracted. The new system was capable of improving performance in the problems at hand such as stock market prediction, credit card/loans approval and fraud detection.

On the other hand, customer relationship management, and more specifically customer churn prediction, is another important use case where skewed class distributions are found. Customer churn prediction is imbalanced because most of the customers tend to remain in the same company. However, detecting customer churn is important in order to improve the relationships with customers and target the right customers to retain. In [3] a comparison among six data sampling techniques and four different rule induction methods for the churn prediction was carried out. Similarly, a comprehensive study with sampling, cost-sensitive and ensemble solutions for the class imbalance problem was developed in [89].

2.2.6 Security

Most of the security applications with imbalanced class distributions are found on biometric authentication and video surveillance. Face recognition was addressed in the work of Radtke et al. [60]. In video surveillance applications, face recognition is used to detect the presence of target individuals of interest in complex and changing scenarios. The problem is that usually, few reference target data is available at learning time, which produces the undesirable class imbalance problem. The authors proposed a new approach based on modifying how base classifiers are combined in an ensemble with a skew-sensitive boolean combination scheme. The new approach is also compared with the performance of two undersampling mechanisms (random undersampling and one-side selection). Their work was focused on face re-identification, which consists of matching facial regions captured in live or archived video streams against facial models of individuals enrolled to a system.

The same face recognition problem was addressed in [68]. In this case, the authors proposed a new way for computing the loss factors in Adaboost, which was applied to existing ensemble-based approaches for the class imbalance problem. The same authors developed a specifically designed Boosting approach named as Progressive Boosting [69] so as to improve the classification performance in face re-identification. This approach was based on progressively inserting uncorrelated groups of examples into the Boosting procedure, which was possible due to the type of application they were dealing with.

Likewise, a similar approach for face recognition was developed in [8], where the main difference laid on the fact that the faces used to learn the classifiers were obtained from still images and hence, a still-to-video face recognition system was designed. Therefore, the authors addressed the problem of detecting specific people in video-cameras starting from images of the target individuals. The system should learn the facial models to be detected from high-quality target face stills and then, it should be able to detect this faces when they appear in videos. As in the case of face re-identification, these kind of recognition systems are usually built as individual-specific detectors, that is, a classifier is constructed for each individual to be tracked. This is why class imbalance becomes a problem, many images and regions of interest (ROIs) can be obtained from non-target persons, whereas the number of images and ROIs from the target individual are scarce. In this work the authors tackled this problem by means of cost-sensitive SVMs, which were then combined with the Random Subspace Method to build an ensemble.

In [77], the problem of multimodal biometric authentication was considered. In this scenario, a two-class classification problem is generated from the vector of matching scores, which must be then classified into genuine user or impostor user. In order to address this problem, the authors developed a model based on Real AdaBoost and the usage of one-class classification instead of combining the ensemble model with sampling strategies as many other authors have previously done.

2.2.7 Education

Educational DM is a recent research field where DM techniques are used to improve such an important service for the society. In this field, there are also problems when the class distribution is uneven, for example, in the problem of detecting early school dropout [53]. In this work, several data gathered from the students at the start of the course was used to learn a model able to detect whether students will leave the school during the course or not. In order to build a interpretable rule-based model they proposed the usage of genetic programming where the fitness function was modified so as to manage the imbalance that was inherent to the problem (most of the student do not dropout the school). Moreover, their algorithm was compared with oversampling via SMOTE.

2.3 Case Studies on Imbalanced Classification

The ultimate goal of any DM process is to be applied to real life problems. Since testing a technique in every existing problem is infeasible, the common procedure is to evaluate the technique in a set of publicly available DM problems (or datasets). In this case, we are focused on the class imbalance problem and hence, these datasets should have this property. In this section we will introduce the most commonly used datasets for the comparison of the methods developed to address the class imbalance problem.

The most well-known repository for imbalanced datasets is the KEEL dataset repository [2], which supports the KEEL DM tool (that will be extensively used in this book). The datasets that can be found in this repository were gathered from different well-known sources such as UCI repository [46]. In order to facilitate the comparison among proposals, datasets are provided with the cross-validation partitions which helps in reducing the differences between algorithms that can be attributed to the usage of different partitioning schemes. Moreover, in this repository there is an specific section devoted to imbalanced problems. In fact, this is the one in which we are interested.

In order to obtain two-class imbalanced problems, originally multi-class datasets were modified so that the union of one or more classes became the positive class and the union of one or more of the remaining classes was labeled as the negative class. This way, datasets with different IRs were obtained: from low imbalance to highly imbalanced datasets. Table 2.2 summarizes the properties of the datasets in this repository, including the most relevant information about the data set:

- The name of the dataset, which encodes how the dataset was obtained. For example, *pima* dataset is originally a two-class imbalanced dataset and hence,

Table 2.2 Benchmark datasets in the KEEL dataset repository

Name	#Atts. (R/I/N)	#Ex.	#Min.	#Maj.	IR
Imbalance ratio between 1.5 and 9					
glass1	9 (9/0/0)	214	76	138	1.82
ecoli-0_vs_1	7 (7/0/0)	220	77	143	1.86
wisconsin	9 (0/9/0)	683	239	444	1.86
pima	8 (8/0/0)	768	268	500	1.87
iris0	4 (4/0/0)	150	50	100	2
glass0	9 (9/0/0)	214	70	144	2.06
yeast1	8 (8/0/0)	1484	429	1055	2.46
haberman	3 (0/3/0)	306	81	225	2.78
vehicle2	18 (0/18/0)	846	218	628	2.88
vehicle1	18 (0/18/0)	846	217	629	2.9
vehicle3	18 (0/18/0)	846	212	634	2.99
glass-0-1-2-3_vs_4-5-6	9 (9/0/0)	214	51	163	3.2
vehicle0	18 (0/18/0)	846	199	647	3.25
ecoli1	7 (7/0/0)	336	77	259	3.36
new-thyroid1	5 (4/1/0)	215	35	180	5.14
new-thyroid2	5 (4/1/0)	215	35	180	5.14
ecoli2	7 (7/0/0)	336	52	284	5.46

(continued)

Table 2.2 (continued)

Name	#Atts. (R/I/N)	#Ex.	#Min.	#Maj.	IR
segment0	19 (19/0/0)	2308	329	1979	6.02
glass6	9 (9/0/0)	214	29	185	6.38
yeast3	8 (8/0/0)	1484	163	1321	8.1
ecoli3	7 (7/0/0)	336	35	301	8.6
page-blocks0	10 (4/6/0)	5472	559	4913	8.79
Imbalance ratio higher than 9 – Part I					
yeast-2_vs_4	8 (8/0/0)	514	51	463	9.08
yeast-0-5-6-7-9_vs_4	8 (8/0/0)	528	51	477	9.35
vowel0	13 (10/3/0)	988	90	898	9.98
glass-0-1-6_vs_2	9 (9/0/0)	192	17	175	10.29
glass2	9 (9/0/0)	214	17	197	11.59
shuttle-c0-vs-c4	9 (0/9/0)	1829	123	1706	13.87
yeast-1_vs_7	7 (7/0/0)	459	30	429	14.3
glass4	9 (9/0/0)	214	13	201	15.47
ecoli4	7 (7/0/0)	336	20	316	15.8
page-blocks-1-3_vs_4	10 (4/6/0)	472	28	444	15.86
abalone9-18	8 (7/0/1)	731	42	689	16.4
glass-0-1-6_vs_5	9 (9/0/0)	184	9	175	19.44
shuttle-c2-vs-c4	9 (0/9/0)	129	6	123	20.5
yeast-1-4-5-8_vs_7	8 (8/0/0)	693	30	663	22.1
glass5	9 (9/0/0)	214	9	205	22.78
yeast-2_vs_8	8 (8/0/0)	482	20	462	23.1
yeast4	8 (8/0/0)	1484	51	1433	28.1
yeast-1-2-8-9_vs_7	8 (8/0/0)	947	30	917	30.57
yeast5	8 (8/0/0)	1484	44	1440	32.73
ecoli-0-1-3-7_vs_2-6	7 (7/0/0)	281	7	274	39.14
yeast6	8 (8/0/0)	1484	35	1449	41.4
abalone19	8 (7/0/1)	4174	32	4142	129.44
Imbalance ratio higher than 9 – Part II					
ecoli-0-3-4_vs_5	7 (7/0/0)	200	20	180	9
ecoli-0-6-7_vs_3-5	7 (7/0/0)	222	22	200	9.09
ecoli-0-2-3-4_vs_5	7 (7/0/0)	202	20	182	9.1
glass-0-1-5_vs_2	9 (9/0/0)	172	17	155	9.12
yeast-0-3-5-9_vs_7-8	8 (8/0/0)	506	50	456	9.12
yeast-0-2-5-7-9_vs_3-6-8	8 (8/0/0)	1004	99	905	9.14
yeast-0-2-5-6_vs_3-7-8-9	8 (8/0/0)	1004	99	905	9.14
ecoli-0-4-6_vs_5	6 (6/0/0)	203	20	183	9.15
ecoli-0-1_vs_2-3-5	7 (7/0/0)	244	24	220	9.17
ecoli-0-2-6-7_vs_3-5	7 (7/0/0)	224	22	202	9.18
glass-0-4_vs_5	9 (9/0/0)	92	9	83	9.22
ecoli-0-3-4-6_vs_5	7 (7/0/0)	205	20	185	9.25
ecoli-0-3-4-7_vs_5-6	7 (7/0/0)	257	25	232	9.28
ecoli-0-6-7_vs_5	6 (6/0/0)	220	20	200	10

(continued)

Table 2.2   (continued)

Name	#Atts. (R/I/N)	#Ex.	#Min.	#Maj.	IR
ecoli-0-1-4-7_vs_2-3-5-6	7 (7/0/0)	336	29	307	10.59
led7digit-0-2-4-5-6-7-8-9_vs_1	7 (7/0/0)	443	37	406	10.97
glass-0-6_vs_5	9 (9/0/0)	108	9	99	11
ecoli-0-1_vs_5	6 (6/0/0)	240	20	220	11
glass-0-1-4-6_vs_2	9 (9/0/0)	205	17	188	11.06
ecoli-0-1-4-7_vs_5-6	6 (6/0/0)	332	25	307	12.28
cleveland-0_vs_4	13 (13/0/0)	177	13	164	12.62
ecoli-0-1-4-6_vs_5	6 (6/0/0)	280	20	260	13
Imbalance ratio higher than 9 – Part III					
dermatology-6	34 (0/34/0)	358	20	338	16.9
zoo-3	16 (0/0/16)	101	5	96	19.2
shuttle-6_vs_2-3	9 (0/9/0)	230	10	220	22
lymphography-normal-fibrosis	18 (0/3/15)	148	6	142	23.67
flare-F	11 (0/0/11)	1066	43	1023	23.79
car-good	6 (0/0/6)	1728	69	1659	24.04
car-vgood	6 (0/0/6)	1728	65	1663	25.58
kr-vs-k-zero-one_vs_draw	6 (0/0/6)	2901	105	2796	26.63
kr-vs-k-one_vs_fifteen	6 (0/0/6)	2244	78	2166	27.77
winequality-red-4	11 (11/0/0)	1599	53	1546	29.17
poker-9_vs_7	10 (0/10/0)	244	8	236	29.5
kddcup-guess_passwd_vs_satan	41 (26/0/15)	1642	53	1589	29.98
abalone-3_vs_11	8 (7/0/1)	502	15	487	32.47
winequality-white-9_vs_4	11 (11/0/0)	168	5	163	32.6
kr-vs-k-three_vs_eleven	6 (0/0/6)	2935	81	2854	35.23
winequality-red-8_vs_6	11 (11/0/0)	656	18	638	35.44
abalone-17_vs_7-8-9-10	8 (7/0/1)	2338	58	2280	39.31
abalone-21_vs_8	8 (7/0/1)	581	14	567	40.5
winequality-white-3_vs_7	11 (11/0/0)	900	20	880	44
winequality-red-8_vs_6-7	11 (11/0/0)	855	18	837	46.5
kddcup-land_vs_portsweep	41 (26/0/15)	1061	21	1040	49.52
abalone-19_vs_10-11-12-13	8 (7/0/1)	1622	32	1590	49.69
kr-vs-k-zero_vs_eight	6 (0/0/6)	1460	27	1433	53.07
winequality-white-3-9_vs_5	11 (11/0/0)	1482	25	1457	58.28
poker-8-9_vs_6	10 (0/10/0)	1485	25	1460	58.4
shuttle-2_vs_5	9 (0/9/0)	3316	49	3267	66.67
winequality-red-3_vs_5	11 (11/0/0)	691	10	681	68.1
abalone-20_vs_8-9-10	8 (7/0/1)	1916	26	1890	72.69
kddcup-buffer_overflow_vs_back	41 (26/0/15)	2233	30	2203	73.43
kddcup-land_vs_satan	41 (26/0/15)	1610	21	1589	75.67
kr-vs-k-zero_vs_fifteen	6 (0/0/6)	2193	27	2166	80.22
poker-8-9_vs_5	10 (0/10/0)	2075	25	2050	82
poker-8_vs_6	10 (0/10/0)	1477	17	1460	85.88
kddcup-rootkit-imap_vs_back	41 (26/0/15)	2225	22	2203	100.14

it has not suffered any transformation. However, the name *glass1* indicates that class 1 is used as the minority class whereas the union of the rest of the classes is used as majority class. Similarly, in the case of *yeast-2_vs_4* only two of the classes of the originally multi-class dataset are considered in a one-vs-one manner. The same nomenclature is used for the rest of the datasets.

- #Atts. (R/I/N) is the number of attributes/features in the problem and their type. R stands for the number of real-valued attributes, I refers to the number of integer attributes and N indicates the number of nominal attributes.
- #Ex. is the number of examples/instances in the data set.
- #Min. indicates the number of minority class examples in the dataset.
- #Maj. is the number of majority class examples in the dataset.
- IR is the ratio of imbalance in the dataset.

All datasets are publicly available on the corresponding web-page.[1]

For the sake of completeness, the complete list of available datasets is listed (Table 2.2). Notice that the table is divided into four groups. The first one corresponds to datasets with imbalance ratio between 1.5 and 9, which are considered to have a moderate degree of imbalance. The rest of the groups correspond to the datasets with imbalance ratio greater than 9, but they are separated because they have been made available at different times. In fact, the last one corresponds to the latest addition to the KEEL dataset repository and has not been extensively used in the literature yet.

We should recall that all the datasets listed in this section are binary datasets with only two classes. The KEEL dataset repository also has a section devoted to multi-class imbalanced datasets, which is introduced in the corresponding chapter, that is, Chap. 8.

Apart from the KEEL dataset repository, there is another complementary benchmark set with fewer datasets. The HDDT collection[2] contains 20 binary imbalanced datasets that were originally used in [17] to validate the proposed model. Most of these datasets are also transformations of multi-class datasets. Table 2.3 summarizes the properties of these datasets following the same scheme as in Table 2.2.

Comparing the KEEL dataset repository and the HDDT collection, the former one is the most extended in the literature for the comparison of algorithms, for instance, see [21–23, 27, 28, 51]. Anyway, HDDT collection has also been used in several works [17, 21, 22].

Apart from these datasets, there is also another repository containing several specific datasets for defect prediction in software development, an application that we have already reviewed in Sect. 2.2.2. These datasets were originally made available by the NASA Metrics Data Program. However, we do not report their complete details because there is some controversy regarding the different versions of these datasets that can be found in the literature [67] and the misuse that they

---

[1]http://www.keel.es/dataset.php
[2]https://www3.nd.edu/~dial/hddt/

Table 2.3 Benchmark datasets in the HDDT collection

Name	#Atts. (R/I/N)	#Ex.	#Min.	#Maj.	IR
boundary	175 (0/0/175)	3505	123	3382	27.5
breast-y	9 (0/0/9)	286	85	201	2.36
cam	132 (0/0/132)	18,916	942	17,974	19.08
compustat	20 (20/0/0)	13,657	520	13,137	25.26
covtype	10 (10/0/0)	38,500	2746	35,754	13.02
credit-g	20 (7/0/13)	1000	300	700	2.33
estate	12 (12/0/0)	5322	636	4686	7.37
german-numer	24 (24/0/0)	1000	300	700	2.33
heart-v	13 (5/0/8)	200	51	149	2.92
hypo	25 (7/0/18)	3163	151	3012	19.95
ism	6 (6/0/0)	11,180	260	10,920	42
letter	16 (16/0/0)	20,000	789	19,211	24.35
oil	49 (49/0/0)	937	41	896	21.85
optdigits	64 (64/0/0)	5620	554	5066	9.14
page	10 (10/0/0)	5473	560	4913	8.77
pendigits	16 (16/0/0)	10,992	1141	9851	8.63
phoneme	5 (5/0/0)	5404	1585	3819	2.41
PhosS	480 (480/0/0)	11,411	613	10,798	17.62
satimage	36 (36/0/0)	6430	625	5805	9.29
segment	19 (19/0/0)	2310	330	1980	6

have suffered [31]. That is, there is no a clear benchmark where all the algorithms are tested with exactly the same datasets. There exist different versions of the same datasets with different preprocessing, which makes it difficult to use them as a common benchmark. One should use these datasets carefully and attending at their specific properties. Anyway, since they can be of interest for the analysis or development of new methods on this area, we refer the reader to the current [55] and also the old [66] PROMISE dataset repository, where different versions of these datasets can be found.

References

1. Acharya, U.R., Chowriappa, P., Fujita, H., Bhat, S., Dua, S., Koh, J.E.W., Eugene, L.W.J., Kongmebhol, P., Ng, K.: Thyroid lesion classification in 242 patient population using gabor transform features from high resolution ultrasound images. Knowl. Based Syst. **107**, 235–245 (2016)
2. Alcalá-Fdez, J., Fernández, A., Luengo, J., Derrac, J., García, S., Sánchez, L., Herrera, F.: KEEL data–mining software tool: data set repository, integration of algorithms and experimental analysis framework. J. Multi–Valued Logic Soft Comput. **17**(2–3), 255–287 (2011)
3. Amin, A., Anwar, S., Adnan, A., Nawaz, M., Howard, N., Qadir, J., Hawalah, A., Hussain, A.: Comparing oversampling techniques to handle the class imbalance problem: a customer churn prediction case study. IEEE Access **4**, 7940–7957 (2016)

4. Azari, A., Janeja, V.P., Levin, S.: Imbalanced learning to predict long stay emergency department patients. In: IEEE International Conference on Bioinformatics and Biomedicine (BIBM), Washington, DC, pp. 807–814 (2015)
5. Bach, M., Werner, A., Żywiec, J., Pluskiewicz, W.: The study of under- and over-sampling methods utility in analysis of highly imbalanced data on osteoporosis. Inf. Sci. **384**, 174–190 (2017)
6. Bae, S.H., Yoon, K.J.: Polyp detection via imbalanced learning and discriminative feature learning. IEEE Trans. Med. Imaging **34**(11), 2379–2393 (2015)
7. Barandela, R., Sánchez, J.S., García, V., Rangel, E.: Strategies for learning in class imbalance problems. Pattern Recogn. **36**(3), 849–851 (2003)
8. Bashbaghi, S., Granger, E., Sabourin, R., Bilodeau, G.A.: Dynamic ensembles of exemplar-svms for still-to-video face recognition. Pattern Recogn. **69**, 61–81 (2017)
9. Batista, G.E.A.P.A., Prati, R.C., Monard, M.C.: A study of the behavior of several methods for balancing machine learning training data. SIGKDD Explor. Newslett. **6**, 20–29 (2004)
10. Bermejo, P., Gámez, J.A., Puerta, J.M.: Improving the performance of naive bayes multinomial in e-mail foldering by introducing distribution-based balance of datasets. Expert Syst. Appl. **38**(3), 2072–2080 (2011)
11. Cao, P., Yang, J., Li, W., Zhao, D., Zaiane, O.: Ensemble-based hybrid probabilistic sampling for imbalanced data learning in lung nodule CAD. Comput. Med. Imaging Graph. **38**(3), 137–150 (2014)
12. Chawla, N.V., Japkowicz, N., Kolcz, A. (eds.): Special issue on learning from imbalanced datasets. ACM SIGKDD Explor. Newslett. **6**(1), 1–6 (2004)
13. Chawla, N., Cieslak, D., Hall, L., Joshi, A.: Automatically countering imbalance and its empirical relationship to cost. Data Min. Knowl. Disc. **17**, 225–252 (2008)
14. Chen, L.S., Cai, S.J.: Neural-network-based resampling method for detecting diabetes mellitus. J. Med. Biol. Eng. **35**(6), 824–832 (2015)
15. Chen, Z., Yan, Q., Han, H., Wang, S., Peng, L., Wang, L., Yang, B.: Machine learning based mobile malware detection using highly imbalanced network traffic. Inf. Sci. **433–434**, 346–364 (2018)
16. Cheng, L.C., Hu, Y.H., Chiou, S.H.: Applying the temporal abstraction technique to the prediction of chronic kidney disease progression. J. Med. Syst. **41**(5), 85 (2017)
17. Cieslak, D.A., Hoens, T.R., Chawla, N.V., Kegelmeyer, W.P.: Hellinger distance decision trees are robust and skew-insensitive. Data Min. Knowl. Disc. **24**(1), 136–158 (2012)
18. Dai, H.L.: Imbalanced protein data classification using ensemble FTM-SVM. IEEE Trans. NanoBiosci. **14**(4), 350–359 (2015)
19. Dean, J., Ghemawat, S.: Mapreduce: simplified data processing on large clusters. Commun. ACM **51**(1), 107–113 (2008)
20. Deeba, F., Mohammed, S.K., Bui, F.M., Wahid, K.A.: An empirical study on the effect of imbalanced data on bleeding detection in endoscopic video. In: 38th Annual International Conference of the IEEE Engineering in Medicine and Biology Society (EMBC), Orlando, pp. 2598–2601 (2016)
21. Díez-Pastor, J.F., Rodríguez, J.J., García-Osorio, C., Kuncheva, L.I.: Random balance: ensembles of variable priors classifiers for imbalanced data. Knowl. Based Syst. **85**, 96–111 (2015)
22. Díez-Pastor, J.F., Rodríguez, J.J., García-Osorio, C.I., Kuncheva, L.I.: Diversity techniques improve the performance of the best imbalance learning ensembles. Inf. Sci. **325**, 98–117 (2015)
23. Fernández, A., García, S., del Jesus, M.J., Herrera, F.: A study of the behaviour of linguistic fuzzy rule based classification systems in the framework of imbalanced data–sets. Fuzzy Sets Syst. **159**(18), 2378–2398 (2008)
24. Fernández, A., García, S., del Jesus, M.J., Herrera, F.: A study of the behaviour of linguistic fuzzy rule based classification systems in the framework of imbalanced data-sets. Fuzzy Sets Syst. **159**(18), 2378–2398 (2008)
25. Fernández-Navarro, F., Hervás-Martínez, C., Gutiérrez, P.A.: A dynamic over-sampling procedure based on sensitivity for multi-class problems. Pattern Recogn. **44**(8), 1821–1833 (2011)

26. Galar, M., Fernández, A., Barrenechea, E., Bustince, H., Herrera, F.: An overview of ensemble methods for binary classifiers in multi-class problems: experimental study on one-vs-one and one-vs-all schemes. Pattern Recogn. **44**(8), 1761–1776 (2011)

27. Galar, M., Fernández, A., Barrenechea, E., Bustince, H., Herrera, F.: A review on ensembles for class imbalance problem: bagging, boosting and hybrid based approaches. IEEE Trans. Syst. Man Cybern. Part C Appl. Rev. **42**(4), 463–484 (2012)

28. Galar, M., Fernández, A., Barrenechea, E., Herrera, F.: Eusboost: enhancing ensembles for highly imbalanced data-sets by evolutionary undersampling. Pattern Recogn. **46**(12), 3460–3471 (2013)

29. García, V., Mollineda, R., Sánchez, J.: On the k-nn performance in a challenging scenario of imbalance and overlapping. Pattern. Anal. Appl. **11**, 269–280 (2008)

30. Garg, S., Sarje, A.K., Peddoju, S.K.: Improved detection of p2p botnets through network behavior analysis. In: Martínez Pérez, G., Thampi, S.M., Ko, R., Shu, L. (eds.) Recent Trends in Computer Networks and Distributed Systems Security: Second International Conference, SNDS 2014, Trivandrum, 13–14 Mar 2014, Proceedings, pp. 334–345. Springer, Berlin/Heidelberg (2014)

31. Gray, D., Bowes, D., Davey, N., Sun, Y., Christianson, B.: The misuse of the nasa metrics data program data sets for automated software defect prediction. In: 15th Annual Conference on Evaluation Assessment in Software Engineering (EASE 2011), Durham, pp. 96–103 (2011)

32. Haddad, B.M., Yang, S., Karam, L.J., Ye, J., Patel, N.S., Braun, M.W.: Multifeature, sparse-based approach for defects detection and classification in semiconductor units. IEEE Trans. Autom. Sci. Eng. **15**(1), 144–159 (2017)

33. Haixiang, G., Yijing, L., Shang, J., Mingyun, G., Yuanyue, H., Bing, G.: Learning from class-imbalanced data: review of methods and applications. Expert Syst. Appl. **73**, 220–239 (2017)

34. He, H., Garcia, E.A.: Learning from imbalanced data. IEEE Trans. Knowl. Data Eng. **21**(9), 1263–1284 (2009)

35. Iannello, G., Percannella, G., Soda, P., Vento, M.: Mitotic cells recognition in HEp-2 images. Pattern Recogn. Lett. **45**, 136–144 (2014)

36. Japkowicz, N., Stephen, S.: The class imbalance problem: a systematic study. Intell. Data Anal. **6**, 429–449 (2002)

37. Khreich, W., Granger, E., Miri, A., Sabourin, R.: Iterative boolean combination of classifiers in the ROC space: an application to anomaly detection with hmms. Pattern Recogn. **43**(8), 2732–2752 (2010)

38. Krawczyk, B., Schaefer, G., Woźniak, M.: A hybrid cost-sensitive ensemble for imbalanced breast thermogram classification. Artif. Intell. Med. **65**(3), 219–227 (2015)

39. Krawczyk, B., Galar, M., Jeleń, L., Herrera, F.: Evolutionary undersampling boosting for imbalanced classification of breast cancer malignancy. Appl. Soft Comput. **38**, 714–726 (2016)

40. Kubat, M., Matwin, S.: Addressing the curse of imbalanced training sets: one-sided selection. In: Proceedings of the 14th International Conference on Machine Learning, pp. 179–186. Morgan Kaufmann, San Francisco (1997)

41. Kubat, M., Holte, R., Matwin, S.: Learning when negative examples abound. In: van Someren, M., Widmer, G. (eds.) Proceedings of the 9th European Conference on Machine Learning, pp. 146–153. Springer, Berlin/Heidelberg (1997)

42. Kubat, M., Holte, R.C., Matwin, S.: Machine learning for the detection of oil spills in satellite radar images. Mach. Learn. **30**(2), 195–215 (1998)

43. Laradji, I.H., Alshayeb, M., Ghouti, L.: Software defect prediction using ensemble learning on selected features. Inf. Softw. Technol. **58**, 388–402 (2015)

44. Lee, T., Lee, K.B., Kim, C.O.: Performance of machine learning algorithms for class-imbalanced process fault detection problems. IEEE Trans. Semicond. Manuf. **29**(4), 436–445 (2016)

45. Lertampaiporn, S., Thammarongtham, C., Nukoolkit, C., Kaewkamnerdpong, B., Ruengjitchatchawalya, M.: Heterogeneous ensemble approach with discriminative features and modified-smotebagging for pre-mirna classification. Nucleic Acids Res. **41**(1), e21 (2013)

46. Lichman, M.: UCI machine learning repository. School of Information and Computer Sciences, University of California, Irvine (2013). http://archive.ics.uci.edu/ml
47. Lin, Y., Lee, Y., Wahba, G.: Support vector machines for classification in nonstandard situations. Mach. Learn. **46**, 191–202 (2002)
48. Ling, C., Sheng, V., Yang, Q.: Test strategies for cost-sensitive decision trees. IEEE Trans. Knowl. Data Eng. **18**(8), 1055–1067 (2006)
49. Liu, Y.H., Chen, Y.T.: Total margin based adaptive fuzzy support vector machines for multiview face recognition. In: IEEE International Conference on Systems, Man and Cybernetics, Waikoloa, vol. 2, pp. 1704–1711 (2005)
50. Liu, B., Ma, Y., Wong, C.: Improving an association rule based classifier. In: Zighed, D., Komorowski, J., Zytkow, J. (eds.) Principles of Data Mining and Knowledge Discovery. LNCS, vol. 1910, pp. 293–317. Springer, Berlin/Heidelberg (2000)
51. López, V., Fernández, A., García, S., Palade, V., Herrera, F.: An insight into classification with imbalanced data: empirical results and current trends on using data intrinsic characteristics. Inf. Sci. **250**(20), 113–141 (2013)
52. Lu, W., Li, Z., Chu, J.: A novel computer-aided diagnosis system for breast {MRI} based on feature selection and ensemble learning. Comput. Biol. Med. **83**, 157–165 (2017)
53. Márquez-Vera, C., Cano, A., Romero, C., Noaman, A.Y.M., Mousa Fardoun, H., Ventura, S.: Early dropout prediction using data mining: a case study with high school students. Expert Syst. **33**(1), 107–124 (2016)
54. Mazurowski, M.A., Habas, P.A., Zurada, J.M., Lo, J.Y., Baker, J.A., Tourassi, G.D.: Training neural network classifiers for medical decision making: the effects of imbalanced datasets on classification performance. Neural Netw. **21**(2–3), 427–436 (2008)
55. Menzies, T., Krishna, R., Pryor, D.: The promise repository of empirical software engineering data. Department of Computer Science, North Carolina State University (2015). http://www.openscience.us/repo
56. Napierała, K., Stefanowski, J., Wilk, S.: Learning from imbalanced data in presence of noisy and borderline examples. In: Kryszkiewicz, M., et al. (eds.) Rough Sets and Current Trends in Computing, pp. 158–167. Springer, Berlin/Heidelberg (2010)
57. Orriols-Puig, A., Bernadó-Mansilla, E.: Evolutionary rule-based systems for imbalanced data sets. Soft Comput. **13**, 213–225 (2009)
58. Pérez-Ortiz, M., Gutiérrez, P., Ayllón-Terán, M., Heaton, N., Ciria, R., Briceño, J., Hervás-Martínez, C.: Synthetic semi-supervised learning in imbalanced domains: constructing a model for donor-recipient matching in liver transplantation. Knowl. Based Syst. **123**, 75–87 (2017)
59. Polikar, R.: Ensemble based systems in decision making. IEEE Circuits Syst. Mag. **6**(3), 21–45 (2006)
60. Radtke, P.V., Granger, E., Sabourin, R., Gorodnichy, D.O.: Skew-sensitive boolean combination for adaptive ensembles – an application to face recognition in video surveillance. Inf. Fusion **20**, 31–48 (2014)
61. Ren, F., Cao, P., Li, W., Zhao, D., Zaiane, O.: Ensemble based adaptive over-sampling method for imbalanced data learning in computer aided detection of microaneurysm. Comput. Med. Imaging Graph. **55**, 54–67 (2017). Special Issue on Ophthalmic Medical Image Analysis
62. Rodriguez, D., Herraiz, I., Harrison, R., Dolado, J., Riquelme, J.C.: Preliminary comparison of techniques for dealing with imbalance in software defect prediction. In: Proceedings of the 18th International Conference on Evaluation and Assessment in Software Engineering, EASE '14, pp. 43:1–43:10. ACM, New York (2014)
63. Santos, P., Maudes, J., Bustillo, A.: Identifying maximum imbalance in datasets for fault diagnosis of gearboxes. J. Intell. Manuf. **29**(2), 333–351 (2018)
64. Sanz, J.A., Bernardo, D., Herrera, F., Bustince, H., Hagras, H.: A compact evolutionary interval-valued fuzzy rule-based classification system for the modeling and prediction of real-world financial applications with imbalanced data. IEEE Trans. Fuzzy Syst. **23**(4), 973–990 (2015)

65. Sanz, J., Fernandez, J., Bustince, H., Gradin, C., Fortun, M., Belzunegui, T.: A decision tree based approach with sampling techniques to predict the survival status of poly-trauma patients. Int. J. Comput. Intell. Syst. **10**(1), 440–455 (2017)
66. Sayyad Shirabad, J., Menzies, T.: The PROMISE repository of software engineering databases. School of Information Technology and Engineering, University of Ottawa, Canada (2005). http://promise.site.uottawa.ca/SERepository
67. Shepperd, M., Song, Q., Sun, Z., Mair, C.: Data quality: some comments on the nasa software defect datasets. IEEE Trans. Softw. Eng. **39**(9), 1208–1215 (2013)
68. Soleymani, R., Granger, E., Fumera, G.: Loss factors for learning boosting ensembles from imbalanced data. In: 23rd International Conference on Pattern Recognition (ICPR), Cancún, pp. 204–209 (2016)
69. Soleymani, R., Granger, E., Fumera, G.: Progressive boosting for class imbalance and its application to face re-identification. Expert Syst. Appl. **101**, 271–291 (2018)
70. Stefanowski, J., Wilk, S.: Selective pre-processing of imbalanced data for improving classification performance. In: Song, I.Y., Eder, J., Nguyen, T. (eds.) Data Warehousing and Knowledge Discovery. LNCS, vol. 5182, pp. 283–292. Springer, Berlin/Heidelberg (2008)
71. Sun, Y., Wong, A.C., Kamel, M.S.: Classification of imbalanced data: a review. Int. J. Pattern Recognit. Artif. Intell. **23**(4), 687–719 (2009)
72. Sun, Z., Song, Q., Zhu, X.: Using coding-based ensemble learning to improve software defect prediction. IEEE Trans. Syst. Man Cybern. Part C Appl. Rev. **42**(6), 1806–1817 (2012)
73. Tang, M., Ding, S.X., Yang, C., Cheng, F., Shardt, Y.A.W., Long, W., Liu, D.: Cost-sensitive large margin distribution machine for fault detection of wind turbines. Clust. Comput. 1–13 (2018). https://doi.org/10.1007/s10586-018-1854-3
74. Tavallaee, M., Stakhanova, N., Ghorbani, A.: Toward credible evaluation of anomaly-based intrusion-detection methods. IEEE Trans. Syst. Man Cybern. Part C Appl. Rev. **40**(5), 516–524 (2010)
75. Tax, D.M.J.: One-class classification: concept learning in the absence of counter-examples. Ph.D. thesis, Technische Universiteit Delft (2001)
76. Tomek, I.: Two modifications of CNN. IEEE Trans. Syst. Man Cybern. **SMC-6**(11), 769–772 (1976)
77. Tran, Q.D., Liatsis, P.: Raboc: an approach to handle class imbalance in multimodal biometric authentication. Neurocomputing **188**, 167–177 (2016). Advanced Intelligent Computing Methodologies and Applications
78. Triguero, I., del Río, S., López, V., Bacardit, J., Benítez, J.M., Herrera, F.: ROSEFW-RF: the winner algorithm for the ECBDL–14 big data competition: An extremely imbalanced big data bioinformatics problem. Knowl. Based Syst. **87**, 69–79 (2015). Computational Intelligence Applications for Data Science
79. Wang, S., Yao, X.: Multiclass imbalance problems: analysis and potential solutions. IEEE Trans. Syst. Man Cybern. B Cybern. **42**(4), 1119–1130 (2012)
80. Wei, H., Sun, B., Jing, M.: Balancedboost: a hybrid approach for real-time network traffic classification. In: 23rd International Conference on Computer Communication and Networks (ICCCN), Shanghai, pp. 1–6 (2014)
81. Weiss, G.M., Provost, F.: Learning when training data are costly: the effect of class distribution on tree induction. J. Artif. Intell. Res. **19**, 315–354 (2003)
82. Wu, Q., Ye, Y., Zhang, H., Ng, M.K., Ho, S.S.: Forestexter: an efficient random forest algorithm for imbalanced text categorization. Knowl. Based Syst. **67**, 105–116 (2014)
83. Wu, Z., Lin, W., Ji, Y.: An integrated ensemble learning model for imbalanced fault diagnostics and prognostics. IEEE Access **6**, 8394–8402 (2018)
84. Yang, Z., Tang, W., Shintemirov, A., Wu, Q.: Association rule mining-based dissolved gas analysis for fault diagnosis of power transformers. IEEE Trans. Syst. Man Cybern. Part C Appl. Rev. **39**(6), 597–610 (2009)
85. Yang, P., Yoo, P.D., Fernando, J., Zhou, B.B., Zhang, Z., Zomaya, A.Y.: Sample subset optimization techniques for imbalanced and ensemble learning problems in bioinformatics applications. IEEE Trans. Cybern. **44**(3), 445–455 (2014)

86. Zhang, S., Liu, L., Zhu, X., Zhang, C.: A strategy for attributes selection in cost-sensitive decision trees induction. In: IEEE 8th International Conference on Computer and Information Technology Workshops, Sydney, pp. 8–13 (2008)
87. Zhang, X., Zhuang, Y., Wang, W., Pedrycz, W.: Transfer boosting with synthetic instances for class imbalanced object recognition. IEEE Trans. Cybern. **48**(1), 357–370 (2018)
88. Zhu, Z.B., Song, Z.H.: Fault diagnosis based on imbalance modified kernel fisher discriminant analysis. Chem. Eng. Res. Des. **88**(8), 936–951 (2010)
89. Zhu, B., Baesens, B., vanden Broucke, S.K.L.M.: An empirical comparison of techniques for the class imbalance problem in churn prediction. Inf. Sci. **408**, 84–99 (2017)
90. Zhu, L., Lu, C., Dong, Z.Y., Hong, C.: Imbalance learning machine based power system short-term voltage stability assessment. IEEE Trans. Ind. Inf. **13**(5), 2533–2543 (2017)
91. Zieba, M., Tomczak, J.M., Lubicz, M., Światek, J.: Boosted SVM for extracting rules from imbalanced data in application to prediction of the post-operative life expectancy in the lung cancer patients. Appl. Soft Comput. **14, Part A**, 99–108 (2014)

Chapter 3
Performance Measures

Abstract Analyzing the performance of learning algorithms under presence of class imbalance is a difficult task. For some widely-used measures, such as accuracy, the prevalence of more frequent classes may mask a poor classification performance in infrequent classes. To alleviate this problem, the choice of suitable measures is of fundamental importance. This chapter presents some performance measures that can be used to evaluate classification performance under presence of class imbalance, highlighting their advantages and drawbacks. With aims at presenting this content, the chapter is organized as follows: First, Sect. 3.1 sets the background on the evaluation procedure. Then, Sect. 3.2 presents performance measures for crisp, nominal predictions. Section 3.3 discuss evaluation methods for scoring classifiers. Finally, Sect. 3.4 discuss probabilistic evaluation, and Sect. 3.5 concludes the chapter.

3.1 Introduction

The quality of learning algorithms is generally evaluated by analyzing how well they perform on test data [18]. To this end, the predictions of the learned classifiers are compared to the true classes of test data (which are hidden from the models for evaluation purposes), and some performance measures are calculated. Depending on the scale of information given by the classifiers, or how do we interpret them, we have three possible cases:

1. **Nominal class predictions:** in which the predicted class labels are compared to the actual true class values for evaluating the model.
2. **Numerical scoring predictions:** considers some numerical score associated to the predictions to grade test examples according to the likelihood of pertaining to a class.
3. **Probabilistic predictions:** where the numerical outputs associated to the prediction are interpreted as probabilities of the examples belonging to the class.

Some scales are intrinsically related to some classifiers. For instance, the NN classifier [8] only make nominal predictions (the class of the nearest example in

© Springer Nature Switzerland AG 2018
A. Fernández et al., *Learning from Imbalanced Data Sets*,
https://doi.org/10.1007/978-3-319-98074-4_3

the training set). Standard SVM predictions [5] are a scoring function related to the distance of the new instance to the hyperplane which maximizes the margin between classes. Naïve Bayes [21] predictions are the posterior probability of the instance belonging to a class, under the naive assumption of independence among features. However, some post-processing techniques can be used to convert from one scale to another. For example, one can use the distance to the NN [13] as a score in the classifier; use of scaling [23] to convert SVM outputs to probabilities; or use the argmax function to convert from probabilities to nominal class predictions in Naïve Bayes [11], among other possible alternatives.

Regarding evaluation, considering only the nominal predictions in the evaluation is the simplest approach. However, it is not possible to differentiate predictions within the same class, as there is no way to differentiate between more or less likely nominal predictions with the same class value. Probabilistic output allows to think probabilistically, adding some degree of confidence on the prediction. However, this requires the probabilistic output to be well calibrated.[1] Scoring information is between these two approaches, where the scores given by classifiers are used to give some ordering among instance predictions, without committing to a probabilistic interpretation. However, there is no a standard way to interpret the scores, as in the case of probability outputs.

3.2   Nominal Class Predictions

When considering nominal class predictions, a convenient way to summarize the performance of classifiers is to do a cross-tabulation between actual and predicted classes. The resulting cross-tabulation is a matrix, called confusion matrix. The columns of the confusion matrix represent the counts of instances in the predicted classes while the rows represent the counts of instances in the actual classes (or vice versa). An example of a confusion matrix for a binary class problem (where without loss of generality classes are generically named positive and negative, and the minority class is the negative one) is shown in Table 3.1. In this matrix, TP and

Table 3.1 Confusion matrix for a binary class problem

		Predicted class		
		Positive	Negative	Total
Actual class	Positive	TP	FN	POS
	Negative	FP	TN	NEG
	Total	$PPOS$	$PNEG$	N

---

[1]In a well calibrated classifier, the percentage of examples with a similar predicted probability value should approximately match the probability value (e.g., among the samples to which the classifier give a probability value of 0.8 of being of some class, 80% of the instances should belong to that class).

TN (for true positives/true negatives) indicate correct classification of positive and negative instances, respectively, and FN and FP (for false negatives/false positives) indicate positive/negative instances misclassified as negative/positive, respectively.

Different performance measures can be derived based on the confusion matrix. These measures correspond to different views of what constitute a good classifier, aiming to summarize the confusion matrix into performances metrics so that they can be used in the assessment of the strengths and weakness of the classifiers.

A common performance metric and widely used to evaluate classification performance is accuracy (or its complement, the error rate). Accuracy (Eq. 3.1) is the percentage of correctly classified instances. It corresponds to the sum of diagonal elements in the confusion matrix (which in the binary case is $TP + TN$) divided by the total number of instances. Error rate (Eq. 3.2) is the percentage of incorrectly classified instances. It corresponds to the sum of off-diagonal elements in the confusion matrix (in the binary case is $FP + FN$) divided by the total number of instances.

$$Acc = \frac{TP + TN}{N} \tag{3.1}$$

$$Error = 1 - Acc = \frac{FP + FN}{N} \tag{3.2}$$

Although accuracy and error rate are widely used and are easy to calculate and interpret, it has some drawbacks in imbalanced data sets [26]. Firstly, it is easy to obtain high accuracy (or low error rate) under highly imbalanced problems. For example, a trivial classifier which systematically assign the majority class to new instances will achieve 99% of accuracy (1% error rate) in a problem where the majority class is 99% prevalent. Secondly, it assumes that errors are equally cost. However, in imbalanced classification, misclassifying instances of the minority class is generally much costlier than misclassifying instances of the majority class. In a medical domain, for instance, failing to predict a rare disease is costlier (the patient may die) than a false alarm (the false diagnostic may be revised in the future). Finally, it assumes that the class proportion is static, and may not change. In a classifier for SPAM filtering, for instance, the percentage of SPAM may vary from user to user or may change over time.

To illustrate these drawbacks, consider the three confusion matrices shown in Fig. 3.1. The three matrices lead to the same accuracy value: 99%. The matrix to the left (M_1) corresponds to the trivial classifier of always predicting the majority class. The matrix in the center (M_2) correctly classify all the 10 minority instances, although it trespasses into 10 false positives (i.e., 10 negative instances which are mistakenly classified as positives). The matrix to the right (M_3) have a different class proportion than the other two. It also correctly classifies 10 positive instances, although other 10 are mistakenly classified as negative (i.e., they are false negatives).

The Cohen's kappa could be used to reduce some of these drawbacks [2]. The main idea of kappa is to "compensate" from the accuracy the portion due to chance,

$$M_1 = \begin{pmatrix} 0 & 10 \\ 0 & 990 \end{pmatrix} \quad M_2 = \begin{pmatrix} 10 & 0 \\ 10 & 980 \end{pmatrix} \quad M_3 = \begin{pmatrix} 10 & 10 \\ 0 & 980 \end{pmatrix}$$

Fig. 3.1 Three confusion matrices with the same accuracy

i.e., the portion that a random classifier would achieve. This portion is called expected accuracy, as shown in Eq. 3.3,

$$Acc_e = \frac{\mathbf{E}(TP) + \mathbf{E}(TN)}{N} \tag{3.3}$$

where $\mathbf{E}(TP)$ and $\mathbf{E}(TN)$ are the product of their marginal distributions, as shown in Eqs. 3.4 and 3.5.

$$\mathbf{E}(TP) = \frac{POS*PPOS}{N} \tag{3.4}$$

$$\mathbf{E}(TN) = \frac{NEG*PNEG}{N} \tag{3.5}$$

In the kappa metric, defined in Eq. 3.6, the accuracy[2] is subtracted from the expected accuracy (Eq. 3.3). This value is then normalized by $1 - Acc_e$. The values of kappa ranges from -1 to 1, and values lower than zero indicate that the performance of the classifier is lower than random guessing.

$$\kappa = \frac{Acc_o - Acc_e}{1 - Acc_e} \tag{3.6}$$

The values of kappa for the matrices M_1, M_2 and M_3 in Fig. 3.1 are 0, 0.66 and 0.66, respectively. Observe that by using kappa, it is possible to differentiate the performance of the classifier which confusion matrix is M_1 in Fig. 3.1. However, the performance of classifiers with matrices M_2 and M_3 have the same kappa value. This is because the same misclassification costs and hit rewards are being applied to both types of errors/hits.

Unsymmetrical costs/rewards can be incorporated by means of a cost matrix, as shown in Table 3.2 for binary classification problems. $C(+|+)$ and $C(-|-)$ represents the rewards of correctly classifying positive/negative instances, respectively, while $C(-|+)$ and $C(+|-)$ corresponds the costs of misclassifying positive and negative instances, respectively.

By multiplying each cell of the cost matrix by the corresponding cell in the confusion matrix we can define a loss function L (Eq. 3.7). Observe that accuracy

---

[2]In Eq. 3.6, the accuracy as defined in Eq. 3.1 is designed as Acc_o (for observed accuracy) to distinguish from expected accuracy Acc_e.

Table 3.2 Cost matrix for a binary class problem

		Predicted class	
		Positive	Negative
Actual class	Positive	$C(+|+)$	$C(-|+)$
	Negative	$C(+|-)$	$C(-|-)$

and error rate are special cases of the loss function by setting costs/rewards to 0 and 1 for accuracy or 1 and zero for error rate.

$$L = \frac{TP \cdot C(+|+) + FP \cdot C(+|-) + FN \cdot C(-|+) + TN \cdot C(-|-)}{N} \quad (3.7)$$

Similarly, it is possible to define a weighted kappa version [3], in which the values from the cost matrix are the weights, as shown in Eq. 3.9. The expected loss (L_e), shown in Eq. 3.8, is calculated by multiplying each cell of the cost matrix by the corresponding expected values (Eq. 3.8).

$$L_e = \frac{\mathbf{E}(TP) \cdot C(+|+) + \mathbf{E}(FP) \cdot C(+|-) + \mathbf{E}(FN) \cdot C(-|+) + \mathbf{E}(TN) \cdot C(-|-)}{N}$$

$$(3.8)$$

$$\kappa_w = 1 - \frac{L_o}{L_e} \quad (3.9)$$

Although costs and rewards in the cost matrix are domain specific, with their values defined by the end-user, a possible approach is to set the rewards as zero (i.e., there is any reward by correct classifying an instance) and misclassification costs proportional to the inverse of class proportion: $C(+|-) = N/NEG$ and $C(-|+) = N/POS$. The idea of these values is that the weighted proportion matches a balanced class distribution. By using these cost values for the matrices in Fig. 3.1, L assume the values 1, 0.1, and 0.5 (the lower, the better), and κ_w assume the values 0, 0.98, 0.5 (the higher, the better).

The MCC [20] is a measure that comes from the field of Bioinformatics, where class imbalance occurs very often. It is also used in text classification. It is an adaptation of the Pearson correlation coefficient to evaluate the correlation in confusion matrices, and it related to the χ^2 statistic for contingency tables. It is a measure that takes into account all values of the confusion matrix, considering errors and correct classification in both classes. The formulation of MCC is shown in Eq. 3.10. MCC ranges from 1 (when the classification is always wrong) to 0 (when it is no better than random) to 1 (when it is always correct).

$$MCC = \frac{TP \cdot TN + FP \cdot FN}{\sqrt{POS \cdot NEG \cdot PPOS \cdot PNEG}} \quad (3.10)$$

Another possibility is to use measures which focus in single classes, separately. Basic measures that do this divide each cell in the confusion matrix by their marginal distributions. For binary class problems, the measures in Eqs. 3.11, 3.12, 3.13 and 3.14 divides the cells row-wise. These measures are named as True Positive Rate (TPR—Eq. 3.11), False Positive Rate (FPR—Eq. 3.12), False Negative Rate (FNR—Eq. 3.13) and True Negative Rate (TNR—Eq. 3.14). On the other hand, the measures in Eqs. 3.15, 3.16, 3.17, and 3.18 divides the cells column-wise. These measures are named Positive Predictive Value (PPV—Eq. 3.15), False Discovery Rate (FDR—Eq. 3.16), False Omission Rate (FOR—Eq. 3.17) and Negative Predictive Value (NPV—Eq. 3.18).

$$TPR = {}^{TP}/_{POS} \tag{3.11}$$

$$FPR = {}^{FP}/_{NEG} \tag{3.12}$$

$$FNR = {}^{FN}/_{POS} \tag{3.13}$$

$$TNR = {}^{TN}/_{NEG} \tag{3.14}$$

$$PPV = {}^{TP}/_{PPOS} \tag{3.15}$$

$$FDR = {}^{FP}/_{PPOS} \tag{3.16}$$

$$FOR = {}^{FN}/_{PNEG} \tag{3.17}$$

$$NPV = {}^{TN}/_{PNEG} \tag{3.18}$$

Considering the classes individually allow the analysis of particular aspects of each class. However, it is difficult to analyze them separately, as there are several measures for each class, which difficulties the analysis of possible compromises among classes. Some performance measures which combine these basic measures were designed summarize different compromises among the individual performance measures for each class.

F-measure is a measure that focus on the analysis of positive class, and is widely used in information retrieval [1]. Its objective is to analyze the trade-offs between correctness and coverage in classifying positive instances. To this end, the measure uses a weighed harmonic mean between positive predictive value and true positive rate, also known as precision and recall, respectively, in the literature. Precision evaluates the fraction of correct classified instances among the ones classified as positive, while recall is the fraction of total positive instances correctly classified as positive. Equation 3.19 shows the general F_β formulation of F-measure, where β is a parameter that controls the importance given to each term. A common choice is setting $\beta = 1$, leading to the F_1 measure, shown in Eq. 3.20.

$$F_\beta = (1 + \beta^2) \frac{precision \cdot recall}{(\beta^2 \cdot precision) + recall} \tag{3.19}$$

$$F_1 = 2 \frac{precision \cdot recall}{precision + recall} \tag{3.20}$$

A variation of F-Measure is G-Measure, which uses the geometric mean instead of the harmonic mean to trade-off precision and recall. The formula for G-measure is shown in Eq. 3.21.

$$G\text{-}measure = \sqrt{precision \cdot recall} \qquad (3.21)$$

Another measure that uses the geometric mean, but uses information from both classes, is the geometric mean of true positive and true negative rates (*G-mean*) [19]. This measure aims at a balance between classification performances on the majority and minority classes. A poor performance in prediction of the positive examples will lead to a low *G-mean* value, even if the negative examples are correctly classified. *G-mean* formulation is shown in Eq. 3.22. A simpler version is the balanced accuracy [6, 30], which is the arithmetic average of true positive and true negative rates, as shown in Eq. 3.23. When the classifier has equal performance in both classes, or when the classes are equally balanced, this measure is equivalent to conventional accuracy (Eq. 3.1). However, if the conventional accuracy is high only because the classifier takes advantage of an imbalanced test set, then the balanced accuracy will be lower.

$$G\text{-}mean = \sqrt{TPR \cdot TNR} \qquad (3.22)$$

$$BAC = \frac{TPR + TNR}{2} \qquad (3.23)$$

3.3 Scoring Predictions

Let's consider a classifier that gives a numeric score for an instance to be classified in the positive class. Therefore, instead of a simple positive or negative prediction, the score introduces a level of granularity: instances with a higher score are more likely to have to be classified as positive. Indeed, almost all classifiers generate positive or negative predictions by applying a threshold to a score. The choice of this threshold will have an impact in the trade-offs of positive and negative errors. A higher threshold will reduce the false positive rate, as less instances will be classified as positive. However, the false negative rate would increase, as we are very restrictive in classifying an instance as positive. On the other hand, a lower threshold will reduce the false negative rate, as more instances are classified as positive. However, a larger false positive rate is expected, as we are more lenient in classifying instances as positive.

For evaluating a scoring classifier, we may choose an arbitrary threshold and use the metrics discussed in Sect. 3.2. However, by using this approach, we throw away the granularity given by the scores, as we cannot differentiate between more or less likely instances within each class, and we are committed to this arbitrary threshold. To avoid these drawbacks, it would be interesting to evaluation the scoring classifications without having to select a specific threshold.

The methods discussed in this section uses the ordering given by the score to rank the instances. For doing this, the instances are ordered according to the decreasing predicted likelihood (the score) of being positive. This ranked list is compared to the true class of the test instances, and graphical performance evaluation methods [24] are often used to evaluated classification performance.

The ROC curve [14] is a graphical evaluation method that is not dependent of a specific threshold. A ROC graph is a plot of False Positive Rate (FPR) on the x-axis, and True Positive Rate (TPR) on the y-axis. Given the ranked list of instances according to scores, to draw the graph, the threshold is varied from the most restrictive (highest score) to the most lenient (lowest score). For each possible value of the threshold, there is a point in the ROC space based on the values of FPR and TPR for that threshold. The curve is drawn by linear interpolation among these points. Table 3.3 shows an example of ranked list of instances according to the predicted score, together to the true actual class value, the corresponding FPR and FPR values, and an identifier to the point in the ROC space. The corresponding ROC curve is shown in Fig. 3.2.

In the ROC space, a good classifier should reach as close to the top left corner as possible. This corner corresponds to perfect classification. The upward diagonal indicates random performance. Ideally, all points in the ROC curve should lie above this diagonal, as points below the diagonal indicates performance worse than random. The lower left corner corresponds to a classifier which always predict the wrong class. The lower left corner (origin) corresponds to always predicting the negative class, while the top right corner corresponds to always predicting the positive class.

The AUC_{ROC}, highlighted in gray in the Fig. 3.2, is a summary index about the ROC graph. AUC_{ROC} can be interpreted as the probability that the scores given by a classifier will rank a randomly chosen positive instance higher than a randomly chosen negative one. AUC_{ROC} is also related to the MannWhitney U statistic, which tests to what extent positives are ranked higher than negatives. The AUC_{ROC} can be calculated using the trapezoidal rule. The AUC_{ROC} of random guessing is

Table 3.3 Ranked instances for drawing a ROC graph

Rank	Score	Actual class	FPR	TPR	ROC point
#1	1.0	Positive	0.0	0.2	p_1
#2	0.9	Positive	0.0	0.4	p_2
#3	0.85	Negative	0.2	0.4	p_3
#4	0.7	Positive	0.2	0.6	p_4
#5	0.6	Positive	0.2	0.8	p_5
#6	0.45	Negative	0.4	0.8	p_6
#7	0.35	Positive	0.4	1.0	p_7
#8	0.3	Negative	0.6	1.0	p_8
#9	0.2	Negative	0.8	1.0	p_9
#10	0.05	Negative	1.0	1.0	p_{10}

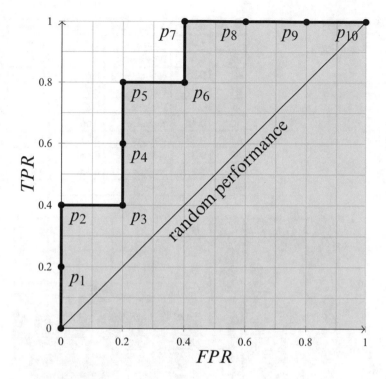

Fig. 3.2 Example of a ROC graph

0.5, so it is expected that AUC_{ROC} for useful classifier is higher than 0.5. However, it should be noted that AUC_{ROC} does not necessarily means random classification. The ideal classifier would achieve an AUC_{ROC} equals to 1.

Although ROC graphs are widely used to evaluate classifiers under presence of class imbalance, it has a drawback: under class rarity, that is, when the problem of class imbalance is associated to the presence of a low sample size of minority instances, as the estimates can be unreliable [16]. Some researchers have argued the Precision-Recall (PR) graphs are more adequate under this context [27].

The process of drawing the PR graphs are similar to ROC graphs, but uses in the x-axis the *Recall* (also known as *TPR*), and *Precision* (also known as *PPV*) in the y-axis. PR curves are often used in information retrieval, and focus only in the positive class. Table 3.4 shows the same instances used in drawing the ROC graph, with the metrics modified for drawing the PR graph. The corresponding PR graph is shown in Fig. 3.3.

The interpretation of PR graph is slightly different from the ROC graph. Good classifiers should be as close as possible to the top right, as this corner represents the best trade-off between precision and recall. As can be seen from the Fig. 3.3, the PR curve is not monotone. Furthermore, the interpolation between consecutive points could not be linear when the classes are not balanced [9, 28].

Table 3.4 Ranked instances for drawing a Precision-Recall graph

Rank	Score	Actual class	Precision	Recall	point
#1	1.0	Positive	1.0	0.2	p_1
#2	0.9	Positive	1.0	0.4	p_2
#3	0.85	Negative	0.66	0.4	p_3
#4	0.7	Positive	0.75	0.6	p_4
#5	0.6	Positive	0.8	0.8	p_5
#6	0.45	Negative	0.66	0.8	p_6
#7	0.35	Positive	0.71	1.0	p_7
#8	0.3	Negative	0.63	1.0	p_8
#9	0.2	Negative	0.55	1.0	p_9
#10	0.05	Negative	0.5	1.0	p_{10}

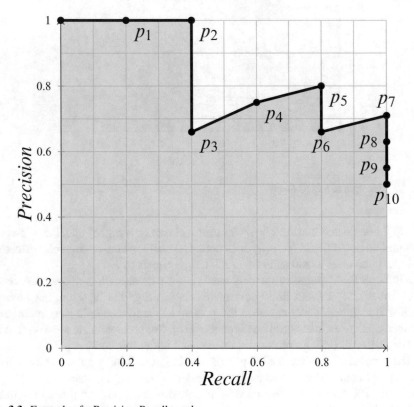

Fig. 3.3 Example of a Precision-Recall graph

As in the ROC case, the AUC_{PR} can be used as a summary statistic for the PR graph. AUC_{PR} does not have a probabilistic interpretation as AUC_{ROC} does. The AUC_{PR} of the random classifier varies with the prevalence of the positive class, and its expected value is close to the proportion of positive instances in the test set. It should be keep in mind that, although AUC_{ROC} and AUC_{PR} are useful summary index, visually inspecting the curves are more informative.

3.4 Probabilistic Predictions

The methods discussed in Sect. 3.3 only uses the scores to rank the instances. Nonetheless, in some applications, it is interesting to interpret the scores as probabilities. A necessary but not sufficient requirement for this is that the scores are within the range 0–1. Furthermore, to be usefully interpreted as probabilities, the scores should be calibrated. In a well calibrated classifier, the proportion of proportion of instances with score similar score should closely match the score value. For instance, in the subset of instances whose predicted score is near 0.8, the proportion of positive instances should be close to 0.8. Some approaches have been proposed in the literature to transform uncalibrated scores into calibrated probabilities [22, 23, 33].

The evaluation of probabilistic scores is generally performed by means of the Brier Score. The basic idea is to compute the mean squared error (MSE) between predicted probability scores and the true class indicator, where the positive class is coded as 1, and negative class 0. The most common formulation of the Brier Score is shown in Equation 3.24.

$$BS = \frac{1}{N} \sum_{i=1}^{N} (p_i - o_i)^2 \tag{3.24}$$

The Brier score is a loss function, meaning the lower its value, the better. It is a proper scoring rule [25], meaning that the expected accuracy is maximized if the true distribution probability is used for prediction. If a positive instance has a predicted probability of being positive, its Brier score is 0 (the best score for a single instance. On the other hand, if the predicted probability is 0, its Brier score is 1 (the worst value score for a single instance). If a negative instance is predicted with a 0.7 probability of being positive, its Brier score is 0.49. The same negative instance with 0.3 predicted probability of being positive has a Brier score of 0.09. An 0.5 of predicted probability has a Brier score of 0.25, no matter the class. The overall Brier score index is the average over all instances. These values can be understood as a "penalty" to the confidence in which the classifier asserts its prediction. If the classifier predicts the wrong class with high probability, it should be heavily penalized. Thus, the lower the Brier score, the lower the average penalties imposed to the classifier.

The Brier score can be decomposed into calibration and refinement [7, 10]. Roughly speaking, the calibration term indicates how close is the evaluation of the probabilities predicted by the classifier for the positive class to the observed frequency of actual positive instances. In a well-calibrated classifier is one with the calibration term close to 0. The refinement term is linked to the utility of the predictions. If a classifier always predicts a probability score equal to the percentage of the positive instances in the test set, the classifier is well calibrated although useless for classifying new instances. The more concentrated the predicted scores towards 0 or 1, the more refined the classifier. To minimize the overall Brier score, the predicted probabilities of the classifier should minimize both calibration and refinement terms. Therefore, for two classifiers with the same calibration term, the one with lower refinement will have lower Brier score [7]. The decomposition of Brier score in calibration and refinement is shown in Eq. 3.25, where K is the total number of unique probabilistic score predictions, n_k is the number of instances with score k, $\mathbf{f_k}$ the vector of instances with score k, and $\mathbf{\bar{o}_k}$ is the ratio of positive instances with score k.

$$BS = \underbrace{\frac{1}{N} \sum_{k=1}^{K} n_k (\mathbf{f_k} - \mathbf{\bar{o}_k})^2}_{\text{calibration}} + \underbrace{\frac{1}{N} \sum_{k=1}^{K} n_k (\mathbf{\bar{o}_k}(1 - \mathbf{\bar{o}_k}))}_{\text{refinement}} \qquad (3.25)$$

The two components of the Brier score can be visualized in two graphs The Reliability diagram [24], also known as probability classification diagram, is a relatively simple technique for visualizing the quality of the calibrated scores. To plot the diagram, the scores are first discretized into bins (generally 10 bins). For each bin, the mean predicted value is plotted against the true fraction of positive cases. In a well calibrated model, the points will fall near the upward diagonal line. The refinement term can be visualized by a histogram of the score. A classifier with good resolution will have an "U"-shaped aspect. An example of these plots is shown in Fig. 3.4.

Bin	Mean score	# instances	Fraction of positives
[0–0.1)	0.07	100	0.10
[0.1–0.2)	0.16	20	0.10
(0.2–0.3)	0.25	10	0.20
(0.3–0.4)	0.37	16	0.32
(0.4–0.5)	0.48	15	0.33
(0.5–0.6)	0.55	10	0.40
(0.6–0.7)	0.68	15	0.66
(0.7–0.8)	0.75	20	0.80
(0.8–0.9)	0.85	33	0.91
(0.9–1.0)	0.96	45	0.93

3.5   Summarizing Comments

In this section, we pose a discussion on some issues related to the evaluation of a classifier's performance in the presence of class imbalance. Our intent was to introduce the most commonly used approaches, so that the reviewed measures and evaluation procedures presented here are not an exhaustive list. This section was

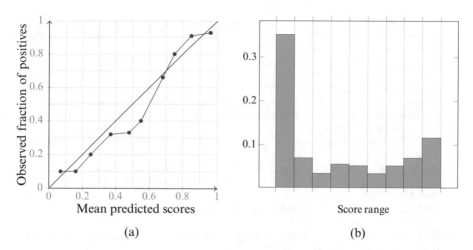

Fig. 3.4 Visualizing the calibration and refinement terms of the Brier score. (**a**) Reliability (calibration) diagram. (**b**) Histogram of scores

also focused on binary classification performance, as these problems appear more often in the literature. For details on Multi-class evaluation reader could refer to Chap. 8.

Regarding the evaluation of nominal class predictions, other measures are also suggested in the specialized literature [15, 29]. Furthermore, it should be keep in mind that there is no universally performance measure, as they consider different and often conflicting criteria. The choice of adequate performance measure is domain dependent, and it should take into account the adequate objectives in the comparison. Different approaches have also been proposed for evaluating ranked predictions. With respect to graphical-based evaluating techniques we have stressed the use of Cost curves [12] and Lift charts [24], together with other alternative summary measures [17, 31]. Finally, we must refer to few works that use different measures to evaluate probabilistic scores [4, 32], although their use is less frequent in ML community.

References

1. Baeza-Yates, R., Ribeiro-Neto, B.: Modern Information Retrieval, vol. 463. ACM Press, New York (1999)
2. Ben-David, A.: A lot of randomness is hiding in accuracy. Eng. Appl. Artif. Intell. **20**(7), 875–885 (2007)
3. Ben-David, A.: Comparison of classification accuracy using Cohen's weighted Kappa. Expert Syst. Appl. **34**(2), 825–832 (2008)
4. Bickel, J.E.: Some comparisons among quadratic, spherical, and logarithmic scoring rules. Decis. Anal. **4**(2), 49–65 (2007)

5. Boser, B.E., Guyon, I., Vapnik, V.: A training algorithm for optimal margin classifiers. In: Haussler, D. (ed.) Proceedings of the Fifth Annual ACM Conference on Computational Learning Theory, (COLT'1992), pp. 144–152. ACM, Baltimore (1992)

6. Brodersen, K.H., Ong, C.S., Stephan, K.E., Buhmann, J.M.: The balanced accuracy and its posterior distribution. In: 2010 20th International Conference on Pattern Recognition (ICPR), pp. 3121–3124. IEEE, Piscataway (2010)

7. Cohen, I., Goldszmidt, M.: Properties and benefits of calibrated classifiers. In: European Conference on Principles of Data Mining and Knowledge Discovery, pp. 125–136. Springer, Berlin/Heidelberg (2004)

8. Cover, T., Hart, P.: Nearest neighbor pattern classification. IEEE Trans. Inf. Theory 13(1), 21–27 (1967)

9. Davis, J., Goadrich, M.: The relationship between precision-recall and ROC curves. In: Proceedings of the 23rd International Conference on Machine Learning, pp. 233–240. ACM, New York (2006)

10. DeGroot, M.H., Fienberg, S.E.: The comparison and evaluation of forecasters. The Statistician 32(1–2), 12–22 (1983)

11. Domingos, P., Pazzani, M.: On the optimality of the simple bayesian classifier under zero-one loss. Mach. Learn. 29(2), 103–130 (1997)

12. Drummond, C., Holte, R.C.: Cost curves: an improved method for visualizing classifier performance. Mach. Learn. 65(1), 95–130 (2006)

13. Dudani, S.A.: The distance-weighted k-nearest-neighbor rule. IEEE Trans. Syst. Man Cybern. SMC-6(4), 325–327 (1976)

14. Fawcett, T.: An introduction to ROC analysis. Pattern Recogn. Lett. 27(8), 861–874 (2006)

15. Ferri, C., Hernández-Orallo, J., Modroiu, R.: An experimental comparison of performance measures for classification. Pattern Recogn. Lett. 30(1), 27–38 (2009)

16. Hanczar, B., Hua, J., Sima, C., Weinstein, J., Bittner, M., Dougherty, E.R.: Small-sample precision of ROC-related estimates. Bioinformatics 26(6), 822–830 (2010)

17. Hand, D.J.: Measuring classifier performance: a coherent alternative to the area under the ROC curve. Mach. Learn. 77(1), 103–123 (2009)

18. Japkowicz, N., Shah, M.: Evaluating learning algorithms: a classification perspective. Cambridge University Press, Cambridge (2011)

19. Kubat, M., Matwin, S., et al.: Addressing the curse of imbalanced training sets: one-sided selection. In: ICML, Nashville, vol. 97, pp. 179–186 (1997)

20. Matthews, B.W.: Comparison of the predicted and observed secondary structure of t4 phage lysozyme. Biochimica et Biophysica Acta (BBA)-Protein Structure 405(2), 442–451 (1975)

21. Mitchell, T.M.: Bayesian learning. In: Machine Learning. McGraw-Hill, Boston (1997)

22. Niculescu-Mizil, A., Caruana, R.: Predicting good probabilities with supervised learning. In: Proceedings of the 22nd International Conference on Machine Learning, pp. 625–632. ACM, New York (2005)

23. Platt, J., et al.: Probabilistic outputs for support vector machines and comparisons to regularized likelihood methods. Adv. Large Margin Classif. 10(3), 61–74 (1999)

24. Prati, R.C., Batista, G.E.A.P.A., Monard, M.C.: A survey on graphical methods for classification predictive performance evaluation. IEEE Trans. Knowl. Data Eng. 23(11), 1601–1618 (2011)

25. Predd, J.B., Seiringer, R., Lieb, E.H., Osherson, D.N., Poor, H.V., Kulkarni, S.R.: Probabilistic coherence and proper scoring rules. IEEE Trans. Inf. Theory 55(10), 4786–4792 (2009)

26. Provost, F.J., Fawcett, T.: Robust classification for imprecise environments. Mach. Learn. 42(3), 203–231 (2001)

27. Saito, T., Rehmsmeier, M.: The precision-recall plot is more informative than the ROC plot when evaluating binary classifiers on imbalanced datasets. PloS One 10(3), e0118432 (2015)

28. Saito, T., Rehmsmeier, M.: Precrec: fast and accurate precision–recall and ROC curve calculations in R. Bioinformatics 33(1), 145–147 (2017)

29. Sokolova, M., Lapalme, G.: A systematic analysis of performance measures for classification tasks. Inf. Process. Manag. 45(4), 427–437 (2009)

30. Velez, D.R., White, B.C., Motsinger, A.A., Bush, W.S., Ritchie, M.D., Williams, S.M., Moore, J.H.: A balanced accuracy function for epistasis modeling in imbalanced datasets using multifactor dimensionality reduction. Genet. Epidemiol. **31**(4), 306–315 (2007)
31. Walter, S.: The partial area under the summary ROC curve. Stat. Med. **24**(13), 2025–2040 (2005)
32. Winkler, R.L.: Scoring rules and the evaluation of probability assessors. J. Am. Stat. Assoc. **64**(327), 1073–1078 (1969)
33. Zadrozny, B., Elkan, C.: Transforming classifier scores into accurate multiclass probability estimates. In: Proceedings of the Eighth ACM SIGKDD International Conference on Knowledge Discovery and Data Mining, pp. 694–699. ACM, New York (2002)

Chapter 4
Cost-Sensitive Learning

Abstract Cost-sensitive learning is an aspect of algorithm-level modifications for class imbalance. Here, instead of using a standard error-driven evaluation (or 0–1 loss function), a misclassification cost is being introduced in order to minimize the conditional risk. By strongly penalizing mistakes on some classes, we improve their importance during classifier training step. This pushes decision boundaries away from their instances, leading to improved generalization on these classes. In this chapter we will discuss the basics of cost-sensitive methods, introduce their taxonomy, and describe how to deal with scenarios in which misclassification cost is not given beforehand by an expert. Then we will describe most popular cost-sensitive classifiers and talk about the potential for hybridization with other techniques. Section 4.1 offers background and taxonomy of cost-sensitive classification algorithms. The important issue of how to obtain the cost matrix is discussed in Sect. 4.2. Section 4.3 describes MetaCost, a popular wrapper approach for adapting any classifier to a cost-sensitive setting, while Sect. 4.4 discusses various aspects of cost-sensitive decision trees. Other cost-sensitive classification models are described in Sect. 4.5, while Sect. 4.6 shows the potential advantages of using hybrid cost-sensitive algorithms. Finally Sect. 4.7 concludes this chapter and presents future challenges in the field of cost-sensitive solutions to class imbalance.

4.1 Introduction

Cost-sensitive learning refers to a specific set of algorithms that are sensitive to different costs associated with certain characteristics of considered problems. These costs can originate from various aspects related to a given real-life problem and be provided by a domain expert, or learned during the classifier training phase. Two distinct views on cost-sensitive classifiers exist in the literature. On the one hand 'cost associated with features and, on the other hand cost associated with classes.

1. **Cost associated with features.** This scenario assumes that acquiring a certain feature is connected with a given cost, being also known as test cost [47].

© Springer Nature Switzerland AG 2018
A. Fernández et al., *Learning from Imbalanced Data Sets*,
https://doi.org/10.1007/978-3-319-98074-4_4

This can be viewed from the monetary perspective (e.g., a feature is more expensive to extract, as it requires additional resources or laboratory tests), time perspective (e.g., a feature takes more time to extract and therefore may cause a bottleneck in the classification system), or other difficulties perspective (e.g., obtaining a feature involves invasive tests on humans, or the measurement procedure is unpleasant, painful, or difficult to perform) [65].

This aspect of cost-sensitive learning aims at creating a classifier that obtains the best possible predictive performance, while utilizing features that can be obtained at lowest possible cost (or the sum of costs being below a given threshold) [68].

This can be seen as a multi-objective learning, where we try to strike a balance between performance and cost of used features [29, 60]. In many cases they more costly features offer higher predictive power, leading to a problem of whether to use several cheaper features or few more expensive ones [23].

This can also be viewed as a feature selection task, but many cost-sensitive classifiers (e.g., decision trees) have the cost optimization procedure inbuilt [48].

2. **Cost associated with classes.** This scenario assumes that making errors on instances coming from certain classes causes is connected with a higher cost.

This can be viewed from a monetary perspective (e.g., giving a credit to a person with a bad credit score will potentially cause higher loses to a bank than declining credit to a person with a good score), or priority/health/ethical issues (e.g., sending a sick patient home is much more costly and dangerous for a hospital than assigning additional tests to a healthy person) [32].

This aspect of cost-sensitive learning aims to train a classifier in such a way that it will focus on classes that have higher costs assigned to them. They can be seen as priority ones and we want to influence the training procedure by treating them differently.

While over the last decade cost-sensitive learning gained most attention for problems with skewed class distributions [39], it is also often used in balanced scenarios, where incorrect classification outcomes may lead to severe consequences.

In the context of class imbalance, the cost-sensitive learning can be seen as a specific type of algorithm-level approach [27, 42]. It assumes asymmetric misclassification costs between classes, defined in a form of a cost matrix. Standard machine learning methods most commonly use so-called 0–1 loss function, which assigns value 0 to a correctly classified instance and value 1 to an incorrectly classified one. Then the training procedure aims at minimizing the overall cost, i.e., minimizing the number of wrong predictions. As 0–1 loss function uses the same cost associated with a wrong classification for all classes considered, it is highly susceptible to skewed class distributions [36]. The 0–1 loss function over imbalanced data can be easily minimized by focusing on majority class and overlooking (or in extreme cases even completely ignoring) minority class. This problem is getting more prevalent with increasing imbalance ratio.

Table 4.1 Cost matrix for a two-class problem

	True positive	True negative
Predicted positive	$C(0, 0)$	$C(0, 1)$
Predicted negative	$C(1, 0)$	$C(1, 1)$

Cost-sensitive learning aims at alleviate this problem by adapting a different loss function, with different costs associated with each class. Such a cost can be seen as a penalty factor introduced during a classifier training procedure (or in some cases during prediction step), aiming at increasing the importance of difficult (e.g., minority) classes. By stronger penalization of errors on a given class, we force the classifier training procedure (aiming to minimize the overall cost) to focus on instances coming from this distribution. An example of a cost matrix for a two-class problem is given in Table 4.1.

With a provided cost matrix, a new instance should be classified as the one belonging to a class characterized by the lowest expected cost. This is known as the minimum expected cost principle. The expected cost (conditional risk) $R(i|x)$ of classifying instance x as belonging to i-th class can be expressed as:

$$R(i|x) = \sum_{j=1}^{M} P(j|x) \cdot C(i, j),$$ (4.1)

where $P(j|x)$ is the probability estimation of classifying instance x as belonging to class j from a set of M classes.

For a standard two-class problem a cost-sensitive classifier will classify given instance x as belonging to positive class if and only if:

$$P(0|x) \cdot C(1, 0) + P(1|x) \cdot C(1, 1) \leq P(0|x) \cdot C(0, 0) + P(1|x) \cdot C(0, 1),$$ (4.2)

which is equivalent to:

$$P(0|x) \cdot (C(1, 0) - C(0, 0)) \leq P(1|x) \cdot (C(0, 1) - C(1, 1)).$$ (4.3)

This shows that any cost matrix can work under an assumption that $C(0, 0)$ = $C(1, 1)$ = 0 (and analogically for multi-class problems). This allows to reduce the number of cost parameters to be established, as one is only interested in misclassification cost among classes.

Following this assumption, a cost-sensitive classifier will classify given instance x as belonging to positive class if and only if:

$$P(0|x) \cdot C(1, 0) \leq P(1|x) \cdot C(0, 1).$$ (4.4)

By following the fact that $P(0|x) = 1 - P(1|x)$, we may obtain a threshold $p*$ for classifying an instance x as belonging to positive class if $P(1|x) \geq p*$, where:

$$p* = \frac{C(1, 0)}{C(1, 0) - C(0, 1)}. \tag{4.5}$$

Cost-sensitive learning algorithms can be separated into two main groups:

- **Direct approaches.** This methodology is based on directly introducing the misclassification cost into the training procedure of a classifier. This directly corresponds to other algorithm-level approaches, with difference of utilizing the cost matrix.
- **Meta-learning approaches.** This methodology is based on modifying either the training data or the outputs of a classifier. It does not modify the underlying training algorithm, thus making this a suitable approach for almost any type of a classifier. Meta-learning solutions can be applied during two different steps of the classification process:

    - **Preprocessing.** Here we aim at modifying the training set, similarly to data-level solutions discussed in previous chapters. The most popular approach includes weighting the instances according to a provided cost matrix, thus allowing for assigning higher importance to minority objects.
    - **Postprocessing.** Here we aim at modifying the outputs of a classifier during the classification phase. It does not involve any modification before or during training and the entire effort is moved to introducing the cost factor when a decision about a new instance is being made.

4.2   Obtaining the Cost Matrix

The effectiveness of cost-sensitive learning relies strongly on the supplied cost matrix. Parameters provided there will be of crucial importance to both training and predictions steps. Incorrectly initialized costs can impair the learning process [64]. Too low costs will not allow to properly adjust the classification boundaries, while too high cost will lead to loss of generalization capabilities on the remaining classes. In case of class imbalance wrongly set costs can actually mirror a bias towards the majority class into a bias towards minority class – while we should aim to get a balanced performance on both of them. But how does one obtain such a cost matrix? There are two possible scenarios:

1. **Cost matrix provided by an expert.** In this case the supplied data is accompanied by the cost matrix that comes directly from the nature of a problem. This usually requires an access to a domain expert that can assess the most realistic cost values. As an example of an application with a predefined cost matrix we may take credit card fraud detection [45]. Here cost is given directly as an average monetary loss in a case of accepting a fraudulent transaction (this is $C(i, j)$) and in case of losing a customer after rejecting a valid transaction (this is $C(j, i)$).

2. **Cost matrix estimated using training data.** In many cases we do not have an access to a domain expert and no a priori information on cost matrix is available during classifier training. This is a common scenario when we want to apply cost-sensitive learning as a method for solving imbalanced problems, especially over a wide range of different datasets. This requires either heuristic setting of cost values or learning them from training data.

The most popular heuristic approach lies in utilizing the IR as a direct way to estimate the cost. In this set-up $C(i, j) = $ IR and $C(j, i) = 1$, where minority is the i-th and majority is the j-th class (to allow for cases with multiple classes). The reasoning behind this approach is that the higher IR the more difficult the learning problem. While this is very easy to apply and gives the cost matrix very quickly, one must be aware of significant limitations of it. The major one lies in the fact that IR is not the sole source of learning difficulties in imbalanced data [27]. One must take into an account instance-level characteristics, such as small sample size, class overlapping [56], or presence of noisy and borderline instances [58]. Therefore, two problems with similar IR may pose drastically different challenges to a classifier and using similar cost matrices for them will be an oversimplification.

Popular way of training a cost-sensitive classifier without know cost matrix is to put emphasis on modifying the classification outputs when predictions are being made on new data. This is usually done by setting a threshold on the positive class, below which the negative one is being predicted. The value of this threshold is optimized using a validation set and thus the cost matrix can be learned from training data [18]. This approach has been criticized for creating a division between training and cost-sensitive evaluation, as the trained classifier in the first phase (when costs are unknown) is error-driven and not cost-driven [6]. Therefore, the estimation of the cost parameters is initialized with a method that is not cost-sensitive and the outcome may be biased.

This problem has been addressed by incorporating ROC-based criterion for classifier training. As ROC analysis allows to handle performance on both classes simultaneously, it is a highly suitable tool for cost-sensitive learning. Values of cost matrix are then found using a ROC space with iso-performance lines [17]. The best threshold (cost parameter) is defined by the operating point for which the iso-performance line is tangent to the ROC curve. ROC-based training can be easily applied to various classification algorithms, making their cost-sensitive adaptations possible in scenarios without explicitly stated cost matrix [19, 46]. At the same time, we must remember that ROC-based cost tuning is sub-optimal, as there are no guarantees for the obtained classifier to be optimal over all possible misclassification costs.

This problem can be alleviated by using an ensemble-based strategy and training a pool of classifiers, where each individual one is being specialized in a given misclassification cost settings. Additionally, this allows to predict multiple potential scenarios in the prediction phase, allowing for handling cases where testing set has different properties than training set (which is known as dataset shift). Then we may select single best classifier that is most suitable for discovered cost matrix, or combine more classifiers to achieve better classification performance by exploring diversity among their cost settings [31]. One of the first ensemble approaches was based on generating a grid of cost pairs and training an individual classifier on each of them [3]. A multi-objective genetic algorithm is applied for optimizing base classifiers with respect to estimated cost matrix. This idea was extended as ROC Front [8], where authors proposed to use multi-objective optimization to train ensemble of SVMs by adapting hyperparameter values to the misclassification cost. An interesting alternative was proposed in [53], where authors used Precision-Recall Operating Characteristic (P-ROC).

ROC-based tuning of cost matrix has also been considered in multi-class scenarios, by working in a $M \times (M - 1)$ dimensional ROC space (for M classes). Then weights are assigned to individual outputs per class in order to control the decision making process and make it cost-sensitive. However, the number of possible weight combinations with different values of thresholds becomes computationally prohibitive [5, 35]. Therefore, using the divide-and-conquer approach with a pairwise combination of classes attracted more attention [26]. This approach has been used for Volume Under the Surface estimation [21], as well as for optimization of parameters used in classifier training [33, 34]. Ensemble-based approaches for multi-class cost matrix estimation are not that popular, yet one should point out to very interesting works by Everson and Fieldsen [16], as well as by Bernard et al. [4]

4.3   MetaCost

MetaCost algorithm [12] will be discussed firstly, due to its unique flexibility in adapting classifiers to cost-sensitive scenarios. It works as a wrapper method that can be applied to any type of classifier, regardless of the type of output it returns (either class labels or probability estimates). This makes it stand out from the remaining algorithms discusses in this chapter, as they are focusing on modifying only a specific type of classifiers.

MetaCost is based on the assumption that with the introduction of a cost matrix, the classification boundary should be adapted in favor of the classes with a higher cost assigned. This translates to expanding regions in the decision space assigned to these classes, even if the a priori probabilities do not change. Hence, class labels provided for the instances in the training set may in fact coincide with optimal predictions for them according to a provided cost matrix. MetaCost postulates that if these instances would be relabeled to their optimal classes suggested by the cost matrix, then there is no further need for data preprocessing and a standard classifier using 0–1 loss function can be used. Modified training set should allow any classifier to find optimal decision boundaries that will minimize the misclassification cost.

MetaCost is a preprocessing meta-learning approach that utilizes ensemble-based data manipulation [20]. The original training set is used to learn multiple classifiers by bootstrapping instances (following Bagging idea). Then a probability for each instance belonging to each of classes is being estimated using a fraction of votes

---

Algorithm 1 MetaCost algorithm

Require: S: Training set; S': relabeled training set; L: Number of Bagging iterations; n: Bootstrap size; Ψ: classification algorithm; M: # of classes.

1:
2: **for** $l = 1$ to L **do**
3:     $S_l \leftarrow \text{RandomSampleReplacement}(n, S)$
4:     $\Psi_l \leftarrow \text{train } \Psi \text{ on } S_l$
5: **end for**
6:
7: **for** $s = 1$ to $|S|$ **do**
8:     **for** $i = 1$ to M **do**
9:         **if** Ψ returns probabilistic outputs **then**
10:             obtain $P(i|x_s, \Psi_l)$
11:         **else**
12:             $P(i|x_s, \Psi_l) = 1$ for the class predicted and 0 for others
13:         **end if**
14:         **if** use all bootstraps for each instance **then**
15:             l ranges over all Ψ_l
16:         **else**
17:             l ranges over all Ψ_l such that $x_s \notin S_l$
18:         **end if**
19:         $P(i|x_s) = \frac{1}{\sum_l 1} \sum_l P(i|x_s, \Psi_l)$
20:     **end for**
21:     $x'_s \leftarrow \text{relabel } x_s$ according to $\text{argmin}_l \sum_j^M P(m|x_s) C(i, j)$
22:     $S' \leftarrow S' \cup x'_s$
23: **end for**
24:
25: $\Psi_{final} \leftarrow \text{train } \Psi \text{ on } S'$

---

it receives from the ensemble. Then training instances are relabeled to minimize the conditional risk (see Eq. 4.1). Finally, the ensemble is being discarded (as it was used only for preprocessing step) and a new classifier is being trained on the modified set of instances. The pseudo-code of MetaCost is given in Algorithm 1.

4.4 Cost-Sensitive Decision Trees

Among all of the classifiers, induction of cost-sensitive decision trees has arguably gained the most attention [13, 37, 52, 57]. This can be attributed to the ease of modification of their training [38, 59] and pruning algorithms [14, 25, 66], as well as plethora of ways to apply meta-learning principles. Let us provide general frameworks for two most important approaches to cost-sensitive decision tree induction: splitting criterion modification (Sect. 4.4.1) and instance weighting (Sect. 4.4.2).

4.4.1 Direct Approach with Cost-Sensitive Splitting

Induction of a cost-sensitive tree takes into account two different costs – test cost of a-th feature $tc(a)$ and misclassification cost of instance $mc(x)$ [38]. Both of these costs are to be minimized, allowing to eliminate the skew towards majority class, while reducing the cost of used features [40, 41]. As for many imbalanced problems we do not have costs assigned to features, then one should assume an uniform value of $tc(a)$, which will allow for the training algorithm to focus on minimization of $mc(x)$. The following five-step process allows for the computation of the average total cost associated with a given decision tree.

Step 1. Denote the inducted decision tree as T, training set as S, selected training instance as $x \in S$, and set of features describing this instance as $B(x)$.

Step 2. Calculate the test cost associated with x using the subset of features $B'(x)$ that are used by path from the root of T to one of its leaves to which x belongs:

$$tc(x) = tc\left(B'(x)\right) = \sum_{a \in S'} tc(a). \tag{4.6}$$

Step 3. Denote the set of instances in a given leaf node l as $S'(l)$ and the decision value of instance $x \in S'(l)$ as $d(x)$. Let $|S'_i(l)|$ and $|S'_j(l)|$ be the number of instances from i-th and j-th class in this l-th node. To minimize the misclassification cost, a one class $d_c(x)$ is assigned for all of instances in $S'(l)$, based on:

$$mc(S'(l)) = \min(|S'_i(l)| \times C(i, j), |S'_j(l)| \times C(j, i)). \tag{4.7}$$

Then for any $x \in S'(l)$ the assigned class is calculated as:

$$d_c(x) = \begin{cases} i\text{-th class} & \text{if } |S'_j(l)| \times C(j, i), \\ j\text{-th class} & \text{if } |S'_i(l)| \times C(i, j). \end{cases} \tag{4.8}$$

Step 4. Calculate the misclassification cost. Despite each leaf node l is now being associated with only a single class label, there still may be instances within it that have their true class labels different. We denote the true class label of x as $d_t(x)$, while the label assigned to it by a given leaf node as $d_c(x)$. For each instance x in S' that has different true class label than the label associated with this node, calculate:

$$mc(x) = \begin{cases} C(i, j) & \text{if } d_t(x) = i \text{ and } d_c(x) = j, \\ C(j, i) & \text{if } d_t(x) = j \text{ and } d_c(x) = i. \end{cases} \tag{4.9}$$

Step 5. Calculate the average total cost ATC that takes into account both the cost associated with misclassified instances ($mc(x)$) and features used by them

$(tc(x))$. This metric is calculated for the entire training set U:

$$ATC(U) = \frac{\sum_{x \in U} (tc(x) + mc(x))}{|S|}. \tag{4.10}$$

This approach can be used with any splitting measure that has been adapted to take into account feature costs.

4.4.2   Meta-learning Approach with Instance Weighting

An alternative solution to using the cost directly when creating splits lies in weighting the training instances [59]. Higher weights is assigned to instances coming from the class with higher value of misclassification cost. This is done instead of sampling procedures, thus the size of the training set is not altered. The following four-step process allows for modifying any decision tree induction scheme to take into account misclassification costs expressed as weighted instances.

Step 1. Convert the cost matrix into a cost parameter for each class. For a two-class problem $C_i = C(i, j)$ and $C_j = C(j, i)$, while for multi-class problems with M classes one may use the following conversion:

$$C(i) = \sum_{j}^{M} C(i, j). \tag{4.11}$$

Step 2. Calculate weight associated to instances coming from i-th class:

$$w_i = C_i \frac{|S|}{\sum_j C_j |S_j|}, \tag{4.12}$$

where $|S_j|$ is the number of training instances belonging to j-th class and $\sum_i w(i)|S_i| = |U|$. For $C(i) \geq 1$, w_i takes the smallest value bounded within $0 \leq \frac{|S|}{\sum_j C_j |S_j|}, \leq 1$ when $C_i = 1$, and takes the following largest value when $C_i = \max_j C_j$:

$$w_i = \frac{C_i |S_i|}{\sum_j C_j |S_j|} \geq 1. \tag{4.13}$$

Step 3. Calculate the ratio of the total weight of i-th class in leaf node l to the overall total weight of all instances in l:

$$p_w(i|l) = \frac{W_i(l)}{\sum_j W_j(l)} = \frac{w_i |S_i'(l)|}{\sum_j w_j |S_j'(l)|}. \tag{4.14}$$

Step 4. Use any selected training procedure for induction decision trees. $W_i(l)$ must be used instead of $|S'_j(l)|$ when calculating splitting criterion value in each node in the tree growing process, as well as and the error estimation in the pruning process. Therefore, no algorithm-level modifications are required.

4.5 Other Cost-Sensitive Classifiers

While MetaCost and decision trees are the most popular approaches to cost-sensitive classification, plethora of other methods have also been adapted to work with varying misclassification costs [10, 15, 43]. Below we will shortly discuss the most important cost-sensitive versions of popular classification models, namely SVMs (Sect. 4.5.1), ANNs (Sect. 4.5.2), and NN classifiers (Sect. 4.5.3).

4.5.1 Support Vector Machines

SVMs can be easily adjusted to work with cost-sensitive setting [11, 24]. One of the main reasons behind their sensitivity to skewed datasets lies in soft margin objective function assigning identical costs (parameter C) for both positive and negative class. Different Error Cost (DEC) approach [61] uses the provided (or estimated) cost matrix to assign separate misclassification costs to each of classes. Therefore, for positive class we use parameter $C^+ = C(1, 0)$ and for negative we use $C^- = C(0, 1)$. This modifies the calculation of soft margin objective function to:

$$
\min \left(\frac{1}{2} w \cdot w + C^+ \sum_{i | y_i = +1}^{l} \xi_i + C^- \sum_{i | y_i = -1}^{l} \xi_i \right)
$$

$$
\text{subject to} \underset{i=1,\cdots,l}{\forall} \underset{\xi_i \geq 0}{\forall} y_i (w \cdot \Phi(x_i) + b) \geq 1 - \xi_i,
$$

(4.15)

The dual Lagrangian optimization problem can be then represented as follows:

$$
\max_{\alpha_i} \left(\sum_{i=1}^{l} \alpha_i - \frac{1}{2} \sum_{i=1}^{l} \sum_{j=1}^{l} \alpha_i \alpha_j y_i y_j K(x_i, x_j) \right)
$$

$$
\text{subject to} \underset{i=1,\cdots,l}{\forall} \underset{0 \leq \alpha_i^+ \leq C^+}{\forall} \underset{0 \leq \alpha_i^- \leq C^-}{\forall} \sum_{i=1}^{l} y_i \alpha_i = 0,
$$

(4.16)

where α_i^+ and α_i^- stand for Lagrangian multipliers for positive and negative classes. When misclassification costs are unknown DEC uses the IR to initialize C^+ and C^-.

4.5.2   Artificial Neural Networks

Cost-sensitive modifications of ANNs [67] involve alternation of weight update functions [7], sampling solutions [2], and moving threshold approaches. The latter one is a post-processing meta-learning solution to cost-sensitive learning. We denote the real-valued output of an ANN if a form of support for instance x belonging to i-th class as $O_i(x)$(for$i \in M$), where $\sum_{i=1}^{M} O_i(x) = 1$ and $0 \leq O_i(x) \leq 1$. Standard ANNs use Winner-Take-All approach for determining the final predicted class: $\text{argmax}_i O_i(x)$. However, moving threshold approach modifies the values of outputs by including the misclassification cost:

$$O_i^*(x) = \eta \sum_{j=1}^{M} O_i(x)C(i, j),\qquad(4.17)$$

where *eta* is a normalization term in order to scale cost-sensitive outputs to $\sum_{i=1}^{M} O_i^* = 1$ and $0 \leq O_i^* \leq 1$. A cost-sensitive ANN with moving threshold makes its predictions based on $\text{argmax}_i O_i^*(x)$. Threshold-moving approaches for ANNs have been overlooked for a long time and are not as popular as sampling-based methods for class imbalance. However, some studies report its high usefulness for dealing with datasets with skewed distributions [30, 44, 67]. Other works report that simply changing the data distribution without considering the imbalance effect on the classification threshold (and thus adjusting it properly) may be misleading [50].

4.5.3   Nearest Neighbors

The popular k-NN classifier also finds its usage in cost-sensitive learning [22, 51]. It uses the minimization of conditional risk, similarly to decision tree approaches, as cost parameter modifies the probabilities of assigning new instance x to each of classes. However, k-NN utilizes the proportion of k-NN of x belonging to i-th class to estimate $P(i|x)$. Cost-sensitive k-NN rescales the cost matrix parameters, so that for a two-class problems we have $C(1, 0) + C(0, 1) = 1$. Then the classification rule assigns x to class 1 if $k_1/k > C(0, 1)$ and to class 0 otherwise, where k_1 is the number of instances from class 1 among k-NN of x.

4.6   Hybrid Cost-Sensitive Approaches

While sampling methods seem attractive due to their requirements of modifying (rebalance) only training set (and thus a flexibility of applying any type of classifier afterwards), they may suffer from problems related to loss of information after removing some instances, increasing noise or overlapping with introduction of new instances, or even causing a data set shift (more details on data-level approaches can be found at Chap. 5). Cost-sensitive methods may suffer from incorrectly estimated parameters of cost matrix. This tend to happen when the search procedure get stuck in a local minimum, or the search space is too big to efficiently find a (sub)optimal solution.

A potentially attractive solution lies in using a hybrid approach that will combine advantages of its components, while alleviating their drawbacks. One idea lies in conducting a small-scale sampling of the training set before learning a cost-sensitive classifier. This will reduce the IR, leading to a reduction of misclassification costs for minority instances and thus making the search process less biased. As we introduce/remove lower number of instances, we reduce the risk of deleting important information or introducing noise. Finally, cost-sensitive classifiers are usually faster than sampling approaches. Thus a hybrid methodology allows for a computational speed-up when compared with a scenario that uses only sampling.

Abkani et al. [1] proposed SMOTE with Different Costs (SDC) algorithm that works in three steps. Firstly, no undersampling of the majority class is conducted, thus not allowing for any loss of information. Secondly, a SVM with different misclassification costs is being trained on supplied dataset in order to reduce the bias towards the majority class. Finally, SMOTE is applied on minority distances in order to improve the definition of the learned class boundary. Similar idea was proposed by Wang et al. [62].

Chawla et al. [9] developed a wrapper approach that automatically learns sampling ratios individually for each dataset via evaluation function optimization. One can plug-in misclassification cost into this evaluator. An internal cross-validation on training data is used to establish undersampling and oversampling ratios, apply it to all instances and train a classifier on the modified data set.

Peng [49] proposed an adaptive undersampling and oversampling, where a pool of classifiers is being trained using different sampling ratios and estimated misclassification costs, and a weighted combination function is used for fusion of base classifiers.

4.7 Summarizing Comments

This chapter discussed the idea of cost-sensitive learning in the context of varying misclassification costs and class imbalance. Taxonomy of cost-sensitive approaches was presented and most representative algorithms were described in details, with a special emphasis on meta-learning solutions and decision trees. Despite over two decades of progress in this field, there are many directions to be pursued by researchers in this domain. Let us conclude this chapter by discussing the most important open issues and future challenges that cost-sensitive learning from imbalanced data must face in years to come.

- **Cost-sensitive solutions for data-level difficulties**: cost-sensitive solutions used so far associate on the level of classes. Yet, instances within the minority class may pose different levels of difficulty and mistakes on some of them should be penalized stronger than on the others. Developing methods that could induce cost-sensitive classifiers that take into account intrinsic data characteristics seems as a promising direction.
- **Hybrid cost-sensitive learning**: combining cost-sensitive approaches with sampling (please refer to Chap. 5), or potentially other algorithm-level solutions, is a worthwhile, yet larger unexplored area. It is necessary to gain a deeper insight into scenarios in which one of these approaches outperforms the other, in order to be able to create a more versatile compound algorithm.
- **Cost matrix estimation from non-stationary data**: learning misclassification costs is challenging on its own, but is even more challenging when conducted on non-stationary data streams [28] (see also Chap. 11). There is a need to develop new online cost-sensitive approaches that can combine advantages of ROC-based analysis with low computational complexity and capabilities of tackling concept drift.
- **Cost-sensitive approaches for other learning paradigms**: cost-sensitive learning should be expanded to other learning domains where class imbalance is present, such as multi-label/multi-instance problems [63], regression [54], or time-series analysis [55]. A complete description of these areas can be found at Chap. 12.

We envision that next decade will bring significant developments in this area, as many contemporary real-world applications call for existence of such machine learning methods.

References

1. Akbani, R., Kwek, S., Japkowicz, N.: Applying support vector machines to imbalanced datasets. In: Machine Learning: ECML 2004, 15th European Conference on Machine Learning, Pisa, Proceedings, pp. 39–50, 20–24 Sept 2004
2. Alejo, R., Toribio, P., Sotoca, J.M., Valdovinos, R.M., Gasca, E.: Resampling methods versus cost functions for training an MLP in the class imbalance context. In: Advances in Neural Networks – ISNN 2011 – 8th International Symposium on Neural Networks, ISNN 2011, Guilin, Proceedings, Part II, pp. 19–26, 29 May–1 June 2011
3. Anastasio, M.A., Kupinski, M.A., Nishikawa, R.M.: Optimization and FROC analysis of rule-based detection schemes using a multiobjective approach. IEEE Trans. Med. Imaging **17**(6), 1089–1093 (1998)
4. Bernard, S., Chatelain, C., Adam, S., Sabourin, R.: The multiclass ROC front method for cost-sensitive classification. Pattern Recogn. **52**, 46–60 (2016)
5. Bourke, C., Deng, K., Scott, S.D., Schapire, R.E., Vinodchandran, N.V.: On reoptimizing multiclass classifiers. Mach. Learn. **71**(2–3), 219–242 (2008)
6. Cao, P., Zhao, D., Zaïane, O.R.: An optimized cost-sensitive SVM for imbalanced data learning. In: Advances in Knowledge Discovery and Data Mining, 17th Pacific-Asia Conference, PAKDD 2013, Gold Coast, Proceedings, Part II, pp. 280–292, 14–17 Apr 2013

7. Castro, C.L., de Pádua Braga, A.: Novel cost-sensitive approach to improve the multilayer perceptron performance on imbalanced data. IEEE Trans. Neural Netw. Learn. Syst. **24**(6), 888–899 (2013)
8. Chatelain, C., Adam, S., Lecourtier, Y., Heutte, L., Paquet, T.: A multi-model selection framework for unknown and/or evolutive misclassification cost problems. Pattern Recogn. **43**(3), 815–823 (2010)
9. Chawla, N.V., Cieslak, D.A., Hall, L.O., Joshi, A.: Automatically countering imbalance and its empirical relationship to cost. Data Min. Knowl. Discov. **17**(2), 225–252 (2008)
10. Cheng, F., Zhang, J., Wen, C., Liu, Z., Li, Z.: Large cost-sensitive margin distribution machine for imbalanced data classification. Neurocomputing **224**, 45–57 (2017)
11. Datta, S., Das, S.: Near-Bayesian support vector machines for imbalanced data classification with equal or unequal misclassification costs. Neural Netw. **70**, 39–52 (2015)
12. Domingos, P.M.: Metacost: a general method for making classifiers cost-sensitive. In: Proceedings of the Fifth ACM SIGKDD International Conference on Knowledge Discovery and Data Mining, San Diego, pp. 155–164, 15–18 Aug 1999
13. Drummond, C., Holte, R.C.: C4.5, class imbalance, and cost sensitivity: why under-sampling beats over-sampling. In: ICML Workshop on Learning from Imbalanced Datasets II, Washington, DC, pp. 1–8 (2003)
14. Du, J., Cai, Z., Ling, C.X.: Cost-sensitive decision trees with pre-pruning. In: Advances in Artificial Intelligence, 20th Conference of the Canadian Society for Computational Studies of Intelligence, Canadian AI 2007, Montreal, Proceedings, pp. 171–179, 28–30 May 2007
15. Ducange, P., Lazzerini, B., Marcelloni, F.: Multi-objective genetic fuzzy classifiers for imbalanced and cost-sensitive datasets. Soft Comput. **14**(7), 713–728 (2010)
16. Everson, R.M., Fieldsend, J.E.: Multi-class ROC analysis from a multi-objective optimisation perspective. Pattern Recogn. Lett. **27**(8), 918–927 (2006)
17. Fawcett, T.: Roc graphs: notes and practical considerations for researchers. Technical report (2004)
18. Fawcett, T.: An introduction to ROC analysis. Pattern Recogn. Lett. **27**(8), 861–874 (2006)
19. Ferri, C., Flach, P.A., Hernández-Orallo, J.: Learning decision trees using the area under the ROC curve. In: Proceedings of the Nineteenth International Conference on Machine Learning (ICML 2002), University of New South Wales, Sydney, pp. 139–146, 8–12 July 2002
20. Garcia, L.P.F., Lorena, A.C., Matwin, S., de Leon Ferreira de Carvalho, A.C.P.: Ensembles of label noise filters: a ranking approach. Data Min. Knowl. Discov. **30**(5), 1192–1216 (2016)
21. Hand, D.J., Till, R.J.: A simple generalisation of the area under the ROC curve for multiple class classification problems. Mach. Learn. **45**(2), 171–186 (2001)
22. Hand, D.J., Vinciotti, V.: Choosing k for two-class nearest neighbour classifiers with unbalanced classes. Pattern Recogn. Lett. **24**(9–10), 1555–1562 (2003)
23. Jackowski, K., Krawczyk, B., Wozniak, M.: Cost-sensitive splitting and selection method for medical decision support system. In: 13th International Conference on Intelligent Data Engineering and Automated Learning – IDEAL 2012, Natal, Proceedings, pp. 850–857, 29–31 Aug 2012
24. Katsumata, S., Takeda, A.: Robust cost sensitive support vector machine. In: Proceedings of the Eighteenth International Conference on Artificial Intelligence and Statistics, AISTATS 2015, San Diego, 9–12 May 2015 (2015)
25. Knoll, U., Nakhaeizadeh, G., Tausend, B.: Cost-sensitive pruning of decision trees. In: Machine Learning: ECML-94, European Conference on Machine Learning, Catania, Proceedings, pp. 383–386, 6–8 Apr 1994
26. Krawczyk, B.: Cost-sensitive one-vs-one ensemble for multi-class imbalanced data. In: 2016 International Joint Conference on Neural Networks, IJCNN 2016, Vancouver, pp. 2447–2452, 24–29 July 2016
27. Krawczyk, B.: Learning from imbalanced data: open challenges and future directions. Prog. AI **5**(4), 221–232 (2016)

28. Krawczyk, B., Skryjomski, P.: Cost-sensitive perceptron decision trees for imbalanced drifting data streams. In: European Conference on Machine Learning and Knowledge Discovery in Databases, ECML PKDD 2017, Skopje, Proceedings, Part II, pp. 512–527, 18–22 Sept 2017
29. Krawczyk, B., Woźniak, M.: Designing cost-sensitive ensemble – genetic approach. In: 3rd International Conference on Image Processing and Communications Challenges 3, IP&C 2011, Proceedings, pp. 227–234 (2011)
30. Krawczyk, B., Woźniak, M.: Cost-sensitive neural network with ROC-based moving threshold for imbalanced classification. In: 16th International Conference on Intelligent Data Engineering and Automated Learning – IDEAL 2015, Wroclaw, Proceedings, pp. 45–52, 14–16 Oct 2015
31. Krawczyk, B., Woźniak, M., Schaefer, G.: Cost-sensitive decision tree ensembles for effective imbalanced classification. Appl. Soft Comput. **14**, 554–562 (2014)
32. Krawczyk, B., Schaefer, G., Woźniak, M.: A hybrid cost-sensitive ensemble for imbalanced breast thermogram classification. Artif. Intell. Med. **65**(3), 219–227 (2015)
33. Landgrebe, T., Duin, R.P.W.: Approximating the multiclass ROC by pairwise analysis. Pattern Recogn. Lett. **28**(13), 1747–1758 (2007)
34. Landgrebe, T., Duin, R.P.W.: Efficient multiclass ROC approximation by decomposition via confusion matrix perturbation analysis. IEEE Trans. Pattern Anal. Mach. Intell. **30**(5), 810–822 (2008)
35. Landgrebe, T., Paclík, P.: The ROC skeleton for multiclass ROC estimation. Pattern Recogn. Lett. **31**(9), 949–958 (2010)
36. Landgrebe, T., Paclík, P., Tax, D.M.J., Verzakov, S., Duin, R.P.W.: Cost-based classifier evaluation for imbalanced problems. In: Structural, Syntactic, and Statistical Pattern Recognition, Joint IAPR International Workshops, SSPR 2004 and SPR 2004, Lisbon, Proceedings, pp. 762–770, 18–20 Aug 2004
37. Li, F., Zhang, X., Zhang, X., Du, C., Xu, Y., Tian, Y.: Cost-sensitive and hybrid-attribute measure multi-decision tree over imbalanced data sets. Inf. Sci. **422**, 242–256 (2018)
38. Ling, C.X., Yang, Q., Wang, J., Zhang, S.: Decision trees with minimal costs. In: Proceedings of the Twenty-first International Conference on Machine Learning (ICML 2004), Banff, 4–8 July 2004
39. Liu, X., Zhou, Z.: The influence of class imbalance on cost-sensitive learning: an empirical study. In: Proceedings of the 6th IEEE International Conference on Data Mining (ICDM 2006), Hong Kong, pp. 970–974, 18–22 Dec 2006
40. Liu, M., Xu, C., Luo, Y., Xu, C., Wen, Y., Tao, D.: Cost-sensitive feature selection by optimizing f-measures. IEEE Trans. Image Process. **27**(3), 1323–1335 (2018)
41. Liu, Z., Ma, C., Gao, C., Yang, H., Lan, R., Luo, X.: Cost-sensitive collaborative representation based classification via probability estimation with addressing the class imbalance. Multimed. Tools Appl. **77**(9), 10835–10851 (2018)
42. López, V., Fernández, A., Moreno-Torres, J.G., Herrera, F.: Analysis of preprocessing vs. cost-sensitive learning for imbalanced classification. Open problems on intrinsic data characteristics. Expert Syst. Appl. **39**(7), 6585–6608 (2012)
43. López, V., del Río, S., Benítez, J.M., Herrera, F.: Cost-sensitive linguistic fuzzy rule based classification systems under the mapreduce framework for imbalanced big data. Fuzzy Sets Syst. **258**, 5–38 (2015)
44. Maloof, M.A.: Learning when data sets are Imbalanced and when costs are unequal and unknown. In: International Conference on Machine Learning, Washington, DC (2003)
45. Moepya, S.O., Akhoury, S.S., Nelwamondo, F.V.: Applying cost-sensitive classification for financial fraud detection under high class-imbalance. In: 2014 IEEE International Conference on Data Mining Workshops, ICDM Workshops 2014, Shenzhen, pp. 183–192, 14 Dec 2014
46. Narasimhan, H., Agarwal, S.: Support vector algorithms for optimizing the partial area under the ROC curve. Neural Comput. **29**(7), 1919–1963 (2017)
47. Núñez, M.: The use of background knowledge in decision tree induction. Mach. Learn. **6**, 231–250 (1991)

48. Penar, W., Woźniak, M.: Cost-sensitive methods of constructing hierarchical classifiers. Expert. Syst. **27**(3), 146–155 (2010)
49. Peng, Y.: Adaptive sampling with optimal cost for class-imbalance learning. In: Proceedings of the Twenty-Ninth AAAI Conference on Artificial Intelligence, Austin, pp. 2921–2927, 25–30 Jan 2015
50. Provost, F.: Machine learning from imbalanced data sets 101. In: Proceedings of the AAAI 2000 Workshop on Imbalanced Data Sets, pp. 1–3 (2000)
51. Qin, Z., Wang, A.T., Zhang, C., Zhang, S.: Cost-sensitive classification with k-nearest neighbors. In: 6th International Conference on Knowledge Science, Engineering and Management, KSEM 2013, Dalian, Proceedings, pp. 112–131, 10–12 Aug 2013
52. Qiu, C., Jiang, L., Li, C.: Randomly selected decision tree for test-cost sensitive learning. Appl. Soft Comput. **53**, 27–33 (2017)
53. Radtke, P.V.W., Granger, E., Sabourin, R., Gorodnichy, D.O.: Skew-sensitive boolean combination for adaptive ensembles – an application to face recognition in video surveillance. Inf. Fusion **20**, 31–48 (2014)
54. Riccardi, A., Fernández-Navarro, F., Carloni, S.: Cost-sensitive adaboost algorithm for ordinal regression based on extreme learning machine. IEEE Trans. Cybern. **44**(10), 1898–1909 (2014)
55. Roychoudhury, S., Ghalwash, M.F., Obradovic, Z.: Cost sensitive time-series classification. In: European Conference on Machine Learning and Knowledge Discovery in Databases, ECML PKDD 2017, Skopje, Proceedings, Part II, pp. 495–511, 18–22 Sept 2017
56. Sáez, J.A., Krawczyk, B., Woźniak, M.: Analyzing the oversampling of different classes and types of examples in multi-class imbalanced datasets. Pattern Recogn. **57**, 164–178 (2016)
57. Sheng, S., Ling, C.X.: Hybrid cost-sensitive decision tree. In: Knowledge Discovery in Databases: PKDD 2005, 9th European Conference on Principles and Practice of Knowledge Discovery in Databases, Porto, Proceedings, pp. 274–284, 3–7 Oct 2005
58. Skryjomski, P., Krawczyk, B.: Influence of minority class instance types on SMOTE imbalanced data oversampling. In: First International Workshop on Learning with Imbalanced Domains: Theory and Applications, LIDTA@PKDD/ECML 2017, Skopje, pp. 7–21, 22 Sept 2017
59. Ting, K.M.: An instance-weighting method to induce cost-sensitive trees. IEEE Trans. Knowl. Data Eng. **14**(3), 659–665 (2002)
60. Turney, P.D.: Cost-sensitive classification: empirical evaluation of a hybrid genetic decision tree induction algorithm. J. Artif. Intell. Res. **2**, 369–409 (1995)
61. Veropoulos, K., Campbell, C., Cristianini, N.: Controlling the sensitivity of support vector machines. In: Proceedings of the International Joint Conference on AI, Stockholm, pp. 55–60 (1999)
62. Wang, S., Li, Z., Chao, W., Cao, Q.: Applying adaptive over-sampling technique based on data density and cost-sensitive SVM to imbalanced learning. In: The 2012 International Joint Conference on Neural Networks (IJCNN), Brisbane, pp. 1–8, 10–15 June 2012
63. Wang, X., Liu, X., Japkowicz, N., Matwin, S.: Resampling and cost-sensitive methods for imbalanced multi-instance learning. In: 13th IEEE International Conference on Data Mining Workshops, ICDM Workshops, Dallas, pp. 808–816, 7–10 Dec 2013
64. Zhang, X., Hu, B.: A new strategy of cost-free learning in the class imbalance problem. IEEE Trans. Knowl. Data Eng. **26**(12), 2872–2885 (2014)
65. Zhang, S., Qin, Z., Ling, C.X., Sheng, S.: "Missing is useful": missing values in cost-sensitive decision trees. IEEE Trans. Knowl. Data Eng. **17**(12), 1689–1693 (2005)
66. Zhao, H., Li, X., Xu, Z., Zhu, W.: Cost-sensitive decision tree with probabilistic pruning mechanism. In: 2015 International Conference on Machine Learning and Cybernetics, ICMLC 2015, Guangzhou, pp. 81–87, 12–15 July 2015
67. Zhou, Z., Liu, X.: Training cost-sensitive neural networks with methods addressing the class imbalance problem. IEEE Trans. Knowl. Data Eng. **18**(1), 63–77 (2006)
68. Zhou, Q., Zhou, H., Li, T.: Cost-sensitive feature selection using random forest: selecting low-cost subsets of informative features. Knowl. Based Syst. **95**, 1–11 (2016)

Chapter 5
Data Level Preprocessing Methods

Abstract The first mechanism to address the problem of imbalanced learning was the use of sampling methods. They consists of modifying a set of imbalanced data using different procedures to provide a balanced or more adequate data distribution to the subsequent learning tasks. In the specialized literature, many studies have shown that, for several types of classifiers, rebalancing the dataset significantly improves the overall performance of the classification compared to a non-preprocessed data set. Over the years, this procedure has been common and the use of sampling methods for imbalanced learning has been standardized. Still, classifiers do not always have to use this kind of preprocessing because many of them are able to directly deal with imbalanced datasets. There is no clear rule that tells us which strategy is best, whether to adapt the behavior of learning algorithms or to use data preprocessing techniques. However, data sampling and preprocessing techniques are standard techniques in imbalanced learning, they are widely used in Data Science problems. They are simple and easily configurable and can be used in synergy with any learning algorithm. This chapter will review the techniques of sampling, undersampling (the classical ones in Sect. 5.2 and advanced approaches in Sect. 5.3) and oversampling such as SMOTE in Sect. 5.4, as well as the most-known algorithm SMOTE and its derivatives in Sect. 5.5. Some hybridizations of undersampling and oversampling are described in Sect. 5.6. Experiments with graphical illustrations will be carried out to show the behavior of these techniques.

5.1 Introduction

The hitch with imbalanced datasets is that standard classification learning algorithms are often biased towards the majority classes (known as "negative") and therefore there is a higher misclassification rate in the minority class instances (called the "positive" class) [15, 19]. Therefore, throughout the last years, many solutions have been proposed to deal with this problem, both for standard learning algorithms and for ensemble techniques [44, 75]. They can be categorized into three major groups [5, 21, 55]:

© Springer Nature Switzerland AG 2018
A. Fernández et al., *Learning from Imbalanced Data Sets*,
https://doi.org/10.1007/978-3-319-98074-4_5

- **Data sampling**: in which the training instances are modified in such a way as to produce a more balanced class distribution that allow classifiers to perform in a similar manner to standard classification.
- **Algorithmic modification**: this procedure is oriented towards the adaptation of base learning methods to be more attuned to class imbalance issues
- **Cost-sensitive learning**: this type of solutions incorporate approaches at the data level, at the algorithmic level, or at both levels jointly, considering higher costs for the misclassification of examples of the positive class with respect to the negative class, and therefore, trying to minimize higher cost errors.

In the specialized literature, we can find some papers about resampling techniques studying the effect of changing the class distribution to deal with imbalanced datasets. Those works have proved empirically that, applying a preprocessing step in order to balance the class distribution, is usually an useful solution [22, 30, 39]. Furthermore, the main advantage of these techniques is that they are independent of the underlying classifier.

Resampling techniques can be categorized into three groups or families [10]:

- **Undersampling methods**, which create a subset of the original dataset by eliminating instances (usually majority class instances).
- **Oversampling methods**, which create a superset of the original dataset by replicating some instances or creating new instances from existing ones.
- **Hybrids methods**, which combine both sampling approaches.

Among these categories, there are several proposals where the simplest preprocessing are non heuristic methods such as random undersampling and random oversampling. In the first case, the major drawback is that it can discard potentially useful data, that could be important for the induction process. For random oversampling, several authors agree that this method can increase the likelihood of occurring overfitting, since it makes exact copies of existing instances. Section 5.2 is devoted to describe all the basic techniques for undersampling and oversampling in imbalanced learning.

Regarding undersampling, most of the proposed approaches are based in data cleaning techniques [54]. Some representative works in this area include the Wilson's edited nearest neighbor (ENN) rule [81], which removes examples that differ from two of its three NNs, the OSS [50], an integration method between the condensed NN rule and Tomek Links [79] and the NCR, which is based on the ENN technique [81]. In addition, there are many advanced approaches for undersampling that deserve to be mentioned here. Section 5.3 will be devoted to this goal.

According to the previous facts, more sophisticated methods have been proposed. Among them, the "Synthetic Minority Oversampling Technique" (SMOTE) [20] has become one of the most renowned approaches in this area. Briefly, its main idea is to create new minority class examples by interpolating several minority class instances that lie together for oversampling the training set. More insight about SMOTE will be given in this chapter, please see the Sect. 5.4.

Fig. 5.1 Chessboard data set

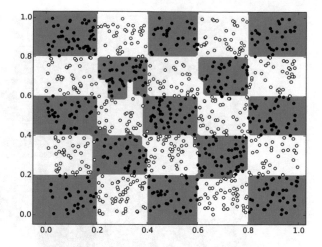

As a drawback, in oversampling techniques, and especially for the SMOTE algorithm, the problem of over generalization is largely attributed to the way in which it creates synthetic samples. Precisely, SMOTE generates the same number of synthetic data samples for each original minority example and does so without consideration to neighboring examples, which increases the occurrence of overlapping between classes. To this end, various adaptive sampling methods have been proposed to overcome this limitation; some representative works include the Borderline-SMOTE [42], Adaptive Synthetic Sampling (ADASYN) [45], Safe-Level-SMOTE [16] and MWMOTE [8] algorithms. More details will be given in Sect. 5.5.

Finally, the combination of different data preprocessing such as undersampling and oversampling or even cleaning techniques could lead to diminish the overlapping that is introduced from sampling methods, i.e. the integrations of SMOTE with ENN [81] and SMOTE with Tomek links [79], or a wrapper technique introduced in that defines the best percentage to perform both undersampling and oversampling. These hybridizations will be considered in Sect. 5.6 of this chapter.

Throughout this chapter, we will resort to figures representing a simple data set whose examples belong to two classes and are distributed as a 5×5 squares chessboard.[1] The original data set, depicted in Fig. 5.1, contains 1,000 data points and it is 100% balanced, hence it has 500 examples per class. In addition, the borders and areas modeled by a decision tree (more specifically, the CART algorithm [14, 82]) are drawn to make easier the visualization of the shape and possible loss of information in the chessboard. In fact, CART is not able to perfectly model the chessboard, as we can see in Fig. 5.1, due to lack of some critical data points in certain places.

---

[1]We would like to thank Sergio González for the development of a visualization module for this task. See more at https://github.com/sergiogvz/imbalanced_synthetic_data_plots

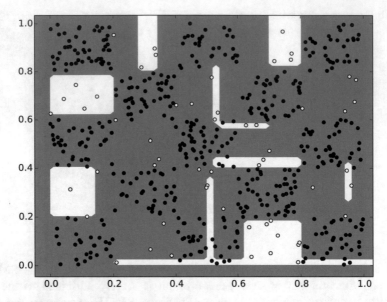

Fig. 5.2 Imbalanced chessboard data set

By using the chessboard data set, we can see the effects of the imbalanced learning problem once a class is assumed to be underrepresented regarding to the other. If we reduce the class represented by white points (from now, the minority or positive class) to only a 10% by using a random sampling, the outcome can be visualized in Fig. 5.2. Now, the chessboard shape is practically lost with CART, only five white squares are partially maintained. Another major fact is that many white points are completely ignored, indicating that they have been considered as harmful data points to avoid the overfitting of the model.

The data set depicted in Fig. 5.2 will be the basis from which we set out to illustrate the behavior of other data level techniques we will see in this chapter.

5.2 Undersampling and Oversampling Basics

As we mentioned before, sampling approaches can be categorized into two approaches: *undersampling*, that consists of reducing the data by eliminating examples belonging to the majority class with the objective of equalizing the number of examples of each class; and *oversampling*, that aims to replicate or generate new positive examples in order to gain importance.

As classical methods, we consider a total of nine techniques. Two of these methods, random undersampling and random oversampling, are non-heuristic methods that were initially included in this evaluation as baseline methods. However, they usually obtain good results in a very low response time [10].

- **Random Undersampling (RUS):** It is a non-heuristic method that aims to balance class distribution through the random elimination of majority class examples to get a balanced instance set. The final ratio of balancing can be adjusted.
- **Random Undersampling (ROS):** It is another non-heuristic method that aims to balance class distribution through the random replication of minority class examples.

The major drawback of random undersampling is that this method can discard potentially useful data that could be important for the induction process. The removal of data is a critical decision to be made, hence many the proposal of undersampling use heuristics in order to overcome the limitations of the non-heuristics decisions. On the other hand, the random oversampling may increase the likelihood of occurring overfitting, since it makes exact copies of the minority class examples. In this way, a symbolic classifier, for instance, might construct rules that are apparently accurate, but actually cover one replicated example.

Next, we will describe other classical undersampling techniques which use heuristic procedures to decide the data points to be removed. The well-known SMOTE oversampling and hybridizations will be presented in Sects. 5.4 and 5.5 of this chapter.

Regarding the notation used, let us assume that there is a training set TR with N instances which consists of pairs $(x_i, y_i), i = 1, \ldots, N$, where x_i defines an input vector of attributes and y_i defines the corresponding class label. Each of the N instances have M input attributes and they should belong to the positive or negative class. Let $\hat{E} \subseteq E$ be the subset of selected examples resulted in the run of a undersampling technique.

- **Tomek Links (TL):** TL [79] can be defined as follows: given two examples $E_i = (x_i, y_i)$ and $E_j = (x_j, y_j)$ where $y_i \neq y_j$ and $d(E_i, E_j)$ being the distance between E_i and E_j. A pair (E_i, E_j) is called Tomek link if there is not an example E_l, such that $d(E_i, E_l) < d(E_i, E_j)$ or $d(E_j, E_l) < d(E_i, E_j)$. Tomek links can be used as an undersampling method eliminating only examples belonging to the majority class in each Tomek link found.
- **Condensed Nearest Neighbor Rule (US-CNN):** Hart's CNN[43] is used to find a consistent subset of examples. A subset $\hat{E} \subset E$ is consistent with E if using a 1-nearest neighbor [25], $\hat{E}$ correctly classifies the examples in E. An algorithm to create a subset $\hat{E}$ from E as an undersampling method is the US-CNN. First, it randomly draws one majority class example and all examples from the minority class and put these examples in $\hat{E}$. Afterwards, use a 1-NN over the examples in $\hat{E}$ to classify the examples in E. Every misclassified example from E is moved to $\hat{E}$. It is important to note that this procedure does not find the smallest consistent subset from E. The idea behind this implementation of a consistent subset is to eliminate the examples from the majority class that are distant from the decision border, since these kind of examples might be considered less relevant for learning.

- **One-Sided Selection (OSS):** OSS [50] is an undersampling method resulting from the application of Tomek links [79] followed by the application of US-CNN. Tomek links are used as an undersampling method and removes noisy and borderline majority class examples. Borderline examples can be considered "unsafe" since a small amount of noise can make them fall on the wrong side of the decision border. US-CNN aims to remove examples from the majority class that are distant from the decision border. The remainder examples, i.e. "safe" majority class examples and all minority class examples are used for learning.
- **US-CNN + TL:** This hybridization [10] is similar to OSS, but the method US-CNN is applied before the Tomek links [79]. As finding Tomek links is computationally demanding, it would be computationally cheaper if it was performed on a reduced data set.
- **Neighborhood Cleaning Rule (NCL):** NCL [51] uses the *Wilson's Edited Nearest Neighbor Rule (ENN)* [81] to remove majority class examples. ENN removes any example whose class label differs from the class of at least two of its three NNs. NCL modifies the ENN in order to increase the data cleaning. For a two-class problem the algorithm can be described in the following way: For each example $E_i = (x_i, y_i)$ in the training set, its three nearest neighbors are found. If E_i belongs to the majority class and the classification given by its three NNs contradicts the original class of E_i, then E_i is removed. If E_i belongs to the minority class and its three NNs misclassify E_i, then the NNs that belong to the majority class are removed.
- **Class Purity Maximization (CPM):** CPM [87] attempts to find a pair of centers, one being a minority class instance while the other is a majority class instance. Using these centers, it partitions all the instances into two clusters C_1 and C_2. If either of the clusters have less class impurity than its parent's impurity (Imp) then we have found our clusters. The impurity of a set of instances is simply the proportion of minority class instances. It then recursively partitions each of these clusters into subclusters. Thus, it forms a hierarchical clustering. If the impurity cannot be improved then we stop the recursion. The algorithm is described in the algorithm described in the Fig. 5.3.
- **Undersampling Based on Clustering (SBC):** It was proposed in [84, 85]. Considering that the number of samples in the class-imbalanced data set is N, within it, the number of samples belonging to the majority class is N^- and the number of minority class samples is N^+. SBC first clusters all samples in the data set into K clusters. The number of majority class and minority class samples is N_i^- and N_i^+, respectively. Therefore, the ratio of the number of majority class samples to the number of minority class samples in the i-th cluster is N_i^-/N_i^+. If the ratio of N_i^- to N_i^+ in the training data set is set to be $m : 1$, the number of selected majority class samples in the i-th cluster is shown in expression (5.1):

$$SN_i^- = (m \cdot N^+) \cdot \frac{N_i^-/N_i^+}{\sum_{i=1}^{K}(N_i^-/N_i^+)} \tag{5.1}$$

Input: *Imp*: cluster impurity of parent cluster

      parent: parent cluster ID

Output: subclusters C_i rooted at parent

CPM(*Imp,parent*)

1. *impurity* $\leftarrow \infty$

2. While *Imp* $\leq$ *impurity*

    3. If all the instance pairs in *parent* were tested then return

    4. Pick a pair of majority and minority class instances as centers

    5. Partition all instances into 2 clusters C_1 and C_2

      according to nearest center

    6. *impurity* $\leftarrow min(impurity\,(C_1), impurity\,(C_2))$

    7. CPM$(impurity\,(C_1), C_1)$

    8. CPM$(impurity\,(C_2), C_2)$

Fig. 5.3 Pseudocode of CPM algorithm

After determining the number of majority class samples in each cluster, it randomly chooses majority class samples in the i-th cluster.

- *NearMiss* **approaches:** This is a family of four methods based on informed heuristics [90]. The first "NearMiss-1" method selects samples from the majority class that are close to some of the minority class samples. In this way, samples of the majority class are selected when their average distances to three samples of the closest minority class are the smallest. The second "NearMiss-2" method selects the samples of the majority class, when their average distances to the three samples of the most distant minority class are the smallest. The third "NearMiss-3" method extracts a given number of the closest majority class samples for each sample of the minority class. Finally, the fourth "More distant" method selects the majority class samples whose mean distances to the three nearest minority class samples are the largest.

We want to show the results offered by two of these classical methods applied on the imbalanced chessboard data set. The first technique is OSS [50], Fig. 5.4 illustrates the final outcome after OSS was run. As you can see, many black dots are removed, belonging either to the borderline places or internal parts of the chessboard squares. The first part of this method runs a *Tomek Links* procedure [79], which achieves the removal of some examples closer to minority examples. This procedure does not produce a very high reduction, only few examples are removed. The second step is accomplished by a condensation process taken by CNN, which removes several examples placed in internal parts of the squares. Here, we started with 100 negative examples in order to have enough representatives in all the black squares of the data set. In spite of this, the quantity of examples removed is higher, reducing the density of black dots within the squares. The final results is quite accurate, eight squares are almost recovered and other four squares are partially recovered with the CART decision tree.

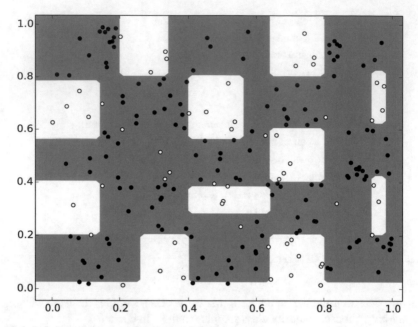

Fig. 5.4 Imbalanced chessboard treated with OSS

The second technique we want to illustrate is NCL [51]. Figure 5.5 depicts the results of applying NCL on the imbalanced chessboard data set. As we have mentioned, NCL is an editing-based technique that works similarly to ENN [81], but focused on majority examples. In order to exaggerate the results, the neighborhood considered during its run is large: 20 neighbors to perform majority voting. The graphic shows how the density of black dots are reduced and they almost maintain the decision frontiers given by CART. However, it is not enough for the positive class, only four squares are more or less completely modeled by CART and the final frontiers lose the initial form of a chessboard. This is a symptom of that this mechanism works in detrimental to the majority class, extending the decision borderlines for the positive class in some cases. As recommendation, a fine-grained NCL with small neighborhoods (3 or 5 neighborhood) may be very useful to be applied after some oversampling procedure which generates noisy examples. Section 5.6 will refer to the benefits of combining oversampling and undersampling as a unique treatment.

5.3   Advanced Undersampling Techniques

In this section, we will review the advanced undersampling techniques which use more complex mechanism to address the data sampling, such as evolutionary algorithms, ensembles or clustering. The most representative techniques will be described in detail for each group mentioned.

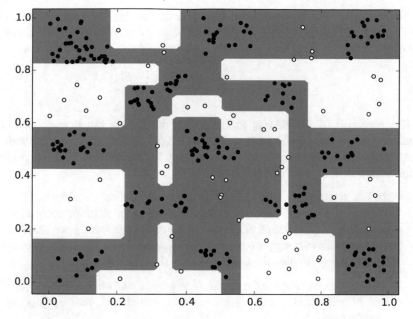

Fig. 5.5 Imbalanced chessboard treated with NCL

5.3.1   Evolutionary Undersampling

Undersampling can be considered as a search problem in which Evolutionary Algorithms (EAs) can be applied [29]. To accomplish this, two important issues must be taken into account: the specification of the representation of the solutions, the definition of the fitness function and the description of the main evolutionary scheme used, which will be the CHC model.

- *Representation of solutions:* The search space associated is constituted by all the subsets of TR. This is accomplished by using a binary representation. A chromosome consists of N genes (one for each instance in TR) with two possible states: 0 and 1. If the gene is 1, its associated instance is included in the subset of TR represented by the chromosome. If it is 0, this does not occur.
- *Fitness Function:* Let S be a subset of instances of TR and be coded by a chromosome. Classically, we define a fitness function that combines two values: the classification rate (*clas_rat*) associated with S and the percentage of reduction (*perc_red*) of instances of S with regards to TR.

$$Fitness(S) = \alpha \cdot clas\_rat + (1 - \alpha) \cdot perc\_red. \tag{5.2}$$

Any classifier can be used as wrapper for measuring the classification rate, $clas\_rat$, associated with S. It denotes the percentage of correctly classified objects from TR using only S to train the learner. $perc\_red$ is defined as

$$perc\_red = 100 \cdot \frac{|TR| - |S|}{|TR|}. \tag{5.3}$$

The objective of the EAs is to maximize the fitness function defined, i.e., maximize the classification rate and minimize the number of instances obtained.

- As the evolutionary computation method, the CHC model was chosen to perform the selection of data examples.

  - CHC is a classical evolutionary model that introduces different features to obtain a trade-off between exploration and exploitation; such as incest prevention, reinitialization of the search process when it becomes blocked and the competition among parents and offspring into the replacement process. During each generation the CHC develops the following steps.

    · It uses a parent population of size N to generate an intermediate population of N individuals, which are randomly paired and used to generate N potential offspring.
    · Then, a survival competition is held where the best N chromosomes from the parent and offspring populations are selected to form the next generation.

    CHC also implements a form of heterogeneous recombination using HUX, a special recombination operator. HUX exchanges half of the bits that differ between parents, where the bit position to be exchanged is randomly determined. CHC also employs a method of incest prevention. Before applying HUX to the two parents, the Hamming distance between them is measured. Only those parents who differ from each other by some number of bits (mating threshold) are mated. The initial threshold is set at $L/4$, where L is the length of the chromosomes. If no offspring are inserted into the new population then the threshold is reduced by one.
    No mutation is applied during the recombination phase. Instead, when the population converges or the search stops making progress (i.e., the difference threshold has dropped to zero and no new offspring are being generated which are better than any member of the parent population) the population is reinitialized to introduce new diversity to the search. The chromosome representing the best solution found over the course of the search is used as a template to reseed the population. Reseeding of the population is accomplished by randomly changing 35% of the bits in the template chromosome to form each of the other $N-1$ new chromosomes in the population. The search is then resumed.

In [35], we presented a taxonomy for Evolutionary Undersampling methods, identifying the main issues used for the classification of the respective models and including each method in its corresponding place. We established two ways of division, the objective that they pursue and the way they do the selection of instances. Regarding the main objective, there are two goals of interest in these methods:

- Aiming for an optimal balancing of data without loss of effectiveness in classification accuracy. Evolutionary undersampling models that follow this tendency are called Evolutionary Balancing undersampling (EBUS).
- Aiming for an optimal power of classification without taking into account the balancing of data, considering the latter as a sub-objective that may be an implicit process. The models that follow this tendency are called Evolutionary undersampling guided by Classification Measures (EUSCM).

With respect to the types of IS that can be carried out in evolutionary undersampling [18], we distinguished:

- If the selection scheme proceeds over any kind of instance, then it is called Global Selection (GS). That is, the chromosome contains the state of all instances belonging to the training data set and removals of minority class instances (those belonging to positive class) are allowed.
- If the selection scheme only proceeds over majority class instances then it is called Majority Selection (MS). In this case, the chromosome saves the state of instances that belong to the negative class and a removal of a positive or minority class instance is not allowed.

This categorization produced a total number of eight evolutionary undersampling methods based on the CHC algorithm. More details on the taxonomy and their reported performance can be found in [35] for KNN classifiers, [37] for decision trees based classifiers and [38] for nested generalized learning algorithms.

5.3.1.1 ACOSampling

In the study [88], a meta-heuristic based undersampling method was introduced based on the idea of ant colony optimization (ACO), which is called ACOSampling. First, the original training data set is randomly and repeatedly divided into two groups: training data set and validation data set. Then, for each partition, ACOSampling is performed to find the subset of the corresponding optimal majority class examples. Unlike traditional ACO, ACOSampling forces the ants to leave the nest, then pass all samples of the majority class one by one, either by a value of 0 or a value of 1, to reach the food source, where 0 indicates that the corresponding sample is useless and should be removes, and 1 indicates that it is important and should be selected. Taking into account the particularity of the imbalanced classification tasks, the overall precision is calculated by three weighted indicative metrics, namely F-measure, G-mean and AUC [13, 47, 65]. Then, many subsets of local optimal majority samples can be generated by iterative partitions, so the significance of each major sample must be estimated according to its selection frequency; i.e., the higher the selection frequency, the more information the sample will provide. Finally, you can then create a globally balanced sample set by combining the highly sorted samples from the majority class with all minority class examples. The fitness function used in ACOSampling is:

$$\text{fitness} = \alpha \times \text{F-measure} + \beta \times \text{G-mean} + \gamma \times \text{AUC} \qquad (5.4)$$

subject to $\alpha + \beta + \gamma = 1$.

5.3.1.2 IPADE-ID

Instance generation has been also applied to perform undersampling tasks with EAs. The original purpose of instance generation is to obtain an instance generated set GS, which consists of $\mathbf{r}$, $\mathbf{r} < \mathbf{n}$, instances $\mathbf{p}_u$ where $\mathbf{p}_u = (\mathbf{p}_{u1}, \mathbf{p}_{u2}, \ldots, \mathbf{p}_{um}, \mathbf{p}_{u\omega})$, which are either selected or generated from the examples of TR. The instances of the generated set are determined to efficiently represent the distributions of the classes and to discriminate well when used to classify the training objects.

IPADE-ID [56] is an extension of the IPADE instance generation algorithm to imbalanced domains. It follows an iterative scheme, in which it determines the most appropriate number of instances per class and their best positioning for a determined classifier, focusing on the positive class. In particular, IPADE-ID is organized into three different stages: initialization, optimization and addition of instances.

1. Initialization: Although IPADE-ID iteratively learns instances to find the most appropriate structure of GS, a good initialization process can lead the search to better results specially when it is dependent on the target classifier. IPADE-ID develops two different initialization processes for KNN and decision tress respectively.
2. Optimization: In IPADE-ID, a Differential Evolution algorithm (specifically, it is a *DE/CurrentToRand/1* strategy) is employed to optimize the outcome. Here, each individual in the population encodes a single instance without the class label and, as such, the dimension of the individuals is equal to the number of attributes of the specific problem. The fitness function used to guide the search process is measured as the AUC obtained with the target classifier using GS as training set and TR as validation set.
3. Addition of Instances: In order to reduce the classification error of the minority class, IPADE-ID extracts a random example of this class from TR and adds this to the current GS in a new trial set. This addition forces the re-positioning of the instances by using the optimization process again and its corresponding evaluation of predictive AUC.

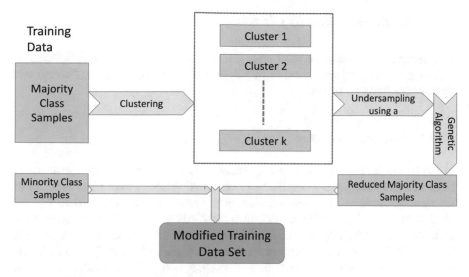

Fig. 5.6 CBEUS algorithm flowchart

5.3.1.3 CBEUS: Cluster-Based Evolutionary Undersampling

The CBEUS method is a undersampling technique that combines clustering and genetic algorithms to address the data imbalance problem [49]. The general process of this algorithm is shown in Fig. 5.6. The process of this method consists of the following steps: The first step is to divide the examples of the majority class into several clusters using the k-means clustering. Next, we calculate the distance between an instance and centroid within each cluster using the Euclidean distance function. The second step is to find the thresholds that represent the distance from the centroid of each group using a genetic algorithm.

CBEUS selects relevant instances of the majority class based on the assumption of removing noisy instances that are far from the centroid of the cluster. This approach is expected to have advantages over previous undersampling techniques. First, it eliminates noisy instances by considering distances between an instance of a majority class and the centroid of each group. The data set that eliminates noisy instances results in improved and stable classification performance. Second, a relatively intelligent undersampling technique is used based on the survival of the most suitable cases in the optimization. The disadvantage of random undersampling is that potentially useful instances can be discarded. Thus, CBEUS uses the geometric mean, which considers the balance and precision of both the majority and minority classes to compensate for these drawbacks.

5.3.2   Undersampling by Cleaning Data

This section will review the most representative undersampling methods based on cleaning harmful majority samples by different criteria, mainly in similarities and other data related measures.

5.3.2.1   Weighted Sampling

In [3] a weighted sampling based approach was proposed. Instances located far from decision limits are more likely to be classified correctly. The examples of the two classes close to each other are more likely to be misclassified by any classifier and the decision boundary is also likely to be in the neighborhood of these border examples. This approach uses this property to select representative negative samples. If the chosen instances are far from the decision limit and if the instances located near the true decision boundary are not chosen by a random selection process, the optimal separation hyperplane obtained by a typical statistical classifier may be wrongly positioned resulting in an increased number of misclassifications. The weighted sampling proposed is described as follows:

1. Calculate the weighted Euclidean distance of each negative sample from each of the positive samples. All features are weighted by its Fishers discriminant score, which measures the overlapping per attribute and it is usually known as F1 measure [9].
2. For each positive sample, sort negative samples in ascending order of distance from the positive sample.
3. For each positive sample, select a user-defined number of negative samples. The user-defined number indicates the desired ratio of negative samples to positive samples. At this stage, special care is taken to avoid repetitive selection of negative samples. If a particular negative sample has been already selected, the next available negative sample is selected.

5.3.2.2   IHT: Instance Hardness Threshold

The article [73] presents a way to compute the difficulty of classifying an instance and provide a measure called *instance hardness* that can be used with a set of thresholds to decide when and why filter a certain instance depending on the training data and the classifier to be used.

Table 5.1 lists the hardness measures considered in [73]. For more details, it is convenient to read the original paper.

Figure 5.7 depicts the result of the method IHT implemented in *Imbalanced-learn* [52] by using the default configuration applied on the imbalanced chessboard data set. As we can see, many black spots have been removed to increase the easiness of classifation for the surrounding white points. The majority examples removed

Table 5.1 List of hardness measures and what they measure. The "+" and "−" symbols distinguish which hardness measures are positively and negatively correlated with instance hardness

Abbr.	+/−	Measure	Insight
kDN	+	k-disagreeing neighbors	Overlap of an instance using all of the data set features on a subset of the instances
DS	−	Disjunct size	Complexity of the decision boundary for an instance
DCP	−	Disjunct class percentage	Overlap of an instance using a subset of the features and a subset of the instances
TD	+	Tree depth	The description length of an instance in an induced C4.5 [67] decision tree
CL	−	Class likelihood	Overlap of an instance using all of the features and all of the instances
CLD	−	Class likelihood difference	Relative overlap of an instance using all of the features and all of the instances
MV	+	Minority value	Class skew
CB	−	Class balance	Class skew

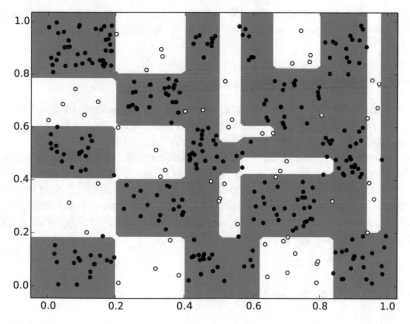

Fig. 5.7 Imbalanced chessboard treated with IHT

were mainly located in the overlapping regions, near to the square limits. Five white squares are perfectly recovered by CART on the left side and two on the right side. The rest of white squares are partially recovered motivated by the lack of positive examples and the overfitting avoiding mechanism of CART. The final outcome is

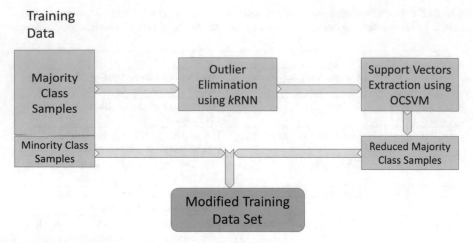

Fig. 5.8 Hybrid undersampling algorithm flowchart

very promising, indicating us that IHT is a very successful undersampling approach which combines local data complexity with class skewing.

5.3.2.3 Hybrid Undersampling

In [76], the authors proposed a hybrid undersampling method by removing the atypical values first from the majority class using a k reverse NNs technique. After, from the resulting dataset without outlier data [4] it extracts the support vectors using an one-class SVMs. They particularly chose SVM, as it performs an IS (through the collection of support vectors), while classifying the data sets. Therefore, they implicitly carry out the undersampling by selecting some important samples from the majority class. These resulting samples are merged with samples from the minority class, resulting in a modified balanced data set. The block diagram of the proposed approach is showed in Fig. 5.8.

5.3.3 Ensemble Based Undersampling

Another trend to carry out undersampling is through the combination of multiple designs in form of ensembles [33, 71]. These distinct designs can be achieved by changing the distribution of the training data set or some parameters that configure them.

5.3.3.1 IRUS: Inverse Random Undersampling

IRUS [77] is a method based on Bagging [28] motivated by the following facts. Suppose we manipulate the data set to the extreme and reverse the imbalance between the two classes. Indeed, we would have to draw sets of negative class samples of proportional size to P^2 where P is the previous probability of the positive class. This would lead to very small sample sets for the negative class and, therefore, a poor definition of the boundary between the two classes. However, the frontier would favor the positive class with a high rate of true positives since the number of negative class samples is much lower than the number of positive class samples. Moreover, since the number of samples of the negative class is very small relative to the dimensionality of the feature space, the ability of each boundary to completely separate the classes is high. In addition, since the number of samples drawn is proportional to P^2, the number of independent sets that can be drawn will be of the order of $1 = P^2$. This large number of designs could be used to control the rate of false positives using a completely different mechanism. By combining the detectors designed by fusion, we can control the false positive error rate. In short, the main idea behind IRUS is to maintain a very high positive rate by reversing the imbalance, that is, by making the majority (negative) subsets of classes have fewer examples than the (positive) minority class. Then to control the rate of false positives by a bagging classifier, i.e. by creating several subsets with each subset having all examples of the positive class and very few samples of the negative class.

The pseudocode presented in Algorithm 1 describes the IRUS algorithm in detail.

Algorithm 1 IRUS algorithm

1: **function** IRUS($TR_{N+}, TR_{N-}, S, Sets, t$)

  Require: TR_{N+}; TR_{N-}; S; $Sets$; t ▷ Training set with N^+ minority samples and N^- majority samples; S is the number of samples from TR_{N-} for each model, $S < N^+$; $Sets$ is the number of classifiers, default is $1.5 \times ceil(N^-/S)$; t is a test sample

  Ensure: $conf(t)$ ▷ confidence score of t

2:     $conf(t) = 0$

3:     **for** $i = 1$ to $Sets$ **do**

4:         $TR'_{N-} \Leftarrow$ Randomly pick S samples without replacement from TR_{N-}

5:         $T_s \Leftarrow TR'_{N-} \cup TR_{N+}$

6:         Train base classifier h_i using T_s samples

7:         $D =$ Probability of positive class assigned by h_i to the test sample t

8:         $D_{norm} = $ z-score normalization of D

9:         $conf(t) = conf(t) + D_{norm}$

10:     **end for**

11:     $conf(t) = conf(t)/Sets$

12: **end function**

Algorithm 2 OligoIS algorithm

1: **function** OLIGOIS(TR, s, r)
   Require: $TR; s; r$ ▷ A training set $TR; s$ is the subset size and r the number of rounds
   Ensure: S ▷ Set of selected instances $S \subset TR$
2:    **for** $i = 1$ to r **do**
3:        Divide instances into n_s disjoint subsets
4:        $D_i : \bigcup_i D_i = TR$ of size s
5:        **for** $j = 1$ to n_s **do**
6:            Apply IS algorithm to D_j
7:            Store votes of selected instances from D_j
8:        **end for**
9:    **end for**
10:   Obtain thresholds of votes to keep an instance from the minority, t^+, and the majority, T^-, classes
11:   $S = \{x_i \in TR | (\text{votes}(x_i) \geq t^+ \text{ and } x_i \in C^+) \text{ or } (\text{votes}(x_i) \geq t^- \text{ and } x_i \in C^-)\}$
12:   Undersample the class with more instances in S to obtain $S^{balanced}$ removing instances with fewer votes
13:   **if** $f(S^{balanced}) \geq f(S)$ **then**
14:        $S = S^{balanced}$
15:   **end if**
16:   **return** S
17: **end function**

5.3.3.2 OligoIS: Oligarchic Instance Selection

This technique is mainly based on the divide and conquer approach [40]. Instead of applying an IS method to the entire data set, it first randomly partitions the instances and applies the selection to each of the obtained subsets. This partition is repeated for several rounds, and the results are combined through a voting process. To account for the imbalanced class property of the datasets, the subsets used always contain the same number of instances of both classes. Any IS method can be used in the subset in the same way that any classifier can be used in a set. Because of this method unfairly treats the examples of the majority class, favoring instances of minority classes, it is called oligarchic IS. By itself, each round would not be able to achieve a good performance. However, combining several rounds using a voting scheme is able to improve the performance of an IS algorithm applied to the entire dataset with a large reduction in runtime of the algorithm.

The pseudocode presented in Algorithm 2 describes the OligoIS method.

5.3.4 Clustering Based Undersampling

Clustering becomes a successful technique to address sampling processes. They take into account both inter and intra-class imbalance distribution and are supported by the borderlines given by a set of clusters and the examples belonging to them.

5.3.4.1 ClusterOSS

It arises as an enhancement of the OSS procedure [6]. OSS [50] assumes that it is sufficient to choose only one random majority instance to initiate the undersampling process. However, the final result of the undersampling method will depend on that random choice. More importantly, OSS does not explicitly take into account the fact that there may be subsets within the majority class, and that subsampling might not work as well on all these subsets, given its random start.

The first difference with respect to OSS is that ClusterOSS can initiate the undersampling process from more than one instance. This already addresses the drawback of OSS that quality results depend heavily on the choice of the instance chosen to initiate the subsampling. The second difference is that it does not start the random undersampling process. Instead, the algorithm defines how many and which instances will be chosen to initiate that process. More specifically, it looks for subsets in the majority class, applying a clustering procedure. Then, the instance in the center of each subset is chosen to be one of the instances that will initiate the subsampling. By doing this, we improve the effectiveness of undersampling, since undersampling will start from points in different regions in the feature space.

ClusterOSS is described in these three steps:

1. At the beginning of the algorithm, a clustering procedure (for example, k-means) is used to group the instances belonging to the majority class.
2. Then, for each group, it finds the instances closest to the center. These instances are used to initiate the undersampling process, which is identical to the OSS.
3. Finally, as in OSS, the *Tomek Links* [79] data cleansing technique is used.

5.3.4.2 DSUS: Diversified Sensitivity Undersampling

DSUS consists of three main components [62]: (1) clustering samples in the majority class; (2) undersampling through a selection of samples using the stochastic sensitivity measure (*SM*); And (3) a trained Radial-basis function neural network (RBFNN) using training samples selected by the *SM*. Figure 5.9 shows the DSUS workflow. Both clustering and RBFNN use off-the-shelf methods. In addition, k-means is used although it could be replaced by other clustering methods. The number of clusters k was set to $k = \sqrt{N^+}$ for the minority class and N^+ for the majority class.

DSUS selects a sample closer to the center of each of these N^+ clusters as representative samples and then calculates their *SM* values. The k samples that produce the highest values of *SM* will be selected from the majority class. Likewise, k samples that produce the highest values of *SM* are also selected from the minority class. These $2k$ samples are added to the initial training set to form a balanced training data set for the RBFNN. At each iteration turn, the training dataset consists of samples $2tk$, where t denotes the number of iterations including the initial spin. The value of t is at most equal to k. The *SM* measure was proposed in [86].

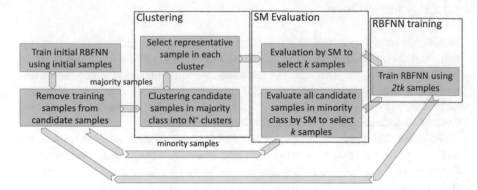

Fig. 5.9 DSUS algorithm flowchart

Fig. 5.10 An illustration of
how to create the synthetic
data points in the SMOTE
algorithm

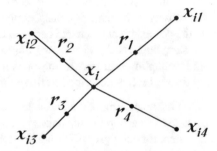

5.4   Synthetic Minority Oversampling TEchnique (SMOTE)

The SMOTE algorithm carries out an oversampling approach to rebalance the
original training set [20]. Instead of applying a simple replication of the minority
class instances, the key idea of SMOTE is to introduce synthetic examples. These
new examples are created by interpolation between several positive instances that
lie together. For this reason, the procedure is said to be focused on the "feature
space" rather than on the "data space". A simple example of this oversampling
process is illustrated in Fig. 5.10. An x_i positive instance is selected as basis to
create new synthetic data points. Based on a distance metric, several NNs of the
same class (points x_{i1} to x_{i4}) are chosen from the training set. Finally, a randomized
interpolation is carried out in order to obtain new instances r_1 to r_4.

The formal procedure works as follows. First, the total amount of oversampling
N (an integer value) is set up, which usually is defined to obtain an approximate
1:1 class distribution. Then, an iterative process is carried out, composed of several
steps. First, a positive class instance is selected at random from the training set. Next,
its KNN (5 by default) are obtained. Finally, N of these K instances are randomly
chosen to compute the new instances by interpolation. To do so, the difference
between the feature vector (sample) under consideration and each neighbor is taken.
This difference is multiplied by a random number drawn between 0 and 1, and then

---

Algorithm 3 SMOTE algorithm

1: **function** SMOTE(T, N, k)
    Input: T; N; k ▷ #minority class examples, Amount of oversampling, #NNs
    Output: (N/100) * T synthetic minority class samples
    Variables: $Sample[][]$: array for original minority class samples;
    $newindex$: keeps a count of number of synthetic samples generated, initialized to 0;
    $Synthetic[][]$: array for synthetic samples
2:    **if** $N < 100$ **then**
3:        Randomize the T minority class samples
4:        $T = (N/100)*T$
5:        $N = 100$
6:    **end if**
7:    $N = (int)N/100$ ▷ The amount of SMOTE is assumed to be in integral multiples of 100.
8:    **for** $i = 1$ to T **do**
9:        Compute KNN for i, and save the indices in the $nnarray$
10:     POPULATE(N, i, $nnarray$)
11:    **end for**
12: **end function**

Algorithm 4 Function to generate synthetic samples

1: **function** POPULATE(N, i, $nnarray$)
    Input: N; i; $nnarray$ ▷ #instances to create, original sample index, array of NNs
    Output: N new synthetic samples in $Synthetic$ array
2:    **while** $N \neq 0$ **do**
3:        nn = random(1,k)
4:        **for** attr = 1 to numattrs **do**   ▷ $numattrs$ = Number of attributes
5:           Compute: $dif = Sample[nnarray[nn]][attr] - Sample[i][attr]$
6:           Compute: $gap = random(0, 1)$
7:           $Synthetic[newindex][attr] = Sample[i][attr] + gap \cdot dif$
8:        **end for**
9:        $newindex + +$
10:     $N - -$
11:    **end while**
12: **end function**

---

it is added to the previous feature vector. This causes the selection of a random point along the "line segment" between the features. In case of nominal attributes, one of the two values are selected at random. The whole process is summarized in Algorithm 3.

Finally, Fig. 5.11 shows a simple example of the SMOTE application in order to understand how synthetic instances are computed.

As we mentioned before, SMOTE has served as inspiration for almost all the oversampling methods proposed for imbalance learning. In [31], the authors surveyed all the issues and further developments based on SMOTE in recognition of the 15 years since the original proposal.

Continuing with the graphical representations of the data-level algorithms, Fig. 5.12 depicts the results of the imbalanced chessboard data set after running SMOTE by using its standard configuration ($k = 5$, 100% of balancing). The results

```
Consider a sample (6,4) and let (4,3) be its NN.
(6,4) is the sample for which KNN are being
identified (4,3) is one of its KNN.
Let: f1_1 = 6 f2_1 = 4,   f2_1 - f1_1 = -2
f1_2 = 4  f2_2 = 3,   f2_2 - f1_2 = -1
The new samples will be generated as
f1',f2' = (6,4) + rand(0-1) * (-2,-1)
rand(0-1) generates a random number between 0 and 1.
```

Fig. 5.11 Example of the SMOTE application

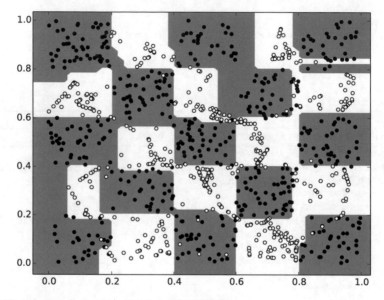

Fig. 5.12 Imbalanced chessboard treated with SMOTE

is quite surprising, due to the fact that the complete chessboard seems to be totally recovered by the CART decision tree. Only three white squares are partially drawn and all the remaining black squares are almost maintained from the original data set. This shows the usefulness of SMOTE, although the algorithm is not perfect [57]. Several drawbacks, which have been pointed out since the development of SMOTE, can be easily exhibited in this figure. First, the modeling of these three partial white squares is due to the location of the positive examples. Each white square in a chessboard has from two or four diagonal adjacent white squares. If the positive examples are distributed or oriented by a certain side of the square, the interpolations will be done focusing on creating new synthetic points in the middle of this adjacent points. This produces the negative effect of keeping away when no points are closer in two diagonal adjacent squares. This explains the three half white squares modeled by CART. Secondly, lots of new artificial examples are created in the same direction, that is, following an artificial connecting line between diagonal squares. This may complicate the modeling of decision surfaces because it produces lots of borderline examples. Finally, SMOTE clearly generates noisy points. They can be easily identified due to they fall into black squares and they are surrounded by black dots.

Motivated by the drawbacks of the original SMOTE idea, many extensions have been proposed to fix and obtain a more robust oversampling mechanism based on the generation of synthetic examples. The next chapter of this book is devoted to describe and show the most relevant SMOTE extensions proposed in the specialized literature.

5.5 Extensions of SMOTE

In this section, we present the most significant SMOTE-based extensions proposed in the specialized literature. Currently, there are more than 90 extensions published in scientific journals and conferences. Here, we will give all the details of the most-known and used extensions of SMOTE as oversampling approach. Other SMOTE extensions proposed for the interested reader are: LLE-SMOTE [80], Distance-SMOTE [26], Polynom-Fit-OS [41], MSMOTE [53], CE-SMOTE [23], Edge-Det-SMOTE [48], CBSO [7], DSRBF [32], TRIM-SMOTE [66], NRSBoundary-SMOTE [46], LVQ-SMOTE [61], BKS [63], PDFOS [34], RWO-Sampling [89], NEATER [2], DAE [11], wRACOG [27], MOT2LD [83], OEFS [64], OUPS [70], SMOTE-FRST-2T [69], CURE-SMOTE [58], among many others. For an exhaustive list, reader may refer to [31].

5.5.1 Borderline-SMOTE

To achieve a better prediction, most of the classification algorithms try to learn the limit of each class as accurately as possible in the training process. Examples at the border and boundary examples are more likely to be misclassified than those that are far from the border, and therefore more important for classification.

Based on the above analysis, those examples away from the borders may contribute little to classification. Therefore, two new methods of oversampling of minority examples, Borderline-SMOTE1 and Borderline-SMOTE2 were proposed [42], in which only the limit examples of the minority class will be oversampled. These methods are different from the existing ones of oversampling in which all minority examples or a random subset of the minority class are oversampled.

These methods are based on SMOTE. SMOTE generates synthetic minority examples to oversample the minority class. For each minority example, its k (which is set to 5 in standard SMOTE) NNs of the same class are estimated, then some examples are randomly selected from them according to the oversampling rate. After that, new synthetic examples are generated along the line between the example of the minority and their closest selected neighbors. Like existing methods of oversampling, these new methods only strengthen minority limit examples. First the borderline minority examples are found; then, synthetic examples are generated from them and added to the original training set.

Let us assume that the whole training set is denoted by TR, the set of minority or positive class examples is P and the set of majority examples is M. The number of minority and majority examples is denoted by N^+ and N^- respectively. the procedure Borderline-SMOTE1 is as follows:

1. For every p_i, $(i = 1, 2, \ldots, N^+)$ in P, we calculate its KNN from the whole training set TR. The number of majority examples among the m NNs is denoted by m' $(0 \leq m' \leq m)$.
2. If $k' = k$ i.e. all the m nearest neighbors of p_i are majority examples, p_i is considered to be noise and is not operated in the following steps. If $m/2 \leq m' \leq m$, namely the number of p_i's majority NNs is larger than the number of its minority ones, p_i is considered to be easily misclassified and put into a set $DANGER$. If $0 \leq m' \leq m/2$, p_i is safe and needs not to participate in the follows steps.
3. The examples in $DANGER$ are the borderline data of the minority class P, and we can see that $DANGER \subset P$. We set $DANGER = \{p'_1, p'_2, \ldots, p'_D\}$, $0 \leq D \leq N^+$. For each example in $DANGER$, we calculate its KNN from P.
4. In this step, $D \times s$ synthetic positive examples are generated from the data in $DANGER$, where s is an integer between 1 and k. For each (p'_i), it randomly selects s NNs from its KNN in P. Firstly, it calculates the differences, dif_j, $(j = 1, 2, \ldots, s)$ between p'_i and its s NNs from P, then multiply dif_j by a random number r_j $(j = 1, 2, \ldots, s)$ between 0 and 1, finally, s new synthetic minority examples are generated between p'_i and its NNs: $synthetic_j = p'_i + r_j \times dif_j$, $(j = 1, 2, \ldots, s)$.

The algorithm repeats the above mechanism for each p'_i in $DANGER$ and it can at tain $D \times s$ synthetic examples. This step is similar to SMOTE's one.

According to the authors, Borderline-SMOTE2 does not only generate synthetic examples from each example in $DANGER$ and its positive NNs in P, but also does that from its nearest negative neighbor in M. The difference between it and its nearest negative neighbor is multiplied a random number between 0 and 0.5, thus the new generated examples are closer to the minority class.

We can see the effects of Borderline-SMOTE1 on the imbalanced chessboard data set in Fig. 5.13. The differences in the outcome with respect to the original SMOTE (Fig. 5.13) are evident in the sense of the change of distribution of the synthetic white points generated. The points are generated especially following the lines accross the diagonals of the squares, even drawing a circular shape. The denser an area, the higher the number of points are generated around. This explains how some white squares located in external places have been missed or reduced during the learning of CART decision tree, producing a less accurate chessboard modeling. It is also interesting to note that the number of white dots generated in black squares is less than that generated by SMOTE.

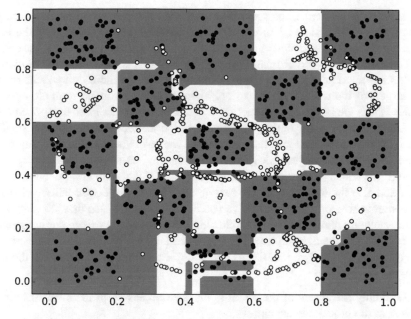

Fig. 5.13 Imbalanced chessboard treated with borderline-SMOTE1

5.5.2   *Adjusting the Direction of the Synthetic Minority ClasS Examples: ADOMS*

According to the authors [78], when analyzing the SMOTE algorithm, the impact of the synthetic examples on the original feature space is restricted to the local space by interpolating the synthetic between the minor class example processing and one of its NNs. When the neighbor is far from the center, which means that there are only few examples in the local space near the center and the true underlying distribution of the class will simply be expressed unreliable, the example of the synthetic minority class should be inserted in the space from the center to occupy the space comparatively better defined. In contrast, when the neighbor is near the center, which means that there are already enough examples in the local space to finely express the underlying class distribution, the synthetic example must be inserted closer to the center to avoid disrupting the well definite space. The previous generation mechanism of examples of synthetic minority classes sounds reasonable, however in SMOTE, only one of the neighbors of the center is chosen at random to represent the local space, and the mechanism is performed only in 1-dimension defined by the center and the selected neighbor. It is obvious that the mechanism must be performed in all space more appropriately.

Note that the real-world data space is little isotropic, and the interpolation mechanism must be considered in all directions in the feature space, respectively. When a synthetic example is generated in the direction in which the projections of the local data are scarce, the projection of the synthetic must be further from the center and; on the contrary, in the direction in which the projections of the local data are dense, the projection of the synthetic examples must be closer to the center.

The local space could be rebuilt using PCA. The first axis of the main component retains the maximum variance, and the next axis of the main component retains the largest of the remainder, and so on. Therefore, the synthetic example must be furthest from the center in the direction of the first axis of the main component, and must therefore be closer in the direction in which its occupied variance is smaller, to the nearest to the center in the direction of the last axis of the main component. When the synthetic is generated directly on the first axis of the main component through the center, its projection on the first axis of the main component must be itself and also the farthest from the center, and then its projection will be closer to the center in which it has a smaller variance, so it is easy to see that the generation of the synthetic minority class example along the axis of the first major component of the local data distribution would fit better with the interpolation mechanism.

Following this motivation, the ADOMS algorithm can be described in the next steps:

1. Randomly select one of the minority class examples p_i in the original training data as the processing example.
2. Define the neighbor number k, $(k = 1, 2, 3, \ldots)$, and calculate the KNN of p_i in the feature space using the Euclidean distance.
3. Calculate the first principal component axis of local data distribution which composed of p_i and its k neighbors in the feature space.
4. Select one of its neighbors m_j randomly and calculate the Euclidean distance d between p_i and m_j, then a *scaling* is obtained from $Random(0, 1)$.
5. Generate a new synthetic minority class example p_i' in the feature space, where p_i' is generated along the direction from p_i to the projection of m_j on the first principal component axis through p_i, and the Euclidean distance between p_i' and p_i is *scaling* $\times d$.

5.5.3 ADASYN: Adaptive Synthetic Sampling Approach

ADASYN [45] is based on the idea of adaptively generating minority examples according to their distributions: more synthetic data are generated for samples of minority classes that are more difficult to learn compared to samples of minorities that are easier to learn. The ADASYN method can not only reduce the learning bias introduced by the original unbalance data distribution, but can also adaptively change the decision boundary to focus on those samples difficult to learn.

The algorithm ADASYN is described next.

Input

Training data set TR with N samples $\{x_i, y_i\}$, $i = 1, \ldots, N$, where x_i is an instance in the m dimensional feature space M and $y_i \in C = \{pos, neg\}$ is the class identity label associated with x_i. Define N^+ and N^- as the number of minority class examples and the number of majority class examples, respectively. Therefore, $N^+ \leq N^-$ and $N^+ + N^- = N$.

Procedure

1. Calculate the degree of class imbalance as $d = N^+/N^-$, where $d \in (0, 1]$.
2. Set d_{th} a preset threshold for the maximum tolerated degree of class imbalance ratio. If $d < d_{th}$:

   (a) Calculate the number of synthetic data examples that need to be generated for the minority class as $G = (N^- - N^+) \times \beta$, where $\beta \in [0, 1]$ is a parameter used to specify the desired balance level after generation of the synthetic data. $\beta = 1$ means a fully balanced data set is created after the generalization process.
   (b) For each minority example p_i, find KNN based on the Euclidean distance in m dimensional space, and calculate the ratio r_i defined as $r_i = \Delta_i/k$, $i = 1, \ldots, N^+$, where Δ_i is the number of examples in the KNN of p_i that belong to the majority class, therefore $r_i \in [0, 1]$.
   (c) Normalize r_i according to $\hat{r}_i = r_i / \sum_{i=1}^{N^+} r_i$, so that $\hat{r}_i$ is a density distribution ($\sum_i \hat{r}_i = 1$).
   (d) Calculate the number of synthetic data examples that need to be generated for each minority example p_i as $g_i = \hat{r}_i \times G$, where G is the total number of synthetic data examples that need to be generated for the minority class as defined in step 2a.
   (e) For each minority class data example p_i, generate g_i synthetic data examples according to the next loop. Do the Loop from 1 to g_i:

      i. Randomly choose one minority data example, p_{zi}, from the KNN for data p_i.
      ii. Generate the synthetic data example s_i with $s_i = p_i + (p_{zi} - p_i) \times \Lambda$, where $(p_{zi} p_i)$ is the difference vector in the m dimensional space, and Λ is a random number $\Lambda \in [0, 1]$.

In Fig. 5.14 we can appreciate the result of applying ADASYN with its standard configuration on the imbalanced chessboard data set. Here, the synthetic points are generation with a more suitable distribution. The first effect we can observe is that the previous behavior of generating new points following the diagonals of connected squares is not present. CART is not able to model full-connected squares, but the chessboard is almost completely restored. It is important to mention that there are some isolates minority points created within the black squares and that it

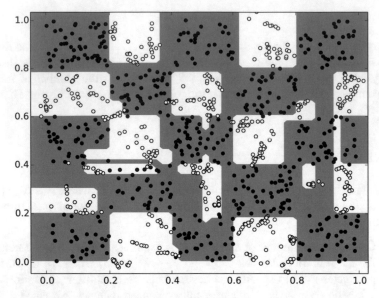

Fig. 5.14 Imbalanced chessboard treated with ADASYN

is noticeable to see a considerable separation between the points of different classes, which supports significantly to the later learning tasks.

5.5.4   ROSE: Random Oversampling Examples

ROSE provides a unified framework to deal simultaneously with the model estimation and accuracy evaluation in imbalanced learning [60]. It builds on the generation of new artificial examples from the classes, according to a smoothed bootstrap approach.

Let be a training data set TR with N samples $\{x_i, y_i\}$, $i = 1, \ldots, N$, where x_i is an instance in the m dimensional feature space M and the class label $y_i \in C = \{Y_0, Y_1\}$. x_i are some related attributes supposed to be realizations of a random vector x defined on R^d, with an unknown probability density function $f(x)$. Let N_j the number of examples belonging to the class Y_j. ROSE consists of the following steps:

1. Select $y^* = Y_j$ with probability π_j.
2. Select $\{x_i, y_i\} \in TR$, such that $y_i = y^*$, with probability $1/N_j$.
3. Sample x^* from $K_{\mathbf{H}_j}(\cdot, x_i)$, with $K_{\mathbf{H}_j}$ a probability distribution centered at x_i and covariance matrix $\mathbf{H}_j$.

Basically, it draws from the training set an observation belonging to one of the two classes, and generate a new example $\{x^*, y'*\}$ in its neighborhood, where the shape of the neighborhood is determined by the shape of the contour sets of K and its width is governed by $\mathbf{H}_j$. The generation of new examples from Y_j, corresponds to the generation of data from the kernel density estimate of $f(x|Y_j)$, with kernel K and smoothing matrix $\mathbf{H}_k$. The choices of K and $\mathbf{H}_k$ may be then addressed by the large specialized literature on kernel density estimation. The repetition of steps from 1 to 3 allows you to generate as many new instances as you want, and changing the value of the probability π_j associated with the class choice allows you to balance the new data set as desired.

The behavior of ROSE is depicted in Fig. 5.15. The values of the optional shrink factor to be multiplied by the smoothing parameters to estimate the conditional kernel density of both the majority and minority classes was set to 0.15. For illustration purposes on how ROSE works, this graphic only shows the artificial generated points for both classes, and the original points coming from the imbalanced chessboard data sets are not included. Thus it is not a real scenario in which we can only generate synthetic points from the minority class and a small set of points from the majority class. The result is very satisfactory, allowing us to sample a new data set from lots of possible configurations depending on the later DM algorithm to be applied.

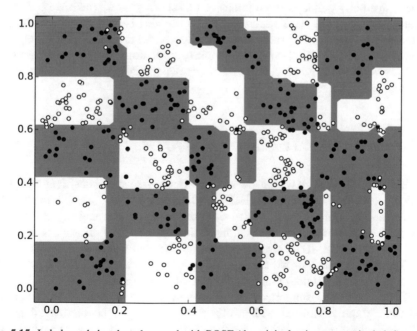

Fig. 5.15 Imbalanced chessboard created with ROSE (the original points are not included)

5.5.5   Safe-Level-SMOTE

Inspired on SMOTE, Safe-Level-SMOTE assigns each positive instance its safe level before generating synthetic instances [16]. Each synthetic instance is positioned closer to the highest secure level, so all synthetic instances are generated only in secure regions.

The safe level (sl) is defined as formula (5.5). If the safe level of an instance is close to 0, the instance is almost noise. If it is near k, the instance is considered safe. The safe level relationship is defined as formula (5.6). It is used to select safe positions for generating synthetic instances. The algorithm Safe-Level-SMOTE is describe in Algorithm 5.

$$\text{safe level}(sl) = \text{the number of a positive instances in } k \text{ nearest neighbours.} \tag{5.5}$$

$$\text{safe level ratio} = sl \text{ of a positive instances}/sl \text{ of a NNs.} \tag{5.6}$$

The result of applying Safe-Level-SMOTE (default parameters) to the imbalanced chessboard data set is depicted in Fig. 5.16. Its behavior is quite similar to BorderLine-SMOTE [42], although the performance is clearly inferior in this case. The shape of the chessboard is not completely recovered and the generation of new synthetic points is more intensive in certain places where we can find a greater density of white points. Even though the idea behind safe level instances sounds interesting, the algorithm does not worry about the quantity of examples to be generated as ADASYN does. Furthermore, some noisy synthetic instances can be also viewed in the graphic, hence a complementary edition process may be very useful to be combined with it.

5.5.6   DBSMOTE: Density-Based SMOTE

The DBSMOTE [17] development was inspired by several consistent and paradoxical concepts in Borderline-SMOTE [42]. DBSMOTE broadly follows the Borderline-SMOTE approach, which operates in an overlapping region [36], but DBSMOTE over-examines this region to maintain the majority class detection rate. However, DBSMOTE also incorporates a different approach than Borderline-SMOTE, which does not work in secure regions. Instead, DBSMOTE overviews this region to improve detection rates for minority examples.

This algorithm is supported by a data structure called the directly density-reachable graph associated with a cluster C which can be discovered by the DBSCAN clustering algorithm. Algorithm 6 represents the pseudocode of the DBSMOTE method.

DBSCAN begins to produce l disjoint clusters $C_1, C_2, \ldots, C_l$, and detects a set of noise instances, which reduces in the next step from a minority class D^+.

Algorithm 5 Safe-level-SMOTE algorithm

1: **function** SAFE-LEVEL-SMOTE(P)
   Input: P ▷ a set of all original positive instances
   Output: P' ▷ a set of all synthetic positive instances
2:   $P' = \emptyset$
3:   **for** each positive instance p in P **do**
4:       compute KNN for p in P and select a random neighbor n from the k nearest neighbours
5:       sl_p = the number of positive instances in k nearest neighbours for p in P
6:       sl_n = the number of positive instances in k nearest neighbours for n in P
7:       **if** $sl_n \neq 0$ **then**   ▷ sl is safe level
8:           $sl\_ratio = sl_p/sl_n$ ▷ sl_ratio is safe level ratio
9:       **else**
10:          $sl\_ratio = \infty$
11:      **end if**
12:      **if** $sl\_ratio = \infty$ and $sl_p = 0$ **then**
13:          does not generate positive synthetic instance
14:      **else**
15:          **for** $m_i = 1$ to M **do**   ▷ M is the total number of attributes
16:              **if** $sl\_ratio = \infty$ and $sl_p \neq 0$ **then**
17:                  $gap = 0$
18:              **else if** $sl\_ratio = 1$ **then**
19:                  $gap = random(0, 1)$
20:              **else if** $sl\_ratio > 1$ **then**
21:                  $gap = random(0, 1/sl\_ratio)$
22:              **else if** $sl\_ratio < 1$ **then**
23:                  $gap = random(1 - sl\_ratio, 1)$
24:              **end if**
25:              $dif = n[m_i] - p[m_i]$
26:              $s[m_i] = p[m_i] + gap \times dif$
27:          **end for**
28:          $P' = P' \cup \{s\}$
29:      **end if**
30: **end for**
31: return P'
32: **end function**

DBSMOTE subsequently generates l sets of synthetic instances $C'_1, C'_2, \ldots, C'_l$. Eventually, these l sets are merged with an original dataset TR to create an oversampled dataset TR'.

Figure 5.17 draws the outcome as a consequence of running DBSMOTE over the imbalanced chessboard data set. After DBSMOTE the picture is again similar to a original chessboard once modeled by CART. Almost all the white squares have been recovered although the located in the center of the grid present some deficiencies. the picture clearly shows how the graph guides and determines the interpolation of synthetic examples in this algorithm. Note that the graph usually connects the diagonals of the squares as expected, but it obviously depends on the quantity and distribution of points. Curiously, we can observe that the graph draw a line intersecting a black square, producing harmful white dots that fortunately were ignored by CART.

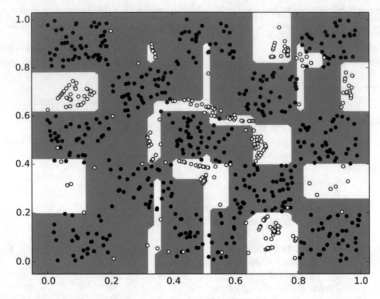

Fig. 5.16 Imbalanced chessboard treated with Safe-Level-SMOTE

Algorithm 6 DBSMOTE algorithm

1: **function** DBSMOTE(C_i, ϵ, k)
    Input: $C_i; \epsilon; k$ ▷ a cluster i of positive instances, Eps and $MinPts$ parameters for the construction of the graph
    Output: C_i' ▷ a set i of synthesis instances
2:     $C_i' = \emptyset$
3:     $G = construct\_directly\_density\text{-}reachable\_graph(C_i, \epsilon, k)$
4:     $c = determine\_pseudo\text{-}centroid(C_i)$ ▷ the nearest instance from a mean of C_i
5:     $\pi = Dijkstra(G, c)$ ▷ to build a predecessor list π where a given source node is c in G
6:     **for** each $p \in C_i$ **do**
7:         $\S = retrieve\_shortest\_path(\pi, p, c)$
8:         $e = select\_random\_edge(\S)$
9:         $(v_1, v_2) = get\_connected\_nodes(e)$
10:        **for** $m_j = 1$ to M **do**   ▷ M is the total number of attributes
11:           $diff = v_2[m_j] - v_1[m_j]$
12:           $gap = random(0, 1)$
13:           $s[m_j] = v_1[m_j] + gap \times diff$
14:        **end for**
15:        $C_i' = C_i' \cup \{s\}$
16:     **end for**
17:     return C_i'
18: **end function**

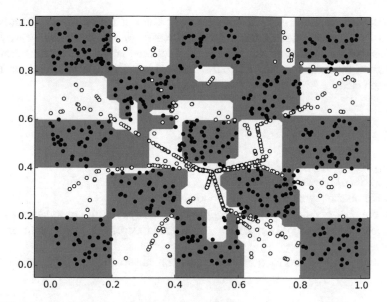

Fig. 5.17 Imbalanced chessboard treated with DBSMOTE

5.5.7 MWMOTE: Majority Weighted Minority Oversampling TEchnique

The authors claimed that in some circumstances, many of the previous extensions of SMOTE become inappropriate and do not generate useful synthetic minority class samples [8]. For instance, the parameter dth of ADASYN defining the number of the majority class samples among the KNN of the minority class example may encounter the some problems, like:

- It is inappropriate for assigning weights to the minority class samples located near the decision boundary.
- It is insufficient to distinguish the minority class samples with regard to their importance in learning.
- It may favor noisy samples.

Also, the authors criticize the KNN based interpolation employed in SMOTE, alleging that this approach may create duplicate and wrong synthetic minority class examples coming from the members of dense and small-sized clusters.

Motivated by the problems mentioned above, a new oversampling method called MWMOTE is developed. The aim of the method is twofold: to improve the sample selection scheme and to improve the synthetic sample generation scheme. MWMOTE is organized around three phases. In the first phase, MWMOTE identifies the most important and difficult-to-learn minority class samples of the original minority set and constructs a new set for the identified samples. In the second phase, each member of the new set is given a selection weight according to its importance within the set. In the third stage, MWMOTE generates the synthetic samples using the previous weights and produces the output set resulting from the addition of the synthetic samples to the original set. The MWMOTE algorithm is described next:

Input

1. S_{maj}: Set of majority class examples.
2. S_{min}: Set of minority class examples.
3. N: Number of synthetic samples to be generated.
4. $k1$: Number of neighbors used for predicting noisy minority class samples.
5. $k2$: Number of majority neighbors used for constructing informative minority set.
6. $k3$: Number of minority neighbors used for constructing informative minority set.

Procedure

1. For each minority example $x_i \in S_{min}$, compute the NN set, $NN(x_i)$ consisting of the nearest $k1$ neighbors of x_i according to euclidean distance.
2. Construct the filtered minority set, S_{minf} by removing those minority class samples which have no minority example in their neighborhood: $S_{minf} = S_{min} - \{x_i \in S_{min} : NN(x_i)$ contains no minority example$\}$.
3. For each $x_i \in S_{minf}$, compute the nearest majority set, $N_{maj}(x_i)$ consisting of the nearest $k2$ majority samples from x_i according to euclidean distance.
4. Find the borderline majority set, $S_{bmaj} = \bigcup_{x_i \in S_{minf}} N_{maj}(x_i)$.
5. For each majority example $y_i \in S_{maj}$, compute the nearest minority set, $N_{min}(y_i)$ consisting of the nearest $k3$ minority examples from y_i according to euclidean distance.
6. Find the informative minority set, $S_{imin} = \bigcup_{y_i \in S_{bmaj}} N_{min}(y_i)$.
7. For each $y_i \in S_{bmaj}$ and for each $x_i \in S_{imin}$, compute the information weight, $I_w(y_i, x_i)$. This measure is directly proportional to a closeness factor and a density factor explained in the original paper.
8. For each $x_i \in S_{imin}$, compute the selection weight $S_w(x_i) = \sum_{y_i \in S_{bmaj}} I_w(y_i, x_i))$.
9. Convert each $S_w(x_i)$ into selection probability $S_p(x_i) = S_w(x_i)/\sum_{z_i \in S_{imin}} S_w(z_i)$.
10. Find the clusters of S_{min}. Let, M clusters are formed which are $L_1, L_2, \ldots, L_M$.
11. Initialize the set $S_{oamin} = S_{min}$.
12. Do for $j = 1 \ldots N$.

(a) Select a sample x from S_{imin} according to probability distribution $S_p(x_i)$. x is a member of the cluster l_k, $1 \leq k \leq M$.
(b) Select randomly another sample y, from the members of the cluster L_k.

(c) Generate one synthetic data s, according to $s = x + \alpha \times (y - x)$, where α is a random number in the range $[0, 1]$.

(d) $S_{omin} = S_{omin} \cup \{s\}$

13. End For.

Output: The oversampled minority set S_{omin}.

Figure 5.18 depicts the result of MWMOTE applied on the imbalanced chessboard data set after generating 400 minority synthetic examples. The picture show how this technique is able to recover almost the original chessboard shape with a complete balanced data set. The use of clustering is easily observed as there are very few white spots out of place, suggesting that the drawback on the use of KNN pointed out by the authors is well addressed. Besides, the quantity of points generated in each place seems to be accurate because all the white squares are recovered. It is true that three of have been partially extracted, but this is due to the original localization of the minority examples in the imbalanced data set. MWMOte os quite conservative and prefer not to generate points in the line intersection of two remote points, explaining why these three squares are partially modeled by CART. In summary, Fig. 5.18 shows us that MWMOTE is one of the best extensions of SMOTE.

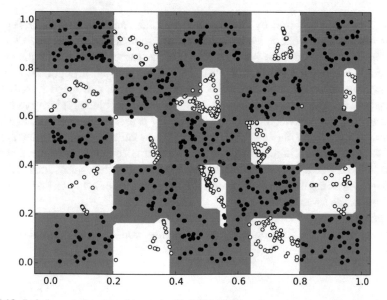

Fig. 5.18 Imbalanced chessboard treated with MWMOTE

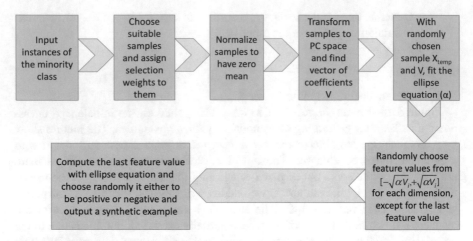

Fig. 5.19 MDO algorithm flowchart

5.5.8   MDO: Mahalanobis Distance-Based Oversampling Technique

This algorithm is inspired by the distance of Mahalanobis[59]. MDO [1] over-samples the minority examples by considering each sample of the minority class to generate a new synthetic instance that has the same Mahalanobis distance as the average of the class considered with the sample chosen. It generates synthetic samples towards the variation of the corresponding class and helps to reduce the overlap between different class regions. In multi-class problems, it is very common to find overlapping between different regions. By preserving the covariance structure of data in minority classes, MDO can create new suitable examples that are very useful in learning algorithms. MDO selects those minority class candidates who are placed in the dense areas of the corresponding class. In other words, new synthetic samples are generated towards the probability boundaries of samples that have more neighbors in the same class.

A general scheme describing the MDO framework is showed in Fig. 5.19. For more details on its implementation, please consult the original paper of MDO.

5.6   Hybridizations of Undersampling and Oversampling

Hybridizations of undersampling and oversampling arise from the drawbacks mentioned in the previous sections associated with each family of methods. They pursue the optimal balance of removing majority examples and generating new minority examples to achieve the best possible performance in any imbalance data set.

As classical methods, we consider 2 techniques proposed in the early study of Batista et al. [10] in which SMOTE is linked with two classical undersampling approaches. Over the years, they have become a standard because they almost always enhance the performance of the original SMOTE by using a very simple extra step.

- **SMOTE + Tomek Link:** Although oversampling minority class examples can balance class distributions, some other problems usually present in data sets with skewed class distributions are not solved [10]. Frequently, class clusters are not well defined since some majority class examples might be invading the minority class space. The opposite can also be true, since interpolating minority class examples can expand the minority class clusters, introducing artificial minority class examples too deeply in the majority class space. Inducing a classifier under such a situation can lead to overfitting. In order to create better-defined class clusters, Tomek links [79] can be applied to the oversampled training set as a data cleaning method. Thus, instead of removing only the majority class examples that form Tomek links, examples from both classes are removed. Thus, this method works as follows: first, the original data set is oversampled with SMOTE, and then Tomek links are identified and removed, producing a balanced data set with well-defined class clusters.

- **SMOTE + ENN:** The motivation behind this method is similar to SMOTE + Tomek links [10]. ENN [81] tends to remove more examples than the Tomek links does [79], so it is expected that it will provide a more in depth data cleaning. Differently from NCL which is an undersampling method [51], ENN is used to remove examples from both classes. Thus, any example that is misclassified by its KNN is removed from the training set.

Both algorithms work similarly, they can remove examples belonging to either the majority or minority class. Figure 5.20 represents the effects of applying ENN after SMOTE in the chessboard data set (the result offered by Tomek Links after SMOTE is more or less similar, thus we do not draw it). At first glance, the result seems to be a bit worse than using SMOTE isolate, but this is mainly motivated by the data set characteristics and CART modeling. We can see that the previous existing points connecting the diagonals between squares have completely disappeared, which limitates an accurate modelling of the squares. The area devoted to white points is significantly reduced in general, showing us the negative effects that can be achieved if some important minority examples are removed. This is a defect of ENN, it may consider as noisy points some positive points that support the modeling of correct decisions boundaries. In addition, all the white dots falling inside the black squares are removes without any undesired effect. It is noteworthy to mention that both ENN and Tomek Links are basic approaches and more sophisticated hybridizations have been proposed to overcome the problems drawn from this figure.

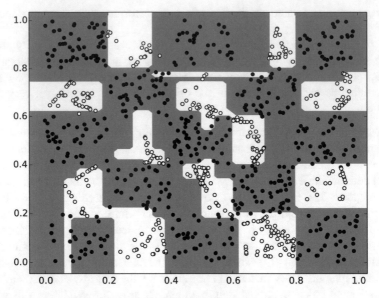

Fig. 5.20 Imbalanced chessboard treated with SMOTE + ENN

Next, we will describe other hybrid sampling methods utilizing more complex mechanisms:

- **Agglomerative Hierarchical Clustering (AHC):** AHC was one of the first attempts to use clustering to balance the data [24]. The K-means algorithm was used to undersample the majority examples and agglomerative hierarchical clustering was used to oversample the minority examples. Here, the clusters are gathered from all levels of the resulting dendograms and their centroids are interpolated with the original positive examples.
- **SPIDER:** It is an original method for selective preprocessing [12, 74]. It combines the elimination of these objects from the majority classes that can result in the misclassification of objects of the minority class, with local sampling of these objects of the minority class that are "overwhelmed" by objects surrounding the majority classes. On the one hand, this filtering is less greedy than the one used by NCL, and on the other hand, the oversampling is more focused than that used by SMOTE. SPIDER offers three filtering options that affect minority class modification and lead to ever greater degree and scope changes: weak amplification, weak amplification and re-labeling, and strong amplification.
- **SMOTE-RSB$_*$:** Here, a new hybrid proposal is introduced based on two steps [68]: (1) constructing new synthetic examples of the minority class using SMOTE, (2) improving the quality of these new samples through editing techniques based on Rough Set Theory (RST) and the smaller approximation of a subset, acting on the artificial instances of the minority class created by the SMOTE algorithm. The main contribution is to introduce a new preprocessing

method using SMOTE to generate synthetic examples and RST as a cleaning method. The elimination of any synthetic example that does not belong to the lower approximation (B_*) of the minority class is encouraged, considering these examples in the boundary region as noisy and not useful for classification.

- **SMOTE-IPF:** It is a SMOTE hybridization in which the IPF noise filter is applied as post-processing [72]. Their suitability to handle noisy and minority examples in imbalanced data was a particular focus of evaluation as these are one of the main sources of difficulty for the learning algorithms. The IPF method eliminates noisy examples in multiple iterations until a stopping criterion is reached. The iterative process stops when, for a series of consecutive iterations, the number of noisy examples identified in each of these iterations is less than a percentage of the size of the original training dataset.

5.7 Summarizing Comments

In this chapter, data preparation level solutions for class imbalance were presented and analyzed as a useful and widely used alternative for treatment in classification with imbalanced classes. The approaches we have presented are organized around two main trends: undersampling and oversampling. We have also seen several hybrid techniques and how they can offer better performance and more targeted assistance to the problem of imbalance learning.

Although many data level techniques have been introduced, new challenges remain. In the paper [31], a detailed overview is made of the oversampling techniques that have emerged from SMOTE as inspiration. It is easy to see how there are many mechanisms that have been previously incorporated in derivatives techniques that have not yet been merged or explored into new algorithms. Likewise, undersampling techniques and their hybrids with oversampling are maturing and much remains to be explored. Moreover, the study of the intrinsic properties of data (which we will also study in this book) can incorporate interesting mechanisms for the creation of new data level strategies. There is still a long way to go in this field and this is shown by the interest of the scientific community in proposing new techniques at the data level that are increasingly achieving better results in imbalanced learning.

References

1. Abdi, L., Hashemi, S.: To combat multi-class imbalanced problems by means of over-sampling techniques. IEEE Trans. Know. Data Eng. **28**(1), 238–251 (2016)
2. Almogahed, B.A., Kakadiaris, I.A.: NEATER: filtering of over-sampled data using non-cooperative game theory. Soft Comput. **19**(11), 3301–3322 (2015)
3. Anand, A., Pugalenthi, G., Fogel, G.B., Suganthan, P.N.: An approach for classification of highly imbalanced data using weighting and undersampling. Amino Acids **39**(5), 1385–1391 (2010)

4. Angiulli, F., Basta, S., Pizzuti, C.: Distance-based detection and prediction of outliers. IEEE Trans. Know. Data Eng. **18**(2), 145–160 (2006)
5. Barandela, R., Sánchez, J.S., García, V., Rangel, E.: Strategies for learning in class imbalance problems. Pattern Recogn. **36**(3), 849–851 (2003)
6. Barella, V., Costa, E., Carvalho, A.C.P.L.F.: ClusterOSS: a new undersampling method for imbalanced learning. Technical report (2014)
7. Barua, S., Islam, M.M., Murase, K.: A novel synthetic minority oversampling technique for imbalanced data set learning. In: 18th International Conference on Neural Information Processing, ICONIP, Shanghai, pp. 735–744 (2011)
8. Barua, S., Islam, M.M., Yao, X., Murase, K.: MWMOTE-majority weighted minority oversampling technique for imbalanced data set learning. IEEE Trans. Know. Data Eng. **26**(2), 405–425 (2014)
9. Basu, M., Ho, T.K. (ed.): Data Complexity in Pattern Recognition. Springer, London (2006)
10. Batista, G.E.A.P.A., Prati, R.C., Monard, M.C.: A study of the behaviour of several methods for balancing machine learning training data. SIGKDD Explor. **6**(1), 20–29 (2004)
11. Bellinger, C., Drummond, C., Japkowicz, N.: Beyond the boundaries of SMOTE – a framework for manifold-based synthetically oversampling. In: European Conference on Machine Learning and Knowledge Discovery in Databases (ECML PKDD), Riva del Garda, pp. 248–263 (2016)
12. Błaszczyński, J., Deckert, M., Stefanowski, J., Wilk, S.: Integrating selective pre-processing of imbalanced data with ivotes ensemble. In: Szczuka, M., Kryszkiewicz, M., Ramanna, S., Jensen, R., Hu, Q. (eds.) Rough Sets and Current Trends in Computing. LNSC, vol. 6086, pp. 148–157. Springer, Berlin/Heidelberg (2010)
13. Bradley, A.P.: The use of the area under the roc curve in the evaluation of machine learning algorithms. Pattern Recogn. **30**(7), 1145–1159 (1997)
14. Breiman, L., Friedman, J.H., Olshen, R.A., Stone, C.J.: Classification and Regression Trees. Chapman and Hall, New York/Wadsworth and Inc., Belmont (1984)
15. Brodley, C.E., Friedl, M.A.: Identifying mislabeled training data. J. Artif. Intell. Res. **11**, 131–167 (1999)
16. Bunkhumpornpat, C., Sinapiromsaran, K., Lursinsap, C.: Safe–level–SMOTE: safe–level–synthetic minority over–sampling TEchnique for handling the class imbalanced problem. In: Proceedings of the 13th Pacific–Asia Conference on Advances in Knowledge Discovery and Data Mining PAKDD'09, Bangkok, pp. 475–482 (2009)
17. Bunkhumpornpat, C., Sinapiromsaran, K., Lursinsap, C.: DBSMOTE: density-based synthetic minority over-sampling TEchnique. Appl. Intell. **36**(3), 664–684 (2012)
18. Cano, J.R., Herrera, F., Lozano, M.: Using evolutionary algorithms as instance selection for data reduction in KDD: an experimental study. IEEE Trans. Evol. Comput. **7**(6), 561–575 (2003)
19. Chawla, N.V.: Data mining for imbalanced datasets: an overview. In: Maimon, O., Rokach, L. (eds.) Data Mining and Knowledge Discovery Handbook, pp. 853–867. Springer, New York (2005)
20. Chawla, N.V., Bowyer, K.W., Hall, L.O., Kegelmeyer, W.P.: SMOTE: synthetic minority over–sampling technique. J. Artif. Intell. Res. **16**, 321–357 (2002)
21. Chawla, N.V., Japkowicz, N., Kotcz, A.: Editorial: special issue on learning from imbalanced data sets. SIGKDD Explor. **6**(1), 1–6 (2004)
22. Chawla, N.V., Cieslak, D.A., Hall, L.O., Joshi, A.: Automatically countering imbalance and its empirical relationship to cost. Data Min. Knowl. Disc. **17**(2), 225–252 (2008)
23. Chen, S., Guo, G., Chen, L.: A new over-sampling method based on cluster ensembles. In: 7th International Conference on Advanced Information Networking and Applications Workshops, Perth, pp. 599–604 (2010)
24. Cohen, G., Hilario, M., Sax, H., Hugonnet, S., Geissbuhler, A.: Learning from imbalanced data in surveillance of nosocomial infection. Artif. Intell. Med. **37**, 7–18 (2006)
25. Cover, T.M., Hart, P.E.: Nearest neighbor pattern classification. IEEE Trans. Inf. Theory **13**, 21–27 (1967)

26. de la Calleja, J., Fuentes, O.: A distance-based over-sampling method for learning from imbalanced data sets. In: Proceedings of the Twentieth International Florida Artificial Intelligence, pp. 634–635 (2007)
27. Das, B., Krishnan, N.C., Cook, D.J.: RACOG and wRACOG: two probabilistic oversampling techniques. IEEE Trans. Know. Data Eng. **27**(1), 222–234 (2015)
28. Dietterich, T.G.: An experimental comparison of three methods for constructing ensembles of decision trees: bagging, boosting, and randomization. Mach. Learn. **40**, 139–157 (2000)
29. Drown, D.J., Khoshgoftaar, T.M., Seliya, N.: Evolutionary sampling and software quality modeling of high-assurance systems. IEEE Trans. Syst. Man Cybern. Part A **39**(5), 1097–1107 (2009)
30. Estabrooks, A., Jo, T., Japkowicz, N.: A multiple resampling method for learning from imbalanced data sets. Comput. Intell. **20**(1), 18–36 (2004)
31. Fernández, A., García, S., Herrera, F., Chawla, N.V.: Smote for learning from imbalanced data: progress and challenges, marking the 15-year anniversary. J. Artif. Intell. Res. **61**, 863–905 (2018)
32. Fernández-Navarro, F., Hervás-Martínez, C., Gutiérrez, P.A.: A dynamic over-sampling procedure based on sensitivity for multi-class problems. Pattern Recognit. **44**(8), 1821–1833 (2011)
33. Galar, M., Fernández, A., Barrenechea, E., Bustince, H., Herrera, F.: A review on ensembles for class imbalance problem: bagging, boosting and hybrid based approaches. IEEE Trans. Syst. Man Cybern. Part C Appl. Rev. **42**(4), 463–484 (2012)
34. Gao, M., Hong, X., Chen, S., Harris, C.J., Khalaf, E.: PDFOS: PDF estimation based over-sampling for imbalanced two-class problems. Neurocomputing **138**, 248–259 (2014)
35. García, S., Herrera, F.: Evolutionary under-sampling for classification with imbalanced data sets: proposals and taxonomy. Evol. Comput. **17**(3), 275–306 (2009)
36. García, V., Mollineda, R.A., Sánchez, J.S.: On the k–NN performance in a challenging scenario of imbalance and overlapping. Pattern Anal. Appl. **11**(3–4), 269–280 (2008)
37. García, S., Fernández, A., Herrera, F.: Enhancing the effectiveness and interpretability of decision tree and rule induction classifiers with evolutionary training set selection over imbalanced problems. Appl. Soft Comput. **9**, 1304–1314 (2009)
38. García, S., Derrac, J., Triguero, I., Carmona, C.J., Herrera, F.: Evolutionary-based selection of generalized instances for imbalanced classification. Know. Based Syst. **25**(1), 3–12 (2012)
39. García, V., Sánchez, J.S., Mollineda, R.A.: On the effectiveness of preprocessing methods when dealing with different levels of class imbalance. Knowl. Based Syst. **25**(1), 13–21 (2012)
40. García-Pedrajas, N., Pérez-Rodríguez, J., de Haro-García, A.: Oligois: scalable instance selection for class-imbalanced data sets. IEEE Trans. Cybern **43**(1), 332–346 (2013)
41. Gazzah, S., Amara, N.E.B.: New oversampling approaches based on polynomial fitting for imbalanced data sets. In: The Eighth IAPR International Workshop on Document Analysis Systems, Nara, pp. 677–684 (2008)
42. Han, H., Wang, W.Y., Mao, B.H.: Borderline–SMOTE: a new over–sampling method in imbalanced data sets learning. In: Proceedings of the 2005 International Conference on Intelligent Computing (ICIC'05), Hefei. Lecture Notes in Computer Science, vol. 3644, pp. 878–887 (2005)
43. Hart, P.E.: The condensed nearest neighbor rule. IEEE Trans. Inf. Theory **14**, 515–516 (1968)
44. He, H., Garcia, E.A.: Learning from imbalanced data. IEEE Trans. Know. Data Eng. **21**(9), 1263–1284 (2009)
45. He, H., Bai, Y., Garcia, E.A., Li, S.: ADASYN: adaptive synthetic sampling approach for imbalanced learning. In: Proceedings of the 2008 IEEE International Joint Conference Neural Networks (IJCNN'08), Hong Kong, pp. 1322–1328 (2008)
46. Hu, F., Li, H.: A novel boundary oversampling algorithm based on neighborhood rough set model: NRSBoundary-SMOTE. Math. Probl. Eng. **Article ID 694809**, 10 (2013)
47. Huang, J., Ling, C.X.: Using AUC and accuracy in evaluating learning algorithms. IEEE Trans. Knowl. Data Eng. **17**(3), 299–310 (2005)
48. Kang, Y.I., Won, S.: Weight decision algorithm for oversampling technique on class-imbalanced learning. In: ICCAS, Gyeonggi-do, pp. 182–186 (2010)

49. Kim, H., Jo, N., Shin, K.: Optimization of cluster-based evolutionary undersampling for the artificial neural networks in corporate bankruptcy prediction. Expert Syst. Appl. **59**, 226–234 (2016)
50. Kubat, M., Holte, R.C., Matwin, S.: Learning when negative examples abound. In: van Someren, M., Widmer, G. (eds.) Proceedings of the 9th European Conference on Machine Learning (ECML'97). Lecture Notes in Computer Science, vol. 1224, pp. 146–153. Springer, Berlin/New York (1997)
51. Laurikkala, J.: Improving identification of difficult small classes by balancing class distribution. In: AIME'01: Proceedings of the 8th Conference on AI in Medicine in Europe, Cascais, pp. 63–66 (2001)
52. Lemaitre, G., Nogueira, F., Aridas, C.K.: Imbalanced-learn: a python toolbox to tackle the curse of imbalanced datasets in machine learning. J. Mach. Learn. Res. **18**(17), 1–5 (2017)
53. Liang, Y., Hu, S., Ma, L., He, Y.: MSMOTE: improving classification performance when training data is imbalanced. In: International Workshop on Computer Science and Engineering, Qingdao, vol. 2, pp. 13–17 (2009)
54. Liu, X.Y., Wu, J., Zhou, Z.H.: Exploratory undersampling for class-imbalance learning. IEEE Trans. Syst. Man Cybern. B **39**(2), 539–550 (2009)
55. López, V., Fernández, A., García, S., Palade, V., Herrera, F.: An insight into classification with imbalanced data: empirical results and current trends on using data intrinsic characteristics. Inf. Sci. **250**, 113–141 (2013)
56. López, V., Triguero, I., Carmona, C.J., García, S., Herrera, F.: Addressing imbalanced classification with instance generation techniques: IPADE-ID. Neurocomputing **126**, 15–28 (2014)
57. Luengo, J., Fernández, A., García, S., Herrera, F.: Addressing data complexity for imbalanced data sets: analysis of SMOTE–based oversampling and evolutionary undersampling. Soft Comput. **15**(10), 1909–1936 (2011)
58. Ma, L., Fan, S.: CURE-SMOTE algorithm and hybrid algorithm for feature selection and parameter optimization based on random forests. BMC Bioinf. **18**, 169 (2017)
59. Mahalanobis, P.: On the generalized distance in statistics. Proc. Nat. Inst. Sci. (Calcutta) **2**, 49–55 (1936)
60. Menardi, G., Torelli, N.: Training and assessing classification rules with imbalanced data. Data Min. Knowl. Disc. **28**(1), 92–122 (2014)
61. Nakamura, M., Kajiwara, Y., Otsuka, A., Kimura, H.: LVQ-SMOTE – learning vector quantization based synthetic minority over-sampling technique for biomedical data. BioData Min. **6**, 16 (2013)
62. Ng, W.W.Y., Hu, J., Yeung, D.S., Yin, S., Roli, F.: Diversified sensitivity-based undersampling for imbalance classification problems. IEEE Trans. Cybern. **45**(11), 2402–2412 (2015)
63. Pérez-Ortiz, M., Gutiérrez, P.A., Hervás-Martínez, C.: Borderline kernel based over-sampling. In: 8th International Conference on Hybrid Artificial Intelligent Systems (HAIS), Salamanca, pp. 472–481 (2013)
64. Pérez-Ortiz, M., Gutiérrez, P.A., Tiño, P., Hervás-Martínez, C.: Oversampling the minority class in the feature space. IEEE Trans. Neural Netw. Learn. Syst. **27**(9), 1947–1961 (2016)
65. Prati, R.C., Batista, G.E.A.P.A., Monard, M.C.: A survey on graphical methods for classification predictive performance evaluation. IEEE Trans. Know. Data Eng. **23**(11), 1601–1618 (2011)
66. Puntumapon, K., Waiyamai, K.: A pruning-based approach for searching precise and generalized region for synthetic minority over-sampling. In: 16th Pacific-Asia Conference Advances in Knowledge Discovery and Data Mining (PAKDD), Kuala Lumpur, pp. 371–382 (2012)
67. Quinlan, J.R.: C4.5: Programs for Machine Learning. Morgan Kauffman, San Mateo (1993)
68. Ramentol, E., Caballero, Y., Bello, R., Herrera, F.: SMOTE-RSB*: a hybrid preprocessing approach based on oversampling and undersampling for high imbalanced data-sets using smote and rough sets theory. Know. Inf. Syst. **33**(2), 245–265 (2012)
69. Ramentol, E., Gondres, I., Lajes, S., Bello, R., Caballero, Y., Cornelis, C., Herrera, F.: Fuzzy-rough imbalanced learning for the diagnosis of high voltage circuit breaker maintenance: the SMOTE-FRST-2T algorithm. Eng. Appl. AI **48**, 134–139 (2016)

70. Rivera, W.A., Xanthopoulos, P.: A priori synthetic over-sampling methods for increasing classification sensitivity in imbalanced data sets. Expert Syst. Appl. **66**, 124–135 (2016)
71. Rokach, L.: Ensemble-based classifiers. Artif. Intell. Rev. **33**(1), 1–39 (2010)
72. Sáez, J.A., Luengo, J., Stefanowski, J., Herrera, F.: SMOTE-IPF: addressing the noisy and borderline examples problem in imbalanced classification by a re-sampling method with filtering. Inf. Sci. **291**, 184–203 (2015)
73. Smith, M.R., Martinez, T.R., Giraud-Carrier, C.G.: An instance level analysis of data complexity. Mach. Learn. **95**(2), 225–256 (2014)
74. Stefanowski, J., Wilk, S.: Selective pre-processing of imbalanced data for improving classification performance. In: Proceedings of the 10th International Conference on Data Warehousing and Knowledge Discovery (DaWaK08), Turin, pp. 283–292 (2008)
75. Sun, Y., Wong, A.K.C., Kamel, M.S.: Classification of imbalanced data: a review. Int. J. Pattern Recogn. Artif. Intell. **23**(4), 687–719 (2009)
76. Sundarkumar, G.G., Ravi, V.: A novel hybrid undersampling method for mining unbalanced datasets in banking and insurance. Eng. Appl. Artif. Intell. **37**, 368–377 (2015)
77. Tahir, M.A., Kittler, J., Yan, F.: Inverse random under sampling for class imbalance problem and its application to multi-label classification. Pattern Recogn. **45**(10), 3738–3750 (2012)
78. Tang, S., Chen, S.: The generation mechanism of synthetic minority class examples. In: 5th International Conference on Information Technology and Applications in Biomedicine (ITAB), Shenzhen, pp. 444–447 (2008)
79. Tomek, I.: Two modifications of CNN. IEEE Trans. Syst. Man Commun. **6**, 769–772 (1976)
80. Wang, J., Xu, M., Wang, H., Zhang, J.: Classification of imbalanced data by using the SMOTE algorithm and locally linear embedding. In: 8th International Conference on Signal Processing (ICSP), Beijing, vol. 3, pp. 1–6. IEEE (2006)
81. Wilson, D.L.: Asymptotic properties of nearest neighbor rules using edited data. IEEE Trans. Syst. Man Cybern. **2**(3), 408–421 (1972)
82. Wu, X., Kumar, V. (eds.): The top ten algorithms in data mining. In: Data Mining and Knowledge Discovery Series. Chapman and Hall/CRC Press, London (2009)
83. Xie, Z., Jiang, L., Ye, T., Li, X.: A synthetic minority oversampling method based on local densities in low-dimensional space for imbalanced learning. In: 20th International Conference on Database Systems for Advanced Applications (DASFAA), Hanoi, pp. 3–18 (2015)
84. Yen, S., Lee, Y.: Under-sampling approaches for improving prediction of the minority class in an imbalanced dataset. In: ICIC, Kunming. LNCIS, vol. 344, pp. 731–740 (2006)
85. Yen, S.J., Lee, Y.S.: Cluster-based under-sampling approaches for imbalanced data distributions. Expert Syst. Appl. **36**(3), 5718–5727 (2009)
86. Yeung, D.S., Ng, W.W.Y., Wang, D., Tsang, E.C.C., Wang, X.: Localized generalization error model and its application to architecture selection for radial basis function neural network. IEEE Trans. Neural Netw. **18**(5), 1294–1305 (2007)
87. Yoon, K., Kwek, S.: An unsupervised learning approach to resolving the data imbalanced issue in supervised learning problems in functional genomics. In: HIS'05: Proceedings of the Fifth International Conference on Hybrid Intelligent Systems, Rio de Janeiro, pp. 303–308 (2005)
88. Yu, H., Ni, J., Zhao, J.: Acosampling: an ant colony optimization-based undersampling method for classifying imbalanced dna microarray data. Neurocomputing **101**, 309–318 (2013)
89. Zhang, H., Li, M.: RWO-Sampling: a random walk over-sampling approach to imbalanced data classification. Inf. Fusion **20**, 99–116 (2014)
90. Zhang, J., Mani, I.: KNN approach to unbalanced data distributions: a case study involving information extraction. In: Proceedings of the 20th International Conference on Machine Learning (ICML'03), Workshop Learning from Imbalanced Data Sets (2003)

Chapter 6
Algorithm-Level Approaches

Abstract Algorithm-level solutions can be seen as an alternative approach to data pre-processing methods for handling imbalanced datasets. Instead of focusing on modifying the training set in order to combat class skew, this approach aims at modifying the classifier learning procedure itself. This requires an in-depth understanding of the selected earning approach in order to identify what specific mechanism may be responsible for creating the bias towards the majority class. Algorithm-level solutions do not cause any shifts in data distributions, being more adaptable to various types of imbalanced datasets – at the cost of being specific only for a given classifier type. In this chapter we will discuss the basics of algorithm-level solutions, as well as review existing skew-insensitive modifications. To do so, the background will be introduced first in Sect. 6.1. Then, special attention will be given to four groups of methods. First, modifications of SVMs will be discussed in Sect. 6.2. Section 6.3 will focus on skew-insensitive decision trees. Variants of NN classifiers for imbalanced problems will be presented in Sect. 6.4 and skew insensitive Bayesian in Sect. 6.5. Finally, one-class classifiers will be discussed in Sect. 6.6, whereas Sect. 6.7 will conclude this chapter and will present future challenges in the field of algorithm-level solutions to class imbalance.

6.1 Introduction

Algorithm-level methods concentrate on modifying existing learners to alleviate their bias towards majority class instead on altering the supplied training set [35]. This requires a good insight into the modified learning algorithm and a precise identification of reasons for its failure in mining skewed distributions. While pre-processing algorithms can be seen as more general ones, as any learning algorithm can be trained afterwards such balancing, the group of methods discussed in this chapter is specific to a selected model. This reduces their flexibility, but offers higher specialization potential in tuning the method to the problem at hand.

In order to propose an algorithm-level modification one must firstly understand what hinders the performance of a given classifier on imbalanced data. Often the classification bias is caused by more than a single factor, forcing researchers to

© Springer Nature Switzerland AG 2018
A. Fernández et al., *Learning from Imbalanced Data Sets*,
https://doi.org/10.1007/978-3-319-98074-4_6

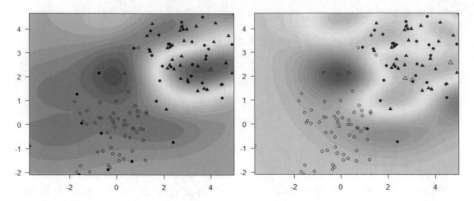

Fig. 6.1 Different decision boundaries given by Support Vector Machine for an imbalanced dataset: (*left*) standard approach; (*right*) instance-level weighting

understand how strong influence holds each of them independently and how their interplay with each other. Usually one of the characteristics of a given learner is most prone to be skewed towards the majority class. An example of this would be a splitting criteria used for decision tree induction. Imbalanced training data may lead to selecting such a criteria that favors majority class instead of minority one. Therefore, to counter this one must analyze the splitting mechanism and decide what can be done to avoid such a scenario. Support Vector Machines are another popular example of algorithm-level solutions. An example of modifying such a classifier by assigning higher importance to minority class instances is depicted in Fig. 6.1.

Algorithm-level solutions are not as popular in the literature, as they are arguably more difficult to design and implement than pre-processing methods [6, 35]. Despite this there exist a number of efficient solutions for class imbalance that rely on direct modifications of learners. Many of popular machine learning algorithms have been subject to such alternations, including SVMS [1] and their variants [52, 73], Decision Trees [11], NN approaches [7], Bayesian classifiers [16], ANNs [17], or kernel machines [62].

In the following sections we will discuss selected skew-insensitive algorithm-level modifications of popular classification algorithms.

6.2   Support Vector Machines

SVMs are among the most popular algorithms for pattern classification, due to their powerful generalization abilities, convergent properties and flexibility in adapting to various learning difficulties. However, in their original form they are highly prone to imbalanced class distributions. There was a substantial effort in understanding what causes such shortcoming and how to alleviate it. This spawned a number of alternative solutions that modified the underlying mechanisms of SVMs in order to make them skew-insensitive. Before discussing them in detail, let us revise the basics behind this classifier.

SVM algorithm aims at finding the optimal hyperplane which separates instances into two classes. As traditional linear classifiers offer many desirable properties, while not being able to cope with complex data structures, a transformation of input instances into higher dimensional artificial feature spaces is being used. Thus by using a non-linear mapping Φ, we are able to achieve a linear separation between classes in the new space, which in turn translates to a non-linear decision boundary in the original feature space. We may represent the potential separating hyperplane constructed in the mentioned higher dimensional space as:

$$w \cdot \Phi(x) + b = 0, \tag{6.1}$$

where w stands for a weight vector normal to this hyperplane. In case of considered data are linearly separable, the decision hyperplane characterized by a maximum margin (highest possible intra-class distance) can be obtained by the following optimization of margin: $\min\left(\frac{1}{2}w \cdot w\right)$, subject to $\forall_{i=1,\cdots,l} y_i (w \cdot \Phi(x_i) + b) \geq 1$, where l stands for the number of training instances.

However, contemporary datasets are rarely linearly separable, thus forcing us to modify the previous statement to include the possibilities of classifying some of training instances, thus achieving greater generalization purposes and reducing the overfitting issue. This is done by using slack variable associated with i-th instance $\xi_i \geq 0$. This allows to rewrite the margin optimization problem as soft margin:

$$\min\left(\frac{1}{2}w \cdot w + C\sum_{i=1}^{l}\xi_i\right) \tag{6.2}$$

$$\text{subject to } \forall_{i=1,\cdots,l} \forall_{\xi_i \geq 0} y_i (w \cdot \Phi(x_i) + b) \geq 1 - \xi_i,$$

where C stands for the regularization parameter that controls the trade-off between maximizing the separation margin between classes and minimizing the number of misclassified instances. The penalty term $\sum_{i=1}^{l}\xi_i$ depicts how many training instances may lie on the wrong side of the decision boundary during the classifier learning procedure.

This is a quadratic optimization problem that can be solved by transforming it into Lagrangian optimization problem with the following dual form:

$$\max_{\alpha_i}\left\{\sum_{i=1}^{l}\alpha_i - \frac{1}{2}\sum_{i=1}^{l}\sum_{j=1}^{l}\alpha_i\alpha_j y_i y_j \Phi(x_i) \cdot \Phi(x_j)\right\} \tag{6.3}$$

$$\text{subject to } \forall_{i=1,\cdots,l} \forall_{0\leq\alpha_i\leq C} \sum_{i=1}^{l} y_i\alpha_i = 0,$$

where α_i are Lagrange multipliers that must satisfy the following Karush-Kuhn-Tucker conditions:

$$\underset{i=1,\cdots,l}{\forall} \quad \alpha_i \left(y_i \left(w \cdot \Phi(x_i) + b \right) - 1 + \xi_i \right) = 0, \tag{6.4}$$

$$\underset{i=1,\cdots,l}{\forall} \quad (C - \alpha_i)\xi_i = 0. \tag{6.5}$$

As learning the mapping function $\Phi(x)$ may be difficult or even impossible, SVMs use kernel functions $K(x_i, x_j) = \Phi(x_i) \cdot \Phi(x_j)$, we are able to write the dual optimization problem in its kernelized form as:

$$\underset{\alpha_i}{\max} \left(\sum_{i=1}^{l} \alpha_i - \frac{1}{2} \sum_{i=1}^{l} \sum_{j=1}^{l} \alpha_i \alpha_j y_i y_j K(x_i, x_j) \right) \tag{6.6}$$

$$\text{subject to} \underset{i=1,\cdots,l}{\forall} \underset{0 \le \alpha_i \le C}{\forall} \sum_{i=1}^{l} y_i \alpha_i = 0.$$

Solving this kernelized dual optimization form and finding optimal values of α_i allows us to calculate $w = \sum i = 1 l \alpha_i y_i \Phi(x_i)$ and determine value of parameter b from Karush-Kuhn-Tucker conditions. Training instances with associated non-zero values of α_i are known as support vectors and deemed as sufficient to represent the training set. Therefore, SVMs achieve instance reduction by relying only on support vectors.

The previous equations allow us to write the SVM classification function as:

$$f(x) = \text{sign}\left(w \cdot \Phi(x) + b \right) = \text{sign}\left(\sum_{i=1}^{l} \alpha_i y_i K(x_i, x) + b \right). \tag{6.7}$$

While this solution is suitable for roughly balanced datasets, it tends to fail for skewed class distributions. As we want to propose an algorithmic-level solution to this problem, we must understand what hinders the performance of SVMs in imbalanced domains. The first answer comes from the soft margin optimization task defined in Eq. (6.2). Here, the regularization parameter C may be seen as a misclassification cost for penalizing errors on the training set. However, it assumes identical cost assigned to both of classes. Therefore, learning algorithm will favor the majority class, as concentrating on it will lead to a better trade-off between classification error and margin maximization. This will come at the expense of minority class, especially when the imbalance ratio is high, as then ignoring the minority class will lead to better optimization results. Therefore, the resulting hyperplane will be shifted towards minority class.

Another potential drawback of SVMs is connected with support vectors derived from imbalanced data. As one may recall, only instances with $\alpha_i \geq 0$ will be preserved and used as support vectors. As this process is also skew-insensitive, the larger imbalance ratio will lead to bigger disproportions in number of support vectors associated to each class. Therefore, trained SVM will display reduced (if any) generalization capabilities on the minority class, caused by further increased disproportion between class instances.

Additional problem may lie in difficult types of minority class instances. Not only the sole disproportion between class distributions may play role in SVM bias. Small number of minority class instances, combined with the fact that they are often overlapping with majority class or distributed in small chunks, will lead to an insufficient density around the area where the actual classification boundary should be estimated.

SVMs have been often combined with dedicated sampling solutions [67] and feature selection [53] to tackle class imbalance, but their true potential lies in modifying their underlying mechanisms. Let us now discuss the algorithm-level approaches to making SVMs skew-insensitive. They are divided into four categories: using specific kernel modifications, weighting training instances according to their importance, using active learning paradigm to select a subset of training instances, and other approaches that do not fit into previous groups.

6.2.1   Kernel Modifications

Used kernel functions play crucial role in the performance of SVMs. Therefore, it seems natural that modifying these underlying functions may alleviate the bias towards the minority class. Let us now discuss several most popular kernel modifications that allow us to train skew-insensitive SVMs.

6.2.1.1   Kernel Boundary and Margin Shift

First possible kernel modification is to directly influence the kernel matrix given by a selected kernel function on training data [87]. The main advantage of this lies in relying directly on the information coming from instances in the transformed feature space, thus making it more flexible. Given kernel modification should improve the spatial resolution along the decision boundary, thus leading to a better intra-class separatio. As it works in the mapped space, it can easily identify the learned boundary as the center hyperplane in the estimated margin. Then, in order to reduce the bias, the boundary between the center hyperplane and the hyperplane formed by majority class support vectors is being magnified [88]. This leads to reduced number of majority class support vectors, and hence alleviates the classification bias. Authors of [92] postulate to shift the margin in order to reduce the classification bias. Their modification re-weights the classes via inversed proportional regularized penalty. Then, a margin compensation is being conducted which leads to lopsided margin. This forces a shift of the decision boundary in favor of minority class.

Similar approach is adopted by [78], where authors use the margin alignment to obtain skew-insensitive ensemble of classifiers. Decision boundary and margin shifts have recently attracted a lot of attention in various different formulations of classifiers based on SVMs. Yu et al. [93] enhanced SVM with optimized decision threshold adjustment strategy that allowed for a self-adaptive decision boundary alignment. Maximum margin and minimum volume hyper-spheres machine with pinball loss, based on twin hyper-sphere SVMs were proposed in [90]. The idea was based on constructing two hyperspheres, one for majority and one for minority class. Then the margin between them was subject to maximization, while pinball loss function was use to combat the presence of potential overlapping and noise. This approach was extended in [89], where authors proposed a new version of their twin hyper-sphere SVM that avoids the matrix inverse operation and offers significant training speed-up compared to other solutions.

6.2.1.2   Kernel Target Alignment

While training SVMs one may use a kernel-alignment approach for model selection purposes [13]. It is a measure of similarity between two kernel functions or between a kernel and a target function. It allows us to quantify the level of agreement between the used kernel and the classification problem at hand. It can be used instead of other measures (such as margins), leading to efficient and simpler SVM tuning. In order to calculate if the used kernel obtains the correct data representation one needs to check the difference between the sum of the inter-class distances with the sum of the intra-class distances. Such a difference can be directly translated into the obtained alignment between the used kernel and a theoretical ideal one (oracle) and thus check the fitness of currently used kernel. This approach was further extended in [98], where authors merged the EulerMaclaurin formula with local and global extremal properties derived from the approximate kernel separability criterion. This allowed to calculate a determined global minimum point for the approximation function. After this, the SVM optimization is being solved without continuously repeating the search with varying starting points to obtain local minimums. Further works examined the applicability of kernel target alignment to optimization of multi-scale kernels, where a different width is chosen for each feature independently [65]. Kernel alignment may be used for class imbalance learning, by taking into account the skewed distributions while calculating the fitness of the kernel [33]. Thus, kernels leading alleviating the bias towards the majority class will be preferred instead of skew-sensitive ones.

6.2.1.3   Kernel Scaling

Yet another approach to improving the performance of SVMs on imbalanced data lies in scaling the underlying kernel. This allows to take as an input the initial approximate solution and then modify such model to better adjust to skewed class distributions. While traditional kernel functions offer some possibilities of feature space geometry re-shaping, applying a conformal transformation leads to an even greater adaptability. A conformal transformation of any geometrical space (like considered here feature space) is defined as such a function that maps given space into a new one, while locally preserving angles between curves. Maratea et al. [56] proposed to use asymmetric kernel scaling based on such a conformal transformation in order to enlarge areas on both sides of the decision boundary in an independent manner. This allows for reducing the bias towards the majority class. Any SVM solution can be used to compute the initial decision boundary and obtained predictions are used to divide the instance set into positive χ^+ and negative χ^- groups. Then a following kernel transformation is used:

$$
D(x) = \begin{cases} e^{-k_1 f(x)^2} & \text{if } x \in \chi^+ \\ e^{-k_1 f(x)^2} & \text{if } x \in \chi^- \end{cases},
\tag{6.8}
$$

where k_1 and k_2 are free scaling parameters that are responsible for the size of the decision area enlargement associated with positive and negative classes. While one can easily see how significant impact their values will have on the final scaled classifiers, only an empirical value selection was presented in [56]. Therefore, a grid-search or other automated parameter tuning procedure must be used in order to determine the proper parameter values. This leads to an increased computational complexity of this method. This was addressed by Zhang et al. [95, 96], where authors used the same transformation as in Eq. (6.8), but added a Chi-Squared test for calculating the scaling parameters, as well as weights associated with training instances. Furthermore, authors showed how to extend their model to multi-class imbalanced problems.

6.2.2 Weighted Approaches

This approach assumes that one may assign higher importance to given training instances (usually to the ones coming from the minority class) in order to boost their influence on the SVM training procedure and increase their chances of becoming support vectors. Additionally, some approaches apply the weighting scheme directly to support vectors to reshape the decision boundary. Let us take a closer look on the most popular weighting-based solutions.

6.2.2.1 Instance Weighting

Standard SVM formulations assume that all of training instances are of equal importance for the training process. This is not a valid assumption in case of imbalanced data. There are several reasons behind such a reasoning. Firstly, as classes are skewed minority instances should compensate in their importance what their lose in their numbers [6]. Secondly, imbalanced datasets are often composed of instances posing various difficulties to learners, such as borderline cases or small disjuncts [77]. Finally, outliers may also come into the scenario, as some imbalanced datasets may consist of many rare examples [69]. To accommodate these factors in SVMs an instance-level weighted modification was proposed [91].

The underlying assumption behind this approach is to assign different weights or penalties to each training instance. This may be achieved by re-writing the soft margin optimization task (see Eq. (6.2)) as:

$$
\min \left(\frac{1}{2} w \cdot w + \sum_{i=1}^{l} C_i \xi_i \right)
$$

(6.9)

$$
\text{subject to} \underset{i=1,\cdots,l}{\forall} \underset{\xi_i \geq 0}{\forall} \underset{C_i \geq 0}{\forall} \; y_i \left(w \cdot \Phi(x_i) + b \right) \geq 1 - C_i \xi_i,
$$

where C_i is the penalty/weight associated with given training instance x_i. Values of weights may be given depending on the imbalance ratio between classes or individual instance complexity factors [75].

While this approach seems highly attractive, one must be aware of its potential limitations. Proper setting of weights plays a crucial role in obtained performance and thus is a highly sensitive and data-dependent process. Additionally, importance of instances may change over time due to non-stationary nature of data [36], or even during the training process as geometry of decision space is being altered [63]. Recalculating weights may be computationally expensive, especially for large-scale datasets. To address this issue a multi-parametric solution-path algorithm for weighted SVMs was proposed in [34]. Authors have extended the standard solution-path algorithm, which was used for single-parameter problems, to multiple parameter formulation (as each weight can be considered as an independent parameter). Additionally, they have dealt with the issue of high-dimensional breakpoints that arise during the parameter search procedure. Another work by Wang et al. proposed weighted SVMs with both 1-norm and 2-norm for imbalanced datasets, where instance weights were derived from boosting procedure [85]. A distributed version of their approach using MapReduce approach for large-scale imbalanced problems was discussed in [84]. An interesting solution to calculating instance weights was proposed by Zhu et al. [100], where authors used extended nearest neighbor chains to locate objects that may potentially lie close to the decision boundary before SVM training. SVMs were also used to determine the difficulty of training instances in imbalanced datasets in order to adjust instance-level weights in AdaBoost ensemble learning [43].

6.2.2.2 Support Vector Weighting

Alternative approach assumes using the original imbalanced dataset to train a SVM classifier and then apply weighting to obtained support vectors in order to shift the decision boundary. One of the first algorithms following this idea was zSVM [31]. It is based on modifying the original SVM decision function (see Eq. (6.7)) in the following way:

$$f(x) = \text{sign}\left(\sum_{i=1}^{l_1}\alpha_i^+ y_i K(x_i, x) + \sum_{j=1}^{l_2}\alpha_j^- y_j K(x_j, x) + b\right), \qquad (6.10)$$

where α_i^+ and α_j^- are coefficients of support vectors of positive and negative class respectively (usually minority class is considered as a positive one here) and l_1 and l_2 stand for the number of training instances in each class. The zSVM method postulates to increase the importance of support vectors assigned to minority class by re-weighting them. This is achieved by multiplying them by a user-set positive-valued parameter z (hence the name of the method). This allows us to rewrite the decision function as:

$$f(x) = \text{sign}\left(z \cdot \sum_{i=1}^{l_1}\alpha_i^+ y_i K(x_i, x) + \sum_{j=1}^{l_2}\alpha_j^- y_j K(x_j, x) + b\right). \qquad (6.11)$$

This will increase the impact of minority class support vectors on the formed decision boundary and thus effectively alleviate the classification bias. As the value of z parameter plays a crucial role in the performance of this method, it must be carefully tuned. Authors [31] propose to tune it independently for each dataset by using performance on training data.

6.2.2.3 Fuzzy Approaches

Alternative formulation to instance-weighting solution was developed with the usage of fuzzy logic. Fuzzy SVM (FSVM) [45] allowed to assign different levels of importance to each training instance by associating them with fuzzy membership functions. FSVM was originally developed to deal with datasets containing noisy instances and outliers [46, 47]. However, the fuzzy membership mechanism became highly attractive for imbalanced domain.

FSVM reformulates the soft margin optimization problem (see Eq. (6.2)) as:

$$\min\left(\frac{1}{2}w \cdot w + C\sum_{i=1}^{l} m_i \xi_i\right) \qquad (6.12)$$

$$\text{subject to} \underset{i=1,\cdots,l}{\forall}\ \underset{\xi_i \geq 0}{\forall}\ y_i\left(w \cdot \Phi(x_i) + b\right) \geq 1 - \xi_i.$$

This allows to adjust to embed the membership function m_i associated with an instance x_i into the SVM penalty function. Therefore, with smaller values of m_i the effects of slack variable ξ_i on the objective function are reduced. A less important object will then have associated smaller values of fuzzy membership, to reduce their impact or even completely exclude them from the decision boundary calculation. This may also be viewed as adding a soft misclassification cost to each training instance, allowing to differentiate the error penalty associated with them [81]. This method was later combined with rough set approach to allow utilizing information granules [8].

While this methods works very well for noisy datasets, it will still be subject to classification bias present in imbalanced domain. Therefore, a modification know as FSVM-CIL was proposed in [3]. Here authors proposed three different strategies for calculating the membership functions in a way that will be relevant for skewed datasets. Fuzzy membership for i-th minority class instance is denoted as m_i^+, while for j-th majority class instance as m_j^-. FSVM-CIL proposes to calculate these membership functions as follows:

$$m_i^+ = f(x_i^+)r^+, \tag{6.13}$$

$$m_j^- = f(x_j^-)r^-, \tag{6.14}$$

where $f(x)$ is a specified decaying function returning values in range [0,1], allowing to calculate the importance of a given instance according to a selected criterion. Parameters r^+ and r^- are used to reflect the disproportion between classes, where $r^+ = 1$ and r^- is set to the minority to majority imbalance ratio.

The decaying function $f(x)$ plays a crucial role in the performance of FSVM-CIL algorithm. As it gives significant freedom in designing the mechanism to reduce the influence of majority instances, several different mechanisms were proposed. First solution associates the value of $f(x_i)$ for i-th instance using the distance from its own class center. Here examples closer to the class centroid have assigned a higher membership function value. Therefore, outliers and noisy instances will be effectively filtered out. One must notice that this strategy may fail for many imbalanced scenarios, as minority classes tend to be characterized by non-homogeneous structure and presence of small disjuncts. Therefore, minority class centroid may not be the most suitable representation.

Second solution associates the value of $f(x_i)$ for i-th instance using the distance from the pre-estimated decision boundary. This step is applied before actual FSVM training and hence requires an estimation of where the decision boundary is most likely to be localized. This is achieved by finding a hyper-sphere covering the overlapping region between classes, as the decision boundary most likely to be put. The distance between a point x_i and a center of this hypersphere is used to calculate $f(x_i)$ using linear or exponential functions. Disadvantage of this approach will lie in potential miscalculations of the overlapping hypersphere, especially in cases of minority classes consisting of many borderline or noisy instances.

The third solution associates the value of $f(x_i)$ for i-th instance using the distance from the calculated decision boundary. This is a post-training approach and requires an input a standard crisp SVM. Then the decision boundary is fuzzified using membership functions calculated for instances. Therefore, it can be seen as a boundary shift method. Here, instances lying closer to the crisp decision boundary are assigned higher weights and later guide the construction of the fuzzy decision boundary. Disadvantage of this approach lies in using a crisp SVM boundary for membership calculations. In case of severely imbalanced datasets it may lay too far within the minority class structure, thus rendering the boundary shift not significant enough.

Fuzzy SVMs for imbalanced data were further developed by the research community. Let us look at some of the most important modifications. A fuzzy total margin based support vector machine was introduced in [14]. Instead of relying on soft margin, a total margin approach was incorporated into the FSVM training procedure. Additionally, authors combined membership function instance weighting with different values of parameter C associated with minority and majority class independently. Another modification known as IBFSVM was developed in [9], where authors calculated membership functions using denoising factors and class compensation factors. The former one allowed to handle differing distributions of objects in minority and majority classes with respect to underlying class structures, while the latter one allowed to incorporate the class imbalance ratio into the decision boundary computation. In [21] authors used entropy to calculate fuzzy membership functions for instances. Additionally, they proposed an automatic solution for automatically associating sufficiently large membership function values to minority class instances in order to effectively alleviate the class bias.

6.2.3 Active Learning

Active learning methods [2] are used to select instances for label query when labeling costs must be taken into account [104], or to select most informative instances from the training set to improve the quality of obtained classifier [24]. In the context of imbalanced data, active learning may be utilized to balance the training set by selecting the most representative instances from majority class [20], removing noisy minority class examples [97] and reducing the overall imbalance ratio [23]. Example of training set selection with active learning from imbalanced dataset and its effect on borderline and overlapping instances is given in Fig. 6.2.

Active learning is a popular addition to SVMs [26, 32], especially in applications where one cannot afford a fully labeled dataset [29, 79]. Although active learning does not directly modify the SVM training procedure, we will consider it as an algorithm-level solution. It is embedded in the training process, as opposite to pre-processing approaches that are executed before the training begins.

First skew-insensitive active learning solution for SVMs was proposed in [19]. This approach starts with small subset of the training set and iteratively selects from the set of unused instances the nearest one to the decision boundary. Then it is added to the training set and SVM is being retrained. This allows to select only the

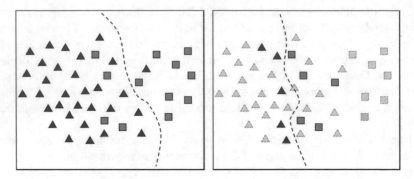

Fig. 6.2 Active learning applied to training set selection for imbalanced dataset with borderline and overlapping instances: (*left*) skewed decision boundary; (*right*) corrected decision boundary after instance selection

most relevant instances and by suing an early stopping criterion achieve a significant training speed up for large-scale datasets. Zieba and Tomczak [103] proposed a combination of SVMs, Boosting and active learning to achieve better elimination of irrelevant instances and better estimation of misclassification costs for each of the base classifiers in the ensemble.

6.3 Decision Trees

Decision trees are highly popular classification algorithms due to their efficiency, simplicity, low computational complexity and interpretability. However, they are highly prone to skewed class distributions and therefore fail in learning from imbalanced data. There is a number of modifications available [11, 64, 71], most of which concentrate on cost-sensitive solutions. From the algorithm-level point of view the most straightforward approach to improving decision trees lies in modifying their key component – split function.

The most efficient solution lies in using Hellinger distance for creating splits proposed by Cieslak et al. [11]. Hellinger distance is a measure of distributional divergence [10] that could be used to measure the distance between two probability distributions P_1 and P_2. In order to calculate it, one must derive the Bhattacharyya coefficient with assumption of working on a measure space (Ω, B, v), where P is a set of all measures on B that are absolutely continuous with respect to v:

$$p(P_1, P_2) = \int_{\Omega} \sqrt{\frac{dP_1}{dv} \frac{dP_2}{dv}} dv. \tag{6.15}$$

This allows to derive the Hellinger distance as:

$$h_H(P_1, P_2) = 2\left[1 - \int_\Omega \sqrt{\frac{dP_1}{dv}\frac{dP_2}{dv}}dv\right] = \sqrt{\int_\Omega \left(\sqrt{\frac{dP_1}{dv}} - \sqrt{\frac{dP_2}{dv}}\right)^2 dv.}$$

(6.16)

As in machine learning we usually deal with countable and not continuous space we may switch to a summation of all values and re-express this for a two-class problems as:

$$d_H(P(m^+), P(m^-)) = \sqrt{\sum_{i \in v}\left(\sqrt{P(Y^+|X_i)} - \sqrt{P(Y^-|X_i)}\right)^2}.$$

(6.17)

One may translate this into a confusion matrix for a two-class problem, obtaining the final formulation of Hellinger distance for binary imbalanced domain:

$$d_H(TPR, FPR) = \sqrt{\left(\sqrt{TPR} - \sqrt{FPR}\right)^2 + \left(\sqrt{1 - TPR} - \sqrt{1 - FPR}\right)^2}.$$

(6.18)

Hellinger allows for an induction of skew-insensitive trees. In [10] this was proven by analyzing the shape of this function. Further proofs are given in [11]. Experimental results back-up these claims, showing that Hellinger Distance Trees built upon a C4.4 algorithm (unpruned and uncollapsed C4.5 with Laplace smoothing at the leaves) leads to much better performance on minority class without sacrificing the effectiveness on majority instances. An example of differences between decision trees using Gini and Hellinger criteria is presented in Fig. 6.3. Hellinger trees tend to form broader, yet enclosed decision boundaries around minority class instances. This allows them to achieve a better generalization over the minority class, without losing the predictive power on majority class.

Limitation of Hellinger distance lies in its binary nature, as it cannot be directly applied to multi-class imbalanced problems. In [28] authors proposed to used a one-vs-all approach to estimate the split value for multi-class cases. However, the obtained results were moderate, as this approximation often failed to properly capture complexities of multiple skewed distributions.

Other splitting criteria were developed as well. Lenca et al. [44] proposed to use an off-centered entropy. This specific formulation takes its maximum value for a distribution fixed by the user. This distribution can be the a priori distribution of the class variable modalities or a distribution taking into account the costs of misclassification. This allows to embed either standard imbalance ratio or user preferences into the tree induction procedure. The use of entropy was further studied by Boonchuay et al. [5]. Here a new impurity measure named minority entropy was proposed. It is based on the information derived from the minority class. Shannon's entropy is applied on a local subset of minority instances, effectively defining the local space for decision tree induction that takes into account given minority class

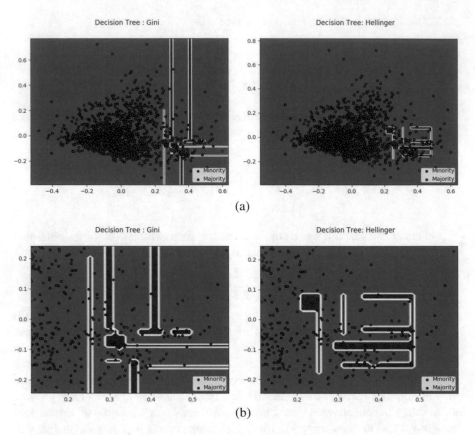

Fig. 6.3 Comparison between decision trees trained using Gini and Hellinger splitting criteria on yeast6 dataset with IR 41.6. (**a**) Differences between learned decision boundaries over entire dataset. (**b**) Detailed look on differences between learned decision boundaries over a part of the decision space

characteristics. Class Confidence Proportion split function was proposed by Liu et al. [50]. A top-down and bottom-up approach using Fisher's exact test to prune branches of the tree was used to develop statistically significant decision rules. Experimental results showed that this algorithm-level modification outperforms decision trees balanced with pre-processing algorithms.

6.4 Nearest Neighbor Classifiers

Lazy classifiers, including the most popular NN approach, offer interesting properties from the imbalanced data classification point of view [25]. However, they seem unlikely to become subject of algorithm-level modifications for imbalanced data domain. They do not create a classification model until a new test instance becomes available, and even then use straightforward approaches to determine its label. Although there is a plethora of works for NN classifiers for imbalanced data, they usually concentrate on prototype selection [83] or prototype generation [51]. As they directly manipulate the training set, they should be considered as pre-processing solutions rather than algorithm-level approaches. However, there exist several solutions for NN classifiers that make them skew-insensitive without referring to prototype modifications.

Cano et al. [7] proposed a gravitational-based algorithm for NN classifier with emphasis on imbalanced data. It aimed to modify the distance function by using a gravitational approach, assuming that the gravitation of minority class instances would be eclipsed by instances belonging to the majority class. Authors proposed to alleviate this problem by weighting a gravitation of each class by the ratio between the number of instances belonging to given group and the total number of instances. This allows to calculate the gravitation function for a given instance as:

$$g(x, m) = \left(1 - \frac{N_m - 1}{N}\right) \sum_{i=1}^{N} \frac{1}{d(x, x_i, m)} \mid \underset{x_i \in m}{\forall}, \tag{6.19}$$

where N and N_i stand for the number of training instances and number of instances in m-th class respectively, and $d(x, x_i, m)$ is a distance function proposed by authors [7]. It takes into account weights assigned to each feature to control its importance, while an evolutionary optimization is being used to automatically adapt these weights to the dataset at hand. This is embedded into a standard NN framework, allowing skew and noise insensitive classification.

The idea of combining gravitation-based computations with NN classifiers was continued in [99]. Instead of relying on popular k-NN solution authors proposed to use fixed-radius NN approach [59]. This was enhanced with pairwise class gravitation calculation in order to remove the class bias.

Another weighted k-NN modification was proposed by Liu and Chawla [48]. Here, prototypes are individually weighted instead of the classes. Their parameters are calculated using the probability of attribute values for a given class. Similar solution was proposed in [18], where weights are assigned to each of the class based on how instances belonging to it are classified in the neighborhood of the test instance by a standard k-NN classifier. Positive-biased NN algorithm [94] postulated not to influence the k-NN classification by the overall imbalance ratio, but rather by the local class distributions in each neighborhood.

NN approaches were also coupled with fuzzy and rough set approaches in order to improve their responsiveness to skewed datasets. Han and Mao proposed a fuzzy-rough k-NN that took into account the fuzziness and roughness of the NNs of a given test instance into consideration [27]. Their solution defines fuzzy membership function that favors the minority class and allows to form a fuzzy equivalent relation between the new instance and its k-NNs. Ramentol et al. [68] extended this idea by proposing Imbalanced Fuzzy-Rough Ordered Weighted Average NN Classification

(IFROWANN). Several strategies for OWA weight vectors were proposed that allowed to better model the neighborhood of the minority class.

Finally, it is important to notice that k-NN method is also frequently used with other classifiers in order to determine the class structure [41] and types of minority class instances in both binary [60] and multi-class imbalanced scenarios [70]. Such an information may be then used to improve the performance of any classifier and to gain a deeper insight into the considered problem.

6.5 Bayesian Classifiers

Bayesian approaches are very popular in data classification, due to their excellent theoretical background, low computational complexity and good performance. They offer an attractive possibility for adaptation to imbalanced data by manipulating class prior probabilities in order to alleviate the class bias. Furthermore, they are very popular in text classification [80], where uneven class distributions are bound to appear [40, 57]. Therefore, several Bayesian-based approaches for skewed datasets were proposed in last years. Let us discuss the most important ones.

Frank et al. developed Locally Weighted Naïve Bayes [22]. Their version of relaxed the standard independence assumption by learning local models at prediction time. Therefore, this is a lazy learning solution that stores the training instances and does not train any model until classification time. For each tested instance a new Naïve Bayes is being constructed using a weighted set of training instances from the neighborhood of the test instance. Although not directly used for imbalanced data, one may see many similarities between this solution and instance-level weighted SVMs (see Sect. 6.2.2). A Bayesian network tuned for imbalanced text classification was proposed in [55]. Authors proposed new structure, which they called mixed Gaussian Bayesian Augmented Naïve Bayes that was able to process both discrete and continuous variables a need for discretization procedure. An undersampling with Tomek links was embedded in the training procedure of this classifier in order to handle skewed classes. An active instance selection method with Naïve Bayes classifier for imbalanced problems was proposed by Lee et al. [42]. Their method trained a Naïve Bayes classifier in an incremental manner, starting with a balanced training subset. Then it proceeds by sequentially adding such informative instances that are characterized by high error rates outputted by the current classifier. A skew-insensitive smoothing method for multinomial Naïve Bayes was introduced in [49]. Their approach was less affected by imbalanced class distributions, leading to improved generalization performance of obtained classifiers. Another skew-insensitive solution is Bayes Vector Quantizer for imbalanced data [16] that aims at minimizing the average misclassification risk, offering an theoretically-sound approach rooted in statistical decision theory.

Interesting usage of Bayesian approaches for improving the interpretability of rule-based classifiers on imbalanced data was developed in [61]. Authors introduced three different approaches for selecting classification rules with descriptive characteristics. They are based on combining Bayesian confirmation measures with rule support. This allows to extract more useful information about the minority class and improve the knowledge discovery from imbalanced datasets.

Bayesian approaches have also been a base for hybrid-based solutions [86] to learning from imbalanced data. Bayesian Support Vector Machines [30] offered an attractive pragmatic expansion scheme of the Bayesian approach to SVM learning and assessing how well the underlying classifier is aligned with the considered imbalanced dataset. This was achieved by developing a model selection scheme that took into account probability estimates, corresponding decision costs, and quadratic program of optimal margin classifier. Another hybrid SVM for imbalanced data was proposed in [15]. Authors introduced Near-Bayesian Support Vector Machines that combined decision boundary shift with varying regularization parameter values for each class. Their approach was further extended to the multi-class scenario and allowed to take into account multi-class cost-sensitive cases.

6.6   One-Class Classifiers

One-class classification (OCC) [72], also known as learning in the absence of counterexamples, was designed for scenarios in which during the training step we have access only to objects coming from a single class. A one-class classifier aims at capturing characteristics of training instances, in order to be able to distinguish between them and potential outliers to appear. OCC assumes that we have no access to any representatives of outliers during training. This may be caused by high cost or difficulty in gathering a meaningful instance set, or because one cannot define the precise nature of outliers. Therefore, OCC finds use in important domains such as novelty detection, fault diagnosis, or target detection. Yet its areas of applicability extend beyond that [4].

In cases when one of the classes is highly underrepresented, or collected samples are far from sufficiently representing the underlying class distribution, training a binary classifier may be difficult [54]. Instead, one may train a one-class classifier on the better represented class and treat the remaining one as outliers [76]. This approach may be directly utilized in imbalanced scenarios, where a majority class will be treated as the target concept and minority class as outliers. This solution has proven to be especially useful when the minority class lack any structure, being predominantly composed of small disjuncts or noisy instances. One-class classifiers are naturally skew-insensitive, as by utilizing only a single class during training they concentrate on creating its data description. Additionally, most of one-class classifiers have inbuilt mechanism to handle noisy instances, thus further increasing their robustness in imbalanced problems. There are three main approaches for tackling imbalanced datasets with OCC:

- Training a one-class classifier on the majority class;
- Training a well-tuned one-class classifier on the minority class;
- Training one-class classifiers on both classes and combining their outputs.

One must remember that the advantages of one-class classifiers come at a price of discarding all of available information about the majority class. Therefore, this solution should be used carefully and may not fit some specific applications.

One of the first works of using OCC for skewed datasets was developed by Cohen et al. [12], where authors proposed to combine one-class SVM with a conformal kernel. Experimental results proven this approach to deliver the best sensitivity among all of tested methods. However, this came at a price of reduced specificity on majority class. This problem is prevailing in many works using OCC for imbalanced data and shows how important a proper tuning of one-class classifiers is. This issue was addressed later [101, 102] by proposing a two-step approach for kernel one-class classifiers, where classifier parameters were established on the basis of minority class instances, but both minority and majority cases were used to tune the classification threshold.

A one-class rule-based symbolic classifier for imbalanced medical datasets was proposed in [58]. Authors showed that it was able to return improved performance than cost-sensitive and data pre-processing methods, while offering good interpretability of decision. An improved one-class rule-based classifier was later developed by Villar et al. [82]. The proposed method used a genetic-fuzzy system to tune rules for target class. The outputted set of rules was characterized by not only good generalization capabilities, but also by its compactness.

Krawczyk et al. [38] proposed a weighted modification of one-class SVM trained on the minority class. A neighborhood-based analysis of the training set was done in the pre-processing step in order to associate minority instances with one of the four predefined difficulty levels. This was used to derive weights for these instances in order to empower the most difficult cases such as small disjuncts or rare examples. Experimental study showed that such an approach in many cases leads to a better performance than training a one-class classifier on the majority class. The importance of proper selection of either majority or minority class as the target concept for OCC was further discussed in [66].

One of the problems in imbalanced class learning is the presence of sub-concepts or class disjuncts within both the majority and minority classes. This, combined with limited number of minority class instances, is the source of a significant learning difficulty for many classifiers. Either decision boundary becomes too complex and generalization capabilities are being lost, or minority sub-concepts are ignored due to not providing enough discriminative information to the classifier. Krawczyk et al. [37] proposed an ensemble approach for one-class classifiers that was able to automatically identify these sub-concepts in all of supplied classes, regardless of their imbalance ratio. Each class was clustered independently with an automatic detection of the proper number of clusters. Then local one-class learners were trained on these concepts in order to encompass complex structure of each class. Authors showed that combining kernel fuzzy clustering with weighted one-class SVMs returns the best performance. Learning over subconcepts with one-class classifiers was later discussed by Sharma et al. [74], where authors proposed to learn one-class classifiers along the lines of underlying domain concepts.

One-class classifiers were also discussed as a tool for solving multi-class imbalanced problems [39], where a separate model was trained on each class. Then a combination solution such as Error-Correcting Output Codes was used to reconstruct the original problem from one-class outputs. Authors stated that such an approach allows to preserve the skew-insensitive advantages of OCC approach, while effectively utilizing information regarding all of available classes.

6.7 Summarizing Comments

This chapter discussed algorithm-level solutions for class imbalance as an alternative to data pre-processing approaches. They required a more in-depth knowledge about the used classifier in order to identify which underlying mechanisms hinder its performance when classes are unequally distributed. Although such modifications are less flexible than data manipulation approaches, they may offer improved performance and more directed alleviation of the imbalance problem.

Although many algorithm-level modifications have been introduced, still new challenges lie ahead. It is important to propose new classifiers that can either directly or indirectly incorporate this background knowledge about objects into their training procedure. Thus, when designing an efficient classifier one must not only alleviate the bias towards the majority class, but also pay attention to difficulties of individual minority examples. Additionally, proposing methods that are able to combine pre-processing and algorithm-level solutions in a guided manner seem as a highly attractive direction.

References

1. Abril, L.G., Núñez, H., Angulo, C., Velasco, F.: GSVM: an SVM for handling imbalanced accuracy between classes inbi-classification problems. Appl. Soft Comput. **17**, 23–31 (2014)
2. Aggarwal, C.C., Kong, X., Gu, Q., Han, J., Yu, P.S.: Active learning: a survey. In: Aggarwal, C.C. (ed.) Data Classification: Algorithms and Applications, pp. 571–606. CRC Press/Taylor & Francis Group, Boca Raton (2014)
3. Batuwita, R., Palade, V.: FSVM-CIL: fuzzy support vector machines for class imbalance learning. IEEE Trans. Fuzzy Syst. **18**(3), 558–571 (2010)
4. Bellinger, C., Sharma, S., Japkowicz, N.: One-class versus binary classification: which and when? In: 11th International Conference on Machine Learning and Applications, ICMLA, Boca Raton, 12–15 Dec 2012, vol. 2, pp. 102–106 (2012)
5. Boonchuay, K., Sinapiromsaran, K., Lursinsap, C.: Decision tree induction based on minority entropy for the class imbalance problem. Pattern Anal. Appl. **20**(3), 769–782 (2017)
6. Branco, P., Torgo, L., Ribeiro, R.P.: A survey of predictive modeling on imbalanced domains. ACM Comput. Surv. **49**(2), 31:1–31:50 (2016)
7. Cano, A., Zafra, A., Ventura, S.: Weighted data gravitation classification for standard and imbalanced data. IEEE Trans. Cybern. **43**(6), 1672–1687 (2013)
8. Chen, D., He, Q., Wang, X.: FRSVMs: fuzzy rough set based support vector machines. Fuzzy Sets Syst. **161**(4), 596–607 (2010)

9. Cheng, J., Liu, G.: Affective detection based on an imbalanced fuzzy support vector machine. Biomed. Signal Proc. Control **18**, 118–126 (2015)
10. Cieslak, D.A., Chawla, N.V.: Learning decision trees for unbalanced data. In: European Conference on Machine Learning and Knowledge Discovery in Databases, ECML/PKDD 2008, Antwerp, 15–19 Sept 2008, Proceedings, Part I, pp. 241–256 (2008)
11. Cieslak, D.A., Hoens, T.R., Chawla, N.V., Kegelmeyer, W.P.: Hellinger distance decision trees are robust and skew-insensitive. Data Min. Knowl. Disc. **24**(1), 136–158 (2012)
12. Cohen, G., Hilario, M., Pellegrini, C.: One-class support vector machines with a conformal kernel. A case study in handling class imbalance. In: Structural, Syntactic, and Statistical Pattern Recognition, Joint IAPR International Workshops, SSPR 2004 and SPR 2004, Lisbon, Proceedings, 18–20 Aug 2004, pp. 850–858 (2004)
13. Cristianini, N., Shawe-Taylor, J., Elisseeff, A., Kandola, J.S.: On kernel-target alignment. In: Advances in Neural Information Processing Systems 14 [Neural Information Processing Systems: Natural and Synthetic, NIPS 2001, Vancouver, 3–8 Dec 2001], pp. 367–373 (2001)
14. Dai, H.: Class imbalance learning via a fuzzy total margin based support vector machine. Appl. Soft Comput. **31**, 172–184 (2015)
15. Datta, S., Das, S.: Near-Bayesian support vector machines for imbalanced data classification with equal or unequal misclassification costs. Neural Netw. **70**, 39–52 (2015)
16. Diamantini, C., Potena, D.: Bayes vector quantizer for class-imbalance problem. IEEE Trans. Know. Data Eng. **21**(5), 638–651 (2009)
17. Dorado-Moreno, M., Pérez-Ortiz, M., Gutiérrez, P.A., Ciria, R., Briceño, J., Hervás-Martínez, C.: Dynamically weighted evolutionary ordinal neural network for solving an imbalanced liver transplantation problem. Artif. Intell. Med. **77**, 1–11 (2017)
18. Dubey, H., Pudi, V.: Class based weighted k-nearest neighbor over imbalance dataset. In: 17th Pacific-Asia Conference on Advances in Knowledge Discovery and Data Mining, PAKDD 2013, Gold Coast, 14–17 Apr 2013, Proceedings, Part II, pp. 305–316 (2013)
19. Ertekin, S., Huang, J., Bottou, L., Giles, C.L.: Learning on the border: active learning in imbalanced data classification. In: Proceedings of the Sixteenth ACM Conference on Information and Knowledge Management, CIKM 2007, Lisbon, 6–10 Nov 2007, pp. 127–136 (2007)
20. Ertekin, S., Huang, J., Giles, C.L.: Active learning for class imbalance problem. In: SIGIR 2007: Proceedings of the 30th Annual International ACM SIGIR Conference on Research and Development in Information Retrieval, Amsterdam, 23–27 July 2007, pp. 823–824 (2007)
21. Fan, Q., Wang, Z., Li, D., Gao, D., Zha, H.: Entropy-based fuzzy support vector machine for imbalanced datasets. Know. Based Syst. **115**, 87–99 (2017)
22. Frank, E., Hall, M.A., Pfahringer, B.: Locally weighted naive bayes. In: UAI'03, Proceedings of the 19th Conference in Uncertainty in Artificial Intelligence, Acapulco, 7–10 Aug 2003, pp. 249–256 (2003)
23. Fu, J., Lee, S.: Certainty-based active learning for sampling imbalanced datasets. Neurocomputing **119**, 350–358 (2013)
24. Fu, Y., Zhu, X., Li, B.: A survey on instance selection for active learning. Know. Inf. Syst. **35**(2), 249–283 (2013)
25. García, V., Mollineda, R.A., Sánchez, J.S.: On the k-nn performance in a challenging scenario of imbalance and overlapping. Pattern Anal. Appl. **11**(3–4), 269–280 (2008)
26. Guo, H., Wang, W.: An active learning-based SVM multi-class classification model. Pattern Recogn. **48**(5), 1577–1597 (2015)
27. Han, H., Mao, B.: Fuzzy-rough k-nearest neighbor algorithm for imbalanced data sets learning. In: Seventh International Conference on Fuzzy Systems and Knowledge Discovery, FSKD 2010, Yantai, 10–12 Aug 2010, pp. 1286–1290 (2010)
28. Hoens, T.R., Qian, Q., Chawla, N.V., Zhou, Z.: Building decision trees for the multi-class imbalance problem. In: 16th Pacific-Asia Conference on Advances in Knowledge Discovery and Data Mining, PAKDD 2012, Kuala Lumpur, Proceedings, Part I, 29 May–1 June 2012, pp. 122–134 (2012)

29. Hoi, S.C.H., Jin, R., Zhu, J., Lyu, M.R.: Semisupervised SVM batch mode active learning with applications to image retrieval. ACM Trans. Inf. Syst. **27**(3), 16:1–16:29 (2009)
30. Hsu, C., Wang, K., Chang, S.: Bayesian decision theory for support vector machines: imbalance measurement and feature optimization. Expert Syst. Appl. **38**(5), 4698–4704 (2011)
31. Imam, T., Ting, K.M., Kamruzzaman, J.: z-SVM: an SVM for improved classification of imbalanced data. In: AI 2006: Advances in Artificial Intelligence, 19th Australian Joint Conference on Artificial Intelligence, Hobart, 4–8 Dec 2006, Proceedings, pp. 264–273 (2006)
32. Jiang, J., Ip, H.H.: Active learning with SVM. In: Rabunal, J.R., Dorado, J., Sierra, A.P. (eds.) Encyclopedia of Artificial Intelligence (3 vol.), pp. 1–7. Information Science Reference, Hershey (2009)
33. Kandola, J.S., Shawe-Taylor, J.: Refining kernels for regression and uneven classification problems. In: Proceedings of the Ninth International Workshop on Artificial Intelligence and Statistics, AISTATS 2003, Key West, 3–6 Jan 2003
34. Karasuyama, M., Harada, N., Sugiyama, M., Takeuchi, I.: Multi-parametric solution-path algorithm for instance-weighted support vector machines. Mach. Learn. **88**(3), 297–330 (2012)
35. Krawczyk, B.: Learning from imbalanced data: open challenges and future directions. Prog. AI **5**(4), 221–232 (2016)
36. Krawczyk, B., Woźniak, M.: One-class classifiers with incremental learning and forgetting for data streams with concept drift. Soft Comput. **19**(12), 3387–3400 (2015)
37. Krawczyk, B., Woźniak, M., Cyganek, B.: Clustering-based ensembles for one-class classification. Inf. Sci. **264**, 182–195 (2014)
38. Krawczyk, B., Woźniak, M., Herrera, F.: Weighted one-class classification for different types of minority class examples in imbalanced data. In: 2014 IEEE Symposium on Computational Intelligence and Data Mining, CIDM 2014, Orlando, 9–12 Dec 2014, pp. 337–344 (2014)
39. Krawczyk, B., Woźniak, M., Herrera, F.: On the usefulness of one-class classifier ensembles for decomposition of multi-class problems. Pattern Recogn. **48**(12), 3969–3982 (2015)
40. Krawczyk, B., McInnes, B.T., Cano, A.: Sentiment classification from multi-class imbalanced twitter data using binarization. In: 12th International Conference on Hybrid Artificial Intelligent Systems, HAIS 2017, La Rioja, 21–23 June 2017, Proceedings, pp. 26–37 (2017)
41. Kriminger, E., Príncipe, J.C., Lakshminarayan, C.: Nearest neighbor distributions for imbalanced classification. In: The 2012 International Joint Conference on Neural Networks (IJCNN), Brisbane, 10–15 June 2012, pp. 1–5 (2012)
42. Lee, M.S., Rhee, J., Kim, B., Zhang, B.: AESNB: active example selection with naive bayes classifier for learning from imbalanced biomedical data. In: Ninth IEEE International Conference on Bioinformatics and Bioengineering, BIBE 2009, Taichung, 22–24 June 2009, pp. 15–21 (2009)
43. Lee, W., Jun, C., Lee, J.: Instance categorization by support vector machines to adjust weights in adaboost for imbalanced data classification. Inf. Sci. **381**, 92–103 (2017)
44. Lenca, P., Lallich, S., Do, T., Pham, N.: A comparison of different off-centered entropies to deal with class imbalance for decision trees. In: Advances in Knowledge Discovery and Data Mining, 12th Pacific-Asia Conference, PAKDD 2008, Osaka, Proceedings, 20–23 May 2008, pp. 634–643 (2008)
45. Lin, C., Wang, S.: Fuzzy support vector machines. IEEE Trans. Neural Netw. **13**(2), 464–471 (2002)
46. Lin, C., Wang, S.: Training algorithms for fuzzy support vector machines with noisy data. In: NNSP 2003, IEEE XIII Workshop on Neural Networks for Signal Processing, Toulouse, 17–19 Sept 2003, pp. 517–526 (2003)
47. Lin, C., Wang, S.: Training algorithms for fuzzy support vector machines with noisy data. Pattern Recogn. Lett. **25**(14), 1647–1656 (2004)

48. Liu, W., Chawla, S.: Class confidence weighted knn algorithms for imbalanced data sets. In: 15th Pacific-Asia Conference on Advances in Knowledge Discovery and Data Mining, PAKDD 2011, Shenzhen, 24–27 May 2011, Proceedings, Part II, pp. 345–356 (2011)
49. Liu, A., Martin, C.E.: Smoothing multinomial naïve bayes in the presence of imbalance. In: 7th International Conference on Machine Learning and Data Mining in Pattern Recognition, MLDM 2011, New York, 30 Aug–3 Sept 2011, Proceedings, pp. 46–59 (2011)
50. Liu, W., Chawla, S., Cieslak, D.A., Chawla, N.V.: A robust decision tree algorithm for imbalanced data sets. In: Proceedings of the SIAM International Conference on Data Mining, SDM 2010, Columbus, 29 April–1 May 2010, pp. 766–777 (2010)
51. López, V., Triguero, I., Carmona, C.J., García, S., Herrera, F.: Addressing imbalanced classification with instance generation techniques: IPADE-ID. Neurocomputing 126, 15–28 (2014)
52. Maldonado, S., López, J.: Imbalanced data classification using second-order cone programming support vector machines. Pattern Recogn. 47(5), 2070–2079 (2014)
53. Maldonado, S., López, J.: Dealing with high-dimensional class-imbalanced datasets: embedded feature selection for SVM classification. Appl. Soft Comput. 67, 94–105 (2018)
54. Maldonado, S., Montecinos, C.: Robust classification of imbalanced data using one-class and two-class SVM-based multiclassifiers. Intell. Data Anal. 18(1), 95–112 (2014)
55. Maragoudakis, M., Kermanidis, K., Tasikas, A., Fakotakis, N., Kokkinakis, G.K.: Bayesian induction of verb sub-categorization frames in imbalanced heterogeneous data. J. Quant. Linguis 12(2–3), 185–211 (2005)
56. Maratea, A., Petrosino, A., Manzo, M.: Adjusted f-measure and kernel scaling for imbalanced data learning. Inf. Sci. 257, 331–341 (2014)
57. McInnes, B.T., Stevenson, M.: Determining the difficulty of word sense disambiguation. J. Biomed. Inf. 47, 83–90 (2014)
58. Mena, L.J., Gonzalez, J.A.: Symbolic one-class learning from imbalanced datasets: application in medical diagnosis. Int. J. Artif. Intell. Tools 18(2), 273–309 (2009)
59. Muja, M., Lowe, D.G.: Scalable nearest neighbor algorithms for high dimensional data. IEEE Trans. Pattern Anal. Mach. Intell. 36(11), 2227–2240 (2014)
60. Napierala, K., Stefanowski, J.: Types of minority class examples and their influence on learning classifiers from imbalanced data. J. Intell. Inf. Syst. 46(3), 563–597 (2016)
61. Napierala, K., Stefanowski, J., Szczech, I.: Increasing the interpretability of rules induced from imbalanced data by using Bayesian confirmation measures. In: New Frontiers in Mining Complex Patterns – 5th International Workshop, NFMCP 2016, Held in Conjunction with ECML-PKDD 2016, Riva del Garda, 19 Sept 2016, Revised Selected Papers, pp. 84–98 (2016)
62. Ohsaki, M., Wang, P., Matsuda, K., Katagiri, S., Watanabe, H., Ralescu, A.: Confusion-matrix-based kernel logistic regression for imbalanced data classification. IEEE Trans. Know. Data Eng. 29(9), 1806–1819 (2017)
63. Pan, B., Chen, W., Xu, C., Chen, B.: A novel framework for learning geometry-aware kernels. IEEE Trans. Neural Netw. Learn. Syst. 27(5), 939–951 (2016)
64. Park, Y., Ghosh, J.: Ensembles of (α)-trees for imbalanced classification problems. IEEE Trans. Know. Data Eng. 26(1), 131–143 (2014)
65. Pérez-Ortiz, M., Gutiérrez, P.A., Sánchez-Monedero, J., Hervás-Martínez, C.: A study on multi-scale kernel optimisation via centered kernel-target alignment. Neural Process. Lett. 44(2), 491–517 (2016)
66. Pérez-Sánchez, B., Fontenla-Romero, O., Sánchez-Maroño, N.: Selecting target concept in one-class classification for handling class imbalance problem. In: 2015 International Joint Conference on Neural Networks, IJCNN 2015, Killarney, 12–17 July 2015, pp. 1–8 (2015)
67. Piri, S., Delen, D., Liu, T.: A synthetic informative minority over-sampling (SIMO) algorithm leveraging support vector machine to enhance learning from imbalanced datasets. Decis. Support. Syst. 106, 15–29 (2018)

68. Ramentol, E., Vluymans, S., Verbiest, N., Caballero, Y., Bello, R., Cornelis, C., Herrera, F.: IFROWANN: imbalanced fuzzy-rough ordered weighted average nearest neighbor classification. IEEE Trans. Fuzzy Syst. **23**(5), 1622–1637 (2015)
69. Razzaghi, T., Xanthopoulos, P., Seref, O.: Constraint relaxation, cost-sensitive learning and bagging for imbalanced classification problems with outliers. Optim. Lett. **11**(5), 915–928 (2017)
70. Sáez, J.A., Krawczyk, B., Woźniak, M.: Analyzing the oversampling of different classes and types of examples in multi-class imbalanced datasets. Pattern Recogn. **57**, 164–178 (2016)
71. Sardari, S., Eftekhari, M., Afsari, F.: Hesitant fuzzy decision tree approach for highly imbalanced data classification. Appl. Soft Comput. **61**, 727–741 (2017)
72. Schölkopf, B., Williamson, R.C., Smola, A.J., Shawe-Taylor, J., Platt, J.C.: Support vector method for novelty detection. In: Advances in Neural Information Processing Systems 12, NIPS Conference, Denver, 29 Nov–4 Dec 1999, pp. 582–588 (1999)
73. Shao, Y., Chen, W., Zhang, J., Wang, Z., Deng, N.: An efficient weighted lagrangian twin support vector machine for imbalanced data classification. Pattern Recogn. **47**(9), 3158–3167 (2014)
74. Sharma, S., Somayaji, A., Japkowicz, N.: Learning over subconcepts: strategies for 1-class classification. Comput. Intell. **34**(2), 440–467 (2018). https://doi.org/10.1111/coin.12128
75. Smith, M.R., Martinez, T.R., Giraud-Carrier, C.G.: An instance level analysis of data complexity. Mach. Learn. **95**(2), 225–256 (2014)
76. Sotiropoulos, D.N., Giannoulis, C., Tsihrintzis, G.A.: A comparative study of one-class classifiers in machine learning problems with extreme class imbalance. In: 5th International Conference on Information, Intelligence, Systems and Applications, IISA 2014, Chania, 7–9 July 2014, pp. 362–364 (2014)
77. Stefanowski, J.: Dealing with data difficulty factors while learning from imbalanced data. In: Matwin, S., Mielniczuk, J. (eds.) Challenges in Computational Statistics and Data Mining, pp. 333–363. Springer, Cham (2016)
78. Sun, T., Jiao, L., Feng, J., Liu, F., Zhang, X.: Imbalanced hyperspectral image classification based on maximum margin. IEEE Geosci. Remote Sens. Lett. **12**(3), 522–526 (2015)
79. Sun, F., Xu, Y., Zhou, J.: Active learning SVM with regularization path for image classification. Multimed. Tools Appl. **75**(3), 1427–1442 (2016)
80. Tang, B., He, H., Baggenstoss, P.M., Kay, S.: A Bayesian classification approach using class-specific features for text categorization. IEEE Trans. Knowl. Data Eng. **28**(6), 1602–1606 (2016)
81. Tao, Q., Wang, J.: A new fuzzy support vector machine based on the weighted margin. Neural Process. Lett. **20**(3), 139–150 (2004)
82. Villar, P., Krawczyk, B., Sánchez, A.M., Montes, R., Herrera, F.: Designing a compact genetic fuzzy rule-based system for one-class classification. In: IEEE International Conference on Fuzzy Systems, FUZZ-IEEE 2014, Beijing, 6–11 July 2014, pp. 2163–2170 (2014)
83. Vluymans, S., Triguero, I., Cornelis, C., Saeys, Y.: EPRENNID: an evolutionary prototype reduction based ensemble for nearest neighbor classification of imbalanced data. Neurocomputing **216**, 596–610 (2016)
84. Wang, X., Liu, X., Matwin, S.: A distributed instance-weighted SVM algorithm on large-scale imbalanced datasets. In: 2014 IEEE International Conference on Big Data, Big Data 2014, Washington, DC, 27–30 Oct 2014, pp. 45–51 (2014)
85. Wang, X., Liu, X., Matwin, S., Japkowicz, N.: Applying instance-weighted support vector machines to class imbalanced datasets. In: 2014 IEEE International Conference on Big Data, Big Data 2014, Washington, DC, 27–30 Oct 2014, pp. 112–118 (2014)
86. Woźniak, M.: Hybrid Classifiers – Methods of Data, Knowledge, and Classifier Combination. Studies in Computational Intelligence, vol. 519. Springer, Berlin/Heidelberg (2014)
87. Wu, G., Chang, E.Y.: Aligning boundary in kernel space for learning imbalanced dataset. In: Proceedings of the 4th IEEE International Conference on Data Mining (ICDM 2004), 1–4 Nov 2004, Brighton, pp. 265–272 (2004)

88. Wu, G., Chang, E.Y.: KBA: kernel boundary alignment considering imbalanced data distribution. IEEE Trans. Know. Data Eng. **17**(6), 786–795 (2005)
89. Xu, Y.: Maximum margin of twin spheres support vector machine for imbalanced data classification. IEEE Trans. Cybern. **47**(6), 1540–1550 (2017)
90. Xu, Y., Yang, Z., Zhang, Y., Pan, X., Wang, L.: A maximum margin and minimum volume hyper-spheres machine with pinball loss for imbalanced data classification. Know. Based Syst. **95**, 75–85 (2016)
91. Yang, X., Song, Q., Wang, Y.: A weighted support vector machine for data classification. IJPRAI **21**(5), 961–976 (2007)
92. Yang, C., Yang, J., Wang, J.: Margin calibration in SVM class-imbalanced learning. Neurocomputing **73**(1–3), 397–411 (2009)
93. Yu, H., Mu, C., Sun, C., Yang, W., Yang, X., Zuo, X.: Support vector machine-based optimized decision threshold adjustment strategy for classifying imbalanced data. Know. Based Syst. **76**, 67–78 (2015)
94. Zhang, X., Li, Y.: A positive-biased nearest neighbour algorithm for imbalanced classification. In: 17th Pacific-Asia Conference on Advances in Knowledge Discovery and Data Mining, PAKDD 2013, Gold Coast, 14–17 Apr 2013, Proceedings, Part II, pp. 293–304 (2013)
95. Zhang, Y., Fu, P., Liu, W., Chen, G.: Imbalanced data classification based on scaling kernel-based support vector machine. Neural Comput. Appl. **25**(3–4), 927–935 (2014)
96. Zhang, Y., Fu, P., Liu, W., Zou, L.: SVM classification for imbalanced data using conformal kernel transformation. In: 2014 International Joint Conference on Neural Networks, IJCNN 2014, Beijing, 6–11 July 2014, pp. 2894–2900 (2014)
97. Zhang, J., Wu, X., Sheng, V.S.: Active learning with imbalanced multiple noisy labeling. IEEE Trans. Cybern. **45**(5), 1081–1093 (2015)
98. Zhong, S., Chen, D., Xu, Q., Chen, T.: Optimizing the gaussian kernel function with the formulated kernel target alignment criterion for two-class pattern classification. Pattern Recogn. **46**(7), 2045–2054 (2013)
99. Zhu, Y., Wang, Z., Gao, D.: Gravitational fixed radius nearest neighbor for imbalanced problem. Know. Based Syst. **90**, 224–238 (2015)
100. Zhu, F., Yang, J., Gao, J., Xu, C.: Extended nearest neighbor chain induced instance-weights for SVMs. Pattern Recogn. **60**, 863–874 (2016)
101. Zhuang, L., Dai, H.: Parameter estimation of one-class SVM on imbalance text classification. In: Advances in Artificial Intelligence, 19th Conference of the Canadian Society for Computational Studies of Intelligence, Canadian AI 2006, Québec City, 7–9 June 2006, Proceedings, pp. 538–549 (2006)
102. Zhuang, L., Dai, H.: Parameter optimization of kernel-based one-class classifier on imbalance text learning. In: PRICAI 2006: Trends in Artificial Intelligence, 9th Pacific Rim International Conference on Artificial Intelligence, Guilin, 7–11 Aug 2006, Proceedings, pp. 434–443 (2006)
103. Zieba, M., Tomczak, J.M.: Boosted SVM with active learning strategy for imbalanced data. Soft Comput. **19**(12), 3357–3368 (2015)
104. Zliobaite, I., Bifet, A., Pfahringer, B., Holmes, G.: Active learning with drifting streaming data. IEEE Trans. Neural Netw. Learn. Syst. **25**(1), 27–39 (2014)

Chapter 7
Ensemble Learning

Abstract In this chapter existing ensemble solutions for the class imbalance problems are reviewed. In Data Science, classifier ensembles, that is, the combination of several classifiers into a single one, are known to improve the accuracy in comparison with the usage of a single classifier. However, ensemble learning techniques by themselves are neither able to solve the class imbalance problem. To deal with the problem in question, ensemble learning algorithms need to be specifically adapted. This is usually done by combining an ensemble learning strategy with any of the methods presented in the previous chapters to deal with the class imbalance such as data-level preprocessing methods or cost-sensitive learning. Different solutions mainly differ on how this hybridization is done and which ones are the methods considered for the construction of the new model. In order to present these models, we first introduce the foundations of ensemble learning and the most commonly considered ensemble methods for imbalanced problems, that is, Bagging and Boosting (Sect. 7.2). Then, we review the existing ensemble techniques in the framework of imbalanced datasets, focusing on two-class problems. Each model is described and classified in a taxonomy depending on the inner ensemble methodology in which it is based (Sect. 7.3). In Sect. 7.4 we develop a brief experimental study aimed at showing the advantages of ensemble models and contrasting the behavior of several representative ensemble approach. Finally, Sect. 7.5 concludes this chapter.

7.1 Introduction

Traditionally, solutions for the class imbalance problem have been divided into three groups. Algorithm level (*internal*) approaches modify existing algorithms or create new ones to take consider class imbalance inside the learning algorithm itself [90, 122, 126]. Data level (*external*) techniques carry out a preprocessing step where the data distribution is balanced so as to decrease the influence of the skewed class distribution during the learning phase of the subsequent classifier [5, 19, 21]. Finally, cost-sensitive methods are a combination of both algorithm and data level approaches, which incorporate different misclassification costs for each class in the

© Springer Nature Switzerland AG 2018
A. Fernández et al., *Learning from Imbalanced Data Sets*,
https://doi.org/10.1007/978-3-319-98074-4_7

learning phase [22, 31]. Any of these approaches to deal with class imbalance can be integrated into an ensemble of classifiers to improve the final performance. This type of approaches are known as ensemble-based solutions for the class imbalance problem and has been widely applied with success [35, 78]

Ensembles [67, 121] are designed to improve the performance of a single classifier by training several different classifiers and combining their outputs to make the final decision. Ensemble methods are well-known in data mining and machine learning for their excellent performance in a wide variety of applications and the class imbalance problem is not an exception (see Chap. 2).

However, ensembles learning algorithms are usually designed to optimize accuracy. Hence, applying them directly to imbalanced datasets do not solve the underlying problem in the classifiers themselves with skewed class distributions. For this reason, they need to be combined with other techniques to tackle class imbalance problem. The resulting ensemble solutions are in some sense algorithm level methods (since the ensemble learning algorithm is slightly modified), but there is no change in the underlying base classifier (used to learn each component classifier of the ensemble), which is one of their advantages. The most common approach for modifying ensemble learning algorithms to deal with class imbalance consists in including a data level approach to preprocess the data before learning each classifier [9, 20, 77, 99]. Another type of hybridization introduces the usage of costs in the ensemble learning process [30, 104, 108]. All the possibilities for using ensembles to deal with imbalanced datasets are described in the rest of this chapter.

7.2   Foundations on Ensemble Learning

In this section we give a brief introduction to the foundations on ensemble learning and also present several classical learning algorithms for constructing sets of classifiers, whose classifiers are complementary.

The main objective of ensemble learning is to improve the performance of single classifiers by constructing several classifiers whose combination, which can be seen as a new classifier, is able to outperform every one of its counterparts. Hence, the basic idea consists of constructing several classifiers from the original data and then combining or aggregating their predictions when classifying new previously unknown examples. That is, in order to classify a new example, it is submitted to all the ensemble members (classifiers); then, the predictions of all the classifiers are considered in the combination phase, which also known as classifier fusion or aggregation [121]. Both the way in which the classifiers are constructed and how they are combined are key factors in ensembles. We should notice that the classifiers of an ensemble are usually referred to as *base classifiers*.

In the literature, the term "ensemble methods" usually refers to those collection of classifiers that are minor variants of the same classifier, whereas "multiple classifier systems" is a broader category that also includes those combinations considering the hybridization of different models [51, 52]. In this chapter, we only cover ensemble methods since all the reviewed approaches for the class imbalance problem are based on classifier ensembles.

This idea of ensembles follows the human natural behavior before making any important decision. It is not uncommon when one has to decide among several alternatives to seek for several experts opinions and to consider all of them in order to take the most suitable alternative. The main motivation for combining classifiers in redundant ensembles is to improve their generalization ability: each classifier is known to make errors, and if we are able to generate classifiers making different errors (e.g., by training them on different datasets or by making them work on different parts of the input space), misclassified examples will not be necessarily the same [59]. Therefore, one can take advantage of this idea and make use of them to complement each other.

This fact directly leads us to one of the key issues when forming an ensemble, the way the base classifiers are constructed. If we are combining several decision trees built with the same learner (e.g., C4.5 or CART) and using the same data, it is clear that all the trees will be equal and hence, their combination will not lead to an improvement of the results, but to the same results as using a single decision tree. This is why creating diverse classifiers (but maintaining their consistency with the training set) is a very important issue to obtain accurate models. This is the only way to create classifiers that can be complementary. *Diversity* is the term used to refer to ensembles where the outputs of their base classifiers differ. However, one should take into account that greater diversity does not always mean greater accuracy.

In the literature, the need of diverse classifiers to compose an ensemble is studied in terms of the statistical concepts of *bias-variance* decomposition [43, 109] and the related ambiguity [65] decomposition. The bias can be characterized as a measure of the ability of the classifier to correctly generalize to a test set; otherwise, the variance can be characterized as a measure of how sensitive are the classifier's prediction to the data on which it was trained. Hence, variance is related to overfitting, whereas bias is related to underfitting. Generally, the performance improvement in ensembles comes from a reduction of variance, because the usual effect of ensemble averaging is to reduce the variance of a set of classifiers. Anyway, there are also some ensemble learning algorithms that are capable of reducing bias, for instance, Boosting [34], which is presented in Sect. 7.2.2. On the other hand, ambiguity decomposition shows that, taking the combination of several predictors is better on average, over several patterns, than a method selecting one of the predictors at random. In any case, these concepts are clearly defined in regression problems where the output is real-valued and the mean squared error is used as loss function. However, in the classification context, those terms are still ill-defined [15, 68], since different authors provide different assumptions [11, 33, 61, 62, 107] and there is no agreement on their definition for generalized loss functions [57].

In addition, there have been several recent advances on the effect of diversity in the ensemble for single class performance measures in the imbalance framework [115]. Wang and Yao extended the work of Kuncheva et al. [70] were the *pattern of success* and the *pattern of failure* were studied, also known as the good and the bad pattern, respectively. These patterns were defined in a majority voting scenario. The former one refers to cases were no votes are wasted in the ensemble, the perfect case where all the correctly classified examples are correctly classified by exactly half of the classifiers plus one, and incorrectly classified examples are incorrectly classified by every ensemble member. The latter case is the other extreme case, were all correctly classified examples are correctly classified by all the classifiers and incorrectly classified ones are correctly classified by half of the classifiers. These patterns were related to Q-statistic diversity measure [125] (the greater the value of Q, the lower the diversity is) and showed that diversity is not always beneficial . In the pattern of success, the overall accuracy is a decreasing function of Q, meaning that diversity is beneficial. Otherwise, in the pattern of failure, the overall accuracy is an increasing function of Q and hence, in this case negatively related classifiers are not beneficial.

In the imbalance scenario, Wang and Yao [115] developed a thorough theoretical study on the effect of Q on single class performance measures such as Recall, Precision and F-measure, which was complemented with an empirical study where the effect of diversity on the GM and the AUC_{ROC} was also considered. In the study, the two original cases from Kuncheva were further divided into three difference scenarios leading to a total of six different patterns were the effect of Q on the three mentioned measures was studied. Mainly, the best and the worst cases remain the same, showing that greater diversity is beneficial in the best case of the good pattern and not beneficial in the worst case of the bad pattern, but intermediate cases were also considered. Anyway, the experimental analysis showed that diversity has a positive effect in classifying imbalanced datasets in general; the performance of both classes is better balanced between recall and precision, identifying more minority class examples. Besides, diversity was shown to be beneficial to the accuracy of the minority class, but harmful to that of the majority class. Interestingly, the last part of the study showed that there was a strong negative correlation between Q and GM and AUC_{ROC} performance measures. Hence, in this imbalanced framework, classifier ensembles with greater diversity should be preferred as they should provide better performance.

Once we have stated the importance of diversity in classifier ensembles, and more specifically in the imbalanced scenario, the different ways to reach the required diversity can be presented. Different ensemble learning mechanisms are simply different ways of generating diverse classifiers. An important point when aiming at constructing a diverse ensemble is that the base classifiers should be *weak learners*; a classifier learning algorithm is said to be weak when low changes in data produce big changes in the model obtained. This is why the most commonly used base classifiers are tree induction algorithms.

Considering a weak learning algorithm, different techniques can be used to construct an ensemble. The most widely used ensemble learning algorithms are AdaBoost [32] and Bagging [10], whose applications in several classification problems have led to significant improvements [87]. These methods provide a way in which the classifiers are strategically generated to reach the diversity needed, by manipulating the training set before learning each classifier. For this reason, they are also known as data variation-based ensembles.

In the next sections, we describe the most well-known ensemble techniques, that is, Bagging (including the modification called pasting small votes with importance sampling) and Boosting (AdaBoost and its variants AdaBoost.M1 and AdaBoost.M2) ensemble learning algorithms. We put our focus on this alternatives because they have been the most used ones to deal with imbalanced datasets. Moreover, we also introduce other techniques to increase diversity in classifier ensembles as they will be considered later in this chapter.

Before introducing the ensemble learning techniques, we should mention the other key point in classifier ensembles, that is, classifier combination or classifier fusion [121]. How to combine the classifiers in an ensemble can greatly modify its output. However, few algorithms in our framework have considered the modification of this component. Hence, we refer the reader to [67] for a deeper discussion on the topic. Briefly, in classifier combination techniques can be divided into two groups:

- *Classifier fusion*: In this case, all the classifiers of the ensemble are aggregated to obtain the final decision. All classifiers are supposed to be competent in the whole feature space and expected to misclassify different examples. Two different types of classifier fusion can be considered.

  1. Non-trainable combiners, where the way to combine the classifiers is prefixed, for example, the majority or weighted majority voting. In this cases, each classifier gives a vote (or a weighted vote) for the predicted class, all the votes are summed up and the class achieving the largest number of votes is predicted.
  2. Trainable combiners, where the combiner itself is trained aiming at improving accuracy, for instance, Decision Templates [69] or Stacking [119].

- *Classifier/ensemble selection*: These methods [46] perform the combination in a different way. Instead of combining all the classifiers of the ensemble, classifier selection tries to select only those (or that) leading to the best classification performance. Hence, classifier selection assumes that the classifiers are complementary, being experts on classifying the instances from a part of the input space; therefore, when a new instance is submitted, the most competent classifiers (one or more) are selected, which are the ones used to perform the classification. Also in this case two types of selections are commonly distinguished [66].

  1. *Static*: A region of competence is defined in training time for each classifier. Then, before classifying a new example, its region is found and the corresponding classifier is used to decide its class [3, 76, 110].
  2. *Dynamic*: In this case, the classifier that classify the new instance is decided during the classification [14]. First, the competence (accuracy) of each classifier for classifying the instance is estimated, and only the winner's output will be used to label the instance [6, 28, 60, 118, 120].

Anyway, both types can be seen as a unique classifier selection paradigm where, in the first case, the classification phase is accelerated by pre-computing the competence of the classifiers. These selection procedures mainly focus on defining the competence of the classifiers by its accuracy [100, 120] or by the region of the input space in which they are the experts [3, 66].

In any case, it should be mentioned that data variation-based ensembles are more commonly used in conjunction with classifier fusion strategies, whereas classifier/ensemble selection strategies are usually designed in conjunction with the ensemble creation model.

Additionally ensemble pruning [80] is another topic very related to classifier combination. Classifier pruning can be considered as a classifier selection technique, which is done prior to be used for testing. In this case, unnecessary, redundant or inaccurate classifiers are removed from the ensemble aiming at improving the generalization performance, reducing the storage necessity and the testing times. As we explain in Sect. 7.3 (Other family), pruning techniques have already been successfully applied to ensembles for the class imbalance problem [37, 63].

7.2.1 Bagging

Breiman [10] introduced the concept of *bootstrap aggregating* to construct ensembles. These ensemble learning model consists of training several classifiers with different bootstrapped replicas of the original training dataset. That is, to train each classifier a new dataset is formed by randomly drawing (with replacement) instances from the original dataset. The most usual practice is to maintain the original dataset size, which means that approximately 63.2% of the instances will be present in each bag (with some of them appearing more than once)

Hence, in Bagging diversity is obtained through the resampling procedure by training each classifier with a different data subset. Assuming that the corresponding classifier is weak, the resulting models should differ due to the changes in the data.

Finally, when an unknown instance is going to be classified, a majority or weighted vote is used to obtain the class. Weighted majority voting is usually performed by using the confidence given by each classifier in the prediction. One of the advantages of Bagging is its simplicity. Moreover, Bagging reduces variance, since the effect of voting is similar to that of averaging in regression where the reduction of overfitting becomes easier to be observed.

The complete pseudo-code of Bagging is shown in Algorithm 1.

Algorithm 1 Bagging

Input: S: Training set; T: Number of iterations; n: Bootstrap size; I: Weak learner

Output: Bagged classifier: $H(x) = sign \left(\sum_{t=1}^{T} h_t(x) \right)$ where $h_t \in [-1, 1]$ are the induced

   classifiers
1: **for** $t = 1$ to T **do**
2:     $S_t \leftarrow \text{RandomSampleReplacement}(n, S)$
3:     $h_t \leftarrow \text{I}(S_t)$
4: **end for**

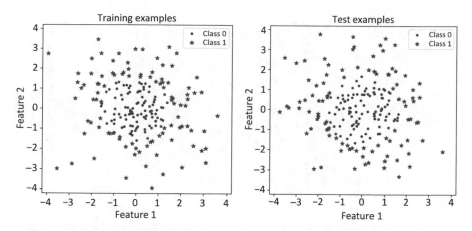

Fig. 7.1 Traning (*left*) and testing (*right*) sets for the illustrative examples on Bagging and Boosting. Both sets have been generated from the same distribution

For the sake of understanding of the two principal ensemble learning methods that are considered in this chapter, we consider an illustrative example for each one considering the same bi-dimensional two-class problem. We have generated two different datasets of 200 examples coming from the same distribution so as to be used as training and testing sets for our toy example. Both datasets are shown in Fig. 7.1.

Since the effect of Bagging is to reduce variance, the base classifiers considered are expected to overfit the training data (different from AdaBoost, Bagging does not tend to work well with high bias classifiers). For this reason, we have considered a Decision Tree without pruning to show its behavior. Figure 7.2 presents the five base classifiers trained using Bagging technique (i.e., each classifier has been trained using a different boostrap replica of the original dataset) and also the final result of the ensemble. This last result is computed using the weighted majority voting where the weights are based on the proportion of instances falling in the leave that made the prediction. Notice that the data presented in the figures corresponds to the training data, but we have computed both the accuracy for the training and testing data.

Figure 7.2 illustrates how Bagging works. It can be observed that most of the base classifier has overtrained a part of the data, whereas Bagging has produced a less overfitted result, achieving the best accuracy both in training and testing (which need not occur in all cases). Notice also that even if the decision trees are overtraining the data, their training accuracy is not as high as that of Bagging because they have not used all the data to be trained, but a boostrap replica with approximately 63.2% of the examples (some of them being repeated).

Pasting Small Votes is a variation of Bagging originally designed for large datasets [12] that has also been applied in the imbalance framework. Large datasets are split into smaller subsets that are used to train different classifiers. There are two variants: (1) *Rvotes* that creates the data subsets at random; (2) *Ivotes* that creates

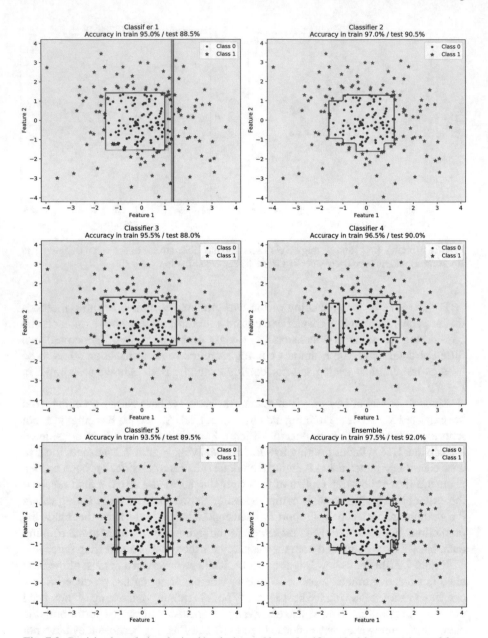

Fig. 7.2 Decision boundaries obtained by the bagged base classifiers (decision trees) learned from the training data (depicted). The last (bottom right) figure corresponds to the ensemble model. For each model, the accuracy in training and testing are presented

consecutive datasets based on the importance of the instances; important instances are those that increase diversity. The way used to create the datasets consists of using a balanced distribution of easy and difficult instances. In order to detect difficult instances *out-of-bag* classifiers [10] are considered. An instance is considered to be difficult when it is misclassified by the ensemble classifier formed of those classifiers which did not use the instance for training. These difficult instances are always added to the next data subset, whereas easy instances have a low chance to be included. The pseudo-code for Ivotes is shown in Algorithm 2.

Algorithm 2 Ivotes

Input: S: Training set; T: Number of iterations; n: Bootstrap size; I: Weak learner

Output: Bagged classifier: $H(x) = sign\left(\sum_{t=1}^{T} h_t(x)\right)$ where $h_t \in [-1, 1]$ are the induced classifiers

1: $e_{new} \leftarrow 0.5$
2: **repeat**
3:      $e_{old} \leftarrow e_{new}$
4:      $S_t \leftarrow \emptyset$
5:      **while** $size(S_t) < n$ **do**   ▷ Importance sampling
6:          $x \leftarrow$ RandomInstance(S)
7:          **if** x misclassified by out-of-bag classifier **then**
8:              $S_t \leftarrow S_t \cup \{x\}$
9:          **else**
10:             $S_t \leftarrow S_t \cup \{x\}$ with probability $\frac{e_{old}}{1-e_{old}}$
11:          **end if**
12:      **end while**
13:      $h_t \leftarrow I(S_t)$
14:      $e_{new} \leftarrow$ error of out-of-bag classifier
15: **until** $e_{new} > e_{old}$

7.2.2 Boosting

Boosting (also known as ARCing, Adaptive Resampling and Combining) was introduced by Schapire in 1990 [96]. Schapire proved that a weak learner (which is slightly better than random guessing) can be turned into a strong learner in the sense of *probably approximately correct* (PAC) learning framework. AdaBoost [32] is the most representative algorithm in this family. It was the first applicable approach of Boosting, and it has been appointed as one of the top ten DM algorithms [123].

In contrast to Bagging, which is only capable of reducing variance, AdaBoost is also known to reduce bias (besides from variance) [34], and similarly to SVMs boosts the margins [95]. Therefore, AdaBoost can allow low bias classifiers to be boosted, highly increasing their performance. The only condition AdaBoost requires to the classifier is that it must be slightly better than a random classifier. In order to understand the power behind AdaBoost, in Fig. 7.3 we have replicated the same experiment as we have done with Bagging in Fig. 7.2. In this case, we

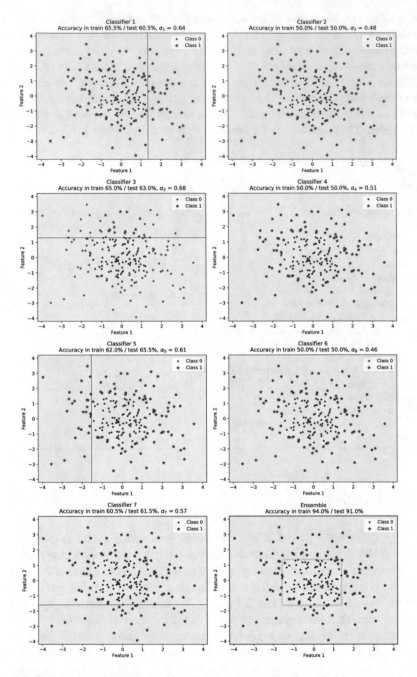

Fig. 7.3 Decision boundaries obtained by the boosted base classifiers (decision stumps) learned from the training data (depicted). The last (bottom right) figure corresponds to the ensemble model. For each model, the accuracy in training and testing and its weight in the final ensemble are presented

have considered decision stumps [56] as base classifiers, that is, decision trees with a single internal node (the root node). Hence, their prediction is based on the value of a single feature. As a result, their bias is high since they lack of flexibility so as to get adapted to the whole training data.

Looking at the different figures one can observe that the decision stumps were far from being accurate classifiers. In fact, their accuracy is a only a bit more than 60%, i.e., they are slightly better than a random classifier (whose accuracy would be 50% as we have a balanced dataset). However, even with these poor base classifiers, AdaBoost has been able to boost their performance achieving an accuracy of 95% in training and 90% in test when all the classifiers are combined in the ensemble. Hence, it has clearly improved the high bias of the base algorithm. Next, we explain how this effect is achieved, because in this case, different from Bagging, classifiers are learned sequentially depending on how well the previous ones has performed in classifying each example. Besides, not all the classifiers vote with the same weight and therefore, in Fig. 7.3, we should not assume that all the classifiers are equally weighted in the final ensemble. In fact, the term α_t (where t is the classifier number) that appears together with the accuracy in training and testing of each classifier is the weight assigned to each base classifier by AdaBoost. Moreover, notice that classifiers 2, 4 and 6 are apparently totally trivial classifiers, classifying everything as class 1. Even with that behavior, the final ensemble is able to achieve a result almost as accurate as Bagging in this dataset. We will explain the reason why these classifiers are learned this way after introducing the complete algorithm.

Unlike Bagging, AdaBoost does not introduce diversity by resampling. It works with weighted examples, where each example is assigned a weight that measures its importance or difficulty in being learned. Initially, all examples are given the same weight. AdaBoost then uses the whole dataset to train each classifier iteratively, but after each iteration, the weights given to each example are modified. More focus is given to difficult instances, with the goal of correctly classifying examples in the next iteration which were incorrectly classified during the current iteration. Hence, the main objective of the next classifier is to better learn the examples that were harder to classify in previous iterations. In order to give more focus to these instances, after each iteration, the weights of misclassified instances are increased; on the contrary, the weights of correctly classified instances are decreased. Furthermore, another weight is assigned to each individual classifier depending on its overall accuracy (α_t) which is then used in test phase to perform a weighted voting; more confidence is given to more accurate classifiers. It is interesting to note that the classifier confidence is estimated with the weights of the instances in the current iteration and hence, it need not reflect the accuracy over the global training set. Finally, when a new instance is submitted, each classifier gives a weighted vote, and the class label is selected by majority.

In this chapter, we will use the original two-class AdaBoost (show in Algorithm 3) and two of its very-well known modifications [32, 97] that have been employed in imbalanced domains: AdaBoost.M1 and AdaBoost.M2.

We first focus on AdaBoost algorithm in Algorithm 3. The first step corresponds to the initialization of the weight distribution (D_t, where t is the current iteration

---

Algorithm 3 AdaBoost

Input: Training set $S = \{x_i, y_i\}, i = 1, \ldots, N$; and $y_i \in \{-1, +1\}$; T: Number of iterations; I: Weak learner

Output: Boosted classifier: $H(x) = sign\left(\sum_{t=1}^{T} \alpha_t h_t(x)\right)$ where h_t, α_t are the induced classifiers

  (with $h_t(x) \in \{-1, 1\}$) and their assigned weights, respectively
  1: $D_1(i) \leftarrow 1/N$ for $i = 1, \ldots, N$
  2: **for** $t = 1$ to T **do**
  3:     $h_t \leftarrow I(S, D_t)$
  4:     $\varepsilon_t \leftarrow \sum\limits_{i, y_i \neq h_t(x_i)} D_t(i)$
  5:     **if** $\varepsilon_t > 0.5$ **then**
  6:         $T \leftarrow t - 1$
  7:         **return**
  8:     **end if**
  9:     $\alpha_t = \frac{1}{2} \ln\left(\frac{1-\varepsilon_t}{\varepsilon_t}\right)$
  10:     $D_{t+1}(i) = D_t(i) \cdot e^{(-\alpha_t h_t(x_i) y_i)}$ for $i = 1, \ldots, N$
  11:     Normalize D_{t+1} to be a proper distribution
  12: **end for**

---

or classifier number). Afterwards, a weak learner is used to obtain a classifier using D_t. The error is computed as the weighted sum of misclassified instances and the condition in line 5 refers to the fact that AdaBoost requires that the base classifiers should be slightly better than random ones. Finally, the weight for each classifier is computed depending on the error committed in the weighted training set and the new distribution of weights is assigned. With this algorithm in mind, we can analyze the behavior of AdaBoost in Fig. 7.3. One can better understand why classifiers 2, 4 and 6 are trivial classifiers. The first classifier has correctly classified almost all examples from class 0, whereas many examples from class 1 are misclassified. As a consequence, these examples will get their weights increased, whereas those of class 0 and the ones from class 1 correctly classified will get their weights decreased. Hence, classifier 2 needs to focus on correctly classifying the Class 1 examples misclassified in the first iteration; due to the spherical shape of the classes and the high bias of decision stumps, the way to minimize the weighted error is to classify every example as from Class 1. Notice that even if the accuracy in training is 50%, the weighted error leading to a classifier weight (α_2) of 0.48 is 0.3817, which is better than a random classifier. Hence, AdaBoost can continue working on the problem. The case with classifiers 4 and 6 is similar to the one explained. In fact, in this example, AdaBoost is focused on learning the examples from Class 0 in the odd classifiers, whereas the focus changes to Class 1 in the even classifiers.

Regarding AdaBoost.M1 and AdaBoost.M2, the former is the first extension to multi-class classification where a different weight changing mechanism is applied. The pseudo-code of AdaBoost.M1 is presented in Algorithm 4.

The latter is the second extension to multi-class, which is reduced to AdaBoost.M1 when two classes are considered except for one interesting characteristic. In this case, AdaBoost makes use of base classifiers' confidence rates. The pseudo-code of this method is shown in Algorithm 5.

Algorithm 4 AdaBoost.M1

Input: Training set $S = \{\mathbf{x}_i, y_i\}$, $i = 1, \ldots, N$; and $y_i \in \mathbb{C}, \mathbb{C} = \{c_1, \ldots, c_m\}$; T: Number of iterations; I: Weak learner

Output: Boosted classifier: $H(x) = \arg\max_{y \in \mathbb{C}} \sum_{t=1}^{T} \ln\left(\frac{1}{\beta_t}\right) [h_t(x) = y]$ where h_t, β_t are the induced classifiers (with $h_t(x) \in \mathbb{C}$) and their assigned weights, respectively

1: $D_1(i) \leftarrow 1/N$ for $i = 1, \ldots, N$
2: **for** $t = 1$ to T **do**
3:     $h_t \leftarrow I(S, D_t)$
4:     $\varepsilon_t \leftarrow \sum_{i=1}^{N} D_t(i)[h_t(\mathbf{x}_i) \neq y_i]$
5:     **if** $\varepsilon_t > 0.5$ **then**
6:        $T \leftarrow t - 1$
7:        **return**
8:     **end if**
9:     $\beta_t = \frac{\varepsilon_t}{1-\varepsilon_t}$
10:    $D_{t+1}(i) = D_t(i) \cdot \beta_t^{1-[h_t(\mathbf{x}_i) \neq y_i]}$ for $i = 1, \ldots, N$
11:    Normalize D_{t+1} to be a proper distribution
12: **end for**

Algorithm 5 AdaBoost.M2

Input: Training set $S = \{\mathbf{x}_i, y_i\}$, $i = 1, \ldots, N$; and $y_i \in \mathbb{C}, \mathbb{C} = \{c_1, \ldots, c_m\}$; T: Number of iterations; I: Weak learner

Output: Boosted classifier: $H(x) = \arg\max_{y \in \mathbb{C}} \sum_{t=1}^{T} \ln\left(\frac{1}{\beta_t}\right) h_t(x, y)$ where h_t, β_t (with $h_t(x, y) \in$ [0, 1]) are the classifiers and their assigned weights, respectively

1: $D_1(i) \leftarrow 1/N$ for $i = 1, \ldots, N$
2: $w_{i,y}^1 \leftarrow D(i)/(m - 1)$ for $i = 1, \ldots, N$, $y \in \mathbb{C} - \{y_i\}$
3: **for** $t = 1$ to T **do**
4:     $W_i^t \leftarrow \sum_{y \neq y_i} w_{i,y}^t$
5:     $q_t(i, y) \leftarrow \frac{w_{i,y}^t}{W_i^t}$ for $y \neq y_i$
6:     $D_t(i) \leftarrow \frac{W_i^t}{\sum_{i=i}^{N} W_i^t}$
7:     $h_t \leftarrow I(S, D_t)$
8:     $\epsilon_t \leftarrow \frac{1}{2} \sum_{i=1}^{N} D_t(i) \left(1 - h_t(\mathbf{x}_i, y_i) + \sum_{i, y \neq y_i} q_t(i, y) h_t(\mathbf{x}_i, y)\right)$
9:     $\beta_t = \frac{\epsilon_t}{1 - \epsilon_t}$
10:    $w_{i,y}^{t+1} = w_{i,y}^t \cdot \beta_t^{\frac{1}{2}(1 + h_t(\mathbf{x}_i, y_i) - h_t(\mathbf{x}_i, y))}$ for $i = 1, \ldots, N$, $y \in \mathbb{C} - \{y_i\}$
11: **end for**

Notice that neither of these algorithms by itself deals with the imbalance problem directly; all of them have to be changed or combined with another technique, since they focus their attention on difficult examples without differentiating the class they belong to. In an imbalanced dataset, majority class examples contribute more to the accuracy measure, so the likelihood of being considered as difficult examples is greater than that of minority class instances. Hence, rather than trying to improve the True Positives, it is easier to improve the True Negatives that also leads to increasing the False Negatives, which is not a desired characteristic in the class imbalance framework. Therefore, in the Sect. 7.2.2 the different work that have tackled this aspect to deal with class imbalance using classifier ensembles are reviewed.

7.2.3   Techniques to Increase Diversity in Classifier Ensembles

Bagging and Boosting are the most commonly used techniques in the imbalance framework for constructing ensembles. However, there are many other ways of achieving the required diversity. In fact, many of those techniques can be considered together with the mentioned methods. Even thought these diversity enhancing techniques has not been widely applied in the imbalance framework, a recent work [27] showed that their usage in existing ensemble models can lead to more accurate models. Hence, hereafter we briefly review these kind of techniques, which can be divided into four main groups depending on how they try to add diversity to the ensemble [27]:

- *Guided random sampling* – In the Random Oracle ensemble [71] diversity is added by dividing the instances into two groups using a random hyperplane. This way, in each iteration, instead of learning a single classifier, two classifiers are learned, one for each group of instances. The hyperplanes considered can be either linear or spherical.
- *New attributes* – In this type of methods, the feature space is expanded by adding new attributes to the dataset that were not originally present. For example, in the Disturbing Neighbors (DNs) method [81] before learning each base classifier N randomly instances are selected, which are named as DNs. Then these instances are used together with a 1-NN classifier to create $N + 1$ new binary attributes. The first N attributes codifies whether the corresponding DN is the NN to the corresponding instance (1) or not (0). Otherwise, the last attribute is a nominal attribute with the predicted class for the instance by the 1-NN classifier only using the DNs.
- *Random weights* – Another way of introducing diversity is by modifying the importance/weight of each attribute before learning each classifier in the ensemble. The well-known Random Subspace Method (RSM) [50] can be considered in this category. In the RSM, each classifier is learned using a random set of attributes; that is, random binary weights are considered for each base classifier. Notice that RSM is usually combined with bagging. Another popular ensemble method in this category is Random Forest (RF) [13], which also considers bagging but combined with random trees. RF is similar to RSM but instead of randomly selecting attributes for each base classifier, the attributes are randomly selected in each node when constructing the decision tree. That is, a random tree

is a standard decision tree where a random subset of attributes is considered for splitting in each node. Random Feature Weights (RFWs) ensemble [82] considers real-valued weights instead of binary ones to randomly vary the importance of the attributes for learning each base decision tree. The dataset is not directly modified, but the weights are used when the merit function of the attributes is computed by weighting the merit of each attribute by the corresponding weight. As a result, a bias is introduced in favor of attributes with higher weights, which combined with the usage of different weights for each classifier produces the expected diversity. The weights are randomly drawn for each base classifier.

- *Projections* – These methods are based on modifying the dataset by creating a dataset composed of a new set of features obtained as a transformation of the original ones. Therefore, projections can be used as a source of diversity if different projections of the data are considered for each base classifier. Rotation Forest [92] is an ensemble models making use of Principal Component Analysis (PCA) to project different groups of attributes for each base classifier. Differently, supervised projections combined with boosting has also been proposed [41]. Finally, random projections have also demonstrated their ability to boost diversity [98]. Notice that the RSM could also be considered in this category.

7.3 Ensemble Learning for Addressing the Class Imbalance Problem

Proposals to deal with imbalanced classes have been traditionally classified into three categories, depending on how they deal with the skewed class distribution. As stated in Chap. 2, Algorithm level (*internal*) approaches create or modify existing algorithms to take into account the significance of positive examples [90, 122, 126]. Data level (*external*) techniques add a preprocessing step where the data distribution is rebalanced in order to decrease the effect of the skewed class distribution in the learning process [5, 19, 21]. Finally, cost-sensitive methods combine both algorithm and data level approaches to incorporate different misclassification costs for each class in the learning phase [22, 31].

Ensemble-based methods techniques dealing with imbalanced classes usually consist in a combination between an ensemble learning algorithm and one of the techniques above, specifically, data level and cost-sensitive ones. Adding a data level approach to the ensemble learning algorithm, the new hybrid method usually preprocesses the data before training each classifier. On the other hand, cost-sensitive ensembles instead of modifying the base classifier in order to accept costs in the learning process, guide the cost minimization via the ensemble learning algorithm. This way, the modification of the base learner is avoided, but the major drawback (i.e., costs definition) is still present.

For the sake of completeness of this chapter, since many of the ensemble methods are based on combining a data preprocessing method with an ensemble learning model, we briefly recall most of the preprocessing methods used in conjunction with ensemble models. For more details we refer the reader to Chap. 5.

- *Random Undersampling (RUS)*: It aims at balancing class distribution through the random elimination of majority class examples. Its major drawback is that it can discard potentially useful data, which could be important for the induction process.
- *Random Oversampling (ROS)*: In the same way as random undersampling, it tries to balance class distribution, but in this case, randomly replicating minority class instances.
- *Synthetic Minority Oversampling Technique* (SMOTE) [19]: It is an oversampling method, which main idea is to create new minority class examples by interpolating several minority class instances that lie together. SMOTE creates instances by randomly selecting one (or more depending on the oversampling ratio) of the KNN of a minority class instance and generating the new instance values from a random interpolation of both instances.
- *Modified Synthetic Minority Oversampling Technique* (MSMOTE) [55]: It is a modified version of SMOTE. This algorithm divides the instances of the minority class into three groups, *safe*, *border* and *latent noise* instances by calculating the distances among all examples. When MSMOTE generates new examples, the strategy to select the NNs is changed with respect to SMOTE depending on the group previously assigned to the instance. For safe instances, the algorithm randomly selects a data point from the kNN (same way as SMOTE); for border instances, it only selects the NN; finally, for latent noise instances, it does nothing.
- *Selective Pre-processing of Imbalanced Data* (SPIDER) [102]: It combines local oversampling of the minority class with filtering difficult examples from the majority class. It consists in two phases, identification and preprocessing. The first one identifies which instances are flagged as noisy (misclassified) by kNN. The second phase depends on the option established (*weak, relabel* or *strong*); when weak option is settled, it amplifies minority class instances; for relabel, it amplifies minority class examples and relabels majority class instances (i.e., changes class label); finally, using strong option, it strongly amplifies minority class instances. After carrying out these operations, the remaining noisy examples from the majority class are removed from the dataset.
- *Random Balance* (RB) [26]: It is a data level algorithm oriented to the construction of ensembles. The total number of instances of the sampled dataset is always the same as that of the original dataset. The number of examples that are going to be taken from the minority class is decided randomly and therefore, the remaining examples until reaching the number of the original dataset examples are obtained from the majority class. In order to carry out this sampling, the examples from the class from which more examples are needed to reach the specified number are created with SMOTE. In the case of the other class from which more examples than the required ones are available, RUS is applied. Notice that both cases may occur with both classes.

From this point, our aim is to review the different ensemble learning methods designed to deal with the class imbalance problem. In order to do so, we will complete the taxonomy presented in [35], where all these techniques were categorized and compared in a thorough experimental study.

To start with the description of the taxonomy, we show its categories and the methods in each category in Table 7.1. Next, these categories are described.

- *Cost-Sensitive Ensemble.* In this type of ensembles, combinations of classifiers learned with the usage of costs for each classes in the problem are considered. Two different ways to manage these costs have been considered in the literature.

  - *Cost-Sensitive Boosting:* These approaches are similar to cost-sensitive methods, but instead of introducing the management of the costs into the classifier learning algorithm the costs minimization is guided by the boosting algorithm.
  - *Ensembles with Cost-Sensitive Base Classifiers:* Different from cost-sensitive boosting approaches, these ensemble models make use of cost-sensitive classifiers in order to make the ensemble capable of dealing with imbalanced classes.

- *Data Preprocessing + Ensemble Learning.* Ensembles in this category share a common characteristic. All of them consist of embedding a data preprocessing technique in an ensemble learning algorithm. The main difference lies in the base ensemble learning algorithm considered and the preprocessing method selected.

  - *Boosting-based:* These methods use AdaBoost or any of its variants as ensemble method where a data level technique is introduced.
  - *Bagging-based:* In this case, Bagging is the ensemble method considered to be combined with a data level technique.
  - *Hybrid:* In hybrid approaches both Bagging and Boosting are considered together and in combination with preprocessing mechanisms.

- *Other.* This last category groups the proposals that do not fall in any of the previous groups. They are mainly ways of improving ensembles from the rest of the categories by adding some extra feature to their working procedure.

Next, we look over these families, reviewing the existing works.

7.3.1 Cost-Sensitive Boosting

As we have already explained, AdaBoost is an accuracy-oriented algorithm. Hence, when the class distribution is uneven, this strategy biases the learning (i.e., the weights) toward the majority class, since it contributes more to the overall accuracy. For this reason, there have been several proposals modifying the weight update of AdaBoost, which corresponds to line 10 in Algorithm 3 and, as a consequence, the

Table 7.1 Applications of ML and DM where the class imbalance problem is present

Ensembles to address class imbalance problem		
Main category	Subcategory	Method
Cost-sensitive	Cost-sensitive	AdaCost [30]
Ensembles	Boosting	CSB1, CSB2 [108]
		RareBoost [58]
		AdaC1 [104]
		AdaC2 [104]
		AdaC3 [104]
	Ensembles with	BoostedCS-SVM [112]
	Cost-sensitive	BoostedWeightedELM [75]
	Base classifiers	CS-DT-Ensemble [64]
		BayEnsBNN [72]
		AL-BoostedCS-SVM [127]
		IC-BoostedCS-SVM [73]
Data preprocessing +	Boosting-based	SMOTEBoost [20]
Ensemble learning		MSMOTEBoost [55]
		MSMOTEBoost [55]
		RUSBoost [99]
		DataBoost-IM [47]
		RAMOBoost [23]
		Adaboost.NC [114]
		EUSBoost [36]
		GESuperPBoost [42]
		BalancedBoost [116]
		RB-Boost [26]
		Balanced-St-GrBoost [8]
		RHBoost [44]
	Bagging-based	OverBagging [113]
		− SMOTEBagging [113]
		UnderBagging [4]
		− QuasiBagging [18]
		− Asymetric Bagging [106]
		− Roughly Balanced Bagging [49]
		− Partitioning [17, 124]
		− Bagging Ensemble Variation [74]
		− IRUS [105]
		− α-TreeEnsembles [88]
		− PUSB [63]
		UnderOverBagging [113]
		IIVotes [9]

(continued)

Table 7.1 (continued)

Ensembles to address class imbalance problem		
Main category	Subcategory	Method
		RB-Bagging [26]
		EPRENNID [111]
		USwitchingNED [45]
	Hybrid	EasyEnsemble [77]
		BalanceCascade [77]
		HardEnsemble [86]
		StochasticEnsemble [8]
Other		MOGP-GP [7]
		RandomOracles [93]
		Loss factors [101]
		GOBoost [79]
		OrderingBasedPruning [37]
		Diversity enhancing techniques for improving ensembles [27]
		PT-Bagging [24]
		IMCStacking [16]
		DynamicSelection [94]

modification of line 9 is also required. In such a way, the algorithm is modified so that examples from the different classes are unequally treated. To reach this unequal treatment, cost-sensitive boosting approaches keep the general learning framework of AdaBoost, but at the same time introduce cost items into the weight update formula. This way, they also avoid the modification of the weak learner. However, as in any other cost-sensitive approach, the main problem is that the costs that should be assigned to each class are not predefined, being a difficult choice in practical applications. The proposals in this category usually differ in the way that they modify the weight update rule. Among this family AdaCost [30], CSB1, CSB2 [108], RareBoost [58], AdaC1, AdaC2 and AdaC3 [104] are the most representative approaches that we describe hereafter.

7.3.1.1 AdaCost

In this algorithm [30], the weight update is modified by adding a *cost adjustment function* φ. This function, for an instance with a higher cost factor increases its weight "more" if the instance is misclassified, but decreases its weight "less" otherwise. Being C_i the cost of misclassifying the ith example, the authors provide their recommended function as: $\varphi_+ = -0.5C_i + 0.5$ and $\varphi_- = 0.5C_i + 0.5$. The weighting function and the computation of α_t are replaced by the following formulas:

$$D_{t+1}(i) = D_t(i) \cdot exp(-\alpha_t y_i h_t(\mathbf{x}_i)\varphi_{\text{sign}(h_t(\mathbf{x}_i),y_i)}) \tag{7.1}$$

$$\alpha_t = \frac{1}{2}\ln\frac{1 + \sum_i D_t(i) \cdot exp(-\alpha_t y_i h_t(\mathbf{x}_i)\varphi_{\text{sign}(h_t(\mathbf{x}_i),y_i)})}{1 - \sum_i D_t(i) \cdot exp(-\alpha_t y_i h_t(\mathbf{x}_i)\varphi_{\text{sign}(h_t(\mathbf{x}_i),y_i)})} \tag{7.2}$$

7.3.1.2   CSB

Two methods were proposed inside CSB family [108], but neither CSB1 nor CSB2 use an adjustment function as AdaCost does. Moreover, these approaches only consider the costs in the weight update formula, avoiding any changes in the computation of α_t. In the case of CSB1, because it does not use α_t anymore ($\alpha_t = 1$), whereas in CSB2, because it uses the same α_t computed by AdaBoost (this is the different between both methods). In these cases, the weight update is replaced by:

$$D_{t+1}(i) = D_t(i)C_{\text{sign}(h_t(\mathbf{x}_i),y_i)} \cdot exp(-\alpha_t y_i h_t(\mathbf{x}_i)) \tag{7.3}$$

where $C_+ = 1$ and $C_- = C_i \geq 1$ are the costs of misclassifying a positive and a negative example, respectively.

7.3.1.3   RareBoost

RareBoost [58] is a modification of AdaBoost that tries to tackle the class imbalance problem by simply changing the computation of α_t term (Algorithm 3, line 9). In order to do so, RareBoost make use of the confusion matrix in each iteration. Moreover, two different values of α_t are computed in each iteration. This way, False Positives (FP_t is the weights' sum of FP in the tth iteration) are scaled in proportion to how well they are distinguished from True Positives (TP_t), whereas False Negatives (FN_t) are scaled in proportion to how well they are distinguished from True Negatives (TN_t). On the one hand, $\alpha_t^p = TP_t/FP_t$ is computed for examples predicted as positives. On the other hand, $\alpha_t^n = TN_t/FN_t$ is computed for the ones predicted as negatives. Finally, the weight update is done separately using both factors depending on the predicted class of each instance. Therefore, even if the weight update formula is not changed, the resulting weights will be different since the α_t term is considered inside the formula. Notice that, despite we have include RareBoost in cost-sensitive boosting family, it does not directly make use of costs, which can be an advantage, but it modifies AdaBoost algorithm in a similar way to the rest of the approaches in this family. In any case, this algorithm has a handicap, TP_t and TN_t are reduced, and FP_t and FT_t are increased only if $TP_t > FP_t$ and $TN_t > FN_t$, that is equivalent to require an accuracy of the positive class greater than 50%:

$$TP_t/(TP_t + FP_t) > 0.5 \tag{7.4}$$

This constraint is not trivial when dealing with class imbalance problem; moreover, it is a strong condition. Without satisfying this condition, the algorithm will collapse.

7.3.1.4   AdaC1

This algorithm is one of the three modifications of AdaBoost that were proposed in [104]. The authors proposed different ways in which the costs could be embedded into the weight update formula (Algorithm 3, line 10). As a result, they derived different wasy of computing α_t depending on where they introduced the costs. In the case of AdaC1, the cost factors are introduced within the exponent part of the formula:

$$D_{t+1}(i) = D_t(i) \cdot exp(-\alpha_t C_i h_t(\mathbf{x}_i) y_i) \tag{7.5}$$

where $C_i \in [0, +\infty)$. Hence, the computation of the classifiers' weight is done as follows:

$$\alpha_t = \frac{1}{2} \ln \frac{1 + \sum\limits_{i, y_i = h_t(\mathbf{x}_i)} C_i D_t(i) - \sum\limits_{i, y_i \neq h_t(\mathbf{x}_i)} C_i D_t(i)}{1 + \sum\limits_{i, y_i = h_t(\mathbf{x}_i)} C_i D_t(i) + \sum\limits_{i, y_i \neq h_t(\mathbf{x}_i)} C_i D_t(l)} \tag{7.6}$$

Notice that AdaCost is a variation of AdaC1 where there is a cost adjustment function instead of a cost item inside the exponent. Though, in the case of AdaCost, it does not reduce to AdaBoost algorithm when both classes are equally weighted (contrary to AdaC1).

7.3.1.5   AdaC2

Similarly to AdaC1, AdaC2 [104] integrates the costs in the weight update formula. But the procedure is different; the costs are introduced outside the exponent part:

$$D_{t+1}(i) = C_i D_t(i) \cdot exp(-\alpha_t h_t(\mathbf{x}_i) y_i) \tag{7.7}$$

In consequence, α_t's computation is changed:

$$\alpha_t = \frac{1}{2} \ln \frac{\sum\limits_{i, y_i = h_t(\mathbf{x}_i)} C_i D_t(i)}{\sum\limits_{i, y_i \neq h_t(\mathbf{x}_i)} C_i D_t(i)} \tag{7.8}$$

7.3.1.6 AdaC3

This modification [104] considers the idea of AdaC1 and AdaC2 at the same time. The weight update formula is modified by introducing the costs both inside and outside the exponent part:

$$D_{t+1}(i) = C_i D_t(i) \cdot exp(-\alpha_t C_i h_t(\mathbf{x}_i) y_i) \tag{7.9}$$

In this manner, over again α_t changes:

$$\alpha_t = \frac{1}{2} \ln \frac{\sum\limits_{i} C_i D_t(i) + \sum\limits_{i, y_i = h_t(\mathbf{x}_i)} C_i^2 D_t(i) - \sum\limits_{i, y_i \neq h_t(\mathbf{x}_i)} C_i^2 D_t(i)}{\sum\limits_{i} C_i D_t(i) - \sum\limits_{i, y_i = h_t(\mathbf{x}_i)} C_i^2 D_t(i) + \sum\limits_{i, y_i \neq h_t(\mathbf{x}_i)} C_i^2 D_t(i)} \tag{7.10}$$

7.3.2 Ensembles with Cost-Sensitive Base Classifiers

This is a new category that was not considered in [35]. In fact, in this category ensembles are considered, but the ensembles are not really the ones adapted to the class imbalance scenario; the base classifiers used under Boosting framework are the ones managing the costs in this case. Hence, they consider the original structure of AdaBoost algorithm but uses cost-sensitive base classifiers that are not only capable of dealing with the weights of AdaBoost algorithm, but they can also make use of the costs assigned to each class. One of the disadvantages of the algorithms in this category is that they are less versatile than cost-sensitive Boosting approaches as they are oriented to the usage of a specific base classifier, whereas in the previous category the algorithms were developed independently of the base classifier considered. The main difference between these proposals lie in the cost-sensitive approach considered to be used inside Boosting. The most representative methods in this category are BoostedCS-SVM [112], BoostedWeightedELM [75], CS-DT-Ensemble [64], BayEnsBNN [72], AL-BoostedCS-SVM [127] and IC-BoostedCS-SVM [73], which are described next.

7.3.2.1 BoostedCS-SVM

In [112], the authors propose to introduce a cost-sensitive SVM into the Adaboost algorithm. This was aimed at reducing the overfitting found in previous cost-sensitive SVM models. Moreover, the new algorithm modifies Adaboost algorithm by considering a specific empirical parameter λ used to tune the magnitude of the penalty for each iteration. In this way, the new computation of $alpha_t$ considering the new term is as follows.

$$\alpha_t = \lambda \ln \frac{1 - \varepsilon_t}{\varepsilon_t} \text{ with } \lambda \in (0, 1]. \tag{7.11}$$

Moreover, the original stopping criterion of AdaBoost is also modified. In this method, the g-mean is considered to stop the algorithm. The new criterion considers the g-mean performance on a validation set, and the algorithm is stopped when the g-mean on this set was no longer improved. Furthermore, the weights of correctly classified examples is never explicitly decreased.

7.3.2.2 BoostedWeightedELM

An extension of the weighted Extreme Learning Machine (ELM) is proposed and named as BoostedWeightedELM in [75]. In this method, the weighted ELM classifier is used inside the Adaboost.M1 algorithm to overcome the class imbalance problem. This way, the costs of AdaBoost are directly considered in the weighted ELM. Moreover, AdaBoost is also modified in two ways: (1) The initial distribution of weights is modified so as to give more weights to the instance of the minority class and less to those of the majority class; (2) the weight update is done separately for each class. Hence, an alpha is computed for each class and applied in the weight update such that the weights examples of each class sum up the same weight in the final distribution of AdaBoost (in each iteration). For the classifier aggregation, the same formula to compute $alpha_t$ as in AdaBoost.m1 is considered.

7.3.2.3 CS-DT-Ensemble

The authors of this work presents a new ensemble model formed of cost-sensitive decision trees [64]. In this case, first, a pool of classifiers is constructed following the RSM method after which decision trees are learned with the predefined costs. Finally, a classifier selection/weighting step is performed by meas of a genetic algorithm.

7.3.2.4 BayEnsBNN

A Bayesian Ensemble of Bayesian Neural Networks (BayEnsBNNs) [72] is proposed in this work. Even though cost-sensitive learning is not mentioned, it could be considered a kind of cost-sensitive approach. Several Bayesian Neural Networks are learned using different costs for each one. Afterwards, a Bayesian combination is considered, where another term for managing the imbalance is introduced.

7.3.2.5   AL-BoostedCS-SVM

This is a improvement of cost-sensitive SVMs where the authors aimed at avoiding the setting of the costs for each class [127], which is a very difficult task and one of the main drawbacks of cost-sensitive approaches. In order to do so, they introduced AL strategies into the learning framework to select the most informative examples and more accurately estimate the costs. In this way, each base learner was trained on a reduced number of instances, which were labeled as significant by the previously created classifier (for the first iteration OSS was performed). Since the considered dataset is composed only of examples situated near the borderline, the training sets becomes more balanced and avoids redundant and noisy cases.

7.3.2.6   IC-BoostedCS-SVM

IC-BoostedCS-SVM (Instance Categorization BoostedCS-SVM) [73] introduces an additional weighting procedure to estimate the weights of each example in Adaboost before using these weights to learn the next classifier. This new adjustment factor is applied to instances that are inside the margin of the previously learned SVM (initially they are set to 1) and those who are on the margin boundaries. This new factor is afterwards multiplied by the original weights of Adaboost and used to learn the next cost-sensitive SVM. The adjustment factors are only used for the classifier learning and not in the rest of the AdaBoost algorithm in order to preserve the theoretical foundations of AdaBoost.

7.3.3   Boosting-Based Ensembles

In this family, we review those algorithms which embed techniques for data preprocessing into Boosting algorithms. This way, these methods alter and bias the weight distribution used to train the next classifier toward the minority class every iteration. Inside this family, we include SMOTEBoost [20], MSMOTEBoost [55], RUSBoost [99], DataBoost-IM [47], GESuperPBoost [42], BalancedBoost [116], RB-Boost [26], Balanced-St-GrBoost [8] and RHBoost [44] algorithms.

7.3.3.1   SMOTEBoost/MSMOTEBoost

Both SMOTEBoost [20] and SMOTEBagging [55] introduce synthetic instances just before Step 4 of AdaBoost.M2 (Algorithm 5), using the SMOTE and MSMOTE data preprocessing algorithms, respectively. The weights of the new instances are proportional to the total number of instances in the new dataset. Hence, their weights are always the same (in all iterations and for all new instances), whereas original dataset's instances weights are normalized in such a way that they form a distribution with the new instances. After training a classifier, the weights of the original dataset instances are updated, then another sampling phase is applied (again, modifying the weight distribution). The repetition of this process also brings along more diversity in the training data, which generally benefits the ensemble learning.

7.3.3.2 RUSBoost

RUSBoost [99] performs similarly to SMOTEBoost, but it removes instances from the majority class by random undersampling the dataset in each iteration. In this case, it is not necessary to assign new weights to the instances. It is enough with simply normalizing the weights of the remaining instances in the new dataset with respect to their total sum of weights. The rest of the procedure is the same as in SMOTEBoost.

7.3.3.3 DataBoost-IM

This approach [47] is slightly different to the previous ones. Its initial idea is not different, it combines AdaBoost.M1 algorithm with a data generation strategy. Its major difference is that it first identifies hard examples (seeds) and then carries out a rebalance process, always for both classes. At the beginning, the N_s instances (as many as misclassified instances by the current classifier) with the largest weights are taken as seeds. Considering that N_{min} and N_{maj} are the number of instances of the minority and majority class, respectively; whereas N_{smin} and N_{smaj} are the number of seed instances of each class; $M_L = \min(N_{maj}/N_{min}, N_{smaj})$ and $M_S = \min((N_{maj} \cdot M_L)/N_{min}, N_{smin})$ minority and majority class instances are used as final seeds. Each seed produce N_{maj} or N_{min} new examples, depending on its class label. Nominal attributes' values are copied from the seed and the values of continuous attributes are randomly generated following a normal distribution with the mean and variance of class instances. Those instances are added to the original dataset with a weight proportional to the weight of the seed. Finally, the sums of weights of the instances belonging to each class are rebalanced, in such a way that both classes' sum is equal. The major drawback of this approach is its incapability to deal with highly imbalanced datasets, because it generates an excessive amount of instances which are not manageable for the base classifier (i.e., $N_{maj} = 3000$ and $N_{min} = 29$ with $Err = 15\%$, there will be 100 seed instances, which 71 have to be from the majority class and at least $71 \cdot 3000 = 213,000$ new majority instances are generated in each iteration). For this reason, we will not analyze it in the experimental study.

7.3.3.4   RAMOBoost

RAMOBoost [23] stands for Ranked Minority Oversampling in Boosting. It is similar to SMOTEBoost, but it is based on the instance generation mechanism of ADASYN [48], where the number of instances to be generated depends on how many instances from the majority class are in the KNN of each minority class instance. The more instances from the majority class are, the more synthetic examples will be generated, since the instance is assumed to be nearer to the decision boundary. In summary, RAMOBoost uses AdaBoost.M2; first, it carries out a sampling of the dataset following the weight distribution D_t of AdaBoost; then, the instances from the minority class are oversampled by generating synthetic examples depending on the number of examples from the majority class in their neighborhood. That is, the more neighbors from the other class, the more probability the instance has to be used for oversampling. This is achieved by resampling with replacement the minority class examples, giving more probability of being selected to those with greater number of majority class NNs. Afterwards, for each instance selected to be oversampled, new instances are generated by interpolation as in SMOTE in order to balance the dataset (a predefined number of instances are generated in this case). Finally, the base classifier is learned using the dataset resampled using D_t and the generated minority class examples. Afterwards, AdaBoost.M2 algorithm continues its execution without the synthetic examples.

7.3.3.5   Adaboost.NC

Adaboost.NC [114] was developed aiming at combining the benefits of Negative Correlation Learning (NCL) and Boosting. The same authors extended the usage of this method to two-class imbalanced problems by randomly oversampling the dataset before applying the Adaboost.NC algorithm. In order to improve diversity and performance at the same time, Adaboost.NC introduces a penalty term $p_t = 1 - |amb_t|$ for each training example where amb_t assesses the disagreement degree of the classification within the ensemble in iteration t :

$$amb_t = \frac{1}{t} \sum_{i=1}^{t} (||H_t = y|| - ||h_i = y||) \tag{7.12}$$

The magnitude of amb_t indicates a "pure" disagreement. This penalty term is then introduced into the $alpha_t$ computation as well as in the weight update giving more attention to examples with small $|amb_t|$ in order to force negative correlation. Notice that although this method is classified in this category as it is using Boosting and data preprocessing, they are combined one after the other and not one inside the other as in the rest of the methods.

7.3.3.6   EUSBoost

EUSBoost (Evolutionary Undersampling Boosting) [36] is similar to RUSBoost model, but evolutionary undersampling (EUS) is considered instead of RUS in order to select the majority class instances to be used in each iteration in a supervised manner. In this way, both the classification performance can be improved as well as the diversity of the classifiers, which is promoted by a mechanism introduced in the fitness function of EUS. This way, not only the best subset of majority class instances is selected in each phase but also the subset with the greatest diversity compared with the ones already selected.

7.3.3.7   GESuperPBoost

The idea of the GESuperPBoost (Genetically Evole Supervised Projection Boosting) [42] algorithm is based on AdaBoost. However, instead of optimizing the weights of AdaBoost in an aggressive manner (learning a classifier that minimizes the cost), the authors propose to transform the dataset in each iteration by non-linear projections. That is, no data-preprocessing method for the class imbalance problem is considered (such as undersampling or oversampling) but data is transformed to a new feature space where examples become more separable. This is done by learning an adequate non-linear transformation using a genetic algorithm which takes into account the weight distribution of Adaboost in a weighted g-mean measure (the one optimized by the genetic algorithm). Afterwards, a classifier is learned in the new feature space without considering the weights of AdaBoost (which were considered for the feature transformation). Hence, supervised non-linear projections are considered as a data preprocessing step. These types of projections are constructed using both the inputs and the label of the patterns and with the aim of improving the classification accuracy of any given learner.

7.3.3.8   BalancedBoost

BalancedBoosts [116] consists of a modification of RUSBoost, where instead of applying RUS, the authors consider the undersampling of the majority class and the oversampling of the minority one in such a way that the new dataset is balanced and has the same number of majority and minority class instances. Moreover, the sampling process is carried out following the weights of AdaBoost.M2 algorithm, which is the one considered by the authors.

7.3.3.9   RB-Boost

RandomBalanace Boosting [26] is based on the same idea as RUSBoost and SMOTEBoost, but in this case RandomBalance data level technique is considered.

That is, an hybrid between RUSBoost and SMOTEBoost is achieved because RandomBalance randomly selects the number of instances from each class to be present in the dataset and then, RUS or SMOTE are applied depending on the necessity. As it is done in RUSBoost or SMOTEBoost, RandomBalance sampling is also combined with Adaboost.M2 algorithm to create an ensemble capable of dealing with imbalanced classes. To do so, RandomBalance preprocessing was introduced just before step 4 of Adaboot.M2 (Algorithm 5). New instances in the dataset receive a weight of $1/N$ (the weight initially given to all instances), whereas the instances remaining in the dataset maintain their original weights.

7.3.3.10 Balanced-St-GrBoost

Focused on high dimensional datasets where class imbalance is present, the authors considered the usage of Gradient Boosted Trees [8]. Gradient Boosted Trees generalize the idea of Boosting by allowing the optimization of an arbitrary differentiable loss function. However, as many other classifiers they are also biased toward the majority class. Hence, they proposed three different variations, which were analogous to existing methods for the class imbalance but changing the inner classification method. In the case of Boosting-based family, they proposed the Balanced-St-GrBoost method, which is an Stochastic Gradient Boosting ensemble that uses RUS to balance the dataset in each iteration.

7.3.4 Bagging-Based Ensembles

Due to its simplicity and good generalization ability many approaches have been developed using bagging ensembles to deal with class imbalance problems. The integration of data preprocessing techniques in bagging is usually simpler than their hybridization with boosting. In bagging, in contrast to boosting, there is no need of recompute any kind of weights; therefore, neither is necessary to adapt the weight update formula nor to change the computations in the algorithm. In bagging-based methods, the key factor is the way in which each bootstrap replica is obtained (Step 2 of Algorithm 1), that is, how the class imbalance problem is dealt to obtain a useful classifier in each iteration without forgetting the importance of the diversity. Many of the algorithms in this category have proposed to change the original bootstrapping of Bagging by the usage of a data preprocessing method, which by itself should also be able to provide the required diversity.

In this category, we distinguish two main algorithms because they have been the basis for many others: OverBagging [113] and UnderBagging [4]. Moreover, algorithms such as UnderOverBagging [113], IIVotes [9], RB-Bagging [26], EPRENNID [111] or USwitchingNED [45] also belong to this family. Notice that, there are other algorithms that have being grouped into OverBagging and Under-Bagging due to their similarity, for instance, SMOTEBagging [113], QuasiBagging

[18], Asymetric Bagging [106], Roughly Balanced Bagging [49], Partitioning [17, 124], Bagging Ensemble Variation [74], IRUS [105], α-TreeEnsembles [88] and PUSB [63]. Hereafter, we explain all these approaches.

7.3.4.1   OverBagging

An easy way to overcome class imbalance problem when facing the resampling stage in bagging is to take the classes of the instances into account when they are randomly drawn from the original dataset. Hence, instead of performing a random sampling (with replacement) of the whole dataset, an oversampling process can be carried out before training each classifier (OverBagging). This procedure can be developed in at least two ways. Oversampling consists in increasing the number of minority class instances by their random replication. Regarding majority class instances, they can directly be included in the new bootstrap, but another option is to resample with replacement them aiming at increasing diversity. Notice that in OverBagging all instances will probably take part in at least one bag, but each bootstrapped replica will contain many more instances than the original dataset.

- **SMOTEBagging [113]**. The oversampling of the minority class instances can also be carried out using a different algorithm such as SMOTE preprocessing algorithm. Nevertheless, SMOTEBagging [113] differs from OverBagging not only due the usage of a different preprocessing method (SMOTE instead of ROS), it also follows a significantly different strategy to create each bag. As well as in OverBagging, in this method both classes contribute to each bag with N_{maj} instances. But, a SMOTE resampling rate ($a\%$) is set in each iteration (ranging from 10% in the first iteration to 100% in the last, always being multiple of 10) and this ratio defines the number of positive instances ($a\% \cdot N_{maj}$) randomly resampled (with replacement) from the original dataset in each iteration. The rest of the positive instances are generated by SMOTE algorithm. Besides, the set of negative instances is bootstrapped in each iteration in order to form a more diverse ensemble.

7.3.4.2   UnderBagging

In contrast to OverBagging, UnderBagging procedure uses undersampling instead of oversampling. However, in the same manner as OverBagging, it can be developed in at least two ways. The undersampling procedure is usually only applied to the majority class; however, a resampling with replacement of the minority class can also be applied in order to obtain a priori more diverse ensembles. Nonetheless, doing so can be more risky as relevant information from the minority class may be lost (which in OverBagging is unlikely to happen with the majority class). Also, point out that, in UnderBagging it is more probable to ignore some useful negative instances, but each bag has less instances than the original dataset (on the contrary to OverBagging).

In the following, we also describe different variations of UnderBagging that can be found in the literature.

- **Asymmetric Bagging [106]/QuasiBagging [18]**. Even if these methods are named differently, these methods maintain the same functional structure of UnderBagging and can be therefore considered to be the same algorithm.
- **Roughly-balanced Bagging [49]** is quite similar to UnderBagging, but it does not bootstrap a totally balanced bag. The number of positive examples is always kept fixed (using all of them or resampling them), whereas the number of negative examples drawn in each iteration varies slightly following a negative binomial distribution (with $q = 0.5$ and $n = N_{min}$). Hence, each bag is not force to be totally balanced.
- **Partitioning [17, 124]/Bagging Ensemble Variation [74]** is another way to develop the undersampling, in this case, the instances of the majority class are divided into IR disjoint datasets and each classifier is trained with one of those bootstraps (mixed with the minority class examples). As a consequence, the number of classifiers to be trained is given by the IR of the dataset.
- **IRUS[105]**. IRUS (Inverse Random UnderSampling) is very similar to Under-Bagging, but it is named as inverse random undersampling because in each undersampling phase, the imbalanced distribution is inverted. That is, all the minority class examples are selected but few majority class examples are randomly drawn (without replacement). In this way, the new dataset will have more instances from the minority class than from the majority one. As a result, a high true positive rate is expected due to the imbalance inversion. On the contrary, the false positive rate can clearly affect this method. However, false positives are expected to decrease due to the averaging effect of bagging. Since the number of examples from the majority class in each iteration is very small, the diversity should be boosted, alleviating the number of false positives. Moreover, for the classifier fusion phase, the outputs of each classifier are normalized by their mean and variance instead of directly using the output of each classifier to perform a weighted voting.
- **α-TreeEnsembles[88]** α-trees introduce a new splitting criterion based on alpha-divergence, which generalizes well-known criteria such as the ones used in C4.5 or CART. With this new splitting, different trees can be constructed using different values for the α scalar. The authors take advantage of this fact and use it to construct ensembles for the class imbalance problem, where the values of alpha are changed. Moreover, this is combined with undersampling. Hence, these ensembles can be seen as UnderBagging where α-trees are considered in order to increase diversity.

7.3.4.3 UnderOverBagging

The methodology followed by *UnderBagging to OverBagging* is different from that of OverBagging and UnderBagging. In fact, it is more similar to SMOTEBagging in the way to create each bag. Both oversampling and undersampling techniques are applied. A resampling rate ($a\%$) is set in each iteration (ranging from 10% to 100% always being multiple of 10), which defines the number of instances that are randomly taken from each class ($a\% \cdot N_{maj}$ instances). Hence, the first classifiers are trained with a lower number of instances than the last ones. This way, the diversity is boosted.

7.3.4.4 IIVotes

Imbalanced IVotes [9] is based on the same combination idea of introducing a data level algorithm into bagging. In this case, SPIDER is the data preprocessing technique considered and instead of being combined with bagging, the ensemble learning model considered is IVotes. Therefore, a preprocessing phase is applied in each iteration of IVotes before Step 13 of Algorithm 2. This method has the advantage of not needing to define the number of bags, since the algorithm stops when the out-of-bag error estimation no longer decreases.

7.3.4.5 RB-Bagging

Likewise its boosting version, RandomBalance Bagging [26] is an hybrid between SMOTEBagging and UnderBagging, in the sense that RandomBalance preprocessing uses both RUS and SMOTE to create the new dataset. In RB-Bagging, each new bag is obtained by RandomBalance and hence, all the bags always have the same number of instances as the original dataset. However, the number of instances from each class is randomly selected. Depending on the number of instances to be taken from each class either RUS or SMOTE is applied.

7.3.4.6 EPRENNID

EPRENNID (Evolutionary Prototype Reduction based Ensemble for Nearest Neighbor classification of Imbalanced Data) [111] is a classifier specific ensemble model based on data preprocessing. The authors make use of k-NN classifier to create an ensemble. In order to do so, the reference sets for k-NN needs to be different, which is achieved by the hybridization of prototype selection (where few instances from the original set are selected) and prototype generation (where those instances are moved in the feature space aiming at improving the generalization performance). In this model, both techniques are developed using evolutionary algorithms. The first one is based on a memetic algorithm, where a local search is included in the genetic algorithm looking for the best set of instances to be selected. Likewise, prototype generation is developed by means of differential evolution. Both approaches take into account the class imbalance in order to perform well in this framework. This is mainly carried out by considering appropriate performance measures in the fitness functions (such as g-mean or AUC_{ROC}). Moreover, in order to obtain a diverse set of k-NN classifiers, diversity is taken into account when selecting the final reference sets. It should be noted that different from classic UnderBagging approaches, in this method, both the majority and minority class examples are undersampled in each final reference set, but this is done in a guided manner. Finally, classifiers in the ensemble are combined using a dynamic classifier weighting approach.

7.3.4.7 USwitchingNED

USwitchingNED [45] stands for Undersampling Switching Nearest Enemy Distance. This method is similar to UnderBagging, but it adds an extra step for increasing the diversity of the ensemble members. In order to do so, Class Switching ensembles are considered. In these ensembles, diversity is achieved by randomly switching the classes of selected instances. The authors adapted this methodology to the class imbalance framework by only switching the labels of majority class instances. Moreover, these instance were selected depending on a probability, whose value is inversely proportional to the distance to its nearest enemy (instance from the minority class). However, as with every other ensemble technique, some kind of preprocessing was needed in order to address highly imbalanced datasets and hence, they combined their method with random undersampling that gave the best results (also SMOTE and random oversampling were considered). As a consequence, the algorithm works as follows: in each iteration, a fraction of examples from the majority class are switched (the fraction is a parameter of the method); afterwards, if the dataset is still unbalanced, random undersampling is applied to completely balance the dataset. The final prediction is given by majority voting of the ensemble members.

7.3.5 Hybrid Ensembles

The main difference of the algorithms in this category with respect to the previous ones is that they carry out a double ensemble learning, that is, they combine both bagging and boosting (also with a preprocessing technique). Algorithms using this kind of hybridization were first proposed in [77] (EasyEnsemble and BalanceCascade, referred to as exploratory undersampling techniques). Other similar approaches are HardEnsemble [86] and StochasticEnsemble [8]. All these approaches use Bagging as main ensemble learning method, but instead of training a classifier for each new bag, they train each bag using AdaBoost. Hence, the final classifier is an ensemble of ensembles. The specific details of each method are explained in the following.

7.3.5.1 EasyEnsemble

In the same manner as UnderBagging, each balanced bag is constructed by randomly undersampling instances from the majority class and using all the instances from the minority class. Afterwards, instead of simply learning a classifier, in EasyEnsemble [77] AdaBoost learning algorithm is considered to learn an ensemble from the undersampled dataset. Hence, this method can be seen as an UnderBagging where the base learner used is AdaBoost. If we fix the number of classifiers, EasyEnsemble will train less bags than UnderBagging, but more classifiers will be assigned to learn each single bag. Finally, classifier combination is made by the combination of all classifiers with the corresponding weights assigned by AdaBoost to each one of them.

7.3.5.2 BalanceCascade

BalanceCascade [77] is similar to EasyEnsemble as they are based on the same model. However, in BalanceCascade the removal of negative instances is considered after each bagging iteration (that is, after learning the AdaBoost classifier). Hence, differently EasyEnsemble, the AdaBoost classifiers cannot be run in parallel as each one depends on the previous models. In each bagging iteration after learning the AdaBoost classifier, the majority class examples that are correctly classified with higher confidences by the current trained classifiers are removed from the dataset, and they are not taken into account in further iterations. The rest of the method, including the classifier combination is the same as in EasyEnsemble.

7.3.5.3 HardEnsemble

HardEnsemble [86] is also an ensemble of ensembles. A similar strategy to EasyEnsemble is followed, but in this case both oversampled and undersampled datasets are considered. HardEnsemble is composed of a total of 150 classifiers, 50 of which are constructed from oversampled datasets and 100 from undersampled datasets. As oversampling method a new modification of SMOTE named as Critical SMOTE is considered, which is proposed in the same work. For undersampling the authors proposed the usage of Reward-Punishment technique [85], which removes the cases in the overlapping regions. Preprocessed datasets were afterwards used to learn a RUSBoost ensemble (10 iterations). Therefore, this is similar to EasyEnsemble but as the preprocessed datasets may not be totally balanced, RUSBoost is applied instead of directly using AdaBoost algorithm. Finally, all the classifiers learned were combined by weighted voting strategy (as in EasyEnsemble).

7.3.5.4 StochasticEnsemble

StochasticEnsemble was proposed in the same work as Balance-St-GrBoost [8], which we have already reviewed. Both models were focused on addressing high dimensional datasets. The authors make use of Gradient Boosted Trees, which are also biased to the majority class and hence, preprocessing techniques are required. If Balanced-St-GrBoost can be considered as a variation of RUSBoost where the base classifiers used are Gradient Boosted Trees, then StochasticEnsemble follows the same idea but replicating the behavior of EasyEnsemble. Hence, it performs UnderBagging were each bag is learned using Gradient Boosted Trees.

7.3.6 Other

This family of methods differs from the previous ones in the sense that they are not new ensemble methods as whole but they propose a set of techniques to improve existing models by mainly either increasing the diversity of the ensemble (RandomOracles [93], diversity enhancing techniques for improving ensembles [27] and OrderingBasedPruning [37]) or adapting the AdaBoost algorithm to better learn in the imbalance framework (Loss factors [101] and GOBoost [79]). The only exception is MOGP-GP [7], which is an ensemble method based on multi-objective genetic programming and hence, they way of building the ensemble highly differs from the ones already reviewed. Hereafter, the approaches in this category are described one by one.

7.3.6.1 MOGP-GP

The authors of [7] proposed a completely different approach based on evolutionary computation. First, a multi-objective genetic programming (GP) was considered to evolve a set of GP classifiers to form the ensemble by trading-off the performance over the minority and majority classes. This way, any kind of resampling or data preprocessing phase is avoided. Afterwards, an ensemble selection approach was developed also using GP to finally select the members of the ensemble.

7.3.6.2 RandomOracles

In [93], Random Oracles are considered to improve the capabilities of existing ensembles for the class imbalance problem such as SMOTEBoost, SMOTEBagging and RUSBoost. In such a way, Random Oracles are used as base classifiers instead of directly considering the selected classifier. The truth is that in Random Oracles, two base classifiers are learned instead of one in each iteration of the ensemble, because the feature space is randomly divided into two (via linear or spherical oracles) and one classifier is then learned for each part of the feature space. In any case, the rest of the ensemble model remains unchanged and this is why this method is considered as a possible improvement of existing ones.

7.3.6.3 Loss Factors

Two new loss factors based on F-measure and G-mean are proposed for AdaBoost algorithm [101] based on the fact that AdaBoost aims at decreasing the overall classification error, being not totally adequate for the imbalance framework even if data is preprocessed in each iteration. Therefore, instead of the loss factor based on standard accuracy, specific loss factors for the class imbalance problem are introduced. As a consequence, both $alpha_t$ and therefore the weight update formula are changed, taking into account both classes equally. These new loss schemes are considered together with existing ensembles such as SMOTEBoost, RUSBoost and RB-Boost.

7.3.6.4 GOBoost

This work also deals with the loss factors of AdaBoost [79]. The authors modify AdaBoost algorithm changing the function to be minimized by AdaBoost. Instead of the error rate, they consider the maximization of the g-mean, which is much more adequate for the imbalance framework. As a result, they derive the new GOBoost algorithm where the g-mean is maximized. This new algorithm is tested in combination with existing approaches for the class imbalance such as RUSBoost, EasyEnsemble, ROSBoost, SMOTEBoost and AdaC2. Hence, it is aimed at complementing existing approaches by making AdaBoost more conscious of the problem.

7.3.6.5 OrderingBasedPruning

Pruning for classifier ensembles consists of removing classifiers from the ensemble in order to improve the generalization performance of the final ensemble, reduce the storage necessity and the testing times. In the case of ordering-based ensemble pruning, classifiers are ordered an added one by one to the final ensemble (instead of removing classifiers, they are added). In this way, the key factor is the measure considered to decide which one is the next classifier to be added to the ensemble. In [37], the authors considered a general framework that was applied to existing classifiers for the class imbalance problem such as SMOTEBagging, UnderBagging, RUSBoost, EUSBoost and EasyEnsemble, among others. Existing measures for ensemble pruning in standard classification scenarios were adapted to the specific properties of imbalanced datasets. Five new metrics were proposed as an adaptation of existing ones. The authors showed that the usage of pruning highly enhanced the results of existing models. Among them, the combination of UnderBagging with the Reduced-Error with Geometric Mean (RE-GM) ensemble pruning achieved remarkable results, being one of the simplest pruning models. The original RE model consisted of adding the classifiers that achieve the largest reduction of the classification error (which is the same as those with the greatest accuracy improvement). Therefore, the error has the same problems as the accuracy measure when dealing with imbalanced problems, being biased toward the majority class. The g-mean performance measure is considered to solve this problem by adding the classifier leading to the ensemble with largest g-mean.

7.3.6.6 Diversity Enhancing Techniques for Improving Ensembles

In [27], the authors developed an extensive experimental study where several diversity enhancing techniques for classifier ensembles were considered to improve existing ensemble models for the class imbalance problem. They focused on the four groups of techniques already introduced in Sect. 7.2.3. More specifically, they performed experiments with Random Linear Oracles, Disturbing Neighbors, RFW and Rotation Forest (one method from each category). These diversity enhancing techniques were combined with methods like SMOTEBagging, UnderBagging, SMOTEBoost, RUSBoost, RAMOBoost, RB-Boost and RB-Bagging. They concluded that the diversity added by the new introduced techniques paid off with an increase in the overall performance of the classifiers.

7.3.6.7 PT-Bagging

On the contrary to most of the ensemble-based method presented for addressing the class imbalance problem, PT-Bagging [24] aims to avoid the rebalancing of the dataset, which can introduce its own biases. The authors propose to substitute the adaptation of the learning phase by the adaptation of the testing phase introducing a simple threshold-moving technique. This technique consists in selecting the best threshold for predicting each class (instead of the predefined 0.5 that is commonly considered). Since Bagging is known to provide good probability estimates, the authors propose different ways of adjusting the threshold depending on the measure to be optimized. More specifically, the original averaged output probabilities given by Bagging are transformed to scores dividing them by the respective class threshold. These thresholds can be adapted to maximize the measure of interest. In this case, both the average accuracy and F-measure are considered to be optimized.

7.3.6.8 IMCStacking

Similarly to PT-Bagging, the authors of this work avoided rebalancing the dataset [16]. They considered the usage of Stacking to combine the different base classifier that were learned from the original training data. Stacking [119] makes use of another classifier in order to combine the outputs of the previous ones, this way, the outputs of the base classifiers are the inputs of the stacked classifier used to finally predict the output of the ensemble. In order to handle the imbalance, cost-sensitive logistic regression is used for the combination of the base classifiers. Moreover, the probabilities given by the base classifiers are transformed by a method named as inverse feature mapping before using them as input for the cost-sensitive logistic regression. These feature transformation is based on an exponential transformation of the probabilities, whose exponentiation parameter is fitted by cross-validation. As base classifiers Linear Discriminant Analysis, Logistic Regression, Random Forest, Extremely randomized Trees and Gradient Based Decision Trees are considered.

7.3.6.9   DynamicSelection

In [94], the authors focused on showing the goodness of applying dynamic selection [14] in the combination phase of the ensemble. Four different dynamic selection methods were considered together with different Bagging-based ensembles for the class imbalance problem (RB-Bagging, SMOTE-Bagging and a Bagging version of RAMO-Boost). Recall that dynamic selection methods can either select a single classifier or a group of classifiers. In this case, both types were considered. Another key factor in dynamic selection is the reference dataset used to establish the competence of each classifier to classify a given test instance. Accordingly, the authors proposed to apply SMOTE or RAMO to ensure that the resulting dataset will have enough instances so as to be reliable, and at the same time handle the class imbalance.

7.4   An Illustrative Experimental Study on Ensembles for the Class Imbalance Problem

To end this chapter, in this last section we develop a brief experimental study comparing several selected ensemble methods that we have carefully selected. In fact, our objective is two-fold: (1) We want to show the effectiveness of ensemble methods by comparing them against the usage of preprocessing (without considering ensembles); (2) We present a comparison among ensemble methods and show the usefulness of ensemble pruning methods to enhance their results. In order to develop this study, first, we introduce the experimental framework in Sect. 7.4.1. Then, we present the results obtained and discuss them in Sect. 7.4.2

7.4.1 Experimental Framework

7.4.1.1 Datasets and Performance Measures

For the experimental analysis we have considered the complete set of imbalanced datasets in the KEEL data-set repository [1, 2], which is publicly available on the corresponding web-page.[1] The table with the properties of the 66 datasets in this repository is presented in Chap. 2. We recall that they are binary class imbalanced problem with IR ranging from 1.5 to 129.

In order to measure the performance of each approach we consider the g-mean, which requires both classes to be properly distinguished without favoring any of them. The estimates for this metrics are obtained by means of a Distribution Optimally Balanced Stratified Cross-Validation (DOB-SCV) [84], as suggested in the specialized literature for working in imbalanced classification [78]. DOB-SCV avoids dataset shift [83], which hinders the results obtained in the experimental analysis. This procedure is carried out using fivefolds, aiming to include enough positive class instances in the different folds. In this way, we avoid additional problems in the data distribution, especially for highly imbalanced datasets. In accordance with the stochastic nature of the learning methods, these fivefolds are generated with five different seeds, and each one of the five-fold cross-validation is run 5 times. Therefore, experimental results for each method and dataset are computed with the average of 125 runs.

7.4.1.2 Algorithms and Parameters

In first place, the baseline classifier that will be used in all the ensembles needs to be defined. With this goal, we will use C4.5 decision tree generating algorithm [91]. We should note that the majority of the ensemble methodologies that are tested in this section were proposed using C4.5 as base classifier. Moreover, it has been widely used to deal with imbalanced datasets [29, 39, 103], and C4.5 has also been included as one of the top-ten data-mining algorithms [123]. Therefore, from our point of view it is the most appropriate base learning for these experiments. C4.5 learning algorithm constructs the decision tree top-down using the normalized information gain (difference in entropy) that results from choosing an attribute for splitting the data. The attribute with the highest normalized information gain is the one used to make the decision. In Table 7.2, we show the configuration parameters that we have used to run C4.5.

For the experiments we have selected several representative methods from the different families that we have analyzed. Regarding Bagging-, Boosting-based and Hybrid ensemble methods, we have considered the best performers in the comparison carried out in [35]. Therefore, UnderBagging and SMOTEBagging

---

[1]http://www.keel.es/dataset.php

Table 7.2 Parameter
specification for C4.5

Parameters
Prune = True
Confidence level = 0.25
Minimum number of item-sets per leaf = 2
Confidence = Laplace smoothing [89]

from Bagging-based ensembles, RUSBoost and SMOTEBoost from Boosting-based ensembles and EasyEnsemble as Hybrid method are considered. Additionally, we have considered EUSBoost as another more recent Boosting-based method specifically developed for highly imbalanced datasets. Ensemble methods are complemented with the best performing ordering-based pruning model in [37] as a representative of the family Other. Notice that in this case, a base ensemble model is considered (UnderBagging) together with a post-processing mechanism to reduced the size of the ensemble (RE-GM). This method is denoted as UnderBagging_RE in the following. The parameters considered for all the algorithms are the ones recommended by the authors. The same parameters are used for every dataset.

Regarding the number of classifiers considered for the ensembles, all the methods should have the same opportunities to achieve their best performance, but avoiding the fine-tuning of their parameters depending on the dataset. In [35], it was shown that Boosting-based ensembles work better with only 10 classifiers, whereas Bagging-based ones need 40 to reach their maximum potential. Hence, we consider 10 classifiers for the former ensembles and 40 for the latter and Hybrid ones. For the case of UnderBagging_RE, following the recommendations of the authors, 100 classifiers are initially built, but the final pruned ensemble will only consists of 21 classifiers.

We should notice that the only category not included in the comparison is the cost-sensitive ensembles. We prefer not to include models in this category because previous experiments [35] have shown that setting the costs with a general pattern do not allow them to achieve their maximum potential and hence, the comparison may be not totally fair in this case.

Finally, in order to compare the performance of ensemble methods with data level ones, we have considered the most commonly used methods for data preprocessing in classifier ensembles, that is, RUS and SMOTE. SMOTE configuration is the standard one with a 50% class distribution, 5 neighbors for generating the synthetic samples, and Heterogeneous Value Difference Metric for computing the distance among the examples.

All experiments have been developed under KEEL software [1, 2]. We must stress that the implementations of the algorithms in the comparison are publicly available in KEEL source code.

7.4.1.3 Statistical Analysis

In order to compare the different algorithms appropriately a statistical analysis of
the results needs to be carried out. Non-parametric tests are considered as suggested
in the literature [25, 38, 40]. Any interested reader can find additional information
on the Website http://sci2s.ugr.es/sicidm/. We consider two different tests.

- *Pairwise comparisons.* Wilcoxon paired signed-rank test [117] is used to find out
  whether significant differences exist between a pair of algorithms.
- *Multiple comparisons.* Friedman aligned-ranks test [53] is used to detect statistical differences among a set of algorithms. Then, if significant differences are
  found, Holm post-hoc test [54] is used to check if the control algorithm (the best
  one) is significantly better than the others (that is, $1 \times n$ comparison).

Moreover, we show the p-value for each comparison, which represents the lowest
level of significance of a hypothesis resulting in a rejection. In such a manner, we
are able to know how different two algorithms are.

In addition, the average aligned-ranks of each algorithm (used in the Friedman
aligned-ranks test) are considered in order to compare at a first glance the behavior
of each algorithm with respect to the others. These rankings are computed by first
calculating the difference between the performance obtained by the algorithm and
the mean performance of all algorithms in the corresponding data-set. Then, these
differences are ranked from 1 to $k \cdot n$ (being k the number of data-sets and n the
number of methods), assigning the corresponding rank to the method from which
the difference has been computed. Hence, the lower the rank is, the better the method
is. At last, the average ranking of each algorithm in all data-sets can be computed to
show their global performance.

7.4.2 Experimental Results and Discussion

Table 7.3 presents the g-mean results obtained in test by each method for each
dataset considered. Moreover, the average performance of each method is presented
in the last row. The first two columns of methods correspond to preprocessing
approaches (RUS and SMOTE) without considering ensembles, whereas the rest
of them are ensemble methods. Notice that the last one is an ensemble model with
a post-processing mechanism to prune classifiers. The best result in each row is
stressed in bold-face.

At a first glance, it can be observed that the overall performance of RUS and
SMOTE is considerably lower than that of the ensemble models. Among ensemble
models, in this framework, SMOTEBagging and SMOTEBoost are the ones with
the worst overall performance, whereas EUSBoost and UnderBagging_RE perform
the best. Anyway, one should notice that there are datasets were the worst methods
overall perform better than the rest, which is in accordance with the no free lunch
theorem.

Table 7.3 Test results for the selected preprocessing and ensemble methods using the g-mean performance measure

Data-set	RUS	SMOTE	UnderBagging	SMOTEBagging	RUSBoost	SMOTEBoost	EUSBoost	EasyEnsemble	UnderBagging_RE
abalone19	0.6510	0.2946	0.6942	0.2756	0.6648	0.2428	0.6702	**0.7023**	0.6956
abalone918	0.6854	0.6442	**0.7533**	0.6802	0.7335	0.6322	0.7264	0.7176	0.7320
cleveland0vs4	0.7335	0.6932	0.8420	0.7330	**0.8609**	0.7229	0.8557	0.8594	0.8583
ecoli0137vs26	0.6706	0.7797	0.7078	0.7625	0.7269	0.7790	0.7602	**0.8044**	0.7897
ecoli0146vs5	0.8247	0.8753	0.8880	0.8791	**0.9145**	0.8936	0.9022	0.8937	0.9046
ecoli0147vs2356	0.7953	0.8356	0.8272	0.8599	0.8514	0.8627	0.8539	0.8380	**0.8632**
ecoli0147vs56	0.8180	0.8652	0.8707	0.8590	0.8822	**0.8994**	0.8919	0.8812	0.8907
ecoli01vs235	0.8355	0.8438	0.8791	0.8943	0.8811	0.8653	0.8858	0.8836	**0.9025**
ecoli01vs5	0.8234	0.8614	0.8676	0.8808	0.9017	0.8887	**0.9188**	0.9049	0.9102
ecoli0234vs5	0.8061	0.8830	0.8549	0.8913	**0.8987**	0.8831	0.8925	0.8868	0.8876
ecoli0267vs35	0.8125	0.8537	0.8488	0.8528	**0.8596**	0.8503	0.8488	0.8525	0.8545
ecoli0346vs5	0.8174	0.8727	0.8722	0.8779	0.8839	0.8778	**0.8892**	0.8794	0.8856
ecoli0347vs56	0.8165	0.8529	0.8721	0.8492	0.8875	0.8836	0.8848	0.8714	**0.8923**
ecoli034vs5	0.8278	0.8840	0.8861	0.9053	**0.9115**	0.9001	0.9087	0.9052	0.9047
ecoli046vs5	0.8316	0.8871	0.8816	0.9071	**0.9098**	0.8904	0.8950	0.8921	0.9059
ecoli067vs35	0.8182	0.8421	0.8517	0.8495	0.8535	0.8541	0.8480	0.8552	**0.8565**
ecoli067vs5	0.8471	0.8535	0.8781	0.8832	0.8851	**0.8879**	0.8778	0.8646	0.8847
ecoli0vs1	0.9740	0.9766	0.9803	**0.9810**	0.9736	0.9750	0.9730	0.9719	0.9772
ecoli1	0.8753	0.8838	0.8965	**0.9043**	0.8896	0.8677	0.8996	0.8998	0.9035
ecoli2	0.8680	0.8888	0.9046	0.9131	0.9061	**0.9154**	0.9037	0.9048	0.9044
ecoli3	0.8441	0.8333	**0.8791**	0.8400	0.8562	0.8296	0.8645	0.8736	0.8682
ecoli4	0.8243	0.8989	0.8923	0.9197	0.9234	0.9035	0.9218	0.9256	**0.9271**
glass0123vs456	0.9061	0.9125	0.9327	**0.9395**	0.9276	0.9168	0.9295	0.9391	0.9366
glass0146vs2	0.6125	0.6680	0.6981	0.6245	0.6176	0.6860	0.6730	0.7003	**0.7363**
glass015vs2	0.5766	0.6539	**0.7093**	0.6457	0.6134	0.6813	0.6745	0.6611	0.6889
glass016vs2	0.5791	0.6436	0.6751	0.6073	0.6282	0.6499	0.6855	0.6525	**0.7024**
glass016vs5	0.9044	0.8827	0.9411	**0.9863**	0.9462	0.8914	0.9570	0.9497	0.9759
glass04vs5	**0.9939**	0.9295	**0.9939**	0.9908	**0.9939**	0.9757	**0.9939**	0.9835	**0.9939**
glass06vs5	0.9081	0.9061	0.9106	0.9924	0.9901	0.9811	**0.9947**	0.9462	0.9921
glass0	0.7783	0.7886	0.8214	0.8328	0.8397	0.8377	**0.8449**	0.8322	0.8437
glass1	0.7041	0.7414	0.7664	0.7620	0.7932	**0.8126**	0.7842	0.8059	0.7939
glass2	0.6101	0.6424	0.7418	0.7084	0.6615	0.6668	0.6812	0.6726	**0.7468**
glass4	0.8375	0.8343	**0.9030**	0.9004	0.8697	0.7922	0.8776	0.8640	0.8915
glass5	0.9392	0.9438	0.9473	**0.9748**	0.9556	0.9235	0.9717	0.9518	0.9659
glass6	0.8808	0.8944	0.9079	**0.9269**	0.9239	0.9157	0.9224	0.9121	0.9245
haberman	0.6241	0.6443	**0.6554**	0.6551	0.6476	0.6489	0.6226	0.6491	0.6528

(continued)

Table 7.3 (continued)

Data-set	RUS	SMOTE	UnderBagging	SMOTEBagging	RUSBoost	SMOTEBoost	EUSBoost	EasyEnsemble	UnderBagging_RE
iris0	**0.9897**	**0.9897**	**0.9897**	0.9877	**0.9897**	**0.9897**	**0.9897**	**0.9897**	**0.9897**
led7digit02456789vs1	0.8176	0.7978	0.8139	0.8336	**0.8381**	0.6222	0.8253	0.8159	0.8209
newthyroid1	0.9156	0.9514	0.9471	0.9548	0.9541	**0.9757**	0.9597	0.9531	0.9471
newthyroid2	0.9267	0.9595	0.9593	0.9630	0.9703	**0.9764**	0.9650	0.9626	0.9618
pageblocks13vs4	0.9497	0.9897	0.9802	**0.9952**	0.9800	0.9911	0.9828	0.9610	0.9941
pageblocks0	0.9457	0.9483	0.9609	0.9579	0.9558	0.9410	0.9511	0.9620	**0.9633**
pima	0.7085	0.7212	**0.7576**	0.7556	0.7275	0.7326	0.7426	0.7361	0.7513
segment0	0.9833	0.9920	0.9866	0.9917	0.9920	**0.9933**	0.9916	0.9925	0.9898
shuttlec0vsc4	**1.0000**	0.9998	**1.0000**	0.9999	**1.0000**	0.9998	**1.0000**	**1.0000**	**1.0000**
shuttlec2vsc4	0.9712	0.9992	**1.0000**	**1.0000**	**1.0000**	**1.0000**	**1.0000**	0.9881	**1.0000**
vehicle0	0.9264	0.9312	0.9485	0.9632	0.9573	0.9642	0.9541	**0.9653**	0.9547
vehicle1	0.7229	0.7394	0.7963	0.7837	0.7669	0.7641	0.7752	**0.7998**	0.7941
vehicle2	0.9408	0.9510	0.9703	0.9721	0.9738	**0.9809**	0.9744	0.9794	0.9734
vehicle3	0.7185	0.7351	**0.7994**	0.7774	0.7701	0.7459	0.7762	0.7971	0.7953
vowel0	0.9465	0.9753	0.9585	**0.9877**	0.9725	0.9860	0.9741	0.9758	0.9684
wisconsin	0.9562	0.9587	0.9689	0.9706	0.9685	0.9676	0.9656	**0.9752**	0.9700
yeast0256vs3789	0.7704	0.7640	0.8087	0.7916	0.7878	0.7728	0.7941	0.7910	**0.8126**
yeast02579vs368	0.8984	0.9004	0.9142	**0.9169**	0.9011	0.8937	0.9032	0.9040	0.9116
yeast0359vs78	0.6692	0.6800	**0.7330**	0.6993	0.7047	0.6164	0.7192	0.7175	0.7217
yeast05679vs4	0.7703	0.7834	0.8189	0.8138	0.8126	0.7713	0.8133	**0.8288**	0.8210
yeast1289vs7	0.6048	0.6445	**0.7279**	0.6498	0.6912	0.5658	0.7075	0.6919	0.7076
yeast1458vs7	0.5155	0.5040	**0.6270**	0.5458	0.6039	01.3651	0.6004	0.6157	0.6225
yeast1vs7	0.6664	0.6495	0.7617	0.7245	0.7373	0.7086	0.7599	0.7506	**0.7647**
yeast2vs4	0.9116	0.8911	**0.9428**	0.9262	0.9255	0.8747	0.9230	0.9386	0.9396
yeast2vs8	0.7142	0.7480	0.7366	**0.7815**	0.7610	0.7258	0.7549	0.7598	0.7439
yeast1	0.6922	0.7074	0.7297	0.7253	0.7136	0.7175	0.7222	0.7151	**0.7306**
yeast3	0.9169	0.9105	0.9306	0.9326	0.9233	0.8828	0.9235	0.9285	**0.9340**
yeast4	0.8107	0.7562	0.8375	0.8125	0.8269	0.7151	0.8303	0.8441	**0.8502**
yeast5	0.9425	0.9540	0.9587	0.9615	0.9543	0.8984	0.9481	0.9584	**0.9632**
yeast6	0.8280	0.8019	0.8664	0.8243	0.8501	0.7518	0.8475	0.8485	**0.8688**
Average	0.8076	0.8222	0.8536	0.8421	0.8554	0.8312	0.8606	0.8577	**0.8691**

Table 7.4 Wilcoxon test to compare the preprocessing techniques (RUS and SMOTE) $[R^+]$ against the ensemble-based models $[R^-]$ using the g-mean performance measure

Comparison		R^+	R^-	p-value	
RUS vs.	SMOTE	528.5	1682.5	0.00024	Rejected for SMOTE at 95%
	UnderBagging	9.0	2202.0	0.00000	Rejected for UnderBagging at 95%
	SMOTEBagging	99.0	2112.0	0.00000	Rejected for SMOTEBagging at 95%
	RUSBoost	7.0	2204.0	0.00000	Rejected for RUSBoost at 95%
	SMOTEBoost	645.5	1565.5	0.00338	Rejected for SMOTEBoost at 95%
	EUSBoost	12.0	2199.0	0.00000	Rejected for EUSBoost at 95%
	EasyEnsemble	15.5	2195.5	0.00000	Rejected for EasyEnsemble at 95%
	UnderBagging_RE	3.0	2208.0	0.00000	Rejected for UnderBagging_RE at 95%
SMOTE vs.	UnderBagging	260.5	1950.5	0.00000	Rejected for UnderBagging at 95%
	SMOTEBagging	211.0	2000.0	0.00000	Rejected for SMOTEBagging at 95%
	RUSBoost	222.5	1988.5	0.00000	Rejected for RUSBoost at 95%
	SMOTEBoost	838.5	1372.5	0.09370	Rejected for SMOTEBoost at 90%
	EUSBoost	109.5	2101.50	0.00000	Rejected for EUSBoost at 95%
	EasyEnsemble	78.5	2132.5	0.00000	Rejected for EasyEnsemble at 95%
	UnderBagging_RE	35.5	2175.5	0.00000	Rejected for UnderBagging_RE at 95%
RUS vs.	SMOTE	528.5	1682.5	0.00024	Rejected for SMOTE at 95%

In order to gain more insights into the results, we first perform a comparison between data-level methods and ensemble ones. In order to do so, we carry out a Wilcoxon test between each data-level method (RUS and SMOTE) and the ensemble models. These tests are presented in Table 7.4.

As it can be observed, all the tests are rejected with high confidence in favor of the corresponding ensemble method. Hence, it can be concluded that the usage of ensemble methods pays off although the increase in the complexity of the algorithms and the final models. We should also notice that we have included the comparison between RUS and SMOTE. The test is rejected in favor of SMOTE, which could be expected as SMOTE performs a more complex guided sampling than RUS, which can discard important information from the majority class. We should keep this result in mind because we will show how this result changes when these approaches are considered to build ensembles.

In the second part of this experimental study, we aim to compare the different ensemble approaches. Table 7.5 summarizes the overall g-mean performance of these approaches together with the results of the Friedman Aligned-ranks test and the corresponding Holm post-hoc test.

Focusing on the overall g-mean test and the final ranked position following aligned-ranks, one can observe that UnderBagging_RE is the best performing approach. EUSBoost is the second best performing algorithm, which is based on evolutionary undersampling in combination with Boosting. Then, all the methods based on RUS are the ones achieving the best performances: EasyEnsemble (Hybrid model using RUS), UnderBagging (RUS in Bagging) and RUSBoost (RUS in Boosting). Finally, the worst performing models are SMOTEBagging (SMOTE in

Table 7.5 Average results (g-mean), ranks (Friedman aligned test) and adjusted p-values (Holm test) for the comparison among ensemble-based methods. Control method is pointed out with asterisks in the Holm test column. Symbol * near the p-value implies significant differences at 95%, whereas symbol + sets the confidence degree at 90%

Ensemble model	g-mean in test	Ranking (Friedman aligned)	APV (Holm test)
UnderBagging	0.8536	231.83 (4)	0.00039*
SMOTEBagging	0.8421	247.30 (6)	0.00004*
RUSBoost	0.8554	240.99 (5)	0.00010*
SMOTEBoost	0.8312	316.35 (7)	0.00000*
EUSBoost	0.8606	215.17 (2)	0.00189*
EasyEnsemble	0.8577	225.92 (3)	0.00071*
UnderBagging_RE	**0.8691**	142.95 (1)	********

Bagging) and SMOTEBoost (SMOTE in Boosting). This ranking is remarkable in comparison with the result that we have previously analyzed were SMOTE was clearly outperforming RUS. However, when moving to ensemble where these approaches are used to create diversity and at the same time to balance the dataset, it seems that RUS is much more appropriate than SMOTE. This fact could be due to the greater diversity that RUS provides to the ensemble, since its totally random nature can benefit this aspect.

Anyway, we should also pay attention to the results of the statistical test. UnderBagging_RE is the control method as it achieves the larges number of ranks. It is interesting to observe that this method is capable of statistically outperforming all the other ones. This fact puts into perspective that the methods in Other family that we have reviewed in the previous section have really something to give to existing ensemble methods. Hence, using these kinds of models together with existing ensemble can make a difference. In this case, the only difference with respect to UnderBagging is that the ensemble has been pruned using an ordering-based method following an adapted measure that considers the g-mean. Regarding the rest of the ensemble methods, one can observe that all of them except for SMOTEBoost have a similar number of ranks and there may not be statistical differences among them.

7.5 Summarizing Contents

In this chapter, solutions based on the usage of ensembles of classifiers for class imbalance were presented and analyzed as a powerful and widely considered alternative to deal with imbalanced datasets. The existing models can be classified into three main categories: cost-sensitive approaches, data preprocessing-based ensembles and others. Although many methods have been proposed combining data preprocessing with ensemble learning techniques, recently, several methods that cannot be clearly classified into this category have emerged, as they consider more complex combinations.

According to the brief experimental study carried out there is no doubt about the superiority of ensemble-based models against simple data preprocessing algorithms. However, there are still challenges that require new ensemble solutions to further improve current approaches. Most of the research effort has gone to how to build diverse classifiers in this scenario, but few attempts have been made on how to improve the way the classifiers in the ensemble are combined: either considering dynamic ensemble selection models or advanced aggregation strategies.

References

1. Alcalá-Fdez, J., Sánchez, L., García, S., del Jesus, M.J., Ventura, S., Garrell, J.M., Otero, J., Romero, C., Bacardit, J., Rivas, V.M., Fernández, J., Herrera, F.: KEEL: a software tool to assess evolutionary algorithms for data mining problems. Soft Comput. **13**(3), 307–318 (2008)
2. Alcalá-Fdez, J., Fernández, A., Luengo, J., Derrac, J., García, S., Sánchez, L., Herrera, F.: KEEL data-mining software tool: data set repository, integration of algorithms and experimental analysis framework. J. Multiple-Valued Logic Soft Comput. **17**(2–3), 255–287 (2011)
3. Avnimelech, R., Intrator, N.: Boosted mixture of experts: an ensemble learning scheme. Neural Comput. **11**(2), 483–497 (1999)
4. Barandela, R., Valdovinos, R.M., Sánchez, J.S.: New applications of ensembles of classifiers. Pattern Anal. Appl. **6**, 245–256 (2003)
5. Batista, G.E.A.P.A., Prati, R.C., Monard, M.C.: A study of the behavior of several methods for balancing machine learning training data. SIGKDD Explor. Newsl. **6**, 20–29 (2004)
6. Batista, L., Granger, E., Sabourin, R.: Dynamic selection of generative-discriminative ensembles for off-line signature verification. Pattern Recogn. **45**(4), 1326–1340 (2012)
7. Bhowan, U., Johnston, M., Zhang, M., Yao, X.: Reusing genetic programming for ensemble selection in classification of unbalanced data. IEEE Trans. Evol. Comput. **18**(6), 893–908 (2014)
8. Blagus, R., Lusa, L.: Gradient boosting for high-dimensional prediction of rare events. Comput. Stat. Data Anal. **113**, 19–37 (2017)
9. Błaszczyński, J., Deckert, M., Stefanowski, J., Wilk, S.: Integrating selective pre-processing of imbalanced data with ivotes ensemble. In: Szczuka, M., Kryszkiewicz, M., Ramanna, S., Jensen, R., Hu, Q. (eds.) Rough Sets and Current Trends in Computing. LNSC, vol. 6086, pp. 148–157. Springer, Berlin/Heidelberg (2010)
10. Breiman, L.: Bagging predictors. Mach. Learn. **24**, 123–140 (1996)
11. Breiman, L.: Bias, variance, and arcing classifiers. Technical report, University of California Berkeley (1996)
12. Breiman, L.: Pasting small votes for classification in large databases and on-line. Mach. Learn. **36**, 85–103 (1999)
13. Breiman, L.: Random forests. Mach. Learn. **45**(1), 5–32 (2001)
14. Britto, A.S., Sabourin, R., Oliveira, L.E.: Dynamic selection of classifiers-a comprehensive review. Pattern Recogn. **47**(11), 3665–3680 (2014)
15. Brown, G., Wyatt, J., Harris, R., Yao, X.: Diversity creation methods: a survey and categorisation. Inf. Fusion **6**(1), 5–20 (2005). Diversity in Multiple Classifier Systems
16. Cao, C., Wang, Z.: IMCStacking: cost-sensitive stacking learning with feature inverse mapping for imbalanced problems. Know. Based Syst. **150**, 27–37 (2018)
17. Chan, P.K., Stolfo, S.J.: Toward scalable learning with non-uniform class and cost distributions: a case study in credit card fraud detection. In: Proceedings of the 4th International Conference on Knowledge Discovery and Data Mining (KDD-98), New York, pp. 164–168 (1998)

18. Chang, E., Li, B., Wu, G., Goh, K.: Statistical learning for effective visual information retrieval. In: Proceedings of the International Conference on Image Processing (ICIP 2003), Barcelona, vol. 3 (2), pp. 609–612 (2003)
19. Chawla, N.V., Bowyer, K.W., Hall, L.O., Kegelmeyer, W.P.: SMOTE: synthetic minority over-sampling technique. J. Artif. Intell. Res. **16**, 321–357 (2002)
20. Chawla, N.V., Lazarevic, A., Hall, L.O., Bowyer, K.W.: SMOTEBoost: improving prediction of the minority class in boosting. In: Knowledge Discovery in Databases (PKDD'03), pp. 107–119. Springer, Berlin/Heidelberg (2003)
21. Chawla, N. V., Japkowicz, N., Kotcz, A. (eds.): Special issue on learning from imbalanced data sets. ACM SIGKDD Explor. Newsl. **6**(1), 1–6 (2004)
22. Chawla, N., Cieslak, D., Hall, L., Joshi, A.: Automatically countering imbalance and its empirical relationship to cost. Data Min. Knowl. Disc. **17**, 225–252 (2008)
23. Chen, S., He, H., Garcia, E.A.: Ramoboost: ranked minority oversampling in boosting. IEEE Trans. Neural Netw. **21**(10), 1624–1642 (2010)
24. Collell, G., Prelec, D., Patil, K.R.: A simple plug-in bagging ensemble based on threshold-moving for classifying binary and multiclass imbalanced data. Neurocomputing **275**, 330–340 (2018)
25. Demšar, J.: Statistical comparisons of classifiers over multiple data sets. J. Mach. Learn. Res. **7**, 1–30 (2006)
26. Díez-Pastor, J.F., Rodríguez, J.J., García-Osorio, C., Kuncheva, L.I.: Random balance: ensembles of variable priors classifiers for imbalanced data. Know. Based Syst. **85**, 96–111 (2015)
27. Díez-Pastor, J.F., Rodríguez, J.J., García-Osorio, C.I., Kuncheva, L.I.: Diversity techniques improve the performance of the best imbalance learning ensembles. Inf. Sci. **325**, 98–117 (2015)
28. Dos Santos, E., Sabourin, R., Maupin, P.: A dynamic overproduce-and-choose strategy for the selection of classifier ensembles. Pattern Recogn. **41**(10), 2993–3009 (2008)
29. Drown, D., Khoshgoftaar, T., Seliya, N.: Evolutionary sampling and software quality modeling of high-assurance systems. IEEE Trans. Syst. Man Cybern. A Syst. Hum. **39**(5), 1097–1107 (2009)
30. Fan, W., Stolfo, S.J., Zhang, J., Chan, P.K.: Adacost: misclassification cost-sensitive boosting. In: Proceedings of the 6th International Conference on Machine Learning, ICML'99, San Francisco, pp. 97–105 (1999)
31. Freitas, A., Costa-Pereira, A., Brazdil, P.: Cost-sensitive decision trees applied to medical data. In: Song, I., Eder, J., Nguyen, T. (eds.) Data Warehousing and Knowledge Discovery. LNCS, vol. 4654, pp. 303–312. Springer, Berlin/Heidelberg (2007)
32. Freund, Y., Schapire, R.E.: A decision-theoretic generalization of on-line learning and an application to boosting. J. Comput. Syst. Sci. **55**(1), 119–139 (1997)
33. Friedman, J.H.: On bias, variance, 0/1-loss, and the curse-of-dimensionality. Data Min. Knowl. Disc. **1**, 55–77 (1997)
34. Friedman, J., Hastie, T., Tibshirani, R.: Additive logistic regression: a statistical view of boosting. Ann. Stat. **28**, 337–407 (1998)
35. Galar, M., Fernández, A., Barrenechea, E., Bustince, H., Herrera, F.: A review on ensembles for the class imbalance problem: bagging-, boosting-, and hybrid-based approaches. IEEE Trans. Syst. Man Cybern. C Appl. Rev. **42**(4), 463–484 (2012)
36. Galar, M., Fernández, A., Barrenechea, E., Herrera, F.: Eusboost: enhancing ensembles for highly imbalanced data-sets by evolutionary undersampling. Pattern Recogn. **46**(12), 3460–3471 (2013)
37. Galar, M., Fernández, A., Barrenechea, E., Bustince, H., Herrera, F.: Ordering-based pruning for improving the performance of ensembles of classifiers in the framework of imbalanced datasets. Inf. Sci. **354**, 178–196 (2016)
38. García, S., Herrera, F.: An extension on "statistical comparisons of classifiers over multiple data sets" for all pairwise comparisons. J. Mach. Learn. Res. **9**, 2677–2694 (2008)

39. García, S., Fernández, A., Herrera, F.: Enhancing the effectiveness and interpretability of decision tree and rule induction classifiers with evolutionary training set selection over imbalanced problems. Appl. Soft Comput. **9**(4), 1304–1314 (2009)
40. García, S., Fernández, A., Luengo, J., Herrera, F.: Advanced nonparametric tests for multiple comparisons in the design of experiments in computational intelligence and data mining: experimental analysis of power. Inf. Sci. **180**, 2044–2064 (2010)
41. García-Pedrajas, N., Maudes-Raedo, J., García-Osorio, C., Rodríguez-Díez, J.J.: Supervised subspace projections for constructing ensembles of classifiers. Inf. Sci. **193**, 1–21 (2012)
42. García-Pedrajas, N., García-Osorio, C.: Boosting for class-imbalanced datasets using genetically evolved supervised non-linear projections. Prog. Artif. Intell. **2**(1), 29–44 (2013)
43. Geman, S., Bienenstock, E., Doursat, R.: Neural networks and the bias/variance dilemma. Neural Comput. **4**, 1–58 (1992)
44. Gong, J., Kim, H.: RHSBoost: improving classification performance in imbalance data. Comput. Stat. Data Anal. **111**, 1–13 (2017)
45. Gónzalez, S., García, S., Lázaro, M., Figueiras-Vidal, A.R., Herrera, F.: Class switching according to nearest enemy distance for learning from highly imbalanced data-sets. Pattern Recogn. **70**, 12–24 (2017)
46. Gunes, V., Ménard, M., Loonis, P., Petit-Renaud, S.: Combination, cooperation and selection of classifiers: a state of the art. Int. J. Pattern Recogn. Artif. Intell. **17**(8), 1303–1324 (2003)
47. Guo, H., Viktor, H.L.: Learning from imbalanced data sets with boosting and data generation: the DataBoost-IM approach. SIGKDD Explor. Newsl. **6**, 30–39 (2004)
48. He, H., Bai, Y., Garcia, E.A., Li, S.: ADASYN: Adaptive synthetic sampling approach for imbalanced learning. In: 2008 IEEE International Joint Conference on Neural Networks (IEEE World Congress on Computational Intelligence), Hong Kong, pp. 1322–1328 (2008)
49. Hido, S., Kashima, H., Takahashi, Y.: Roughly balanced bagging for imbalanced data. Stat. Anal. Data Min. **2**, 412–426 (2009)
50. Ho, T.K.: The random subspace method for constructing decision forests. IEEE Trans. Pattern Anal. Mach. Intell. **20**(8), 832–844 (1998)
51. Ho, T.K.: Multiple classifier combination: lessons and next steps. In: Kandel, A., Bunke, H. (eds.) Hybrid Methods in Pattern Recognition, pp. 171–198. World Scientific, Singapore (2002)
52. Ho, T.K., Hull, J.J., Srihari, S.N.: Decision combination in multiple classifier systems. IEEE Trans. Pattern Anal. Mach. Intell. **16**(1), 66–75 (1994)
53. Hodges, J.L., Lehmann, E.L.: Rank methods for combination of independent experiments in analysis of variance. Ann. Math. Stat. **33**, 482–497 (1962)
54. Holm, S.: A simple sequentially rejective multiple test procedure. Scand. J. Stat. **6**, 65–70 (1979)
55. Hu, S., Liang, Y., Ma, L., He, Y.: MSMOTE: Improving classification performance when training data is imbalanced. In: 2nd International Workshop on Computer Science and Engineering (WCSE'09), Qingdao, vol. 2, pp. 13–17 (2009)
56. Iba, W., Langley, P.: Induction of one-level decision trees. In: Proceedings of the Ninth International Workshop on Machine Learning, ML'92, pp. 233–240. Morgan Kaufmann Publishers Inc., San Francisco (1992)
57. James, G.M.: Variance and bias for general loss functions. Mach. Learn. **51**, 115–135 (2003)
58. Joshi, M., Kumar, V., Agarwal, R.: Evaluating boosting algorithms to classify rare classes: comparison and improvements. In: Proceedings of the IEEE International Conference on Data Mining (ICDM 2001), San Jose, pp. 257–264 (2001)
59. Kittler, J., Hatef, M., Duin, R., Matas, J.: On combining classifiers. IEEE Trans. Pattern Anal. Mach. Intell. **20**(3), 226–239 (1998)
60. Ko, A., Sabourin, R., Britto, A., Jr.: From dynamic classifier selection to dynamic ensemble selection. Pattern Recogn. **41**(5), 1735–1748 (2008)
61. Kohavi, R., Wolpert, D.H.: Bias plus variance decomposition for zero-one loss functions. In: Proceedings of the 13th International Conference on Machine Learning, Bari (1996)

62. Kong, E.B., Dietterich, T.G.: Error-correcting output coding corrects bias and variance. In: Proceedings 12th International Conference on Machine Learning, Tahoe City, pp. 313–321 (1995)
63. Krawczyk, B., Schaefer, G.: An improved ensemble approach for imbalanced classification problems. In: 2013 IEEE 8th International Symposium on Applied Computational Intelligence and Informatics (SACI), Timisoara, pp. 423–426 (2013)
64. Krawczyk, B., Wozniak, M., Schaefer, G.: Cost-sensitive decision tree ensembles for effective imbalanced classification. Appl. Soft Comput. **14**, 554–562 (2014)
65. Krogh, A., Vedelsby, J.: Neural network ensembles, cross validation, and active learning. In: Advances in Neural Information Processing Systems, Denver, vol. 7, pp. 231–238 (1995)
66. Kuncheva, L.I.: Switching between selection and fusion in combining classifiers: an experiment. IEEE Trans. Syst. Man Cybern. B Cybern. **32**(2), 146–156 (2002)
67. Kuncheva, L.I.: Combining Pattern Classifiers: Methods and Algorithms. Wiley-Interscience, Hoboken (2004)
68. Kuncheva, L.I.: Diversity in multiple classifier systems. Inf. Fusion **6**(1), 3–4 (2005). Diversity in Multiple Classifier Systems
69. Kuncheva, L.I., Bezdek, J.C., Duin, R.P.W.: Decision templates for multiple classifier fusion: an experimental comparison. Pattern Recogn. **34**(2), 299–314 (2001)
70. Kuncheva, L., Whitaker, C., Shipp, C., Duin, R.: Limits on the majority vote accuracy in classifier fusion. Pattern Anal. Appl. **6**(1), 22–31 (2003)
71. Kuncheva, L.I., Rodriguez, J.J.: Classifier ensembles with a random linear oracle. IEEE Trans. Knowl. Data Eng. **19**(4), 500–508 (2007)
72. Lázaro, M., Herrera, F., Figueiras-Vidal, A.R.: Classification of binary imbalanced data using a bayesian ensemble of bayesian neural networks. In: Engineering Applications of Neural Networks, Communications in Computer and Information Science, pp. 304–314. Springer, Cham (2015). https://doi.org/10.1007/978-3-319-23983-5_28
73. Lee, W., Jun, C.H., Lee, J.S.: Instance categorization by support vector machines to adjust weights in AdaBoost for imbalanced data classification. Inf. Sci. **381**, 92–103 (2017)
74. Li, C.: Classifying imbalanced data using a bagging ensemble variation (BEV). In: Proceedings of the 45th Anual Southeast Regional Conference, ACM-SE 45, New York, pp. 203–208 (2007)
75. Li, K., Kong, X., Lu, Z., Wenyin, L., Yin, J.: Boosting weighted {ELM} for imbalanced learning. Neurocomputing **128**, 15–21 (2014)
76. Liu, R., Yuan, B.: Multiple classifiers combination by clustering and selection. Inf. Fusion **2**(3), 163–168 (2001)
77. Liu, X.Y., Wu, J., Zhou, Z.H.: Exploratory undersampling for class-imbalance learning. IEEE Trans. Syst. Man Cybern. B Cybern. **39**(2), 539–550 (2009)
78. López, V., Fernández, A., Herrera, F.: On the importance of the validation technique for classification with imbalanced datasets: addressing covariate shift when data is skewed. Inf. Sci. **257**, 1–13 (2014)
79. Lu, Y., Cheung, Y.M., Tang, Y.Y.: GOBoost: G-mean optimized boosting framework for class imbalance learning. In: 12th World Congress on Intelligent Control and Automation (WCICA), pp. 3149–3154 (2016)
80. Martínez-Munoz, G., Hernández-Lobato, D., Suárez, A.: An analysis of ensemble pruning techniques based on ordered aggregation. IEEE Trans. Pattern Anal. Mach. Intell. **31**(2), 245–259 (2009)
81. Maudes, J., Rodríguez, J.J., García-Osorio, C.: Disturbing neighbors diversity for decision forests. In: Okun, O., Valentini, G. (eds.) Applications of Supervised and Unsupervised Ensemble Methods, pp. 113–133. Springer, Berlin/Heidelberg (2009)
82. Maudes, J., Rodríguez, J.J., García-Osorio, C., García-Pedrajas, N.: Random feature weights for decision tree ensemble construction. Inf. Fusion **13**(1), 20–30 (2012)
83. Moreno-Torres, J.G., Raeder, T., Aláiz-Rodríguez, R., Chawla, N.V., Herrera, F.: A unifying view on dataset shift in classification. Pattern Recogn. **45**(1), 521–530 (2012)

84. Moreno-Torres, J.G., Sáez, J.A., Herrera, F.: Study on the impact of partition-induced dataset shift on k-fold cross-validation. IEEE Trans. Neural Netw. Learn. Syst **23**(8), 1304–1313 (2012)
85. Nanni, L., Franco, A.: Reduced reward-punishment editing for building ensembles of classifiers. Expert Syst. Appl. **38**(3), 2395–2400 (2011)
86. Nanni, L., Fantozzi, C., Lazzarini, N.: Coupling different methods for overcoming the class imbalance problem. Neurocomputing **158**, 48–61 (2015)
87. Oza, N.C., Tumer, K.: Classifier ensembles: select real-world applications. Inf. Fusion **9**(1), 4–20 (2008)
88. Park, Y., Ghosh, J.: Ensembles of ($alpha$)-trees for imbalanced classification problems. IEEE Trans. Knowl. Data Eng. **26**(1), 131–143 (2014)
89. Provost, F., Domingos, P.: Tree induction for probability-based ranking. Mach. Learn. **52**, 199–215 (2003)
90. Quinlan, J.R.: Improved estimates for the accuracy of small disjuncts. Mach. Learn. **6**, 93–98 (1991)
91. Quinlan, J.R.: C4.5: Programs for Machine Learning, 1st edn. Morgan Kaufmann Publishers, San Mateo (1993)
92. Rodriguez, J.J., Kuncheva, L.I., Alonso, C.J.: Rotation forest: a new classifier ensemble method. IEEE Trans. Pattern Anal. Mach. Intell. **28**(10), 1619–1630 (2006)
93. Rodríguez, J.J., Díez-Pastor, J.F., García-Osorio, C.: Random oracle ensembles for imbalanced data. In: Zhou, Z.H., Roli, F., Kittler, J. (eds.) Multiple Classifier Systems: 11th International Workshop, MCS 2013, Nanjing, 15–17 May 2013, Proceedings, pp. 247–258. Springer, Berlin/Heidelberg (2013)
94. Roy, A., Cruz, R.M.O., Sabourin, R., Cavalcanti, G.D.C.: A study on combining dynamic selection and data preprocessing for imbalance learning. Neurocomputing **286**, 179–192 (2018)
95. Rudin, C., Daubechies, I., Schapire, R.E.: The dynamics of adaboost: cyclic behavior and convergence of margins. J. Mach. Learn. Res. **5**, 1557–1595 (2004)
96. Schapire, R.E.: The strength of weak learnability. Mach. Learn. **5**, 197–227 (1990)
97. Schapire, R.E., Singer, Y.: Improved boosting algorithms using confidence-rated predictions. Mach. Learn. **37**, 297–336 (1999)
98. Schclar, A., Rokach, L.: Random projection ensemble classifiers. In: Filipe, J., Cordeiro, J. (eds.) Enterprise Information Systems: 11th International Conference, ICEIS 2009, Milan, 6–10 May 2009. Proceedings, pp. 309–316. Springer, Berlin/Heidelberg (2009)
99. Seiffert, C., Khoshgoftaar, T., Van Hulse, J., Napolitano, A.: Rusboost: a hybrid approach to alleviating class imbalance. IEEE Trans. Syst. Man Cybern. A Syst. Hum. **40**(1), 185–197 (2010)
100. Shin, H., Sohn, S.: Selected tree classifier combination based on both accuracy and error diversity. Pattern Recogn. **38**(2), 191–197 (2005)
101. Soleymani, R., Granger, E., Fumera, G.: Loss factors for learning boosting ensembles from imbalanced data. In: 23rd International Conference on Pattern Recognition (ICPR), Cancun, pp. 204–209 (2016)
102. Stefanowski, J., Wilk, S.: Selective pre-processing of imbalanced data for improving classification performance. In: Song, I.Y., Eder, J., Nguyen, T. (eds.) Data Warehousing and Knowledge Discovery. LNCS, vol. 5182, pp. 283–292. Springer, Berlin/Heidelberg (2008)
103. Su, C.T., Hsiao, Y.H.: An evaluation of the robustness of MTS for imbalanced data. IEEE Trans. Knowl. Data Eng. **19**(10), 1321–1332 (2007)
104. Sun, Y., Kamel, M.S., Wong, A.K., Wang, Y.: Cost-sensitive boosting for classification of imbalanced data. Pattern Recogn. **40**(12), 3358–3378 (2007)
105. Tahir, M.A., Kittler, J., Yan, F.: Inverse random under sampling for class imbalance problem and its application to multi-label classification. Pattern Recogn. **45**(10), 3738–3750 (2012)
106. Tao, D., Tang, X., Li, X., Wu, X.: Asymmetric bagging and random subspace for support vector machines-based relevance feedback in image retrieval. IEEE Trans. Pattern Anal. Mach. Intell. **28**(7), 1088–1099 (2006)

107. Tibshirani, R.: Bias, variance and prediction error for classification rules. Technical reports, Department of Statistic, University of Toronto (1996)
108. Ting, K.M.: A comparative study of cost-sensitive boosting algorithms. In: Proceedings of the 17th International Conference on Machine Learning (ICML'00), Stanford, pp. 983–990 (2000)
109. Ueda, N., Nakano, R.: Generalization error of ensemble estimators. In: IEEE International Conference on Neural Networks, Washington, DC, vol. 1, pp. 90–95 (1996)
110. Verikas, A., Lipnickas, A., Malmqvist, K., Bacauskiene, M., Gelzinis, A.: Soft combination of neural classifiers: a comparative study. Pattern Recogn. Lett. 20(4), 429–444 (1999)
111. Vluymans, S., Triguero, I., Cornelis, C., Saeys, Y.: Eprennid: an evolutionary prototype reduction based ensemble for nearest neighbor classification of imbalanced data. Neurocomputing 216, 596–610 (2016)
112. Wang, B.X., Japkowicz, N.: Boosting support vector machines for imbalanced data sets. Knowl. Inf. Syst. 25(1), 1–20 (2010)
113. Wang, S., Yao, X.: Diversity analysis on imbalanced data sets by using ensemble models. In: IEEE Symposium on Computational Intelligence and Data Mining (CIDM'09), Nashville, pp. 324–331 (2009)
114. Wang, S., Yao, X.: Multiclass imbalance problems: analysis and potential solutions. IEEE Trans. Syst. Man Cybern. B (Cybern.) 42(4), 1119–1130 (2012)
115. Wang, S., Yao, X.: Relationships between diversity of classification ensembles and single-class performance measures. IEEE Trans. Knowl. Data Eng. 25(1), 206–219 (2013)
116. Wei, H., Sun, B., Jing, M.: Balancedboost: a hybrid approach for real-time network traffic classification. In: 2014 23rd International Conference on Computer Communication and Networks (ICCCN), Shanghai, pp. 1–6 (2014)
117. Wilcoxon, F.: Individual comparisons by ranking methods. Biom. Bull. 1(6), 80–83 (1945)
118. Woloszynski, T., Kurzynski, M.: A probabilistic model of classifier competence for dynamic ensemble selection. Pattern Recogn. 44(10–11), 2656–2668 (2011)
119. Wolpert, D.H.: Stacked generalization. Neural Netw. 5(2), 241–260 (1992)
120. Woods, K., Philip Kegelmeyer, W., Bowyer, K.: Combination of multiple classifiers using local accuracy estimates. IEEE Trans. Pattern Anal. Mach. Intell. 19(4), 405–410 (1997)
121. Wozniak, M., Grana, M., Corchado, E.: A survey of multiple classifier systems as hybrid systems. Inf. Fusion 16, 3–17 (2014)
122. Wu, G., Chang, E.: KBA: kernel boundary alignment considering imbalanced data distribution. IEEE Trans. Knowl. Data Eng. 17(6), 786–795 (2005)
123. Wu, X., Kumar, V., Ross Quinlan, J., Ghosh, J., Yang, Q., Motoda, H., McLachlan, G.J., Ng, A., Liu, B., Yu, P.S., Zhou, Z.H., Steinbach, M., Hand, D.J., Steinberg, D.: Top 10 algorithms in data mining. Knowl. Inf. Syst. 14, 1–37 (2007)
124. Yan, R., Liu, Y., Jin, R., Hauptmann, A.: On predicting rare classes with SVM ensembles in scene classification. In: Proceedings of the IEEE International Conference on Acoustics, Speech, and Signal Processing (ICASSP'03), Hong Kong, vol. 3, pp. 21–4 (2003)
125. Yule, G.: On the association of attributes in statistics. Philos. Trans. A 194, 257–319 (1900)
126. Zadrozny, B., Elkan, C.: Learning and making decisions when costs and probabilities are both unknown. In: Proceedings of the 7th ACM SIGKDD Internaional Conference on Knowledge Discovery and Data Mining, KDD'01, New York, pp. 204–213 (2001)
127. Zieba, M., Tomczak, J.M.: Boosted SVM with active learning strategy for imbalanced data. Soft Comput. 19(12), 3357–3368 (2015)

Chapter 8
Imbalanced Classification with Multiple Classes

Abstract Dealing with multi-class problems is a hard issue, which becomes more severe in the presence of imbalance. When facing multi-majority and multi-minority classes, it is not straightforward to acknowledge a priori which ones should be stressed during the learning stage, as it was done in the binary case study. Additionally, most of the techniques proposed for binary imbalanced classification are not directly applicable for multiple classes. To analyze in detail all these issues, the chapter is structured as follows. First, Sect. 8.1 introduces the general characteristics on multi-class imbalanced classification. Section 8.2 describes decomposition based approaches and how standard preprocessing techniques can be directly applied. Then, Sect. 8.3 presents the ad-hoc approaches for both preprocessing and classification methods. The performance metrics employed in the context of multi-class imbalanced problems are enumerated in Sect. 8.4. Next, a brief experimental study to contrast some of the state-of-the-art and promising approaches in this area is carried out in Sect. 8.5. Finally, the concluding remarks are given in Sect. 8.6.

8.1 Introduction

The topic of imbalanced classification has been traditionally related to binary datasets [9, 47, 67, 78, 92] Specifically, it is common to refer to a minority or "positive" class, and a majority or "negative" class. Therefore, most of the research carried out in this topic has been focused to stress the recognition of the less represented class.

However, in several real applications practitioners must deal with more than two classes. Some clear examples are microarray research [105], protein classification [112], medical diagnosis [16], activity recognition [41], target detection [83] and video mining [42]. All these problems have one thing in common: the distribution of examples among the classes is not homogeneous.

In this sense, we must refer to the extension of the imbalanced classification problem to the multi-class scenario [27, 45, 55] And as the number of classes increases, so does the challenges of representing the whole problem space accurately. In a general case study we must refer to the restriction for the larger

© Springer Nature Switzerland AG 2018
A. Fernández et al., *Learning from Imbalanced Data Sets*,
https://doi.org/10.1007/978-3-319-98074-4_8

number of boundaries to consider. But concretely in the imbalanced scenario, the most significant issue that must be taken into account is the presence of multi-minority and multi-majority classes [98]. This implies that is no longer possible to focus on just a single class to reinforce the learning models towards it. But this is not the only difficulty when addressing multiple class imbalanced datasets. All data intrinsic characteristics that caused a performance degradation in the binary case [67, 90], are now further accentuated. Among others, the dependency among classes (including overlapping) and relations between same-class examples must be analyzed in depth [94].

These facts arise a simple yet significant question: how can multi-class imbalanced datasets be properly addressed? However, there is not a simple answer to that. We must face the challenge to extend standard solutions designed for binary-class to be applied in this scenario. On the one hand, data level solutions (preprocessing) are not directly applicable as the search space is increased, i.e. to determine the proper sampling rate for each class [30]. On the other hand, algorithmic level solutions become more complicated since there can be more than one minority class [113].

To address all these issues, we must stress one simple, yet effective way to maintain traditional binary-class imbalanced approaches to be applied in multi-class problems: by means of decomposition strategies [35]. Specifically, original datasets are divided into binary ones following the divide-and-conquer paradigm. As a result, a set of classifiers must be learned, each one being responsible for one of the novel binary problems. In the testing phase, the outputs of all the classifiers for a given instance are aggregated to make the final decision [58]. Therefore, the difficulty in addressing the multi-class problem is shifted from the classifier itself to the combination stage.

Among decomposition strategies, the most popular techniques are the One-vs-One (OVO) [46, 53] and One-vs-All (OVA) [5, 18] schemes. The former approach divides the original problem in as many pairs of classes as possible, ignoring the examples that do not belong to the related classes. Then, these are learned in an independent way by the so called base learners or base classifiers of the ensemble [33]. The latter takes one class as "positive" and the joint of the remaining ones as "negative". Therefore, there are as many classifiers as classes, one of each devoted to recognize a single class.

Class decomposition is not the only option in this case. There are many ad-hoc approaches that are also able to learn directly from the entire dataset. These type of methods thus consider the class distribution globally in the search of a more robust modeling, both from the perspective of preprocessing [1] and algorithmic modification [100]. Another possibility is incorporating misclassification costs as a general cost-sensitive learning scheme [91].

In addition to the structural modifications in the approaches' design, the validation of the results must be also adapted in the context of multi-class imbalanced datasets. In this sense, general metrics of performance must be applied to guarantee a good sensitivity for all represented classes [89]. Therefore, and following a similar strategy than for the learning scheme, we must focus on both ad-hoc measures and aggregation of binary ones, particularly via micro- and macro-averages [31].

8.2   Multi-class Imbalanced Learning via Decomposition-Based Approaches

An intuitive approach for handling multi-class imbalanced datasets is to apply a decomposition strategy [35]. When the original problem is reduced to a set of two-class subsets, then it can be directly solved by one of existing techniques for the binary imbalanced scenario, such as those already described in previous chapters.

In this section, the different decomposition strategies for multi-class problems, namely OVO and OVA, will be first introduced (Sect. 8.2.1). Then, some representative examples of research works that have applied this methodology will be presented (Sect. 8.2.2). Finally, a brief discussion on both the advantages and future directions in this field of research will be provided (Sect. 8.2.3).

8.2.1   Reducing Multi-class Problems by Binarization Techniques

Many proposals have been developed under the label of binarization for multi-classification [35]. The underlying idea is to undertake the multi-classification using binary classifiers with a divide and conquer strategy. Binary problems are simpler to solve than the original multicategory problem. However, drawbacks exist, as the outputs from each new classifier have to be combined in order to make the final decision of the predicted class. Hence, a correct management of the outputs is crucial to produce a correct prediction.

The most common decomposition strategies include OVO [33] and OVA [85]. Below, we describe the main characteristics of both approaches.

8.2.1.1   The One-vs-One Scheme (OVO)

In the OVO strategy, an m-class problem is divided into $m(m-1)/2$ two-class problems (one for each possible pair of classes). Each binary classification sub-problem is face up by a different classifier. The learning phase is thus carried out using a subset of the original training instances considering only those that contain any of the two classes considered, whereas the instances with different class labels are simply ignored. This methodology is illustrated in Fig. 8.1.

In validation phase, a pattern is presented to each one of the binary classifiers. An easy way of organizing the outputs of these base classifiers for an instance is by means of a score-matrix R^M, from which different combination models can be applied:

$$R^M = \begin{pmatrix} - & r_{12} & \cdots & r_{1m} \\ r_{21} & - & \cdots & r_{2m} \\ \vdots & & & \vdots \\ r_{m1} & r_{m2} & \cdots & - \end{pmatrix} \tag{8.1}$$

Fig. 8.1 Example of the
OVO binarization technique
for a 3-class problem

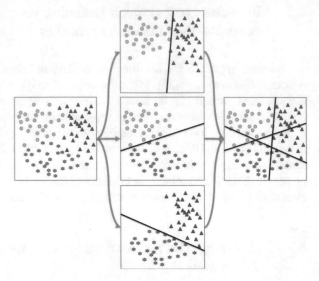

where $r_{ij} \in [0, 1]$ represents the confidence of the classifier discriminating classes
i and j in favor of the former; whereas the confidence for the latter is computed by
$r_{ji} = 1 - r_{ij}$ (if the classifier does not provide it[1]).

The final output of the system is derived from the score matrix by different
aggregation models. The weighted voting strategy is the widest used strategy, where
confidences are aggregated class by class (by rows) and the one with the largest sum
of confidences is predicted.

8.2.1.2   The One-vs-All Scheme (OVA)

OVA decomposition divide an m class problem into m binary problems. Each
problem is face up by a binary classifier which is responsible of distinguishing one
of the classes from all other classes. The learning step of the classifiers is done using
the whole training data, considering the patterns from the single class as positives
and all other examples as negatives. This methodology is illustrated in Fig. 8.2.

In validation phase, a pattern is presented to each one of the binary classifiers
and then, the classifier which gives a positive output indicates the output class. In
many cases, the positive output is not unique and some tie-breaking techniques are
required. The most common approach uses the confidence of the classifiers to decide
the final output, predicting the class from the classifier with the largest confidence.
Instead of having a score matrix, when dealing with the outputs of OVA classifiers
(where $r_i \in [0, 1]$ is the confidence for class i) a score vector R^V is used:

---

[1]If the classifier provides both confidence degrees, one must ensure that they are normalized such
that $r_{ij} + r_{ji} = 1$.

Fig. 8.2 Example of the
OVA binarization technique
for a 3-class problem

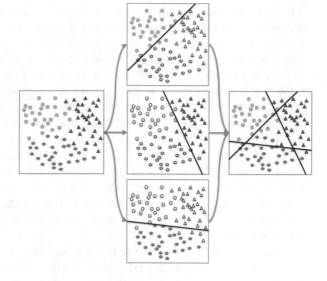

$$R^V = (r_1, r_2, \ldots, r_i, \ldots, r_m) \qquad (8.2)$$

As in the case of OVO decomposition, the most straightforward approach to determine the final output label is by considering the index with the maximum value from the score vector R^V.

8.2.2 Binary Imbalanced Approaches for Multi-class Problems

As we have stressed previously, binarization techniques are very useful in overcoming the gap between two-class and multi-class imbalanced datasets. In particular, they make it possible to apply any of the standard solutions, particularly those that rebalance the training set.

One of the most representative research works in this context, can be found in [27]. In this paper, authors made use of both OVO and OVA in conjunction with well-known preprocessing techniques for both over- and under-sampling, as well as a weighting procedure for cost-sensitive learning. By means of a thorough experimental study they analyzed which binarization is more appropriate for imbalanced classification. Then, they compared all possible combinations with the imbalanced technique in order to determine the best synergy between strategies. As baseline classifiers, they selected algorithms based on different paradigms; namely, decision trees, SVMs and instance-based learning, with aims at providing a better generalization. Using a strong validation procedure, results shown that OVO and oversampling was the most robust approach overall.

In [63], authors presented a similar study but focusing on the problem of weld-flaws classification. They investigated the behavior of several distance-based classification algorithms in conjunction with different preprocessing techniques, namely undersampling, oversampling, and hybrid approaches. To cope with multiple classes, they applied the OVA scheme, considering that some of the classes of the problem contained less than 10 examples. They found out that nearest-neighbors classifiers are well suited for this task, especially the 1-NN classifier with agglomerative hierarchical clustering based preprocessing [19].

A cost-sensitive ANN approach embedded into OVO learning scheme was introduced in [54]. The rationale to use such a decomposition scheme is based on the findings made in [27]. Regarding the inner procedure, the cost is computed based on the Receiver Operating Characteristic (ROC) curve analysis [113], moving the threshold seeking the best ration between the True Positive rate and False Positive rate. As stated previously, estimates of the cost matrix were obtained for each class pair independently.

Among different solutions for addressing the binary-class imbalanced problem, ensemble learning approaches have also to be excelled [36]. However, as in the case of standard preprocessing mechanisms and algorithmic approaches, the most well-known ensembles for imbalanced classification are limited to the binary case study. Taking this issue into account, authors from [110] developed a complete experimental analysis to contrast the performance of different ensemble techniques from the state-of-the-art [36], when embedded into an OVO learning workflow. To check the flexibility of the proposed approach we have tested it with three different base classifiers from the field of rule learning, ANNs and SVMs. They stressed the goodness of three ensemble techniques, namely Easy-Ensemble [66], SMOTE-Bagging [99] and RUS-Boost [87], for empowering OVO techniques in multi-class imbalance scenarios. Apart from the discovery of this positive synergy, this research opened the way for interesting future work, both regarding the aggregation mechanisms (for both OVO and ensembles), and the building of the ensembles.

Other authors have also combined decomposition techniques with ensemble learning. For example, in [112] a hybrid sampling technique is proposed as a committee of classifiers for the biological problem of protein identification. First, the OVA scheme is considered to focus on each class separately. Then, if the subset of data contains a high degree of imbalance (IR), a preprocessing stage that combines both over- and undersampling balanced the input instances. Finally, to carry out the learning of the classifiers, three different sub-feature spaces are considered via feature extraction process. Finally, a majority vote is applied during the testing phase to the different classifiers in the ensemble.

A similar idea can be found in [88]. Following also the OVA scheme, the training set is divided into as many subsets as number of classes. Then, for each class, the classifier is built iteration by iteration focusing on the hardest instances, thus following a boosting mechanism [32], to overcome somehow the class-imbalance that is created when contrasting one class versus the rest. To emphasize the recognition of misclassified instances, a resampling procedure is applied to add multiple copies of such data, i.e. increasing their weight. In addition to the former, the SMOTE oversampling technique is also considered on the misclassified data for including more information to problem space. However, the use of SMOTE is only taken into account after several iterations of the process, for the sake of avoiding overfitting. The efficacy of this novel framework was shown by extensive simulations conducted using different base classifiers.

Focusing on the OVO learning scheme itself, several approaches have been designed with aims at empowering the recognition of the most difficult classes. In particular, some authors pointed out that standard aggregation procedures have a bias towards "easily separable" classes, i.e. the confidence degrees for those instances belonging to that classes are likely to be much higher than that of the remaining ones [39]. In the aforementioned work, authors propose a new aggregation model based on similarity measures, in particular via Restricted Equivalence Functions (REF) [10]. REFs enables the modification of the decision boundaries of the base classifiers, thus boosting the values in the score matrix without changing the underlying base classifiers. Parameters of the REFs are optimized via a genetic procedure in order to adapt them in favor of the difficult classes.

A recent work also considers a smart adaptation of the aggregation step for improving the global recognition of all classes represented in the problem [96]. The premise is that each OVO classifier loses some information by reducing the dataset to two classes. This loss is somehow counteracted by aggregating the local scores over all classifiers to obtain a final prediction. However, to improve the enhance the recognition ability of the system, some global summary information should also be included. Specifically, for a test instance the summary terms evaluate its global affinity with all candidate classes. As these values are computed following fuzzy rough set theory, this aggregation scheme is called Weighted Voting with Fuzzy ROugh Summary Terms or WV-FROST for short, whereas the whole methodology was named as FROVOCO.

A work that combined cost-sensitive learning with OVO decomposition can be found in [111]. Specifically, authors make use of a Cost-Sensitive Back-Propagation Neural Network (CSBPNN) [113], which in contrast to over-sampling and under-sampling to change the training data distribution, is based on the threshold-moving method to alter the output of different nodes in the final layer of the network. The goodness of the binarization procedure was tested throughout a complete experimental study, in particular due to the higher quality of sophisticated aggregation approaches when combining the outputs of the binary CSBPNN classifiers.

A multi-model method for multiclass cost-sensitive classification was proposed in [7]. It is based on a previous approach for binary datasets named as ROC front [13]. The method carries out a multi-objective optimization strategy that considers both kinds of classification errors (false positive and false negative) as objectives,in order to build a Pareto-optimal pool of classifiers. During the decision stage, the best classifier can be selected according to the environment using iso-performance lines. Due to the constraints in the multi-class context, two extensions were developed. On the first hand, a OVO pairwise decomposition is used to transform the original problem and thus to apply the computation of the misclassification costs. On the other hand, several classifiers are related to the same pair of classes, i.e. for each ROC point. This fact suppose a complication for determining the best combination of pairwise classifiers among the different possibilities. To solve this problem, first, a greedy algorithm is used for sequentially choosing the classifiers of each ROC front, according to their decreasing AUC. All the ROC Front classifiers are evaluated through their multiclass performance when combined with other pairwise classifiers. For sub-problems that have already been processed, the retained classifier is taken into account in the combination, whereas for remaining sub-problems (with a greater AUC),the default classifier is used for combination. For a more detailed description of this process, reader may refer to [7].

Finally, we must refer to an alternative to address the multi-class problem as suggested in [12]. In this research, authors focused on associative based classifiers, whose rules are mined according to both their support (noted as frequency) and confidence (correct coverage). The bias towards majority classes in such scenario is clear. When considering the OVA decomposition scheme, a further degradation on the performance is caused by the union of many instances into a single "negative" class. In OVO, conflicting rules may appear for different pair of classes. For this reason, authors define the OVE (One-Versus-Each) framework. It follows a similar procedure than in OVA, i.e. focusing on one-class for the rule generation, but instead of joining instances as a single negative class, the frequency of the rule is computed independently for each class. Then, frequencies are compared with a parameter matrix that contains both the "positive" frequency threshold and the "infrequency" ones. If the rule values are within the appropriate ranges, it is stored in the final model. In order to achieve the best performance, the parameter matrix is computed via an optimization method.

8.2.3   Discussion on the Capabilities of Decomposition Strategies

In this part of the chapter we have reviewed some of the most significant approaches to deal with multi-class imbalanced problems via class decomposition. We have stressed two different strategies to be taken into account: OVO and OVA.

OVA is one of the widest used schemes not only in this context, but for binarization purposes in general. This popularity is probably due to several factors. First, its simplicity in its working procedure, i.e. it requires less decomposition and a direct aggregation mechanism. This issue also affects the efficiency of the learning stage, especially in the case of a high number of classes. Finally, since all classifiers are trained with the complete dataset, they provide a robust output confidence degree.

In spite of these good capabilities of OVA, it comprises one great drawback for the classification of imbalanced datasets: extremely uneven distributions may appear when contrasting the less represented classes versus the rest. In addition to the former, some of the data-level difficulties that degrade the performance, such as overlapping or class noise [67] are still present in the training set.

For this reason, OVO strategy is recommended be applied in the event of skewed class distributions. The most significant advantage in this case is the simplification of the boundary areas of the problem, as shown in Fig. 8.1. This way, those aforementioned intrinsic data characteristics, especially overlapping, can be properly addressed. Furthermore, the required time for the training can be even lower than in the case of OVA as fewer examples are considered for each binary classifier.

However, we must state that the goodness in training the classifiers by pairs of classes can be also be a disadvantage. In testing phase, every new pattern is submitted to all binary classifiers. However, we must be aware that some of them have been trained with a subset of data that did not contain any instance with the actual class label. Therefore, the output given by these classifiers cannot be relevant to the final prediction, leading to what has been defined as the *non-competent* examples problem [34, 51]. Usually, OVO aggregations suppose that the base classifiers will do a correct prediction in the cases where the new pattern is one of the considered pair of classes, and therefore considering a voting strategy, the class with the largest number of votes would be the correct class. However, the assumption about the base classifiers is not always fulfilled and the global performance can be hindered.

Fortunately, several authors have proposed different solutions to overcome this undesirable situation [29, 37, 40, 96]. The basis of all these methods is common: to take into account not only the confidence degrees of the score-matrix during the decision stage, but also to compute the "competence" of the confidence degrees that are given for the aggregation. To do so, the most straightforward approach is to measure the similarity of the query instance to each of the classes, and then to weight the former score values.

In addition to the former, it seems worthwhile to design new fusion approaches suitable for cases with skewed distributions. This way it may be possible to compensate for the imbalance both on decomposed class level and on final output combination level.

Another possible improvement in this framework is to utilize a different approach for each pair of classes, leading to a more flexible learning. All solutions reviewed in this Section are quite naive in this sense, as they not comprise that pairwise relationships may vary. Calculating the cost penalties or oversampling ratios individually for each pairs is a good starting direction, but the true challenge lies in proposing a framework that will be able to select specific data or algorithm-level solution on the basis of subproblem characteristics [69].

In addition to the standard OVO and OVA decomposition strategies, more sophisticated binarization techniques can seen as a promising direction. In particular, we may refer a broader framework known as Error Correcting Output Codes (ECOC) [4, 23]. In this context, aggregation of classes are given within a "code-matrix"; then, the final output is obtained by decoding the code word given by the outputs of the classifiers for a new input pattern. The challenge in this case is to found an automatic designing of this code-matrix [43, 80], and using different error correcting codes [72, 75]. The final goal is being able to build hierarchical methods by aggregating classes according to their similarities or dissimilarities. Then, as suggested throughout this section any solution must be taken into account to alleviate the uneven class distribution at each level. Finally, using a sequential, step-wise approach will allow to determine the final class. Alternatively, decomposition with one-class classifiers can be considered, as they are robust to class imbalance and can serve as an efficient tool for dealing with difficult multi-class datasets [57].

8.3 Ad-hoc Approaches for Multi-class Imbalanced Classification

In previous sections, we have stressed the excellent properties of applying a decomposition strategy for addressing multi-class imbalanced datasets. However, the global outlook on the problem space is somehow rejected. In other words, pairwise relations may be a too strong over-simplification, hiding some complex relations among the classes.

For this reason, some researchers have focused on a general perspective with aims at finding specific solutions, rather than adapting standard ones to the multi-class context. In this section, we present an overview of those ad-hoc approaches for multi-class imbalanced classification, both on preprocessing (Sect. 8.3.1), algorithmic modifications (Sect. 8.3.2), cost-sensitive learning (Sect. 8.3.3) and ensemble methodologies (Sect. 8.3.4). Finally, we carry out a short discussion on those findings extracted throughout this part of the chapter (Sect. 8.3.5).

8.3.1 Multi-class Preprocessing Techniques

The majority of the proposals for rebalancing the training set are focused on the binary problem. As reported in Sect. 8.2, most of these cannot be directly extended to the multi-class case study, mainly due to the multi-majority and multi-minority examples. There are some exceptions, such as the random oversampling and random undersampling, from which all examples are iteratively replicated or removed (in each case) until the class distribution is completely balanced.

A more sophisticated approach, but following similar guidelines, is the Static-SMOTE resampling procedure [28]. As its name suggests, it is based on the well-known SMOTE algorithm [14], which generates new synthetic data based on the neighborhood instances of the same class. To cope with the multi-class problem, the procedure is applied in M steps, being M the number of classes in the dataset. In each iteration, the class with the lower number of instances is selected, and it is oversampled at 100%, i.e. examples are duplicated. It is possible that the same class is selected in different iterations. In such case, only the original instances are considered for generating synthetic data.

Different from SMOTE related techniques, the MDO was proposed in [1]. As already explained in Chap. 5, the core idea of this approach is to not generate synthetic minority instances at random, but rather to guarantee that an artificial instance has the same Mahalanobis distance [70] to its class mean as the seed element from which it was constructed. By considering this restriction, synthetic samples are expected to be placed in dense areas of the minority class regions. In this sense, MDO may reduce the risk of overlapping among different classes. In this sense, it also aims at avoiding the possible over-generalization that is present in other over-sampling techniques. In the context of multiple classes, the MDO procedure is iterated class by class considering a complete balanced output, i.e. the number of new generated instances is equal to $n_{maj} - n_i$ where the former stands for the number of instances of the majority class and the latter for the number of instances of the current class.

Finally, we must refer to the research made in [94], where authors analyze the effect of oversampling techniques in multi-class problems focusing on different types of instances, namely safe, borderline, rare, and outliers. This categorization was first defined in [74], where the neighborhood of the instances is considered. Safe examples are those surrounded by those of the same class, whereas borderline are close-by to a similar ratio of different class examples. The last two groups of examples were used to characterized those ones in homogeneous areas belonging to a different classes. The main difference between rare and outlier examples is that the former are located within a small cluster of examples, where the latter are isolated.

Experimental results obtained in this work [94] showed that the oversampling of some classes and examples may cause either an improvement or a deterioration of the performance depending on their characteristics, instead of indiscriminately preprocessing all the classes. In general terms, the best configurations found by the authors were characterized by not preprocessing safe examples, although the magnitude of their presence may affect the preprocessing of other types of examples. For borderline examples, preprocessing should be always carried out. Applying oversampling on outliers depends on whether the safe examples are representative enough within the core of the class: if the amount of safe examples is rather low, preprocessing outliers is usually a good alternative. Finally, preprocessing of rare examples mainly depends on the amounts of safe examples and outliers. If both quantities are similar enough (either higher or lower) their preprocessing can be recommended.

8.3.2   Algorithmic Solutions on Multi-class

Several authors have focused on adapting the core procedure of the learning algorithms in order to design skew-insensitive approaches. For example, in decision trees a Hellinger distance modification were proposed in [17]. By means a thorough experimental analysis, authors show the good properties of the Hellinger distance in imbalanced domains over popular alternatives such as entropy (gain ratio). In order to adapt the binary Hellinger distance to multi-class problems, all possible pairs are considered, similar to the OVO decomposition scheme. Finally, authors suggested the use of such Hellinger distance decision trees as ensemble of classifiers.

There are also some proposals that generalize learning algorithms into multi-class cases with SVMs. The reason for not considering these approach within Sect. 8.2 (a simple adaptation in decomposition scheme) is because of the mandatory use of binarization in these cases, due to nature of SVMs. For example, a model based on Support Vector Data Description (SVDD) [95] (initially designed for outlier detection) and binary trees (BTs) was proposed in [24]. To determine the structure of the BTs the Mahalanobis distance was applied as separability measure to consider both the distance between each dataset and imbalanced degree (which can be used to calculate the separability degree among different datasets). Then, a different classifier was built by describing the boundary of the target via SVDD.

In [21] we may found a new variant named as Near-Bayesian SVMs (NBSVMs). It focus on minimizing the asymmetric-cost scaled Bayes error. Being based on SVMs, this was achieved by combining decision boundary shifting within the margin with cost-sensitivity. While the shifting is expected to achieve better inductive performance, even for training datasets that are linearly separable; the unequal regularization penalties (higher penalty for minority class) are expected to ensure that the shift does not result in undue misclassification of the minority class. NBSVM is extended to the inherently imbalanced OVA approach for multi-class classification and also to cases where the two classes have different misclassification costs.

In the context of ANNs, a learning paradigm that has gained much attention for both standard and imbalanced classification is Extreme Learning Machines (ELMs) [50]. However, the decision boundary of ELM tends to be pushed towards the region of the minority class [115]. A thorough study for the causes and factor that influence this behavior in ELMs is carried out in [106]. In addition, authors propose an optimal decision output compensation-based ELM (ODOC-ELM) for improving the recognition of the minority class examples. To do so, the geometric mean is used to determine the proper decision boundary, representing it as an optimization problem. In the case of multiple minority classes, the space turns in to a multi-variate one, so that a Particle Swarm Optimization [52] is applied for the task.

Following the ideas from boosting [32], dynamic sampling approaches can be regarded as a mixture of preprocessing and algorithmic adaptation. They are based on the integration between preprocessing process (either sampling or cost matrix setting) and training process. This way, several drawbacks can be avoided, such as excessive training times and/or overfitting due to oversampling, loss of information due to undersampling, and misleading costs that can affect the learning stage. One good example of a dynamic sampling approach can be found at [64]. In this research paper, authors make use of Multilayer perceptrons (MLPs) due to a twofold reason: it can be directly used for multi-class problems, and the sequential training model based in epochs allows the application of the aforementioned approach. To avoid the initial bias of the majority class instances, the training set is completely balanced by random oversampling prior learning. Then, a heuristic mechanism was proposed to determine whether a training example should be learned (i.e., be used to update the weights of an MLP) in a training epoch. To determine its value, an a combination between the class ratio (minority classes should be stressed) and the current error of the MLP (difficult examples are "boosted") is taken into account.

A very similar approach was developed in [3], where proposed a dynamic method that allows the efficient use of oversampling strategy on severe multi-class imbalanced problems. In this particular case, the method is based on the back-propagation mean square error (MSE) for automatically identifying the oversampling rate for the SMOTE technique. To achieve this goal, the class ratios are first computed as the fraction between the number of examples of a class and the majority one. These values will be used as a probability threshold for the selection of the examples as inputs to the ANN. Then, the training set is balanced applying SMOTE class by class to reach a 1:1 ratio for all classes. Finally, the ANN is trained selecting examples at random depending on the initial computed class ratios, following the same scheme than in [64]. When a epoch is finished, class ratios (probability thresholds) are updated according to the MSE obtained for each class. Their values are increased when the error in a given class is higher than for the majority class.

8.3.3   Multi-class Cost-Sensitive Learning

The use of a cost-matrix to guide the learning is a straightforward option to force the modeling of minority class instances by providing them a higher penalty value. However, as it happened with resampling strategies, while determining an optimal value in the binary context can be difficult, the case study with multiple classes impose higher constraints.

A trivial solution to this issue was first given in [114]. Specifically, authors applied a instance weighting mechanism. To allow each class to become equally important, a factor of N_i / N_{max} was considered, being N_i the number of examples of the i-th class and N_{max} the number of examples for the majority class of the problem. The robustness of this approach was tested in the thorough experimental study made in [27].

Following a different perspective for approaching the problem, authors from [2] proposed a data expansion technique taking into account different costs associated with several ways to misclassify examples. Specifically, each training example is map in K new examples, each for a given class represented in the initial problem. With a given weight assigned to each of these examples, there are more degrees of freedom to obtain all the misclassification costs for the original instance.

A similar approach can be found in [104], where authors not only considered the influence of cost on labels, but their reduction further computed the influence of cost on features. In addition, the cost-sensitive learning problem was reduced to a standard classification one. By operating on the cost matrix, authors derived well-behaved reductions to simplify the previous translation, helping to gain understanding of the nature of cost-sensitive multi-class classification.

Finally, with aims at obtaining a robust cost matrix for the training of Deep Belief Networks [49] in imbalanced problems, the proposal in [109] used a differential evolution algorithm [81], where each individual represented a different cost matrix. Although the experimental validation is carried out only in binary problems, this algorithm can be easily extended to the multi-class case study.

8.3.4 Ensemble Approaches

Ensemble-based classifiers, also known as multiple classifier systems [76] of classifiers have excelled as a powerful solution for both standard [103] and imbalanced classification [36], as it was pointed out already in Chap. 7. This fact implies their spread use also for multi-class problems.

Whereas boosting algorithms were initially designed for binary classification, these can be easily extended to multi-class problems following the AdaBoost.M1 generalization first presented in [32]. Among different cost-sensitive ensemble classifiers for imbalanced problems, authors from [91] selected the weighting strategy of AdaC2 algorithm to obtain the AdaC2.M1 ensemble methodology. Finally, in order to determine the cost setups to be applied, a Genetic Algorithm was used.

A very relevant algorithm also based in AdaBoost is AdaBoost.NC. The binary version of this method was proposed in [97] and incorporates negative correlation learning. It is based on the AdaBoost algorithm and extends it by introducing diversity between the constructed classifiers. The instance weights are not solely used to better recognize misclassified elements in later iterations, but also to enhance the diversity. The methodology was extended to handle more than two classes in [101]. In their study, authors noted that the application of random oversampling is required to improve the recognition of minority instances. To avoid increasing the training time, we incorporate this instruction by a modified initialization of the ensemble weights, in order to give a higher significance to smaller classes.

In spite most of the solutions for the class imbalance problems aims at rebalance or weight the training instances, a quite different scheme was proposed in [44]. Specifically, and following the suggestions made in [56], a parallel FS is applied. The removal of irrelevant and/or redundant features may allow to diminish the noise in the input data, especially for the minority class instances. This way, a conjunction between Adaboost and a wrapper FS is applied using KNN as the baseline classifier, being the complete methodology named as BPSO-Adaboost-KNN. To adapt this procedure to the multi-class problem, authors considered a novel AUC metric known as AUCarea [44].

Same authors from BPSO-Adaboost-KNN propose an Adaptive Multiple Classifier System [62]. This classification algorithm is composed of three different ensemble learning algorithms, namely AdaBoost.M1 [32], Under-Sampling Balanced Ensemble [56, 93] and Over-Sampling Balanced Ensemble (SMOTEBoost) [15]. For the latter algorithms, different aggregation rules are considered. Finally, and following the findings extracted in the authors' previous work [44], an FS is applied to address the possible noise present in the dataset. In order to select the most appropriate synergy of methodologies for the final classification, imbalanced data is categorized into eight different types based on their IR; dimension and number of classes.

In [59] an extension of the Roughly Balanced Bagging [8, 48] for multi-class problems was proposed, known as MRBBag. In such method, the main modification concerns a construction of bootstrap samples. Whereas in the original approach the number of majority examples is decided probabilistically according to the negative binomial distribution (all minority ones are included in all bags), now a mulinomial distribution is considered by using the classes' prior probabilities. This way, minority class instances will be more likely to be replicated than majority ones within each bag. Two versions of this model are suggested, depending on the size of the bags. On the one hand, oMRBBags considers each bag to contain the same number of instances than the original dataset. On the other hand, uMRBBag will limit the size of the bags to that of the minority class.

A more recent approach known as "Ensemble classifier from a Feature and Instance Selection by means of Multi-Objective Evolutionary Algorithm" (EFIS-MOEA) was proposed in [26]. This novel approach addressed learning on difficult classes focusing on the uneven class distribution and the overlapping simultaneously. To do so, the C4.5 decision tree [82] was embedded in a wrapper procedure, applying the well-known NSGA-II multi-objective optimization algorithm [22]. The basis for this methodology involves several components. First, FS was devoted to simplify the overlapping areas easing the generation of rules to distinguish between the classes. Second, selection of instances from all classes addressed the imbalance itself by finding the most appropriate class distribution for the learning task, as well as possibly removing noise and difficult borderline examples. Finally, the non-dominated solutions of the Pareto front from the MOEA could be directly combined into an ensemble of classifiers [84]. Additionally, before the use of the NSGA-II procedure, three different approaches to address imbalance are considered in synergy with EFIS-MOEA, namely (i) acting directly over the original training set; (ii) using a weighting cost-sensitive scheme; and (iii) applying SMOTE preprocessing.

The use of Deep Learning [60] has been also investigated for multiclass imbalanced data with ensemble learning. In particular, the research made in [107] combines the application of stratified random undersampling together with a regularization parameter for the weighting of the classifiers during the learning of the boosting ensemble. This synergy is the strongest point of the methodology, as it allows to better focus on the borderline examples.

Finally, we must stress a recent work that analyze the dynamic selection of ensembles [86]. It is based on the fact that during the generation stage classifiers are "local" to their training data. Therefore, it is reasonable to determine the true competence of the classifiers during the inference process. With this premise, authors applied preprocessing for the generation of the ensemble to deal with the intrinsic imbalance, and then exploit the local competency of base classifiers in the integration step. An extensive experimental study allow authors to validate the premise that both techniques together provide a significant enhancement of the results.

8.3.5 Summary and Future Prospects on Ad-hoc Approaches

The goodness of ad-hoc solutions for the multi-class imbalanced problems over decomposition techniques is clear: the problem can addressed as a whole taking into account the relationship among the classes, instead of "losing" some information due to the binarization, and depending on the robustness of the final aggregation mechanism. However, the task of designing such type of direct solutions is far to be straightforward. Implementing inbuilt mechanisms requires in-depth knowledge about the nature of the classifiers and underlying reasons of their failure in minority class recognition. Below, we discuss on the capabilities and challenges for the ad-hoc approaches on multi-class imbalanced classification.

8.3.5.1 Preprocessing Techniques

Regarding preprocessing techniques, simple re-balancing towards the biggest or smallest class is not a proper approach, as shown by the experimental results obtained in [27, 96]. Instead, one should focus on those areas of the problem that actually need to be reinforced. We basically refer to small disjuncts and overlapping, which now may appear with more than two groups. Additionally, other possible difficulties may arise, such as the class label noise that causes the problem boundaries to be poorly defined. All these issues clearly affect in more severe way in the presence of multiple classes. Therefore, it will be positive to define a clear taxonomy for the different type of instances present in each class, as well as their relations to other classes [62, 94].

In accordance with the former, new data cleaning and sampling procedures must be developed to handle presence of these varying characteristics of the classes and to their mutual relations. The final goal is to balance the performance on all represented concepts. Therefore, hybrid approaches, utilizing more than one method seem as an attractive solution.

From another perspective the indiscriminate discarding of overlapping instances for a given set of classes may deteriorate the correct boundary learning from the others. A possible way to address such task is to consider projections to new spaces to alleviate the overlapping, in a similar way than kernels are applied for SVMs.

Finally, a proper identification of the class noise is also mandatory due to its strong influence in the classifiers' performance. This preprocessing stage may not only redefine class boundaries, but also to rebalance the classes (in case wrong labels are assigned to majority classes). The hitch in this case is not only being able to detect and filtering noise data, but also to develop strategies for the relabeling process.

8.3.5.2 Algorithmic Approaches

When addressing algorithmic approaches, we must consider a deeper insight into how multiple skewed distributions affect the forming of decision boundaries in classifiers. This way, it is possible to adapt some well-performing state-of-the-art classifiers to this scenario by incorporating some ot the capabilities that have shown to be quite effective for addressing the class imbalance. A first example is the Hellinger distance [17], which can be applied to other distance-based classifiers. The paradigm of ELM has also gained much attention in the last years [61, 65, 108], and the output weights can be shifted towards the most difficult classes [106]. Finally, density-based methods should be explored in combination with those trying to overcome the class overlapping [26].

8.3.5.3 Cost-Sensitive Learning

For cost-sensitive multi-class learning, the different importance among original samples can be a crucial factor for the performance of learning algorithms, but how to deal with it remains unexplored. Some approaches try to optimize the costs in a wrapper scheme by means of evolutionary algorithms [91, 109]. However, rather than focusing on the performance to guide the search, additional objectives may be considered to avoid the overfitting.

8.3.5.4 Ensemble Systems

Finally, ensemble solutions should be investigated in depth. These are known to provide very robust solutions by focusing on "different" parts of the problem, either by bagging or boosting. However, this is achieved in exchange of higher training times and a poor interpretability of the final models. In addition to the former, there is a necessity in maintaining the diversity and compactness in the ensemble system [38] as well as a proper selection of useful base learners.

8.4 Performance Metrics in Multi-class Imbalanced Problems

Carrying our a proper comparison among classification models is a complex and still open challenge. This task depends not only on what type of understanding of the committed error is aimed to be evaluated, but also on the nature of the problem itself, to avoid a wrong bias of the evaluation. This is exactly the case of imbalanced problems, from which the single performance for each class must be taken into account in order to analyze whether a given class is boosted in detriment of the other.

From the binary confusion matrix, several metrics have been proposed to deal with the imbalanced class distribution, namely the AUC_{ROC}, the Geometric Mean of the true rates (GM) or the F-measure, as shown in Chap. 3. However, the extension of the former metrics to the context of multi-class problems must be carefully regarded. Several research papers have studied this generalization such in [31, 89] and [11]. In the work from Ferri et al. [31], authors also propose a taxonomy of existing performance metrics, organized into three groups, where many of them share the second and third types:

1. Qualitative metrics that are used when the minimization of the number of classification errors is seek. Some examples are accuracy, GM, macro-averaged accuracy, mean F-measure, Kappa statistic and minimum sensitivity.
2. Probabilistic metrics that aim at testing the reliability of the model. Mean absolute error, mean squared error or the LogLoss error (cross-entropy) are examples of this type.
3. Raking metrics that are based on how the model ranks the examples, such as the AUC metric.

This organization of measures is totally consistent to that shown in previous Chap. 3 for imbalanced binary classification. In addition to the former, and as it was pointed out also in Chap. 3.2, prior to the introduction of the different metrics of performance that might be used for multi-class imbalanced problems, we must recall the misleading use of standard accuracy. Since correct classifications count the same, disregard the class label, it is impossible to determine if the good or bad behavior of the model is due to a certain subset of the classes [39]. Unfortunately, there are still many research works that keep using this performance metric in imbalanced domains [45].

Throughout this section, we follow a similar notation as shown in [31]. Given a dataset, we denote by m the number of examples, and c as the number of classes. $f(i, j)$ represents the actual probability of example i to be of class j. We assume that $f(i, j)$ always takes values in 0,1 and, strictly, it is not a probability but an indicator function. With $m_j = \sum_{i=1}^{m} f(i, j)$, we denote the number of examples of class j.

Given a classifier, $p(i, j)$ represents the estimated probability of example i to be of class j taking values in $[0, 1]$. $C_\theta(i, j)$ is 1 iff j is the predicted class for i obtained from $p(i, j)$ using a given threshold or decision rule θ (especially in multiclass problems). Otherwise, $C_\theta(i, j)$ is 0. We will omit θ in what follows.

- Kappa statistic: (KapS) compensates for random hits [6, 20]. In contrast to accuracy rate, kappa evaluates the portion of hits that can be attributed to the classifier itself (i.e., not to mere chance), relative to all the classifications that cannot be attributed to chance alone. This metric was also introduced for binary classification in Chap. 3.2, but it is more commonly applied for multi-class classification. Following the current notation, KapS is computed as.

$$KapS = \frac{P(A) - P(E)}{1 - P(E)}$$

(8.3)

where $P(A)$ is the relative observed agreement among classifiers, and $P(E)$ is the probability that agreement is due to chance. As shown in Chap. 3.2, $P(A)$ is just the accuracy of the classifier, and $P(E)$ is the expected accuracy, defined for multiple classes as follows:

$$P(E) = \frac{\sum_{k=1}^{c} \left(\left[\sum_{j=1}^{c} \sum_{i=1}^{m} f(i,k)C(i,j) \right] \cdot \left[\sum_{j=1}^{c} \sum_{i=1}^{m} f(i,j)C(i,k) \right] \right)}{m^2}$$

(8.4)

- Mean F-Measure (MFM): In the binary case (please refer to Chap. 3.2), the standard F-measure (with $\beta = 1$) computes a trade-off between precision and recall of both classes:

$$FM_j = \frac{2 \cdot Recall_j \cdot Precision_j}{Recall_j + Precision_j}$$

(8.5)

$$Recall_j - \frac{\sum_{i=1}^{m} f(i,j)C(i,j)}{m_j}$$

(8.6)

$$Precision_j = \frac{\sum_{i=1}^{m} f(i,j)C(i,j)}{m_j \sum_{i=1}^{m} C(i,j)}$$

(8.7)

In the multi-class case, the average for the F-measure achieved for each class (taken as positive) and the remaining ones (taken as a whole as negative) is usually computed.

$$MFM = \frac{\sum_{j=1}^{c} FM_j}{c}$$

(8.8)

- Minimum sensitivity (MS): Is the minimum value of the sensitivities for each class. Therefore, it allows to determine which is the class that hinders the classification ability of the whole model:

$$MS = \min_{j=1,\ldots,c} Recall_j \qquad (8.9)$$

- Macro average arithmetic (MAvA): Also known as average accuracy, average recall, or balanced accuracy, it is computed as the mean of the individual hits for each class.

$$MAvA = \frac{1}{c} \sum_{j=1}^{c} Recall_j \qquad (8.10)$$

- Macro average geometric (MAvG): Also known as the geometric mean, it is more "strict" in the sense that the global value is highly affected in case of low performing classes.

$$\sqrt[c]{\prod_{j=1}^{c} Recall_j} \qquad (8.11)$$

- Mean Probabilistic AUC (MPAUC): In most cases, the AUC metric is computed using a single point from the ROC-Curve, i.e. without taking into account the a-posteriori probabilities given by the classifier. However, when the confidence degrees of each output are given, it is preferable to calculate the AUC approximating the continuous ROC-curve by a finite number of points [25] (see also Chap. 3.3). In such way, a model in which true positives relay on high confidences, whereas false positives are related to low confidences, will present a higher performance value.

  This way, the coordinates of these points in ROC-space are taken as false positive $(1 - Precision_j)$ and true positive rates $(Recall_j)$ obtained by varying the threshold of the probability above which an instance is classified as positive. The curve itself is approximated by linear interpolation between the calculated points. The AUC can therefore be determined as the sum of the areas of the successive trapezoids. This method is referred to as the trapezoid rule and is also described in e.g. [71].

$$PAUC(j,k) = \frac{\sum_{i=1}^{m} \frac{f(i,j)p(i,j)}{m_j} - \sum_{i=1}^{m} \frac{f(i,k)p(i,j)}{m_k} + 1}{2} \qquad (8.12)$$

Finally, MPAUC is computed as the macro-average of the pairwise AUC values of all pairs of classes.

$$MPAUC = \frac{2}{c(c-1)} \sum_{j<k} PAUC(j,k) \qquad (8.13)$$

To summarize this section, we must refer to the problem in the aggregation of the metrics. By using macro averages, the individual recognition degree reached for each class is somehow diluted. This is of extreme significance in case of a large number of classes, where high accuracy rates compensate low classifications. Furthermore, it is still not possible to identify the source of difficulty of the problem. These facts imply the relevance of general metrics that directly combine the values from the confusion matrix, as well as considering the global information shown in the former.

However, regarding the use of different metrics, one must be aware of the high level of correlation that is shown among them. This issue was reported in both [31] and [11]. Therefore, one should focus on the most informative metrics, as well as those ones that are widely used so as to be able to be able to compare the quality of the novel proposals with respect to the state-of-the-art.

Finally, the advantages of representation metrics such as AUC or cost-curves must be also taken into account [77]. However, being initially designed for the binary case study, their representational comprehensibility for the analysis of multi-class problems is lost, as well as increasing the computational complexity. For this reason, at present few alternatives have been proposed to clear this gap [44, 79], so that the effort of research should be addressed in this way.

8.5   A Brief Experimental Analysis for Imbalanced Multi-class Problems

This section is devoted to put in value all the topics presented throughout the chapter. Specifically, the behavior among some state-of-the-art solutions, both considering a decomposition strategy or a direct approach, will be contrasted. Also, it contains some evaluation metrics with aims at analyzing the possible correlation of the results. To do so, in Sect. 8.5.1 the selected benchmark data, the algorithms for comparison and their parameters, and the performance metrics are introduced. Then, Sect. 8.5.2 shows the experimental results and contains a brief discussion.

8.5.1   Experimental Setup

For this study, 18 multi-class datasets with different properties have been selected. These are shown in Table 8.1, were the number of instances, features (numeric and nominal) and classes are listed. We also provide the distribution of the instances over the classes to give an indication of their imbalance.

To carry out a fair evaluation, the 10-fold DOB-SCV partitioning scheme from [73] was used. The main reason is to avoid the data-shift problem, the issue of having different distributions in the training and test partitions of the evaluation. In

Table 8.1 The 18 multi-class imbalanced datasets used in our experimental study. The number of features is divided between numeric and nominal ones, e.g. the automobile dataset has 15 numeric features and 10 nominal features

Dataset	ID	# inst	# feat	m	Class distribution
Automobile	aut	150	25 (15/10)	6	3/20/48/46/29/13
Balance	bal	625	4 (4/0)	3	288/49/288
Cleveland	cle	297	13 (13/0)	5	164/55/36/35/13
Contraceptive	con	1473	9 (9/0)	3	629/333/511
Dermatology	der	358	34 (34/0)	6	111/60/71/48/48/20
Ecoli	eco	336	7 (7/0)	8	143/77/2/2/35/20/5/52
Glass	gla	214	9 (9/0)	6	70/76/17/13/9/29
Led7digit	led	500	7 (7/0)	10	45/37/51/57/52/52/47/57/53/49
Lymphography	lym	148	18 (3/15)	4	2/81/61/4
Newthyroid	new	215	5 (5/0)	3	150/35/30
Pageblocks	pag	5472	10 (10/0)	5	4913/329/28/87/115
Satimage	sat	6435	36 (36/0)	6	1533/703/1358/626/707/1508
Shuttle	shu	58000	9 (9/0)	7	45586/49/171/8903/3267/10/13
Thyroid	thy	7200	21 (21/0)	3	166/368/6666
Wine	win	178	13 (13/0)	3	59/71/48
Winequality-red	wqr	1599	11 (11/0)	6	10/53/681/638/199/18
Winequality-white	wqw	4898	11 (11/0)	7	20/163/1457/2198/880/175/5
Yeast	yea	1484	8 (8/0)	10	244/429/463/44/51/163/35/30/20/5

the fold construction of DOB-SCV, regions of same-class elements are divided over different folds, to guarantee a proper representation of such a region in all partitions. The use of this partitioning scheme for imbalanced data was advised in [68].

The full datasets and all partitions are available from the KEEL dataset repository (http://www.keel.es) for any interested reader that wishes to repeat the current analysis.

With the sake of including a representative algorithm from each type discussed in Sects. 8.2 and 8.3, we have selected four different approaches. Specifically, as multi-class imbalanced learning via decomposition-based approaches we have considered one method from preprocessing and one novel methodology, namely OVO with SMOTE-C4.5 classifier for the first type, and FROVOCO for the second type. Regarding ad-hoc approaches for multi-class imbalanced classification, we have also chosen one preprocessing method and one ensemble, namely the MDO preprocessing in combination with C4.5 as well, and AdaBoost.NC.

All parameters are the recommended ones from the authors. In AdaBoost.NC, we have set the penalty strength λ to 2, as done in earlier work e.g. [27, 100]. The number of classifiers in the ensemble was set to 10, which is a lower value than the one used by these referenced studies. In a preliminary evaluation, we observed that this value provides better average results on our selected datasets.

For the C4.5 with OVO learning in combination with SMOTE, the classifier was used with pruning mechanism, using a confidence level of 0.25, and minimum number of item-sets per leaf $= 2$. SMOTE considered a balance rate of 1, with 5 neighbors to create artificial data, and the HVDM distance functions [102]. Finally, the MDO preprocessing needs only one parameter, i.e. the balance rate, which was set to 1.

Finally, to evaluate the performance of the included methods, we apply two different evaluation measures. On the one hand, the average accuracy (MAvA) as qualitative metric. The second measure is the mean AUC (MAUC) so as to include a ranking metric that take into account the output probabilities of the classifier.

8.5.2   Experimental Results and Discussion

In Table 8.2 we show the experimental results for the four selected classification methods. Abbreviations are as follows: "Ada" for AdaBoost.NC, "SMT" for OVO+C4.5-SMOTE, "MDO" for MDO+C4.5 and "FROVO" for FROVOCO.

The table is divided into two parts, the left-hand side contains the results computed with MAvA and the right-hand side those computed with MAUC.

First of all, we must stress in first place the necessity of adapting the learning methodology to the context of imbalanced data. Specifically, the results of the standard C4.5 decision tree are quite far from the average shown by the remaining approaches. Therefore, as it was stressed in the binary case study, for multiple classes it is even more important to apply different techniques to boost the minority classes if we aim to identify all concepts included in the problem.

Regarding the absolute comparison among the methods that are designed to address the imbalance, we may observe the high quality of FROVOCO in contrast with the remaining algorithms. AdaBoost.NC also obtains very good average results for both MAvA and MAUC. Both methods include an ensemble of classifier, thus boosting the recognition ability for every single model. In the case of FROVOCO the advantages rely on the class division, focusing on finding a good separation pair by pair. For AdaBoost.NC, the classifier focuses on the difficult examples iteration by iteration. We have shown that both approaches imply a clear advantage for achieving a robust performance.

In the case of the preprocessing algorithms (OVO+C4.5-SMOTE and MDO+C4.5) results are good on average, but not so high as in the previous case. The first approach (OVO+C4.5-SMOTE) is a straightforward adaptation of the solution for binary problems, and artificial instances are built disregard the relations among classes, just focusing on the different pairs. For MDO, although the Malanahobis distance is well suited to cope with overlapping, the generated synthetic instances do not allow the classifier to make a difference with respect to learning using the original dataset.

Finally, we must remark that the two evaluation measures capture complementary performance information. The MAvA solely focuses on the number of hits and misses, while the MAUC takes the confidence of the predictions of a classifier

Table 8.2 Full MAvA and MAUC results for the imbalanced multi-class state-of-the-art classifiers. For each dataset, for each measure, the highest value is printed in bold

Data	MAvA					MPAUC				
	C4.5	Ada	SMT	MDO	FRST	C4.5	Ada	SMT	MDO	FROVO
aut	73.2889	79.9444	**80.6444**	76.4778	77.1556	.8490	.9370	.9299	.8928	.9633
bal	56.3743	65.8900	55.2701	56.4819	**78.8514**	.7057	.8609	.5901	.6768	.8854
cle	29.2003	26.8750	26.1917	29.0417	**33.7833**	.5702	.5834	.5772	.5610	**.6981**
con	50.2750	47.9522	**51.7246**	48.7521	47.4449	.6422	**.6669**	.6560	.6529	.6485
der	94.9793	94.6845	96.2096	95.3709	**97.1553**	.9725	.9857	.9861	.9727	**.9966**
eco	61.5362	76.2654	71.4609	71.1481	**77.2723**	.7922	.9162	.8990	.8556	.9304
gla	66.7817	**71.5516**	75.1885	63.0437	67.0694	.8136	.9246	.9204	.8534	.9325
led	**72.2393**	54.3621	63.5466	64.1728	64.7918	.8536	.7640	.9134	.8780	.9189
lym	68.7945	72.4355	72.2222	73.2093	**86.2401**	.7684	.7847	.7717	.8231	**.9108**
new	89.3968	**94.7222**	91.3889	90.4444	91.1111	.9391	.9972	.9563	.9276	**.9981**
pag	84.4919	**91.9105**	89.2398	83.7520	9.0399	.9127	**.9876**	.9739	.9446	.9736
sat	83.4618	87.5570	85.2928	84.7142	**89.4955**	.9043	**.9817**	.9619	.9214	**.9817**
shu	91.8788	**98.4803**	96.8439	91.3154	91.8527	.9592	.9911	.9979	.9600	**.9987**
thy	97.6168	99.4186	**99.2688**	97.9360	66.4500	.9834	**.9998**	.9965	.9894	.8494
win	93.4468	94.7579	95.2698	92.9881	**98.2143**	.9558	.9818	.9788	.9482	**1.0000**
wqr	34.0128	39.6884	34.1986	31.8371	**43.7544**	.6066	.7581	.7495	.6432	**.8342**
wqw	33.7716	47.6684	39.3455	39.3391	**47.8895**	.6201	.7856	.7772	.6811	**.8309**
yea	55.2475	49.0789	51.8083	53.3381	**58.8178**	.7560	.8279	.8472	.7693	**.8810**
Mean	68.7108	71.8468	70.8397	69.0757	**72.6327**	.8114	.8741	.8602	.8306	**.9018**

into account. Based on the analysis presented in Table 8.2, we may stress that the prediction confidences of FROVOCO are significantly more reliable than those of the remaining algorithms.

8.6 Summarizing Comments

In this chapter, we have carried out a thorough review on the topic of multi-class imbalanced datasets. First, we have stressed the importance of this framework, as it comprises an additional level of difficulty with respect to the binary case study. In particular, we have referred to the problem of multi-majority and multi-minority classes, the inner relations among the classes, and the higher incidence of the data intrinsic characteristics.

Then, we have enumerated the main ways of addressing this issue. On the one hand, we may proceed by applying binarization techniques to transform the original problem into several two-class datasets. This way, standard solutions for the imbalanced class distribution may be directly applied, shifting the problem of addressing the multi-class dataset to the final combination stage. On the other hand, we have introduced several ad-hoc solutions (from preprocessing, algorithmic and cost-sensitive learning) that are directly applied to the multi-class problem. Additionally, we have stressed the significance of ensemble-based approaches in this context. For both binarization and ad-hoc approaches, we have carried out an in depth discussion for analyzing the goodness and drawbacks of both types of solutions, also providing some topics that should be considered as future work.

Next, we have presented some useful metrics of performance for multi-class imbalanced learning, allowing readers to select the one that better suites to his/her validation procedure. Finally, a short experimental study has been carried out in order to show the behavior for some state-of-the-art techniques, as well as understanding the differences between the MAvA and the MPAUC metrics of performance.

References

1. Abdi, L., Hashemi, S.: To combat multi-class imbalanced problems by means of over-sampling techniques. IEEE Trans. Knowl. Data Eng. **28**(1), 238–251 (2016)
2. Abe, N., Zadrozny, B., Langford, J.: An iterative method for multi–class cost–sensitive learning. In: Proceedings of the 10th ACM SIGKDD International Conference on Knowledge Discovery and Data Mining, KDD'04, Seattle, pp. 3–11 (2004)
3. Alejo, R., García, V., Pacheco-Sánchez, J.H.: An efficient over-sampling approach based on mean square error back-propagation for dealing with the multi-class imbalance problem. Neural Process. Lett. **42**(3), 603–617 (2015)
4. Allwein, E.L., Schapire, R.E., Singer, Y.: Reducing multiclass to binary: a unifying approach for margin classifiers. J. Mach. Learn. Res. **1**, 113–141 (2000)

5. Anand, R., Mehrotra, K., Mohan, C.K., Ranka, S.: Efficient classification for multiclass problems using modular neural networks. IEEE Trans. Neural Netw. **6**(1), 117–124 (1995)
6. Ben-David, A.: A lot of randomness is hiding in accuracy. Eng. Appl. Artif. Intell. **20**, 875–885 (2007)
7. Bernard, S., Chatelain, C., Adam, S., Sabourin, R.: The multiclass ROC front method for cost-sensitive classification. Pattern Recognit. **52**, 46–60 (2016)
8. Blaszczynski, J., Stefanowski, J.: Neighbourhood sampling in bagging for imbalanced data. Neurocomputing **150**, 529–542 (2015)
9. Branco, P., Torgo, L., Ribeiro, R.P.: A survey of predictive modelling under imbalanced distributions. ACM Comput. Surv. **49**(2), 31:1–31:50 (2016)
10. Bustince, H., Barrenechea, E., Pagola, M.: Restricted equivalence functions. Fuzzy Sets Syst. **157**(17), 2333–2346 (2006)
11. Carbonero-Ruz, M., Martínez-Estudillo, F.J., Fernández-Navarro, F., Becerra-Alonso, D., Martínez-Estudillo, A.C.: A two dimensional accuracy-based measure for classification performance. Inf. Sci. **382–383**, 60–80 (2017)
12. Cerf, L., Gay, D., Selmaoui-Folcher, N., Crémilleux, B., Boulicaut, J.F.: Parameter-free classification in multi-class imbalanced data sets. Data Knowl. Eng. **87**, 109–129 (2013)
13. Chatelain, C., Adam, S., Lecourtier, Y., Heutte, L., Paquet, T.: A multi-model selection framework for unknown and/or evolutive misclassification cost problems. Pattern Recognit. **43**(3), 815–823 (2010)
14. Chawla, N.V., Bowyer, K.W., Hall, L.O., Kegelmeyer, W.P.: SMOTE: synthetic minority over–sampling technique. J. Artif. Intell. Res. **16**, 321–357 (2002)
15. Chawla, N.V., Lazarevic, A., Hall, L.O., Bowyer, K.W.: Smoteboost: improving prediction of the minority class in boosting. In: Lavrac, N., Gamberger, D., Blockeel, H., Todorovski, L. (eds.) Proceedings of the 7th European Conference on Principles and Practices on Knowledge Discovery in Databases (PKDD). Lecture Notes in Computer Science, vol. 2838, pp. 107–119. Springer, Berlin/Heidelberg (2003)
16. Chen, Y.S.: An empirical study of a hybrid imbalanced-class DT-RST classification procedure to elucidate therapeutic effects in uremia patients. Med. Biol. Eng. Comput. **54**, 983–1001 (2016)
17. Cieslak, D.A., Hoens, T.R., Chawla, N.V., Kegelmeyer, W.P.: Hellinger distance decision trees are robust and skew-insensitive. Data Min. Knowl. Disc. **24**(1), 136–158 (2012)
18. Clark, P., Boswell, R.: Rule induction with CN2: some recent improvements. In: EWSL'91: Proceedings of the European Working Session on Machine Learning, pp. 151–163. Springer, London (1991)
19. Cohen, G., Hilario, M., Sax, H., Hugonnet, S., Geissbühler, A.: Learning from imbalanced data in surveillance of nosocomial infection. Artif. Intell. Med. **37**(1), 7–18 (2006)
20. Cohen, J.A.: Coefficient of agreement for nominal scales. Educ. Psychol. Meas. **20**, 37–46 (1960)
21. Datta, S., Das, S.: Near-bayesian support vector machines for imbalanced data classification with equal or unequal misclassification costs. Neural Netw. **70**, 39–52 (2015)
22. Deb, K., Pratap, A., Agarwal, S., Meyarivan, T.: A fast and elitist multiobjective genetic algorithm: NSGA-II. IEEE Trans. Evol. Comput. **6**(2), 182–197 (2002)
23. Dietterich, T.G., Bakiri, G.: Solving multiclass learning problems via error-correcting output codes. J. Artif. Intell. Res. **2**, 263–286 (1995)
24. Duan, L., Xie, M., Bai, T., Wang, J.: A new support vector data description method for machinery fault diagnosis with unbalanced datasets. Expert Syst. Appl. **64**, 239–246 (2016)
25. Fawcett, T.: An introduction to ROC analysis. Pattern Recognit. Lett. **27**(8), 861–874 (2006)
26. Fernandez, A., Carmona, C.J., del Jesus, M.J., Herrera, F.: A pareto based ensemble with feature and instance selection for learning from multi-class imbalanced datasets. Int. J. Neural Syst. **27**(6), 1–21 (2017)
27. Fernandez, A., Lopez, V., Galar, M., del Jesus, M.J., Herrera, F.: Analysing the classification of imbalanced data-sets with multiple classes: binarization techniques and ad-hoc approaches. Knowl.-Based Syst. **42**, 97–110 (2013)

28. Fernández-Navarro, F., Hervás-Martínez, C., Gutiérrez, P.A.: A dynamic over-sampling procedure based on sensitivity for multi-class problems. Pattern Recognit. **44**, 1821–1833 (2011)
29. Fernández, A., Elkano, M., Galar, M., Sanz, J.A., Alshomrani, S., Bustince, H., Herrera, F.: Enhancing evolutionary fuzzy systems for multi-class problems: distance-based relative competence weighting with truncated confidences (DRCW-TC). Int. J. Approx. Reason. **73**, 108–122 (2016)
30. Fernández-Navarro, F., Hervás-Martínez, C., Antonio Gutiérrez, P.: A dynamic over-sampling procedure based on sensitivity for multi-class problems. Pattern Recognit. **44**(8), 1821–1833 (2011)
31. Ferri, C., Hernández-Orallo, J., Modroiu, R.: An experimental comparison of performance measures for classification. Pattern Recognit. Lett. **30**, 27–38 (2009)
32. Freund, Y., Schapire, R.: A decision-theoretic generalization of on-line learning and an application to boosting. J. Comput. Syst. Sci. **55**(1), 119–139 (1997)
33. Fürnkranz, J.: Round robin classification. J. Mach. Learn. Res. **2**, 721–747 (2002)
34. Fürnkranz, J., Hüllermeier, E., Vanderlooy, S.: Binary decomposition methods for multipartite ranking. In: Buntine, W.L., Grobelnik, M., Mladenic, D., Shawe-Taylor, J. (eds.) Machine Learning and Knowledge Discovery in Databases. Lecture Notes in Computer Science LNCS, vol. 5781(1), pp. 359–374. Springer, Berlin/New York (2009)
35. Galar, M., Fernandez, A., Barrenechea, E., Bustince, H., Herrera, F.: An overview of ensemble methods for binary classifiers in multi-class problems: experimental study on one-vs-one and one-vs-all schemes. Pattern Recognit. **44**(8), 1761–1776 (2011)
36. Galar, M., Fernandez, A., Barrenechea, E., Bustince, H., Herrera, F.: A review on ensembles for class imbalance problem: bagging, boosting and hybrid based approaches. IEEE Trans. Syst. Man Cybern. Part C Appl. Rev. **42**(4), 463–484 (2012)
37. Galar, M., Fernández, A., Barrenechea, E., Bustince, H., Herrera, F.: Dynamic classifier selection for one-vs-one strategy: avoiding non-competent classifiers. Pattern Recognit. **46**(12), 3412–3424 (2013)
38. Galar, M., Fernandez, A., Barrenechea, E., Bustince, H., Herrera, F.: Ordering-based pruning for improving the performance of ensembles of classifiers in the framework of imbalanced datasets. Inf. Sci. **354**, 178–196 (2016)
39. Galar, M., Fernandez, A., Barrenechea, E., Herrera, F.: Empowering difficult classes with a similarity-based aggregation in multi-class classification problems. Inf. Sci. **264**, 135–157 (2014)
40. Galar, M., Fernandez, A., Barrenechea, E., Herrera, F.: DRCW-OVO: distance-based relative competence weighting combination for one-vs-one strategy in multi-class problems. Pattern Recognit. **48**(1), 28–42 (2015)
41. Gao, X., Chen, Z., Tang, S., Zhang, Y., Li, J.: Adaptive weighted imbalance learning with application to abnormal activity recognition. Neurocomputing **173**, 1927–1935 (2016)
42. Gao, Z., Zhang, L., Chen, M.-yu., Hauptmann, A.G., Zhang, H., Cai, A.N.: Enhanced and hierarchical structure algorithm for data imbalance problem in semantic extraction under massive video dataset. Multimed. Tools Appl. **68**(3), 641–657 (2014)
43. Garcia-Pedrajas, N., Fyfe, C.: Evolving output codes for multiclass problems. IEEE Trans. Evol. Comput. **12**(1), 93–106 (2008)
44. Guo, H., Li, Y., Li, Y., Liu, X., Li, J.: Bpso-adaboost-knn ensemble learning algorithm for multi-class imbalanced data classification. Eng. Appl. Artif. Intell. **49**, 176–193 (2016)
45. Guo, H., Li, Y., Shang, J., Mingyun, G., Yuanyue, H., Bing, G.: Learning from class-imbalanced data: review of methods and applications. Expert Syst. Appl. **73**, 220–239 (2017)
46. Hastie, T., Tibshirani, R.: Classification by pairwise coupling. Ann. Stat. **26**(2), 451–471 (1998)
47. He, H., Garcia, E.A.: Learning from imbalanced data. IEEE Trans. Knowl. Data Eng. **21**(9), 1263–1284 (2009)
48. Hido, S., Kashima, H., Takahashi, Y.: Roughly balanced bagging for imbalanced data. Stat. Anal. Data Mining **2**(5–6), 412–426 (2009)

49. Hinton, G.E., Osindero, S., Teh, Y.W.: A fast learning algorithm for deep belief nets. Neural Comput. **18**, 1527–1554 (2006)
50. Huang, G.B., Wang, D.H., Lan, Y.: Extreme learning machines: a survey. Int. J. Mach. Learn. Cybern. **2**(2), 107–122 (2011)
51. Hüllermeier, E., Vanderlooy, S.: Combining predictions in pairwise classification: an optimal adaptive voting strategy and its relation to weighted voting. Pattern Recognit. **43**(1), 128–142 (2010)
52. Kennedy, J., Eberhart, R.: Particle swarm optimization. In: Proceedings of the IEEE International Conference on Neural Networks, ICNN'95, Perth, vol. 4, pp. 1942–1948 (1995)
53. Knerr, S., Personnaz, L., Dreyfus, G.: Single-layer learning revisited: a stepwise procedure for building and training a neural network. In: Fogelman Soulié, F., Hérault, J. (eds.) Neurocomputing: Algorithms, Architectures and Applications. NATO ASI Series, vol. F68, pp. 41–50. Springer, Berlin/Heidelberg (1990)
54. Krawczyk, B.: Cost-sensitive one-vs-one ensemble for multi-class imbalanced data. In: 2016 International Joint Conference on Neural Networks (IJCNN), Vancouver, pp. 2447–2452. IEEE (2016)
55. Krawczyk, B.: Learning from imbalanced data: open challenges and future directions. Progress Artif. Intell. **5**(4), 221–232 (2016)
56. Krawczyk, B., Schaefer, G.: An improved ensemble approach for imbalanced classification problems. In: IEEE International Symposium on Applied Computational Intelligence and Informatics (SACI), Timisoara, pp. 423–426. IEEE (2013)
57. Krawczyk, B., Wozniak, M., Herrera, F.: On the usefulness of one-class classifier ensembles for decomposition of multi-class problems. Pattern Recognit. **48**(12), 3969–3982 (2015)
58. Kuncheva, L.I.: Combining Pattern Classifiers: Methods and Algorithms. Wiley-Interscience, Hoboken (2004)
59. Lango, M., Stefanowski, J.: Multi-class and feature selection extensions of roughly balanced bagging for imbalanced data. J. Intell. Inf. Syst. **50**(1), 97–127 (2018)
60. Lecun, Y., Bengio, Y., Hinton, G.: Deep learning. Nature **521**(7553), 436–444 (2015)
61. Li, K., Kong, X., Lu, Z., Wenyin, L., Yin, J.: Boosting weighted ELM for imbalanced learning. Neurocomputing **128**, 15–21 (2014)
62. Li, Y., Guo, H., Liu, X., Li, Y., Li, J.: Adapted ensemble classification algorithm based on multiple classifier system and feature selection for classifying multi-class imbalanced data. Knowl.-Based Syst. **94**, 88–104 (2016)
63. Liao, T.W.: Classification of weld flaws with imbalanced class data. Expert Syst. Appl. **35**(3), 1041–1052 (2008)
64. Lin, M., Tang, K., Yao, X.: Dynamic sampling approach to training neural networks for multiclass imbalance classification. IEEE Trans. Neural Netw. Learn. Syst. **24**(4), 647–660 (2013)
65. Liu, P., Huang, Y., Meng, L., Gong, S., Zhang, G.: Two-stage extreme learning machine for high-dimensional data. Int. J. Mach. Learn. Cybern. **7**(5), 765–772 (2016)
66. Liu, X.Y., Wu, J., Zhou, Z.H.: Exploratory undersampling for class-imbalance learning. IEEE Trans. Syst. Man Cybern. B **39**(2), 539–550 (2009)
67. Lopez, V., Fernandez, A., Garcia, S., Palade, V., Herrera, F.: An insight into classification with imbalanced data: empirical results and current trends on using data intrinsic characteristics. Inf. Sci. **250**(20), 113–141 (2013)
68. Lopez, V., Fernandez, A., Herrera, F.: On the importance of the validation technique for classification with imbalanced datasets: addressing covariate shift when data is skewed. Inf. Sci. **257**, 1–13 (2014)
69. Luengo, J., Herrera, F.: An automatic extraction method of the domains of competence for learning classifiers using data complexity measures. Knowl. Inf. Syst. **42**(1), 147–180 (2015)
70. Mahalanobis, P.: On the generalized distance in statistics. Proc. Natl. Inst. Sci. (Calcutta) **2**, 49–55 (1936)
71. Mason, S.J., Graham, N.E.: Areas beneath the relative operating characteristics (ROC) and relative operating levels (ROL) curves: statistical significance and interpretation. Q. J. R. Meteorol. Soc. **128**(584), 2145–2166 (2002)

72. Masulli, F., Valentini, G.: Effectiveness of error correcting output coding methods in ensemble and monolithic learning machines. Pattern Anal. Appl. **6**(4), 285–300 (2003)
73. Moreno-Torres, J., Sáez, J., Herrera, F.: Study on the impact of partition-induced dataset shift on-fold cross-validation. IEEE Trans. Neural Netw. Learn. Syst. **23**(8), 1304–1312 (2012)
74. Napierala, K., Stefanowski, J.: Identification of different types of minority class examples in imbalanced data. In: Corchado, E., Snásel, V., Abraham, A., Wozniak, M., Graña, M., Cho, S.B. (eds.) 7th International Conference on Hybrid Artificial Intelligence Systems (HAIS-2012). Lecture Notes in Computer Science, vol. 7209, pp. 139–150. Springer, Berlin (2012)
75. Passerini, A., Pontil, M., Frasconi, P.: New results on error correcting output codes of kernel machines. IEEE Trans. Neural Netw. **15**(1), 45–54 (2004)
76. Polikar, R.: Ensemble based systems in decision making. IEEE Circuits Syst. Mag. **6**(3), 21–45 (2006)
77. Prati, R.C., Batista, G.E.A.P.A., Monard, M.C.: A survey on graphical methods for classification predictive performance evaluation. IEEE Trans. Knowl. Data Eng. **23**(11), 1601–1618 (2011)
78. Prati, R.C., Batista, G.E.A.P.A., Silva, D.F.: Class imbalance revisited: a new experimental setup to assess the performance of treatment methods. Knowl. Inf. Syst. **45**(1), 247–270 (2015)
79. Provost, F.J., Fawcett, T.: Robust classification for imprecise environments. Mach. Learn. **42**(3), 203–231 (2001)
80. Pujol, O., Radeva, P., Vitria, J.: Discriminant ECOC: a heuristic method for application dependent design of error correcting output codes. IEEE Trans. Pattern Anal. Mach. Intell. **28**(6), 1007–1012 (2006)
81. Qin, A.K., Huang, V.L., Suganthan, P.N.: Differential evolution algorithm with strategy adaptation for global numerical optimization. IEEE Trans. Evol. Comput. **13**(2), 398–417 (2009)
82. Quinlan, J.: C4.5: Programs for Machine Learning. Morgan Kaufmann Publishers Inc., San Francisco (1993)
83. Razakarivony, S., Jurie, F.: Vehicle detection in aerial imagery: a small target detection benchmark. J. Vis. Commun. Image Represent. **34**, 187–203 (2016)
84. Ren, Y., Zhang, L., Suganthan, P.N.: Ensemble classification and regression-recent developments, applications and future directions. IEEE Comput. Intell. Mag. **11**(1), 41–53 (2016)
85. Rifkin, R., Klautau, A.: In defense of one-vs-all classification. J. Mach. Learn. Res. **5**, 101–141 (2004)
86. Roy, A., Cruz, R.M.O., Sabourin, R., Cavalcanti, G.D.C.: A study on combining dynamic selection and data preprocessing for imbalance learning. Neurocomputing **286**, 179–192 (2018)
87. Seiffert, C., Khoshgoftaar, T.M., Hulse, J.V., Napolitano, A.: Rusboost: A hybrid approach to alleviating class imbalance. IEEE Trans. Syst. Man Cybern. Part A **40**(1), 185–197 (2010)
88. Sen, A., Islam, M.M., Murase, K., Yao, X.: Binarization with boosting and oversampling for multiclass classification. IEEE Trans. Cybern. **46**(5), 1078–1091 (2016)
89. Sokolova, M., Lapalme, G.: A systematic analysis of performance measures for classification tasks. Inf. Process. Manag. **45**(4), 427–437 (2009)
90. Stefanowski, J.: Dealing with data difficulty factors while learning from imbalanced data. In: Matwin, S., Mielniczuk, J. (eds.) Challenges in Computational Statistics and Data Mining. Studies in Computational Intelligence, vol. 605, pp. 333–363. Springer, Cham (2016)
91. Sun, Y., Kamel, M.S., Wang, Y.: Boosting for learning multiple classes with imbalanced class distribution. In: ICDM, pp. 592–602. IEEE Computer Society (2006)
92. Sun, Y., Wong, A.K.C., Kamel, M.S.: Classification of imbalanced data: a review. Int. J. Pattern Recognit. Artif. Intell. **23**(4), 687–719 (2009)
93. Sun, Z., Song, Q., Zhu, X., Sun, H., Xu, B., Zhou, Y.: A novel ensemble method for classifying imbalanced data. Pattern Recognit. **48**(5), 1623–1637 (2015)
94. Sáez, J.A., Krawczyk, B., Wozniak, M.: Analyzing the oversampling of different classes and types of examples in multi-class imbalanced datasets. Pattern Recognit. **57**, 164–178 (2016)

95. Tax, D.M., Duin, R.P.W.: Support vector domain description. Pattern Recognit. Lett. **20**, 1191–1199 (1999)
96. Vluymans, S., Fernandez, A., Saeys, Y., Cornelis, C., Herrera, F.: Dynamic affinity-based classification of multi-class imbalanced data with one-vs-one decomposition: a fuzzy rough set approach. Knowl. Inf. Syst. **56**(1), 55–84 (2018)
97. Wang, S., Chen, H., Yao, X.: Negative correlation learning for classification ensembles. In: 2010 International Joint Conference on Neural Networks (IJCNN), pp. 1–8. IEEE (2010)
98. Wang, S., Minku, L.L., Yao, X.: Dealing with multiple classes in online class imbalance learning. In: IJCAI International Joint Conference on Artificial Intelligence, pp. 2118–2124 (2016)
99. Wang, S., Yao, X.: Diversity analysis on imbalanced data sets by using ensemble models. In: Proceedings of the 2009 IEEE Symposium on Computational Intelligence and Data Mining, CIDM'09, pp. 324–331 (2009)
100. Wang, S., Yao, X.: Multiclass imbalance problems: analysis and potential solutions. IEEE Trans. Syst. Man Cybern. Part B **42**(4), 1119–1130 (2012)
101. Wang, S., Yao, X.: Multiclass imbalance problems: analysis and potential solutions. IEEE Trans. Syst. Man Cybern. Part B Cybern. **42**(4), 1119–1130 (2012)
102. Wilson, D., Martinez, T.: Improved heterogeneous distance functions. J. Artif. Intell. Res. **6**, 1–34 (1997)
103. Wozniak, M., Graña, M., Corchado, E.: A survey of multiple classifier systems as hybrid systems. Inf. Fusion **16**, 3–17 (2014)
104. Xia, F., Yang, Y., Zhou, L., Li, F., Cai, M., Zeng, D.: A closed-form reduction of multi-class cost-sensitive learning to weighted multi-class learning. Pattern Recognit. **42**(7), 1572–1581 (2009)
105. Yu, H., Hong, S., Yang, X., Ni, J., Dan, Y., Qin, B.: Recognition of Multiple imbalanced cancer types based on DNA microarray data using ensemble classifiers. BioMed Res. Int. **2013**, 1–13 (2013)
106. Yu, H., Sun, C., Yang, X., Yang, W., Shen, J., Qi, Y.: ODOC-ELM: Optimal decision outputs compensation-based extreme learning machine for classifying imbalanced data. Knowl.-Based Syst. **92**, 55–70 (2016)
107. Yuan, X., Xie, L., Abouelenien, M.: A regularized ensemble framework of deep learning for cancer detection from multi-class, imbalanced training data. Pattern Recognit. **77**, 160–172 (2018)
108. Zhai, J., Zhang, S., Wang, C.: The classification of imbalanced large data sets based on MapReduce and ensemble of ELM classifiers. Int. J. Mach. Learn. Cybern. **8**, 1–9 (2015)
109. Zhang, C., Tan, K.C., Ren, R.: Training cost-sensitive deep belief networks on imbalance data problems. In: International Joint Conference on Neural Networks (IJCNN), Vancouver, pp. 4362–4367. IEEE (2016)
110. Zhang, Z., Krawczyk, B., García, S., Rosales-Pérez, A., Herrera, F.: Empowering one-vs-one decomposition with ensemble learning for multi-class imbalanced data. Knowl.-Based Syst. **106**, 251–263 (2016)
111. Zhang, Z.L., Luo, X.G., García, S., Herrera, F.: Cost-sensitive back-propagation neural networks with binarization techniques in addressing multi-class problems and non-competent classifiers. Appl. Soft Comput. J. **56**, 357–367 (2017)
112. Zhao, X.M., Li, X., Chen, L., Aihara, K.: Protein classification with imbalanced data. Proteins Struct. Funct. Bioinf. **70**(4), 1125–1132 (2008)
113. Zhou, Z.H., Liu, X.Y.: Training cost-sensitive neural networks with methods addressing the class imbalance problem. IEEE Trans. Knowl. Data Eng. **18**(1), 63–77 (2006)
114. Zhou, Z.H., Liu, X.Y.: On multi-class cost-sensitive learning. Comput. Intell. **26**(3), 232–257 (2010)
115. Zong, W., Huang, G.B., Chen, Y.: Weighted extreme learning machine for imbalance learning. Neurocomputing **101**, 229–242 (2013)

Chapter 9
Dimensionality Reduction
for Imbalanced Learning

Abstract One of the most successful data preprocessing techniques used is the reduction of the data dimensionality by means of feature selection and/or feature extraction. The key idea is to simplify the data by replacing the original features with new created that extract the main information or simply select a subset of original set. Although this topic has been carefully studied in the specialized literature for the classical predictive problems, there are also several approaches specifically devised to deal with imbalance learning scenarios. Again, their main purpose is to exploit the most informative features to preserve as much as possible the concept related to the minority class. This chapter will describe the most-known techniques of feature selection and feature extraction developed to tackle imbalance data sets. We will consider these two main families of techniques separately and we will also provide the recent advances in feature selection and feature extraction by non-linear methods. In addition, we will mention a recently proposed discretization approach which is able to reduce the numeric features into categories. The chapter is organized as follows. After a short introduction in Sect. 9.1, we will review in Sect. 9.2 the straightforward solutions devised in feature selection for tackling imbalanced classification. Next, we will delve deeper into describing more advanced techniques for feature selection in Sect. 9.3. Section 9.4 will be devoted to explain the redefined feature extraction techniques based on linear models. In Sects. 9.5 and 9.6, a non-linear feature extraction technique based on autoencoders and a discretization method will be outlined, respectively. Finally, Sect. 9.7 will conclude this chapter.

9.1 Introduction

High dimensional data can be very usual in imbalanced learning. A common characteristic of high dimensional data is that the number of variables far exceeds the number of samples. As we know, classical classifiers are thought to train from datasets in which the number of samples in each class is not equal. The fact that high dimensionality can pose additional challenges when it comes to a balanced prediction in the class has been investigated. In particular, several studies have

© Springer Nature Switzerland AG 2018

A. Fernández et al., *Learning from Imbalanced Data Sets*,

https://doi.org/10.1007/978-3-319-98074-4_9

been done on the prediction of microarray data, which are high-dimensional tools commonly used in the biomedical field.

An important aspect that specifically characterizes the classification for high dimensional data is the need to make some type of DR, either through FS or feature extraction. The former consists of identifying a subset of features that will be used to learn the classification model, and can be done before the classifier is developed or can be incorporated into the classification method. In feature extraction, a reduced set of artificial attributes is created from the most informative aspects of the original features and this new set will replace the original one to perform learning tasks.

The importance of DR for high dimensional data is based on two facts: some classification models cannot be derived if the number of features is greater than the number of observations, and the removal of features that are redundant or have clear correlations with others will improve the predictive accuracy.

In the literature, the results show that the naive use of classifiers in imbalanced high-dimensional data can produce highly biased classification results towards the majority class [1]. The extent of this bias depends on the classification method, the magnitude of the class difference and the level of class imbalance, and is further increased when standard methods of FS are used; the standardization of attributes generally increases the bias and should be avoided, unless the class imbalance is equal in training and testing group. In addition, the use of a balanced training data set is suggested as a good option for the design of accurate model by using data-level sampling techniques. In [1], the authors evaluated the performance of six classification algorithms and three sampling approaches (over- and undersampling and undersampling ensemble) and an algorithm-based threshold approach for logistic regression modeling and Random Forests.

According to [17], these analyses and interpretations are incomplete. For example, they did not take into account the correlation structure between genes in their simulation studies and completely omitted to investigate the effect of lack of data, which is the main factor contributing to the low performance of standard classification algorithms. These reasons motivated the analytic study in [17], where they stated that the classification performance of high-dimensional imbalanced data is affected by the imbalance ratio, the distributions of minority and majority class data, the sample size and FS, as well as the classification algorithm and the correction strategy. A standard classifier could perform well in classifying imbalanced data when the sample size is large enough.

The standard recommendations given to tackle high-dimensional imbalanced data sets are summarized as: (1) to gather the samples for each class as balanced as possible, (2) to estimate the implications of class imbalance using standard classifiers and (3) a suitable classifier can be selected based on the effect of class imbalance and the pre-specified misclassification costs.

Before we begin to mention DR techniques, it is worth mentioning the study of high dimensionality in two widely known pillars of imbalanced classification: SMOTE and KNN.

A proper investigation on the effects of high-dimensional data on SMOTE oversampling was conducted in [2]. The conclusions achieved were the following ones:

- In the low-dimension environment, SMOTE is effective in reducing the class balance problem for most classifiers.
- SMOTE barely influences most of the classifiers trained in high dimensional data.
- When the data is large, SMOTE is beneficial for k-NN classifiers if a FS is carried out before.
- SMOTE is not beneficial for discriminant analysis classifiers even in the low-dimension configuration.
- Undersampling is preferred for some kind of classifier in high dimensional settings.

KNN suffers from hubness which is usually associated with the high dimensional feature spaces present in data. Hubs are small groups of samples that account for most of the observed neighbor situations, and they are very common in KNN. The phenomenon of hubness gets worse in high dimensional data and it influences the bias of the classification rule. In [23], the authors attempted to correlate hubness as an aspect of the imbalance high dimensional classification problems. Their analysis showed some surprising results, such that the minority class induces a high misclassification of the majority class in high dimensional data sets, unlike the low dimensional case.

9.2   Feature Selection

The FS is a data preprocessing task that selects a subset of features or attributes from the entire feature set and eliminates redundant features that do not contribute to performance [9]. FS methods have been introduced to avoid the "curse of dimensionality", meaning that the required number of calculations becomes enormous as the number of dimensions increases, maintaining or even improving the performance of predictor.

There are three main approaches for FS: filtering, wrapping and embedding. Filter methods select high-range features based on statistical or information measures. The wrapper approach makes the selection by using the classifier as a black box and classifying the subset of characteristics by their predictive outcome. Because a complete search requires 2^n different evaluations, greedy or test and trial techniques are more convenient to explore the best solutions. A sensitivity analysis could be used to calculate the relevance of each characteristic according to each classifier. Embedded methods, unlike wrapping approaches, select features while taking into account the design of the classifier and local information, and they are integrated in the modeling process.

This section will be divided into two parts. First, we will mention the first studies carried out in FS for imbalanced scenarios. Next, we will describe the most representative feature selectors devised or updated to address imbalance classification.

9.2.1 Studies of Classical Feature Selection in Imbalance Learning

There are several FS methods studied in the imbalance learning problem. First, the standard methods proposed as they are were analyzed to check whether or not they are beneficial in the performance of imbalanced classification. In [8], three FS methods were analyzed in the prediction of diabetic nephropathy with imbalanced data: ReliefF, sensitivity analysis with SVM and Recursive feature elimination with SVM (SVMRFE).

The key idea in ReliefF is to evaluate the contribution of each feature to the class difference and intraclass similarity [15]. With a randomly selected data, the algorithm looks for the closest k hits (those with the same class label) and errors (those with a different class label). After that, it updates the quality of the contribution of the features with regard to the difference between the features values of the selected data and the closest ones. The pseudocode is shown in Algorithm 1. The diff(f, I_i, I_j) function calculates the difference between the values of the characteristics of two instances. Therefore, the weight vector $\mathbf{W}[f]$ increases when the characteristic value of the selected instance is different from that of the nearest $M_j(C)$. On the other hand, it decreases when there is a difference between the characteristic values of the selected instance and the nearest H_j. Finally, according

---

Algorithm 1 ReliefF algorithm

---

  function RELIEFF(All the instances and their class labels)
      Set all weights $\mathbf{W}[f] = 0$
      Set arbitrary iteration number a
      for $i = 1$ to a **do**
          Randomly select an Instance I_i
          Find the k nearest hits H_j
          Find the k nearest misses $M_j(C)$ for each class $C \neq Class(I_i)$
          for $f = 1$ to number of features **do**
             $\mathbf{W}[f] = \mathbf{W}[f] - \sum_{j=1}^{k} \text{diff}(f, I_i, H_j)/m \cdot k+$

             $\sum_{C \neq Class(I_i)} \left[\frac{P(C)}{1-P(class(I_i))} \sum_{j=1}^{k} \text{diff}(j, I_i, M_j(C)) \right]/(m \cdot k)$
          end for
      end for
      return Weight vector $\mathbf{W}[f]$.
  end function

Algorithm 2 Sensitivity analysis method

---
function SA(A predictive model $F(x)$)
    Set all weights $\mathbf{W}[f] = 0$
    Set $\mathbf{O}[a] = 0$
    for $f = 1$ to number of features **do**
        Initialize an instance $\mathbf{x} = [x_1 = \text{mean}(x_1), x_2 = \text{mean}(x_2), \ldots, x_n = \text{mean}(x_n)]$.
        for $j = \min(x_f)$ to $\max(x_f)$ **do**
            Set $x_f = j$
            Set $\mathbf{O}[j] = F(x)$
        end for
        $\mathbf{W}[f] = \max(\mathbf{O}) - \min(\mathbf{O})$
    end for
    return Weight vector $\mathbf{W}[f]$.
end function

Algorithm 3 SVM-RFE method

---
function SVM-RFE(Training instances $\mathbf{x}_o$ and their class labels $\mathbf{y}$)
    Initialize subsets of surviving features $\mathbf{s} = [1, 2, \ldots, n]$
    Initialize feature ranking list $\mathbf{r} = []$
    while $\mathbf{s} \neq []$ **do**
        Restrict training instances to the subset of surviving features $\mathbf{X} = \mathbf{X}_o(:, \mathbf{s})$
        Train the SVM with the restricted instances and their class labels
        Compute the weight vector of the SVM model $\mathbf{w} = \sum_i^{sc} y_i \alpha_i \mathbf{x}_i$
        Compute the ranking criteria $C_k = (\mathbf{w}_k)^2$, for all k
        Update the feature ranking list according to the criteria
        Eliminate features with the lowest ranking
    end while
    return Feature ranking list $\mathbf{r}$
end function

---

to the weight values in $\mathbf{W}[f]$, the ranking of each feature can be identified and then to carry out the FS by removing those with the smallest weight values.

Sensitivity analysis is another method that has been widely used to rank input features in terms of their contribution to the output discrimination as wrapper [22]. It involves varying each input feature over a reasonable range with the fixed ones and observing the relative changes in the outputs. As a result, the features that produce the greatest deviation in output are considered most important. Algorithm 2 shows the pseudocode of the sensitivity analysis method. The algorithm calculates the difference between the maximum and minimum output of the predictive model when a feature value varies from its minimum possible to its maximum with the other features remaining fixed.

SVM-RFE is an example of embedded method and a similar approach that eliminates less important features recursively [10]. It uses the weight magnitude as ranking criterion. The algorithm scheme is presented in Algorithm 3.

The main conclusion achieved in [8] is that ReliefF had advantages in computation because they do not interact with classifiers. By contrast, the wrapper and embedded methods were more computationally expensive, but offered better performances than ReliefF in imbalance classification.

The imbalance nature of the software defect prediction was also studied in [13]. Some filter-based feature ranking were studied in this contribution: chi-square (CS), information gain (IG), gain ratio (GR), two types of ReliefF (RF and RFW), and symmetrical uncertainty (SU). The authors considered four scenarios covering several questions in imbalance classification: (1) FS based on original data and training data based on original data; (2) FS based on original data and training data based on sampled data; (3) FS based on sampled data and training data based on original data; and (4) FS based on sampled data and training data based on sample data. The results showed that FS based on sampled data resulted in significantly better performance than FS based on original data.

The paradigm of text classification was explored in [18]. Again, several feature ranking based algorithms are analyzed from the point of view of three main draw-backs detected: they are highly problem dependent, they are univariate functions and they fail in multiple class problems with imbalanced class distribution because of the bias to the majority class. The analysis included IG, normalized IG and CS as information-theoretic scoring measures; Document frequency (DF), odds ratio (OR) and precision and recall for information-retrieval scoring measures. Regarding imbalanced learning, most feature ranking methods fail when applied to multiple class problems with non-uniform class distributions. Feature ranking methods can select relevant features for easy classes, while they cannot learn in difficult or small classes. They pay more attention to easy and large classes to compensate for their weakness facing difficult classes. This behavior compensate their overall accuracy, even though there are a large number of negative results for small and difficult classes. As the authors recommend, one approach to reducing the destructive impact of the imbalance is to make use of the classification of local characteristics rather than a global scheme.

A comprehensive experimental study involving the most representative datasets in microarray data using well-known FS methods is presented in [3]. As expected, the authors devote a major part of the experimental analysis to the imbalance nature of microarray data sets. Seven classical feature selectors were used using many configurations. The results obtained in this experimental study are highly dependent on the classifier, the FS method, and in particular the dataset. A general recommendation on the careful study of the particularities of each problem and classifier is given before tackling an imbalance learning problem.

9.2.2   Ad-hoc Feature Selection Techniques for Tackling Imbalance Classification

There are many attempts to select the best features when dealing with imbalanced classification problems. In this section, we will describe the most relevant presented in the specialized literature.

9.2.2.1 Feature Selection with Biased Sample Distribution

As we have seen, ReliefF is essentially an instance-based filtering method. This means that ReliefF's ability to estimate the quality of attributes depends largely on the number of instances of different classes in the data set. Although the algorithm depends on the class distribution of the instances, it does not consider the class distribution while classifying the attributes. For balanced datasets, this filtering procedure works well. However, performance degrades significantly when the data set is imbalanced or biased towards a specific class. Since many applications often provide users with unbalanced datasets, it is strongly recommended that a filtering approach take into account data imbalance issues to improve the performance of imbalanced datasets.

Three enhancements of ReliefF were devised in [12] to handle imbalance classification:

- **Higher Weight (HW) feature selection**
  In HW (see Algorithm 4), the class distributions are firstly calculated. When updating the weight for each feature, if the randomly selected instance x_i is from the minority class, we add a higher weight by using the next equation instead of the original.

$$\mathbf{W}[a] = \mathbf{W}[a] - \sum_{j=1}^{k} \text{diff}(a, x_i, h_i)/(m \cdot k) +$$

$$\sum_{C \neq class(x_i)} \left[\left(\frac{P(C)}{1 - P(class(x_i))} \right) \times \sum_{j=1}^{k} \text{diff}(a, x_i, M_j(C)) \left(1 + \left(1 - \frac{\min}{m} \right) \right) \right] /(m \cdot k)$$

Algorithm 4 Higher weight ReliefF FS

---

  function HW(D a training set with m instances and n attributes)
    $\mathbf{W}[] = 0 \, for all attributes$
    min = number of minority class examples
    for $f = 1$ to m **do**
      Randomly select an instance x_i from D.
      Find x_i's k nearest instances $H_i j$, $j = 1, \ldots, k$ with the same label as x_i
      for each class $C \neq$ class(x_i) **do**
        Find x_i's k nearest $M_j(C)$, $j = 1, \ldots, k$ labeled as class C
      end for
      for each attribute $a = 1$ to n **do**
        if x_i is a minority class example **then**
          Use new equation to update weight $\mathbf{W}[a]$
        else
          Use original equation to update weight $\mathbf{W}[a]$
        end if
      end for
    end for
    return Weight vector $\mathbf{W}$.
  end function

Algorithm 5 Differential minority repeat FS

---

function DMR(D a training set with m instances)

　$\{S_{majority}, S_{minority}\} \leftarrow$ build majority and minority subsets from D.

　$N_{majority} \leftarrow$ number of instances in $S_{majority}$

　$N_{minority} \leftarrow$ number of instances in $S_{minority}$

　$D_n \leftarrow N_{majority} - N_{minority}$

　$D_{minority} \leftarrow$ randomly sample D_n from $S_{minority}$

　$S'_{minority} \leftarrow S_{minority} \bigcup D_{minority}$

　$S' \leftarrow S_{minority} \bigcup D_{minority} \bigcup S_{majority}$

　$\mathbf{W}[] \leftarrow$ apply ReliefF to S'

　return Weight vector $\mathbf{W}$.

end function

Algorithm 6 Balanced minority repeat FS

---

function BMR(D a training set with m instances)

　$\{S_{majority}, S_{minority}\} \leftarrow$ build majority and minority subsets from D.

　$N_{majority} \leftarrow$ number of instances in $S_{majority}$

　$N_{minority} \leftarrow$ number of instances in $S_{minority}$

　$S_1, S_2, \ldots, S_N \leftarrow$ randomly split $S_{majority}$ into N subsets with

　$N = \frac{N_{majority}}{N_{minority}}$ and $S_{majority} = S_1 \bigcup S_2 \bigcup \ldots \bigcup S_N$

　for each subset $i = 1$ to N **do**

　　$S'_i = S_i \bigcup S_{minority}$

　　$\mathbf{W}_i[] \leftarrow$ apply ReliefF to the S'_i

　　for each attribute $j = 1$ to n **do**

　　　$\mathbf{W}[j] \leftarrow \mathbf{W}[j] + \mathbf{W}_i[j]$

　　end for

　end for

　return Weight vector $\mathbf{W}$.

end function

On the other hand, if x_i is from the majority class, we keep the original weight function to estimate the weight for the attributes. In doing so, we assign a higher weight value to genes that are able to differentiate a minority class example from a majority class example.

- **Differential Minority Repeat (DMR)**. This method, illustrated in Algorithm 5, alters the original dataset in such a way that it becomes relatively balanced, so that the minority class examples are not neglected while calculating the weight for attributes. If we compute the difference between the number of majority and minority class examples, we can update the minority instance subset by randomly selecting and duplicating as many instances from the minority instance as necessary and then adding and merging these to a new built example dataset.
- **Balanced Minority Repeat (BMR)**. In this technique, which is shown in Algorithm 6, we undersample and decompose the majority class examples into a number of small subsets, each of which has almost the same number of instances as the minority class example set. The number of the newly created subsets is estimated by the ceiling of the ratio between the ratio of number of examples in the majority set and minority set, let us call it N. After it, each created subset

is aggregated with the original minority subset, obtaining a total of N relatively balanced subsets. At the last step, ReliefF is applied to each subset, and the a sum of the weight values for each gene over all N subsets is computed.

9.2.2.2 Combating the Small Sample Class Imbalance Problem Using Feature Selection

Most of the content in [27] examines the performance of various FS metrics and how they address the problem of class imbalance. Because there are two other general approaches to dealing with this problem, we must also examine the performance of sampling techniques and algorithms. They selected a representative example of each of these approaches to compare it to the FS methods. The FS metrics are single-sided or double-sided. They differ according to whether they select only positive features or a combination of positive and negative features. Positive features are those that, when present, indicate class membership, while negative features indicate non-membership of a class. A one-sided metric uses the signed value of a feature's score and will therefore only select positive features. A two-sided metric ignores the punctuation mark of a feature and only considers the absolute value; you can select both positive and negative features.

The authors evaluated binary and continuous FS methods. Within the continuous family, there are several attempts to directly deal with imbalanced classification problems:

- **Pearson Correlation Coefficient (PCC)** measures the strength and degree of the linear relationship between a feature and the class labels. It is a one-sided metric; a two-sided version can easily be created by taking the square value of the scores.
- **Feature Assessment by Sliding Thresholds (FAST)** is an algorithm designed to find the ROC curve representing a features predictions for the class labels. It selects those features with the greatest area under the ROC. This is a two-sided metric.
- **Feature Assessment by Sliding Thresholds (FAIR)**: Precision-Recall uses a modification of the FAST algorithm that instead finds the Precision-Recall curve associated with a features predictions for the class labels. Those features with the greatest area under the P-R curve are selected. This is a two-sided metric.
- **Signal-to-Noise Correlation Coefficient (S2N)** measures the ratio of some desired signal (i.e., the class labels) to the background noise in a feature. While this ratio is originally an electrical engineering concept, in the ML community. It is a one-sided metric.

According to [27], the best FS metrics are S2N, FAST and PCC. These metrics do not discretize the attributes; the conversion of continuous noisy characteristics into binary characteristics seems to amplify the noise and makes the binary feature selectors to work worse with a small number of attributes. In contrast, continuous metrics were not so affected by noise and separated the classes slightly better.

9.2.2.3   Discriminative Feature Selection by Nonparametric Bayes Error
Minimization

There is an algorithmic framework that employs a nonparametric estimator to minimize the Bayes error rate when a subset of features is being selected. It was proposed in [29] with the goal of studying the underlying properties of the subset of margin-based FSs algorithms such as Relief, revealing their weaknesses and the way of how to mitigate them. As a consequence, the authors devised two alternative algorithms:

- **Parzen-Relief**, which resembles the standard Relief algorithm, but instead of kNN, it uses the Parzen window method to estimate the Bayes error.
- **MAP-Relief**, which incorporates the class distribution into the margin maximization objective function and thus effectively captures the imbalanceness among classes.

9.2.2.4   Feature Selection for High-Dimensional Imbalanced Data

Two promising approaches were developed in [31] to cope with high-dimensional data in imbalance classification problems. As it is well-known, the samples belonging to the larger classes have more influence on the FS method. By contrast, the samples of the minority class are crucial to achieve a good performance in imbalanced learning but they have less dominance in the FS process. Because of that, two procedures were proposed to solve these problems in FS. The former is a class decomposition based FS and the latter is a FS based on the Hellinger distance.

- **Decomposition-based Feature Selection**. In [31], authors proposed a framework based on decomposition for FS. Specifically, as shown in Algorithm 7, there are three phases in this frame. In Phase I, they used K-means clustering in class i ($i = 1, 2, \ldots, C$) according to the number of $K(i)$ clusters preset by the user to break down the majority class into relatively balanced pseudo-subclasses. Then it changes the instance labels of class i to the subclass labels provided by the K-means clustering, thus forming a multi-class data set with $\sum_{i=1}^{C} K(i)$ subclasses. After, the pseudo-labels for the samples with the pseudo-subclasses are got. For some smaller classes, decomposition is unnecessary, which means that $K(i) = 1$. In Phase II, the procedure measures the goodness of each feature with pseudo-labels and the traditional measurement of the goodness of each feature. It then ranks the features according to the goodness based on the calculated scores. Then, the good features of the top k are selected and the pseudo-labels to the original labels are released. Finally, in Phase III, we can do the classification or other task with the selected features and the labels released.
- **Feature Selection based on the Hellinger Distance**. Here, we describe an alternative method of FS based on Hellinger's distance for imbalanced data, also proposed in [31]. Hellinger's distance is a measure of distributive divergence. Let

---

Algorithm 7 Decomposition based framework for FS

---

function DFFS(D a training set with M features and C classes. L is the label set. K is a vector
that specifies the number of local clusters.)
    Phase I: local clustering
    for class $i = 1$ to C **do**
        clusterLabel(i) = Clustering($D(i),K(i)$)
        $L(i)$ = changeLabel($L(i)$,clusterLabel(i))
    end for
    Phase II: score calculation
    for feature $j = 1$ to M **do**
        score(j) = scoreMeasure(feature(j),L)
    end for
    ranking features according to score
    features with higher scores coming first
    $D' = D$(sample set with the top-M-scores features)
    Phase III: validation
    learningModel = build(D',L)
    return D' as the training set after FS.
end function

P and Q denote two measures of probability that are continuous distributions with respect to a third measure of probability λ. The definition of Hellinger's distance can be given as

$$d_H(P,q) = \sqrt{\int_\Omega (\sqrt{P} - \sqrt{Q})^2 d\lambda}.$$

This definition does not depend on λ. It can also be defined for a countable space θ:

$$d_H(P,q) = \sqrt{\sum_{\theta \in \Theta} (\sqrt{P(\theta)} - \sqrt{Q(\theta)})^2}.$$

Hellinger's distance range is in $[0, \sqrt{2}]$. It is symmetrical and not negative, which implies $d_H(P, Q) = d_H(Q, P)$. Hellinger's distance allows us to capture the notion of "affinity" between probability measures in a space of finite events. If $P = Q$, then the distance is 0, and if P and Q are completely disjoint, the distance will be $\sqrt{2}$. Therefore, the best feature we want to select is the one that carries the minimum affinity between the class. The minimum affinity means that this feature is more discriminatory between classes. Thus, the Hellinger's distance can be used to measure the predictive power of the features to classify the samples.

For computing efficiency, we discretize all continuous features into p intervals. Assuming a two-class problem, let X_+ be positive class and X_- be the negative one, we want to calculate the distance at the aggregated normalized frequencies on all partitions. Thus, Hellinger's distance between X_+ and X_- is:

$$d_H(X_+, X_-) = \sqrt{\sum_{j=1}^{p} \left(\sqrt{\frac{|X_{+j}|}{X_+}} - \sqrt{\frac{|X_{-j}|}{X_-}} \right)^2}.$$

9.2.2.5   Iterative Feature Selection

There is a proposal in [14] where an iterative method is designed for processing the FS for imbalanced data. Algorithm 8 presents the procedure of this approach. It consists of two basic steps:

1. Use of the random subsampling technique (RUS) to balance data. RUS creates the balanced data by randomly removing examples from the majority class. In this algorithm, they look at two postsampling ratios: 35:65 (RUS35) and 50:50 (RUS50), meaning that the ratio between the minority and majority examples is 35:65 and 50:50, respectively, after sampling.
2. Applying a filter-based FS technique to the sampled data and ranking all features according to their predictive capacity (scores). They explored 18 filter-based FS techniques.

The filter-based FS techniques used are: Chi-Squared, Gain Ration, Information Gain, Relief, ReliefW, Symmetrical Uncertainty, F-Measure, Odds-Ratio, Power, Probability Ratio, Gini Index, MI, Kolmogorov-Smirnov Statistic, Deviance, Geometric Mean, AUC_{ROC}, AUC_{PR}, Signal-to-noise ratio.

Algorithm 8 Iterative FS algorithm

---

function IFS(D a training set with features F^j, $j = 1, \ldots, M$ and two classes $\in \{fp, nfp\}$. A filter-based feature ranking technique ω. A data sampling technique Σ. A predefined threshold: number (percentage) of the features to be selected.)

    for $i = 1$ to k **do**

        Use Σ to balance D and get the balanced data D_i.

        Employ ω to rank features on D_i, and get new rankings $\omega_i(F^j)$, $j = 1, \ldots, M$.

    end for

    Create feature ranking $\mathbb{R}$ by combining the k different rankings $\omega_i(F^j)|i = 1, \ldots, k \; \forall j$ with mean (average).

    return Select features according to $\mathbb{R}$ and a predefined threshold.

end function

9.3   Advanced Feature Selection

This section is devoted to enumerate and briefly describe several FS techniques used in imbalanced learning, mainly divided into two groups: ensemble and/or wrapper based techniques and evolutionary-based techniques.

9.3.1   Ensemble and Wrapper-Based Techniques

The main approaches based on ensembles or sophisticated wrappers are the following ones:

- In [30], an ensemble-based wrapper approach is proposed for the selection of features from highly imbalanced datasets. The proposed algorithm retains the advantages of wrapper FS while maximizing data usage and reducing the FS bias simultaneously by forming multiple base classifiers with balanced subsets of samples. A hybrid multisampling procedure is used to create balanced sample subsets. At the same time, they introduce a unified framework that incorporates the ensemble FS and multiple sampling in a mutually beneficial way.
- FS using SVMs [19]: here, it is presented a family of embedded methods for selecting features in a backward fashion using vector support machines that are inspired by the algorithm SVM-RFE [10] backward selection procedure. The reason for this approach is that it removes those features whose elimination has less impact on the final solution, considering a problem of imbalance classification. To do this, the algorithm tries to recreate the main objective of this task: to achieve the best predictive performance in an unseen subset, using a cost sensitive metric.
- The Ensemble FS (EFS) is a type of ensemble learning approach based on FS. Unlike the traditional selection of features, EFS seeks not only to find an appropriate subset for learning, but from the perspective of the ensemble to obtain the best ensemble. The selected subsets of features usually have a strong impact on the performance of the final ensembles. If these subsets are prone to the minority class, then the whole will be beneficial to the minority class. In [32], the authors proposed the Imbalanced Ensemble FS (IEFS), which imports costs into feature subset evaluation functions using weight-based evaluation methods and adds penalty-reward factors. During the process of searching for subsets of characteristics, a reward will be given while increasing the classification accuracy of the minority class. Otherwise, a punishment will be imposed.

9.3.2   Evolutionary-Based Techniques

Regarding evolutionary-based FS techniques, we may find in the literature several proposals:

- Joint optimization of granularity learning and FS in genetic-based fuzzy rule systems (GA-FS+GL) [25]: it is a proposal based on an standard generational genetic algorithm for the database definition that allows us to carry out FS and learn an adequate number of labels for each selected variable (granularity learning).
- In [21], a genetic algorithm that combines four tasks; namely IS, instance weighting, FS and feature weighting; was used to optimize the performance of the NN rule. The individuals of the population are represented by hybrid arrays formed by binary and real numbers and the operators to recombine individuals are the classical from binary genetic algorithms and differential evolution in real coded parts.
- The ECBL'14 Big Data competition consisted of an huge imbalanced classi-fication problem of bioinformatics. The winner algorithm was ROSEFW-RL [24], based on several MapReduce approaches to balance the classes distribution through random oversampling, detect the most relevant features via an evolu-tionary feature weighting process and a threshold to choose them and to build an appropriate Random Forest model. The feature weighting was performed by using a differential evolution algorithm guided by the NN rule. After the process, the associated weights are obtained and a threshold is used to decide which features will be selected to build the model.

9.4   Linear Models for Feature Extraction

Feature extraction involves reducing the quantity of resources needed to explain an oversized set of information. Feature extraction can be seen as a transformation of the original feature space to a smaller feature space to reduce the dimensionality. It is well-known [6] that feature extraction can significantly reduce the dimensions of the feature space compared with FS. When carrying out analysis of complex data, one of the foremost issues stems from the amount of features concerned. Analysis with an outsized variety of variables typically needs an oversized quantity of memory and computation power, additionally it should cause a classification algorithm to overfit to training samples and generalize poorly to new samples. Feature extraction may be a general term for methods of constructing mixtures of the variables to induce around these issues while still describing the information with sufficient accuracy. Many data scientist practitioners believe that a properly optimized feature extraction is the key to achieve an effective model construction.

The results will be improved using created sets of application-dependent features, usually built by an expert. One such method is termed feature engineering. As an alternative, general DR techniques are used such as: Independent component analysis, Latent semantic analysis, Partial least squares or Principal component analysis.

This section will describe the major proposals for feature extraction based on linear models in imbalanced learning. Although there are many applications of these techniques in this topic, they are used as secondary processes to improve a part of a whole algorithm or methodology. Thus, these applications will not be mentioned here; instead, we will describe the ad-hoc linear features extraction techniques thought for dealing with imbalanced class distributions.

9.4.1   Asymmetric Principal Component Analysis

Given q n−dimensional column vectors for training where the positive class ω_0 has q_0 samples and the negative class ω_c has q_c samples, $q = q_0 + q_c$, compute the class-conditional mean vectors M_0, M_c, and covariance matrices Σ_0, Σ_c. The covariance matrix of the class mean is computed as

$$\Sigma_m = \frac{1}{q}[q_0(M_0 - M)(M_0 - M)^T + q_c(M_c - M)(M_c - M)^T],$$

where M is the mean over all training samples. It is not difficult to get the covariance matrix of the total training data by

$$\Sigma_t = \frac{1}{q}(q_0\Sigma_0 + q_c\Sigma_c) + \Sigma_m. \tag{9.1}$$

If the a priori probabilities of the two classes are estimated by $p_0 = q_0/q$ and $p_c = q_c/q$, the covariance matrix of the total training data can be expressed as

$$\Sigma_t = p_0\Sigma_0 + p_c\Sigma_c + \Sigma_m. \tag{9.2}$$

In the literature, Σ_t is often called total scatter matrix, Σ_m is called between-class scatter matrix, and $\Sigma_w = p_0\Sigma_0 + p_c\Sigma_c$ is often called within-class scatter matrix.

PCA applies eigen-decomposition on Σ_t, i.e., $\Sigma_t = \Phi\Lambda\Phi^T$, and keeps the m eigenvectors Φ_m, $\Phi_m \in \mathbb{R}^{\kappa \times \triangleright}$, corresponding to the m largest eigenvalues. An n−dimensional pattern vector X is transformed to an m−dimensional feature vector $\hat{X}$ by $\hat{X} = \Phi_m^T X, m < n$. The role of PCA in the classification is far beyond the low-dimensional data representation or solving the singularity problem of Σ_w. For a quantitative analysis of the role of PCA in classification, we can model the class-conditional distributions by multivariate Gaussian density functions. The Bayes optimal decision rule detects a positive sample X if

$$(X - M_c)^T \Sigma_c^{-1}(X - M_c) - (X - M_0)^T \Sigma_0^{-1}(X - M_0) > b, \tag{9.3}$$

where $b = \ln(|\Sigma_0|/|\Sigma_c|) + 2(\ln p_c - \ln p_0)$. After applying eigen-decomposition, the Bayes decision rule (9.3) is simplified as

$$\sum_{k=1}^{n} \frac{g_k^2}{\lambda_k^c} - \sum_{k=1}^{n} \frac{h_k^2}{\lambda_k^0} > b, \tag{9.4}$$

where g_k is the projection of $(X - M_c)$ on the eigenvector Φ_k^c corresponding to the eigenvalue λ_k^c of Σ_c and h_k is the projection of $(X - M_0)$ on the eigenvector Φ_k^0 corresponding to the eigenvalue λ_k^0 of Σ_0.

Many approaches modify the above optimal decision rule into

$$\sum_{k=1}^{m} \frac{g_k^2}{\lambda_k^c} + \sum_{k=m+1}^{n} \frac{g_k^2}{p_c} - \sum_{k=1}^{m} \frac{h_k^2}{\lambda_k^0} - \sum_{k=m+1}^{n} \frac{h_k^2}{p_0} > b, \tag{9.5}$$

which replaces the $n - m$ smallest eigenvalues of both classes by two constants p_c and p_0, respectively, and often $m << n$.

Eigenvalue λ_k^c or λ_k^0 is the variance of the positive or negative training samples projected on the eigenvector Φ_k^c or Φ_k^0. It is an estimate of the class true ensemble variance based on the available training data. If the eigenvalues deviate from the ensemble variances, the decision rule (9.3) and (9.4) overfits the training samples and therefore there will be a poor generalization over test data.

Thus, similar to (9.5) that replaces the smallest eigenvalues by a constant, removing the subspace spanned by the eigenvectors of Σ_0 and Σ_c corresponding to the smallest eigenvalues improves the generalization of the classifier. However, the principal components of Σ_m should not be removed as they contain the discriminative information. Hence, it is obvious that PCA on $\Sigma_t = p_0\Sigma_0 + p_c\Sigma_c + \Sigma_m$ plays an important role in classification. It alleviates the overfitting problem or improves the generalization capability by removing the subspace spanned by eigenvectors of Σ_0 and Σ_c corresponding to the small eigenvalues while keeping the principal components of Σ_m.

However, in (9.1) and (9.2), Σ_0 and Σ_c are weighted by q_0/q and q_c/q or by p_0 and p_c. These weights are required for PCA to achieve the least-mean-square reconstruction error. In classification, the goal is to remove dimensions in which the sample-based class-conditional variables are unreliable. The reliability of a covariance matrix is not dependent on the class prior probability. The Bayes optimal decision rule (9.3) minimizes the sum of the two errors weighted by p_0 and p_c do that the threshold b depends on p_0 and p_c. More training samples of a class may results in a more reliable covariance matrix if they are properly collected. However, it is not the more but the less reliable covariance matrix that should be heavily weighted so that more dimensions characterized by the small variances of this class can be removed. It is thus clear that PCA on the total data scatter matrix Σ_t (9.1) or (9.2) does not effectively remove the unreliable dimensions because Σ_t is not constructed from a classification point of view.

To address this problem, the author in [11] proposed to construct an asymmetric pooled covariance matrix by

$$\Sigma_\alpha = \alpha_0 \Sigma_0 + \alpha_c \Sigma_c + \Sigma_m, \tag{9.6}$$

where α_0 and α_c are determined by the reliability of the covariance matrices Σ_0 and Σ_c, $\alpha_0 + \alpha_c = 1$. Different from (9.1) and (9.2), α_0 and α_c are unrelated to the class a priori probabilities. The objective of the proposed asymmetric pooled covariance matrix Σ_α is to facilitate an effective removal of the unreliable dimensions. Hence, larger values of α_0 or α_c should be assigned to the less reliable covariance matrix so that more dimensions characterized by the small variances of the less reliable class can be removed by eigen-decomposition of Σ_α.

If there is no prior knowledge about the class characteristics and the data collection procedure, less training samples in general result in a less reliable covariance matrix. Thus, it was suggested to construct the asymmetric pooled covariance matrix in the form of

$$\Sigma_\alpha = \frac{1}{q}(q_c \Sigma_0 + q_0 \Sigma_c) + \Sigma_m, \tag{9.7}$$

In sharp contrast to the scatter matrix Σ_t (9.1) that weights the covariance matrices proportionally to the number of training samples, the proposed Σ_α (9.7) pools them with weights inversely proportional to the number of training samples.

The asymmetric principal component analysis (APCA) applies eigen-decomposition on Σ_α (9.6), i.e.,

$$\alpha_0 \Sigma_0 + \alpha_c \Sigma_c + \Sigma_m = \Phi \Lambda \Phi^T, \tag{9.8}$$

and extract the m eigenvectors $\hat{\Phi}$ from Φ corresponding to the m largest eigenvalues in Λ. It aims at removing the unreliable dimensions to alleviate the overfitting problem and hence to achieve a better classification performance in imbalanced problems.

9.4.2   Extraction of Minimum Positive and Maximum Negative Features

In [26], the authors proposed a method for extracting, in terms of absolute values, the minimum positive and maximum negative feature in binary imbalanced classification. This means that the positive features extracted are expected to be in an interval $[-\xi, \xi]$, and the negative features fall into $(-\infty, -\xi) \cup (\xi, +\infty)$, where ξ is a positive scalar. Two models were developed to perform the feature extraction.

The technique is mainly oriented to linear classifiers (LDA, SVM, etc.), which classify a sample x based on the sign of the value

$$f(x) = x^T w + w_o, \tag{9.9}$$

where w is the coefficient vector and w_0 is the threshold. Linear classifiers have bad issues related to the assumed presence of a hyperplane that perfectly could separate the data into two classes, which rarely occurs and with the trend of misclassifying outliers.

Thus, the basic idea of the method proposed in [26] is to seek for a pair of parallel hyperplanes $h^{\pm}(x) : w^T x = \pm \xi$ for classification. The positive samples are expected to be clustered in the belt area A defined as:

$$A : -\xi \leq w^T x \leq +\xi. \tag{9.10}$$

The negative samples are expected to be in the area $\overline{A}$ defined as:

$$\overline{A} : w^T x > +\xi \cup w^T x < -\xi. \tag{9.11}$$

Compared with the negative samples, the positive samples are nearer to the hyperplane $h^0(X) : w^T x = 0$. This methods assigns two asymmetrical areas to these two classes instead of assigning two symmetric half-spaces to the positive and negative class. The outcome is to assign a larger area to the negative class.

The scalar $w^T x$ is the feature of sample x after projecting onto the feature extractor w. From Eqs. 9.9 and 9.10, we know that the positive features fall into the interval $[-\xi, \xi]$, and the negative features fall into $(-\infty, -\xi) \cup (\xi, +\infty)$. In order to enlarge the separation, the method seeks the minimum possible and maximum negative features in terms of absolute value for imbalanced classification.

Correctly, we can obtain the feature extractor w by solving the following l inequalities, where l denote the total number of samples and l_1 are the number of samples from the positive class:

$$\begin{cases} |w^T x_i| \leq \xi, i = 1, 2, \ldots, l_1 \\ |w^T x_i| > \xi, i = l_1 + 1, l_1 + 2, \ldots, l \end{cases} \tag{9.12}$$

Nevertheless, there are three problems in solving these inequalities: (1) there is no solution in some cases, (2) when they are solvable and have infinite solutions there is a not straightforward way to choose the best ones and (3) it is high time consuming.

Next, the authors in [26] proposed two modifications of the model in Eq. 9.12.

9.4.2.1 Model 1

It is an special case of the model in Eq. 9.12 where the parameter ξ is set to zero. This model minimizes the positive features to be zero and maximizes the negative features, as follows:

$$\max_{w} ||X_2^T w||_2 \quad s.t. \quad ||X_1^T w||_2 = 0, \tag{9.13}$$

where the matrices X_1 and X_2 are the positive and negative samples, respectively.

To solve Eq. 9.13 efficiently, they designed a two-step procedure. The first step generates a set of candidate feature extractors onto which the positive samples have zero projections. From this set, the second step takes the vectors onto which the negative samples have the maximum projections as the feature extractors.

9.4.2.2 Model 2

They proposed the next model

$$\min_{max||X_2^T v||_2} ||X_1^T v||_2. \tag{9.14}$$

Among all the vectors v onto which the negative samples have maximum projections, this model picks out the ones onto which the positive samples have minimum projections and takes them as the feature extractors. Again, there is a two.step procedure to solve this model. This first step generates a set of vectors onto which the negative samples have projections as large as possible. From this set, the second step picks out the vector onto which the positive samples have minimum projections.

9.5 Non-linear Models for Feature Extraction: Autoencoders

Deep learning tools have been also used for imbalanced learning, such as the case of autoencoders. An autoencoder produces useful feature representation when the number of neurons in the hidden layer is different from the number of inputs, allowing a change of dimensionality to the input data. DR can be also done as well with autoencoders.

In [20], the authors propose the Dual Autoencoding Features (DAF), which is a feature learning method based on stacked autoencoders, providing a new form to solve imbalance classification problems. Two stacked autoencoders with different activation functions are used to learn features from the input space with imbalanced data to extract important characteristics from data. They are concatenated to form the DAF.

First of all, we have to introduce the concept of autoencoder used in [20]. A single autoencoder consists of the input layer, the encoding layer and the decoding layer. For each sample x_i in the training dataset D, where x_i and N denote the n-dimension input vector of the i-th sample and the number of samples, respectively, we can define the encoding layer as:

$$f(x) = s_e(W_e x + b_e), \tag{9.15}$$

where W_e, b_e, and $S_e(\cdot)$ denote the weight matrix, the bias vector and the activation function of the encoding layer, respectively. Similarly, the decoding layer is defined as:

$$g(x) = s_d(W_d x + b_d), \tag{9.16}$$

where W_d, b_d, and $S_d(\cdot)$ denote the weight matrix, the bias vector and the activation function of the decoding layer, respectively.

The output of the autoencoder is:

$$y = g(f(x)) \tag{9.17}$$

The aim of the autoencoder is to learn a feature representation in the encoding layer such that the outputs of the autoencoder reconstruct the inputs. Thus, the learning problem of an autoencoder is to find a set of parameters $\theta = \{W_e, b_e, W_d, b_d\}$ to minimize the reconstruction error between the inputs and the outputs of the autoencoder:

$$\arg \min_\theta \sum_{i=1}^{N} L(x_i, g(f(x_i))), \tag{9.18}$$

where

$$L(x, y) = ||y - x||_2. \tag{9.19}$$

To avoid overfitting, the l_2 weight decay penalty us added to restrict the magnitudes of weights. Then, the optimization problem is rewritten as follows:

$$\arg \min_\theta \frac{1}{2} \sum_{i=1}^{N} L(x_i, g(f(x_i))) + \frac{1}{2}\lambda ||W||_2, \tag{9.20}$$

where λ and W denote the regularization parameter and the matrix consisting of two weight matrices (W_e and W_d) respectively. The parameter θ of an autoencoder is usually optimized using back-propagation, but in this case, the desired outputs are the same than the inputs.

The autoencoder can be stacked together to derive deeper and more abstract features to support better representation of patterns. In stacked autoencoders, the outputs of the encoding layer of an autoencoder are fed to the next autoencoder as their inputs [5].

In the following, we will describe the framework of DAF. It combines the feature learned from two stacked autoencoders which use the *sigmoid* and the *tanh* functions as activation functions, respectively. Figure 9.1 shows the overall

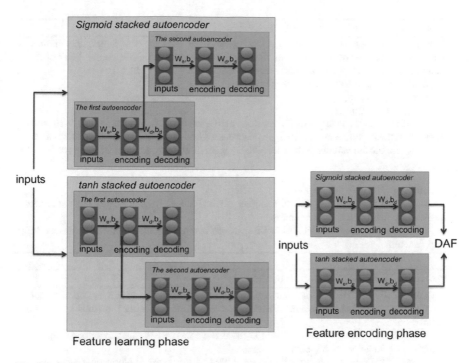

Fig. 9.1 DAF framework

procedure of the DAF over all datasets, distinguishing the feature learning from the feature encoding. Both functions are defined as follows:

$$sigmoid(x) = \frac{1}{1 + e^{-x}},\tag{9.21}$$

$$tanh(x) = \frac{e^x - e^{-x}}{e^x + e^{-x}}\tag{9.22}$$

DAF uses 2-layer stacked autoencoders to learn features, but it does not limit the number of autoencoders to being stacked. According to the authors, a single layer autoencoder may not be powerful enough to learn useful features, and the stacked autoencoders with more than 2 layers may not yield much better representation at the cost of slower training time. For these reasons, they justify the need of using stacked autoencoders with 2-layers with different activation functions.

Algorithm 9 shows the feature learning procedures for the DAF and Algorithm 10 shows the feature encoding procedures for a given sample set. The training dataset will be used to train with Algorithm 9 and then samples in both the training and the testing sets are encoded using Algorithm 10 to get the DAF for both sets. The DAF of the training set is used to train the classifier for solving an imbalanced classification problem.

Algorithm 9 Feature learning of the DAF

---

function DAF LEARNING(N, n, l, m_j, D denote the number of samples, the number of features, the number of autoencoders, the number of neurons on the encoding layer of the j-th autoencoder, and the $n \times M$ input feature matrix.)

    Scale each input feature to the range [0, 1].

    Set $\varphi = D$, and $m_0 = n$.

    for $j = 1$ to l **do**

        Train an autoencoder with the $sigmoid$ activation function using σ and Eq. 9.20 with m_j neurons on the encoding layer and $m_{(j-1)}$ neurons on both the input and the decoding layer.

        Compute the outputs of the encoding layer for all training samples to get $m_j \times N$ matrix H_j.

        Set $\varphi = H_j$

    end for

    Repeat the previous loop to train another stacked autoencoder by replacing the $sigmoid$ activation function by the $tanh$ function.

    return Two stacked autoencoders with $sigmoid$ and $tanh$ activation function, respectively.

end function

Algorithm 10 Feature encoding of the DAF

---

function DAF ENCODING(X denotes the $n \times N_X$ input feature matrix of a five set of samples)

    Get two stacked autoencoders with $sigmoid$ and $tanh$ activation functions by the Algorithm 9.

    Compute the values of the encoding layer of the l_{th} $sigmoid$ stacked autoencoder for all samples in X to get $m_l \times N_X$ matrix $H_{sigmoid}$.

    Compute the values of the encoding layer of the l_{th} $tanh$ stacked autoencoder for all samples in X to get $m_l \times N_X$ matrix H_{tanh}.

    Concatenate $H_{sigmoid}$ and H_{tanh} by rows to get the learned feature matrix H_{DAF}.

    return $2m_l \times N_X$ learned feature matrix H_{DAF}.

end function

9.6 Discretization in Imbalanced Data: ur-CAIM

To the best of our knowledge, there is only an attempt of ad-hoc discretization technique thought for dealing with imbalance learning problems. This algorithm, denoted by ur-CAIM, is an extension of the well-known CAIM [16] discretizer.

CAIM stands for Class-Attribute Interdependency Maximization criterion, which measures the dependency between the class variable C and the discretized variable D for attribute A. The method requires the computation of the quanta matrix [7], which, in summary, collects a snapshot of the number of real values of A within each interval and for each class of the corresponding example. The criterion is calculated as:

$$\text{CAIM}(C, D, A) = \frac{\sum_{r=1}^{n} \frac{\max_r^2}{M_{+r}}}{m},$$

where m is the number of intervals, r iterates through all intervals, i.e. $r = 1, 2, \ldots, m$, $\max_r$ is the maximum value among all q_{ir} values (maximum value within the rth column of the quanta matrix), M_{+r} is the total number of continuous values of attribute A that are within the interval $(d_{r-1}, d_r]$.

The CAIM criterion formula is biased towards the majority class instances and it is not capable of handling such imbalanced data. In [4], the authors present a new algorithm, called ur-CAIM, that solves the above mentioned problems of the original CAIM algorithm, analyzing the behavior and performance of the original CAIM on imbalanced data. The ur-CAIM algorithm is a free parameter algorithm, which means that it does not require any user-entered parameter settings. The algorithm is capable of automatically selecting the most appropriate number of discrete intervals. In addition, it overcomes the bias of the CAIM algorithm of choosing a number of intervals very close to the number of classes, which provides more flexible discretization schemes.

The ur-CAIM criterion is defined as:

$$\text{ur-CAIM} = \text{CAIM}_N \cdot \text{CAIR} \cdot (1 - \text{CAIU}),$$

where CAIM_N stands for a normalized version of the standard CAIM criterion to the range [0, 1], CAIR is the class-attribute interdependence redundancy criterion [28] with a modification in the MI to handle imbalance data more appropriately, and CAIU is the class attribute interdependence uncertainty criterion [4].

The criterion ur-CAIM represents a compensation for processing the number of intervals. The CAIM part of the formula advocates a more generalized scheme with fewer intervals, while the CAIR and CAIU advocate a greater number. The ur-CAIM criterion thus makes it possible to evaluate different behaviors of different metrics and presents a unique quality measure of the discretization scheme that works well with imbalanced data.

The rest of the algorithm works exactly like the original CAIM.

9.7 Summarizing Comments

DR is an important aspect of imbalanced classification. We have seen that numerous studies have been published that analyze the deterioration in the behavior of classical algorithms, such as SMOTE, when undertaking high-dimensional data.

The most commonly used and analyzed techniques in DR are the FS. Again, much emphasis has been placed on analyzing the properties of classical ranking-based methods when dealing with high-dimensionality problems and combining them with all kinds of sampling techniques. The ReliefF algorithm is particularly noteworthy, with several adaptations specifically designed for imbalanced classification.

Feature extraction techniques have just been developed in this area. While there are many applications and they have been combined in more complex processes, in this chapter we have mentioned two linear and one non-linear proposals based on stacked autoencoders. There is still much to be done in this discipline, since the nature of imbalanced learning makes it conducive to devising new techniques of feature extraction that take into account the classes of examples acting in a supervised manner.

Finally, a discretization proposal has been presented that comes as an adaptation to the classic CAIM technique and that helps to preserve the intervals that contain minority examples and shows better behavior in this type of problems. Discretization is a field that has also been underdeveloped and requires more effort to improve the algorithms that require it to work.

References

1. Blagus, R., Lusa, L.: Class prediction for high-dimensional class-imbalanced data. BMC Bioinf. **11**(1), 523 (2010)
2. Blagus, R., Lusa, L.: Smote for high-dimensional class-imbalanced data. BMC Bioinf. **14**, 106 (2013)
3. Bolón-Canedo, V., Sánchez-Maroño, N., Alonso-Betanzos, A., Benítez, J.M., Herrera, F.: A review of microarray datasets and applied feature selection methods. Inf. Sci. **282**, 111–135 (2014)
4. Cano, A., Nguyen, D.T., Ventura, S., Cios, K.J.: ur-CAIM: improved CAIM discretization for unbalanced and balanced data. Soft Comput. **20**(1), 173–188 (2016)
5. Charte, D., Charte, F., García, S., del Jesús, M.J., Herrera, F.: A practical tutorial on autoencoders for nonlinear feature fusion: taxonomy, models, software and guidelines. Inf. Fusion **44**, 78–96 (2018)
6. Chen, M.C., Chen, L.S., Hsu, C.C., Zeng, W.R.: An information granulation based data mining approach for classifying imbalanced data. Inf. Sci. **178**(16), 3214–3227 (2008)
7. Ching, J.Y., Wong, A.K.C., Chan, K.C.C.: Class-dependent discretization for inductive learning from continuous and mixed-mode data. IEEE Trans. Pattern Anal. Mach. Intell. **17**, 641–651 (1995)
8. Cho, B.H., Yu, H., Kim, K.W., Kim, T.H., Kim, I.Y., Kim, S.I.: Application of irregular and unbalanced data to predict diabetic nephropathy using visualization and feature selection methods. Artif. Intell. Med. **42**(1), 37–53 (2008)
9. Guyon, I., Elisseeff, A.: An introduction to variable and feature selection. J. Mach. Learn. Res. **3**(Mar), 1157–1182 (2003)
10. Guyon, I., Weston, J., Barnhill, S., Vapnik, V.: Gene selection for cancer classification using support vector machines. Mach. Learn. **46**(1–3), 389–422 (2002)
11. Jiang, X.: Asymmetric principal component and discriminant analyses for pattern classification. IEEE Trans. Pattern Anal. Mach. Intell. **31**(5), 931–937 (2009)
12. Kamal, A.H.M., Zhu, X., Pandya, A.S., Hsu, S., Narayanan, R.: Feature selection for datasets with imbalanced class distributions. Int. J. Softw. Eng. Knowl. Eng. **20**(2), 113–137 (2010)
13. Khoshgoftaar, T.M., Gao, K., Seliya, N.: Attribute selection and imbalanced data: problems in software defect prediction. In: 22nd IEEE International Conference on Tools with Artificial Intelligence, ICTAI, Arras, 27–29 Oct 2010, vol. 1, pp. 137–144 (2010)
14. Khoshgoftaar, T.M., Gao, K., Napolitano, A., Wald, R.: A comparative study of iterative and non-iterative feature selection techniques for software defect prediction. Inf. Syst. Front. **16**(5), 801–822 (2014)
15. Kononenko, I.: Estimating attributes: analysis and extensions of relief. In: Bergadano, F., Raedt, L.D. (eds.) European Centre for Modern Languages. Lecture Notes in Computer Science, vol. 784, pp. 171–182. Springer, Berlin/Heidelberg (1994)

16. Kurgan, L.A., Cios, K.J.: CAIM discretization algorithm. IEEE Trans. Knowl. Data Eng. **16**(2), 145–153 (2004)
17. Lin, W.J., Chen, J.J.: Class-imbalanced classifiers for high-dimensional data. Briefings Bioinf. **14**(1), 13–26 (2012)
18. Makrehchi, M., Kamel, M.S.: Impact of term dependency and class imbalance on the performance of feature ranking methods. Int. J. Pattern Recogn. Artif. Intell. **25**(7), 953–983 (2011)
19. Maldonado, S., Weber, R., Famili, F.: Feature selection for high-dimensional class-imbalanced data sets using support vector machines. Inf. Sci. **286**, 228–246 (2014)
20. Ng, W.W., Zeng, G., Zhang, J., Yeung, D.S., Pedrycz, W.: Dual autoencoders features for imbalance classification problem. Pattern Recogn. **60**(C), 875–889 (2016)
21. Pérez-Rodríguez, J., Arroyo-Peña, A.G., García-Pedrajas, N.: Simultaneous instance and feature selection and weighting using evolutionary computation. Appl. Soft Comput. **37**(C), 416–443 (2015)
22. Stevenson, M., Winter, R., Widrow, B.: Sensitivity of feedforward neural networks to weight errors. IEEE Trans. Neural Netw. **1**(1), 71–80 (1990)
23. Tomašev, N., Mladenić, D.: Class imbalance and the curse of minority hubs. Knowl.-Based Syst. **53**, 157–172 (2013)
24. Triguero, I., del Río, S., López, V., Bacardit, J., Benítez, J.M., Herrera, F.: ROSEFW-RF: the winner algorithm for the ECBDL'14 big data competition: an extremely imbalanced big data bioinformatics problem. Knowl.-Based Syst. **87**, 69–79 (2015)
25. Villar, P., Fernández, A., Carrasco, R.A., Herrera, F.: Feature selection and granularity learning in genetic fuzzy rule-based classification systems for highly imbalanced data-sets. Int. J. Uncertainty Fuzziness Knowl.-Based Syst. **20**(3), 369–397 (2012)
26. Wang, J., You, J., Li, Q., Xu, Y.: Extract minimum positive and maximum negative features for imbalanced binary classification. Pattern Recogn. **45**(3), 1136–1145 (2012)
27. Wasikowski, M., Chen, X.: Combating the small sample class imbalance problem using feature selection. IEEE Trans. Knowl. Data Eng. **22**(10), 1388–1400 (2010)
28. Wong, A., Liu, T.: Typicality, diversity, and feature pattern of an ensemble. IEEE Trans. Comput. **24**, 158–181 (1975)
29. Yang, S., Hu, B.: Discriminative feature selection by nonparametric Bayes error minimization. IEEE Trans. Knowl. Data Eng. **24**(8), 1422–1434 (2012)
30. Yang, P., Liu, W., Zhou, B.B., Chawla, S., Zomaya, A.Y.: Ensemble-based wrapper methods for feature selection and class imbalance learning. In: Pei, J., Tseng, V.S., Cao, L., Motoda, H., Xu, G. (eds.) Pacific Asia Knowledge Discovery and Data Mining (1). Lecture Notes in Computer Science, vol. 7818, pp. 544–555. Springer, Berlin/Heidelberg (2013)
31. Yin, L., Ge, Y., Xiao, K., Wang, X., Quan, X.: Feature selection for high-dimensional imbalanced data. Neurocomputing **105**, 3–11 (2013)
32. Yin, H., Gai, K., Wang, Z.: A classification algorithm based on ensemble feature selections for imbalanced-class dataset. In: 2016 IEEE 2nd International Conference on Big Data Security on Cloud (BigDataSecurity), IEEE International Conference on High Performance and Smart Computing (HPSC), and IEEE International Conference on Intelligent Data and Security (IDS), New York, pp. 245–249. IEEE (2016)

Chapter 10
Data Intrinsic Characteristics

Abstract Although class imbalance is often pointed out as a determinant factor for degradation in classification performance, there are situations in which good performance can be achieve even in the presence of severe class imbalance. The identification of situation where the class imbalance is a complicating factor is an important research question. These situations are often associated to some data intrinsic characteristics. This chapter describes some of these characteristics. Section 10.2 discuss some studies using data complexity measures for categorizing imbalanced datasets. Section 10.3 discuss the relationship between class imbalance and small disjuncts. Section 10.4 analyses the problem of data rarity or lack of data. Section 10.5 discuss the problem of class overlapping, a complicating factor for class imbalance. Section 10.6 discuss the problem of noise in the context of class imbalance. The influence of borderline instances is discussed in Sect. 10.7. Section 10.8 analyses the problem on shifting between training and deployment datasets. Section 10.9 describes problems with imperfect data. Finally, Sect. 10.10 concludes this chapter.

10.1 Introduction

Class imbalance was widely acknowledged as a complicating factor for classification. However, some studies also argue that the imbalance ratio is not the only cause of performance degradation in learning from imbalanced data [46, 60]. These and other studies point out that many data intrinsic characteristics, in conjunction of an imbalanced class distribution, may account for the poor performance in classification problems.

As a matter of fact, standard classifiers may achieve good performance in some highly imbalanced domains, as long as the data at hand can be considered linearly separable (or of low complexity). Furthermore, state of the art techniques for dealing with class imbalance may fail in some problems, where other factors (such as noise or class overlapping) are complicating factors for classification.

Understanding these data intrinsic characteristics, as well as their relationship with class imbalance, is crucial for applying existing and developing new techniques

© Springer Nature Switzerland AG 2018
A. Fernández et al., *Learning from Imbalanced Data Sets*,
https://doi.org/10.1007/978-3-319-98074-4_10

to deal with imbalance data. Studies alongside this line of research include the estimation of the inherent complexity of the data set, the presence of sub-concepts and small disjuncts, the lack of sufficient data, the overlapping among class regions, noisy instances, class boundaries and rare borderline examples, data shifts between training and testing data, and data imperfection. This chapter discuss some of these data intrinsic characteristics can be considered when dealing with class imbalance.

10.2   Data Complexity for Imbalanced Datasets

Possible causes for degradation in performance of learning algorithms include deficiencies in the algorithms, mismatch between methods and problems, and intrinsic difficulties in the data [34]. Understanding some characteristics in the data may help in identifying families of algorithms which are more adequate to data with some properties, pointing out some difficulties in data as well as identify intrinsic difficulties in the data.

Unfortunately, developing measures for evaluating the characteristics in a dataset is not a trivial task, as classification difficulty may have different natures [33]. Several approaches have been developed aiming to evaluate the complexity of a dataset based on the overlapping of values within a single feature; estimates of the separability of classes and measures of geometry, topology, and density of manifolds [33, 49, 72].

Some research work has been conducted to study the relationship of classification complexity and class imbalance. In [90], the authors have used data complexity measures to gain some insights about the behavior of a data sampling method based on data projection in two text classification tasks. Complexity measures were computed globally for the entire dataset and in a per class basis. In [2], a complexity measure based on kNN rule is proposed. Roughly speaking, this measure is high if, in the training set, a large proportion of minority class instances is misclassified by kNN. The proposed measure has a strong linear correlation with sensitivity, unlike other measures presented in [33].

In [47], the authors study the relationship between Fisher discriminant ratio [33] with the class imbalance ratio, and the performance of classifiers with and without treatment for class imbalance. This measure aims to measure the degree of class overlapping, considering each feature of the dataset in isolation. Their main result is that the imbalance ratio by itself cannot justify the degradation in performance, and the Fisher discriminant ratio can help in characterizing the behavior of classifiers under presence of class imbalance. The relationship of class overlapping and class imbalance under the context of software defect prediction was studied in [11].

The proportion of class labels in the neighborhood of an instance was used in [51] for characterizing the minority class instances into different types. The proportion of kNN from the same class compared to neighbors from different classes can range from $k : 0$ (all neighbors are from the same class as the analyzed instance) to $0 : k$ (all neighbors belong to the different classes). Depending on this proportion minority class instances are divided into:

- **Safe instances:** where the majority of NNs' instances belongs to the same class.
- **Borderline instances:** where the proportion of instances in the neighborhood is close to a balanced distribution.
- **Rare instances:** when the majority of neighbors belongs to a different class.
- **Outliers:** when the all the NNs belong to a different class.

An ad-hoc and a parametric kernel approach for delimiting the thresholds for each category were proposed in [51]. The ad-hoc approach is suitable for small values of k (e.g., 5), whereas the kernel approach can be applied to larger values. The authors advocate the idea that different types of instances should have different treatments, and focus on rare and outliers' cases. Experiments for tuning the number of neighbors depending on other data characteristics was carried out in [6].

An approach for estimating the complexity of individual instances was proposed in [73]. The instance hardness measure is based on the frequency that the instance is misclassified by different classifiers. Authors claim that the one of the factors that contributes to instance hardness is the degree of imbalance. Instance hardness can be used for undersampling by removing from the training set the instances of majority class with high degree of hardness. Figure 10.1 shows an example of this approach for an artificial dataset where the instances from the majority class were undersampled according to the instance hardness until some desired imbalance ratio is achieved. In Fig. 10.1, the original imbalance ratio is 1:9 (one minority to nine majority) and is undersampled to the ratios 1:4, 1:2 and 1:1 (top right, bottom left and bottom right, respectively). The majority, minority and removed instances are shown in blue, red and cyan, respectively.

10.3 Sub-concepts and Small-Disjuncts

A common problem faced by learning algorithms is that instances from the same class normally do not belong to a homogeneous region in the input space. Indeed, it is common that the "concept" beneath a class is split into several sub-concepts, spread over the input space. This lack of homogeneity is particularly problematic in algorithms based on the strategy of dividing-and-conquering (e.g., as in decision trees) and set covering (e.g., as in rule induction), where the sub-concepts lead to the creation of small disjuncts [36]. The name is related to the fact that, in divide-and-conquer and set covering approaches, the models are divided in several pieces, and a concept class is represented as disjunction of different pieces for each class.

Figure 10.2 shows graphical representations of two different datasets. In the figure to the left (Fig. 10.2a), only one large concept is present for each class. However, in the figure to the right (Fig. 10.2b), the concept represented by blue dots is split into two groups. In this case, the learned model is composed by two pieces, where one of them is small disjunct. The presence of sub-concepts (and small disjunct) may accentuate the problem of class imbalance, as different levels of imbalance may exist for each sub-concept.

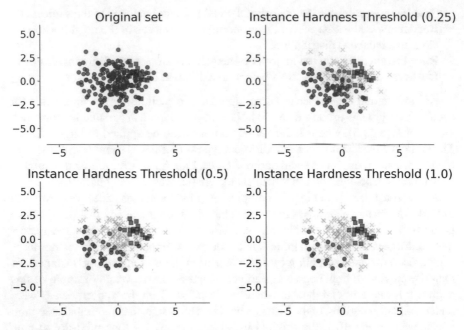

Fig. 10.1 Instance hardness used for undersampling

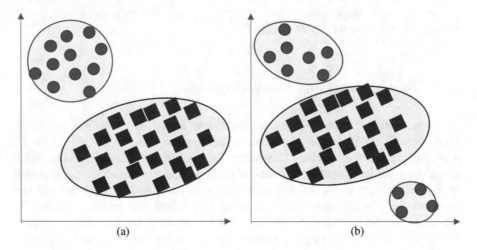

Fig. 10.2 Datasets with and without sub-concepts. (**a**) No sub-concepts. (**b**) Sub-concepts

It is reported in the literature that small disjuncts are problematic because they concentrate most of the errors of a classifier [36, 88]. One possible reason for this ER is the degree of imbalance between disjuncts of different sizes [39, 61, 86]. Class imbalance may also lead to generation of small disjuncts which are not necessarily related to sub-concepts.

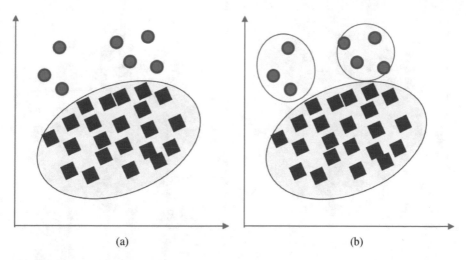

(a)   (b)

Fig. 10.3 Imbalanced Datasets with and without sub-concepts. (**a**) Dataset without small disjuncts. (**b**) Sub-concepts

In some case, the formation of small disjuncts appear due to the sparsity and scarcity of data, a situation common in class imbalance [46]. Figure 10.3 illustrates this situation. In this figure, the same dataset is shown in both sides. In the figure to the left (Fig. 10.3a) one (relatively) large disjuncts for each class exists. However, as the dataset is imbalanced (the number of red squares is much larger than the number of blue circles), the blue circle class is scarce, and a ML algorithm may found two small disjuncts rather than the larger disjunct, as shown in the figure to the right (Fig. 10.3b).

Besides class imbalance, small disjuncts may also be caused by other reasons, such as the inability of the algorithm to properly represent the class boundaries, the occurrence of class overlapping and noise instances, among others.

Figure 10.4 shows the small disjunct formation due to the inability of ML algorithms which can only represent models by splitting the input space by axis-parallel lines, such as most regular decision tree learning algorithms. In this situation, small disjuncts were created as a way of the algorithm to approximate the oblique decision boundary. In the figure to the left (Fig. 10.4a), the class boundary is correctly identified as an oblique line (e.g., as in a logistic regression or SVMs), whereas in the figure to the right (Fig. 10.4b), the decision boundaries are composed by axis-parallel splits (e.g., as in a decision tree learner).

Small disjuncts may also appears when there is a class overlap in some regions of the input space. Figure 10.5 illustrates this situation. To avoid creating larger overlapped disjuncts, as in the figure to the left (Fig. 10.5a), the learning algorithm may prefer to generate smaller disjuncts, as in the figure to the right (Fig. 10.5b).

Another possible reason for the appearance of small disjuncts is the presence of noisy instances. If noisy instances occur in a similar region in the input space, they me mistakenly interpreted as a small disjunct. Figure 10.6 illustrates this. The figure

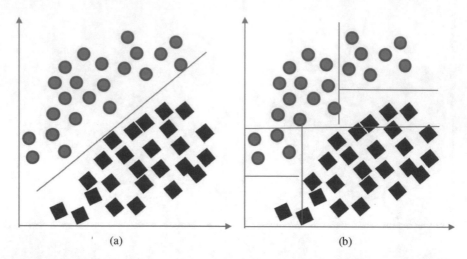

Fig. 10.4 Formation of small disjuncts due to the inability of a decision tree to handle oblique class boundaries. (**a**) Oblique decision boundary. (**b**) Axis-parallel splits cannot approximate well the boundary

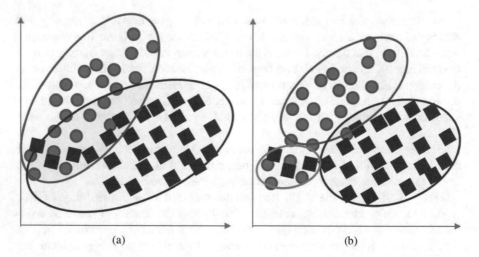

Fig. 10.5 Formation of small disjuncts for avoiding overlapping regions. (**a**) Large overlapped disjuncts found. (**b**) Sub-concepts created to avoid overlapping areas

to the left (Fig. 10.6a) represents a dataset with two noisy instances. In the figure to the right (Fig. 10.6b), these two noisy instances are mistakenly interpreted as a small disjunct. The occurrence of noise may also split a larger disjunct, if the noisy instances invades the boundaries of a different class [46].

In [86], a graphical evaluation approach was proposed to evaluate the concentration of errors towards small disjuncts, for classifiers which allows a piecewise evaluation of each disjunct. The main idea is to order the disjuncts by the disjunct

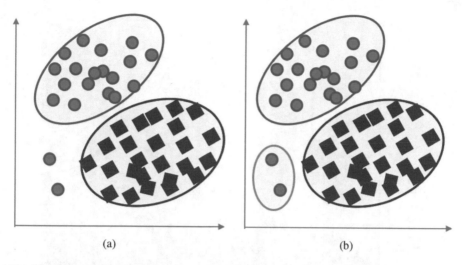

(a)   (b)

Fig. 10.6 Formation of small disjuncts due to the presence of noisy data. (**a**) Instances outside the class boundaries are due to noise. (**b**) Noisy instance are mistakenly identified as a small disjunct

size, and plotting the percentage of correctly classified instances in the x-axis *versus* the percentage or errors in the y-axis for each disjunct. Figure 10.7 shows an example of an ER Curve. The curve is generated by starting with the smallest disjunct from the classifier and then progressively adding larger disjuncts, according to the disjunct size. The diagonal line represents a classifier in which classification errors are distributed uniformly across the disjuncts. If the ER curve is above this diagonal, then errors are more concentrated in the smaller disjuncts. The area under this curve is the EC index. Values of EC granter than 0.5 indicates that errors are majority concentrated in small disjuncts.

To alleviate the problem with small disjuncts, several approaches were proposed in the literature [86, 88]:

- **Obtaining more training data.** Poorly represented classes may lead to the apparition of small disjuncts, specially in the minority class. Acquiring new data in under-represented regions could alleviate the problem [38].
- **Use adequate inductive bias.** To avoid the introduction of artificial small disjuncts in caused by a mismatch between the algorithm bias and the data at hand, richer inductive bias may be required [9, 22, 23].
- **Using more appropriate metrics.** Adequate metrics could help in properly identifying disjuncts when classes overlaps or in the presence of noisy instances [35]. Another possible option is to use different metrics independent of class imbalance [13, 18, 59]
- **Better control pruning.** Correctly determining pruning parameters could help in establishing an appropriate trade-off between disjunct sizes and classification performance. A strong pruning strategy will eliminate most small disjuncts by

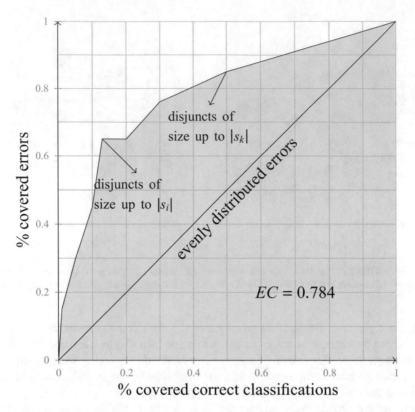

Fig. 10.7 Example of ER curve. Disjuncts are ordered by size, such that $|s_i| < |s_j|$, and the percentage of correct classified instances is plotted against the percentage of incorrectly classified instances

generalizing the classification rules, while no pruning will highly increase the likelihood of smaller (and maybe spurious) disjuncts.

- **Using ensembles** Different ensemble techniques have been proposed to overcome the problem of class imbalance [10, 28, 68, 84]. As ensembles work by combining the output of different classifiers, the detrimental effect of small disjuncts may be averaged out by using ensembles.

A method developed to handle both class imbalance and small disjuncts have been proposed in [39]. It uses a cluster based oversampling. Authors argument that handling both problems together is an interesting and worthy approach to improve performance.

10.4   Lack of Data

A problem that often arises in classification is the small number of training
instances. This issue, often reported as data rarity [87] or lack of data [65], is
related to the "lack of density" or "insufficiency of information". In these scenarios,
learning algorithms do not have enough data to make generalizations about the
underlying concept, producing poor models. This is because a sufficient amount of
data is required by learning algorithms to make generalizations about the datasets.
Without a sufficient large training set, a classifier may not generalize characteristics
of the data. Furthermore, the classifier could also overfit the training data, with a
poor performance in out-of-sample tests instances [65].

The lack of data problem is intensified in the presence of class imbalance. To
gain some insight of the reasons, consider the artificial dataset shown in Fig. 10.8.
In both plots the ratio between positive (blue dots) and negative (red squares) is the
same: 1/10. However, the number of instances in the figure to the left (Fig. 10.8b) is
about 10% of the number of instances in the figure to the right (Fig. 10.8b).

In the former case, we have an absolute rarity of the positive instances, due to
the small sample size. Besides an imbalance proportion, very few instances of the
positive class were available for training a classifier. In the latter case, however, we
have a relative rarity. Even though the dataset is imbalanced the number of positive
instances may be sufficient to train a reasonable classification model. Indeed, an
experimental framework developed in [89] shows that performance increases as
more training set instances where available, for the same imbalance ratio.

Although the relative rarity may be a problem in some domains, absolute rarity is
a much worse problem. It has been shown that sampling techniques, a method often

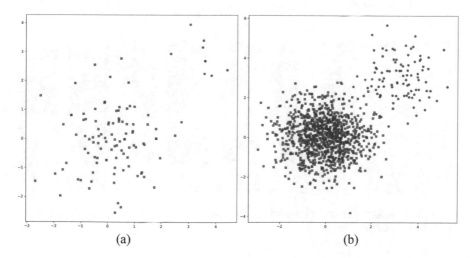

(a)   (b)

Fig. 10.8 Imbalance dataset with and without lack of data. (**a**) Lack of data to represent the
problem. (**b**) Data of the problem is well represented

used in to deal with class imbalance, may fail in the case of absolute rarity [20]. FS can be used to reduce the data sparsity, and thus improve results of learning in presence of class imbalance and small sample size [20, 85].

10.5   Overlapping and Separability

Class overlapping occurs when the input features are not sufficient to correctly differentiate among instances of different classes, and the same regions of the input space contains instances from more than one class. Therefore, the class boundaries overlap in these regions.

It has been shown, using artificially generated datasets, that class overlapping is complicating factor for imbalanced classes [60]. The experiments conducted by the authors, using the learning algorithm C4.5, support the claim that when the class overlapping is larger, the influence of class imbalance in the degradation in performance of the induced classifiers is stronger.

Figures 10.9 and 10.10 shows a simplified version of these experiments for different learning algorithms. In both figures, data is artificially generated from a bivariate Gaussian distribution with a uniform covariance. In Fig. 10.9, the center of mass of each class is one standard deviation apart from each other, resulting in a high class overlapping. The data from Fig. 10.10 were generated using the same pattern, although the center of mass is located two standard deviations apart from each other, thus the classes are less overlapped. In both figure, the first line corresponds to data generated from the same class proportion (a balanced dataset), whereas in the second line the class ratio is $1/5$ (an imbalanced dataset). The values in the lower right corner indicate the AUC_{ROC}.

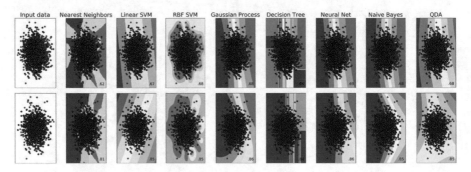

Fig. 10.9 A comparison of decision boundaries induced by different learning algorithms for highly overlapped datasets

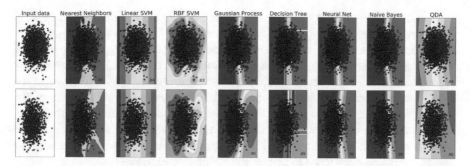

Fig. 10.10 A comparison of decision boundaries induced by different learning algorithms for low overlapped datasets

Analyzing both figures, we can observe the influence of class imbalance and class overlapping in each dataset. In the former case, where the datasets are more overlapped, the deterioration in performance comparing balanced and imbalanced datasets is much stronger than in the latter, where the datasets are less imbalanced. The stronger deterioration can be observed for all classifiers in the highly overlapped case (Fig. 10.9). The induced class boundaries changes considerably, and we can see a much larger influence of the majority class in imbalanced case. On the other hand, in the less overlapped datasets, the influence is much lower (Fig. 10.10). In this particular case, RBF SVM and kNN are more affected, but the influence region of both classes changes less for the other learning algorithms.

These figures show that class overlapping do play an important role in the performance degradation when associated to class imbalance, as the highly overlapped dataset is stronger affected by class imbalance when compared to the lower overlapped dataset. Other studies have drawn similar conclusion using different experimental evaluation.

In [73], authors conjectured that instance complexity is affected by class imbalance and class overlapping. However, the relationship between these two components is unknown, and other sources may contribute to the degree of hardness of instances.

The relationship between the performance and complexity of learned models and the problems of overlapping and class imbalance was studied in [16]. The authors show that overlapping and imbalance, as well as the training set, have interdependent effects in the model complexity and performance and that it is not possible characterize their effects by considering them only in isolation. However, the analysis of the overlap problem in isolation shows it is a much more serious issue than imbalance.

A comparative study of kNN and other four learning algorithms in the context of overlapped and imbalanced classes was performed in [25]. They investigate problems where the degree of imbalance differs according to the degree of imbalance, including in an inverse rate to the original imbalance degree. They conclude that algorithms with a local scope (like kNN) are more dependent of changes in the local imbalance ratio. In this case, the local imbalance ratio and the size of the overlap region are more important than the overall imbalance ratio. Furthermore, their results also show that the influence of the class with more instances in the overlap reviews is are better classified by global learning algorithms, whereas the less predominant class tends to be better classified by local methods.

A measure proposes a measure for estimating the degree of overlap in a region of the input space was proposed in [7]. The measure is based on the R-value, proposed in [55], which considers the number of instances of different classes in the k neighborhood of each instance from a given class, averaged over all classes. The extension proposed in [7] also consider the imbalance ratio. This and other measures are used as meta-features for a meta-learning for predicting an adequate learning algorithm for a dataset.

10.6 Noisy Data

Real world data generally present many inconsistencies that negatively affects data quality. These inconsistencies are generally denominated as noise, and can decrease the performance of learning algorithms [94]. Two types of noise are distinguished in the literature: feature (or attribute) and class noise. Class noise is generally assumed to be more harmful than attribute noise in ML [21]. Instance noise alters the observed values of features (e.g., adding a Gaussian noise to a continuous feature) while class noise somehow affects the observed class values (e.g., by somehow flipping the label of a minority class instance to the majority class label).

Considering the context of class imbalance, the presence of class noise can be much problematic than in balanced scenarios, highlighting the necessity to deal with these noisy instances. Mislabeled minority class instances will contribute to increase the perceived imbalance ratio, as well as introduce mislabeled noisy instances inside the class region of the minority class. On the other hand, mislabeled majority class instances may lead the learning algorithm, or imbalanced treatment methods, focus on wrong areas of input space.

Several algorithms originally developed to deal with class noise have been used as, adapted for, or combined with sampling techniques. In [3], e.g., noise cleaning algorithms were adapted for undersampling by only removing instances from the majority class. Author investigate five data cleaning methods adapted for undersampling:

- **Tomek Links** Give a pair of instances (e_i, e_j) from different classes, this pair is called a Tomek link [80] if, for a given distance measure d, there is not another instance e_z such that $d(e_i, e_z) < d(e_i, e_j)$ or $d(e_j, e_z) < d(e_i, e_j)$. For undersampling, the majority class instance from Tomek links are removed.

- **Condensed Nearest Neighbor Rule (CNN)** is based on the construction of a consistent subset. A subset $\hat{E} \subset E$ is said consistent if 1NN rule using $\hat{E}$ correctly classify the instances from E [30]. The adaptation for working as an undersample by forming $\hat{E}$ by the union of a randomly draw positive instance with the minority instances. The 1NN rule is used to classify the remaining instances and incorrectly classified instances are added to $\hat{E}$. The set $\hat{E}$ corresponds to the undersampled set.
- **One-sided selection (OSS)** Consists in the application of Tomek links followed by the CNN Rule [41].
- **CNN + Tomek** Similar to OSS, but first apply the CNN rule followed by the application of Tomek links.
- **Neighborhood Cleaning Rule (NCL)** is based on the Edited NN rule [43], which for noise cleaning removes instances which at least two out of three instances belong to a different class. For undersampling, this was adapted to remove majority class instances. If the instance belongs to the majority class and at least two out of three NNs are from the other class, then the instance is removed. However, if the instance belongs to the minority class and the instance is misclassified by its three NNs, the neighbors from the majority class are removed.

Figure 10.11 shows a pictorial comparison of these data cleaning methods adapted for undersampling, for an artificial dataset. Blue dots represent majority class instances, red squares minority class instances, and green crosses removed instances. These techniques have in common that they perform an informed sampling. Some methods focus on removing instances from regions that the presence of one class is abundant, and others near the decision boundaries.

The association between the oversampling technique SMOTE with Tomek links removal and the Edited Neighborhood Rule was also explored in [3]. In this case, these methods are used as data cleaning methods, aiming to remove potentially noise instances from both classes after the synthetic instances were generated. The idea is that artificially generated instances may also introduce noise, that can be removed by the cleaning process.

An empirical investigation about the impact of class imbalance and class noise was performed in [81]. Authors conducted a series of experiments to answer six research questions: (1) what is the impact of class noise in presence of class imbalance? (2) is the noisy class location significant? (3) are the effects of class noise in imbalanced datasets similar in different learning algorithms? (4) the sampling algorithms performs well in the presence of class noise? (5) are there differences in sampling techniques with different levels of noise? and (6) can we derive some guidance rules to improve noise dealing techniques in presence of class imbalance? Authors conclude that there is considerable impact class noise in the performance in presence of class imbalance, although some algorithms are relatively robust to the presence of noise. This is particular true for noise in the minority

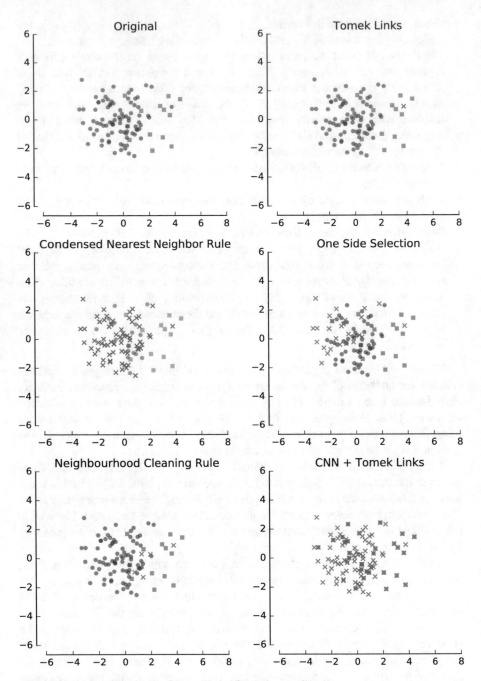

Fig. 10.11 Noise cleaning algorithms adapted for undersampling

class. The sampling techniques do help some algorithms, although Naïve Bayes, 2NN, 5NN and MLP ANN are little benefited by sampling. Among the compared sampling algorithms, ENN and random oversampling techniques tend to perform better for high levels of class noise and filtering techniques are not adequate to remove noise, because correctly labeled instances from the minority class filtered out sensible degrade performance.

A similar research procedure under the context of software quality data was performed in [69]. Authors analyzed the impact of class noise and class imbalance comparing 11 different learning algorithms and 7 different data sampling techniques in the task of predicting the modules system failure in 12 software quality datasets. Authors conclude that, within this domain, class noise is more harmful than class imbalance to classification algorithms. Furthermore, simple undersampling techniques such as random undersampling and ENN were the most robust to noise, and OSS is relatively unaffected by the increase in noise level. Random oversampling and SMOTE obtained good results on average, but were outperformed by the undersampling techniques. Finally, Naïve Bayes and SVMs performed best in this domain.

A combination of oversampling, threshold calibration and noise filtering was used in [64] for improving performance of educational data to predict student performance. They use random forest as classifier, SMOTE for over sampling, cost sensitive threshold adjustment and removal of instances near the class boundaries, and achieves significant improvement in terms of AUC.

A recent study [66] proposed a new oversampling technique that focuses on noise reduction and selective sampling of the minority for synthetic generation of new instances. Their approach first marks potentially noise class instances for removal, and uses the estimate of the probability of instances belonging to the minority class to selective choose instance seeds to generate new synthetic instances. Experimental evaluation using 40 datasets indicates an increasing trend in the sensitivity in majority class and G-mean.

Clustering has been used to identify noise instances prior to oversampling in [48]. To cluster instances, the adaptive hierarchical clustering algorithm CURE [27] is applied. Besides clustering, CURE is capable of identifying potential noise instances which are not assigned to generated clusters. Each cluster has a representative instance, and artificial instances are generated between instances belonging to a cluster and the representative instance.

10.7 Borderline Examples

It is interesting to differentiate among different types of instances, according to their location with respect to the decision boundaries [41, 51]. A common categorization is the division in instances near the class boundaries (borderline instances), instances in class homogeneous regions (safe instances) and instances of a different class inside homogeneous regions of another class (class noisy instances). It has been

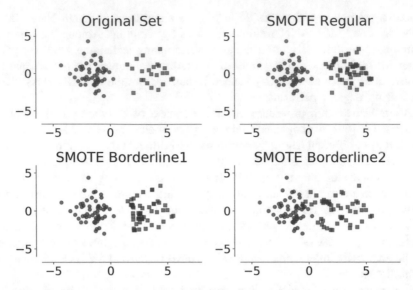

Fig. 10.12 A visual comparison among traditional SMOTE and the two borderline-SMOTE variations

empirically shown that the degradation in performance of a classifier is strongly affected by the number of borderline examples [52].

Different class imbalance treatment methods have been proposed to explore these different types of instances. Applying SMOTE to instances near the borderline was investigated in [29]. Authors developed two strategies, Borderline-SMOTE1 and Borderline-SMOTE2, which apply oversampling only to instances near the class boundaries. If all the NNs of a instance of the minority class belongs to a different class, the instance is considered noise. Instances which are not considered noise but the number of instances from the majority class outnumbers the number of instances from the minority class are considered borderline, and SMOTE is applied to these instances. The main difference between Borderline-SMOTE1 and Borderline-SMOTE2 consists in the generation of artificial instances: while, for each minority class instance, Borderline-SMOTE1 generates a new artificial instance considering only the NN from the minority class to interpolate, Borderline-SMOTE2 also interpolates to the NN from the majority class.

Figure 10.12 shows a graphical example of traditional SMOTE and the two versions of Borderline-SMOTE. Observe that in the two borderline variations, artificial instances are generated closer to the class boundaries. Moreover, as Borderline-SMOTE2 also generate artificial instances considering instances from the other class, the generated instances are closer to the decision boundaries of the majority class.

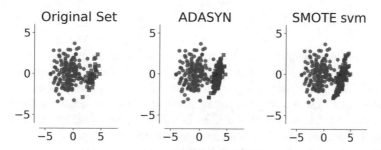

Fig. 10.13 A visual comparison between ADASYN and SMOTE SVM

Two approaches that use an adaptive synthetic sampling for instances near the class boundaries are ADASYN [31] and SMOTE SVM [53]. ADASYN generates artificial instances based on the density distribution of class skew ratio in the neighborhood. For each instance, the local class imbalance degree is computed as the fraction of majority instances in its k-nearest neighborhood. This local imbalance degree is normalized to represent a density function. The density function is then used to calculated the number of artificial instances that should be generated. The main idea is that a larger number of instances are generated near the class boundaries, as these instances have a higher local imbalance degree. SMOTE SVM uses the support vectors generate by learning a classifier with SVM to approximate the class boundaries. The artificial instances are generated using two approaches. The first one is by randomly interpolating the instance to a NN of the same class. This is used if most of the NNs of the minority class instance also belongs to the minority class. The second approach is by extrapolating the instance towards the class boundaries by interpolating to a NN of opposite class with the restriction of not crossing the class boundaries given by the support vector.

Figure 10.13 shows a visual comparison between ADASYN and SMOTE SVM. ADASYN concentrates in generating instances near the class boundaries and dense instances, while the extrapolation process of SMOTE SVM concentrate in generating instances following the support vectors found by SVM.

Safe-level SMOTE [8] and SPIDER [75] are also two sampling techniques which deals with different instance differently. Safe-level smote is somehow opposite to borderline SMOTE. Instead of oversampling instances near the class boundaries, safe-level smote oversample instances in "safe" regions. The rationale is that oversampling near class boundaries may introduce spurious instances, and in some cases, degrade performance. SPIDER is a hybrid undersampling and oversampling approach. It combines majority class noise instance filtering with (optional) relabeling of majority instances near class boundaries, with informed oversampling by replicating negative instances near the class boundaries.

A hierarchical fuzzy rule learning approach which assigns higher granularity to subspace in borderline areas was proposed in [19]. This approach was shown to be competitive in highly imbalanced datasets, where the difficult in classifying minority class instances in the borderline is accentuated.

10.8   Dataset Shift

In many real-world applications, the conditions in which we draw data for learning the model is different from the conditions in which the learned model will be deployed. This phenomenon is called dataset shift, and occurs when the testing (unseen) data suffers a change in the distribution of a single feature, a combination of features, or the class boundaries [50]. In this case, the common assumption that training and testing data follow the same distributions is violated.

In [76], six reasons for dataset shift are discussed:

1. **Simple Covariate Shift:** Given a data generative process that can be modeled as $P(y|x)P(x)$, simple covariate shift occurs when only the distributions of covariates x change and everything else is the same. For instance, suppose we want to predict the likelihood of fraudulent purchases (y), given different payment methods (x). The model is learned using *past* historical data, but due to a large adoption of some modern payment methods (e.g, an increase in mobile e-wallets apps payments), the distribution of different payment methods is affected. Theoretically, a covariate shift in $P(x)$ should have no effect in $P(y|x)$, but the data available at training time may not provide complete information for the deployment scenario, and thus with some side effect in classification performance [77].

2. **Prior Probability Shift:** Prior probability shift occurs when only the $P(y)$ distribution changes over time, while everything else stays the same. A classic example is SPAM detection: a user uses her past historical income messages to train a classifier for tagging new e-mail messages as SPAM or NO-SPAM. However, latter on the classifier is trained, her e-mail address may be placed in a spammer's list, increasing the number of SPAM messages she receives. Thus, the prior probabilities of receiving SPAM messages has been changed between train and test time. In general, a change in $P(y)$ between training and testing time will affect the prediction. However, for a known shift in $P(y)$, prior probability shift can be corrected by adjustments to the posterior class probabilities and decision thresholds [17, 92].

3. **Sample Selection Bias:** This type of shift occurs when the distributions differ as a result of the training data sampling process. Generally, it is assumed that training data is an independent and independently distributed sample of the population. However, in many situations, this unbiased sampling process is impractical or even unfeasible. For instance, in some medical applications, an arbitrarily defined number of healthy and sick patients is normally used, even though this ratio does not match the illness prevalence in the entire population. Some sentiment analysis studies use a similar number of positive and negative opinionated messages despite the true ratio of these messages. The number of genes for some organisms is unknown, thus a sample which matches the true prevalence could not be drawn. Some strategies for coping with sample selection bias in ML are presented in [93].

4. **Imbalanced Data:** The data sampling process for dealing with imbalanced data is a form of deliberately introduce a dataset shift for computational or modeling purposes. Due to this sampling process, the data distribution in the training dataset no longer matches the imbalanced test scenario. Although sampling techniques may improve classification performance and favor the minority class, a decrease in performance of the majority class may occur. A thorough discussion about data sampling methods was presented in Chap. 5.

5. **Domain Shift:** It is often the case that data acquisition or representation processes may change over time. For instance, in a camera surveillance system, a camera of a higher resolution may replace an older camera. Although the underline data generation process remains the same, the higher resolution camera uses a different representation for the captured images. If the learning algorithm is trained with data acquired with the older camera, the introduction of the new one implies in a domain shift. Different approaches for domain shift adaptation have been proposed, among them [5, 14, 24, 56].

6. **Source Component Shift:** This type of shift is related to data coming from multiple sources, and there is a difference between sources used for training and sources where the models will be applied. This kind of shift occurs quite often. For instance, in a retailer chain a sale predictive model could be developed from data for stores of some region, but it is applied to all stores of the chain. Source component shift can be further divided into three categories. Mixture Component shift occurs when the sources are not identified, and there is a difference in the proportion of instances coming from different sources between train and test scenarios. Mixing component shift has a similar scenario as mixture component shift, but with an additional issue that data is somehow aggregated in each source. In factor component shift, data is dependent on some factors, where the "strength" of each factor changes from training ant test time.

Although artificial data shift introduction by data sampling are often used as a technique for improving performance with imbalance data, other types of data shift may have a negative impact in the performance classifiers under imbalanced scenarios. In simple covariate shift, for instance, the minority class may provide insufficient information for fully characterize the concept, leading to a poor performance of classifying the new minority instances when the shift occurs. Prior probability shift may also pose some issues for performance evaluation. Some metrics such as ROC curves (see Chap. 3) are less sensitive to shifts in prior probabilities, as they decouple the performance by considering a probabilistic framework for each class independently. However, in many real-world applications, only focusing on the probabilistic model without also considering the trade-offs among class for decision purposes is not enough [32]. Prior probability shift should be taken into account when incorporating some utility loss function for converting likelihoods into crisp class predictions [42]. Domain shift and source component shift may lead to higher instability and variance in the low prevalent classes, in comparison to higher prevalent classes. Identifying the occurrence of data shifts may also be difficult under imbalance datasets, due to low prevalence of minority classes.

Dealing with dataset shift is a challenging problem on itself, with significant real world implications. However, this problem is even more challenging under the presence of class imbalance. The possible failures that arise from not taking into account the occurrence of dataset shift (e.g. sample selection bias, prior probability shift) have been explored in the literature, but few studies focus on particularities of class imbalance. Furthermore, models that work well in static scenarios may fail in situations of non-stationary environments. These issues are interesting venues for future research work.

10.9   Imperfect Data

Imperfect data are prevalent in real world applications. Several studies have aimed to classify the different types of data imperfections and their possible sources [57]. Some problems correlated to data imperfection include incompleteness, imprecision, inconsistency and uncertainty. These problems are originated from many reasons, such as faulty sensors, inadequate data transcription, unreliable data acquisition or transmission sources, data collection errors and the lack of data representation standards, and many methods for improving data quality prior to data modeling have been proposed [1, 44, 58, 67].

The possible drawbacks of dealing with imperfect and imbalanced data are twofold: First, methods aimed to cope with imbalanced data may have their performance reduce due to the bad quality of data [62, 63, 82, 87]. Second, imbalance data may influence the performance of methods to deal with imperfect data [12, 15, 40].

Traditionally, data imperfection and class imbalance are treated separately. However, few attempts try to deal with imperfection and imbalance jointly. Data clustering combined with under-sampling has been used in [74] for identifying spurious data points.

In the context of MV handling in [79], a method for tackling datasets with MVs and class imbalance is presented. The method uses 1NN in minority class instances to input the MVs. The method performed better than data imputation techniques which does not take class imbalance into account. Class stratification was used in [15] as a strategy to improve imputation in the presence of class imbalance. The fuzzy rule learning classifier FURIA [37] was also used to handle uncertainty. The degree of class imbalance was used as a feature in a meta-learning approach for recommending a imputation method in [71].

To handle label uncertainty, in [91] a method which explores label correlation for the task of label distribution learning. This task aim to quantify the percentage of each class label in a given instance. In label distribution tasks, there is a natural uncertainty in label assignments, and the label correlation approach they propose can alleviate the problem of rarity of some labels. In [54, 78], cross-conformal prediction [83] for predicting label confidences. Cross conformal prediction combines conformal prediction [70] with cross-fold calibration for improving estimates for imbalance datasets. Some approaches incorporate fuzzy theory [4, 26] and rough sets [45] for handling data uncertainty in imbalanced contexts.

Another important kind of imperfection are data scarcity and noisy instances, which were discussed in Sects. 10.4 and 10.6, respectively.

10.10 Summarizing Comments

Class imbalance has been widely acknowledged in the literature as a factor which may decrease performance of learning algorithms. However, it is also acknowledged in the literature that real-world data present other characteristics that, in conjunction with class imbalance, can potentially worsen the performance of learning algorithms. In this chapter, we discuss data complexity, sub-concepts and small disjuncts, data scarcity, data overlapping, noisy data, borderline examples, dataset shift and imperfect data. These issues are important complicating factors for class imbalance, as well as challenging problems for successful application of learning algorithms on itself.

References

1. Aggarwal, C.C., Philip, S.Y.: A survey of uncertain data algorithms and applications. IEEE Trans. Knowl. Data Eng. **21**(5), 609–623 (2009)
2. Anwar, N., Jones, G., Ganesh, S.: Measurement of data complexity for classification problems with unbalanced data. Stat. Anal. Data Min. ASA Data Sci. J. **7**(3), 194–211 (2014)
3. Batista, G.E., Prati, R.C., Monard, M.C.: A study of the behavior of several methods for balancing machine learning training data. ACM Sigkdd Explor. Newslett. **6**(1), 20–29 (2004)
4. Batuwita, R., Palade, V.: FSVM-CIL: fuzzy support vector machines for class imbalance learning. IEEE Trans. Fuzzy Syst. **18**(3), 558–571 (2010)
5. Ben-David, S., Blitzer, J., Crammer, K., Kulesza, A., Pereira, F., Vaughan, J.W.: A theory of learning from different domains. Mach. Learn. **79**(1–2), 151–175 (2010)
6. Błaszczyński, J., Stefanowski, J.: Local data characteristics in learning classifiers from imbalanced data. In: Gawñeda, A.E., Kacprzyk, J., Rutkowski, L., Yen, G.G. (eds.) Advances in Data Analysis with Computational Intelligence Methods, pp. 51–85. Springer, Cham (2018)
7. Borsos, Z., Lemnaru, C., Potolea, R.: Dealing with overlap and imbalance: a new metric and approach. Pattern Anal. Appl. **21**(2), 381–395 (2018)
8. Bunkhumpornpat, C., Sinapiromsaran, K., Lursinsap, C.: Safe-level-smote: safe-level-synthetic minority over-sampling technique for handling the class imbalanced problem. Adv. Knowl. Disc. Data Min. **5476**, 475–482 (2009)
9. Carvalho, D.R., Freitas, A.A.: A hybrid decision tree/genetic algorithm method for data mining. Inf. Sci. **163**(1), 13–35 (2004)
10. Chawla, N.V., Lazarevic, A., Hall, L.O., Bowyer, K.W.: Smoteboost: improving prediction of the minority class in boosting. In: Proceedings of the Principles of Knowledge Discovery in Databases, PKDD-2003, Cavtat-Dubrovnik, Croatia, pp. 107–119 (2003)

11. Chen, L., Fang, B., Shang, Z., Tang, Y.: Tackling class overlap and imbalance problems in software defect prediction. Softw. Qual. J. **26**(1), 97–125 (2018)
12. Chowdhury, A., Alspector, J.: Data duplication: an imbalance problem? In: ICML'2003 Workshop on Learning from Imbalanced Data Sets (II), Washington, DC (2003)
13. Cieslak, D.A., Hoens, T.R., Chawla, N.V., Kegelmeyer, W.P.: Hellinger distance decision trees are robust and skew-insensitive. Data Min. Knowl. Disc. **24**(1), 136–158 (2012)
14. Cortes, C., Mohri, M.: Domain adaptation and sample bias correction theory and algorithm for regression. Theor. Comput. Sci. **519**, 103–126 (2014)
15. Davis, D., Rahman, M.: Missing value imputation using stratified supervised learning for cardiovascular data. J. Inf. Data Min. **1**(2), 1–13 (2016)
16. Denil, M., Trappenberg, T.P.: Overlap versus imbalance. In: Farzindar, A., Keselj, V. (eds.) 23rd Canadian Conference on Artificial Intelligence (Canadian AI 2010), Ontario. Lecture Notes in Computer Science, vol. 6085, pp. 220–231. Springer (2010)
17. Elkan, C.: The foundations of cost-sensitive learning. In: International Joint Conference on Artificial Intelligence, Seattle, Washington, pp. 973–978. Lawrence Erlbaum Associates Ltd (2001)
18. Fawcett, T.: PRIE: a system for generating rulelists to maximize ROC performance. Data Min. Knowl. Disc. **17**(2), 207–224 (2008)
19. Fernández, A., del Jesus, M.J., Herrera, F.: Hierarchical fuzzy rule based classification systems with genetic rule selection for imbalanced data-sets. Int J. Approx. Reason. **50**(3), 561–577 (2009)
20. Forman, G., Cohen, I.: Learning from little: comparison of classifiers given little training. Knowledge Discovery in Databases, PKDD 2004, Pisa, pp. 161–172 (2004)
21. Frénay, B., Verleysen, M.: Classification in the presence of label noise: a survey. IEEE Trans. Neural Netw. Learn. Syst. **25**(5), 845–869 (2014)
22. Friedman, J.H., Kohavi, R., Yun, Y.: Lazy decision trees. In: Association for the Advancement of Artificial Intelligence/Innovative Applications of Artificial Intelligence Conference, vol. 1, pp. 717–724 (1996)
23. Fürnkranz, J., Gamberger, D., Lavrac, N.: Foundations of rule learning. Springer, London (2012)
24. Ganin, Y., Ustinova, E., Ajakan, H., Germain, P., Larochelle, H., Laviolette, F., Marchand, M., Lempitsky, V.: Domain-adversarial training of neural networks. J. Mach. Learn. Res. **17**(1), 2096–2030 (2016)
25. García, V., Mollineda, R.A., Sánchez, J.S.: On the k-NN performance in a challenging scenario of imbalance and overlapping. Pattern Anal. Appl. **11**(3–4), 269–280 (2008)
26. Gu, X., Ni, T., Wang, H.: New fuzzy support vector machine for the class imbalance problem in medical datasets classification. Sci. World J. **2014**, 1–12 (2014)
27. Guha, S., Rastogi, R., Shim, K.: Cure: an efficient clustering algorithm for large databases. ACM SIGMOD Record **27**(2), 73–84 (1998)
28. Guo, H., Viktor, H.L.: Learning from imbalanced data sets with boosting and data generation: the DataBoost-IM approach. ACM SIGKDD Explor. Newslett. **6**(1), 30–39 (2004)
29. Han, H., Wang, W.Y., Mao, B.H.: Borderline-SMOTE: a new over-sampling method in imbalanced data sets learning. In: Huang, D.S., Zhang, X.P., Huang, G.B. (eds.) International Conference on Intelligent Computing, ICIC'2005, Hefei, China. Lecture Notes in Computer Science, vol. 3644, pp. 878–887. Springer, Berlin/Heidelberg (2005)
30. Hart, P.: The condensed nearest neighbor rule. IEEE Trans. Inf. Theory **14**(3), 515–516 (1968)
31. He, H., Bai, Y., Garcia, E.A., Li, S.: Adasyn: adaptive synthetic sampling approach for imbalanced learning. In: IEEE International Joint Conference on Neural Networks (IJCNN 2008), Hong Kong, pp. 1322–1328. IEEE (2008)
32. Hernández-Orallo, J., Flach, P., Ferri, C.: A unified view of performance metrics: translating threshold choice into expected classification loss. J. Mach. Learn. Res. **13**, 2813–2869 (2012)
33. Ho, T.K., Basu, M.: Complexity measures of supervised classification problems. IEEE Trans. Pattern Anal. Mach. Intell. **24**(3), 289–300 (2002)

34. Ho, T., Basu, M., Law, M.: Measures of geometrical complexity in classification problems. In: Basu, M. (ed.) Data Complexity in Pattern Recognition, pp. 1–23. Springer, London (2006)
35. Holte, R.C.: Very simple classification rules perform well on most commonly used datasets. Mach. Learn. **11**(1), 63–90 (1993)
36. Holte, R.C., Acker, L.E., Porter, B.W.: Concept learning and the problem of small disjuncts. In: Proceedings of the 11th International Joint Conference on Artificial Intelligence, IJCAI'89, Detroit, vol. 1, pp. 813–818. Morgan Kaufmann Publishers Inc., San Francisco (1989)
37. Hühn, J., Hüllermeier, E.: Furia: an algorithm for unordered fuzzy rule induction. Data Min. Knowl. Disc. **19**(3), 293–319 (2009)
38. Japkowicz, N.: Concept-learning in the presence of between-class and within-class imbalances. In: Stroulia, E., Matwin, S. (eds.) 14th Biennial Conference of the Canadian Society for Computational Studies of Intelligence, AI'2001, Ottawa, pp. 67–77. Springer, Berlin/Heidelberg (2001)
39. Jo, T., Japkowicz, N.: Class imbalances versus small disjuncts. ACM Sigkdd Explor. Newslett. **6**(1), 40–49 (2004)
40. Kołcz, A., Alspector, J.: Asymmetric missing-data problems: overcoming the lack of negative data in preference ranking. Inf. Retr. **5**(1), 5–40 (2002)
41. Kubat, M., Matwin, S., et al.: Addressing the curse of imbalanced training sets: one-sided selection. In: International Conference on Machine Learning, Nashville, vol. 97, pp. 179–186 (1997)
42. Kull, M., Flach, P.: Novel decompositions of proper scoring rules for classification: score adjustment as precursor to calibration. In: Joint European Conference on Machine Learning and Knowledge Discovery in Databases, Porto, pp. 68–85. Springer (2015)
43. Laurikkala, J.: Improving identification of difficult small classes by balancing class distribution. In: Artificial Intelligence in Medicine, Cascais, pp. 63–66 (2001)
44. Leung, C.K.S.: Mining uncertain data. Wiley Interdiscip. Rev. Data Min. Knowl. Disc. **1**(4), 316–329 (2011)
45. Liu, J., Hu, Q., Yu, D.: A weighted rough set based method developed for class imbalance learning. Inf. Sci. **178**(4), 1235–1256 (2008)
46. López, V., Fernández, A., García, S., Palade, V., Herrera, F.: An insight into classification with imbalanced data: empirical results and current trends on using data intrinsic characteristics. Inf. Sci. **250**, 113–141 (2013)
47. Luengo, J., Fernández, A., García, S., Herrera, F.: Addressing data complexity for imbalanced data sets: analysis of smote-based oversampling and evolutionary undersampling. Soft Comput. **15**(10), 1909–1936 (2011)
48. Ma, L., Fan, S.: Cure-smote algorithm and hybrid algorithm for feature selection and parameter optimization based on random forests. BMC Bioinf. **18**(1), 169 (2017)
49. Morais, G., Prati, R.C.: Complex network measures for data set characterization. In: 2013 Brazilian Conference on Intelligent Systems (BRACIS), Fortaleza, pp. 12–18. IEEE (2013)
50. Moreno-Torres, J.G., Raeder, T., Alaiz-RodríGuez, R., Chawla, N.V., Herrera, F.: A unifying view on dataset shift in classification. Pattern Recogn. **45**(1), 521–530 (2012)
51. Napierala, K., Stefanowski, J.: Types of minority class examples and their influence on learning classifiers from imbalanced data. J. Intell. Inf. Syst. **46**(3), 563–597 (2016)
52. Napierała, K., Stefanowski, J., Wilk, S.: Learning from imbalanced data in presence of noisy and borderline examples. In: Kryszkiewicz, M., Jensen, R., Hu, Q., Szczuka, M. (eds.) Rough Sets and Current Trends in Computing, Warsaw, pp. 158–167. Springer, Berlin/Heidelberg (2010)
53. Nguyen, H.M., Cooper, E.W., Kamei, K.: Borderline over-sampling for imbalanced data classification. Int. J. Knowl. Eng. Soft Data Paradigms **3**(1), 4–21 (2011)
54. Norinder, U., Boyer, S.: Binary classification of imbalanced datasets using conformal prediction. J. Mol. Graph. Model. **72**, 256–265 (2017)
55. Oh, S.: A new dataset evaluation method based on category overlap. Comput. Biol. Med. **41**(2), 115–122 (2011)

56. Pan, S.J., Tsang, I.W., Kwok, J.T., Yang, Q.: Domain adaptation via transfer component analysis. IEEE Trans. Neural Netw. **22**(2), 199–210 (2011)
57. Parsons, S.: Current approaches to handling imperfect information in data and knowledge bases. IEEE Trans. Knowl. Data Eng. **8**(3), 353–372 (1996)
58. Pearson, R.K.: Mining Imperfect Data: Dealing with Contamination and Incomplete Records, vol. 93. SIAM, Philadelphia (2005)
59. Prati, R.C., Flach, P.A.: Roccer: an algorithm for rule learning based on ROC analysis. In: International Joint Conference on Artificial Intelligence, Edinburgh, pp. 823–828 (2005)
60. Prati, R.C., Batista, G., Monard, M.C., et al.: Class imbalances versus class overlapping: an analysis of a learning system behavior. In: 4th Mexican International Conference on Artificial Intelligence, MICAI'2004. Lecture Notes in Computer Science, Mexico City, vol. 2972, pp. 312–321. Springer (2004)
61. Prati, R.C., Batista, G.E.A.P.A., Monard, M.C.: Learning with class skews and small disjuncts. In: 17th Brazilian Symposium on Artificial Intelligence, SBIA'2004, São Luis. Lecture Notes in Computer Science, vol. 3171, pp. 296–306. Springer (2004)
62. Pruengkarn, R., Wong, K.W., Fung, C.C.: Data cleaning using complementary fuzzy support vector machine technique. In: International Conference on Neural Information Processing, Barcelona, pp. 160–167. Springer(2016)
63. Pruengkarn, R., Wong, K.W., Fung, C.C.: Imbalanced data classification using complementary fuzzy support vector machine techniques and smote. In: IEEE International Conference on Systems, Man, and Cybernetics (SMC), Banff (2017)
64. Radwan, A.M., Cataltepe, Z.: Improving performance prediction on education data with noise and class imbalance. Intell. Autom. Soft Comput. 1–8 (2017). https://doi.org/10.1080/10798587.2017.1337673
65. Raudys, S.J., Jain, A.K., et al.: Small sample size effects in statistical pattern recognition: recommendations for practitioners. IEEE Trans. Pattern Anal. Mach. Intell. **13**(3), 252–264 (1991)
66. Rivera, W.A.: Noise reduction a priori synthetic over-sampling for class imbalanced data sets. Inf. Sci. **408**, 146–161 (2017)
67. Schubert, E., Koos, A., Emrich, T., Züfle, A., Schmid, K.A., Zimek, A.: A framework for clustering uncertain data. Proc. VLDB Endow. **8**(12), 1976–1979 (2015). Waikoloa, Hawai
68. Seiffert, C., Khoshgoftaar, T.M., Van Hulse, J., Napolitano, A.: Rusboost: a hybrid approach to alleviating class imbalance. IEEE Trans. Syst. Man Cybern. Part A Syst. Humans **40**(1), 185–197 (2010)
69. Seiffert, C., Khoshgoftaar, T.M., Van Hulse, J., Folleco, A.: An empirical study of the classification performance of learners on imbalanced and noisy software quality data. Inf. Sci. **259**, 571–595 (2014)
70. Shafer, G., Vovk, V.: A tutorial on conformal prediction. J. Mach. Learn. Res. **9**, 371–421 (2008)
71. Sim, J., Lee, J.S., Kwon, O.: Missing values and optimal selection of an imputation method and classification algorithm to improve the accuracy of ubiquitous computing applications. Math. Prob. Eng. Art. ID. 538613, 1–14 (2015)
72. Singh, S.: Multiresolution estimates of classification complexity. IEEE Trans. Pattern Anal. Mach. Intell. **25**(12), 1534–1539 (2003)
73. Smith, M.R., Martinez, T., Giraud-Carrier, C.: An instance level analysis of data complexity. Mach. Learn. **95**(2), 225–256 (2014)
74. Sowah, R.A., Agebure, M.A., Mills, G.A., Koumadi, K.M., Fiawoo, S.Y.: New cluster undersampling technique for class imbalance learning. Int. J. Mach. Learn. Comput. **6**(3), 205 (2016)
75. Stefanowski, J., Wilk, S.: Improving rule based classifiers induced by MODLEM by selective pre-processing of imbalanced data. In: Proceedings of the RSKD Workshop at ECML/PKDD, Warsaw, pp. 54–65 (2007)

76. Storkey, A.: When training and test sets are different: characterising learning transfer, chap. 1. In: Lawrence, C.S.S. (ed.) Dataset Shift in Machine Learning, pp. 3–28. MIT Press, Cambridge (2009)
77. Sugiyama, M., Müller, K.R.: Input-dependent estimation of generalization error under covariate shift. Stat. Decis. **23**(4), 249–279 (2005)
78. Sun, J., Carlsson, L., Ahlberg, E., Norinder, U., Engkvist, O., Chen, H.: Applying mondrian cross-conformal prediction to estimate prediction confidence on large imbalanced bioactivity data sets. J. Chem. Inf. Model. **57**(7), 1591–1598 (2017)
79. Takum, J., Bunkhumpornpat, C.: Parameter-free imputation for imbalance datasets. In: International Conference on Asian Digital Libraries, Chiang Mai, pp. 260–267. Springer (2014)
80. Tomek, I.: Two modifications of CNN. IEEE Trans. Syst. Man Cybern. **6**, 769–772 (1976)
81. Van Hulse, J., Khoshgoftaar, T.: Knowledge discovery from imbalanced and noisy data. Data Knowl. Eng. **68**(12), 1513–1542 (2009)
82. Van Hulse, J., Khoshgoftaar, T.M., Napolitano, A.: Evaluating the impact of data quality on sampling. J. Inf. Knowl. Manag. **10**(03), 225–245 (2011)
83. Vovk, V.: Cross-conformal predictors. Ann. Math. Artif. Intell. **74**(1–2), 9–28 (2015)
84. Wang, S., Yao, X.: Diversity analysis on imbalanced data sets by using ensemble models. In: IEEE Symposium on Computational Intelligence and Data Mining, CIDM'09, Nashville, pp. 324–331. IEEE (2009)
85. Wasikowski, M., Chen, X.W.: Combating the small sample class imbalance problem using feature selection. IEEE Trans. Knowl. Data Eng. **22**(10), 1388–1400 (2010)
86. Weiss, G.M.: Learning with rare cases and small disjuncts. In: Proceedings of the Twelfth International Conference on Machine Learning, Tahoe City, pp. 558–565. Morgan Kaufmann (1995)
87. Weiss, G.M.: Mining with rarity: a unifying framework. ACM Sigkdd Explor. Newslett. **6**(1), 7–19 (2004)
88. Weiss, G.M.: The impact of small disjuncts on classifier learning. In: Stahlbock, R., Crone, S.F., Lessmann, S. (eds.) Data Mining – Special Issue in Annals of Information Systems. Annals of Information Systems, vol. 8, pp. 193–226. Springer, Boston (2010)
89. Weiss, G.M., Provost, F.: Learning when training data are costly: the effect of class distribution on tree induction. J. Artif. Intell. Res. **19**, 315–354 (2003)
90. Weng, C.G., Poon, J.: A data complexity analysis on imbalanced datasets and an alternative imbalance recovering strategy. In: Proceedings of the 2006 IEEE/WIC/ACM International Conference on Web Intelligence, pp. 270–276. IEEE Computer Society, Hong Kong (2006)
91. Xu, M., Zhou, Z.H.: Incomplete label distribution learning. In: Proceedings of the 26th International Joint Conference on Artificial Intelligence, Melbourne, pp. 3175–3181. AAAI Press (2017)
92. Xue, J.C., Weiss, G.M.: Quantification and semi-supervised classification methods for handling changes in class distribution. In: Proceedings of the 15th ACM SIGKDD International Conference on Knowledge Discovery and Data Mining, Paris, pp. 897–906. ACM (2009)
93. Zadrozny, B.: Learning and evaluating classifiers under sample selection bias. In: Proceedings of the Twenty-First International Conference on Machine Learning, Banff, p. 114. ACM (2004)
94. Zhu, X., Wu, X.: Class noise vs. attribute noise: a quantitative study. Artif. Intell. Rev. **22**(3), 177–210 (2004)

Chapter 11
Learning from Imbalanced Data Streams

Abstract Mining data streams is one of the most vital fields in the contemporary ML. Increasing number of real-world problems are characterized by both volume and velocity of data, as well as by evolving characteristics. Learning from data stream assumes that new instances arrive continuously and that their properties may change over time due to a phenomenon known as concept drift. In order to achieve good adaptation to such non-stationary problems, classifiers must not only be accurate and able to continuously accommodate new instances, but also be characterized by high speed and low computational costs. A very challenging subfield of this domain is imbalanced data stream mining. It combined difficulties from streaming and imbalanced data, as well as introduce a plethora of new ones. Algorithms designed for such scenarios must be flexible enough to quickly adapt to changing decision boundaries, imbalance ratios, and roles of classes. In this chapter we will discuss the basics of data stream mining methods, as well as review existing skew-insensitive algorithms. Background in data streams is given in Sect. 11.1. Section 11.2 discusses in-depth learning difficulties present in imbalanced data streams. Data-level and algorithm level methods for skewed data streams are discussed in Sect. 11.3, while ensemble learners are overview in Sect. 11.4. Section 11.5 concentrates on issue of emerging and disappearing classes, while Sect. 11.6 deals with the limited access to ground truth in streaming scenarios. Finally, Sect. 11.7 concludes this chapter and presents future challenges in the field of learning from imbalanced data streams.

11.1 Introduction

The analysis of huge volumes of data is recently the focus of intense research, because such methods could give a competitive advantage for a given company. For contemporary enterprises, the possibility of making appropriate business decisions on the basis of knowledge hidden in stored data is one of the critical success factors. Similar interests in exploring new types of data are present in many other areas of human activity. In many of these applications, one should also take into consideration that data usually comes continuously in the form of *data streams* [15].

© Springer Nature Switzerland AG 2018
A. Fernández et al., *Learning from Imbalanced Data Sets*,
https://doi.org/10.1007/978-3-319-98074-4_11

Representative examples include network analysis, financial data prediction, traffic control, sensor measurement processing, ubiquitous computing, GPS and mobile device tracking, user's click log mining, sentiment analysis, and many others.

A data stream is a potentially unbounded, ordered sequence of data items which arrive over time. The time intervals between the arrival of each data item may vary. These data items can be simple attribute-value pairs like relational database tuples, or more complex structures such as graphs. A data stream is a sequence $< S_1, S_2, \ldots, S_n, \ldots >$, where each element S_j is a set of instances (or a single instance in case of online learning), where each of them is independent and randomly generated according to some stationary probability distribution D_j.

The main differences between data streams and conventional static datasets include:

- data items in the stream appear sequentially over time,
- there is no control over the order in which data items arrive and the processing system should be ready to react at any time,
- the size of the data may be huge (streams are possibly of infinite length); it is usually impossible to store all the data from the data stream in memory,
- usually only one scan of items from a data stream is possible; when the item is processed it is discarded or sometimes stored if necessary, or aggregated statistics or synopses are calculated,
- the data items arrival rate is rapid (relatively high with respect to the processing power of the system),
- data streams are susceptible to change (data distributions generating examples may change on the fly),
- the data labeling may be very costly (or even impossible in some cases), and may not be immediate.

These data stream characteristics pose the need for other algorithms than ones previously developed for *batch learning*, where data are stored in finite, persistent data repositories. Typical batch learning algorithms are not capable of fulfilling all of the data stream requirements such as constraints of memory usage, restricted processing time, and one scan of incoming examples. Note that some algorithms, like Naïve Bayes, instance based learning or neural networks are naturally *incremental* ones. However, simple incremental learning is typically insufficient, as it does not meet tight computational demands and does not tackle evolving nature of data sources.

Examples from the data stream are provided either *online*, i.e., instance by instance, or in the form of *data chunks* (portions, blocks). In the first approach, algorithms process single examples appearing one by one in consecutive moments in time, while in the other approach, examples are available only in larger sets called *data blocks* (or *data chunks*). Blocks are usually of equal size and the construction, evaluation, or updating of classifiers is done when all examples from a new block are available. This distinction may be connected with supervised or semi-supervised frameworks. For instance, in some problems data items are more

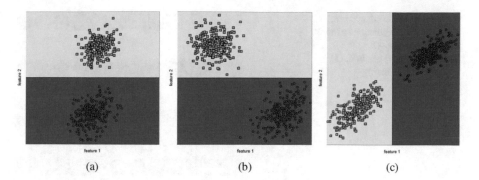

Fig. 11.1 Two main types of concept drift with respect to their influence over decision boundaries. (**a**) Initial distribution. (**b**) Virtual concept drift. (**c**) Real concept drift

naturally accumulated for some time and labeled in blocks while an access to class labels in an online setup is more demanding.

Data streams may evolve over time. By a stationary data stream we will consider a sequence of instances characterized by a transition $S_j \rightarrow S_{j+1}$, where $D_j = D_{j+1}$. However, many real-life problems may be subject to various types of concept drift [18, 35]:

- Drifts may be analyzed from the point of view of their influence on learned decision rules or classification boundaries. Here, we distinguish real and virtual drift (Fig. 11.1). The former has an influence on decision boundaries (posterior probabilities) and additionally may impact unconditional probability density function. Therefore, it poses a challenge for the learning system and must be handled every time it appears. The latter type of drift holds no influence over decision boundaries, yet affects the conditional probability density functions. Therefore, it does not affect currently used classifier. Nevertheless, it still should be detected to understand the reason behind such a change in analyzed stream.
- Drifts can be categorized according to the speed of changes taking place within the stream (Fig. 11.2). Sudden concept drift is characterized by S_j being rapidly replaced by S_{j+1}, where $D_j \neq D_{j+1}$. Gradual concept drift can be considered as a transition phase where examples in S_{j+1} are generated by a mixture of D_j and D_{j+1} with their varying proportions. Incremental concept drift is characterized by a much slower ratio of changes, where the difference between D_j and D_{j+1} is not so significant.
- There is a special type of concept drift, known as recurring drift. In such a case it is possible that a concept from k-th previous iteration may reappear $D_{j+1} = D_{j-k}$, once or periodically.
- Two other types of drifts are connected with potential appearance of incorrect information in the stream: blips and noise. Blips are random changes in stream characteristics that should be ignored (may be seen as outliers). Noise represents

Fig. 11.2 Different types of concept drift according to the ratio of changes. (**a**) incremental, (**b**) gradual, (**c**) sudden, (**d**) recurring

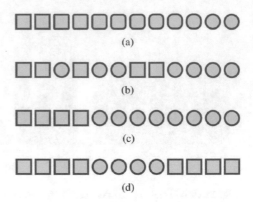

significant fluctuations in feature values or class labels, representing some corruption in received instances.

- One may analyze the impact of the drift on the decision space [42]. Here, we may distinguish local and global drifts. Former ones affect only a small part of the stream, like a certain subset of classes. Latter ones have effect on the entire stream, which actually makes them easier to detect and handle.
- Finally, we must notice that in most real-world problems the nature of changes is far from being well-defined or known, and we must be able to deal with hybrid changes through time, known as mixed concept drift.

Considering the aforementioned problems, one may easily see that tackling concept drift is a major challenge for data stream mining. Thus, we may use one of the following three solutions. First, rebuild the classifier whenever a new instance becomes available, which implies a prohibitive computational cost. Second, monitor the state of the stream, detect incoming change and rebuild the classifier when change becomes too severe. Third, use an adaptive method that will automatically adjust to any changes in the stream. Let us now present three main ways to tackle concept drift that are based on those principles: concept drift detectors, sliding windows, and online learners.

1. **Concept drift detectors** are external algorithms that measure the properties of stream and the accuracy of the classifier over time, which can be used to trigger classifier updates [33]. Characteristics measured by them usually include standard deviation [16] and instance distribution [52]. A change in these characteristics will indicate an appearance of concept drift.
2. **Sliding windows** keep a batch of most recent and relevant examples in a dedicated buffer. The buffer is being used by the classifier and is being constantly updated with new instances [60]. Being of fixed size means that instances are bound to spend there a given amount of time (corresponding to the buffer size) and then being discarded. This allows to store the current state of the stream in the memory. Removal of old instances is achieved by either crisp cutting-off or weighting with applied forgetting factor.

3. **Online learners** exhibit an ability to continuously update their structure instance after instance. This ability allows them to adapt to changes in stream as soon as they appear. To be considered as an online learner, a given algorithm must fulfill a number of requirements. They include processing each instance at most once, working under time and memory constrains, and having a predictive accuracy not lower than a batch model trained on the same set of instances. Some of popular classifiers are actually able to work in online mode, e.g., Neural Networks or Naïve Bayes. However, there exist a plethora of methods modified to provide efficient online mode of operation [10].

An important issue connected with data stream mining is how to compare and evaluate streaming classifiers. In the context of data stream mining, especially in non-stationary environments, canonical metrics and evaluation procedures become no longer applicable. We deal with massive, continuously incoming and evolving data that requires updating the learning model and adjusting to shifts and drifts. New classes may appear, feature space change and decision rules loose relevance over time. Additionally, canonical metrics for measuring the quality of learning process are not sufficient to perform a meaningful evaluation of models. When dealing with streams we cannot assume that all of the data will fit in memory and we must take into consideration limits imposed on the computational resources we have at our disposal. Algorithms must follow certain time and memory constraints. When change appear in a stream not only the accuracy of the updating procedure is important, but also reaction time. Quick change of learning model and gradual recovery is often more reasonable than gathering data for a period of time and trying to rebuild the learner in a single effective but time consuming step. Instead of checking the single performance of algorithm we are more interested in tracking its characteristics over the course of stream progression. The following aspects must always be taken into account during properly executed evaluation of streaming algorithms:

- **Predictive performance**: this is an obvious criterion measured in all learning systems. However, in data streams the relevance of instances is being reduced over time and by using a simple averaged measure we lose information on how a given classifier was able to adapt to changes. Therefore, prequential metrics are commonly used here. They give highest priority to the most recent examples and utilize a forgetting factor to reduce the impact of early stages of stream mining on the final metric. Prequential accuracy [17] is the most commonly used one, although for imbalanced data streams one should use prequential AUC [5], prequential G-mean [56], or class recall [58].
- **Memory consumption**: it is necessary to monitor not only the average memory requirements of each algorithm, but also their change over time with respect to actions being taken.
- **Update time**: here one is interested in the amount of time that an algorithm requires to update its structure and accommodate new data from the stream. In an ideal situation, the update time should be lower than the arrival time of a new example (or chunk of data).

- **Decision time**: amount of time that a model needs to make a decision regarding new instances from the stream. This phase usually comes before the updating procedure takes place. So, any decision latency may result in creating a bottleneck in the stream processing. This is especially crucial for algorithms that cannot update and make predictions regarding new instances at the same time.

These factors make data stream mining a challenging learning scenario.

11.2   Characteristics of Imbalanced Data Streams

Data stream mining is a challenging learning scenario on its own. However, in many real-life scenarios it may simultaneously be affected by the presence of concept drift and class imbalance [26]. Such imbalanced data streams combine difficulties of their respective fields, creating an emerging paradigm in ML. Mining such streams require a combined monitoring of underlying class distributions and drift detection [63]. The general framework for learning from imbalanced data streams is given in Fig. 11.3.

When creating ML algorithms for imbalanced data stream mining, one must take into account the following characteristics unique to this problem [23, 28, 59]:

Simultaneous concept drift and imbalance ratio drift A major challenge lies in the fact that not only characteristics of underlying class generators, but also the ratio of class imbalance may change over time. One needs to detect both of these changes in order to properly adapt the underlying classification system. Drift Detection Method for Online Class Imbalance (DDM-OCI) [55] addresses this issue by an online monitoring of the drops in the minority class recall. After a significant drop has been observed, a drift alarm is being raised. This is a highly efficient solution for drifts occurring in minority class, but tends to overlook changes taking place in the majority class. This issue was addressed by Linear Four Rates (LFR) [54] algorithm that monitors at once four performance metrics derived from the confusion matrix: precision and recall for both minority and majority classes.

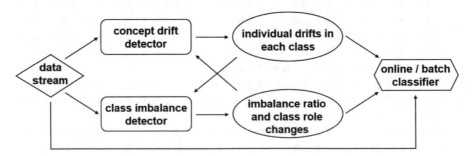

Fig. 11.3 General framework for learning from imbalanced data streams

Dynamic relationship among classes In static binary skewed problems the role of classes is well-defined at the beginning. However, in case of drifting data streams the relationships between the classes may change dynamically. The imbalance ratio may evolve over time, either increasing or decreasing the difficulty of incoming stream. Therefore, methods that take the fixed imbalance ratio under consideration (like cost-sensitive solutions) cannot be used, as a need for adaptation arises. Furthermore, a problem that started as imbalanced may become balanced, making the previous adaptations of a classifier obsolete, or even harmful to the recognition system. When a minority class has been strongly oversampled, the decreasing imbalance ratio will lead towards emergence of a new classification bias, this time towards the starting minority class. Finally, classes may switch roles and minority class may become the majority one and vice versa. This makes usage of any preprocessing or algorithm-level modifications difficult, as their adaptation towards a better recognition of a given class may actually become no longer valid. A classifier that was aiming to alleviate the bias towards a given class (majority at the time), will only empower the imbalance phenomenon when this class suddenly switches to becoming minority. These three difficulties require development of fast and adaptive solutions to imbalanced data streams, augmented with forgetting mechanism allowing a better accommodation of sudden class role switches. The discussed issues become even more challenging in a case of multi-class imbalanced data streams, where relationships among classes are much more difficult to analyze and both multi-minority and multi-majority cases may be present.

Online emergence and disappearance of classes An important issue related to data streams is the possibility of evolving setup of classes. New classes may emerge during the progress of a data stream, while instances from existing ones may start to appear less frequently, or even disappear completely. While the detection of novel patterns in stream is a challenging task itself, it is also strongly connected with the problem of class imbalance. When we are facing initial instances coming from an emerging class, it is very difficult to distinguish them from noise. Furthermore, at the beginning a new class usually will be represented only by a handful of instances, leading to a problem of extreme class imbalance (very high IR). Even if at some point of time classes will reach a roughly balanced distributions, until this happens we must deal with imbalanced scenario. Therefore, one must consider novel class detection and online imbalance learning as highly correlated cases. Algorithms for dealing with skewed data streams will be necessary, even if temporary until we gather enough instances from the new class. Similar situation will happen when one of the classes will start appearing less frequently. What may be initially a balanced problem, will with time increase its IR until the class completely disappears. Usually we do not want to compromise the performance on any of classes and we must account for such a growing IR. Finally, new emerging classes may change the nature of analyzed problem. A binary data stream may evolve into a multi-class one, posing a plethora of new challenges. Therefore, we must take into account not only changes in IR, but also the possible transition between binary and multi-class problems (both

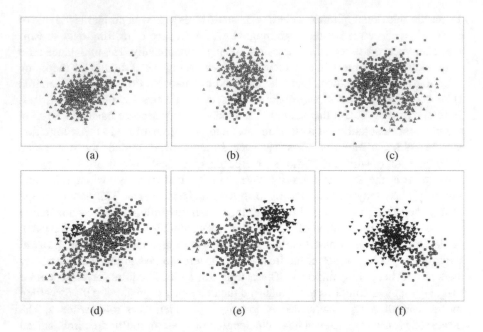

Fig. 11.4 Six states of imbalanced data stream with concept drift and novel class appearance. (**a**) S_1: two-class imbalance. (**b**) S_2: imbalance ratio changes. (**c**) S_3: classes switch roles. (**d**) S_4: new class emerges. (**e**) S_5: three-class imbalance. (**f**) S_6: class disappears

ways). Example of such learning difficulties in drifting imbalanced data streams are given in Fig. 11.4.

Evolving instance characteristics   The instance-level difficulty plays an important role in learning from imbalanced data. The simplest taxonomy is to consider either safe or difficult instances in the minority class. Other works propose a more detailed insight into the nature of difficult instances, categorizing them as borderline, small disjuncts and outliers. In general, minority instances that are overlapping with majority ones and have few neighbors from the same class are pose the highest difficulty for any classifier. While there have been studies on how minority instance characteristics can be used to improve the learning outcomes, they were limited only to static scenarios. In data stream setting, an instance that initially was considered as difficult may turn out to be a safe one when more instances arrive. On the other hand, concept drift may increase the overlapping among classes, in turn changing safe instances into difficult ones. Finally, varying ratios of instance arrival among classes after a concept drift may lead to a small size sample problem, not giving enough instances to derive meaningful decision boundaries.

Limited access to ground truth   Most of works in data stream mining (and especially in imbalanced data streams) assume a fully supervised learning model. Class labels become available right after a model made its prediction and are use to update it. This is a highly unrealistic scenario, especially in case of high-speed and massive data streams. One must assume that either the access to ground truth is highly limited (due to need for a human expert), delayed, or even impossible. While recent years brought a number of active and semi-supervised learning solutions for drifting data streams, vast majority of them assumed that classes are balanced. Skewed distributions will strongly affect these algorithms, increasing the probability of sampling majority instances. This in turn will only further increase the IR. Therefore, sampling mechanisms must be carefully adapted to alleviate this bias and making a fair and efficient sampling of both minority and majority classes possible.

Having discussed the learning difficulties specific to imbalanced data streams, let us present the most important works in this field that aims to tackle these challenges.

11.3   Data-Level and Algorithm-Level Approaches

Adaptation of data-level approaches to imbalanced drifting data streams is not a trivial case. Random under- and oversampling are characterized by a low computational complexity, making them potentially attractive solutions for streaming problems. However, their randomized nature becomes unreliable when dealing with constantly arriving instances and it is easy to lose any control over them when concept drift appears. In case of oversampling, one must take into account the memory requirements necessary for storing additional instances. Guided solutions, especially those based on SMOTE algorithm, are characterized by a high computational and memory complexities. Their required neighborhood analysis may become prohibitive when minimization of latency is crucial. Furthermore, SMOTE-based methods are known to suffer from challenging minority class distributions, often introducing synthetic examples in an unreliable manner. As the structure of minority class constantly evolves, the meaningful creation of new instances becomes far from trivial. Additionally, artificial instances may cause a dataset shift that may incorrectly trigger a drift detector, resulting in a false alarm. In static domain this problem is solved by data cleaning (post-processing), but once again the complexity of this step may prevent it from being applicable to data streams.

11.3.1   Undersampling Naïve Bayes

This online learning framework for Naïve Bayes classifier is based on updating the base classifier with new instances from the stream following an undersampling approach [45]. If the new instance originated from the minority class, then it was always used for updating the classifier. However, if the new instance came from the majority class, then it was used with a given probability equal to the current imbalance ratio. This allowed for balancing the training set for Naïve Bayes classifier. However, authors do not accounted for concept drift presence and assumed that the same class is always the minority one.

11.3.2 Generalized Over-sampling Based Online Imbalanced Learning Framework (GOS-IL)

The proposed model in [3] stores three parameters for each class: the number of instances that were misclassified by the current classifier, the number of instances from this class that arrived from the stream so far, and the number of instances from this class that were used to update the classifier. GOS-IL performs oversampling of only misclassified instances, thus reducing the computational effort and decreasing the chances of introducing noisy synthetic instances. Additionally, oversampling is performed only when the current imbalance ratio calls for it and when the error of the classifier reaches a given threshold. Once again, no specific mechanism for handling concept drift and evolving class characteristics is included.

11.3.3 Sequential SMOTE

Authors from [37] assumed offline (training) and online (streaming) phases. Principal curve was used on the initial batch of training instances to model the shape of the minority class. This allowed for calculating the projection distance of instances to principal curve, which in turn affected the membership function values used for oversampling the minority class and undersampling the majority one. The membership function values were incrementally re-calculated after each new instance, in case of minority ones after oversampling (which pushed the principal curve towards to favor the minority instances). Once again, no drift handling approach was utilized. Authors extended this idea in [38], where they have added several measures for instance-level importance that were used to more efficiently fit the principal curve. Additionally, they have proposed a fast leave-one-out cross-validation for setting the parameters of their method in an online manner.

Algorithm-level approaches seem more naturally applicable to data stream scenario. They are based on combining one of existing techniques for making classifiers skew-insensitive with online learning solutions allowing for a constant adaptation to data stream. Therefore, most of existing learners are based on neural networks, Support Vector Machines and decision trees.

11.3.4 Recursive Least Square Perceptron Model (RLSACP) and Online Neural Network for Non-stationary and Imbalanced Data Streams (ONN)

These classifiers from [21] and [22] are adaptations of neural networks to imbalanced drifting data streams. Both of these models include a forgetting function that allows to discard examples from outdated concepts in an effective manner, as well as weighted error calculation to reduce the bias towards the minority class. The forgetting mechanism can be controlled by the user, allowing to adjust the forgetting ratio to the anticipated type of concept drift. However, authors do not propose any mechanism for automatic adjustment of this parameter, making in impractical in scenarios with mixed concept drift.

11.3.5 Dynamic Class Imbalance for Linear Proximal SVMs (DCIL-IncLPSVM)

This is an incremental SVM training method to handle streaming class imbalance [46]. Authors proposed a simplified and fast weight update strategy, allowing for accommodating new instances from a stream and balancing class distributions. The weight calculation process is guided by the imbalance ratio of the newest chunk, thus achieving adaptation to the current class proportions. However, this method takes into account only the latest set of instances, heavily relying on proper windowing technique being used.

11.3.6 Kernelized Online Imbalanced Learning (KOIL)

This SVM modification uses two buffers of fixed size for storing support vectors learned from minority and majority classes [24]. New support vectors are weighted based on their distance to k-nearest support vectors from the opposite class. This allows for filtering outliers and balancing the influence of support vectors between imbalanced classes. Additionally, KOIL uses a sophisticated scheme for replacing support vectors once the buffer for any of classes becomes full.

11.3.7 Gaussian Hellinger Very Fast Decision Tree (GH-VFDT)

Decision trees are highly popular in data stream mining and therefore they seem as an excellent tool for being modified to handle imbalanced data streams. This algorithm-level modification [36] is based on hybridization between Hellinger distance split measure for skew-insensitive tree induction [9] and Very Fast Decision Tree (VFDT) training algorithm [12]. Hoeffding bound is being used to determine when to conduct a new split in a tree, measuring the error ϵ using the following inequality:

$$\epsilon \leq \sqrt{\frac{R^2 ln(2/\delta)}{2n}}, \tag{11.1}$$

where n is the number of processed instances, R is the range of a real-valued random variable (e.g., for an information gain the range is $\log c$, where c is number of classes) and δ is a standard deviation of this variable. By combining this bound with skew-insensitive splitting criterion, authors created an effective online tree induction algorithm that was not affected by skewed distributions. However, this classifier on its own does not have any drift coping mechanisms and needs to be combined with e.g., drift detector.

11.3.8 Cost-Sensitive Fast Perceptron Tree (CSPT)

This online decision tree [29] is a hybrid solution combining a VFDT with a linear perceptron at each leaf [4], allowing to speed-up the decision making process and improving the overall predictive power. It uses online perceptron approach with sigmoid activation function and squared error optimization. To allow parameter update after each instance, authors use stochastic gradient descent approach, training a single perceptron per each class in the stream.

Contrary to other works, CSPT use a McDiarmid's inequality for controlling the splitting criteria, as recent works pointed out a flaw in the Hoeffding bound [50]. McDiarmid's bound is a generalization of the Hoeffding's bound, being applicable to both numerical and non-numerical data, as well as better describing the split measures:

$$\epsilon \le \sqrt{\frac{8\ln(1/\delta)}{n(S)}}, \tag{11.2}$$

where S is a set of instances in analyzed decision tree node.

CSPT introduces a cost-sensitive modification during the classification step following a moving threshold principle [66], by calculating the output of k-th perceptron in a leaf of our decision tree as:

$$h_{\mathbf{w_k}}^*(\mathbf{x}) = \sum_{l=1}^{K} h_{\mathbf{w_k}}(\mathbf{x}) \cdot cost[k, l], \tag{11.3}$$

where $cost[k, l]$ is the misclassification cost between k-th and l-th class, provided by the user. This solution is highly compatible with data stream mining requirements, as it does not impose significant additional computational needs and do not rely on data preprocessing. Additionally, it is easily applicable for both binary and multi-class data streams, making it a versatile approach. The cost parameter is calculated by monitoring the current imbalance ratio among classes and setting the cost according to local pairwise imbalance ratios. The costs will change with the progress of the stream, as labels of incoming instances will be recorded and used to update the current skewness levels. Such a solution does not require to keep the instances in

Table 11.1 Six levels of
instance difficulty for
minority class

	Safe	Borderline	Borderline+	Rare	Rare+	Outlier
ρ	5	4	3	2	1	0
λ	1	2	3	4	5	6

memory, as only counters for each class are needed. This is combined with a cut-off thresholds that allows to store counters only for most recent instances.

CSPT was also extended to incorporate the information about the evolving structure of classes. An online estimation of instance-level difficulty is conducted using a sliding window approach and defined taxonomy of six levels of difficulty λ that can be assigned to each new minority instance based on how contaminated is its neighborhood. This is measured by parameter ρ that states how many of k neighbors belong to the same minority class. Details are presented in Table 11.1.

In order to accommodate for evolving instance properties, CSPT incorporates information from a drift detector. When a warning signal is being raised, the window will be reduced to 1/4 of its original size. This will allow to accommodate the change that starts to appear by taking into account a reduced subset of recent instances. When a drift is being detected, the window in being flushed in order to not include instances from the previous concepts into the analysis after the change. The same happens when minority classes switch places with majority. To apply this information about instance-level difficulty, authors proposed to use the fact that training procedure of perceptrons used in leafs of CSPT can be influenced by the number of iterations over each instance. Each new minority instance is presented to CSPT λ times, where λ is the difficulty level associated with this instance. This will force CSPT to concentrate on the most difficult instances.

11.4   Ensemble Learning Approaches

Ensemble solutions has gained a significant attention in both static [61] and streaming [30] data classification. They offer excellent predictive performance combined with their flexible line-up of base classifiers that can be used to handle concept drift [42]. Although ensembles have been successfully applied to learning from imbalanced data streams, this field can be seen as still in development.

11.4.1   Stream Ensemble Framework (SE)

This ensemble learning algorithm separates instances from the new data chunk into positive (the minority class) and negative (other classes) subsets [19]. A new classifier is trained by using all of collected positive instances and combining them with a randomly selected subset of the negative instances originating only from the new data chunk. The selected subset size is dynamically calculated using the current class IR. A newly trained classifier is added to the existing ensemble. A standard majority voting technique is used for classifier combination. As data streams may be potentially of an infinite size, SE maintains instances coming from a bounded number of most recent chunks. Two strategies are used for this: fixed (each of stored chunks contributes equal number of instances) or fading (the more recent chunks contribute more instances). SE assumes that all of minority instances are always stored and used to train new classifiers, which makes its usage prohibitive in scenarios with drifting minority class.

11.4.2   Selectively Recursive Approach (SERA)

This is an extension of SE that uses a selective sampling of the minority class [6]. Mahalanobis distance is applied for selecting a subset of most relevant minority instances (originating from the previous chunks) to be combined with the ones from the recent chunk. A Bagging approach is used on the majority class, to achieve reduction of the number of its instances. This allows to alleviate SE limitations on drifting minority classes, at the cost of making SERA highly sensitive to proper selection of the number of minority instances.

11.4.3   Recursive Ensemble Approach (REA)

This is a further extension of SERA [7]. It basically applies the k-NN principle to measure the similarity between old and new minority class instances, in order to retain only the most diverse ones. Each base classifier is assigned a weight reflecting its performance on the most recent chunk.

11.4.4   Boundary Definition Ensemble (BD)

This is a weighted ensemble that uses a propagation of both minority and majority instances to the new chunks, in order to improve the learning process of constantly evolving class boundary [32]. Similarity between two data chunks is being measured using a combination of information gain and Hellinger's distance, allowing for an implicit drift detection. A linear function defined as an inverse of similarity of two chunks is being used for classifier weighting. BD is subject to some limitations, like small weight differences or reduced variance, and authors discuss that this can be resolved by a more advanced combination function.

11.4.5 Learn^{++}.CDC (Concept Drift with SMOTE)

This is an extension of popular Learn^{++} ensemble [48], adapted to an incremental learning from imbalanced data [11]. Learn^{++} is extended with Bagging, balanced using undersampling each bag. In order to achieve a balanced performance on both classes, classifiers are weighted by their predictive capabilities on minority and majority instances. Furthermore, SMOTE may be applied on the minority class. Learn^{++}.CDC assumes that minority class has static properties and the roles of classes do not change over time.

11.4.6 Ensemble of Online Cost-Sensitive Neural Networks (EONN)

It incorporates a cost-sensitive learning scheme during online neural network training [20]. An pool of neural networks is being initially trained using random weights and these models are preserved for the entire data stream processing. New instances are used to update the base classifiers, allowing for adaptation to changes in data. EONN uses a fixed cost-matrix, with cost for errors on minority class being twice as high as for other classes. This limits the applicability of EONN to streams with drifting IR. Classifiers are combined with weighted voting, using a modified Winnow strategy.

11.4.7 Ensemble of Subset Online Sequential Extreme Learning Machines (ESOS-ELM)

Randomized neural networks are used as base classifiers, each trained separately on different balanced subset of instances from the stream [43]. Two types of buffers (short-term and long-term) allow for keeping the members of the ensemble, as well as recording the changes in the stream properties. Two different learning schemes were proposed for moderate and high imbalance ratios (the difference being the way of processing majority class instances). However, the algorithm replicates the limitations of some of the previous methods, assuming that the minority class is never subject to a concept drift.

11.4.8 Oversampling- and Undersampling-Based Online Bagging (OOB and UOB)

This approach takes into an account potential dynamic changes in IR and class roles over time [57]. It combined Online Bagging with sampling that are able to balance the stream instance by instance. A dedicated concept and imbalance drift detector is used to change the sampling ratios of OOB/UOB and their view on minority class when necessary. A further modification, called WEOB, uses a combination of both under and oversampling in order to choose the better strategy for the current state of the stream. An adaptive weighting combination scheme was proposed to accommodate this hybrid solution, where the weights of the sampling strategies are either computed as their G-mean values or are binary (meaning only one of them will be used at a time). A multi-class extension of this method was discussed in [58], where complex relationships among multiple skewed classes are handled by marking them as multi-minority and multi-majority types.

11.4.9   Dynamic Weighted Majority for Imbalance Learning (DWMIL)

Popular Dynamic Weighted Majority ensemble [27] has been adapted to work with imbalanced data streams [34]. Four main characteristics of DWMIL include fast adaptation to various types of concept drift, no need for storing any historical data, requirements for a small number of base classifiers, and using only a single parameter to determine how to manage the minority class.

11.4.10   Gradual Resampling Ensemble (GRE)

In [49], authors propose to apply a sampling only on selected instances from the stream, in order to avoid propagating drifting examples. Additionally, instances that have a low probability of increasing the overlapping with the majority class are selected for the oversampling. This is combined with DBSCAN clustering approach that is used to detect disjuncts in the incoming chunks of data and detect rare instances or outliers. GRE uses continuously updated base classifiers, allowing it to track changes in the stream. Past chunks are also subject to balancing by using newly arriving minority class instances.

11.5   Evolving Number of Classes

As mentioned in Sect. 11.2 emerging and disappearing classes in data streams are strongly connected with the imbalance domain. Although most of works on novel class detection do not concentrate on mechanism how to tackle skewed class distributions, they can be easily utilized in most imbalanced learning frameworks.

11.5.1 Learn^{++}.NovelClass (Learn^{++}.NC)

This algorithm [44] is an extension of Learn^{++} [48] dedicated to handling novel classes appearing in the stream. The main contribution lies in the classifier combination phase. Learn^{++}.NC uses a dynamic weight consult and vote algorithm that allows base classifiers to exchange information regarding potential novel instances. As the most competent classifiers are assigned highest weight, we prevent a situation in which classifier trained on new instances is outvoted by classifiers that did not have access to novel instances.

11.5.2 Enhanced Classifier for Data Streams with Novel Class Miner (ECSMiner)

This approach is dedicated to simultaneous novelty detection and classification in data streams with present time constraints [39]. In high-speed data stream scenarios, new instances must be evaluated within a bounded time frame, to avoid bottlenecking the constantly arriving new data. This is crucial for novelty detection module that is usually characterized by a high computational complexity. ECSMiner takes also into account a delay in an access to true class labels. Three buffers are being used for instance storage: potential novel instances, instances waiting for class labels, and labeled instances to be used in training new classifiers.

11.5.3 Multiclass Miner in Data Streams (MCM)

MCM is an further extension of novel class detection ensembles that take into account evolving feature space [41]. It assumes that new features may appear over time, a common problem in some applications (e.g., new phrases in textual data streams). Each base classifier uses feature space homogenization with lossless conversion, allowing avoiding differences between training and testing sets. The outlier detection module uses an adaptive threshold for changing definitions of novel instances. The novelty detection module was constructed with the usage of Gini coefficient to simultaneously measure the difference among new instance and existing classes, as well as its similarity to other novel instances stored in a buffer. MCM is capable of detecting multiple new emerging classes at the same time, with an usage of graph-based class description.

11.5.4 AnyNovel

This ensemble uses a two-step cluster formation [1]. Firstly, a supervised learning method divides the initial data into clusters, each of which is assigned as a separate class. Next, an unsupervised clustering detects sub-concepts within each class cluster, leading to creation of locally specialized models. AnyNovel is capable of efficiently distinguishing between actual novel concept appearance, drift present in one of the existing sub-concepts or singular outliers appearance. Novel concept are defined as residing outside all existing cluster-based models and consistently moving away from all existing concepts. In order to remove outdated classes that disappear from the stream, a sequential forgetting mechanism was applied. AnyNovel uses an active learning module to reduce the labeling cost during data stream processing.

11.5.5 Class-Based Ensemble for Class Evolution (CBCE)

This algorithm differentiates among three possible scenarios: class emergence, disappearance and re-occurrence. CBCE constructs its ensemble by storing independent online classifiers for every single class that has appeared at a given point of stream progress [53]. This is done via one-vs-all binary decomposition. Additionally, each base classifier is updated with instances after a dynamic undersampling technique that allows for countering the evolving disproportions between instances in classes. CBCE works only with base classifiers that provide decisions in a form of a score, which makes usage of some popular online classifiers impossible. When a novel class emerges, its prior probability is being estimated and a new one-vs-all classifier is trained. Classifiers may be deactivated when a concept disappears and reactivated when its re-occurrence has been detected.

11.5.6 Class Based Micro Classifier Ensemble (CLAM) and Stream Classifier And Novel and Recurring Class Detector (SCARN)

CLAM is an ensemble of micro-classifiers, with each base model is a cluster-based classifier trained using only instances coming from a single class [2]. For each new instance, the ensemble of micro-classifiers checks if it belongs to any of existing classes. If not, then it is considered as a potential novel instance. When the buffer of novel instances becomes full, a new classifier is trained on them and added to the ensemble. SCARN approach utilizes two separate ensembles [2]: a primary one and an auxiliary one. The primary ensemble is responsible for differentiating between known classes and outliers. Each detected outlier is delegated to the auxiliary ensemble that decides whether this is a reoccurring concept from previously known class or a completely new case.

11.6 Access to Ground Truth

Obtaining a true class label for new instance coming from a data stream is far from being a trivial task [40]. If we would have an access to a theoretical oracle that would provide us with such an information every time a new instance becomes available, then there is no need to have any classification procedures. In most real-life applications, a domain expert is required to analyze given instance and label it. While one may theorize that a company developing a specific data stream mining system should have such an expert at their disposal, we cannot forget the costs connected with such a procedure. This can be viewed as a monetary costs, as an expert would require a payment for sharing his knowledge, as well as a time cost, as an expert needs to spend some time analyzing each instance. Therefore, in a real-life scenario neither a constant label query is possible (as a given company would quickly use-up its budget), nor instant label availability. Even if these factors, for various reasons, play less important role, the human throughput must also be considered. A given expert cannot work non-stop and will have limited responsiveness per given time unit. Thus, in cases of massive and high-speed data streams assumption of continuous label availability cannot hold.

Most popular approaches include active learning solutions that allow to select only a limited number of instances for labeling. They are usually selected to offer new information to the classifier, instead of reinforcing old concepts. Although there is a good amount of research on active learning for static scenarios [51], there exist but a few solutions that take into account the drifting and evolving nature of streams [31, 62, 67], label latency [47], or working under assumption that only initial data is being labeled and no further ground truth access is to be expected [13]. This issue becomes even more difficult when dealing with imbalanced drifting data streams. Here, the labeling must be performed in a way that will not concentrate only on one of the classes. While most standard labeling methods will display bias towards majority class, we cannot forget that one cannot do the opposite and sample only minority. A balanced selection from both classes is necessary to maintain an effective data stream classifier.

11.6.1 Online Active Learning with Bayesian Probit

This is one of the first frameworks for skew-insensitive active learning from data streams [8]. For selecting instances, they used importance weighting principle with online Bayesian learning with IID assumptions on non-IID data.

11.6.2   Online Mean Score on Unlabeled Set (Online-MSU)

An unsupervised score is being used to manage and evaluate the performance of multiple active learning algorithms [14]. A prediction mechanism was used to estimate their performance on incoming instances and thus leading to an automatic selection of most competent active learning algorithms from the pool without a need for an evaluation set. Their online learning mechanism is capable of switching among active learning strategies to achieve improved labeling of imbalanced data streams.

11.6.3   Cost-Sensitive Online Active Learning Under a Query Budget (CSOAL)

This method optimizes in an online manner two different cost-sensitive measures [65]: the weighted sum of sensitivity and specificity, and the weighted cost. This is combined with an asymmetric update rule and authors showed the usefulness of their approach to detecting malicious URLs. CSOAL does not take into an account the potential of concept drift occurrence.

11.6.4   Online Active Learning with the Asymmetric Query Model

Two types of evaluations of each new instance are being used, taking into account initial probabilities of which of them may belong to minority and majority classes [64]. During push evaluation only the minority instances are being considered. Push and query evaluation also takes into account the impact of obtaining a label for given instance. Authors optimize their system using F-score, but do not take into an account the possibility of concept drift occurrence.

11.6.5   Genetic Programming Active Learning Framework (Stream-GP)

Genetic programming classifiers are combined with uniform and biased instance sampling to achieve efficient adaptation to imbalanced data streams with limited access to ground truth [25]. Their active learning scheme was based on the output of the best individual from the population. If the elite member predicts that a given instance belongs to a minority class, it is more likely that a ground truth will be obtained for this instance.

11.7 Summarizing Comments

Learning from imbalanced drifting data streams combines the difficulties embedded in data stream mining and imbalanced data classification domains, as well as creates its own unique characteristics. This fascinating domain is still relatively new and many issues still await to be properly analyzed, understood, categorized, and addressed. Let us conclude this chapter by discussing the most important open issues and future challenges that imbalanced data stream mining must face in years to come.

- **Data-level methods**: there is a need for developing new under- and oversampling methods that can adapt to various types of concept drift and are characterized by a low computational complexity.
- **In-depth research into multi-class imbalanced data streams**: there is a need for a detailed taxonomy of learning difficulties that we may encounter in multi-class imbalanced data streams, methods for measuring the relationships among classes, as well as those flexibly adapting to emerging and disappearing classes.
- **Considering online instance difficulty**: in the static data framework, other data difficulty factors such as decomposition of the minority class into rare sub-concepts, overlapping with other classes, and presence of very rare minority cases in the majority class regions are also considered as more influential than the global imbalance between classes. Considering them in drifting scenarios, where sub-concepts or rare cases appear over time and overlapping regions change, is an open research problem.
- **Evaluation measures**: there is not an agreed upon standard what metrics to use for imbalanced data streams, especially in case of multi-class problems. Additionally, new statistical tests of significance must be developed that will take into account multiple predictive metrics, training/testing times, and memory consumption, in order to allow for a truly in-depth comparison of various methods.
- **Benchmark datasets**: the number of real-world publicly available datasets for testing imbalanced stream classifiers is still too small. Additionally, there are no agreed upon benchmarks and data generators that allow to create both binary and multi-class imbalanced data streams with concept drift and various learning difficulties embedded.
- **Open-source code repositories**: algorithms for mining imbalanced data streams are spread upon different languages, personal websites and varying implementations. There is a need for an unifying environment or package that will collect most important methods in order to facilitate reproducible research and easy comparison among different approaches under fair conditions.

We envision that next decade will bring significant developments in this area, as many contemporary real-world applications call for existence of such ML methods.

References

1. Abdallah, Z.S., Gaber, M.M., Srinivasan, B., Krishnaswamy, S.: Anynovel: detection of novel concepts in evolving data streams. Evol. Syst. **7**(2), 73–93 (2016)
2. Al-Khateeb, T., Masud, M.M., Al-Naami, K., Seker, S.E., Mustafa, A.M., Khan, L., Trabelsi, Z., Aggarwal, C.C., Han, J.: Recurring and novel class detection using class-based ensemble for evolving data stream. IEEE Trans. Knowl. Data Eng. **28**(10), 2752–2764 (2016)
3. Barua, S., Islam, M.M., Murase, K.: GOS-IL: a generalized over-sampling based online imbalanced learning framework. In: Neural Information Processing – 22nd International Conference, ICONIP 2015, Proceedings, Part I, Istanbul, 9–12 Nov 2015, pp. 680–687 (2015)
4. Bifet, A., Holmes, G., Pfahringer, B., Frank, E.: Fast perceptron decision tree learning from evolving data streams. In: Advances in Knowledge Discovery and Data Mining, 14th Pacific-Asia Conference, PAKDD 2010, Proceedings. Part II, Hyderabad, 21–24 June 2010, pp. 299–310 (2010)
5. Brzezinski, D., Stefanowski, J.: Prequential AUC: properties of the area under the ROC curve for data streams with concept drift. Knowl. Inf. Syst. **52**(2), 531–562 (2017)
6. Chen, S., He, H.: SERA: selectively recursive approach towards nonstationary imbalanced stream data mining. In: International Joint Conference on Neural Networks, IJCNN 2009, Atlanta, 14–19 June 2009, pp. 522–529 (2009)
7. Chen, S., He, H.: Towards incremental learning of nonstationary imbalanced data stream: a multiple selectively recursive approach. Evol. Syst. **2**(1), 35–50 (2011)
8. Chu, W., Zinkevich, M., Li, L., Thomas, A., Tseng, B.L.: Unbiased online active learning in data streams. In: Proceedings of the 17th ACM SIGKDD International Conference on Knowledge Discovery and Data Mining, San Diego, 21–24 Aug 2011, pp. 195–203 (2011)
9. Cieslak, D.A., Hoens, T.R., Chawla, N.V., Kegelmeyer, W.P.: Hellinger distance decision trees are robust and skew-insensitive. Data Min. Knowl. Discov. **24**(1), 136–158 (2012)
10. Czarnecki, W.M., Tabor, J.: Online extreme entropy machines for streams classification and active learning. In: Proceedings of the 9th International Conference on Computer Recognition Systems CORES 2015, Wroclaw, 25–27 May 2015, pp. 371–381 (2015)
11. Ditzler, G., Polikar, R.: Incremental learning of concept drift from streaming imbalanced data. IEEE Trans. Knowl. Data Eng. **25**(10), 2283–2301 (2013)
12. Domingos, P.M., Hulten, G.: Mining high-speed data streams. In: Proceedings of the Sixth ACM SIGKDD International Conference on Knowledge Discovery and Data Mining, Boston, 20–23 Aug 2000, pp. 71–80 (2000)
13. Dyer, K.B., Capo, R., Polikar, R.: COMPOSE: a semisupervised learning framework for initially labeled nonstationary streaming data. IEEE Trans. Neural Netw. Learn. Syst. **25**(1), 12–26 (2014)
14. Ferdowsi, Z., Ghani, R., Settimi, R.: Online active learning with imbalanced classes. In: 2013 IEEE 13th International Conference on Data Mining, Dallas, 7–10 Dec 2013, pp. 1043–1048 (2013)
15. Gaber, M.M.: Advances in data stream mining. Wiley Interdiscip. Rev. Data Min. Knowl. Disc. **2**(1), 79–85 (2012)
16. Gama, J., Medas, P., Castillo, G., Rodrigues, P.P.: Learning with drift detection. In: Advances in Artificial Intelligence – SBIA 2004, Proceedings of the 17th Brazilian Symposium on Artificial Intelligence, São Luis, Maranhão, 29 Sept–1 Oct 2004. Lecture Notes in Computer Science 3171, Springer (2004). ISBN: 3-540-23237-0
17. Gama, J., Sebastião, R., Rodrigues, P.P.: On evaluating stream learning algorithms. Mach. Learn. **90**(3), 317–346 (2013)
18. Gama, J., Zliobaite, I., Bifet, A., Pechenizkiy, M., Bouchachia, A.: A survey on concept drift adaptation. ACM Comput. Surv. **46**(4), 44:1–44:37 (2014)
19. Gao, J., Ding, B., Fan, W., Han, J., Yu, P.S.: Classifying data streams with skewed class distributions and concept drifts. IEEE Internet Comput. **12**(6), 37–49 (2008)

20. Ghazikhani, A., Monsefi, R., Yazdi, H.S.: Ensemble of online neural networks for non-stationary and imbalanced data streams. Neurocomputing **122**, 535–544 (2013)
21. Ghazikhani, A., Monsefi, R., Yazdi, H.S.: Recursive least square perceptron model for non-stationary and imbalanced data stream classification. Evol. Syst. **4**(2), 119–131 (2013)
22. Ghazikhani, A., Monsefi, R., Yazdi, H.S.: Online neural network model for non-stationary and imbalanced data stream classification. Int. J. Mach. Learn. Cybern. **5**(1), 51–62 (2014)
23. Hoens, T.R., Polikar, R., Chawla, N.V.: Learning from streaming data with concept drift and imbalance: an overview. Prog. AI **1**(1), 89–101 (2012)
24. Hu, J., Yang, H., King, I., Lyu, M.R., So, A.M.: Kernelized online imbalanced learning with fixed budgets. In: Proceedings of the Twenty-Ninth AAAI Conference on Artificial Intelligence, Austin, 25–30 Jan 2015, pp. 2666–2672 (2015)
25. Khanchi, S., Heywood, M.I., Zincir-Heywood, A.N.: Properties of a GP active learning framework for streaming data with class imbalance. In: Proceedings of the Genetic and Evolutionary Computation Conference, GECCO 2017, Berlin, 15–19 July 2017, pp. 945–952 (2017)
26. Khanchi, S., Vahdat, A., Heywood, M.I., Zincir-Heywood, A.N.: On botnet detection with genetic programming under streaming data label budgets and class imbalance. Swarm Evol. Comput. **39**, 123–140 (2018)
27. Kolter, J.Z., Maloof, M.A.: Dynamic weighted majority: an ensemble method for drifting concepts. J. Mach. Learn. Res. **8**, 2755–2790 (2007)
28. Krawczyk, B.: Learning from imbalanced data: open challenges and future directions. Prog. AI **5**(4), 221–232 (2016)
29. Krawczyk, B., Skryjomski, P.: Cost-sensitive perceptron decision trees for imbalanced drifting data streams. In: Machine Learning and Knowledge Discovery in Databases – European Conference, ECML PKDD 2017, Proceedings, Part II, Skopje, 18–22 Sept 2017, pp. 512–527 (2017)
30. Krawczyk, B., Minku, L.L., Gama, J., Stefanowski, J., Woźniak, M.: Ensemble learning for data stream analysis: a survey. Inf. Fusion **37**, 132–156 (2017)
31. Kurlej, B., Woźniak, M.: Active learning approach to concept drift problem. Log. J. IGPL **20**(3), 550–559 (2012)
32. Lichtenwalter, R., Chawla, N.V.: Adaptive methods for classification in arbitrarily imbalanced and drifting data streams. In: New Frontiers in Applied Data Mining, PAKDD 2009 International Workshops, Revised Selected Papers, Bangkok, 27–30 Apr 2009, pp. 53–75 (2009)
33. Liu, A., Lu, J., Liu, F., Zhang, G.: Accumulating regional density dissimilarity for concept drift detection in data streams. Pattern Recog. **76**, 256–272 (2018)
34. Lu, Y., Cheung, Y., Tang, Y.Y.: Dynamic weighted majority for incremental learning of imbalanced data streams with concept drift. In: Proceedings of the Twenty-Sixth International Joint Conference on Artificial Intelligence, IJCAI 2017, Melbourne, 19–25 Aug 2017, pp. 2393–2399 (2017)
35. Lughofer, E., Angelov, P.P.: Handling drifts and shifts in on-line data streams with evolving fuzzy systems. Appl. Soft Comput. **11**(2), 2057–2068 (2011)
36. Lyon, R.J., Brooke, J.M., Knowles, J.D., Stappers, B.W.: Hellinger distance trees for imbalanced streams. In: 22nd International Conference on Pattern Recognition, ICPR 2014, Stockholm, 24–28 Aug 2014, pp. 1969–1974 (2014)
37. Mao, W., Wang, J., Wang, L.: Online sequential classification of imbalanced data by combining extreme learning machine and improved SMOTE algorithm. In: 2015 International Joint Conference on Neural Networks, IJCNN 2015, Killarney, 12–17 July 2015, pp. 1–8 (2015)
38. Mao, W., Jiang, M., Wang, J., Li, Y.: Online extreme learning machine with hybrid sampling strategy for sequential imbalanced data. Cogn. Comput. **9**(6), 780–800 (2017)
39. Masud, M.M., Gao, J., Khan, L., Han, J., Thuraisingham, B.M.: Classification and novel class detection in concept-drifting data streams under time constraints. IEEE Trans. Knowl. Data Eng. **23**(6), 859–874 (2011)

40. Masud, M.M., Woolam, C., Gao, J., Khan, L., Han, J., Hamlen, K.W., Oza, N.C.: Facing the reality of data stream classification: coping with scarcity of labeled data. Knowl. Inf. Syst. **33**(1), 213–244 (2011)
41. Masud, M.M., Chen, Q., Khan, L., Aggarwal, C.C., Gao, J., Han, J., Srivastava, A.N., Oza, N.C.: Classification and adaptive novel class detection of feature-evolving data streams. IEEE Trans. Knowl. Data Eng. **25**(7), 1484–1497 (2013)
42. Minku, L.L., Yao, X., White, A.P.: The impact of diversity on online ensemble learning in the presence of concept drift. IEEE Trans. Knowl. Data Eng. **22**, 730–742 (2009)
43. Mirza, B., Lin, Z., Liu, N.: Ensemble of subset online sequential extreme learning machine for class imbalance and concept drift. Neurocomputing **149**, 316–329 (2015)
44. Muhlbaier, M.D., Topalis, A., Polikar, R.: Learn^{++}.nc: combining ensemble of classifiers with dynamically weighted consult-and-vote for efficient incremental learning of new classes. IEEE Trans. Neural Netw. **20**(1), 152–168 (2009)
45. Nguyen, H.M., Cooper, E.W., Kamei, K.: Online learning from imbalanced data streams. In: Third International Conference of Soft Computing and Pattern Recognition, SoCPaR 2011, Dalian, 14–16 Oct 2011, pp. 347–352 (2011)
46. Pang, S., Zhu, L., Chen, G., Sarrafzadeh, A., Ban, T., Inoue, D.: Dynamic class imbalance learning for incremental LPSVM. Neural Netw. **44**, 87–100 (2013)
47. Plasse, J., Adams, N.M.: Handling delayed labels in temporally evolving data streams. In: 2016 IEEE International Conference on Big Data, BigData 2016, Washington, DC, 5–8 Dec 2016, pp. 2416–2424 (2016)
48. Polikar, R., Upda, L., Upda, S.S., Honavar, V.G.: Learn++: an incremental learning algorithm for supervised neural networks. IEEE Trans. Syst. Man Cybern. Part C **31**(4), 497–508 (2001)
49. Ren, S., Liao, B., Zhu, W., Li, Z., Liu, W., Li, K.: The gradual resampling ensemble for mining imbalanced data streams with concept drift. Neurocomputing **286**, 150–166 (2018)
50. Rutkowski, L., Pietruczuk, L., Duda, P., Jaworski, M.: Decision trees for mining data streams based on the mcdiarmid's bound. IEEE Trans. Knowl. Data Eng. **25**(6), 1272–1279 (2013)
51. Settles, B.: Active learning literature survey. Technical report, University of Wisconsin-Madison (2010)
52. Sobolewski, P., Woźniak, M.: Concept drift detection and model selection with simulated recurrence and ensembles of statistical detectors. J. Univ. Comput. Sci. **19**(4), 462–483 (2013)
53. Sun, Y., Tang, K., Minku, L.L., Wang, S., Yao, X.: Online ensemble learning of data streams with gradually evolved classes. IEEE Trans. Knowl. Data Eng. **28**(6), 1532–1545 (2016)
54. Wang, H., Abraham, Z.: Concept drift detection for streaming data. In: 2015 International Joint Conference on Neural Networks, IJCNN 2015, Killarney, 12–17 July 2015, pp. 1–9 (2015)
55. Wang, S., Minku, L.L., Ghezzi, D., Caltabiano, D., Tiño, P., Yao, X.: Concept drift detection for online class imbalance learning. In: The 2013 International Joint Conference on Neural Networks, IJCNN 2013, Dallas, 4–9 Aug 2013, pp. 1–10 (2013)
56. Wang, S., Minku, L.L., Yao, X.: A learning framework for online class imbalance learning. In: Proceedings of the IEEE Symposium on Computational Intelligence and Ensemble Learning, CIEL 2013, IEEE Symposium Series on Computational Intelligence (SSCI), Singapore, 16–19 Apr 2013, pp. 36–45 (2013)
57. Wang, S., Minku, L.L., Yao, X.: Resampling-based ensemble methods for online class imbalance learning. IEEE Trans. Knowl. Data Eng. **27**(5), 1356–1368 (2015)
58. Wang, S., Minku, L.L., Yao, X.: Dealing with multiple classes in online class imbalance learning. In: Proceedings of the Twenty-Fifth International Joint Conference on Artificial Intelligence, IJCAI 2016, New York, 9–15 July 2016, pp. 2118–2124 (2016)
59. Wang, S., Minku, L.L., Yao, X.: A systematic study of online class imbalance learning with concept drift. IEEE Trans. Neural Netw. Learn. Syst. **PP**(99), 1–20 (2018). https://doi.org/10.1109/TNNLS.2017.2771290
60. Woźniak, M.: A hybrid decision tree training method using data streams. Knowl. Inf. Syst. **29**(2), 335–347 (2011)
61. Woźniak, M., Graña, M., Corchado, E.: A survey of multiple classifier systems as hybrid systems. Inf. Fusion **16**, 3–17 (2014)

62. Woźniak, M., Ksieniewicz, P., Cyganek, B., Kasprzak, A., Walkowiak, K.: Active learning classification of drifted streaming data. In: International Conference on Computational Science 2016, ICCS 2016, San Diego, 6–8 June 2016, pp. 1724–1733 (2016)
63. Yan, Y., Yang, T., Yang, Y., Chen, J.: A framework of online learning with imbalanced streaming data. In: Proceedings of the Thirty-First AAAI Conference on Artificial Intelligence, San Francisco, 4–9, Feb 2017, pp. 2817–2823 (2017)
64. Zhang, X., Yang, T., Srinivasan, P.: Online asymmetric active learning with imbalanced data. In: Proceedings of the 22nd ACM SIGKDD International Conference on Knowledge Discovery and Data Mining, San Francisco, 13–17 Aug 2016, pp. 2055–2064 (2016)
65. Zhao, P., Hoi, S.C.H.: Cost-sensitive online active learning with application to malicious URL detection. In: The 19th ACM SIGKDD International Conference on Knowledge Discovery and Data Mining, KDD 2013, Chicago, 11–14 Aug 2013, pp. 919–927 (2013)
66. Zhou, Z., Liu, X.: Training cost-sensitive neural networks with methods addressing the class imbalance problem. IEEE Trans. Knowl. Data Eng. **18**(1), 63–77 (2006)
67. Žliobaitė, I., Bifet, A., Pfahringer, B., Holmes, G.: Active learning with drifting streaming data. IEEE Trans. Neural Netw. Learn. Syst. **1**, 27–39 (2014)

Chapter 12
Non-classical Imbalanced Classification Problems

Abstract Most of the research in class imbalance are carried out in standard (binary or multi-class) classification problems. However, in recent years, researchers have addressed new classification frameworks beyond standard classification in different aspects. Several variations of class imbalance problem appear within these frameworks. This chapter reviews the problem of class imbalance for a spectrum of these non-classical problems. Throughout this chapter, in Sect. 12.2 some research studies related to class imbalance where only partially labeled data is available (SSL) are reviewed. Then, in Sect. 12.3 the problem of label imbalance in problems where more than a label can be associated to an instance (Multilabel Learning) is discussed. In Sect. 12.4 the problem of class imbalance when labels are associated to bags of instances, rather than individually (Multi-instance Learning), is analyzed. Next, Sect. 12.5 refers to the problem of class imbalance when there exists an ordinal relation among classes (Ordinal Classification). Finally, in Sect. 12.6 some concluding remarks are presented.

12.1 Introduction

Over the past several decades, new real-life problems have motivated the development of new classification frameworks that go beyond standard supervised classification [30]. These frameworks have different constraints on the access or nature of supervised data, such as (1) the inherent relationship between instances and labels of a problem, which may be beyond the one-instance one-label standard, (2) the access of partial class information for the training examples, (3) an ordinal relationship among classes. Class imbalance may have different causes and consequences within these frameworks.

Therefore, new techniques for dealing with peculiarities and specificities of these problems are necessary. This chapter discuss some research related to imbalanced data when not all class labels of the instances are available (Semi-supervised learning), when instances are associated to more than one label (Multilabel learning), when the label is associated to a bag of instances (Multi-instance learning), when classes are ordered (Ordinal classification) and for regression problems.

© Springer Nature Switzerland AG 2018

A. Fernández et al., *Learning from Imbalanced Data Sets*,

https://doi.org/10.1007/978-3-319-98074-4_12

12.2 Semi-supervised Learning

SSL refers to a class of supervised tasks where typically a small set of labeled examples is available, although the learning algorithm also have access to a larger set of unlabeled instances. This scenario is common in situations where collecting data is cheap, however it is expensive to label all the instances to train a classifier. Labeling all instances is costly because it generally requires the know-how of a domain expert (e.g., a linguist specialist to label sentences collected from the web) or some costly procedure (e.g., perform a crash test for testing the resilience of a material). SSL is an interesting way to avoid the cost of having external agents manually labeling data.

The rationale behind SSL is that unlabeled data, when used in conjunction with a small amount of labeled data, can provide important information for improving the learning process. To this end, SSL aims to make use of the combined information in labeled and unlabeled data in such ways that the classification performance is improved when compared to discarding all the unlabeled data and only using the labeled data in the learning process [10, 74].

Similar to the classical supervised learning framework, we are given l labeled instances, were each instance is a pair $< x_i, y_i >$, for $i \in \{1, \ldots, l\}$. Each $x_i \in X$ is associated to its corresponding class label $y_i \in Y$, were X is the input space and Y the set of possible classes. Additionally, we are given u unlabeled instances x_j, for $j \in \{l + 1, \ldots, l + n\}$, where $x_j \in X$.

The general SSL spectrum encompass some specific tasks, depending on the scope and constraints. If the scope of the SSL task is to predict only the class of the u unlabeled instances, without generalizing beyond them, the task is known as transductive learning [61]. In the case the scope includes learning a general function $\mathcal{F} : X \rightarrow Y$, that can be applied to out-of-sample instances, the task in inductive. A special inductive case occurs when we only have instances for one class (the "positive" class). This case is known as PU-learning, for Positive and Unlabelled instances learning. Another related task is AL, where departing from a small labeled sample, the AL algorithm selects instances to be labeled by a human expert.

12.2.1 Inductive Semi-supervised Learning

The most popular inductive SSL algorithms include self-training, EM, co-training [8], and graph-based methods [73]. SSL have been applied to some high-imbalanced domains, including sentiment analysis [40]; author identification [38]; protein splice site prediction [53]; and liver transplantation donor-recipient matching [50]. Due to the imbalanced class ratio in these domains, different techniques have been used to deal with imbalanced data for SSL.

Random subspace generation [33], combined with under-sampling, was used in [40] to deal skewed distributions in sentiment analysis. The approach consists in using under-sampling to generate K balanced samples, where K is proportional to the closest integer approximation of the ratio between the majority and minority classes. For each K sample, two random subspaces are generated by randomly splitting their features, and a classifier is leaned for each subspace. These classifiers are used to choose a pair of instances from the unlabeled set to be labeled as positive and negative, with highest confidence according to the SSL algorithm co-training [8]. These instances are added to the training set, and the process is repeated N times, where N is a parameter set by the user.

In [38], a metric sensitive to class imbalance is used in the Common n-Gram (CNG) [52] profiling approach for author identification. This version of CNG is used as one of the views of a co-training like algorithm [8]. The second view is an SVM classifier, trained over the d most frequent n-grams (d is dynamically chosen based in the intrinsic dimension [39] of the n-grams). When both views agree in the author identification for a text in the unlabeled set, it is added to the training set. The process is repeated until all authors in the unlabeled set are predicted, or when it is both views disagree for all unlabeled texts.

Algorithm level and data level approaches to deal with class imbalance were explored in [53] in conjunction with the SSL algorithm self-training. Self-training first learn a classifier, using any classification algorithm as a base-learner, and use it in a bootstrap sample from the unlabeled sample to select the most confident classified instances to add to the training set. The algorithm retrain itself with the augmented training set. Two data-level and two algorithm level approaches were investigated. At data-level, the first approach consists in applying SMOTE [16] to the training set before each new labeling. The second approach is to select only the instances classified as positive to include in the training set. At the algorithm-level, the first approach consists in using a cost sensitive algorithm as base-learner. The second approach uses an ensemble build using balanced samples from the training data.

To augment the minority class prior to using the SSL algorithm based on label propagation [73], in [50] an over-sampling technique based on the KNN is applied. The approach consists in applying the kNN to classify the instances in the unlabeled set, and use the ones classified as positive, alongside the labeled data, as seeds for propagating the labels in the embedded graph [73].

12.2.2 Transductive Learning

In transductive learning [26], the objective is to, using a set of labeled instances, infer the labels of a fixed test set. This differs from inductive learning in a sense that in inductive learning, the objective is to infer a general model that can be used to classify out-of-the-sample instances.

To overcome the problem of imbalanced data in transductive SVM (TSVM) [35] in the unlabeled instances, progressive transductive SVM (PTSVM) was proposed in [17]. The main idea is to progressively and iteratively label pairs of instances of opposite classes with high confidence. If in one step it is not possible to label a pair with high confidence, the algorithm tries to label, with high confidence, an instance of one of the classes (probably the majority one). When it is not possible to identify instances to label with high accuracy, TSVM is applied to label the remaining instances. In [68], TSVM is associated to sampling techniques to handle the class imbalance problem.

Personalized transductive learning (PTL) [46] builds a unique local model for each instance, by considering their adjacent instances. In [46], this idea was explores using SVM as base learner, and the models are organized hierarchically, in a spanning tree-like fashion. Experimental results conducted by the authors shows good classification performance in imbalanced data sets.

Graph based transductive learning uses a graph embedding approach to label instances by means of label propagation in graph. In [65], a generalized cost function that introduces node normalization terms to incorporate resilience to label imbalances. Also in the context of graph based transduction, in [64] a label regularization method is proposed to handle class imbalance in the task of microscopic image annotation.

12.2.3   PU-Learning

Positive and unlabeled learning, or one-class learning, is related to problems where only instances of one of the classes is available. These problems can be seen as extreme cases of SSL.

One-class SVMs are shown to be useful to deal with extremely unbalanced, high dimensional noise feature spaces such as text classification [51]. In [36], a combination of PU-learning algorithms and resampling methods is proposed with the objective of enriching the training set. A systematic study about the correlation of class imbalance and one class classification under the occurrence of concept drift was carried out in [69].

In a recent study [71], a weighting approach was used to improve classification in PU-learning scenarios. Weights are first determined via Monte-Carlo simulations, and weighted one-class SVMs were used. The difference between class imbalance in the sample set and in the underline distribution was recently investigated in [34].

12.2.4   Active Learning

In AL, the algorithm asks for intervention from the user (or eventually some other information source) to obtain the labels of some unlabeled instances. In the standard configuration, the main idea is to actively ask for external supervision from the selected instances, aiming to improve classification performance. Besides improving classification, the algorithm also aims to minimize the need of external supervision, as this process is costly. To this end, the algorithm should wisely select informative instances that needs external supervision by, e.g., selecting instances that the algorithm may consider ambiguous or hard to classify.

AL can have two different roles in the context of learning from imbalance data [1]. The first role concerns in applying an AL algorithm to an imbalanced data set. In this case, the main challenge is to assure that instances from the minority class are queried to the user. The second role is to reduce, and potentially eliminate, the adverse effects of the class imbalance in the learning process by using AL techniques.

Querying examples from an unlabeled set with substantial class imbalance may pose several difficulties for AL. Indeed, this has been pointed out as one of the obstacles for a larger adoption of AL [3]. Traditional AL techniques often aim to increase diversity by considering.

Under the task of Named Entity Recognition in Natural Language Processing tasks, [58, 75] use sampling techniques associated to AL algorithms during the annotation task to acquire new training instances. A bootstrap sampling approach based on NNs was used in [75] for sampling. When a new unlabeled instance is labeled by the external agent, a sampling technique is applied in the neighborhood in this instance.

In [25], it has been advocated that using SVM's as base learning algorithm for AL is less sensitive to imbalanced data sets. A cost weighted version of SVM's [7], where costs are defined by means of inverse class proportions. The main argument is that cost sensitive SVM's put more preference on the minority class. A drawback is that, in AL applications, the class proportion is often unknown, and difficult to estimate.

Few approaches attempt to use AL techniques to alleviate the class imbalance problem were proposed. In [24], and adaptive mechanism that combined AL and sampling was proposed. The main idea is to use an AL algorithm to suggest the most informative instances for oversampling. Synthetic new instances are generated by linear interpolating between the suggested instances and their NNs.

Another approach is to actively search for new (out-of-sample) instances to alleviate the class imbalance problem [2]. The main idea is to search for instances of the specific class within the unlabeled set of instances [5] or instances in different regions of the input space [6] to improve classification performance.

12.3 Multilabel Learning

In MLL [31], each instance can be associated to a set of relevant labels, instead of a single label per instance.[1] These relevant labels are generally represented as a binary vector, with size equal to the total number of labels, indicating if the corresponding

---

[1]Multilabel learning differs from multi-class classifier as in the latter only one label, from a set larger than two possible classes, is associated to each instance.

label is relevant or not. MLL algorithms were applied to several domains, including text classification, multimedia, and biology.

Three main families of algorithms are generally applied to deal with MLL. The first family uses data transformation to transform a multi-label data set into binary or multi-class data sets. The conversion to binary data sets is generally done in a per-label basis, an approach known as Binary Relevance (BR). The Label Power Set (LP) approach converts a multi-label data set into a multi-class one, by considering each possible label combination which appear in the data set as a class. The second family consists in adapting existent learning algorithms to directly cope with multi-label data sets. Major learning algorithms have been extended, including decision trees, ANNs, KNN, SVMs, to name a few. The third family consists in ensembles of classifiers. See [31] for a detailed overview of these methods.

Class imbalance has an important complication in MLL: different labels may have different degrees of imbalance. In other words, the same data set may have some very frequent labels accompanied of other very infrequent ones. Furthermore, some labels may be correlated, implying some frequent and infrequent labels co-occurring very often.

12.3.1   Imbalance Quantification

In MLL, we are given a set of N examples, where each example is associate to a vector of L possible labels. As there are many labels, there is no a single index for indicating the degree of imbalance. Two traditional measures for indicating the label frequencies are cardinality and density. Label cardinality is the average number of relevant labels per instance, and label density denotes average of label cardinality over the total number of labels. These measures are shown in Eqs. 12.1 and 12.2, respectively.

$$Cardinality = \frac{1}{N} \sum_{i=1}^{N} \sum_{j=1}^{L} l_{ij} \tag{12.1}$$

$$Density = \frac{Cardinality}{L} \tag{12.2}$$

These measures provide an overview of the overall occurrence of labels, but they do not provide information about the degree of imbalance of the labels. In [13], the imbalance ratio per label, $IRLbl(l_i)$ (Eq. 12.3), as the ratio between the most frequent label and each label l_i, as shown in Eq. 12.3, where freq(l) returns the frequency of the label l.

$$IRLbl(l_i) = \frac{\max_{j=1}^{L} \left(\text{freq}(l_j) \right)}{\text{freq}(l_i)} \tag{12.3}$$

To summary the imbalance ratios of the labels, two measure were proposed. The first one, $MeanIR$ (Eq. 12.4), computes the average level of imbalance ratios, while $CVIR$ (Eq. 12.5) measures variation of $IRLbl(l_i)$, i.e., similarity of level of imbalance between all labels. For a nearly balanced data set, all $IRLbl(l_i)$ values are close to 1, which results in values of $MeanIR$ and $CVIR$ close to 1 and 0, respectively.

$$MeanIR = \frac{1}{N} \sum_{i=1}^{L} (IRLbl(l_i)) \tag{12.4}$$

$$CVIR = \frac{IRLbl_\sigma}{MeanIR}, IRLbl_\sigma = \sqrt{\frac{1}{L-1} \sum_{i=1}^{L} (IRLbl(l_i) - MeanIR)^2} \tag{12.5}$$

To assess the concurrence among frequent and infrequent labels, in [12, 15] the authors propose a measure named $SCUMBLE$ (Eq. 12.6). This measure is inspired in the Atkinson index, an econometric measure for measuring social inequality in populations. $SCUMBLE$ measures to what extent labels with different imbalance levels appear jointly. The idea is to use each instance of the data set as a population and each label as an individual. $\overline{IRLbl(l_i)}$ and $\prod_{j=1}^{L} IRLbl(l_{ij})$ are the average and product of the $IRLbl$ relevant to the instance.

$$SCUMBLE = \frac{1}{N} \sum_{i=1}^{N} \left(\frac{1}{\overline{IRLbl(l_i)}} \left(\prod_{j=1}^{L} IRLbl(l_{ij}) \right)^{\frac{1}{L}} \right) \tag{12.6}$$

12.3.2 Methods for Dealing with Imbalance in MLL

Methods for dealing with imbalance labels in MLL can be grouped into three categories: resampling techniques, algorithm adaptation and ensemble. This section describes some of these approaches.

12.3.2.1 Resampling

Some methods under this category follow the problem transformation technique, and then apply some binary or multi-class sampling approach in the transformed problems. In [23], BR is combine with wrapper FS (using C4.5 as wrapper) together with undersampling by removing majority labels participating in a Tomek link [59]. Random undersampling (LP-RUS) and random oversampling (LP-ROS), associated with LP transformation, was explored in [11]. The authors group label sets as frequent and infrequent groups. LD-RUS remove instances from majority group, while LD-ROS duplicate instances from the minority one. Similarly, in [13], random undersampling and random oversampling were used. However, instead of using sets of labels (as in LP-RUS and LP-ROS), labels are group according to the comparison of $IRLbl$ (Eq. 12.3) to $MeanIR$ (Eq. 12.4). The majority group are composed by the labels with $IRLbl$ greater than $MeanIR$, and the minority group by the labels lower than $MeanIR$. ML-RUS remove instances linked to labels in majority group, where ML-ROS duplicate instances from the minority group.

Generation of synthetic instances has also been explored. In [27], SMOTE [16] was used together with three label transformation strategies. The first strategy transforms the instances in which the minority label appears as positive, and the remainder as negative, and runs SMOTE. The second approach is similar to the first, but only the instances in which the minority label appears in isolation are transformed to positive, and the remainder as negative. The third approach considers all the subsets in which the minority label appears, and runs SMOTE several times, one per each subset. An extension of SMOTE, named MLSMOTE, designed to directly cope with multilabel data was proposed in [14]. Instead of transforming the multilabel data set to a binary one, this approach operates directly in the multilabel version. It can operate over a list of minority classes (generally all labels for which $IRLbl$ is greater than $MeanIR$). Instances which belong to one of the labels in the list are used as seeds to generate synthetic instances by interpolating with its NNs. To generate the labels associated to an instance, three approaches were proposed: union and intersection between the labels of the two instances, and a third based on the counting of the labels of the NNs of the two instances.

As the instances may be associated to more than one label, oversampling or undersampling a multilabel data set may produce a side effect: in the first case, oversampling an instance with minority label may also oversample a majority one, while in the latter, undersampling an instance with a majority label may also undersample a minority one, in the case an instance is associated to both labels. To overcome this drawback, an algorithm that takes into account the concurrence among labels, named REMEDIAL [12], is proposed. The algorithm evaluates the $SCUMBLE$ of the instance. If an instance has a high $SCUMBLE$, its labels are decoupled using $MeanIR$ as a threshold. This instance is then replaced by two new instances: one with minority labels and other with majority labels. The rationale behind the decoupling process is that, once labels are separated, oversampling and undersampling techniques would produce better results by avoiding their side effects due to multiple labels associated to the same instance. After the application of REMEDIAL, any sampling algorithm can be applied.

12.3.2.2   Algorithm Adaptation

There are algorithms adapted to MLL which also incorporate mechanisms to deal with imbalanced labels. Some of them are a combination of some data transformation method together a classifier adaptation. In [18], Min-Max modular network was used to split each label into smaller tasks. To derive balanced samples, some projections approaches were considered, including random, clustering and PCA. The simpler tasks are binary, and SVM is used as base classifier. The prediction is a combination of the prediction of the derived tasks, using the Min-Max rule. In [72], a hybrid algorithm, which combines a multi-class data transformation approach with imbalance information labels was developed. This is done by deriving a new multi-class label by cross-coupling its correlation with other randomly chosen label. This new class is ternary, based on the combination of the most infrequent value of the label with the two values of the other label. A scoring multi-class algorithm is applied to predict this new class, and a threshold is automatically set up based on the F-measure. To improve reliability, this process is repeated K times, where K is a parameter. The label prediction is based on voting over the K predictions.

An enrichment process to adjust for label imbalance in ANNs was investigated in [57]. The idea is to first group similar instances, making clusters of different sizes. An initial training set is constructed by selecting the same number of instances in each cluster, and instances are added/removed according to maintain or improve classification performance.

A weighting coefficient was used in [29] to deal with label imbalance in the classification of sub-cellular localization of human proteins. This task present very high levels of label imbalance. The proposed algorithm is based on Gaussian process modeling, allied to latent information from the feature space and correlations among labels. Weights are placed at each instance according to the likelihood of labels in each sample.

For tackling variation among label proportions, in [22] is investigated two ways to maximize macro F-measure. One approach is a plug-in rule for deriving the maximizing F-measure in a probabilistic model and the other is a structured loss, suitable for maximizing the F-measure of training time of structures SVMs.

A two-stage approach based on a multilabel hypernetwork was recently proposed in [54] to handle class imbalance in MLL. In their algorithm, labels of a multi-label data set are divided into two groups based on their imbalance ratios: imbalanced labels and common labels. In the first stage a multi-label hypernetwork is trained for a first prediction of all labels. In the second stage, the predictions obtained in the first stage are further refined utilizing the correlations between common labels and imbalanced labels to improve the learning performance of imbalanced labels.

12.3.2.3 Ensemble Learning

In [56] proposes a method based on a ensemble of binary classifiers. For each label, a bagging of classifiers is induced. Each classifier within the bagging is formed by an "inverse undersampling", a process were all the minority label instances are included, together with a similar sample size of remainder instances. The objective is to generate the bagging with classifiers induced from balanced samples. A combination of heterogeneous multilabel classifiers was used in [55]. To handle class imbalance, different methods for aggregating the different classifiers, as well as different thresholding and weighting mechanisms with tuning carried out by cross-validation.

A recent approach [21] uses a structured forest of Hellinger Decision Trees for addressing the problem o class imbalance under MLL. A structured forest is an ensemble of structured trees. Structured trees apply an on-the-fly transforming approach based on clustering approach that maps multiple labels to a single one. Once transformed, a standard decision tree can be applied. To cope with class imbalance, a splitting criterion based on Hellinger Distance Decision Trees (HDDT) were used. HDDTs are known to be robust to class imbalance [19].

The authors of [45] use a two-layer stack-like ensemble of the MLkNN algorithm for exploiting label associations in MLL. They report an improvement in comparison of MLkNN without stacking, as well as other MLL algorithms.

12.4   Multi-instance Learning

In MIL [32], training examples consist in "bags" (collections of instances) instead of isolated instances. This allows the representation of complex problems, like images, molecules and texts, by means of their decomposition into pieces. For example, consider the case of text classification. In this case, portions of a document (for instance, each sentence of the text) can be represented by instances, whereas the entire document itself is represented as the bag of these instances.

Although multi-class classification may be used [47, 70], the standard model assumes that bags belong to one of two possible classes (generically called positive and negative). Furthermore, only the labels of the bags are known (i.e., the individual labels of the instances within each bag are unknown). For example, in text classification, classes are associated to the entire document, not to each sentence. A bag is labeled as positive if it contains at least one positive instance, and negative otherwise. In the text classification example, a bag is positive if at least one sentence is associate to the positive class, and there is no need of an association for all sentences. More formally, in MIL pairs $\{\mathcal{B}_i, y_i\}$ compose a data set, where $\mathcal{B}_i$ is a bag, and y_i is its class. Moreover, each $\mathcal{B}_i$ is composed by a set containing j instances $\{\mathbf{B}_{i1}, \dots, \mathbf{B}_{ij}\}$ (the index i represents a bag, and the index j instances within the bag) and, generally, the class $y_i \in \{0, 1\}$.

Under MIL context, class imbalance can occur at two levels: instance imbalance and bag imbalance. Label imbalance refers to an imbalanced distribution of instances within each bag. Although, strictly speaking, the classes of individual instances are not known, the actual distribution of classes within the positive bags are likely to be unbalanced, as in the standard model only one instance is required to a bag be considered positive. Furthermore, the class distribution in each bag may vary substantively, depending on the problem. Bag imbalance is a direct generalization of class imbalance in single instance learning to bags. In this case, the number of positive bags is very low when compared to the number of negative bags.

12.4.1 Methods for Dealing with Imbalance in MIL

As in the case of MLL, the approaches to address the imbalance in MIL can be also grouped into three different categories: resampling techniques, algorithm adaptation and ensemble. In the remainder of this section, we introduce some examples for these types of solutions.

12.4.1.1 Resampling

Different resampling techniques have been adapted to MIL problems, for both instance level and bag level.

InstanceSMOTE [66] first converts the MIL data set to single instance data set by assigning to each instance the corresponding class of the bag. The standard SMOTE is then applied to the converted data set to generate new synthetic instances. Finally, the bags are reconstructed back by assigning the new instances to the same bag of the seeds used to generate them.

Three different instance level sampling techniques were investigated in [42]. The approaches rely on kernel density estimation to estimate the degree that each instance can be considered positive. The first approach performs an oversampling within positive bags. A set T^+ containing the "most positive" instance in each positive bag, i.e., the instance which is most likely to be considered positive inside each positive bag, is created. SMOTE oversampling is then used to generate synthetic instances, based seed instances seeds drawn from T^+. These synthetic instances are then added to corresponding bag the seeds belong to. The second approach perform an undersampling within positive bags. The approach is similar, but instead of adding synthetic instances to bags, the idea is to remove negative instances from the positive bags. A set T^- of "most negative" instances is created. The undersampling is based on KNN: when the majority of the neighbors on an instance in T^-, considering all instances in all bags, belongs to negative bags, the instance is considered borderline and it is removed. The third approach is an undersampling within negative bags. The undersampling is also based on KNN: when the majority of neighbors of an instance in a negative bag, considering all instances in all bags, belong to a positive bag, the instance is considered borderline and is removed.

In [66], it was also investigated two ways to apply oversampling techniques at bag level. To balance the data set, Bag_oversampling randomly duplicates minority class bags. BagSMOTE [66] is a SMOTE adaptation to deal with bag level MIL imbalance. The idea is to create one synthetic bags for each minority class (positive) bag. The creation of the instance is performed by interpolating each instance within the seed bag to the NN instance from the instances of all positive bags. The new synthetic bag is formed by the interpolated instances originated from the same seed bag.

Another bag level sampling adaptation was proposed in [43]. As in [42], the approach uses kernel density estimation to identify the most positive instances. The method draw two positive bags at random, and identify the "most positive" instance in each bag. A synthetic instance is created by interpolating these two instances, and put into a new positive bag. The bag is then filled with other instances, until the size is equal to the average bag size. To this end, the "most negative" instance is selected in one of the bags, and new synthetic instances are added by interpolating this instance with random selected instances from the other bag.

12.4.1.2   Problem Adaptation

Cost-based techniques were also investigated in [66, 67]. Their approach is based on boosting (more specifically, AdaBoosting). A cost update weighting scheme was developed by the authors to handle bag imbalance. The class imbalance ratio is used as a proxy to the cost ratio. Four weighting update rules were proposed, with better results reported when compared with sampling.

Two methods based on Fuzzy sets were proposed in [62], to handle the class imbalance problem under MIL: one based on information extracted at bag-level and other at instance-level. They determine the membership degree to the fuzzy rough lower approximation of the two classes. The main difference between then is how they compute the lower approximation values for a bag. The instance-level methods determine the values for instances within the bags. To this, they use similarity between instances, and an affinity degree of instances with bags and of instances with classes. The instance-based values are then aggregated at the bag level. On the other hand, bag-level algorithms try to directly derivate the lower bound approximation from the entire bag, using a metric to measure similarity between bags and the affinity of bags with classes.

In [41], the authors propose a new support vector machine (SVM) multiple-instance formulation that uses a bag-representative selector to train SVMs on bag-level information. Their approach is capable of identifying instances that are highly significant in classification (bag-representatives) for both positive and negative bags while finding the optimal class separation hyperplane. This approach alleviates the influence of class imbalance issues by allowing both positive and negative bags to have at most one representative instance.

12.4.1.3   Ensembles

A recent approach explores combination of MIL classifiers to handle imbalance data in multi-instance classification. The approach combines different multi-instance views aiming to reach a consensus among the weighted class predictions over the multiple views to take advantage of the complementary information these views provide.

12.5 Ordinal Classification and Regression

The ordinal classification, or ordinal regression, is a supervised classification problem in which the objective is to predict the category to which a pattern belongs, having a relation of order between categories [28]. In addition, when the problem clearly manifests an ordinal nature, it is expected that this order will be present somehow in the input space of the data. The data are labeled according to a set of levels so that an order is established between them. The ordinal regression differs from the nominal classification in that there is a relation of order between the categories; and differs from the standard regression in that the number of levels is finite, and the difference between these levels is not defined. In this way, the ordinal classification ranks between classification and regression.

Such sorting problems should not be confused with sorting or ranking problems. The ordering problems are intended to relate all the patterns of the generalization set to a total order. Ranking with rank refers to ordering patterns with relative order. Ordinal classification can also be used to sort patterns, but the aim is to obtain good classification accuracy while maintaining order of patterns.

The problems of ordinal classification present two major questions that must be considered for the design of the learning algorithms. First, the nature of the problem indicates that the order of the classes must be related in some way to the distribution of patterns in the attribute space, as well as to the topological distribution of the classes (although, in general, this relation will be a nonlinear relationship). Consequently, a classifier must exploit this a priori knowledge about the input space. Second, when evaluating the performance of an ordinal classifier, the performance metrics must consider the order of the classes, so that classification errors between adjacent classes should be considered as less important than classification errors between not adjacent classes (more separated on the ordinal scale).

For example, consider a set of prediction data of the size with the target variable taking values in the {*very small, small, medium, large, very large*} set with a clear natural order relationship between classes. It is evident that wrongly predicting the *large* class when the real class is *small* represents a more serious error than the error associated with *very small* prediction. Thus, specific performance measures are required to evaluate the performance of an ordinal classifier.

Imbalanced data naturally appear in ordinal classification problems, since there are usually classes that are naturally less likely (i.e., extreme classes). Several applications have been considered in the specialized literature. For instance, in melanoma image classification problems, there are significantly more patterns associated with benign lesions with respect to melanomas [49] (especially when considered thick). Also, in [37], the authors addressed an application to an emergency and disaster information service considering an ordinal classification problem with 10 types of ranked risks and a weighted KNN method devised for tackling such kind of problems.

While accuracy is the most common metric for standard classification, the Mean Absolute Error (MAE) is the most common measure in the context of ordinal classification [28]. In addition, several alternative measures have been proposed in multi-class classification, for example, to evaluate individual performance in classes [20] (including those worst-ranked classes). Similarly, the mean MAE (average MAE, AMAE) has been proposed by Baccianella et al. [4] to more accurately assess performance in imbalanced data sets. Furthermore, in [63], the authors presented an extension of receiver operating characteristics (ROC) for more than two ordered categories, which fits the ordinal regression setting. The idea behind it is to estimate the volume under an r-dimensional surface (VUS) for r ordered categories. Thus, VUS evaluates the ranking returned by an ordinal regression model instead of measuring the error rate. A comprehensive survey on the state-of-the art of imbalanced classification and, especially, the performance measures used in several settings, can be found in [9].

The state-of-the-art in standard ordinal classification can be found in [28]. In this book, we are interested in those approaches focused on imbalanced learning, either for ordinal classification or regression. Thus, the next two sections will be devoted to describe the available methods proposed for imbalanced regression and imbalanced ordinal classification.

12.5.1   Imbalanced Regression

The prediction of rare extreme values of a continuous variable is very relevant for several real-world domains. The theory of extreme values is a branch of statistics focused on modeling abnormally high and low values in the queues of distributions. This theory describes unsupervised approaches to modeling abnormally high and low values in distribution queues. When we consider supervised approaches, the objective is to obtain a model that relates the values of a set of predictor variables to a numerical target variable for which we are interested in accurately predicting their rare extreme values. These problems can be seen as equivalent to classification problems with imbalanced class distributions that have been studied for a long time within automatic learning. The main difference is that we have a numeric target variable, that is, a regression task. This type of problem is particularly difficult because: (1) there are few examples with rare target values; (2) the errors of the learned models are not equally relevant because the main objective of the user is the predictive accuracy of the rare values; and (3) standard prediction error metrics are not adequate to measure the quality of models given the bias of user preference.

In [60], the first attempts to reformulate the standard resampling approaches to the prediction of extreme values of a continuous variable were described. The authors proposed the problem formulation as follows. Given a data set composed by $\mathbf{x}_i$ input feature vectors and a target continuous variable Y, the goal is to obtain a model that estimates the unknown regression function $Y = f(\mathbf{x})$. However, in predicting rare values, the particularity is to improve as much as possible the predictive accuracy on a certain subset of the domain of Y, called the *rare or extreme values* of Y. In this context, the standard regression estimators (i.e. the mean absolute error) suffer for similar problems to standard accuracy in classification of imbalanced classes.

In prediction of extreme values for regression, we are interested in that our model can accurately predict an extreme value (high precision) and, moreover, our model is able to make value predictions for the cases where the true value is an extreme (high recall). A first idea is to transform the regression problem in an imbalanced classification problem considering that the user is able to provide information on how to distinguish a extreme value from the domain. But it will ignore the numeric difference notion among the output values, achieving a counter-intuitive approach to deal with regression problems. Different formulations were given to deal with the numeric accuracy in extreme values prediction for regression, see [9] for more details.

Another perspective is to preprocess the training data so as the guide the learner to the examples which are of interest for the end user. This change is carried out by balancing the distribution of least represented (even though more relevant) cases with replications, sampling or generation of new instances. Although there are many resampling approaches in the standard imbalanced classification literature, few attempts were made to apply these strategies to equivalent regression tasks. They were proposed in [60] and we next describe the classical under-sampling and the upgrade of SMOTE to tackle regression tasks.

12.5.1.1 Under-sampling for Regression

As we know, the basic idea of under-sampling is to reduce the number of observations with the most common target variable values in order to better balance the ratio between these observations and those with the target values that are less frequent. In classification, this consists in obtaining a random sample of the training cases with the majority (and less interesting) class values.

In regression, we model a continuous objective variable. The concept of importance can be used to determine the values of a continuous target variable that are more relevant to the application or user. We can use the relevance function values to determine what observations are common or non-interesting values that should be under-sampled. That is, the strategy of under-sampling aims at selecting samples whose target value has less relevance than a parameter defined by the user. This threshold will define the set of observations that are relevant according to the user's preference bias:

$$D_r = \{< \mathbf{x}, Y >\in D : \phi(Y) \geq t_E\} \tag{12.7}$$

where t_E is an user defined threshold that measures the relevance and $\phi(Y)$ is a relevance function defined as a continuous function $\phi(Y) : \mathcal{Y} \rightarrow [0, 1]$ that maps the target variable domain Y into a $[0, 1]$ scale of relevance, where 0 represents the minimum and 1 represents the maximum relevance. Please refer to [60] to illustrate how a relevance function works.

Hence, under-sampling will be carried out on the rest of observation $D_i = D/D_r$. The quantity of selected observations will be given according to the size of the set D_r, randomly selecting n_u cases from D_i for each case in D_r. n_u is another user defined parameter which will set the desired ratio between standard and extreme observations.

12.5.1.2 SMOTE for Regression

SMOTE algorithm is another resampling method extended to regression problems [60]. There exist three issues of the SMOTE algorithm that are needed to be adapted if we want to tackle regression tasks: (1) How to define what are the relevant observations and "normal" cases; (2) how to create new synthetic examples; and (3) how to decide the value of the target variable of these new synthetic examples.

The first issue is solved in the original SMOTE algorithm in a straightforward manner due to the fact the user knows the target class to be oversampled, which is usually the minority or positive class. In regression, we have to resort to the definition of a relevance function, as mentioned in previous section, and a user-defined threshold to be applies on the output of this function in order to decide which examples will belong to D_r.

The second issue regarding the generation of new cases, can be solved adapting the same mechanism used in the original SMOTE approach to be suitable to simultaneously handle categorical and numerical attributes.

Finally, the third factor is to decide the output value of the new synthetic point. According to [60], both distances are calculated between the new generated synthetic case and the original case to be over-sampled and the synthetic case and the randomly chosen NNs (in other words, the two seed examples). The output value is estimated by an aggregated average of these two values according to an inverse function of their distances.

As result, the SMOTER proposal to tackle regression tasks with rare cases prediction was developed in [60].

12.5.2 Ordinal Classification of Imbalanced Data

Regarding imbalanced ordinal classification, as far as we known, there are two over-sampling approaches developed for general purposes. The next two sections will describe in brief how they work.

12.5.2.1 Graph-Based Over-sampling

This technique [48] creates synthetic patterns by considering the distribution of minority class data and the ordering of data. The main assumption of this method is that class ordering should be considered when the resampling patterns for an ordinal classification problem and that this order is generally represented by a latent manifold. To exploit this collector, it captures the structure of the data by constructing a pattern based graph and consider the paths that preserve the ordinal constraints of the data for over-sampling. In addition, new patterns are created at the border between adjacent classes, in order to smooth the ordinal nature of the data set.

12.5.2.2 Cluster-Based Weighted Over-sampling

CWOS-Ord [44] is a proposed technique to address ordinal classification with imbalanced data sets. This method aims to address this problem by first clustering the minority classes and then over-sampling them based on their distances and ordering the relationship with the instances of other classes. The final size for over-sampling clusters depends on their complexity and initial size so that more synthetic instances are generated for the more complex and smaller clusters, while fewer instances are generated for less complex and larger clusters.

First, a modified agglomerated hierarchical clustering is introduced to reduce the generation of superimposed synthetic instances during over-sampling. This is achieved by iteratively combining clusters of the same class while considering clusters of instances of other classes. Secondly, a new measure is proposed that quantifies the balance between the complexity of the cluster and the initial size of the cluster. The new measure is used to determine the number of instances oversampled for each cluster. Finally, a new probability distribution that incorporates the distance as well as the range distance to other class instances is presented, so that the instances closest to the nonadjacent classes are over-sampled. As an additional contribution in [44], the existing oversampling methods for binary classification have been extended to ordinal regression.

12.6 Summarizing Comments

Class imbalance has been widely studied for standard classification problems (binary and multi-class classification). However, different variations of class imbalance also occurs in other classification frameworks such as SSL, MLL, MIL and ordinal classification. These frameworks require new techniques aimed to deal with their peculiarities and specificities. This chapter reviewed some recent research work related to class imbalance within these frameworks.

References

1. Attenberg, J., Ertekin, S.: Class imbalance and active learning. In: He, H., Ma, Y. (eds.) Imbalanced Learning: Foundations, Algorithms, and Applications, pp. 101–149. IEEE Press/Wiley, Hoboken (2013)
2. Attenberg, J., Provost, F.: Why label when you can search? Alternatives to active learning for applying human resources to build classification models under extreme class imbalance. In: Proceedings of the 16th ACM SIGKDD International Conference on Knowledge Discovery and Data Mining, San Francisco, pp. 423–432. ACM (2010)
3. Attenberg, J., Provost, F.: Inactive learning? Difficulties employing active learning in practice. ACM SIGKDD Explor. Newsl. 12(2), 36–41 (2011)
4. Baccianella, S., Esuli, A., Sebastiani, F.: Evaluation measures for ordinal regression. In: Ninth International Conference on Intelligent Systems Design and Applications, ISDA'09, Pisa, 30 Nov–2 Dec 2009, pp. 283–287 (2009)
5. Balcan, M.F., Hanneke, S.: Robust interactive learning. In: Conference on Learning Theory, New York, pp. 20–1 (2012)
6. Beygelzimer, A., Hsu, D.J., Langford, J., Zhang, C.: Search improves label for active learning. In: Advances in Neural Information Processing Systems, pp. 3342–3350 (2016)
7. Bloodgood, M., Vijay-Shanker, K.: Taking into account the differences between actively and passively acquired data: the case of active learning with support vector machines for imbalanced datasets. In: Proceedings of Human Language Technologies, New York, pp. 137–140. Association for Computational Linguistics (2009)
8. Blum, A., Mitchell, T.: Combining labeled and unlabeled data with co-training. In: Proceedings of the Eleventh Annual Conference on Computational Learning Theory, Madison, pp. 92–100. ACM (1998)
9. Branco, P., Torgo, L., Ribeiro, R.P.: A survey of predictive modeling on imbalanced domains. ACM Comput. Surv. 49(2), 31:1–31:50 (2016)
10. Chapelle, O., Scholkopf, B., Zien, A.: Semi-supervised learning. IEEE Trans. Neural Netw. 20(3), 542–542 (2009)
11. Charte, F., Rivera, A., del Jesus, M.J., Herrera, F.: A first approach to deal with imbalance in multi-label datasets. In: International Conference on Hybrid Artificial Intelligence Systems, pp. 150–160. Springer, Berlin/Heidelberg (2013)
12. Charte, F., Rivera, A., del Jesus, M.J., Herrera, F.: Concurrence among imbalanced labels and its influence on multilabel resampling algorithms. In: International Conference on Hybrid Artificial Intelligence Systems, Salamanca, pp. 110–121. Springer (2014)
13. Charte, F., Rivera, A.J., del Jesus, M.J., Herrera, F.: Addressing imbalance in multilabel classification: measures and random resampling algorithms. Neurocomputing 163, 3–16 (2015)
14. Charte, F., Rivera, A.J., del Jesus, M.J., Herrera, F.: Mlsmote: approaching imbalanced multilabel learning through synthetic instance generation. Knowl.-Based Syst. 89, 385–397 (2015)
15. Charte, F., Rivera, A.J., del Jesus, M.J., Herrera, F.: Dealing with difficult minority labels in imbalanced mutilabel data sets. Neurocomputing (2017, in press). https://doi.org/10.1016/j.neucom.2016.08.158
16. Chawla, N.V., Bowyer, K.W., Hall, L.O., Kegelmeyer, W.P.: SMOTE: synthetic minority over-sampling technique. J. Artif. Intell. Res. 16, 321–357 (2002)
17. Chen, Y., Wang, G., Dong, S.: Learning with progressive transductive support vector machine. Pattern Recogn. Lett. 24(12), 1845–1855 (2003)
18. Chen, K., Lu, B.L., Kwok, J.T.: Efficient classification of multi-label and imbalanced data using min-max modular classifiers. In: International Joint Conference on Neural Networks (IJCNN'06), Vancouver, pp. 1770–1775. IEEE (2006)

19. Cieslak, D.A., Hoens, T.R., Chawla, N.V., Kegelmeyer, W.P.: Hellinger distance decision trees are robust and skew-insensitive. Data Min. Knowl. Disc. **24**(1), 136–158 (2012)
20. Cruz-Ramírez, M., Hervás-Martínez, C., Sánchez-Monedero, J., Gutiérrez, P.A.: Metrics to guide a multi-objective evolutionary algorithm for ordinal classification. Neurocomputing **135**, 21–31 (2014)
21. Daniels, Z.A., Metaxas, D.N.: Addressing imbalance in multi-label classification using structured Hellinger forests. In: Thirty-First AAAI Conference on Artificial Intelligence, San Francisco (2017)
22. Dembczynski, K., Jachnik, A., Kotlowski, W., Waegeman, W., Hüllermeier, E.: Optimizing the f-measure in multi-label classification: plug-in rule approach versus structured loss minimization. ICML **28**(3), 1130–1138 (2013)
23. Dendamrongvit, S., Kubat, M.: Undersampling approach for imbalanced training sets and induction from multi-label text-categorization domains. In: Pacific-Asia Conference on Knowledge Discovery and Data Mining, Melbourne, pp. 40–52. Springer (2009)
24. Ertekin, S.: Adaptive oversampling for imbalanced data classification. In: Proceedings of the 28th International Symposium on Computer and Information Sciences, Paris. Lecture Notes in Electrical Engineering, vol. 264, pp. 261–269. Springer (2013)
25. Ertekin, S., Huang, J., Bottou, L., Giles, L.: Learning on the border: active learning in imbalanced data classification. In: Proceedings of the Sixteenth ACM Conference on Information and Knowledge Management, pp. 127–136. ACM (2007)
26. Gammerman, A., Vovk, V., Vapnik, V.: Learning by transduction. In: Proceedings of the Fourteenth Conference on Uncertainty in Artificial Intelligence, Madison, pp. 148–155. Morgan Kaufmann Publishers Inc. (1998)
27. Giraldo-Forero, A.F., Jaramillo-Garzón, J.A., Ruiz-Muñoz, J.F., Castellanos-Domínguez, C.G.: Managing imbalanced data sets in multi-label problems: a case study with the smote algorithm. In: Iberoamerican Congress on Pattern Recognition, La Havana, pp. 334–342. Springer (2013)
28. Gutiérrez, P.A., Pérez-Ortiz, M., Sánchez-Monedero, J., Fernández-Navarro, F., Hervás-Martínez, C.: Ordinal regression methods: survey and experimental study. IEEE Trans. Knowl. Data Eng. **28**(1), 127–146 (2016)
29. He, J., Gu, H., Liu, W.: Imbalanced multi-modal multi-label learning for subcellular localization prediction of human proteins with both single and multiple sites. PloS One **7**(6), e37155 (2012)
30. Hernández-González, J., Inza, I., Lozano, J.A.: Weak supervision and other non-standard classification problems: a taxonomy. Pattern Recogn. Lett. **69**, 49–55 (2016)
31. Herrera, F., Charte, F., Rivera, A.J., del Jesus, M.J.: Multilabel Classification: Problem Analysis, Metrics and Techniques. Springer, Cham (2016)
32. Herrera, F., Ventura, S., Bello, R., Cornelis, C., Zafra, A., Sánchez-Tarragó, D., Vluymans, S.: Multiple Instance Learning: Foundations and Algorithms. Springer, Cham (2016)
33. Ho, T.K.: The random subspace method for constructing decision forests. IEEE Trans. Pattern Anal. Mach. Intell. **20**(8), 832–844 (1998)
34. Jacobusse, G., Veenman, C.: On selection bias with imbalanced classes. In: International Conference on Discovery Science, Bari, pp. 325–340. Springer (2016)
35. Joachims, T.: Transductive inference for text classification using support vector machines. In: International Conference on Machine Learning, Bled, pp. 200–209 (1999)
36. Juszczak, P., Duin, R.P.: Uncertainty sampling methods for one-class classifiers. In: Proceedings of the ICML, Washington, DC, vol. 3 (2003)
37. Kim, S., Kim, H., Namkoong, Y.: Ordinal classification of imbalanced data with application in emergency and disaster information services. IEEE Intell. Syst. **31**(5), 50–56 (2016)
38. Kourtis, I., Stamatatos, E.: Author identification using semi-supervised learning. In: CLEF'2011 Conference on Multilingual and Multimodal Information Access Evaluation (Lab and Workshop Notebook Papers), Amsterdam (2011)
39. Levina, E., Bickel, P.J.: Maximum likelihood estimation of intrinsic dimension. Ann Arbor MI **48109**, 1092 (2004)

40. Li, S., Wang, Z., Zhou, G., Lee, S.Y.M.: Semi-supervised learning for imbalanced sentiment classification. In: Proceedings of the 22nd International Joint Conference on Artificial Intelligence IJCAI'2011, Barcelona, pp. 1826–1831 (2011)
41. Melki, G., Cano, A., Ventura, S.: MIRSVM : multi-instance support vector machine with bag representatives. Pattern Recogn. **79**, 228–241 (2018)
42. Mera, C., Orozco-Alzate, M., Branch, J.: Improving representation of the positive class in imbalanced multiple-instance learning. In: International Conference Image Analysis and Recognition, Vilamoura, pp. 266–273. Springer (2014)
43. Mera, C., Arrieta, J., Orozco-Alzate, M., Branch, J.: A bag oversampling approach for class imbalance in multiple instance learning. In: Iberoamerican Congress on Pattern Recognition, pp. 724–731. Springer (2015)
44. Nekooeimehr, I., Lai-Yuen, S.K.: Cluster-based weighted oversampling for ordinal regression (CWOS-Ord). Neurocomputing **218**, 51–60 (2016)
45. Pakrashi, A., Mac Namee, B.: Stacked-MLkNN: a stacking based improvement to multi-label k-nearest neighbours. In: First International Workshop on Learning with Imbalanced Domains: Theory and Applications, pp. 51–63 (2017)
46. Pang, S., Ban, T., Kadobayashi, Y., Kasabov, N.: Personalized mode transductive spanning SVM classification tree. Inf. Sci. **181**(11), 2071–2085 (2011)
47. Pathak, D., Shelhamer, E., Long, J., Darrell, T.: Fully convolutional multi-class multiple instance learning. In: International Conference on Learning Representations (ICLR) Workshop, San Diego, arXiv:1412.7144 (2015)
48. Pérez-Ortiz, M., Gutiérrez, P.A., Hervás-Martínez, C., Yao, X.: Graph-based approaches for over-sampling in the context of ordinal regression. IEEE Trans. Knowl. Data Eng. **27**(5), 1233–1245 (2015)
49. Pérez-Ortiz, M., Sáez, A., Sánchez-Monedero, J., Gutiérrez, P.A., Hervás-Martínez, C.: Tackling the ordinal and imbalance nature of a melanoma image classification problem. In: 2016 International Joint Conference on Neural Networks, IJCNN'2016, Vancouver, 24–29 July 2016, pp. 2156–2163 (2016)
50. Prez-Ortiz, M., Gutirrez, P., Aylln-Tern, M., Heaton, N., Ciria, R., Briceo, J., Hervs-Martnez, C.: Synthetic semi-supervised learning in imbalanced domains. Knowl.-Based Syst. **123**(C), 75–87 (2017)
51. Raskutti, B., Kowalczyk, A.: Extreme re-balancing for SVMS: a case study. ACM SIGKDD Explor. Newsl. **6**(1), 60–69 (2004)
52. Stamatatos, E.: Author identification using imbalanced and limited training texts. In: 18th International Workshop on Database and Expert Systems Applications (DEXA'07), pp. 237–241. IEEE (2007)
53. Stanescu, A., Caragea, D.: Semi-supervised self-training approaches for imbalanced splice site datasets. In: Proceedings of the Sixth International Conference on Bioinformatics and Computational Biology, BICoB'2014, Las Vegas, pp. 131–136 (2014)
54. Sun, K.W., Lee, C.H.: Addressing class-imbalance in multi-label learning via two-stage multi-label hypernetwork. Neurocomputing **266**, 375–389 (2017)
55. Tahir, M.A., Kittler, J., Bouridane, A.: Multilabel classification using heterogeneous ensemble of multi-label classifiers. Pattern Recogn. Lett. **33**(5), 513–523 (2012)
56. Tahir, M.A., Kittler, J., Yan, F.: Inverse random under sampling for class imbalance problem and its application to multi-label classification. Pattern Recogn. **45**(10), 3738–3750 (2012)
57. Tepvorachai, G., Papachristou, C.: Multi-label imbalanced data enrichment process in neural net classifier training. In: IEEE International Joint Conference on Neural Networks (IJCNN'2008), Hong Kong, pp. 1301–1307. IEEE (2008)
58. Tomanek, K., Hahn, U.: Reducing class imbalance during active learning for named entity annotation. In: Proceedings of the Fifth International Conference on Knowledge Capture, Redondo Beach, pp. 105–112. ACM (2009)
59. Tomek, I.: An experiment with the edited nearest-neighbor rule. IEEE Trans. Syst. Man Cybern. **SMC-6**(6), 448–452 (1976)

60. Torgo, L., Branco, P., Ribeiro, R.P., Pfahringer, B.: Resampling strategies for regression. Exp. Syst. **32**(3), 465–476 (2015)
61. Vapnik, V.N.: Statistical Learning Theory. Wiley-Interscience, New York/Chichester (1998)
62. Vluymans, S., Tarragó, D.S., Saeys, Y., Cornelis, C., Herrera, F.: Fuzzy rough classifiers for class imbalanced multi-instance data. Pattern Recogn. **53**, 36–45 (2016)
63. Waegeman, W., Baets, B.D., Boullart, L.: ROC analysis in ordinal regression learning. Pattern Recogn. Lett. **29**(1), 1–9 (2008)
64. Wang, J., Chang, S.F., Zhou, X., Wong, S.T.: Active microscopic cellular image annotation by superposable graph transduction with imbalanced labels. In: IEEE Conference on Computer Vision and Pattern Recognition (CVPR'2008), Anchorage, pp. 1–8. IEEE (2008)
65. Wang, J., Jebara, T., Chang, S.F.: Graph transduction via alternating minimization. In: Proceedings of the 25th International Conference on Machine Learning, Helsinki, pp. 1144–1151. ACM (2008)
66. Wang, X., Liu, X., Japkowicz, N., Matwin, S.: Resampling and cost-sensitive methods for imbalanced multi-instance learning. In: 2013 IEEE 13th International Conference on Data Mining Workshops (ICDMW), Dallas, pp. 808–816. IEEE (2013)
67. Wang, X., Matwin, S., Japkowicz, N., Liu, X.: Cost-sensitive boosting algorithms for imbalanced multi-instance datasets. In: Canadian Conference on Artificial Intelligence, Regina, pp. 174–186. Springer (2013)
68. Wang, A., Liu, L., Jin, X., Li, Y.: Adapting TSVM for fault diagnosis with imbalanced class data. In: Control and Decision Conference (CCDC), 2016 Chinese, Yinchuan, pp. 2919–2923. IEEE (2016)
69. Wang, S., Minku, L.L., Yao, X.: A systematic study of online class imbalance learning with concept drift. IEEE Trans. Neural Netw. Learn. Syst. **29**(10), 4802–4821 (2018)
70. Xu, X., Li, B.: Multiple class multiple-instance learning and its application to image categorization. Int. J. Image Graph. **7**(3), 427–444 (2007)
71. Youngs, N., Shasha, D., Bonneau, R.: Positive-unlabeled learning in the face of labeling bias. In: 2015 IEEE International Conference on Data Mining Workshop (ICDMW), New Jersey, pp. 639–645. IEEE (2015)
72. Zhang, M.L., Li, Y.K., Liu, X.Y.: Towards class-imbalance aware multi-label learning. In: IJCAI, pp. 4041–4047 (2015)
73. Zhou, D., Bousquet, O., Lal, T.N., Weston, J., Schölkopf, B.: Learning with local and global consistency. In: Advances in Neural Information Processing Systems, vol. 16, pp. 321–328. MIT Press, Cambridge (2004)
74. Zhu, X., Goldberg, A.B.: Introduction to semi-supervised learning. Synth. Lect. Artif. Intell. Mach. Learn. **3**(1), 1–130 (2009)
75. Zhu, J., Hovy, E.H.: Active learning for word sense disambiguation with methods for addressing the class imbalance problem. In: EMNLP-CoNLL, vol. 7, pp. 783–790 (2007)

Chapter 13
Imbalanced Classification for Big Data

Abstract New developments in computation have allowed an explosion for both data generation and storage. The high value that is hidden within this large volume of data has attracted more and more researchers to address the topic of Big Data analytics. The main difference between addressing Big Data applications and carrying out traditional DM tasks is scalability. To overcome this issue, the MapReduce framework has arisen as a "de facto" solution. Basically, it carries out a "divide-and-conquer" distributed procedure in a fault-tolerant way (supported by a distributed file system) to adapt for commodity hardware. Apart from the difficulties in addressing the Big Data problem itself, we must take into account that the events of interest might occur infrequently. Having in mind the challenges of mining rare classes in standard classification tasks, adding this to the problem of addressing high volumes of data impose a strong constraint for the development of both accurate and scalable solutions. In order to present this interesting topic, current chapter is organized as follows. First, Sect. 13.1 provides a quick overview on Big Data analytics in the context of imbalanced classification. Then, Sect. 13.2 presents the topic of Big Data in detail, focusing on the MapReduce programming model, the Spark framework, and those software libraries that includes Big Data implementations for ML algorithms. Section 13.3 shows an overview on those works that address imbalanced classification for Big Data problems. Then, Sect. 13.4 presents a discussion on the challenges and open problems on imbalanced Big Data classification. Finally, Sect. 13.5 summarizes and concludes this chapter.

13.1 Introduction

Vast amounts of raw data are surrounding us in nowadays world, implying that data can no longer be directly treated by humans or manual applications. Technologies as the World Wide Web, engineering and science applications and networks, business services and many more generate data in exponential growth thanks to the development of powerful storage and connection tools [1]. Organized knowledge and information cannot be easily obtained due to the management of such Big Data and can neither be easily understood or automatically extracted [20, 40].

© Springer Nature Switzerland AG 2018

A. Fernández et al., *Learning from Imbalanced Data Sets*,
https://doi.org/10.1007/978-3-319-98074-4_13

It is well known that data alone produces information but not knowledge. Its real value lies on the possibility of extracting useful knowledge for decision-making or the exploration and comprehension of the phenomenon that produced the data. Nowadays, the current volume of data managed by our systems has surpassed the processing capacity of traditional methods, and this applies to DM as well [10, 71].

The previous fact is translated into longer training times, or may even make impossible to cope with such data traditional software implementations. It becomes necessary to carry out a migration towards a more efficient framework from which DM algorithms are able to use the whole dataset in a reasonable elapsed time [1, 57]. This framework is known as MapReduce [14], and it mainly consists of two processes: (1) Map, that divides the computation into several parts, one devoted for a different chunk of the total data; and (2) Reduce, that aggregates the partial results from the previous stage. By implementing these two processes, any algorithm will be automatically distributed in a transparent way, and it will be run within a fault-tolerant scheme as supported by a distributed file system.

Several platforms for large-scale processing have been developed including MapReduce capabilities [20, 34]. Two clear and well-known examples are Hadoop[1] [43] and Spark[2] [73, 74]. Whereas the former includes a standard implementation for MapReduce, the latter includes several features that benefit the scalability for iterative processing, thus implying some advantages for ML algorithms.

The emergence of Big Data also brings new problems and challenges for the class imbalance problem [19]. First, standard approaches in preprocessing and cost-sensitive learning must be re-designed (sometimes, entirely) to adapt their procedure to novel MapReduce-style distributed frameworks. Second, the data partitioning associated with this type of process may result on a lack of data of the minority class examples, and/or the generation of small disjuncts (please refer to Chap. 10). Finally, we must refer not only to the increasing data volume, but also to the nature of the problem itself. Regarding current Big Data applications, incoming data may be heterogeneous and/or atypical, i.e. what is known to Variety of data. This issue may force algorithms to be able to handle this graph-based structures (for social networks [35]) or video sequences (for computer vision [11]).

By studying the specialized literature, it can be acknowledged that the topic of imbalanced classification in Big Data is still at an early stage of development [19]. Few research works have been published at present, and some of them are just preliminary proposals that are not able to scale well. Throughout this chapter, the most significant approaches related to preprocessing, cost-sensitive learning, and applications for Big Data will be reviewed. This is made to analyze the inner structure of these methodologies, and so to understand how the imbalanced data problem in Big Data can be overcome.

---

[1]http://hadoop.apache.org
[2]http://spark.apache.org/

Finally, a thorough discussion on the main issues to be addressed for future work on the topic will be presented. This will include several guidelines that may allow researchers to develop high quality solutions in this area of research.

13.2 Big Data: MapReduce Programming Model, Spark Framework and Machine Learning Libraries

In this section, we will first introduce some concepts on Big Data and its strong relationship with the MapReduce programming model to support scalability in data processing (Sect. 13.2.1). Then, we will focus on the Spark programming framework, as it is probably the widest used technology for ML purposes in Big Data (Sect. 13.2.2). Finally, we introduce the Mahout and MLlib libraries that include some state-of-the-art ML algorithms for Big Data (Sect. 13.2.3).

13.2.1 Introduction to Big Data and MapReduce

In the era of information technology, the problem of managing Big Data applications is becoming the main focus of attention in a wide variety of disciplines such as science, business, industry, among others. Data and the ability to process and extract knowledge from it are the "new gold" in the digital economy in which we move [23]. Therefore, the significance of Big Data come along with analytics [41, 57]. Among other benefits, extracting significant value and insight within such data allows to improve the productivity (in business) or to obtain new scientific breakthroughs (in different knowledge domains).

However, Big Data certainly represents "big" challenges for the data analytics community [50]. Currently, researchers must deal with highly distributed data sources, validating data, coping with sampling biases, formats and structures to develop algorithms that consider distributed and highly parallel architectures [31]. This implies that the information retrieving, management, processing, and the knowledge extraction are no longer straightforward to be carried out by means of the classical tools and methodologies [36]. Big Data makes it essential to develop rapid distributed versions that make affordable the learning process, since no batch architecture is able to address such magnitudes [17].

Considering these facts, ML solutions must evolve in order to adopt this data-intensive problems [38]. Many platforms for large-scale processing have been developed to bring closer the distributed technologies to engineers and data scientists. This has been achieved by hiding the technical nuances derived from these distributed environments [20].

The most significant solution to design data processing algorithms for Big Data problems is clearly the MapReduce scheme [14, 15]. It was designed to allow efficient data combination from multiple sources in a transparent way for the programmer, also providing a fault-tolerant execution scheme.

There are just two requirements for using this scheme. On the one hand, it demands algorithms to be expressed into a simple design pattern using two primary functions: Map and Reduce. The first one is devoted to split the data for processing, whereas the second collects and aggregates the results. On the other hand, the MapReduce model is defined with respect to an essential data structure: the <key,value> pair. The processed data, the intermediate and final results work in terms of <key,value> pairs. In this way, the *Map* and *Reduce* are defined as follows:

- **Map function**: first reads data and transforms them into a key-value format. Transformations in this phase may apply any sequence of operations on each record before sending the tuples across the network. Output keys are then shuffled and grouped by key value so that coincident keys are grouped together to form a list of values. Keys are then partitioned and sent to the Reducers according to some key-based scheme previously defined.
- **Reduce function**: it performs some kind of aggregation on the lists to eventually generate a single value for each pair. As an optimization, the reducer is also used as a combiner on the map outputs. This improvement reduces the total amount of data sent across the network by combining each word generated in the Map phase into a single pair.

From another perspective, MapReduce, concretely the Reduce stage, can be seen as a information and/or model fusion process that aggregates partial results to obtain a more coarse-grained outcome. Although the Reduce phase may be skipped in some jobs in order to perform a straightforward parallelization of tasks, it is not the case in most of use cases in Big Data.

To summarize its procedure, Fig. 13.1 illustrates a typical MapReduce program with its *Map* and *Reduce* steps. The terms $k_i : v_j$ refer to the key and value pair that are computed within each Map process. Then, values are grouped linking them to the same key, i.e. $k_i : v_j, \ldots, v_h$, and feed to the same Reduce process. Finally, values are aggregated with any function within the Reduce process to obtain the final result of the algorithm.

Initially released as privative tool from Google [13], an open source counterpart, known as Hadoop, has been traditionally used in academia research [70]. The main idea behind Hadoop was to create a common framework which can process large-scale data on a cluster of commodity hardware, without incurring in a high cost in developing (in contrast to HPC solutions) and execution time. Hadoop MapReduce was originally composed by two elements: the first one was a distributed storage system called Hadoop Distributed File System (HDFS), whereas the second one was a data processing framework that allows to run MapReduce-like jobs. Apart from these goals, Hadoop implements primitives to address cluster scalability, failure recovery, and resource scheduling, among others.

HDFS [3] can be deemed as the main module of Apache Hadoop. It supports distributed storage for large-scale data through the use of distributed files, which

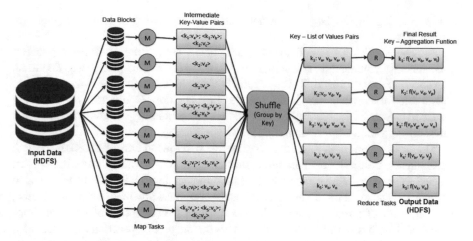

Fig. 13.1 The MapReduce programming model

themselves are composed by fixed-size data blocks. These blocks or partitions are equally distributed among the data nodes in order to balance as much as possible the overall disk usage in the cluster. HDFS also allows replication of blocks across different nodes and racks. In HDFS, the first block is ensured to be placed in the same processing node, whereas the other two replicas are sent to different racks to prevent abrupt ends due to inter-rack issues.

Hadoop MapReduce evolves to a more general component, called **Yet Another Resource Negotiator (YARN)** [72], which provides extra management and maintenance services relied to other components in the past. YARN also acts as a facade for different types of distributed processing engines based on HDFS, such as Spark,[3] Flink[4] or Storm.[5] In short, YARN was intended as a generic purpose system that separates the responsibilities of resource management (performed by YARN), and running management (performed by top-level applications).

13.2.2 Spark: A Novel Technological Approach for Iterative Processing in Big Data

Apache Spark Framework [2] was born in 2010 with the publication of Resilient Distributed Datasets (RDD) structures [73], the keystone behind Spark. Although Spark has a close relationship with Hadoop Ecosystem, it provides specific support

---

[3]http://spark.apache.org
[4]http://flink.apache.org/
[5]http://storm.apache.org/

for every step in the Big Data stack, such as its own processing engine, and ML library.

Apache Spark [30] is defined as a distributed computing platform which can process large volume data sets in memory with a very fast response time due to its memory-intensive scheme. It was originally thought to tackle problems deemed as unsuitable for previous disk-based engines like Hadoop. Continued use of disk is replaced in Spark by memory-based operators that efficiently deal with iterative and interactive problems (prone to multiple I/O operations).

The heart of Spark is formed by **Resilient Distributed Datasets (RDD)**, which transparently controls how data are distributed and transformed across the cluster. Users just need to define some high-level functions that will be applied and managed by RDDs. These elements are created whenever data are read from any source, or as a result of a transformation. RDDs consist of a collection of data partitions distributed across several data nodes. A wide range of operations are provided for transforming RDDs, such as: filtering, grouping, set operations, among others. Furthermore RDDs are also highly versatile as they allows users to customize partitioning for an optimized data placement, or to preserve data in several formats and contexts.

In Spark, fault tolerance is solved by annotating operations in a structure called lineage. Spark transformations annotated in the lineage are only performed whenever a trigger I/O operations appears in the log. In case of failure, Spark re-computes the affected brach in the lineage log. Although replication is normally skipped, Spark allows to spill data in local disk in case the memory capacity is not sufficient.

Spark developers provided another high-level abstraction, called **DataFrames**, which introduces the concept of formal schema in RDDs. DataFrames are distributed and structured collections of data organized by named columns. They can be seen as a table in a relational database or a dataframe in R, or Python (Pandas). As a plus, relational query plans built by DataFrames are optimized by the Spark's Catalyst optimizer throughout the previously defined schema. Also thanks to the scheme, Spark is able to understand data and remove costly Java serialization actions.

A compromise between structure awareness and the optimization benefits of Catalyst is achieved by the novel Dataset API. **Datasets** are strongly typed collections of objects connected to a relational schema. Among the benefits of Datasets, we can find compile-time type safety, which means applications can be sanitized before running. Furthermore, Datasets provide encoders for free to directly convert JVM objects to the binary tabular Tungsten format. These efficient in-memory format improves memory usage, and allows to directly apply operations on serialized data. Datasets are intended to be the single interface in future Spark for handling data.

13.2.3 Machine Learning Libraries for Big Data

As stated throughout this chapter, designing robust and efficient ML solutions based on MapReduce is not an easy task. Fortunately, several libraries have been made available so that researchers and practitioners are able to use some state-of-the-art algorithms for Big Data problems. Two of the most well-known libraries are Mahout (based on Hadoop) and MLlib (based on Spark):

13.2.3.1 Hadoop: Apache Mahout

Since the magnitude of learning problems has been growing exponentially, data scientists demands rapid tools that efficiently extract knowledge from large-scale data. This problem has been solved by MapReduce and other platforms by providing scalable algorithms and miscellaneous utilities in form of ML libraries. These libraries are compatible with the main Hadoop engine, and use as input the data stored in the storage components.

Apache Mahout [48] was the main contribution from Apache Hadoop to this field. Although it can be deemed as mainly obsolete nowadays, Mahout is considered as the first attempt to fill the gap of scalable ML support for Big Data. Mahout comprises several algorithms for plenty of tasks, such as: classification, clustering, pattern-mining, etc. Among a long list of golden algorithms in Mahout, we can highlight Random Forest or Naïve Bayes.

The most recent version (0.13.0) provides three new major features: novel support for Apache Spark and Flink, a vector math experimentation for R, and GPU support based on large matrix multiplications. Although Mahout was originally designed for Hadoop, some algorithms have been implemented on Spark as a consequence of the latter one's popularity. Mahout is also able to run on top of Flink, being only compatible for static processing though.

13.2.3.2 Spark: MLlib and SparkPackages

MLlib project [51] was born in 2012 as an extra component of Spark. It was released and open-sourced in 2013 under the Apache 2.0 license. From its inception, the number of contributions and people involved in the project have been growing steadily. Apart from official API, Spark provides a community package index [12] (Spark Packages) to assemble all open source algorithms that work with MLlib.

MLlib is a Spark library geared towards offering distributed ML support to Spark engine. This library includes several out-of-the-box algorithms for alike tasks, such as: classification, clustering, regression, recommendation, even data preprocessing. Apart from distributed implementations of standard algorithms, MLlib offers:

- Common Utilities: for distributed linear algebra, statistical analysis, internal format for model export, data generators, etc.

- Algorithmic optimizations: from the long list of optimizations included, we can highlight some: decisions trees, which borrow some ideas from PLANET project [53] (parallelized learning both within trees and across them); or generalized linear models, which benefit from employing fast C++-based linear algebra for internal computations.
- Pipeline API: as the learning process in large-scale datasets is tedious and expensive, MLlib includes an internal package (*spark.ml*) that provides an uniform high-level API to create complex multi-stage pipelines that connect several and alike components (preprocessing, learning, evaluation, and so on). *spark.ml* allows model selection or hyper-parameter tuning, and different validations strategies like k-FVC.
- Spark integration: MLlib is perfectly integrated with other Spark components. Spark GraphX has several graph-based implementations in MLlib, like LDA. Likewise, several algorithms for online learning are available in Spark Streaming, such as online k-Means. In any case, most of component in the Spark stack are prepared to effortlessly cooperate with MLlib.

13.3   Addressing Imbalanced Classification in Big Data Problems: Current State

In this section, we discuss the current state-of-the-art on the topic of imbalanced classification for Big Data. These include initial approaches for addressing the problem, making use of those methods and solutions that were mentioned in the previous section. In Table 13.1 we show the list of selected proposal in a taxonomy regarding the type of methodology applied to handle the imbalanced data distribution, or whether they comprise an application paper.

In the remainder of the section we describe each one of these models. Specifically, Sect. 13.3.1 contains the description for those techniques related to data preprocessing. Section 13.3.2 includes those approaches that carry out an algorithmic modification by means of a cost-sensitive learning. Finally, Sect. 13.3.3 presents the application papers on the topic.

Table 13.1 Summary of approaches for imbalanced classification in Big Data

Type of technique	References
Data pre-processing	[4, 29, 33, 39, 42, 58, 59, 65, 66, 75]
Cost-sensitive learning	[46, 59, 61, 67],
Applications on imbalanced Big Data	[16, 21, 27, 55]

13.3.1   Data Pre-processing Studies

Among the different solutions to address imbalanced classification in Big Data, data pre-processing is possibly the one has attracted the highest attention from researchers. Therefore, we may find several approaches that aims at adapting directly the standard undersampling and oversampling techniques to the MapReduce framework. In this sense, both random undersampling, random oversampling and SMOTE are the widest used algorithms, being applied within each Map process seeking for scalability. Furthermore, some ad hoc approaches based on undersampling and oversampling have been also developed, including evolutionary undersampling, a rough set based SMOTE, and an ensemble algorithm. Finally, we will point out a first approach for the multi-class case study.

13.3.1.1   Traditional Data Based Solutions for Big Data

In the first work to be discussed, authors performed a thorough study with the objective of evaluating the performance of traditional solutions for the class imbalance in the context of Big Data [59]. With this aim, several pre-processing techniques were adapted and embedded in a MapReduce workflow. Specifically, the random oversampling (ROS-BigData), random undersampling (RUS-BigData) and the SMOTE (SMOTE-BigData) MapReduce versions were proposed in this research. For every technique, each Map process was responsible for adjusting the class distribution for their data partition, either by the random replication of minority class instances (ROS-BigData), the random removal of majority class instances (RUS-BigData) or the synthetic data generation carried out by SMOTE (SMOTE-BigData). Then, a unique Reduce process was responsible for collecting the outputs generated by each mapper and randomized them to form the balanced dataset. The Random Forest implementation from Mahout[6] [47, 52] was selected as baseline classifier for the experiments, applied over three different imbalanced Big Data problems from the UCI dataset repository [44], with up to 6 millions of instances. One of the outcomes of their study [59] was the observation that random oversampling is more robust than the other techniques when the number of data partitions is increased. In contrast, the performance of SMOTE, random undersampling and cost-sensitive learning methods was not as high as expected.

This literature showed a preliminary study made using Hadoop, which implied a lower scalability in contrast with Spark based approaches. Additionally, all preprocessing and classification methods worked locally within each Map, thus limiting the potential of these algorithms.

A recent approach based on the use of Graphics Processing Units (GPUs) for the parallel computation of SMOTE has been proposed in [29]. The preprocessing

---

[6]http://mahout.apache.org/

technique is adapted to commodity hardware by means of a smart use of the main memory, i.e. by including only the minority class instances, and the neighborhood computation via a fast GPU implementation of the kNN algorithm [28].

Finally, an additional efficient GPU-based implementation was proposed for rapid training and updating of online classifiers, i.e. focused in the area of imbalanced data streams for Big Data. Specifically, an extreme learning machine was used in synergy with undersampling and oversampling [42]. Authors showed that the use of pre-processing allowed the classifier to efficiently adapt to non-stationary properties of incoming objects, while alleviating the influence of skewed distributions on its performance.

13.3.1.2   Random OverSampling with Evolutionary Feature Weighting and Random Forest (ROSEFW-RF)

Another work which showed the success of the application of random oversampling in the scenario of Big Data can be found in [66]. This literature described the methodology followed to achieve the first place of the ECBDL'14 Big Data challenge. This dataset consisted of an imbalance bioinformatics Big Data problem formed by 32 million instances and more than 600 attributes with just a 2% of positive instances. The algorithm, named as ROSEFW-RF, was based on several MapReduce approaches to (1) balance the classes distribution through random oversampling, (2) detect the most relevant features via an evolutionary feature weighting process and a threshold to choose them, (3) build an appropriate Random Forest model from the pre-processed data and finally (4) classify the test data.

In accordance with these issues, this work has two novel contributions with respect to [59]:

- On the one hand, authors stressed that in order to deal with extremely imbalanced Big Data problems such as the one described above, this implies an increment in the density of the underrepresented class by using higher oversampling ratios [58].
- On the other hand, a FS approach was suggested to avoid the curse of dimensionality. Specifically, the authors developed a MapReduce implementation based on the evolutionary approach for Feature Weighting proposed in [63]. In this method, each map task performed a whole evolutionary feature weighting cycle in its data partition and emitted a vector of weights. Then, the Reduce process was responsible of the iterative aggregation of all the weights provided by the maps. Finally, the resulting weights were used with a threshold to select the most important characteristics.

The combination of the instance and feature pre-processing approaches was shown to achieve high quality results in this case study. However, this proposed methodology has the constraint of applying a high ratio of oversampling, thus requiring a high training time.

13.3.1.3 Evolutionary Undersampling

Regarding undersampling approaches, in [65] authors developed a parallel model to enable evolutionary undersampling methods under the MapReduce scheme. Specifically, the aforementioned model consisted of two MapReduce procedures. The first MapReduce task learns a decision tree in each map after performing evolutionary undersampling pre-processing. Then, a second MapReduce job is initiated in order to classify the test set. The evolutionary undersampling step is further accelerated by adding a windowing scheme adapted to the imbalanced scenario. In order to analyze the quality of this proposed method [65], authors carried out an experimental study with the C4.5 decision tree over different versions of the KDDCup'99 dataset, by gradually increasing its number of instances. Results shown the goodness of the global model in terms of accuracy and efficiency. An extension of this model implemented within the Spark framework has been recently presented in [64].

13.3.1.4 Data Cleaning

Another research that carries out a data reduction scheme (data cleaning) can be found in [39]. Specifically, authors proposed a MapReduce based KNN classifier for DNA Big Data problems. As stated previously, authors included a data reduction stage within the Map processes prior to the learning in order to study the best suited option, together with an analysis of the scalability.

13.3.1.5 NRSBoundary-SMOTE

In [33], authors proposed a MapReduce design of the NRSBoundary-SMOTE, an algorithm based on Neighborhood RoughSet Theory [32]. This adaptation consisted of two MapReduce procedures.

The first MapReduce task was responsible for the partition of the dataset, and the second MapReduce task carried out the oversampling of the minority class examples. More specifically, the first MapReduce job divided the training set according to neighborhood relation and it generated three subsets as output, called Positive, Minority and Boundary. The "Positive" subset contained the majority class samples from which its neighbors shown the sample class label. As its name suggests, the "Minority" subset contained the minority samples. Finally, the "Boundary" subset stored those minority samples with any majority class sample in its neighbors. In the second MapReduce job, every map get a data block of the Boundary set and it computed for each sample in its partition the KNNs. Then, the reduce process selected for each sample one of its neighbors randomly to interpolate with it. If the new synthetic sample belonged to the neighbor of samples that in Positive, another neighbor were selected from the list. Otherwise, the synthetic example was generated.

In both MapReduce processes the Positive and Minority sets were added to the Hadoop Distributed Cache [70]. This feature disables the scalability of the algorithm, as long as the training dataset must fit on the Hadoop Distributed Cache.

13.3.1.6 Extreme Learning Machine with Resampling

A MapReduce approach based on ensemble learning and data resampling can be found in [75]. This algorithm consists of four stages: (1) alternately over-sample p times between positive class instances and negative class instances; (2) construct l balanced data subsets based on the generated positive class instances; (3) train l component classifiers with extreme learning machine algorithm on the constructed l balanced data subsets; (4) integrate the l ELM classifiers with simple voting approach.

To carry out the data pre-processing, the algorithm first calculated the center of positive class instances, and then sample instance points along the line between the center and each positive class instance, in a similar style than SMOTE [8]. Next, for each instance point in the new positive class, the method first find its KNN in negative class instances with MapReduce, and then sample instance points along the line between the instance and its k nearest negative neighbors. The process of over-sampling is repeated p times. In the second stage, the algorithm sample instances l times from the negative class with the same size as the generated positive class instances. Each round of sampling, the method put positive class and negative class instances together thus obtain l balanced data subsets.

In order to verify the effectiveness of this proposed method [75], authors selected 7 data sets from UCI repository (with less than half million examples) and compared with three state-of-the-art approaches for classical DM (no Big Data approaches): SMOTE-Vote, SMOTE-Boost and SMOTE-Bagging, showing better speed-up and performance in terms of the g-mean metric. The drawback of this proposal is the iterative oversampling process applied in the first stage, being computationally expensive.

13.3.1.7 Multi-class Imbalance

Finally, a preliminary study regarding multi-class imbalanced classification was introduced in [4]. This methodology consisted of two steps. First, they used the One-vs.-All (OVA) binarization technique [24] for decomposing original dataset into subsets of binary classes. This process was carried out in a sequential way. Then, the SMOTE Big Data approach [59] was applied for each binary subset of imbalanced binary class in order to balance the data distribution, following the same scheme as suggested in [18]. Finally, to carry out the classification step the Random Forest implementation of Mahout was used [47, 52]. This work is interesting as a first step on the topic, but it lacks from a true Big Data experimental framework as all datasets selected contain less than 5,000 examples.

13.3.1.8 Summary

We can see that the recent years have seen a significant interest in adapting current methods to work on Big Data computing paradigms for imbalanced data. Between undersampling and oversampling, the latter is the widest used approach, and it seems to be more robust to the scalability in terms of number of Maps. All these existing implementations can be regarded as the state-of-the-art from which to improve the performance with more sophisticated techniques, both for the binary and multi-class imbalanced datasets.

13.3.2 Cost-Sensitive Learning Studies

In this section we enumerate several methodologies that include algorithmic modifications for taking into account a higher significance for the positive class. Specifically, four approaches are being revised, two of which are based on SVMs, and two for rule based systems, i.e. decision trees (random forest) and fuzzy rule learning.

13.3.2.1 Cost-Sensitive SVM

In [61] a cost-sensitive SVM using randomized dual coordinate descent method (CSVM-RDCD) was proposed. The authors performed an experimental study with several datasets, where they compared their proposed approach with some cost-sensitive SVMs from the state-of-the-art. However, in this paper, the authors did not use any of the existing solutions for the development of algorithms to address massive amounts of data, such as algorithms based on Hadoop or Spark frameworks. The proposal performed iterative calculations that could not be carried out when the problem size grows in size.

13.3.2.2 Instance Weighting SVM

Another approach based on SVMs can be found in [67]. In the aforementioned research, authors combined an instance-weighted variant of the SVM with a Parallel Meta-learning algorithm using MapReduce. Specifically, a symmetric weight boosting method was developed to optimize the instance-weighted SVM. In the MapReduce design, each Map process applies a secuencial Instance Boosting SVM algorithm in the examples of its partition and generates a base learner. Then, the models generated by the all Maps form an ensemble of classifiers. Therefore, no Reduce step is used as no fusion of the models was required. One of the limitations of this MapReduce scheme is the iterative process that is performed in each Map task. In addition, the datasets used in the experiments do not exceed half a million instances, raising the question whether this approach can be scalable for real Big Data problems.

13.3.2.3 Cost-Sensitive Random Forest

In addition to the study of data pre-processing techniques, another contribution made in [59] was the extension of the Random Forest classifier to a cost-sensitive learning approach for enhancing the learning of the minority class examples. In particular, it consisted of two MapReduce process. The first process was devoted to the creation of the model where each map task built a subset of the forest with the data block of its partition and generated a file containing the built trees. Then, the second MapReduce process was initiated to estimate the class associated to a data test set. In this process, each map estimated the class for the examples available in its partition using the previous learned model, and then the predictions generated by each map were concatenated to form the final predictions file.

13.3.2.4 Cost-Sensitive Fuzzy Rule Based Classification System (FRBCS)

In [46] authors extended Chi-FRBCS-BigData, a MapReduce implementation of a FRBCS made in [60], to address imbalanced Big Data. Specifically, they modified the computation of the rule weights during the learning stage by considering the data distribution. This way, the initial fuzzy learning algorithm was transformed to a cost-sensitive learning scheme, which authors noted as Chi-FRBCS-BigDataCS. Following the workflow defined in [60], the Chi-FRBCS-BigDataCS algorithm consisted of two MapReduce procedures: the first MapReduce process was devoted to the creation of the model, then, the second MapReduce process was responsible to estimate the class associated to a dataset. More specifically, in the first MapReduce process, each Map process was responsible for building a rule base using only the data included in its partition, then, the Reduce process was responsible for collecting and combining the rule bases generated by each map task to form the final rule base. When the first MapReduce process devoted to the building of the model had finished, the second MapReduce process was initiated. In this process, each map task estimated the class for the examples included in its data partition using the previous learned model, then, the predictions generated by each map were aggregated to conform the final predictions file. The classification job did not include a reduce step.

In order to analyze the quality of their proposed approach, the authors run the experiments over three datasets up to 6 millions of instances from the UCI repository [44]. The experimental study showed that the proposal is able to handle imbalanced Big Data obtaining competitive results both in the classification performance of the model and the time needed for the computation.

13.3.2.5 Summary

Cost-sensitive classification has not witnessed the body of works as with the data or algorithmic based approaches for directly addressing the issues of class imbalance. This could also imply the complexity of the underlying process of cost-sensitive classification – from procuring costs for different types of errors to the algorithmic complexity.

13.3.3 Applications on Imbalanced Big Data

In addition to novel proposals and experimental analysis, there are also significant applications in the area of imbalanced Big Data. It is of extreme importance not only to design novel approaches for the research community, but also to add a practical perspective that can be of interest for common users and corporations. In this section, we give several examples of real application areas for Big Data. The areas covered are bioinformatics, traffic accident prediction, biomedical purposes, human activity recognition, and fraud detection.

13.3.3.1 Pairwise Ortholog Detection

In [27] authors focused on the Pairwise Ortholog Detection (POD) problem. It combined several gene pairwise features (alignment-based and synteny measures with others derived from the pairwise comparison of the physicochemical properties of amino acids) to address Big Data problems. The methodology followed to address this problem consisted of three steps: (1) the calculation of gene pair features to be combined, (2) the building of the classification model using ML algorithms to deal with Big Data from a pairwise dataset, and (3) the classification of related gene pairs. In order to achieve high quality results, authors made use of several Big Data supervised techniques that manage imbalanced datasets. Specifically, they selected those presented in [59] and [58] such as Random Forest for Big Data with Cost-Sensitive (RF-BDCS), Random Oversampling with Random Forest for Big Data (ROS+RF-BD) and the SVMs for Big Data (SVM-BD) for the Apache Spark MLib [51] combined with Random Oversampling (ROS+SVM-BD). The effectiveness of the supervised approach for POD is compared to the well-known unsupervised Reciprocal Best Hits, Reciprocal Smallest Distance and a Automated Project for the Identification of Orthologs from Complete Genome Data algorithms. For the experiments, the authors focused on benchmark datasets derived from the following yeast genome pairs: S. cerevisiae and K. lactis, S. cerevisiae and C. glabrata and S. cerevisiae and S. pombe. Four datasets were derived from each genome pair comparison with different alignment settings. The authors found that the supervised approach outperformed traditional methods, mainly when they applied ROS combined with SVM-BD.

An extended version of the previous research was recently published in [26]. Authors propose two novel contributions. From the viewpoint of the gene data extracting, authors investigate the goodness of alignment-free protein features. This way, the identification ability of the classifiers for orthologs at the twilight zone is increased. From the viewpoint of the computational scalability, novel approaches based on Spark are applied both in the preprocessing and in classification steps. Thanks to this, exact models can be learned in a very efficient way, also allowing to better capturing the whole information of the dataset.

13.3.3.2   Traffic Accidents Prediction

In [55] authors developed a DM process for classification of imbalance data based on MapReduce to predict traffic accidents with the highway traffic data. More concretely, the previous paper presented a classification analysis process of imbalance data prediction based on Apache Hadoop [70], Hive [62] and Mahout [47]. It consisted of five processing steps: (1) a pre-processing step that combined the datasets and creates training datasets (using Hive), (2) oversampling technique to solve imbalance data problem in the training dataset, (3) cluster classification analysis to discover the numbers of cluster and the data ratio of cluster by using the k-means MapReduce implementation from Mahout, (4) a classification analysis with several clusters using a MapReduce implementation of logistic regression (also from Mahout) and, (5) analysis of the results. In order to validate the classification analysis process, the authors used data form Korea Highway Corporation which contain traffic data created between Jan. 1st, 2011 and Jun. 30th, 2013 on the Gyeongbu line which connects Seoul with Busan, having a total size of about 300 GB. This work was an extension of their previous approach presented in [54] by including a MapReduce implementation of the SMOTE algorithm. The first MapReduce task was responsible to calculate distances among every example. In the second MapReduce job, each Map task was devoted to sort the results by the distances so that every examples k-NN are revealed. Then, in the Reduce phase, the SMOTE calculations were conducted to create synthetic examples using the k-NN and the attributes of the entire dataset from the Hadoop Distributed Cache [70]. This last feature imposes hard constraints for the scalability of the algorithm.

13.3.3.3   Biomedical Data

A large-scale ML classifier based on functional networks was used in [16] for the classification of biomedical data. In their methodology, an iterative process is carried out to sample the data in a MapReduce sampling strategy prior to the learning stage of the model until the accuracy reaches a stable value. The algorithm is based on a ANN using a the Newton-Raphson's method with the maximum likelihood, obtaining more robust results than other well known algorithms such as SVMs, feed forward ANNs, k-NN or random forest techniques.

13.3.3.4   Human Activity Recognition

Holistic data stream mining was investigated in [22], from which authors proposed and developed a stream-based holistic analytics and reasoning in parallel approach (SHARP for short), using decision trees for the classification. It was based on the principles of incremental learning and lightweight processing, being this way capable of induce a prediction model from Big Data. A more recent research was conducted to analyze the behavior of SHARP for imbalanced class distributions [21]. To do so, authors use the human activity recognition as case study, and SMOTE as preprocessing approach to rebalance the uneven data distributions.

13.3.3.5   Fraud Detection

An Scalable Real-time Fraud Finder (SCARFF) was developed as a complete open source solution for the fraud detection problem [7]. It integrates different Big Data tools for a three stage pipeline. First, it uses Kafka for the log data collection of all transactions. Next stage comprises Spark Streaming for the aggregation of the transactions, and carries out both an scalable feature extraction and the online learning and classification. Finally, results are stored in a Cassandra NoSQL database management system for the sake of computing statistics over different time periods.

13.3.3.6   Summary

Addressing real problems is maybe much harder than trying to design and test a given model. In the previous case, we must take into account the specific features of the case study and to adapt or create new models to obtain the highest performance. We have reviewed several case studies. First, the use of random forest and SVM classifiers have been applied in conjunction with data pre-processing and cost-sensitive learning; the final objective was finding the most robust ortholog proteins detection. In the second case study, a combination of several steps, including SMOTE pre-processing, clustering, and logistic regression, allowed the achievement of quality solutions. Next, a data reduction scheme was used for the biomedical data in conjunction with ANNs. Finally, two differente applications were reviewer in the area of data stream mining. On the one hand, and embedded systems that combined decision trees and SMOTE in human activity recognition. On the other hand, a complete open source scalable platform for fraud detection.

13.4   Challenges for Imbalanced Big Data Classification

The general design of Big Data approaches can be regarded from a double perspective [56]: (1) approximative fusion of models (one submodel per partition, eventually fused); and (2) exact fusion for scalable models (compounding model with the same output as the sequential version). This comprises for both learning classifier models and preprocessing techniques.

The "approximative" case is usually the most common, as it just requires to run the standard model over a chunk of the initial data, and then to aggregate the partial results into a single output. However, the quality of the solutions achieved by this type of algorithms is significantly degraded as the number of Maps is increased in the search of efficiency and scalability.

The reason for this behavior is twofold. On the one hand, the use of local data provides only a small view for the global problem space, that also may lead to a different representation of the data in each Map process. On the other hand, fewer positive class instances are included into each subset of data for the Map processes, and models are clearly biased.

As stated in Chap. 10, a problem related to the lack of data is the potential presence of small disjuncts [45, 68] in the data associated to each Map, also as a consequence of the data division process.

When designing SMOTE-based oversampling methods following a direct approximative workflow, the quality of the output data may deteriorate. This is because SMOTE is relying on the positive class neighborhood to generate new examples, and when that neighborhood is sparse and disjointed, it becomes challenging for SMOTE to achieve its potential. Additionally, in a Big Data scenario with a very large number of features, the computation of the actual neighbors become higher, and so it is the variance for the newly created instances [5].

Taking into account all these issues, we must point out several challenges that must be addressed in order to go one step further in the topic of imbalanced classification for Big Data problems:

1. *There is a necessity in a thorough design at the implementation level for current algorithms.* In other words, an effort for the design and development of robust methodologies to address Big Data imbalanced problems has to be made. Novel Big Data programming frameworks such as Spark [73] add different operators that can ease the codification of this kind of solutions, allowing to take advantage of the iterative features of these operators.
2. *The design of novel algorithms for the generation of artificial instances.* To achieve this goal, the different level of partitioning must be taken into account for the sake of maintaining the robustness of the modeling when seeking for a higher level of scalability and predictive performance.

   In addition, other resampling strategies can be considered to counteract simultaneously the between-class imbalance and the within-class imbalance [37]. The main idea is to identify these small regions of data by means of clustering approaches, and to stress the significance of these areas by generating data within this area.

We posit that it is an opportunity to expand SMOTE for a Spark or Hadoop implementation to counter the challenges of small disjuncts, fewer number of positive class examples, and high dimensionality. An appropriate extension of SMOTE will then allow us to leverage the power of SMOTE in the Spark/Hadoop frameworks of tackling Big Data.

3. *Considering different trade-offs for the ratio between classes.* It has been shown that the standard 1:1 might not be the best class distribution to solve the imbalanced classification problem [9, 69]. Therefore, the data fragmentation and locality related to the different subsets in each Map process, can be overcome by means of the generation of additional data. In this sense, we may refer to the findings obtained in [58] and [66] in which a higher ratio of oversampling allows the achievement of better results.

4. *Focus on the MapReduce workflow.* First, we can act on the learning classifier itself with each Map task. Because instances in the small disjuncts are likely to be difficult to predict, one could possibly use Boosting algorithms to improve their classification performance [25].

   Second, we can also take advantage of the MapReduce programming scheme focusing on the Reduce stage. Specifically, we must analyze two different schemes for the classification techniques: (1) carrying out a model aggregation (fusion) from the outputs of every Map process; or (2) building an ensemble system and combine their predictions during the inference process.

   Therefore, we must be aware on the twofold perspective "fusion" versus "ensemble" of models in the MapReduce scheme, and how to introduce diversity within each Map process so that the joint of single models can lead to an optimal solution.

5. *Manage Variety of the data.* Big Data comprises Volume, Velocity, and also Variety of input sources. Regarding this last characteristic, we must be aware of those multiple type of applications in Big Data analytics in which data to process and classify comes in form of graphs, XML structures, video sequences, hyperspectral images, associations, tensors, and so on [6, 49]. Standard ML techniques are not capable of address properly such complex structures, and trying to convert them to numerical values may hinder the final quality of the system. Therefore, it seems appropriate to design both preprocessing and learning algorithms adapted to this novel data representations to achieve the highest advantage in this context.

13.5 Summarizing Comments

This chapter has focused on the topic Big Data problems. The significance of carrying out analytics tasks in this context is beyond all doubts, and imbalanced classification is not an exception. However, obtaining insight and knowledge from such volume of information is not a straightforward process. Standard solutions must be adapted to a novel scalable and fault tolerant distributed scheme known as MapReduce.

To have a complete understanding of this novel framework, the inner details of the MapReduce programming scheme have been presented. Additionally, the most significant technologies that implement it, namely Hadoop-MapReduce and Apache Spark, have been described. Finally, some ML libraries for Big Data in which well-known algorithms MapReduce implementations are available, were also introduced.

Once the concept of Big Data has been make clear, a deep review for those solutions that have been already proposed to deal with imbalanced classification in this scenario have been carried out. These approaches have been organized into three parts considering whether they use a data pre-processing approach, an algorithmic modification via cost-sensitive learning, or they rather aim to solve a given real application.

Finally, we have stressed some open problems related to inner data characteristics such as the lack of data and small disjuncts generated in the data partitions in the Map processes. Taking this into account, we have posited several challenges that must be taken into account in order to develop high quality solutions in this area of research. On the one hand, a detailed design of artificial data generation techniques to improve the behavior of pre-processing approaches. On the other hand, study the different possibilities related to the fusion of models or the management of an ensemble system with respect to the final Reduce task.

References

1. Al-Fuqaha, A., Guizani, M., Mohammadi, M., Aledhari, M., Ayyash, M.: Internet of things: a survey on enabling technologies, protocols, and applications. IEEE Commun. Surv. Tutorials **17**(4), 2347–2376 (2015)
2. Apache Software Foundation: Apache Spark: lightning-fast cluster computing. http://spark.apache.org/ (2016)
3. Apache Software Foundation: Hadoop distributed file system: users guide. https://hadoop.apache.org/docs/stable/hadoop-project-dist/hadoop-hdfs/HdfsUserGuide.html (2018)
4. Bhagat, R.C., Patil, S.S.: Enhanced smote algorithm for classification of imbalanced big-data using random forest. In: Souvenir of the 2015 IEEE International Advance Computing Conference, IACC'2015, Bangalore, pp. 403–408 (2015)
5. Blagus, R., Lusa, L.: SMOTE for high-dimensional class-imbalanced data. BMC Bioinform. **14**(1), 106 (2013)
6. Brzezinski, D., Piernik, M.: Structural XML classification in concept drifting data streams. N. Gener. Comput. **33**(4), 345–366 (2015)
7. Carcillo, F., Dal Pozzolo, A., Le Borgne, Y.A., Caelen, O., Mazzer, Y., Bontempi, G.: Scarff: a scalable framework for streaming credit card fraud detection with spark. Inf. Fusion **41**, 182–194 (2018)
8. Chawla, N.V., Bowyer, K.W., Hall, L.O., Kegelmeyer, W.P.: SMOTE: synthetic minority over-sampling technique. J. Artif. Intell. Res. **16**, 321–357 (2002)
9. Chawla, N.V., Cieslak, D.A., Hall, L.O., Joshi, A.: Automatically countering imbalance and its empirical relationship to cost. Data Min. Knowl. Disc. **17**(2), 225–252 (2008)

10. Chen, C.P., Zhang, C.Y.: Data-intensive applications, challenges, techniques and technologies: a survey on Big Data. Inf. Sci. **275**, 314–347 (2014)
11. Cyganek, B.: Object Detection and Recognition in Digital Images: Theory and Practice, 1st edn. Wiley, New York (2013)
12. Databricks Inc.: Spark Packages: 3rd Party Spark Packages. https://spark-packages.org/ (2018)
13. Dean, J., Ghemawat, S.: MapReduce: simplified data processing on large clusters. In: OSDI04: Proceedings of the 6th Conference on Symposium on Operating Systems Design and Implementation, San Francisco. USENIX Association (2004)
14. Dean, J., Ghemawat, S.: MapReduce: simplified data processing on large clusters. Commun. ACM **51**(1), 107–113 (2008)
15. Dean, J., Ghemawat, S.: MapReduce: a flexible data processing tool. Commun. ACM **53**(1), 72–77 (2010)
16. Elsebakhi, E., Lee, F., Schendel, E., Haque, A., Kathireason, N., Pathare, T., Syed, N., Al-Ali, R.: Large-scale machine learning based on functional networks for biomedical Big Data with high performance computing platforms. J. Comput. Sci. **11**, 69–81 (2015)
17. Fan, J., Han, F., Liu, H.: Challenges of Big Data analysis. Nat. Sci. Rev. **1**(2), 293–314 (2014)
18. Fernández, A., López, V., Galar, M., Del Jesus, M., Herrera, F.: Analysing the classification of imbalanced data-sets with multiple classes: binarization techniques and ad-hoc approaches. Knowl.-based Syst. **42**, 97–110 (2013)
19. Fernandez, A., del Rio, S., Chawla, N.V., Herrera, F.: An insight into imbalanced Big Data classification: outcomes and challenges. Complex Intell. Syst. **3**(2), 105–120 (2017)
20. Fernández, A., Río, S., López, V., Bawakid, A., del Jesus, M.J., Benítez, J., Herrera, F.: Big Data with cloud computing: an insight on the computing environment, MapReduce and programming framework. WIREs Data Min. Knowl. Disc. **4**(5), 380–409 (2014)
21. Fong, S., Liu, K., Cho, K., Wong, R., Mohammed, S., Fiaidhi, J.: Improvised methods for tackling Big Data stream mining challenges: case study of human activity recognition. J. Supercomput. **72**, 3927–3959 (2016)
22. Fong, S., Zhuang, Y., Wong, R., Mohammed, S.: A scalable data stream mining methodology: stream based holistic analytics and reasoning in parallel. In: Proceedings of the 2nd International Symposium on Computational and Business Intelligence, New Delhi, pp. 110–115 (2014)
23. Fosso Wamba, S., Akter, S., Edwards, A., Chopin, G., Gnanzou, D.: How 'Big Data' can make big impact: findings from a systematic review and a longitudinal case study. Int. J. Prod. Econ. **165**, 234–246 (2015)
24. Galar, M., Fernández, A., Barrenechea, E., Bustince, H., Herrera, F.: An overview of ensemble methods for binary classifiers in multi-class problems: experimental study on one-vs-one and one-vs-all schemes. Pattern Recogn. **44**(8), 1761–1776 (2011)
25. Galar, M., Fernández, A., Barrenechea, E., Bustince, H., Herrera, F.: A review on ensembles for class imbalance problem: bagging, boosting and hybrid based approaches. IEEE Trans. Syst. Man Cybern. Part C Appl. Rev. **42**(4), 463–484 (2012)
26. Galpert, D., Fernndez, A., Herrera, F., Antunes, A., Molina-Ruiz, R., Agero-Chapin, G.: Surveying alignment-free features for ortholog detection in related yeast proteomes by using supervised Big Data classifiers. BMC Bioinform. **19**(1), 166:1–166:17 (2018)
27. Galpert, D., Río, S., Herrera, F., Ancede-Gallardo, E., Antunes, A., Agero-Chapin, G.: An effective Big Data supervised imbalanced classification approach for ortholog detection in related yeast species. BioMed Res. Int. **2015**, 1–12 (2015)
28. Gutierrez, P., Lastra, M., Bacardit, J., Benitez, J., Herrera, F.: GPU-SME-kNN: scalable and memory efficient kNN and lazy learning using GPUs. Inf. Sci. **373**, 165–182 (2016)
29. Gutierrez, P.D., Lastra, M., Benitez, J.M., Herrera, F.: SMOTE-GPU: Big Data preprocessing on commodity hardware for imbalanced classification. Prog. Artif. Intell. **6**(4), 347–354 (2017)
30. Hamstra, M., Karau, H., Zaharia, M., Konwinski, A., Wendell, P.: Learning Spark: Lightning-Fast Big Data Analytics. O'Reilly Media, Sebastopol (2015)
31. Hashem, I.A.T., Yaqoob, I., Anuar, N.B., Mokhtar, S., Gani, A., Ullah Khan, S.: The rise of "Big Data" on cloud computing: review and open research issues. Inf. Syst. **47**, 98–115 (2015)

32. Hu, F., Li, H.: A novel boundary oversampling algorithm based on neighborhood rough set model: NRSBoundary-SMOTE. Math. Probl. Eng. **2013**, 1–10 (2013)
33. Hu, F., Li, H., Lou, H., Dai, J.: A parallel oversampling algorithm based on NRSBoundary-SMOTE. J. Inf. Comput. Sci. **11**(13), 4655–4665 (2014)
34. Hu, H., Wen, Y., Chua, T., Li, X.: Toward scalable systems for Big Data analytics: a technology tutorial. IEEE Access **2**, 652–687 (2014)
35. Hurtado, J., Taweewitchakreeya, N., Kong, X., Zhu, X.: A classifier ensembling approach for imbalanced social link prediction. In: 12th International Conference on Machine Learning and Applications, ICMLA'2013, Miami, pp. 436–439. IEEE (2013)
36. Jagadish, H.V., Gehrke, J., Labrinidis, A., Papakonstantinou, Y., Patel, J.M., Ramakrishnan, R., Shahabi, C.: Big Data and its technical challenges. Commun. ACM **57**(7), 86–94 (2014)
37. Jo, T., Japkowicz, N.: Class imbalances versus small disjuncts. ACM SIGKDD Explor. Newsl. **6**(1), 40–49 (2004)
38. Jordan, M.I., Mitchell, T.M.: Machine learning: trends, perspectives, and prospects. Science **349**(6245), 255–260 (2015)
39. Kamal, S., Ripon, S.H., Dey, N., Ashour, A.S., Santhi, V.: A MapReduce approach to diminish imbalance parameters for big deoxyribonucleic acid dataset. Comput. Methods Prog. Biomed. **131**, 191–206 (2016)
40. Kambatla, K., Kollias, G., Kumar, V., Grama, A.: Trends in Big Data analytics. J. Parallel Distrib. Comput. **74**(7), 2561–2573 (2014)
41. Kraska, T.: Finding the needle in the Big Data systems haystack. IEEE Internet Comput. **17**(1), 84–86 (2013)
42. Krawczyk, B.: GPU-accelerated extreme learning machines for imbalanced data streams with concept drift. Proc. Comput. Sci. **80**, 1692–1701 (2016). https://doi.org/10.1016/j.procs.2016.05.509
43. Lam, C.: Hadoop in Action, 1st edn. Manning, Greenwich (2011)
44. Lichman, M.: UCI machine learning repository. University of California, Irvine, School of Information and Computer Sciences (2013). http://archive.ics.uci.edu/ml
45. López, V., Fernández, A., García, S., Palade, V., Herrera, F.: An insight into classification with imbalanced data: empirical results and current trends on using data intrinsic characteristics. Inf. Sci. **250**(20), 113–141 (2013)
46. López, V., Río, S., Benítez, J.M., Herrera, F.: Cost-sensitive linguistic fuzzy rule based classification systems under the MapReduce framework for imbalanced Big Data. Fuzzy Sets Syst. **258**, 5–38 (2015)
47. Lyubimov, D., Palumbo, A.: Apache Mahout: Beyond MapReduce, 1st edn. CreateSpace Independent, Louisville (2016)
48. Mahout, A.: Apache Mahout. https://mahout.apache.org/ (2018)
49. Mardani, M., Mateos, G., Giannakis, G.B.: Subspace learning and imputation for streaming Big Data matrices and tensors. IEEE Trans. Signal Process. **63**(10), 2663–2677 (2015)
50. Marx, V.: The big challenges of Big Data. Nature **498**(7453), 255–260 (2013)
51. Meng, X., Bradley, J., Yavuz, B., Sparks, E., Venkataraman, S., Liu, D., Freeman, J., Tsai, D., Amde, M., Owen, S., Xin, D., Xin, R., Franklin, M.J., Zadeh, R., Zaharia, M., Talwalkar, A.: MLlib: machine learning in Apache Spark. J. Mach. Learn. Res. **17**(34), 1–7 (2016)
52. Owen, S., Anil, R., Dunning, T., Friedman, E.: Mahout in Action, 1st edn. Manning Publications Co., Shelter Island (2011)
53. Panda, B., Herbach, J.S., Basu, S., Bayardo, R.J.: Planet: massively parallel learning of tree ensembles with MapReduce. Proc. VLDB Endow. **2**(2), 1426–1437 (2009)
54. Park, S.H., Ha, Y.G.: Large imbalance data classification based on MapReduce for traffic accident prediction. In: Proceedings – 2014 8th International Conference on Innovative Mobile and Internet Services in Ubiquitous Computing, IMIS'2014, Birmingham, pp. 45–49 (2014)
55. Park, S.H., Kim, S.M., Ha, Y.G.: Highway traffic accident prediction using VDS Big Data analysis. J. Supercomput. **72**, 2815–2831 (2016)

56. Ramírez-Gallego, S., Fernández, A., García, S., Chen, M., Herrera, F.: Big Data: tutorial and guidelines on information and process fusion for analytics algorithms with MapReduce. Inf. Fusion **42**, 51–61 (2018)
57. Reed, D.A., Dongarra, J.: Exascale computing and Big Data. Commun. ACM **58**(7), 56–68 (2015)
58. Río, S., Benítez, J.M., Herrera, F.: Analysis of data preprocessing increasing the oversampling ratio for extremely imbalanced Big Data classification. In: Trustcom/BigDataSE/ISPA, 2015 IEEE, vol. 2, pp. 180–185 (2015)
59. Río, S., López, V., Benítez, J., Herrera, F.: On the use of MapReduce for imbalanced Big Data using random forest. Inf. Sci. **285**, 112–137 (2014)
60. Río, S., López, V., Benítez, J.M., Herrera, F.: A MapReduce approach to address Big Data classification problems based on the fusion of linguistic fuzzy rules. Int. J. Comput. Intell. Syst. **8**(3), 422–437 (2015)
61. Tang, M., Yang, C., Zhang, K., Xie, Q.: Cost-sensitive support vector machine using randomized dual coordinate descent method for big class-imbalanced data classification. Abstr. Appl. Anal. **2014**, 416591:1–416591:9 (2014)
62. Thusoo, A., Sarma, J.S., Jain, N., Shao, Z., Chakka, P., Anthony, S., Liu, H., Wyckoff, P., Murthy, R.: Hive – a warehousing solution over a map-reduce framework. J. Very Large DataBases **2**(2), 1626–1629 (2009)
63. Triguero, I., Derrac, J., García, S., Herrera, F.: Integrating a differential evolution feature weighting scheme into prototype generation. Neurocomputing **97**, 332–343 (2012)
64. Triguero, I., Galar, M., Merino, D., Maillo, J., Bustince, H., Herrera, F.: Evolutionary undersampling for extremely imbalanced Big Data classification under Apache Spark. In: IEEE Congress on Evolutionary Computation (CEC'2016), Vancouver, pp. 640–647 (2016)
65. Triguero, I., Galar, M., Vluymans, S., Cornelis, C., Bustince, H., Herrera, F., Saeys, Y.: Evolutionary undersampling for imbalanced Big Data classification. In: 2015 IEEE Congress on Evolutionary Computation (CEC), pp. 715–722 (2015)
66. Triguero, I., Río, S., López, V., Bacardit, J., Benítez, J.M., Herrera, F.: Rosefw-RF: the winner algorithm for the ECBDL'14 Big Data competition: an extremely imbalanced Big Data bioinformatics problem. Knowl.-Based Syst. **87**, 69–79 (2015)
67. Wang, X., Liu, X., Matwin, S.: A distributed instance-weighted SVM algorithm on large-scale imbalanced datasets. In: Proceedings – 2014 IEEE International Conference on Big Data, IEEE Big Data 2014, Washington, DC, pp. 45–51 (2014)
68. Weiss, G.M.: The impact of small disjuncts on classifier learning. In: Stahlbock, R., Crone, S.F., Lessmann, S. (eds.) Data Mining, Annals of Information Systems, vol. 8, pp. 193–226. Springer, New York (2010)
69. Weiss, G.M., Provost, F.J.: Learning when training data are costly: the effect of class distribution on tree induction. J. Artif. Intell. Res. **19**, 315–354 (2003)
70. White, T.: Hadoop: The Definitive Guide, 4th edn. O'Reilly Media, Sebastopol (2015)
71. Wu, X., Zhu, X., Wu, G.Q., Ding, W.: Data mining with Big Data. IEEE Trans. Knowl. Data Eng. **26**(1), 97–107 (2014)
72. YARN, A.: Apache YARN. https://hadoop.apache.org/docs/current/hadoop-yarn/hadoop-yarn-site/YARN.html (2018)
73. Zaharia, M., Chowdhury, M., Das, T., Dave, A., Ma, J., McCauly, M., Franklin, M.J., Shenker, S., Stoica, I.: Resilient distributed datasets: a fault-tolerant abstraction for in-memory cluster computing. In: Presented as Part of the 9th USENIX Symposium on Networked Systems Design and Implementation (NSDI'12), pp. 15–28. USENIX, San Jose (2012)
74. Zaharia, M., Chowdhury, M., Franklin, M.J., Shenker, S., Stoica, I.: Spark: cluster computing with working sets. In: HotCloud 2010, pp. 1–7 (2010)
75. Zhai, J., Zhang, S., Wang, C.: The classification of imbalanced large data sets based on MapReduce and ensemble of ELM classifiers. Int. J. Mach. Learn. Cybern. **8**(3), 1009–1017 (2015)

Chapter 14
Software and Libraries for Imbalanced Classification

Abstract Researchers in the topic of imbalanced classification have proposed throughout the years a large amount of different approaches to address this issue. To keep on developing this area of study, it is of extreme importance to make these methods available for the research community. This allows for a double advantage: (1) to analyze in depth the features and capabilities of the algorithms; and (2) to carry out a fair comparison with any novel proposal. Taking the former into account, different open source libraries and software packages on imbalanced classification can be found, being built under different tools. In this chapter, we compile the most significant ones focusing on their main characteristics and included methods, from standard DM to Big Data applications. Our intention is to make close to researchers, practitioners and corporations, a non-exhaustive list of the alternatives for applying diverse algorithms to their problem in order to achieve the most accurate results with the lowest effort. To present these software tools, this chapter is organized as follows. First, in Sect. 14.1 the significance of software implementations for imbalanced classification is stressed. Then, Sect. 14.2 introduces the Java tools, i.e. KEEL [2] and WEKA [17]. Next, Sect. 14.3 focus on different R packages. The "imbalanced-learn" Python toolbox [29] from "scikit learn" [39] is described in Sect. 14.4. Big Data solutions under Spark [26] are summarized in Sect. 14.5. Finally, Sect. 14.6 provides some concluding remarks.

14.1 Introduction

The interest for Analytics and DM solutions started as soon as practitioners realized the advantages derived from the knowledge extraction process [22]. This task can be carried out over a myriad of applications, such as finances, medicine, engineering, and many others. However, most of the users from the former areas are non-specialized in computer science, and therefore it might be difficult for them to design and implement the software needed to accomplish their goals.

This fact motivated the rise of many commercial and noncommercial software suites that eases the application of the state-of-the-art algorithms in DM. Many corporations opt for a commercially distributed solution (e.g. SPSS Clementine,

© Springer Nature Switzerland AG 2018

A. Fernández et al., *Learning from Imbalanced Data Sets*,

https://doi.org/10.1007/978-3-319-98074-4_14

Oracle DM or KnowledgeSTUDIO), but the associated licenses are not suitable for other practitioners.

In this sense, there is a strong community that develop a good number of open source tools. There are several advantages related to this type of software [11]. First, it allows implementations to be publicly available for all the research community, who can take advantage of these models for their own applications. Additionally, it supports transparency, meritocracy, and community development, i.e. explicit collaborative participation to gather interesting feedback to improve the capabilities and performance of the initial design. Finally, this collaboration and sharing allow other people to make modifications to the source code and incorporate those changes into their own projects.

Throughout this chapter, we focus on those open source libraries and packages that comprise methods and techniques for addressing imbalanced classification. Specifically, we have selected tools from different programming communities, namely Java,[1] R[2] and Python.[3] Additionally, we include some initial software approaches in the scenario of Big Data [14, 34]. Our aim is that different users may select the most appropriate solution for them, depending on both their previous experience and requirements.

14.2   Java Tools

Java is a high level programming language that gained wide popularity for scientific applications due to some of its advantages. Among others, we may stress that it is stable, portable for several platforms, object-oriented for the ease of use and compatible with novel languages such as Scala or JRuby.

Two of the most well-known software tools for DM purposes are KEEL [2] and WEKA [17]. The reason for their success is basically the inclusion of some of the most significant state-of-the-art algorithms, and their ease of use. Specifically, experiments can be directly designed from a workflow based panel, in which loosely coupled, individual processing nodes can be "bolted together" to permit complex computational operations. This issue implies no need to use any programming environment.

The main difference between KEEL and Weka is that the former provides a complete module for imbalanced classification, whereas the latter is limited to cost-sensitive and simple resampling. In what follows, we will describe in detail KEEL software and the imbalanced module (Sect. 14.2.1), and then we will explain how to address imbalanced problems in Weka (Sect. 14.2.2).

---

[1] https://www.java.com/
[2] https://www.r-project.org/
[3] https://www.python.org/

14.2.1   KEEL Software Suite

The KEEL software[4] was originally developed as a tool pretty much focused on the implementation of evolutionary algorithms and soft computing techniques for standard DM problems such as regression, classification or association rules, as well as data preprocessing techniques [8, 20]. KEEL was launched in 2009 [1] and later upgraded in 2011 [2] as a non-commercial Java suite, so that, it could be on all major platforms.

KEEL provides a simple GUI to design experiments with different data sets and computational intelligence algorithms in order to assess the behavior of the algorithms. Moreover, KEEL was designed with a two-fold goal: research and educational. This suite came along with KEEL-dataset,[5] a repository that includes standardized data set partitions for comparison purposes in the KEEL format and shows some algorithms' results over these data sets. This repository provides researchers with quality well-known data sets, allowing easier comparative experimental studies. Focusing on imbalanced classification, it comprises a total of 167 benchmark problems under different scenarios:

1. 22 datasets with an imbalance ratio between 1.5 and 9. These are considered as low imbalanced problems.
2. 100 datasets with an imbalance ratio higher than 9. These are divided into three different parts, depending on the research papers in which they have been used. All of them are considered to be highly imbalanced problems, i.e. comprising an additional difficulty for the classification task.
3. 15 Multiple class imbalanced problems. These are used to extend the studies in imbalanced classification when several classes are involved.
4. 30 Noisy and Borderline Examples. These are synthetic problems to analyze the behavior in the case of both imbalance and noise.

As mentioned previously, the KEEL Software Suite provides a complete module for the experimentation of this type of problem. Specifically, the implemented solutions came from both external approaches, i.e. data pre-processing, and internal approaches, i.e. algorithmic and cost-sensitive learning classifiers. In addition, it contains a large number of ensemble methods that works either at the data-level or by considering to embed a cost-sensitive framework in the ensemble learning process.

Figure 14.1 summarizes the three main contributions of this module, which are also listed below:

1. Preprocessing techniques: Apart from the existing preprocessing techniques included in the original KEEL Experiment section, this module includes two new categories: Over-Sampling Methods and Under-Sampling techniques. These

---

[4]http://www.keel.es
[5]http://www.keel.es/datasets.php

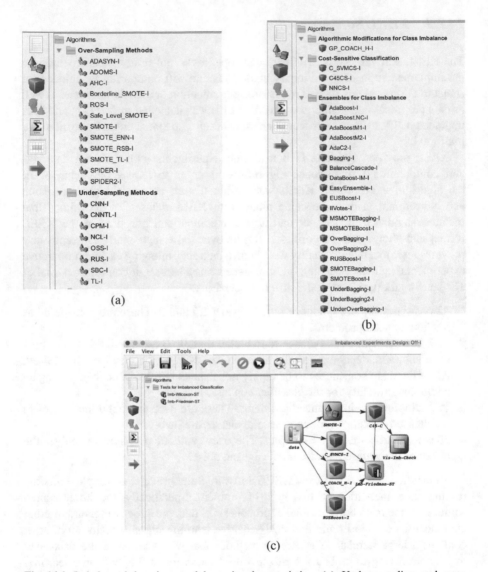

Fig. 14.1 Imbalanced learning module main characteristics. (**a**) Under-sampling and over-sampling models. (**b**) Imbalanced learning algorithms. (**c**) Tailored statistical tests and example of experiment design

preprocessing techniques may be later connected to standard DM models. Reader may recall data level techniques for imbalanced classification in Chap. 5.

2. Methods: KEEL provides tailored algorithm for the class-imbalanced problem. It contains the state-of-the-art in ensemble learning (up to 21 methods, already described in Chap. 7) [18] and cost-sensitive classification such as C.5, ANNs and SVMs (see Chap. 4).

3. Visualisation and Statistical Tests: As in the case of standard classification, KEEL includes a number of visualization and statistical utilities. For this module, these have been modified to take into account the imbalanced problem. Specifically, it uses geometric mean and area under ROC curve (AUC) as more appropriate performance measures for this scenario (see Chap. 3).

The advantages of KEEL with respect to other alternatives to develop experiments on imbalanced classification are enumerated next:

- Its use is independent on previous knowledge on computer science.
- As imbalanced datasets are already available within the tool, initial testing is straightforward. Additionally, it includes an easy-to-use importation window to add user data for further experimentation.
- It contains the largest collection of approaches to address imbalanced classification. Furthermore, these methods come from different families of techniques, namely preprocessing, cost-sensitive, and ensemble learning. Finally, a statistical analysis of the results can be directly carried out within the experimental workflow.

The latest source code version of KEEL (3.0) can be downloaded at https://github.com/SCI2SUGR/KEEL.

14.2.2 Weka

Weka is probably one of the most well-known software tool to perform ML and DM tasks [17]. Its algorithms can either be applied directly to a dataset from its own interface or imported into the users' Java code. Weka contains tools for data pre-processing, classification, regression, clustering, association rules, and visualization. Due to its enormous widespread usage, a complete set of extra packages are available for completing its functionalities.

In the event of addressing imbalanced data, Weka provides two solutions. On the one hand, to carry out a training data rebalancing. On the other hand to perform a cost-sensitive classification.

The rebalancing procedure is selected via instance filtering methods (see Fig. 14.2). By default, Weka includes oversampling (named as "resample") and undersampling (named as "SpreadSubsample"). In addition to these, the SMOTE preprocessing can be included via the package manager.

- *Resample* produces a random subsample of a dataset using either sampling with replacement or without replacement. The main parameter is a bias factor that determines the final ratio of class distribution. This way, the current class distribution may be maintained in the subsample, or it can be biased toward a uniform distribution. The only constraints are that the original dataset must fit entirely in memory and the dataset must have a nominal class attribute, although the unsupervised version might be used in this case.

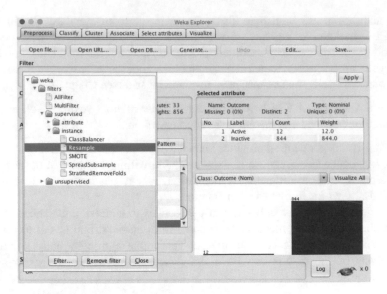

Fig. 14.2 Weka preprocessing techniques

- *SpreadSubsample* allows to randomly subsampling the data by also specifying the spread desired in the classes. For example, user may specify that there be at most a 2:1 difference in class frequencies.
- *SMOTE* implements the original algorithm from [9]. Required parameters are the number of neighbors to build synthetic instances from a given data point, and the percentage of new created examples, that is, if a 100% is chosen, then the minority class will be doubled.

Previous preprocessing filters can be applied in a chain, so that "SpreadSubsample" undersampling can be applied after the "SMOTE" oversampling.

Regarding cost-sensitive learning, there are basically two ways to proceed. The first one is via instance weighting using the "ClassBalancer" filtering. The second one is by importing a user derived cost-matrix. In this case, there are two different options, which are based on meta learning. On the one hand, to use the "CostSensitiveClassifier" approach. On the other hand, to opt for the "MetaCost" scheme. An example is illustrated in Fig. 14.3.

- The goal of "ClassBalancer" is reweighting the instances in each class to obtain a same total class weight. When used in conjunction with "FilteredClassifier," only the training data will be reweighted so that each class has the same total weight, i.e. test data will be left unchanged.
- When using the "CostSensitiveClassifier", two additional methods can be used to introduce cost-sensitivity: reweighting training instances according to the total cost assigned to each class; or predicting the class with minimum expected misclassification cost (rather than the most likely class). Performance can often

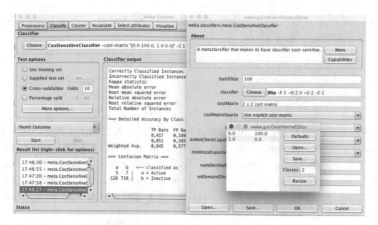

Fig. 14.3 Weka cost-sensitive learning example

be improved by using a Bagged classifier to improve the probability estimates of the base classifier.

Since the classifier normalizes the cost matrix before applying it, it makes it hard coming up with a cost matrix, i.e. to balance out imbalanced data. The most straightforward solution is to set the cost as to equalize the class distributions, i.e. achieving a 1:1 class distribution afterward. The hitch here is that this could be limited to 2-class problems.

- The application of the cost matrix in MetaCost is more intuitive. This classifier should produce similar results to one created by passing the base learner to Bagging, which is in turn passed to a "CostSensitiveClassifier" operating on minimum expected cost. The difference is that MetaCost produces a single cost-sensitive classifier of the base learner, giving the benefits of fast classification and interpretable output (if the base learner itself is interpretable). This implementation uses all bagging iterations when reclassifying training data (the MetaCost paper reports a marginal improvement when only those iterations containing each training instance are used in reclassifying that instance).

MetaCost will compute the costs (*Costs*) based on the class distribution the bagged base learner returns (*Class probs*) and select the class with the lowest cost (*Chosen class*).

Finally, we must remark that apart from these methods to cope with imbalanced distributions, Weka also includes evaluation methods for this scenario, such as the probabilistic AUC metric.

The advantages of the Weka tool for its use in the scenario of imbalanced classification are marginal in contrast to KEEL. In this case, very simple solutions for this area of work are included. Moreover, in the case of cost-sensitive learning, the necessity of setting up a cost-matrix may cause the achievement of sub-optimal models. However, the choice for Weka is well suited when users aim at achieving some preliminary results in the context of imbalanced classification.

Latest version of Weka (3.8.2) may be obtained from http://www.cs.waikato.ac.
nz/ml/weka/downloading.html.

14.3 R Packages

R is an open source programming language made by mathematicians. It is mainly
based on statistical computations that can be used both interactively, through its
command line, and programmatically, through written R scripts. Because of its
flexibility and exploratory data analysis functionality, including rich visualization
skills, R is nowadays one of the most used tool for data science for users of different
communities [44].

R and its libraries implement a wide variety of statistical and graphical techniques. In addition, R is an extensible software tool whose functionality can be
augmented through packages. An R package usually provides an specific functionality, documentation, data, and usage examples. What makes R extensibility different
from other similar tools is the availability of a distributed package repository, named
CRAN (Comprehensive R Archive Network) [25], which eases the automated
download and installation of these packages.

Regarding the packages providing support to imbalanced classification, different oversampling and undersampling preprocessing methods can be found.
Specifically, we will refer to *unbalanced* (Sect. 14.3.1), *smotefamily* (Sect. 14.3.2),
rose (Sect. 14.3.3), *DMwR* (Sect. 14.3.4), and the most recent contribution for R,
the package simply known as *imbalance* (Sect. 14.3.5). Finally, the *mlr* package
supports cost-sensitive classification (Sect. 14.3.6).

14.3.1 Package Unbalanced

The `unbalanced` package was developed by researchers of the ML group from
Université Libre de Bruxelles [12]. It contains some of the most well-known
sampling and distance based methods for imbalanced classification task, which are
listed below:

- Oversampling methods: random oversampling (*ubOver*) and SMOTE
  (*ubSMOTE*).
- Undersampling methods: random undersampling (*ubUnder*), OSS (*ubOSS*),
  CNN (*ubCNN*), ENN (*ubENN*), NCL (*ubNCL*) and Tomek-Links (*ubTomek*).

All these methods can be called by a wrapper function ubBalance that allows
testing all these strategies by simply changing the argument type. A simple example
is illustrated in Fig. 14.4.

Apart from implementing some of the most well-known preprocessing techniques for imbalanced classification, its main feature is to propose a "Racing"

```
#apply oversampling
data <- ubBalance(X=input, Y=output, type="ubOver", k=0)
#oversampled dataset
overData <- data.frame(data$X, Class=data$Y)
#check the frequency of the target variable after oversampling
summary(overData$Class)
```

```
##   0   1
## 225 225
```

(a)

```
#apply undersampling
data <- ubBalance(X=input, Y=output, type="ubUnder", perc=50, method="percPos")
#undersampled dataset
underData <- data.frame(data$X, Class=data$Y)
#check the frequency of the target variable after oversampling
summary(underData$Class)
```

```
##   0   1
## 126 126
```

(b)

Fig. 14.4 R programming steps to carry oversampling and undersampling with unbalanced R package. (**a**) How to carry out oversampling with "ubOver" function. (**b**) How to carry out undersampling with "ubOver" function

algorithm to select adaptively the most appropriate strategy for a given unbalanced task (*ubRacing*). This function compares the 8 previous preprocessing algorithms, plus applying the learning over the original dataset. Candidates are assessed on different subsets of data and, each time a new assessment is made, the Friedman test is used to dismiss significantly inferior candidates. A 10-FCV is used to provide the assessment measure to the race. If a candidate is significantly better than all the others than the race is terminated without the need of using the whole dataset. In case there is not evidence of worse/better methods, the race terminates when the entire dataset is explored and the best candidate is the one with the best average result. Supported algorithms are stated in the *mlr* package.

We may observe an example of the imbalanced Race working procedure in Fig. 14.5.

Finally, in order to test its functionality, the package includes the ubIonosphere dataset. It is a modification of the Ionosphere dataset contained in *mlbench* package. It has only numerical input variables, i.e. the first two variables are removed. The Class variable, originally taking values bad and good, has been transformed into a factor where 1 denotes the minority (bad) and 0 the majority class (good). This variable is our target and it is in the last column of the dataset.

As summary, the advantages of this package is the number of different preprocessing techniques, especially for undersampling, and the use of the meta-learning

```
#use Racing to select the best technique for an imbalanced dataset

#configure sampling parameters
ubConf <- list(type="ubUnder", percOver=200, percUnder=200, k=2, perc=50,
               method="percPos", w=NULL)
#load the classification algorithm that you intend to use inside the Race
#see 'mlr' package for supported algorithms

results <- ubRacing(Class ~., ubIonosphere, "randomForest",
                    positive=1, ubConf=ubConf, ntree=10)


##
##  Racing for unbalanced methods selection in 10 fold CV
##  Number of candidates...........................................9
##  Max number of folds in the CV................................10
##  Max number of experiments..................................100
##  Statistical test...............................Friedman test
##
##                          Markers:
##                             x No test is performed.
##                             - The test is performed and
##                               some candidates are discarded.
##                             = The test is performed but
##                               no candidate is discarded.
##
##  +-+-----------+-----------+-----------+-----------+-----------+
##  | |      Fold|     Alive|      Best| Mean best| Exp so far|
##  +-+-----------+-----------+-----------+-----------+-----------+
##  |x|         1|         9|         2|    0.7745|         9|
##  |=|         2|         9|         4|    0.7473|        18|
##  |-|         3|         5|         4|    0.7585|        27|
##  |=|         4|         5|         1|    0.7668|        32|
##  |=|         5|         5|         4|    0.7585|        37|
##  |=|         6|         5|         1|     0.761|        42|
##  |=|         7|         5|         1|    0.7748|        47|
##  |=|         8|         5|         1|    0.7633|        52|
##  |=|         9|         5|         1|    0.7585|        57|
##  |=|        10|         5|         2|    0.7572|        62|
##  +-+-----------+-----------+-----------+-----------+-----------+
## Selected candidate: ubOver    metric: f1      mean value: 0.7572
```

Fig. 14.5 Automatic selection of the preprocessing procedure with the "Racing" function from unbalanced R package

procedure for selecting the most appropriate algorithm. However, it lacks from a variety of oversampling approaches, which are more commonly used in the specialized literature. Latest version (2.0) can be found at CRAN package repository.[6]

14.3.2   Package Smotefamily

smotefamily is an R package developed with aims at providing a collection of various oversampling techniques, all of which to be considered as SMOTE

---

[6]https://cran.r-project.org/web/packages/unbalanced/index.html

```
data_example = sample_generator(10000,ratio = 0.80)
genData = SMOTE(data_example[,-3],data_example[,3])
genData_2 = ADAS(data_example[,-3],data_example[,3],K=7)
genData_3 = BLSMOTE(data_example[,-3],data_example[,3],K=7,
                    C=5, method = "type2")

## [1] "Borderline-SMOTE done"

genData_4 = SLS(data_example[,-3],data_example[,3],K=7, C=5)

## [1] "SLS done"
```

Fig. 14.6 Example of how to generate oversampled data with different techniques with the smotefamily R package

extensions [42]. Implemented approaches are listed next. SMOTE, ADASYN, Adaptive Neighbor Synthetic Majority Oversampling TEchnique (ANS), Borderline-SMOTE, DBSMOTE, SafeLevels-SMOTE and Relocating Safe-level SMOTE (RSLS) [41]. A simple example of its working procedure is shown in Fig. 14.6

The strongest point of this package is basically compiling some of the best behaving oversampling techniques [32]. However, there is still lots of SMOTE extensions that can provide high quality results depending on the scenario the user is addressing.

Latest version (1.2) can be found at CRAN package repository.[7]

14.3.3   Package ROSE

This R package has its basis on the Random Over-Sampling Examples (ROSE) algorithm [33, 36]. It is a bootstrap-based technique which aids the task of binary classification in the presence of rare classes. It handles both continuous and categorical data by generating synthetic examples from a conditional kernel density estimate of the two classes. Additionally, function *ovun.sample* implements more traditional remedies to the class imbalance, such as oversampling the minority class, undersampling the majority class, or a combination of over and undersampling.

Different metrics to evaluate a learner accuracy are also supplied. Specifically, *roc.curve* function returns the ROC curve and computes the area under the curve (AUC) for binary classifiers; whereas *accuracy.meas* function computes precision, recall and the F measure of a prediction.

---

[7]https://cran.r-project.org/web/packages/smotefamily/index.html

Holdout, bootstrap or cross-validation estimators of these accuracy metrics are computed by means of ROSE and provided by function *ROSE.eval*, to be used in conjunction with virtually any binary classifier.

Finally, it provides the "hacide" simulated training (1,000 instances) and test (200 instances) set for imbalanced binary classification. It is represented by 2 real features. The rare class may be described as a half circle depleted filled with the prevalent class, which is normally distributed and has elliptical contours. The IR is 49 (positive examples are just the 2% of the data).

There are several interesting features for the ROSE package. First, we may find an alternative to the SMOTE-like oversampling approaches, i.e. with ROSE synthetic instances are depending on their density estimation, rather than randomly. Second, it provides a direct way to asses the classification performance with the AUC metric and visualization of the ROC. Finally, a complete validation procedure is also available to simplify this process. However, it lacks from a more complete list of preprocessing algorithms.

A simple usage example is shown in Fig. 14.7. Latest version (0.0–3) can be found at CRAN package repository.[8]

14.3.4   Package DMwR

The functions and data for "DM with R" (DMwR) package comprise a complete list of methods to carry out different DM tasks, from preprocessing, to classification and regression. It was developed to complement the book from L. Torgo [47].

Among the included functions, it supports the SMOTE preprocessing algorithm. It allows to carry out both oversampling (by creating synthetic instances) and undersampling (by random removal of majority instances). The latter value is considered as a percentage of the final number of minority instances in the dataset, i.e. after the oversampling step. The function can also be used to obtain directly the classification model from the resulting balanced data set. This can be done by including the name of the R function that implements the classifier in the parameter learner. A small example is depicted in Fig. 14.8.

The *DMwR* package presents a large collection of functions for those users who want to initiate in the area of DM. It is not specifically designed to address the imbalanced classification task, but the inclusion of the SMOTE algorithm allows to check the behavior of the classifiers in the event of these uneven class distributions.

Latest version (0.4.1) can be found at CRAN package repository.[9]

---

[8]https://cran.r-project.org/web/packages/ROSE/index.html

[9]https://cran.r-project.org/web/packages/DMwR/index.html

```
# loading data
data(hacide)

# check imbalance
table(hacide.train$cls)

##
##   0   1
## 980  20
```

```
# train logistic regression on imbalanced data
log.reg.imb <- glm(cls ~ ., data=hacide.train, family=binomial)

# use the trained model to predict test data
pred.log.reg.imb <- predict(log.reg.imb, newdata=hacide.test,
                            type="response")

# generate new balanced data by ROSE
hacide.rose <- ROSE(cls ~ ., data=hacide.train, seed=123)$data

# check (im)balance of new data
table(hacide.rose$cls)

##
##   0   1
## 507 493
```

```
# train logistic regression on balanced data
log.reg.bal <- glm(cls ~ ., data=hacide.rose, family=binomial)

# use the trained model to predict test data
pred.log.reg.bal <- predict(log.reg.bal, newdata=hacide.test,
                            type="response")

# check accuracy of the two learners by measuring auc
roc.curve(hacide.test$cls, pred.log.reg.imb, plotit = FALSE)
```

```
## Area under the curve (AUC): 0.803
```

```
roc.curve(hacide.test$cls, pred.log.reg.bal, plotit = FALSE)
```

```
## Area under the curve (AUC): 0.910
```

Fig. 14.7 A complete workflow for the experimentation with imbalanced dataset with ROSE R package

```
data(iris)
data <- iris[, c(1, 2, 5)]
data$Species <- factor(ifelse(data$Species == "setosa","rare","common"))

## checking the class distribution of this artificial data set
table(data$Species)

##
## common    rare
##    100      50
## now using SMOTE to create a more "balanced problem"
newData <- SMOTE(Species ~ ., data, perc.over = 600,perc.under=100)
table(newData$Species)

##
## common    rare
##    300     350
## Now an example where we obtain a model with the "balanced" data
classTree <- SMOTE(Species ~ ., data, perc.over = 600,perc.under=100,
                   learner='rpartXse',se=0.5)
```

Fig. 14.8 Example of the SMOTE preprocessing with DMwR R package

14.3.5   Package Imbalance

The software named as `imbalance` is the one of the latest packages for imbalanced classification published at CRAN [10]. This software was developed with the idea of overcoming some of the missing capabilities of the related R packages. First of all, it stresses the significance of oversampling techniques by providing the most recent approaches published in the specialized literature. Additionally, it includes a complete visualization environment, so that the practitioner is now able to determine graphically the influence of the novel synthetic instances in the training data. Finally, it allows for an easier integration of the implemented approaches with the remainder packages on imbalance classification at CRAN.

In this library, there are 5 different novel oversampling algorithms available, plus a filtering method. For the ease of usage, the package also includes the method `oversample` as a *wrapper* for all implemented methods, also including the original SMOTE preprocessing and several well-known extensions. The aforementioned new preprocessing techniques are listed below:

- `mwmote`. The *Majority Weighted Minority Oversampling Technique* (MWMOTE) [4] is an extension of the standard SMOTE algorithm [9, 16]. It is focused on stressing the influence of borderline minority instances, as well as small disjuncts that may be found close to these borderline areas.

- `racog, wracog.` *Rapidly Converging Gibbs* (RACOG) and *wrapper-based RACOG* (wRACOG) [13] are two methods designed for discrete attributes. Instead of using the classical interpolation as in most SMOTE extensions, the generation of novel examples is carried out using a Gibbs Sampler scheme. The difference between both approaches is the stop condition. While RACOG has an a priori number of instances to be generated, wRACOG uses a classifier as in a "wrapper" scheme.
- `rwo.` In *Random Walk Oversampling* (RWO) [52] the idea is to kept new synthetic instances as close as possible to the original ones. This is done by taking into account both the mean and deviation of the numerical attributes.
- `pdfos.` *Probability Distribution density Function estimation based Oversampling* (PDFOS) [19] uses a multivariate Gaussian kernel methods to locally approximate the minority class.
- `neater.` *filteriNg of ovErsampled dAta using non cooperaTive gamE theoRy* (NEATER) [3] that, as the name suggest, is based on game theory. This way, it focus the cleaning procedure on those instances that with higher probability of belonging to the opposite class, based on each instance neighborhood.

To evaluate the oversampling process, a visual method named as `plot Comparison` is included. It plots a pairwise comparative grid of a selected set of attributes, both in the original dataset and the oversampled one. That way, if a proper oversampling has been performed, larger minority clusters in the resulting dataset are expected to be shown.

To evaluate the oversampling process, a visual method named as `plot Comparison` is included. It plots a pairwise comparative grid of a selected set of attributes, both in the original dataset and the oversampled one. That way, if a proper oversampling has been performed, larger minority clusters in the resulting dataset are expected to be shown.

The following example loads a dataset included in this package and applies two different preprocessing techniques, namely MWMOTE and RWO. Both approaches are set to get a completely balanced dataset. For the sake of contrasting the output of both alternatives for oversampling, a pairwise visual comparison between first three attributes of the original and modified datasets is plotted. The output can be observed in Fig. 14.9, and in Fig. 14.10.

```
library("imbalance")
data(yeast4)
dataset=yeast4

imbalanceRatio(dataset)
# 0.03558967

toOversample = as.integer(nrow(dataset) - (nrow(dataset)*
    imbalanceRatio(dataset)))
newSamples <- mwmote(
```

```
dataset,
numInstances = toOversample
)

newDatasetMW <- rbind(
dataset,
newSamples
)

plotComparison(
dataset,
newDatasetMW,
attrs = names(dataset)[1:3]
)

newDatasetRWO <- oversample(dataset,ratio=1,method="RWO")

plotComparison(
dataset,
newDatasetRWO,
attrs = names(dataset)[1:3]
)
```

Latest version (1.0.0) can be found at CRAN repository.[10]

14.3.6   Package mlr: Cost-Sensitive Classification

Up to now, we have reviewed those R packages that include functions to perform a preprocessing step allowing to strengthen the subsequent estimation of any binary classifier. However, cost-sensitive classification is also possible using the ML with R (mlr) package [7]. There are two ways to achieve this. On the one hand, to use class-dependent misclassification cost, where an ordinary *ClassifTask* must be generated. On the other hand, to consider example-dependent misclassification costs, by means of a *CostSensTask* function.

In the first case, mlr supports thresholding and rebalancing. Thresholding is used to turn posterior probabilities into class labels are chosen such that the costs are minimized. This requires a Learner that can predict posterior probabilities. During training the costs are not taken into account. Rebalancing requires the learning

---

[10]https://cran.r-project.org/web/packages/imbalance/index.html

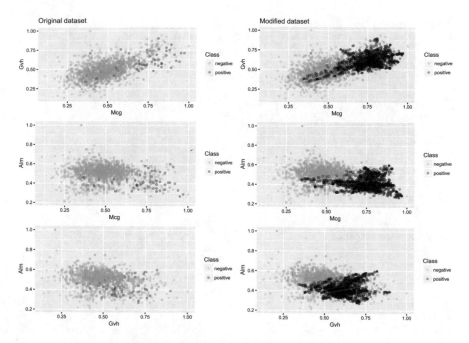

Fig. 14.9 MWMOTE over yeast4

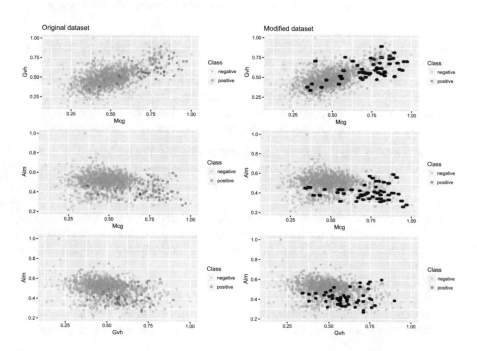

Fig. 14.10 RWO over yeast4

```
data(GermanCredit, package = "caret")
credit.task = makeClassifTask(data = GermanCredit, target = "Class")

#Create cost ad-hoc matrix
costs = matrix(c(0, 1, 5, 0), 2)

#Calculate the theoretical threshold for the positive class
th = costs[2,1]/(costs[2,1] + costs[1,2])

#Thresholding
#Train and predict posterior probabilities
lrn = makeLearner("classif.multinom", predict.type = "prob", trace = FALSE)
mod = train(lrn, credit.task)
pred = predict(mod, task = credit.task)

#Predict class labels according to the theoretical threshold
pred.th = setThreshold(pred, th)

#Rebalancing
#Weight for positive class corresponding to theoretical treshold
w = (1 - th)/th

#Build weighted learner
lrn = makeLearner("classif.multinom", trace = FALSE)
lrn = makeWeightedClassesWrapper(lrn, wcw.weight = w)
```

Fig. 14.11 Cost-sensitive learning by class-dependent misclassification costs with `mlr` R package

classifier that supports class weights or observation weights. Steps for both types of tasks are summarized in Fig. 14.11.

In the case of example-dependent misclassification costs, the feature values x and an $n \times K$ cost matrix that contains the cost vectors for all n examples in the data set are required. *mlr* provides several wrappers to turn regular classification or regression methods into Learners that can deal with example-dependent costs:

- *makeCostSensClassifWrapper* (wraps a classification Learner): This is a naive approach where the costs are coerced into class labels by choosing the class label with minimum cost for each example. Then a regular classification method is used.
- *makeCostSensRegrWrapper* (wraps a regression Learner): An individual regression model is fitted for the costs of each class. In the prediction step first the costs are predicted for all classes and then the class with the lowest predicted costs is selected.
- *makeCostSensWeightedPairsWrapper* (wraps a classification Learner): This is also known as cost-sensitive one-vs-one (CS-OVO) and the most sophisticated of the currently supported methods. For each pair of classes, a binary classifier is fitted. For each observation the class label is defined as the element of the

```
df = iris

#creates cost matrix per example
cost = matrix(runif(150 * 3, 0, 2000), 150) * (1 - diag(3))[df$Species,]+ runif(150, 0, 10)

#creates cost-sensitive task
costsens.task = makeCostSensTask(id = "iris", data = df, cost = cost)

#Finally, the learner is computed
lrn = makeLearner("classif.multinom", trace = FALSE)
lrn = makeCostSensWeightedPairsWrapper(lrn)
mod = train(lrn, costsens.task)
```

Fig. 14.12 Cost-sensitive learning by example-dependent misclassification costs with `mlr` R package

pair with minimal costs. During fitting, the observations are weighted with the absolute difference in costs. Prediction is performed by simple voting.

In Fig. 14.12 and example is shown using the third method commented above. The wrapped Learner is created and trained on the *CostSensTask* defined above.

mlr is one of the widest used packages in R when addressing DM tasks. It contains a large amount of different ML techniques, as well as a vast documentation available in the Web.[11] In spite no preprocessing techniques are explicitly included, they can be integrated with the current *mlr* functions. Finally, it allows different alternatives for cost-sensitive learning, as described throughout this section, adding a good functionality to this package for addressing imbalanced classification.

Latest version (2.12.1) can be found at CRAN package repository.[12]

14.4 Python Libraries

The Python programming language has become one of the most popular tools for scientific computing. There are several reasons for becoming such a wide-spread programming solution. First, we may refer to its high-level interactive nature, being an easy to learn, powerful language. Specifically, it is compound of efficient data structures for object-orient programming. In addition it offers a simple and dynamic typing which, together with its interpreted nature, make it an ideal language for scripting and rapid application development in many areas on most platforms. Furthermore, it has a wide and mature ecosystem of scientific libraries, which adds a higher support for algorithmic development in ML and exploratory data analysis [35, 40].

---

[11]https://mlr-org.github.io/mlr-tutorial/release/html/
[12]https://cran.r-project.org/web/packages/mlr/index.html

The Python interpreter and the extensive standard library are freely available in source or binary form for all major platforms from the Python Web site,[13] and may be freely distributed. The same site also contains distributions of and pointers to many free third party Python modules, programs and tools, and additional documentation.

In spite of the number of different libraries developed for Python, to the best of our knowledge it was not until 2017 when the first solution for the task of imbalanced classification was released. We refer to the `imbalanced-learn` open-source Python toolbox [29].

This toolbox depends only on *numpy*, *scipy*, and *scikit-learn* and is distributed under MIT license. Specifically, it was designed to be fully compatible into the aforementioned `scikit-learn` environment [39], being part of the "scikit-learn-contrib" supported project. Documentation, unit tests as well as integration tests are provided to ease usage and contribution.

The `imbalanced-learn` toolbox provides a wide range of preprocessing methods to cope with the problem of imbalanced dataset. Specifically, authors divided the implemented approaches into four different groups: (i) under-sampling, (ii) over-sampling, (iii) combination of over-and under-sampling, and (iv) ensemble learning methods. All of these are summarized in Table 14.1.

Each sampler class implements three main methods inspired from the *scikit-learn* API: (i) fit computes several statistics which are later needed to resample the data into a balanced set; (ii) sample performs the sampling and returns the data with the desired balancing ratio; and (iii) fit sample is equivalent to calling the method fit followed by the method sample. A class Pipeline is inherited from the *scikit-learn* toolbox to automatically combine samplers, transformers, and estimators.

It also provides a classification report similar to *scikit-learn*,including some specific state-of-the-art metrics that are specific to evaluate the imbalanced learning problem. Specifically, these are recall, specificity, f-measure (F1), geometric mean, Index of Balanced Accuracy (IBA), and support.

Authors of the *imbalanced-learn* toolbox have made available a tutorial with general-purpose and introductory examples in the sphinx-gallery.[14] Specifically, an illustration of the working procedure of all the included algorithms may be found in the aforementioned online documentation site. Figure 14.13 shows different 2D outputs for the application of SMOTE and its variants. Figure 14.14 shows the Python source code used to rebalance a training set with the SMOTE algorithm using the `imbalance-learn` software.

Source code, binaries, and documentation can be downloaded from https://github.com/scikit-learn-contrib/imbalanced-learn. Future versions of this Python library aim to include additional methods based on prototype/instance selection, generation, and reduction. Additionally, user guides are also intended to become more complete.

---

[13] https://www.python.org/

[14] http://contrib.scikit-learn.org/imbalanced-learn/auto_examples/index.html

Table 14.1 List of preprocessing techniques included in the `imbalanced-learn` Python library

Preprocessing	Technique	Ref.
Under-sampling	Random majority under-sampling with replacement	
	Extraction of majority-minority Tomek links	[46]
	Under-sampling with cluster centroids	
	NearMiss-(1 & 2 & 3)	[51]
	Condensed nearest neighbour	[23]
	One-sided selection	[27]
	Neighbourhood cleaning rule	[28]
	Edited nearest neighbours	[50]
	Instance hardness threshold	[43]
	Repeated edited nearest neighbours	[45]
	AllKNN	[45]
Over-sampling	Random majority over-sampling with replacement	
	SMOTE – Synthetic minority over-sampling technique	[9]
	bSMOTE(1 & 2) – Borderline SMOTE of types 1 and 2	[21]
	SVM SMOTE – Support vectors SMOTE	[38]
	ADASYN – Adaptive synthetic sampling approach for imbalanced learning	[24]
Hybrid sampling	SMOTE + TomekLinks	[5]
	SMOTE + ENN	[6]
Ensemble sampling	EasyEnsemble	[30]
	BalanceCascade	[30]

14.5 Big Data Software: Spark Packages

Many platforms for large-scale processing have emerged in the Big Data environment in recent times, as it was introduced in Chap. 13. Apache Spark[15] [26] as one of the most powerful engines in this environment, is aimed at performing faster distributed computing on Big Data by using in-memory primitives. This platform allows user programs to load data into memory and query it repeatedly, making it a well suited tool for online and iterative processing (especially for ML algorithms). It was developed motivated by the limitations in the MapReduce/Hadoop paradigm [31, 49], which forces to follow a linear dataflow that make an intensive disk-usage.

Spark is based on distributed data structures called RDDs. Operations on RDDs automatically place tasks into partitions, maintaining the locality of persisted data. Beyond this, RDDs are an immutable and versatile tool that let programmers persist intermediate results into the memory or disk for re-usability purposes, and customize the partitioning to optimize data placement. RDDs are also fault-tolerant.

---

[15]http://spark.apache.org/

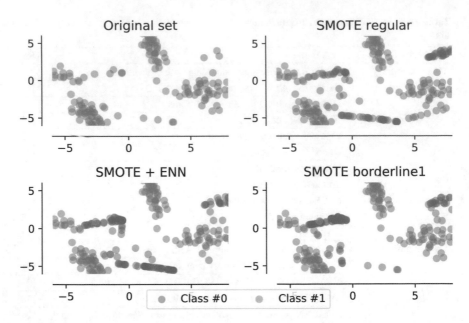

Fig. 14.13 An illustration of the SMOTE method and its variants with `imbalanced-learn` Python toolbox

The lazy operations performed on each RDD are tracked using a "lineage", so that each RDD can be reconstructed at any moment in case of data loss.

In addition to Spark Core, some additional projects have been developed to complement the functionality provided by the core. Among these sub-projects (built on top of the core), we must stress the ML library (MLlib) [37]: is formed by common learning algorithms and statistic utilities. Among its main functionalities includes: classification, regression, clustering, collaborative filtering, optimization, and DR. This library has been especially designed to simplify ML pipelines in large-scale environments.

To address classification with imbalanced data, the *Logistic Regression* classifier from MLlib supports cost-sensitive learning. To do so, weights can be set to the input data by including an additional column. Then, in the command line that creates the classifier it is necessary to three different columns: (i) features; (ii) label; (iii) weights. More details on this functionality can be consulted in the following link: https://issues.apache.org/jira/browse/SPARK-9610. During the writing of this book, the class weighting for the Random Forest algorithm was under development, with a major priority, as stated in the project board at https://issues.apache.org/jira/browse/SPARK-9478.

Apart from the former solution, no preprocessing solution from MLlib is directly related with imbalanced classification. For this reason, some authors on the topic have developed complementary libraries that can be used when facing Big Data imbalanced problems.

```python
from imblearn.over_sampling import SMOTE
from imblearn.combine import SMOTEENN

print(__doc__)

def plot_resampling(ax, X, y, title):
    c0 = ax.scatter(X[y == 0, 0], X[y == 0, 1], label="Class #0", alpha=0.5)
    c1 = ax.scatter(X[y == 1, 0], X[y == 1, 1], label="Class #1", alpha=0.5)
    ax.set_title(title)
    ax.spines['top'].set_visible(False)
    ax.spines['right'].set_visible(False)
    ax.get_xaxis().tick_bottom()
    ax.get_yaxis().tick_left()
    ax.spines['left'].set_position(('outward', 10))
    ax.spines['bottom'].set_position(('outward', 10))
    ax.set_xlim([-6, 8])
    ax.set_ylim([-6, 6])

    return c0, c1

# Generate the dataset
X, y = make_classification(n_classes=2, class_sep=3.5, weights=[0.1, 0.9],
                           n_informative=3, n_redundant=1, flip_y=0.01,
                           n_features=20, n_clusters_per_class=4,
                           n_samples=200, random_state=10)


# Instanciate a PCA object for the sake of easy visualisation
pca = PCA(n_components=2)
# Fit and transform x to visualise inside a 2D feature space
X_vis = pca.fit_transform(X)

# Apply regular SMOTE
kind = ['regular', 'borderline1', 'borderline2', 'svm']
sm = [SMOTE(kind=k) for k in kind]
X_resampled = []
y_resampled = []
X_res_vis = []
for method in sm:
    X_res, y_res = method.fit_sample(X, y)
    X_resampled.append(X_res)
    y_resampled.append(y_res)
    X_res_vis.append(pca.transform(X_res))

#Apply SMOTE+ENN
sm = SMOTEENN()
X_SENN, y_SENN = sm.fit_sample(X, y)
X_SENN_vis = pca.transform(X_SENN)

#Plot graphs
f, ((ax1, ax2), (ax3, ax4)) = plt.subplots(2, 2)
c0, c1 = plot_resampling(ax1, X_vis, y, 'Original set')
plot_resampling(ax2, X_res_vis[0], y_resampled[0], 'SMOTE {}'.format(kind[0]))
plot_resampling(ax3, X_SENN_vis, y_SENN, 'SMOTE + ENN')
plot_resampling(ax4, X_res_vis[1], y_resampled[1], 'SMOTE {}'.format(kind[1]))
f.legend((c0, c1), ('Class #0', 'Class #1'), loc='lower center',
         ncol=2, labelspacing=0.)
plt.tight_layout()
plt.show()
```

Fig. 14.14 Python script for applying SMOTE preprocessing and variants with `imbalanced-learn` Python toolbox

A first example is the evolutionary undersampling proposed by Triguero et al. [48]. Through different iterations, this model is able to find the most appropriate subset of majority instances that, in conjunction with the minority ones, achieve the best results when training a decision tree in imbalanced domains. Through Spark in-memory operations, this model is able to make an efficient use of data. The complete source code can be downloaded at https://github.com/triguero/EUS-BigData.

An easy to use random oversampling and random undersampling built in Scala was one of the contributions made in [15]. It was included in Spark-packages repository at https://spark-packages.org/package/saradelrio/Imb-sampling-ROS_and_RUS, while the complete source code with examples is available at https://github.com/saradelrio/Imb-sampling-ROS_and_RUS. In the oversampling implementation, after the replication of the minority class data points, all examples are repartitioned. This prevents ending up with exactly the same examples in a single partition when carrying out the classification stage.

Finally, we must stress the Spark implementation of the SMOTE and SMOTE-TL preprocessing algorithms, which can be downloaded from https://github.com/adritor7/SMOTE-and-Tomek-Links-in-Spark. It contains its own implementation of the kNN procedure for obtaining the neighborhood when building the new synthetic instances. Similar to the case of random oversampling described above, after filtering out the majority class data points, the minority class examples are repartitioned. This is carried out in order to avoid all minority class data points to be stored in the same data chunk, and thus hindering data parallelism.

14.6 Summarizing Comments

In this chapter, we have compiled the most significant open source tools that provide algorithms to address the imbalanced classification task. We have divided them with respect to their supported language, namely Java, R, Python. Additionally, we have provided some examples of Scala algorithms in Spark for Big Data applications.

KEEL and Weka are two classical Java software tools used by both research and academia for DM with ML algorithms. Specifically, we have stressed the signifi-cance of KEEL for imbalanced classification. This is due to the fact that it provides a complete module with a large amount of approaches from all types of solutions from this area. There is a large set of preprocessing techniques, algorithmic modifications, cost-sensitive learning, and ensemble learning algorithms. The goodness of both KEEL and Weka is their workflow panel, from which any un-experienced user from every area of knowledge can simply build a chain of methods for carrying out the experimentation.

Regarding R-based solutions, we have enumerated an exhaustive list of different libraries that have been either developed ad hoc for the imbalanced classification task, or that support solutions to cope with uneven class distributions. The only hitch in this case is the necessity of writing all the necessary source code in order to include these algorithms.

Together with R, Python is a popular choice for both computer scientists and users from other areas to carry out scientific computations and programs. However, to the best of our knowledge there is only a recent library that allows to carry out data preprocessing to rebalance the training set for imbalanced classification.

Finally, we have focused on the future of Big Data. Being a novel work scenario, there are still few software tools available. Specifically, we have enumerated three approaches, namely an evolutionary undersampling, random over and undersampling and SMOTE. It is therefore of extreme importance to develop a complete library that comprises standard solutions for the imbalanced classification, following the same trend than in for the previous languages.

References

1. Alcalá-fdez, J., Sánchez, L., García, S., Jesus, M.J.D., Ventura, S., Garrell, J.M., Otero, J., Bacardit, J., Rivas, V.M., Fernández, J.C., Herrera, F.: Keel: a software tool to assess evolutionary algorithms for data mining problems. Soft Comput. **13**(3), 307–318 (2009)
2. Alcalá-Fdez, J., Fernández, A., Luengo, J., Derrac, J., García, S.: Keel data-mining software tool: data set repository, integration of algorithms and experimental analysis framework. J. Mult.-Valued Log. Soft Comput. **17**(2–3), 255–287 (2011)
3. Almogahed, B.A., Kakadiaris, I.A.: NEATER: filtering of over-sampled data using non-cooperative game theory. Soft Comput. **19**(11), 3301–3322 (2014)
4. Barua, S., Islam, M.M., Yao, X., Murase, K.: MWMOTE–majority weighted minority over-sampling technique for imbalanced data set learning. IEEE Trans. Knowl. Data Eng. **26**(2), 405–425 (2014)
5. Batista, G.E.A.P.A., Bazzan, A.L.C., Monard, M.C.: Balancing training data for automated annotation of keywords: a case study. In: Lifschitz, S., Almeida Nalvo Jr. F., Joannis Pappas Jr. G., Linden, R. (eds.) Second Workshop Brasileiro de Bioinformática (WOB), pp. 10–18 (2003)
6. Batista, G.E.A.P.A., Prati, R.C., Monard, M.C.: A study of the behavior of several methods for balancing machine learning training data. SIGKDD Explor. **6**(1), 20–29 (2004)
7. Bischl, B., Lang, M., Kotthoff, L., Schiffner, J., Richter, J., Studerus, E., Casalicchio, G., Jones, Z.M.: Mlr: machine learning in R. J. Mach. Learn. Res. **17**(170), 1–5 (2016)
8. Chapelle, O., Schlkopf, B., Zien, A.: Semi-supervised learning, 1st edn. The MIT Press, Cambridge (2010)
9. Chawla, N.V., Bowyer, K.W., Hall, L.O., Kegelmeyer, W.P.: Smote: synthetic minority over-sampling technique. J. Artif. Intell. Res. **16**, 321–357 (2002)
10. Cordn, I., Fernndez, A., Garca, S., Herrera, F.: Imbalance: oversampling algorithms for imbalanced classification in R. Knowl.-Based Syst. (2018, in press). https://doi.org/10.1016/j.knosys.2018.07.035
11. Crowston, K., Wei, K., Howison, J., Wiggins, A.: Free/libre open-source software development: what we know and what we do not know. ACM Comput. Surv. **44**(2), 7 (2012)
12. Dal Pozzolo, A., Caelen, O., Waterschoot, S., Bontempi, G.: Racing for unbalanced methods selection. In: Yin, H., Tang, K., Gao, Y., Klawonn, F., Lee, M., Weise, T., Li, B., Yao, X. (eds.) IDEAL, Hefei, China. Lecture Notes in Computer Science, vol. 8206, pp. 24–31. Springer (2013)
13. Das, B., Krishnan, N.C., Cook, D.J.: RACOG and wRACOG: two probabilistic oversampling techniques. IEEE Trans. Knowl. Data Eng. **27**(1), 222–234 (2015)

14. Fernandez, A., del Ro, S., Lpez, V., Bawakid, A., del Jess, M.J., Bentez, J.M., Herrera, F.: Big data with cloud computing: an insight on the computing environment, mapreduce, and programming frameworks. Wiley Interdisciplinary Rev. Data Min. Knowl. Discov. **4**(5), 380–409 (2014)
15. Fernandez, A., del Rio, S., Chawla, N.V., Herrera, F.: An insight into imbalanced big data classification: outcomes and challenges. Complex Intell. Syst. **3**(2), 105–120 (2017)
16. Fernandez, A., Garcia, S., Herrera, F., Chawla, N.: Smote for learning from imbalanced data: progress and challenges, marking the 15-year anniversary. J. Artif. Intell. Res. **61**, 863–905 (2018)
17. Frank, E., Hall, M.A., Witten, I.H.: The WEKA Workbench. Online Appendix for "Data Mining: Practical Machine Learning Tools and Techniques", 4th edn. Morgan Kaufmann, Burlington (2016)
18. Galar, M., Fernández, A., Barrenechea, E., Bustince, H., Herrera, F.: A review on ensembles for the class imbalance problem: bagging-, boosting-, and hybrid-based approaches. IEEE Trans. Syst. Man Cybern. Part C Appl. Rev. **42**(4), 463–484 (2012)
19. Gao, M., Hong, X., Chen, S., Harris, C.J., Khalaf, E.: PDFOS: PDF estimation based oversampling for imbalanced two-class problems. Neurocomputing **138**, 248–259 (2014)
20. García, S., Luengo, J., Herrera, F.: Data Preprocessing in Data Mining. Intelligent Systems Reference Library, vol. 72. Springer, Cham (2015)
21. Han, H., Wang, W., Mao, B.: Borderline-smote: a new over-sampling method in imbalanced data sets learning. In: Huang, D.S., Zhang, X.P., Huang, G.B. (eds.) ICIC, Hefei, China. Lecture Notes in Computer Science, vol. 3644, pp. 878–887. Springer (2005)
22. Han, J., Kamber, M., Pei, J.: Data Mining: Concepts and Techniques, 3rd edn. Morgan Kaufmann Publishers Inc., Amsterdam (2011)
23. Hart, P.: The condensed nearest neighbor rule. IEEE Trans. Inf. Theory **14**(3), 515–516 (1967)
24. He, H., Bai, Y., Garcia, E.A., Li, S.: Adasyn: adaptive synthetic sampling approach for imbalanced learning. In: IEEE International Joint Conference on Neural Networks (IEEE World Congress on Computational Intelligence), Hong Kong, pp. 1322–1328. IEEE (2008)
25. Hornik, K.: R CRAN (2018). https://CRAN.R-project.org/
26. Karau, H., Konwinski, A., Wendell, P., Zaharia, M.: Learning Spark: lightning-fast big data analytics, 1st edn. O'Reilly Media, Sebastopol (2015)
27. Kubat, M., Matwin, S.: Addressing the curse of imbalanced training sets: one-sided selection. In: Fisher, D.H. (ed.) ICML, vol. 97, pp. 179–186. Morgan Kaufmann, San Mateo (1997)
28. Laurikkala, J.: Improving identification of difficult small classes by balancing class distribution. In: Quaglini, S., Barahona, P., Andreassen, S. (eds.) AIME, Lecture Notes in Computer Science, vol. 2101, pp. 63–66. Springer, Berlin/Heidelberg (2001)
29. Lemaitre, G., Nogueira, F., Aridas, C.K.: Imbalanced-learn: a python toolbox to tackle the curse of imbalanced datasets in machine learning. J. Mach. Learn. Res. **18**, 1–5 (2017)
30. Liu, X.Y., Wu, J., Zhou, Z.H.: Exploratory undersampling for class-imbalance learning. IEEE Trans. Syst. Man Cybern. Part B **39**(2), 539–550 (2009)
31. Lin, J.J.: Mapreduce is good enough? If all you have is a hammer, throw away everything that's not a nail! Big Data **1**(1), 28–39 (2012)
32. López, V., Fernández, A., García, S., Palade, V., Herrera, F.: An insight into classification with imbalanced data: empirical results and current trends on using data intrinsic characteristics. Inf. Sci. **250**, 113–141 (2013)
33. Lunardon, N., Menardi, G., Torelli, N.: ROSE: a package for binary imbalanced learning. R J. **6**, 82–92 (2014)
34. Marx, V.: The big challenges of big data. Nature **498**(7453), 255–260 (2013)
35. McKinney, W.: Python for Data Analysis, 1st edn. O'Reilly, Sebastopol (2012)
36. Menardi, G., Torelli, N.: Training and assessing classification rules with imbalanced data. Data Min. Knowl. Disc. **28**, 92122 (2014)
37. Meng, X., Bradley, J.K., Yavuz, B., Sparks, E.R., Venkataraman, S., Liu, D., Freeman, J., Tsai, D.B., Amde, M., Owen, S., Xin, D., Xin, R., Franklin, M.J., Zadeh, R., Zaharia, M., Talwalkar, A.: Mllib: machine learning in Apache Spark. J. Mach. Learn. Res. **17**(34), 1–7 (2016)

38. Nguyen, H.M., Cooper, E.W., Kamei, K.: Borderline over-sampling for imbalanced data classification. Int. J. Knowl. Eng. Soft Data Paradigms **3**(1), 4–21 (2011)
39. Pedregosa, F., Varoquaux, G., Gramfort, A., Michel, V., Thirion, B., Grisel, O., Blondel, M., Prettenhofer, P., Weiss, R., Dubourg, V., Vanderplas, J., Passos, A., Cournapeau, D., Brucher, M., Perrot, M., Duchesnay, E.: Scikit-learn: machine learning in python. J. Mach. Learn. Res. **12**, 2825–2830 (2011)
40. Raschka, S.: Python Machine Learning, 1st edn. PACKT Publishing, Birmingham (2015)
41. Siriseriwan, W., Sinapiromsaran, K.: The effective redistribution for imbalance dataset: relocating safe-level smote with minority outcast handling. Chiang Mai J. Sci. **43**(1), 234–246 (2014)
42. Siriseriwan, W.: Smotefamily: a collection of oversampling techniques for class imbalance problem based on smote (2018). https://cran.r-project.org/web/packages/smotefamily/index.html
43. Smith, M.R., Martinez, T.R., Giraud-Carrier, C.G.: An instance level analysis of data complexity. Mach. Learn. **95**(2), 225–256 (2014)
44. Tippmann, S.: Programming tools: adventures with R. Nature **517**(7532), 109–110 (2015)
45. Tomek, I.: An experiment with the edited nearest-neighor rule. IEEE Trans. Syst. Man Cybern. **6**(6), 448–452 (1976)
46. Tomek, I.: Two modifications of CNN. IEEE Trans. Syst. Man Cybern. **7**(2), 679–772 (1976)
47. Torgo, L.: Data Mining with R: Learning with Case Studies. Chapman and Hall/CRC Press, Boca Raton (2010)
48. Triguero, I., Galar, M., Merino, D., Maillo, J., Bustince, H., Herrera, F.: Evolutionary undersampling for extremely imbalanced big data classification under Apache Spark. In: IEEE Congress on Evolutionary Computation (CEC 2016), pp. 640–647. Vancouver (2016)
49. White, T.: Hadoop, The Definitive Guide, 1st edn. O'Reilly Media, Inc., Sebastopol (2012)
50. Wilson, D.L.: Asymptotic properties of nearest neighbor rules using edited data. IEEE Trans. Syst. Man Cybern. **2**(3), 408–421 (1972)
51. Zhang, J., Mani, I.: KNN approach to unbalanced data distributions: a case study involving information extraction. In: Proceedings of the ICML'2003 Workshop on Learning from Imbalanced Datasets (2003)
52. Zhang, H., Li, M.: RWO-sampling: a random walk over-sampling approach to imbalanced data classification. Inf. Fusion **20**, 99–116 (2014)

Printed in the United States
By Bookmasters